Heinz Streib, Ralph W. Hood Jr. (eds.)
Faith in Development

BiUP General

Heinz Streib is a senior professor at Universität Bielefeld, Germany, and conducts research in the psychology of religion. He established and directs the *Research Center for Biographical Studies in Contemporary Religion*. He is editor-in-chief of the *International Journal for the Psychology of Religion*. His research focuses on biographical-reconstructive and psychometric assessment of religious change and development over the lifespan, deconversion, fundamentalism, xenophobia and the semantics of spirituality.

Ralph W. Hood Jr. is a professor of psychology, LeRoy A. Martin Distinguished Professor of Religious Studies at the University of Tennessee at Chattanooga, and UT Alumni Association Distinguished Professor. He is a past president of the Division 36 of the American Psychological Association and a recipient of its William James award for research in the psychology of religion.

Heinz Streib, Ralph W. Hood Jr. (eds.)

Faith in Development

Mixed-Method Studies on Worldviews
and Religious Styles

[transcript]

This publication was made possible by grants from the John Templeton Foundation (60806; 61834) and the German Research Foundation (Deutsche Forschungsgemeinschaft). Part of the Open Access book production was funded by a grant from the Publication Fund of Bielefeld University.

Bibliographic information published by the Deutsche Nationalbibliothek
The Deutsche Nationalbibliothek lists this publication in the Deutsche Nationalbibliografie; detailed bibliographic data are available in the Internet

This work is licensed under the Creative Commons Attribution-NonCommercial-NoDerivatives 4.0 (BY-NC-ND) which means that the text may be used for non-commercial purposes, provided credit is given to the author.
https://creativecommons.org/licenses/by-nc-nd/4.0/
To create an adaptation, translation, or derivative of the original work and for commercial use, further permission is required and can be obtained by contacting rights@transcript-publishing.com
Creative Commons license terms for re-use do not apply to any content (such as graphs, figures, photos, excerpts, etc.) not original to the Open Access publication and further permission may be required from the rights holder. The obligation to research and clear permission lies solely with the party re-using the material.

First published in 2024 by Bielefeld University Press, Bielefeld
© Heinz Streib, Ralph W. Hood Jr. (eds.)
An Imprint of transcript Verlag

Cover layout: Maria Arndt, Bielefeld
Print-ISBN: 978-3-8376-7123-0
PDF-ISBN: 978-3-8394-7123-4

Contents

Acknowledgments 9

Introduction.. 11

I. Part A: Conceptual & Methodological Perspectives

Chapter 1
Religious Styles and Types: Studying Change and Development in Worldview and Faith
Heinz Streib & Ralph W. Hood, Jr... 17

Chapter 2
A Common Core? Ideographic and Nomothetic Evidence for Mystical Experience in Relationship to Religious Styles & Types
Ralph W. Hood, Jr. & Heinz Streib 43

Chapter 3
Identity and Narrative across the Adult Life-Span – Concepts and Methods for the Study of Worldview and Religion in Consecutive Autobiographical Reconstructions
Barbara Keller, Ramona Bullik & Anika Steppacher 59

Chapter 4
Mixed-Method and Longitudinal. Background and Profile of Our Research Design
Anika Steppacher, Barbara Keller, Ramona Bullik, Christopher Silver, & Heinz Streib 85

II. Part B: Results of Quantitative Analyses Including Qualitative Data

Chapter 5
The Six Aspects of Faith Development in Longitudinal Analysis
Zhuo Job Chen, Heinz Streib & Ralph W. Hood, Jr. 117

Chapter 6
Religious or Spiritual? Text Analysis of the Free Entries in Defining Religiosity and Spirituality
Zhuo Job Chen, Anika Steppacher, & Heinz Streib 137

Chapter 7
Network Analysis of Case Study Petra S.: A Mixed-Methods Approach
Zhuo Job Chen, Anika Steppacher, & Heinz Streib 153

Chapter 8
Predicting Deconversion. Concurrent and Cross-Time Correlations in Three Samples
Heinz Streib & Zhuo Job Chen 173

III. Part C: Longitudinal Case Studies—Qualitative Analyses Including Quantitative Data

Chapter 9
Reconstructing Individual Trajectories across Time: A Short History and a Guide to Understanding the Case Studies
Barbara Keller & Ramona Bullik 191

Chapter 10
Varieties of Non-Belief in Young Adulthood. A Cross-Cultural Comparison of Nadine and Isabella
Ramona Bullik, Martin Hornshaw, & Daimi Shirck 205

Chapter 11
"The Personal is always Connected to Society." The Pro-Social Values of a Spiritual Atheist. The Case of Petra
Anika Steppacher, Ramona Bullik, & Barbara Keller 237

Chapter 12
Varieties of Being Protestant in the USA and Germany—The Cases of Gisela and George
Ramona Bullik, Matthew Durham, & Barbara Keller 275

Chapter 13
"It's the certainty that my faith reflects a reality that I can't see at the moment, but this is where I'm going" – The Impact of an Exclusivist Faith in Old Age. Comparison of Berthold and Heidemarie
Anika Steppacher, Ramona Bullik, Barbara Keller, & Daimi Shirck 311

IV. Part D: Conclusion

Chapter 14
Longitudinal Mixed-method Study of Worldviews and Religious Styles in the Adult Lifespan – Current Conclusions and Future Directions
Ramona Bullik, Zhuo Job Chen, Matthew Durham, Ralph W. Hood, Jr., Martin Hornshaw, Barbara Keller, Daimi Shirck, Christopher F. Silver, Anika Steppacher, & Heinz Streib 353

APPENDIX A: Sample and Measures in the Three-Wave Longitudinal Data
Heinz Streib, Ralph Hood, Barbara Keller, Ramona Bullik, Matthew Durham, and Zhuo Job Chen ..381

APPENDIX B: The Bielefeld Narrative and Content Coding Scheme (BiNCCS)
Anika Steppacher, Barbara Keller, & Ramona Bullik 389

Acknowledgments

Conducting a study with the goal of gaining a more thorough understanding of how faith and worldview develop across the lifespan is ambitious and would not be possible without the large number of participants who have stayed with us and the project for up to 20 years. We cannot emphasize enough how much we appreciate your interest in this study and your trust in all those working on it. Thank you for continuing to share your life stories and views of the world with us!

We would also like to take this opportunity to thank all those who worked on this phase of the study, by conducting interviews, setting up online surveys, and contributing to the quantitative and qualitative analysis of our data: Veronika Eufinger, Florian Schmidt, Fabian Haefke, Martin Hornshaw, Can David Tobias, Claudia Mahrhofer, Maximilian Schulte, Christin Wiese, William Adkission, William Andrews, Gale Burns, Maylnda Clark, Lauren Drinnon, Matthew Durham, Aaron Eldridge, Jessica Gregg, Adeola Ijiyode, Abbs Kern, Matthew Koonce, Jesse Leslie, Emily Manzano, Olivette Pearson, Nate Scarbeck, Daimi Shirck, Bethany Sikkink, Alexandra Theis, Anna Turner, and Todd Wearner. We are especially grateful to William Andrews and Matthew Durham for language corrections and copy editing.

This publication was made possible by Grants 60806 and 61834 from the John Templeton Foundation. The opinions expressed in this publication are those of the authors and do not necessarily reflect the views of the John Templeton Foundation. The data used in this work were collected in a series of research projects that were funded by generous grants from the German Research Foundation (Deutsche Forschungsgemeinschaft) and the John Templeton Foundation. Part of the Open Access book production was funded by a grant from the Publication Fund of Bielefeld University.

Introduction

This book presents the results of longitudinal investigation of faith development experienced by participants in the United States and Germany. We were interested in the changes in worldview and meaning-making that our respondents associatee with their religious, spiritual, agnostic and atheist identifications. For two decades, research teams in Chattanooga, USA, and Bielefeld, Germany, have invited and re-invited hundreds of people to participate in a personal interview and to complete an extensive questionnaire in order to better understand the reasons for and the consequences of their continuity or discontinuity in religious, spiritual, or nontheistic worldview and meaning-making.

This book presents the current state of conceptual and methodological considerations, quantitative analyses, and typical case studies based on three waves of data collection and analysis. It is the first coherent presentation of findings from our three-wave longitudinal research on faith development. It is not a stand-alone publication: It is the current finale in a concert of publications that began with the overtures on deconversion (Streib et al., 2009) and spirituality (Streib & Hood, 2016) and builds on three recent publications: *Deconversion Revisited* (Streib et al., 2022), which presents findings from a two-wave longitudinal investigation of participants in the Deconversion Study, a dissertation that presents three-wave case studies with focus on narrative identity (Bullik, 2024), and a handbook chapter on leaving high-tension groups (Keller, et al., 2024). In addition, journal publications on religious type construction (Streib et al., 2020), longitudinal modeling of faith development (Streib et al., 2023), mysticism as predictor of spirituality (Streib & Chen, 2021), an analysis of the 'more spiritual than religious' (Chen et al., 2023), and an article focusing on the longitudinal reconstruction of religious biographies (Bullik, 2022) are musical pieces in our current concert.

These publications, including this one, would be unnecessary if religiosity was the dichotomous question of 'Yes, I am religious' and 'No, I am not,' or 'Yes, I am a believer' and 'No, I am not,' and if religiosity, once acquired and accepted, was stable throughout the lifespan. Because we believe—and have been able to document—that it is otherwise, all our research work has focused on the question of change and development. Hence the title *Faith in Development*. Thinking in terms of faith development and religious change was greatly inspired by the work of James Fowler, whose *Stages of Faith* (1981) sparked a lively debate about changes of faith and different styles of faith, which was quite new and provocative, especially for professionals in established religions, such as religious educators, church leaders, and scholars in theology and religious studies. These controversies have calmed down and the idea of faith development has become more widely accepted, and some conceptual and methodological questions were addressed. However, the question of *empirical evidence* and a detailed account of faith in development has not yet been sufficiently resolved, despite many years of research with the Faith Development Interview. Psychology, in contrast, has generally been less reluctant toward thinking in terms of change and development, and has recently presented handbooks that may stimulate the discussion of the dynamics of personality change, including quantitative and qualitative methods (see Chapter 1 for some more details). Against this background, the research question to which our recent publications and the chapters in this book are intended to contribute can be specified: How does faith—in a wide understanding including religious, spiritual, or non-theistic identifications—change and develop in the adult life span, when viewed longitudinally through the lens of psychological methods such as narrative analysis, structural-developmental analysis, and modeling of quantitative variables for personality, well-being and other characteristics?

By inviting you to our concert, we hope to be more than metaphorical. While there is no concert without individual pieces, there is no concert without a score. Which score you focus on will allow you to judge the material of our concert, which, to continue the metaphor, is three movements (Parts A, B, & C below).

The entire score provides an overview of what is to be heard. Part A presents the leitmotif in which the Faith Development Interview dominates. Part B contains the statistical tones that explore changes in faith development in both religious, spiritual, and secular forms. They complement what follows in Part C, individual solos and duets across the lifespan. While readers may chose what whish to hear, our metaphor more than suggests that the concert is best appreciated when it is heard in full by all who attend. Our goal is hopefully reflected in this metaphor, and we are interested in a dialogue with all those who chose to attend this concert. But first, you must attend.

References

Bullik, R. (2024). *Leitmotifs in life stories. Reconstructing subjective religiosity and narrative identity—Developments and stabilities over the adult lifespan*. Bielefeld University Press. https://doi.org/10.14361/9783839471227

Bullik, R. (2022). A faithful journey. Following a married couple's religious trajectory over the adult lifespan. *Religions*, 13(8), 673. https://doi.org/10.3390/rel13080673

Chen, Z., Cowden, R. G., & Streib, H. (2023). More spiritual than religious: Concurrent and longitudinal relations with personality traits, mystical experiences, and other individual characteristics. *Frontiers in Psychology*, Article 1025938. https://doi.org/10.3389/fpsyg.2022.1025938

Fowler, J. W. (1981). *Stages of faith. The psychology of human development and the quest for meaning*. Harper & Row.

Keller, B., Bullik, R., & Streib, H. (2024). Deconversion from high-tension religious groups. In K. Taku & T. K. Shackelford (Eds.), *The Routledge International Handbook of*

Changes in Human Perceptions and Behaviors, pp. 489–507. Routledge https://doi.org/1 0.4324/9781003316602-35 (pre-print: https://doi.org/10.31234/osf.io/kb3te)

Streib, H., & Chen, Z. J. (2021). Evidence for the brief mysticism scale: Psychometric properties, and moderation and mediation effects in predicting spiritual self-identification. *International Journal for the Psychology of Religion*, 31(3), 165–175. https://doi.o rg/10.1080/10508619.2021.1899641 (post-print at: https://doi.org/10.31234/osf.io/6bx 2s)

Streib, H., Chen, Z. J., & Hood, R. W. (2020). Categorizing people by their preference for religious styles: Four types derived from evaluation of faith development interviews. *International Journal for the Psychology of Religion*, 30(2), 112–127. https://doi.org/10.108 0/10508619.2019.1664213 (post-print at: https://doi.org/10.31234/osf.io/d3kbr)

Streib, H., Chen, Z. J., & Hood, R. W. (2023). Faith development as change in religious types: Results from three-wave longitudinal data with faith development interviews. *Psychology of Religion and Spirituality*, 15(2), 298–307. https://doi.org/10.1037/rel00004 40 (post-print at: https://doi.org/10.31234/osf.io/qrcb2)

Streib, H., & Hood, R. W. (Eds.). (2016). *Semantics and psychology of spirituality. A cross-cultural analysis*. Springer International Publishing Switzerland. https://doi.org/10.100 7/978-3-319-21245-6.

Streib, H., Hood, R. W., Keller, B., Csöff, R.-M., & Silver, C. (2009). *Deconversion. Qualitative and quantitative results from cross-cultural research in Germany and the United States of America*. Vandenhoeck & Ruprecht. https://doi.org/10.13109/9783666604393

Streib, H., Keller, B., Bullik, R., Steppacher, A., Silver, C. F., Durham, M., Barker, S. B., & Hood Jr., R. W. (2022). *Deconversion revisited. Biographical studies and psychometric analyses ten years later*. Brill Germany/Vandenhoeck & Ruprecht. https://doi.org/10.13109 /9783666568688

I. Part A: Conceptual & Methodological Perspectives

Chapter 1
Religious Styles and Types: Studying Change and Development in Worldview and Faith

Heinz Streib & Ralph W. Hood, Jr.[1]

Abstract *This chapter outlines the current state of the theory that is the base of our research: faith development theory. From an overview of our past and current Chattanooga-Bielefeld research, we can identify convergencies with other areas in psychology: Change and development in faith relates to recent discussions in personality psychology about an integrative understanding of the dynamics and processes of personality development across the lifespan. Faith development theory has a clear conceptual and empirical focus on styles and types as components of a structural-developmental model. We agree with Fowler's work on a wide conceptualization of 'faith' that corresponds to 'worldview' to encompass religious, spiritual, non-theistic, and secular versions of meaning-making and discovery. The central assumption that development in faith proceeds in progressing styles and types implies that faith in development has a direction and an aim, which is openness to dialog and wisdom in encountering the Unknown; this leads to the consideration of whether and how research on faith development is a contribution to wisdom research.*

Keywords: *religious style; faith development; worldview; religious development; Fowler; personality dynamics; personality process; personality; wisdom; dialectical thinking*

---

1   H. Streib, Bielefeld University, Germany. E-mail: Heinz.Streib@uni-bielefeld.de; R. W. Hood, Jr., University of Tennessee at Chattanooga, USA. © Heinz Streib, Ralph W. Hood Jr. (eds.): Faith in Development. Mixed-Method Studies on Worldviews and Religious Styles. First published in 2024 by Bielefeld University Press, Bielefeld, https://doi.org/10.14361/9783839471234-003

Religious Change and Development – The Focus of Our Research

Our Contributions in Three Areas of Investigation

The central theme of our joint research projects at the University of Tennessee at Chattanooga and Bielefeld University, is *religious change*. This was the focus of a series of major studies: on deconversion, on spirituality, and on faith development in longitudinal perspective. The Deconversion Study (Streib et al., 2009) focused on changes in religious affiliation, centrifugal migrations in the religious fields, and their psychological consequences for the individual. The Spirituality Project (Streib & Hood, 2016) investigated changes in the growing diversity of worldviews, with a focus on the increasing preference for self-identifying as "more spiritual than religious." In our most recent and continuing project we have focused on the longitudinal investigation of change, re-interviewing former participants for a second time (Streib, et al., 2022), and adding a third and fourth wave. Integral to all of these projects is a focus on faith development that attends to cognitive-structural changes and posits increasing openness to dialog as aim of development.

Deconversion

The initial inspiration for our Deconversion Study was the invitation by the Enquête Commission of the German Parliament for an expertise about members and ex-members of new religious and fundamentalist groups (Streib, 1998; 1999). The expertise was based on a dozen case studies which indicated a typology. This initial study made us curious to learn more about the psychology and the well-being of members and former members of so-called sects and other religious groups and organizations. Funds from the German Research Foundation (DFG) enabled the first Bielefeld-Chattanooga project on deconversion (2002–2005). This project had a clear focus on extensive narrative interviews and Faith Development Interviews with deconverts. It included also interviewing members who remained in the religious groups, which the deconverts had left. Both deconverts and (an approximately 10 times higher number of) those remaining in their tradition participated in a questionnaire ($n = 1,196$) that included measures such as the Five Factors Inventory (NEO-FFI) for personality, Ryff's Well-being Scale, and scales for fundamentalism and right-wing authoritarianism. Results include, for deconverts, clearly higher *openness to experience*, slightly lower well-being for Germans but not Americans, advanced faith development, and exceptionally high self-identified "spirituality" of deconverts in both Germany and America (for a comprehensive report of results and case studies, see Streib et al., 2009).

The major result of the evaluation of the many interviews in the Deconversion Study consists in the documentation of a typology of deconversion narratives that includes four types: *Pursuit of autonomy*, *Debarred from paradise*, *Finding a new frame of reference*, and *Life-long quests – late revisions*. This typology is discussed, reflected and advanced in the analysis of two-wave cases in our recent book *Deconversion Revisited* (Streib, et al., 2022), and also in some of the three-wave cases included in this volume. Based on longitudinal three-wave data, we could also quantitatively model the predictors of deconversion (see Chapter 8 in this volume). Thus, our investigation of deconverts can be regarded a contribution to the still relatively young field of deconversion research (Streib, 2021).

Spirituality

The surprisingly high number of "more spiritual than religious" deconverts in the Deconversion Study was the major inspiration to design and conduct the Spirituality Study (2008–2012, DFG-funded). The compilation of the questionnaire already demonstrates our desire for a highly detailed and comprehensive perspective on the semantics of spirituality. Besides items for spiritual/religious self-identification, we also used semantic differentials, including Osgood's (1960; 1962; 1969) classic and our own contextual versions; we also invited participants to note their own subjective definitions of spirituality and of religion in free text entries. Over 1,700 participants entered their definitions. Because we continued the free text entries about spirituality and religion in the questionnaires of the following Wave 2 (n = 677) and Wave 3 (n = 438), we now have unique data sets, and also a small, but interesting longitudinal sample with three consecutive spirituality definitions (n = 122). These are currently analyzed (for first results using thematic analysis, see Chapter 6 in this volume). It may appear paradoxical that advances in faith development dovetail with becoming less religious and more spiritual, and this raises both conceptual and empirical questions regarding the semantics and psychology of spirituality.

One of the remarkable results of the Spirituality Study regards the relation of mysticism and spirituality: *Mysticism*, as measured with Hood's (1975) Mysticism Scale, correlated highly ($r > .42$) with, and predicted, self-rated spirituality (Klein et al., 2016). The predicting effect of *mysticism* for spirituality was confirmed using our longitudinal data set (Streib & Chen, 2021; Streib, Klein, et al., 2021). In the Spirituality Study, we have used *mysticism* and *openness to experience* as axes to map our case studies that analyzed the role of spirituality in the variety of biographical trajectories (Keller et al., 2016). The focus was upon the complex ways in which religion (affiliation), faith (development), and spirituality (self-identification) interact, and what are the psychological correlates and causes that can be uncovered.

Faith Development over Time

The Faith Development Interview (FDI; Fowler, 1981; Streib & Keller, 2018) was included in all our studies, and has moved even more into the center of our research, since we turned to longitudinal investigation and have re-interviewed former participants in Wave 2 (2014–2017, jointly funded by DFG and the John Templeton Foundation, JTF) and Wave 3 (2018–2021, funded by the JTF). This also means that our research now concentrates even more on conceptual and methodological issues in faith development theory. Despite the considerable modifications that Streib (2001; 2003a; 2003b; 2005; 2013; Streib et al., 2020) proposed with the religious styles model, it has deep roots in Fowler's (1981) structural-developmental theory. Our research in faith development continues using an interpretative method of evaluating the FDI with 25 questions—which poses the practical problem that an enormous amount of time and human resources are required. In the structural evaluation of the FDI (rating according to the *Manual*, Streib & Keller, 2018), the interpretative attention is focusing on six aspects: perspective-taking, social horizon, morality, locus of authority, world coherence, symbolic function. These aspects reflect the breadth of information gathered by the FDI and available for aspect-specific rating.

While our attempt to integrate faith development and religious styles research into psychology appears ambitious, we have competed some methodical, statistical and qualitative advancements: (a) An important preparatory step for further analyses was the construction of an algorithm for combining the 25 ratings in an FDI into a single total FDI score that is less vulnerable to methodological criticisms than Fowler's suggestion to calculate a simple average of all 25 ratings (Streib et al., 2020). The religious type is suggested as the final total FDI score, using an algorithm for calculating the religious type that largely converged with (but turned out less prone to error than) Latent Class/Latent Transition Analysis and a machine learning approach (GLMNET). (b) We completed two studies that demonstrate that there *is in fact* (upward and downward) development and to identify predictors that cause faith development (Streib, et al., 2023; Chapter 5 in this volume). These studies need replication using larger samples; nevertheless, they can be regarded as steps in modeling faith development. (c) Turning to the qualitative approach: almost all FDIs are rather long, taking one or two hours; and most interviewees accept the invitation, beginning with the very first question, to tell stories and engage in autobiographical narrating. The FDIs therefore include a wealth of narratives. Thus, analysis for narrative identity has become a major focus of our research. For narrative analysis and content analysis, the Bielefeld team has developed a comprehensive coding system using Atlas.ti that can be analyzed further using approaches such as Network Analysis (see Chapters 4 and 7 in this volume).

The case studies presented in this volume (Chapters 10 through 13) are now based on three consecutive FDIs by one and the same person in their adult lifespan; thus, they are clearly attending to diachronic within-person differences. These case studies reflect the potential of our data for contributing to research in autobiographical reasoning, narrative identity (see Chapter 3 in this volume), and the dynamic and processes of change in personality.

Convergencies: Dynamics and Processes in Personality Psychology

In order to contextualize our research in psychology, we highlight convergencies with selected areas in psychological research, from which we have received inspiration, both conceptually and methodologically. We hope to provide persuasive arguments that faith development research can make a contribution to a genuine dialogue with mainstream psychology.

Contextualizing our line of research with recent proposals in personality psychology, we contend that our research parallels initiatives in psychology that call for greater attention to the dynamics of individual change and development. An important milestone are recent handbooks (Corr & Matthews, 2020; Rauthmann, 2021). The collection of chapters in these handbooks suggests that the personality dynamics and processes may involve personality traits, narrative identity, social interaction, moral behavior, wisdom, or well-being. Atherton et al. (2020), for example, document the continuous development of the person throughout the life span from infancy until death. Revelle and Wilt (2021) explain that the dynamics of the changing personality relate to *within-person differences*, rather than *between-person differences;* they also note that this polarity reflects the tension between nomothetic and idiographic approaches. Thus, research on change and development should clearly focus on the consideration of *within-person differences* using an *idiographic* approach, in order to correct the "prevailing focus on individual difference taxonomies in the personality-psychological landscape" (Kuper et al., 2021, p. 2). These proposals, of course, suggest that both sides need to be integrated. Likewise, a multi-author target article on the dynamics of personality development (Baumert et al., 2017) proposes the integration of structure, process, and development. The authors explain that personality structure is focusing on "patterns of covariation of population-level inter-individual differences" (p. 504), while personality processes "offer potential explanations both for inter-individual differences in behavior and for intra-individual differences across situations" (p. 504), and personality development aims at "understanding enduring changes in individual trait levels across the lifespan, both normative changes as well as deviations from norms" (p. 505). While these authors observe a relative independence of research in the domains, they also see the domains as interdepended and call for an integration.

In the context of these interesting recent discussions on the dynamics of change in personality psychology, our research, which is clearly based on narrative interviews, appears to be positioned at one end of the spectrum that is concerned with the *within-person differences* in narrative identity development. Our interview evaluation has a decisive focus on the idiographic approach. Case studies of individual cases, or two cases in comparison, reconstruct the participants' dynamics of narrative identity construction, and could be even read as stand-alone idiographic portraits. Nevertheless, from the start of our research, we also used comprehensive questionnaires including psychometric scales such as for personality traits or well-being. The results of such mixed-method design (see also Chapter 4 in this volume) opens the opportunity to include individual profiles from diverse psychometric measures—and demonstrate our way for working toward the complementarity of nomothetic and idiographic approaches—which we also see as responding to Lamiell's (2019) sharp criticism of the exclusive use of nomothetic approaches in personality psychology. As noted by Hood and colleagues (2021, p. 100), we take care that, in visualizations such as scatter plots and boxplots for the case studies, the single cases can be identified in a way that "every dot represents a case with a name and a biography," but inter-individual differences and the comparison with the general trend of the groups to which the case belongs remains possible. "We can place diverse biographical trajectories in psychometric spaces, and have interpretations of individual trajectories reflect on these placements" (Hood et al., 2021, p. 100). Thus, we regard our research a demonstration of both the integration of nomothetic and idiographic approaches and of the dynamics and processes in the adult lifespan. Because religiosity, spirituality, and worldview are only addressed at the margins in the recent discussion of personality dynamics and processes,[2] we regard our research an innovative contribution to research in change and development of personality. The other chapters in this volume demonstrate,

---

2   An interesting exception is the study on self-transcendence and life stories of humanistic growth (Reischer et al., 2020) that has identified, in the stories of humanistic growth, among other themes the narrative theme of spiritual pluralism.

and this chapter argues, that also faith, religiosity, spirituality, and worldviews exhibit dynamics of change and development.

With a clear focus on narratives and narrative identity, our research has rather strong convergencies with the proposal of Pasupathi and Adler (2021) in their chapter in Rauthmann's (2021) *Handbook of Personality Dynamics and Processes*. Pasupathi and Adler (2021, p. 387) argue for the integration of "two dominant approaches in the study of narratives, identity and the life story, which we label structural and process approaches." Thereby, *structure* refers to the characteristics of the life story that constitute the person's narrative identity at a specific point in their lifetime, while *process* refers to the evolving capacities for the construction and reconstruction of their own life story. In their discussion, Pasupathi and Adler (2021) refer to McAdams's comprehensive work on narrative identity and the life story. They highlight McAdams's (2013; 2015) model of personality development that distinguishes three lines of development: the self as *actor*, as *agent*, and as *author*. They also emphasize how the three lines of development describe the increasing capacity of the "I" for constructing a "Me."

Pasupathi and Adler (2021, p. 390) however note that "questions remain about the processes by which people's life stories change to accommodate new experiences and roles." They also suggest in their proposal for integrating structure and process in future research in narrative psychology (p. 399) that "one of the critical future directions for this work is to employ longitudinal work that allows for the assessment of ways that situated storytelling may feed into the development of the life story and vice versa." With our third wave of interviews that are presented in this volume, we think that our research on faith development has something to offer.

The three lines of personality in McAdams's (2013) conceptualization roughly parallel the three sorts of data we have in our data base and to the corresponding levels of analysis: (a) data on personality, which in our data include not only the "big five" personality traits, but also a variety of other aspects, including, for example, mystical experiences or intolerance of ambiguity; these correspond to the self as actor; (b) data about worldview and meaning-making, which result from faith development evaluation (styles, types, and schemata) and are primarily related to agentic commitment to life projects; and (c) data on narrative identity, which result from the analysis of autobiographical narratives in the interviews and correspond to the self as author.

The contributions on the dynamics and processes in personality psychology discussed above indicate some correspondence with the structure of our data and our avenues of analysis to arrive at a multi-perspectival portrait of a person's faith in development. This also acknowledges the wisdom of Fowler's strong commitment to the assumption that human beings are "genetically potentiated" with a readiness to develop in faith (1981, p. 303).

The Current Formulation of the Structural-Developmental Model of Faith Development

The faith development model does not only serve as an integrative framework for interpreting a person's narrated change and development in faith (attending to the self as author), but the faith development model has at its core a clear structural focus, which, despite the considerable modifications, has profound roots in Fowler's (1981) theory and research. We continuously have modified and clarified the faith development model. After the advancement from stages of faith to religious styles (Streib, 2001; Streib & Keller, 2018), we have more recently introduced the conceptualization and investigation of development in terms of types (Streib et al., 2020; Streib, et al., 2023). In the remainder of this chapter, we focus on recent considerations—which begins with terminological clarifications.

Conceptual and Terminological Considerations

Faith and Religion

Conceptual and terminological clarity is needed to prevent the risk of misunderstanding our research, as if faith was identical with what is usually meant by, and many measures assess as, 'religiosity.' Faith in our understanding is neither defined by consent to a set of beliefs, nor by ritual observance (service attendance; prayer), nor by belonging to a religious organization, but rather by experiences of transcendence and the meaning we receive from being ultimately concerned (Streib & Hood, 2011; 2013). Thus, faith in this wide understanding denotes not only religious or spiritual, but also agnostic, non-theistic, and non-religious versions of meaning making.

Cantwell Smith (1963; 1979) defined faith as cross-religious human universal that is fundamentally distinct from (the contents of) belief and (organized) religion. And drawing on Cantwell Smith's conceptualization, Fowler (1981, p. 92–93) defined faith as:

> "People's evolved and evolving ways of experiencing self, others and world (as they construct them), as related to and affected by the ultimate conditions of existence (as they construct them), and shaping their lives' purposes and meanings, trusts and loyalties, in the light of the character of being, value and power determining the ultimate conditions of existence (as grasped in their operative images – conscious and unconscious – of them)."

This quote demonstrates Fowler's efforts to avoid the explicit terminology of a particular religious tradition, but instead establish a constructivist and rather formal and universal definition. The "ultimate conditions of existence" is not the language used in religious communities, but a term used in the philosophy of religion by theologians such as H. Richard Niebuhr or Paul Tillich. Interestingly, faith, according to Fowler's definition, originates in *experience*. And these experiences are qualified by their relation to the "ultimate conditions of existence." This echoes Luckmann's (1963; 1991) thought that "experiences of transcendence" are at the origin of religion. And Streib and Hood (2011; 2013) suggest including also Tillich's "ultimate concern" to the definition of religion.

Ironically, what has been discussed for the concept of 'faith,' does also apply for 'religion,' if defined widely in line with Streib and Hood's (2011; 2013) proposal. Transcendence is the essential feature and origin of religion, when understood, as in the social-phenomenological thought of Schütz and Luckmann (Schütz, 1932; Schütz & Luckmann, 1973; 1989), as experience of transcending everyday consciousness. It is especially what Luckmann (1991) later has called the experiences of "great transcendences" in which we are confronted with the extraordinary and largely unknown realms as experienced in mysticism, extasy, or vis a vi our own death. Such experiences of transcendence elicit responses using symbols and narratives for understanding and communication. Transcendence, it should be noted, is not necessarily defined by a relation to a heaven with God or gods (vertical transcendence), but transcendence can be non-theistic or non-religious—featuring horizontal transcendence (Hood, 2016; Hood et al., 2018; Hood & Streib, 2016; Kalton, 2000; Keller et al., 2018; Streib & Hood, 2011; Thurfjell et al., 2019). Fowler (1996) in one of his last major works devotes an entire chapter to a comparison of William James to faith development research. He notes that there is some truth to the view that faith development is a progressive gradual expansion of "once born" as opposed to James's more salutory "twice born." We will develop this more fully later in this chapter and also in Chapter 2.

Unfortunately, such wide definition of religion in the perspectives of Schütz and Luckmann, including Tillich's talk about the ultimate concern, are widely unfamiliar beyond the social-phenomenological and theological discourses. And unfortunately, neither Cantwell Smith's nor Fowler's concepts of faith did constitute a terminological tradition in the scientific study of religion: neither in religious studies, comparative religion, theology, religious education, the psychology of religion—not to speak of other areas in psychology. Therefore, we need to explain again and again our understanding of 'faith' as used in 'faith development.'

Considering 'Worldview'

For this explanation, we may consider another terminological option and relate 'faith' to 'worldview.' The model of religious styles (Streib, 2001; 2005; Streib et al., 2020), and Fowler's (1981) stages of faith alike, can be regarded models of *worldviews*. Eventually, 'worldview' may be regarded wider and more inclusive, since 'worldview' refers not only to religious and spiritual, but clearly also to agnostic, non-theistic, and non-religious versions of meaning construction. While the wide concept of faith—Cantwell Smith, Fowler and ourselves included—appear well integrated in the term worldview, questions arise whether 'worldview' is a term that is used precisely enough. From our reading, 'worldview' is far from well and consensually defined, however, and is often used without much conceptual precision and depth (as, for example, in 'worldview conflict'). Certainly, 'worldview' is much wider and more comprehensive than religion. Worldview is constituted by answers to big questions that address the most fundamental dimensions and ultimate horizons of human meaning making. But this may be also the reason why 'worldview' encounters problems of being used as a concept in psychology. Moreover, empirical studies that include perspectives on worldview do not constitute a coherent line of research in psychology.[3]

---

3   Here is a selection of empirical studies that use 'worldview' and may regarded contributions to worldview research in psychology: The studies by Nilsson and colleagues about the contrast between humanistic and normative worldviews of emerging adults (Nilsson, 2014a; 2014b; 2014c; Nilsson & Strupp-Levitsky, 2016); Gutierrez & Park's (2015) investigation of the change of worldview of emerging adults in the course of a semester; Goplen & Plant's (2015) study of "religious

Nevertheless, there *are* attempts for clarifying the concept of worldview in psychology. And we should consider the few, but remarkable suggestions for a psychology of worldviews: the models of Koltko-Rivera (2000; 2004) and of Johnson, Hill, and Cohen (2011), which Bou Malham (2017) in his dissertation has developed further and advanced into an initial development of a measure for worldview assumptions. Koltko-Rivera (2000; 2004) set the stage for an approach to a psychology of worldviews, which, in agglomeration of outstanding philosophical themes and discussions mainly of the past century, aims toward an integrative and coherent system of categories that characterize worldviews. The immense number of categories could be associated in seven groups (human nature, will, cognition, behavior, interpersonal, truth, and world and life). While Koltko-Rivera (2004) outlined a research agenda for personality and social psychology, in which he specified how certain worldview aspects can be investigated in social and personality psychology, a coherent research program that deserves the name "psychology of worldviews" seems to be a project too ambitious. In a comparable initiative, Johnson, Hill, and Cohen (2011) have modified, reduced and clarified Koltko-Rivera's categories, and they propose six categories that belong to the conceptualization of worldview: ontology, epistemology, semiotics, axiology, teleology, praxeology. This category system looks like an impressive proposal for Johnson and colleagues' project to integrate the study of culture and the study of religion. In Table 1.1, Johnson et al.'s (2011) typology of worldview categories, and also Koltko-Rivera's (2004) category groups (as associated by Johnson et al.) are included.

There are also parallels to the understanding of worldview by Taves and colleagues. Their publications (Taves, 2018a; 2018b; 2020; Taves & Asprem, 2019; Taves et al., 2018) powerfully advocate the inclusiveness of the term worldview, they suggest that using the term worldview may lead beyond the polarity of religion and non-religion, and they strongly invite comparative approaches to the variety of religions in the world (cf. Smart, 1983). Ultimately, under the label worldview, the discipline of religious studies should open up to, and change their name into, *worldview studies*. We regard this proposal as a bit ahead of time but commend the powerful initiative to bridge the gap between religion and non-religion in support of a wide understanding of the variety of ways of human meaning-making facing the big questions. Taves and Asprem (2019) define worldviews in "terms of big questions, such as (1) ontology (what exists, what is real), (2) epistemology (how do we know what is true), (3) axiology (what is the good that we should strive for), (4) praxeology (what actions should we take), and (5) cosmology (where do we come from and where are we going)." These big questions are added in the third column of Table 1.1, which presents the category systems of three approaches discussed here—together with the aspects used in the faith development framework.

When we now return to faith development theory and research with these categorizations that have emerged in the proposals for the (psychological) study of worldviews,

---

worldviews" and how it is protecting the meaning system through religious prejudice; a study investigating conspiracy theory as a specific cognitive style or worldview (Dagnall et al., 2015); or Kosmin & Keysar's (2013) study about the emergence of three distinct worldviews (religious, spiritual and secular) among American college students. While each study is interesting, these studies do not really constitute a coherent line of research.

we note striking parallels to a system of categories introduced by Fowler already in the early publications about the faith development model and the evaluation of the Faith Development Interview. Fowler did not claim his theory being about worldviews, but in his comparison of faith development theory and William James he sought to clarify the dynamic process of transformation of faith, mindful of what James (1985, p. 404) famously referred to as "overbeliefs." Fowler developed a system of categories, which he called the "aspects of faith" (Fowler, 1980; 1981); these aspects or "windows" to a person's faith are visualized in a heptagon (Fowler, 1980, p. 75), and the aspects are detailed in a comprehensive stage-aspect table (Fowler, 1981, pp. 244–245).

Table 1.1: Typologies of Worldview Categorization Compared to the Aspects of Faith

Koltko-Rivera (2004) (adjusted by Johnson et al., 2011)	Johnson et al. (2011)	Taves & Asprem (2019) (Big questions)	Aspects of faith (Fowler, 1981), revised by Streib et al. (2018)
World and life (ontology)	Ontology	ontology (what exists, what is real)	World coherence
Will (teleology)	Teleology	cosmology (where do we come from and where are we going)	
Moral behaviors; human nature (axiology)	Axiology	axiology (what is the good that we should strive for)	Morality; Locus of authority
Interpersonal (praxeology)	Praxeology	praxeology (what actions should we take)	
			Perspective-taking; Social horizon
Orientation behaviors (semiotics)	Semiotics		Symbolic function
Truth; cognition (epistemology)	Epistemology	epistemology (how do we know what is true)	[Form of Logic][4]

These aspects were labelled by Fowler *Form of logic, Role-taking, Form of moral judgment, Bounds of social awareness, Locus of authority, Form of world coherence,* and *Symbolic functioning.* In the fourth column in Table 1.1, we have included the six aspects that we suggest in our current edition of the *Coding Manual* (Streib & Keller, 2018).

---

4   The aspect *Form of logic* has been taken out in our revision of the *Coding Manual* (Streib & Keller, 2018), because we no longer regarded the cognitive domain as the motor of development and found Fowler's stretching of Piaget's descriptions of the development of logic questionable; instead, we intended to place more emphasis on perspective-taking as the first aspect.

Conclusion

Faith is about worldviews, and research about faith can be considered a subdivision of worldview research. Fowler's suggestion of *aspects* that correspond to foundational categories in worldview models and are relevant in a person's "experiences of self, others and world" (definition of faith in Fowler, 1981, p. 92) clearly support the relation of faith development to the study of worldviews. And this is support, once more, for a wide conceptualization of faith that is not confined to a set of beliefs of a particular religious tradition. But 'worldview,' at least at this state of conceptualization and research, may rather serve as an umbrella term to reaffirm a wide understanding of faith and inspire faith development theory and research to think and network outside the box.

Recent Clarifications of the Structural-developmental Model of Styles and Types

Our model of faith development in terms of religious styles is a modified advancement of Fowler's theory, and therefore includes commonalities and disagreements with Fowler's original model. This regards the question of what constitutes the differences between the various stages of faith (Fowler) resp. religious styles (Streib). In addition to disagreements with Fowler's model that were noted at the emergence of the religious styles perspective (Streib, 2001), there are more recent conceptual and empirical clarifications that should be noted here to explicate the conceptual basis for the chapters in this volume.

Summary of Religious Styles

In our current research we discern four styles that, from our experience, occur in adult samples. These can be characterized as follows:

- *The instrumental-reciprocal style* features an ethnocentric and authoritarian structure: challenges and critical questions are answered with reference to an (absolute) authority. Texts and prescriptions are interpreted literally and without the awareness of a semiotic difference in regard to narratives and symbols. Contingent occurrences such as disasters and catastrophes are understood as punishment by (an authoritarian) God or a merciless higher power. Questioning of values is responded with reference to an absolute validity of prescriptions and rules. Outgroups are excluded—with the potential risk to regard them as enemies or evil forces. Ethnocentric authoritarianism is the (potentially toxic) opposite to tolerance and to wisdom, especially to wisdom as xenosophia.
- *The mutual style* is clearly conventional, which means that challenging and critical questions are absent or ignored and, if ignorance is impossible, critical challenges are brushed aside with reference to the conventions of what one ought to believe and how to behave in one's own family, group, or tradition. Consent and harmony in one's own small lifeworld and "family" has top priority. The existence of ethnic, cultural or religious outgroups can be acknowledged, and treated with lower versions of tolerance such as the "permission conception" and the "coexistence conception" (Forst, 2013, pp. 26–29).

- *The individuative-reflective style* features individual autonomous rationality. Authority is located not in an unquestionable tradition, nor in the conventions of one's group, but in one's own judgment as an individual. Controversial questions of morality or world coherence are considered part of legal or scientific discourses in society in which the reflective individual participates. The social horizon is not limited to one's own group but includes societal and potentially global perspectives. The in-group-out-group divide can be integrated in models of ethnic, cultural, and religious pluralism. In case of conflicts, a model of tolerance and respect can be considered.
- *The dialogical style* builds upon the capacity for individuative reflection that characterizes the previous style, but it is ready to adopt a new mode of communication that features intellectual humility and mutual unprejudiced listening. This includes respect for the others' viewpoints and the readiness to revise one's own viewpoint. Thus, this style favors the wisdom that emerges from an open and unprejudiced encounter with the Unknown, Strange or Alien (that we call "xenosophia," see Streib, 2018; 2024; and text below in this chapter). Questions of morality can be appraoched with reference to an ethics that is regarded superior to the legal framework in one's present society such as human rights. Symbols and narratives are appreciated as powerful and, despite the full awareness of the semiotic difference, in a second naïveté (Ricoeur, 1960).

Structure and Structural Differences

We talk about the differences between these styles *in terms of structure* and need to explicate our understanding of structure. This can be done by pointing to agreements and disagreements with Fowler's conceptualization. Fowler understood the typological differences in faith as distinct versions of "operational structures of knowing and valuing in faith" (Fowler, 1981; 1982). This formula indicates Fowler's compromise between two understandings of 'structure.' On the one hand, Fowler made every endeavor to demonstrate agreement with Piaget's genetic epistemology and thus has modeled his definition of 'structure' along the lines of what Kohlberg and colleagues (1983) advocated a proper Piagetian understanding of structural difference. This included that development in the domains of morality and faith were conceptualized based on the assumptions that (a) cognitive operations and their development in a series of accommodations from sensorimotor and preoperational over concrete operational to formal operations were the fundament and motor of development in any developmental domain, and (b) that morality and faith and all of Fowler's additional aspects of faith are a priori assumed to be on the same structural (stage) level, thus forming what Kohlberg and colleagues (1983) called a "structural whole."

On the other hand, Fowler emphasized that faith is more than mere cognitive operations, namely a relation of trust and loyalty to "shared centers of value and power" (Fowler, 1981, p. 17). Consistently, Fowler suggested to move beyond Piaget and to understand 'knowing' as "constitutive knowing" (Fowler, 1980)—knowing that constitutes meaning. Faith development, if defined along these lines, is deemed to exceed the structures of genetic epistemology; and, as stated in Fowler's definition of faith (quoted above), faith is thought to be rooted in *experiences* of self, others and world; and it includes a person's constructions of (ultimate) concern for *values* and relation to *authority*. This is a clear difference to the Piaget/Kohlberg understanding of cognitive structures—and eventually a tension and contradiction in Fowler's work that, to our knowledge, he has never explicitly discussed, let alone solved. Instead, Fowler generally and throughout his work (Fowler, 2001) emphasized agreement with the concept of "structural wholes."

With the development of the religious styles perspective, the assumption of a "structural whole" was called into question (Streib, 2001) for several reasons. One reason is the variance in styles that a person may use in one and the same Faith Development Interview. Unless style assignments that are variant from the majority are regarded outliers and the variance in style assignments is averaged away, empirical investigation of faith development need to take account of the variance of styles in one interview—thus, we drop the "structural whole" as a priori assumption. In our evaluation of the Faith Development Interviews according to our revised *Manual* (Streib & Keller, 2018), we therefore use visualizations of all 25 single ratings in what we call style-aspect maps. These figures present both a general trend and a variety of styles. But the religious styles perspective continues Fowler's second version of understanding structure: The evaluation of religious styles does not attend to the contents and beliefs but discerns different operational structures of meaning-making and valuing, thus different styles of interpreting and responding to experiences, as outlined in the summaries of religious styles.

Type Construction

How can we assign an overall score to the Faith Development Interview, while not streamlining the variance in style assignments? Recently, we have suggested a solution: the construction of types (Streib et al., 2020). The type is the final score for an interview, but this type usually includes two or three style assignment percentages: one is predominant or substantial, the others are lower or marginal, but not ignored. What then is the difference between stages, styles and types? While Kohlberg and Fowler assume that a person can be on only one stage at a time ("structural whole" assumption; averaging all ratings in an interview), we came to the conclusion that a person in fact may have more than one style available, and we account for differences in style assignments. The type reflects the predominant or substantial style in an interview, while each type includes different percentage levels of other style assignments.

The type construction is important especially for statistic modeling. And we have used this type construction to the analysis of faith development in our current longitudinal three-wave sample (Streib et al., 2023). Results indicate that there is progressive faith development over time, but also regression to lower styles. Also, predictors and outcomes for faith development have been modeled—with the result that *openness to experience* (positively) and the Religious Schema subscale *truth of texts and teachings* (negatively) predict the change from a lower to a higher religious type over time, thus they are predictors for progressive faith development.

The type construction further allows addressing the question, whether there is variance between the *aspects* of faith. Thus, the types allow to put the "structural whole" assumption to the empirical test. We have analyzed in our longitudinal sample whether aspect-specific differences in type assignments may result in aspect-specific faith development over time. Results are presented in Chapter 5 in this volume and indicate at least preliminarily that faith development varies in the different aspects of faith, whereby development takes place in the aspect of perspective-taking and (somewhat lower) in social horizon, but not in the other aspects of faith. These results of course need to be repeated using larger samples, but these first results are promising, because they may yield new insight into the variety and the complexity of structural changes that contribute to a person's faith development.

We summarize this section and conclude: Faith development theory and research attend to structural differences in interpreting and communicating experiences of transcendence in terms of ultimate concern. Faith development regards structures (a) in experiencing and interacting with the world, with one's social environment, and with one's own self (perspective-taking; social horizon); (b) structures of being committed to (ultimate) values (morality) and how to relate to, and where to locate, (ultimate) authority (locus of authority); and (c) structures of how to understand symbolic, ritual and narrative representations (world coherence; symbolic function). Structures constitute the differences between styles. The differences in religious styles reflect structural differences between ethnocentric-authoritarian, mutual-conventional, individuative-reflective, or dialogical-xenosophic answers to the big questions that human beings face and the FDI questions elicit. These religious styles are hierarchically ordered.

While with the assumption of a hierarchical order, we are apparently in agreement with Fowler, but also with other developmental theories of the time, it needs to be explained in more detail how our assumptions about the direction and aim of faith development are different. Now we address this question and present new considerations about the direction and aim of faith development.

Direction and Aim of Faith Development

Logic of Development

The religious styles are hierarchically ordered with an obvious strong contrast that spans from the *ethnocentric-authoritarian* to the *dialogical-xenosophic* style. And if, as already noted in the summary description of the dialogical-xenosophic style, the preeminent feature of this highest style is intellectual humility and unprejudiced listening, this would suggest then that the logic of faith development could be described as a developmental line of action and interaction with an endpoint in intellectual humility and unprejudiced listening.

This is a more recent specification of our current state of the theory and should be noted in this chapter. And we can explain this by pointing out agreements and disagreements with what we think is a well-grounded model of a logic of development: Jürgen Habermas's (1983) reconstruction of the logic of development in Kohlberg's moral judgment model and in Selman's (1980) development of perspective-taking in light of his theory of discourse and universal pragmatics. The logic of development, according to Habermas (1983, see Table 4 on p. 166–167), runs from the *preconventional* (including "interaction controlled by authority" and "cooperation based on self-interest") through *conventional* (including "role behavior" and "normatively governed interaction") to *postconventional* action, which is "discourse." A parallel line of development is the change in social perspectives: it begins with an "egocentric perspective," runs over the "primary-group perspective" and the system's point of view in the "perspective of a collectivity," to lead on the postconventional level to a "principled perspective (prior to society)" and finally to the "procedural perspective," which is "ideal role taking" for Habermas.

While, regarding the lower styles or stages, we see clear parallels between Habermas's descriptions and our own model of religious styles, the difference regards the end point of postconventional action and perspective-taking. Habermas's description of the logic of development for moral judgment is tailored from the endpoint of the universal pragmatic in communicative action. And the transition from the conventional to the postconventional level is clearly expressed:

> "As he passes into the postconventional stage of interaction, the adult rises above the naïveté of everyday life practice. Having entered the quasi-natural social world with the transition to the conventional stage of interaction, he now leaves it behind. As he becomes a participant in discourse, the relevance of his experiential context pales, as do the normativity of existing orders and the objectivity of things and events. On the plane of metacommunication the only perspectives on the lived world left to him are retrospective ones. In the light of hypothetical claims to validity the world of existing states of affairs is theorized, that is, becomes a matter of theory, and the world of legitimately ordered relations is moralized, that is, becomes a matter of morality." (Habermas, 1983, p. 161–162)

This quote presents Habermas's understanding of a *decentration* from the life-world that is the necessary precondition for taking part in the ideal discourse for deciding validity claims in morality.[5]

While Habermas's proposal may be an inspiring contribution for defining the logic of development for moral judgment, it cannot be accepted for the conceptualization of faith development and the model of religious styles. Why? Faith is not the result of a communication about validity claims in a discourse of speakers who have risen above the naïveté of everyday life practice, but faith emerges from experiences of transcendence—nonordinary and mystical experiences included—that are interpreted in terms of ultimate concern. Faith, as Streib (1991, p. 113–118) has argued with reference to Ricoeur, is characterized by another understanding of decentration: the reader is taken away, is decentrated and assimilated to what a text, symbol, or narrative has to offer; This requires an attitude of "listening," of "hearkening," of an "active receptivity." Thus, the sharp contrast is between Habermas's emphasis on the *speaker* and *speaker perspectives*, on the one hand, and the *listener* and *listener perspectives*, on the other. And with the *listener perspective* a third reference point is introduced: something unknown before, something "given" by a text, symbol, or narrative. This change of perspectives regarding the postconventional level is in perfect accordance with the features of intellectual humility and unprejudiced listening that we suggested for describing the dialogical-xenosophic style. And it prepares the understanding of xenosophia.

---

5   Of course, Habermas also notes that "these dissociations make contextual application and kind of motivational anchoring of moral insights necessary" (p. 180) and call for "contextual sensitivity and prudence" (p. 181); but his project in this text is the contribution of a clear description of the logic of development for moral judgment.

Dialog and Xenosophia

We characterize the highest style not only as "dialogical," but as "xenosophic." Of course, we are aware that the term 'xenosophia' is used neither in psychology, nor in the scientific study of religion. Nevertheless, we continue to use it since more than a decade: the Religious Schema Scale (RSS; Streib et al., 2010) includes a subscale that we called *xenosophia/inter-religious dialog;* and a volume with research results from Germany published in 2018 has the title *Xenosophia and Religion. Biographical and Statistical Paths for a Culture of Welcome* (Streib & Klein, 2018). Our fascination with xenosophia emerged from considering Waldenfels's philosophy of the alien.[6]

What is indicated by the term 'xenosophia'? What does it add to the characterization of the style 5 as dialogical? Dialog should include an approach characterized by intellectual humility and operationalized, for example, in the Intellectual Humility Scale (Krumrei-Mancuso & Rouse, 2016), which includes the readiness to revise one's own viewpoint, and respect and esteem for the others' viewpoint. But xenosophia goes beyond dialog by introducing a different perspective in which the *other* is *not* the *known* such as the *other* in an out-group, but instead the *other* is the *Unknown, Strange,* and *Alien* (the Greek word, το ξένο translates in the Unknown, the Alien). And this clearly reflects the *unknowable* as in apophatic mysticism and in William James's work (see also Chapter 2 in this volume). This implies that xenosophia is more than compromising or negotiating with a well-identified or well-known other in an ideal-type process of communicative action (Habermas). Instead, xenosophia is based on a perspective non-hermeneutical reservation that is called *epoché* in phenomenological philosophy (Husserl). Thus, xenosophia is characterized by the openness for (the moment of) non-integrable perplexity and irritation. Xenosophia is not about understanding (grasping), but rather about receptivity (being touched) by something un-known (strange/alien). Xenosophia listens to and thus is open to responding to the "demand of the alien," as Waldenfels (1999) says. Xenosophia is the wisdom that emerges from an open and unprejudiced responsivity to the Unknown, Strange or Alien.

This xenosophic process, in which we afford (at least moments of) *epoché* and being touched by the Alien, may open an understanding of the efficiency of prejudice reduction by the encounter (contact hypothesis) with out-groups (Beelmann & Lutterbach, 2020; Francis et al., 2019; Paluck et al., 2018; Tropp et al., 2016), by watching a film about or by mentalizing (McLoughlin & Over, 2019) out-groups, by counter-intuitive intervention against stereotypes or in metacognitive experiments (Moritz et al., 2021; Moritz et al., 2018).[7] This may indicate that xenosophia is not a philosophical glass bead game for the highly educated and that it is not reserved to the generation of the old and wise, but rather a part of real-world wisdom that can be available also in young age.

---

6   Waldenfels's earlier texts (Waldenfels, 1990; 1997; 1999) unfortunately are not translated into English, but some more recent contributions on responsive phenomenology (Waldenfels, 2011; 2016a; 2016b; 2020) are. To our knowledge the term 'xenosophia' was first used and discussed in Nakamura's (2000) dissertation. For a discussion of Waldenfelds and a proposal of how to relate xenosophia to prejudice research and wisdom, see Streib (2018; 2024).

7   For a discussion of more results in prejudice research that may be related to xenosophia, see Streib (2018).

Outlook: Wisdom and Faith Development – Convergent Perspectives?

Theory and research in faith development attend to the changes of styles that the individual applies in interpreting the experience of others, self and world, in answering moral questions, and in finding meaning in their world. The structural differences in faith development thereby present a hierarchical order of styles. Thus, they answer the question about the direction and aim of development: after the styles of ethnocentric authoritarianism, conventional entanglement, and individuative reflection, there may emerge a style of openness for other worldviews, readiness for dialog, and xenosophia at the top of the hierarchy. This characterization of the aim of faith development in the highest style may indicate common ground between faith development theory and wisdom research. Does xenosophia constitute the bridge between faith development theory and wisdom research?

We suppose that xenosophia may be an interesting perspective to consider in research on wisdom. We regard xenosophia an integral aspect of wisdom. Thus, we may expect an interesting, perhaps controversial, but innovative discussion that has already begun in the Special Issue 2/2024 of the journal Possibility Studies & Society in response to the target article "Wisdom and the Other" (Streib, 2024). The conceptual idea that the highest style in faith development has indeed common ground with aspects of wisdom receives support, for example, from the discussion on *dialecticism*. Wisdom research, as noted by Grossmann (2018), needs to include models of dialectical thinking over the lifespan. To arrive at the most appropriate decision or judgment in face of contradictory claims and apparently insoluble options, dialectical thinking suggests the *integration* of contradictory claims on a higher level. Attention to *dialecticism* and to the development of dialectical thinking may be a common feature of both faith development theory and wisdom research. Also, the key role of intellectual humility and the importance of other aspects of perspectival meta-cognition (Grossmann et al., 2020) indicates common ground. This would suggest that our discussion should include a focus on dialectics and dialectical thinking (Grossmann, 2018; Paletz et al., 2018; Spencer-Rodgers et al., 2018) and on post-formal operations and the development of dialectical thinking (Basseches, 2005; Commons & Richards, 2003; Commons et al., 1984; Kallio, 2020; Kramer, 1983), and include the development of emotional complexity and the integration of cognition and emotion in development (Labouvie-Vief, 2015).

How does wisdom develop over the lifespan? Many of the contributions on postformal and dialectical thinking include, implicitly or explicitly, perspectives on the ontogenetic development of wisdom in adolescence and adulthood. Kramer (1983) for example, has developed an ontogenetic model that assumes a developmental sequence toward dialectical thinking, which is a passage through three levels: (a) *absolutistic*, (b) *relativistic*, and *dialectical* thinking that can be expected in late adolescence or emerging adulthood. Labouvie-Vief (2015, p. 102), to mention another example, has worked with a model that differentiates four levels of emotional complexity: pre-systemic, intra-systemic, inter-systemic, and integrated. However, a coherent model of the development of wisdom appears to be an unfinished project so far.

Given our concern with faith development and stage theories, it is noteworthy that Erikson's (1959a; 1959b; 1982) model of psychosocial development is frequently mentioned as one of the early contributions to the ontogeny of wisdom (see, for example, Glück, 2019). As Ardelt and colleagues (2019, p. 152) note, Erikson's model may provide "a framework for the possibility of wisdom development without an over-reliance on cognitive abilities. In his model, even those with lower levels of cognitive comprehension might successfully resolve the eight psychosocial crises that ultimately lead to wisdom." While we find this model of development inspiring, we wonder why wisdom should be reserved for old age or for exceptional exemplars (Glück, 2019).

Finally, as we agree with Ardelt and colleagues (2019, p. 155), we need more longitudinal studies "that analyze in greater detail how and under which circumstances individuals develop wisdom and how wisdom can be nurtured in childhood, adolescence, and adulthood." In the meantime, we may, with all due modesty, note that we are engaged in long-term longitudinal research, and may regard our qualitative and quantitative data a contribution to wisdom research—to the extent, that results from content and narrative analyses of our interviews, from the evaluation for religious styles, and from questionnaire data yield new insight in the development not only of faith, but of wisdom in the adult life span.

References

Ardelt, M., Pridgen, S., & Nutter-Pridgen, K. L. (2019). Wisdom as a personality type. In J. Glück & R. J. Sternberg (Eds.), *The Cambridge handbook of wisdom* (pp. 144–161). Cambridge University Press. https://doi.org/10.1017/9781108568272.008

Basseches, M. (2005). The development of dialectical thinking as an approach to integration. *Integral Review, 1.* https://www.researchgate.net/publication/26507960

Baumert, A., Schmitt, M., Perugini, M., Johnson, W., Blum, G., Borkenau, P., Costantini, G., Denissen, J. J. A., Fleeson, W., Grafton, B., Jayawickreme, E., Kurzius, E., MacLeod, C., Miller, L. C., Read, S. J., Roberts, B., Robinson, M. D., Wood, D., Wrzus, C., & Mõttus, R. (2017). Integrating personality structure, personality process, and personality development. *European Journal of Personality, 31(5),* 503–528. https://doi.org/10.1002/per.2115

Beelmann, A., & Lutterbach, S. (2020). Preventing prejudice and promoting intergroup relations. In L. T. Benuto, M. P. Duckworth, A. Masuda, & W. O'Donohue (Eds.), *Prejudice, stigma, privilege, and oppression. A behavioral health handbook* (pp. 309–326). https://doi.org/10.1007/978-3-030-35517-3_16

Bou Malham, P. (2017). *Investigating the structure and functions of worldview assumptions* [Ph.D. Thesis, University of Oregon].

Cantwell Smith, W. (1963). *The meaning and end of religion.* Fortress Press 1991.

Cantwell Smith, W. (1979). *Faith and belief.* Princeton University Press.

Commons, M. L., & Richards, F. A. (2003). Four postformal stages. In J. Demick & C. Andreoletti (Eds.), *Handbook of Adult Development* (pp. 199–220). Springer.

Commons, M. L., Richards, F. A., & Armon, C. (Eds.). (1984). *Beyond formal operations.* Praeger.

Corr, P. J., & Matthews, G. (Eds.). (2020). *The Cambridge handbook of personality psychology* (2 ed.). Cambridge University Press. https://doi.org/10.1017/9781108264822

Dagnall, N., Drinkwater, K., Parker, A., Denovan, A., & Parton, M. (2015). Conspiracy theory and cognitive style: A worldview. *Frontiers in Psychology*, 6, Article 206. https://doi.org/10.3389/fpsyg.2015.00206

Erikson, E. H. (1959a). Growth and crisis of the healthy personality. In *Identity and the life cycle. Selected papers by Erik H. Erikson* (3rd ed., pp. 50–100). International Universities Press, Inc.

Erikson, E. H. (1959b). The problem of ego identity. In *Identity and the life cycle. Selected papers by Erik H. Erikson* (3rd ed., pp. 101–171). International Universities Press, Inc.

Erikson, E. H. (1982). *The life cycle completed*. W.W. Norton.

Forst, R. (2013). *Toleration in conflict: Past and present*. Cambridge University Press.

Fowler, J. W. (1980). Faith and the structuring of meaning. In C. Brusselmans (Ed.), *Toward moral and religious maturity. First international conference on moral and religious development* (pp. 51–85). Silver Burdett Company.

Fowler, J. W. (1981). *Stages of faith. The psychology of human development and the quest for meaning*. Harper&Row.

Fowler, J. W. (1982). Stages in faith and adults' life cycles. In K. Stokes (Ed.), *Faith development in the adult life cycle* (pp. 178–207). W.H. Sadlier.

Fowler, J. W. (1996). *Faithful change: The personal and public challenges of postmodern life*. Abingdom Press.

Fowler, J. W. (2001). Faith development theory and the postmodern challenges. *International Journal for the Psychology of Religion*, 11(3), 159–172. https://doi.org/10.1207/S15327582IJPR1103_03

Francis, L. J., McKenna, U., & Arweck, E. (2019). Countering anti-Muslim attitudes among Christian and religiously unaffiliated 13- to 15-year-old students in England and Wales: Testing the contact hypothesis. *Journal of Beliefs & Values*, 1–16. https://doi.org/10.1080/13617672.2019.1653062

Glück, J. (2019). The development of wisdom during adulthood. In R. J. Sternberg & J. Glück (Eds.), *The Cambridge handbook of wisdom* (pp. 323–346). Cambridge University Press. https://doi.org/10.1017/9781108568272.016

Goplen, J., & Plant, E. A. (2015). A religious worldview: Protecting one's meaning system through religious prejudice. *Personality and Social Psychology Bulletin*, 41(11), 1474–1487. https://doi.org/10.1177/0146167215599761

Grossmann, I. (2018). Dialecticism across the lifespan. Toward a deeper understanding of the ontogenetic and cultural factors influencing dialectical thinking and emotional experience. In J. Spencer-Rodgers & K. Peng (Eds.), *The psychological and cultural foundations of East Asian cognition: Contradiction, change, and holism* (pp. 135–180). Oxford University Press. https://doi.org/10.1093/oso/9780199348541.003.0005

Grossmann, I., Weststrate, N. M., Ardelt, M., Brienza, J. P., Dong, M. X., Ferrari, M., Fournier, M. A., Hu, C. S., Nusbaum, H. C., & Vervaeke, J. (2020). The science of wisdom in a polarized world: Knowns and unknowns. *Psychological Inquiry*, 31(2), 103–133. https://doi.org/10.1080/1047840x.2020.1750917

Gutierrez, I. A., & Park, C. L. (2015). Emerging adulthood, evolving worldviews: How life events impact college students' developing belief systems. *Emerging Adulthood*, 3(2), 85–97. https://doi.org/10.1177/2167696814544501

Habermas, J. (1983). Moral consciousness and communicative action (C. Lenhardt & S. Weber Nicholsen, Trans.). In J. Habermas (Ed.), Moral consciousness and communicative action (pp. 116–195). MIT Press 1990.

Hood, R. W. Hr. (1975). The construction and preliminary validation of a measure of reported mystical experience. *Journal for the Scientific Study of Religion*, 14, 29–41. https://doi.org/10.2307/1384454

Hood, R. W. Jr. (2016). Mysticism and hypo-egoicism. In K. W. Brown & M. R. Leary (Eds.), *The Oxford handbook of hypo-egoic phenomena*. Oxford University Press. https://doi.org/10.1093/oxfordhb/9780199328079.013.19

Hood, R. W., Hill, P. C., & Spilka, B. (2018). *The psychology of religion: An empirical approach, 5th ed.* Guilford Press.

Hood, R. W. Jr., & Streib, H. (2016). "Fuzziness" or semantic diversification? Insights about the semantics of "spirituality" in cross-cultural comparison (Conclusion). In H. Streib & R. W. Hood (Eds.), *Semantics and psychology of "spirituality". A cross-cultural analysis* (pp. 153–161). Springer International Publishing Switzerland. https://doi.org/10.1007/978-3-319-21245-6_10

Hood, R. W. Jr., Streib, H., & Keller, B. (2021). What is deconversion? Critiques and current conceptualizations from a faith developmental perspective. In H. Streib, B. Keller, R. Bullik, A. Steppacher, C. F. Silver, M. Durham, S. B. Barker, & R. W. Hood Jr. (Eds.), *Deconversion revisited. Biographical studies and psychometric analyses ten years later*. Vandenhoeck & Ruprecht.

James. W. (1985). *The varieties of religious experience: A study in human nature*. Harvard Universiy Press. (Original work published 1902).

Johnson, K. A., Hill, E. D., & Cohen, A. B. (2011). Integrating the study of culture and religion: Toward a psychology of worldview. *Social and Personality Psychology Compass*, 5(3), 137–152. https://doi.org/10.1111/j.1751-9004.2010.00339.x

Kallio, E. K. (Ed.). (2020). *Development of adult thinking. Interdisciplinary perspectives on cognitive development and adult learning*. Routledge. https://doi.org/10.4324/9781315187464

Kalton, M. C. (2000). Green spirituality: Horizontal transcendence. In P. Young-Eisendrath & M. E. Miller (Eds.), *The psychology of mature spirituality: Integrity, wisdom, transcendence* (pp. 187–200). Routledge.

Keller, B., Bullik, R., Klein, C., & Swanson, S. B. (2018). Profiling atheist world views in different cultural contexts: Developmental trajectories and accounts. *Psychology of Religion and Spirituality*, 10(3), 229–243. https://doi.org/doi:10.1037/rel0000212

Keller, B., Klein, C., Swhajor-Biesemann, A., & Streib, H. (2016). Mapping the varieties of "spiritual" biographies. In H. Streib & R. W. Hood (Eds.), *Semantics and psychology of "spirituality". A cross-cultural analysis* (pp. 275–280). Springer International Publishing Switzerland. https://doi.org/10.1007/978-3-319-21245-6_17

Klein, C., Silver, C. F., Coleman, T. J., Streib, H., & Hood, R. W. Jr. (2016). "Spirituality" and mysticism. In H. Streib & R. W. Hood (Eds.), *Semantics and psychology of "spirituality". A cross-cultural analysis* (pp. 165–187). Springer International Publishing. https://doi.org/10.1007/978-3-319-21245-6_11

Kohlberg, L., Levine, C., & Hewer, A. (1983). The current formulation of the theory. In L. Kohlberg (Ed.), *Essays on moral development, Vol. II. The psychology of moral development* (pp. 212–319). Harper&Row 1984.

Koltko-Rivera, M. E. (2000). *The worldview assessment instrument (WAI): The development and preliminary validation of an instrument to assess world view components relevant to counseling and psychotherapy* [Ph.D. Thesis, New York University, School of Education]. New York.

Koltko-Rivera, M. E. (2004). The psychology of worldviews. *Review of General Psychology*, 8(1), 3–58. https://doi.org/10.1037/1089-2680.8.1.3

Kosmin, B. A., & Keysar, A. (2013). Religious, spiritual and secular: The emergence of three distinct worldviews among American college students. A report based on the ARIS 2013 National College Student Survey. http://commons.trincoll.edu/aris/publi cations/2013-2/2013-2/

Kramer, D. A. (1983). Post-formal operations? A need for further conceptualization. *Human Development*, 26, 91–105.

Krumrei-Mancuso, E. J., & Rouse, S. V. (2016). The development and validation of the comprehensive intellectual humility scale. *Journal of Personality Assessment*, 98(2), 209–221. https://doi.org/10.1080/00223891.2015.1068174

Kuper, N., Modersitzki, N., Phan, L., & Rauthmann, J. F. (2021). The dynamics, processes, mechanisms, and functioning of personality: An overview of the field. *British Journal of Psychology*, 112(1), 1–51. https://doi.org/10.1111/bjop.12486

Labouvie-Vief, G. (2015). *Integrating emotions and cognition throughout the lifespan*. Springer International Publishing. https://doi.org/10.1007/978-3-319-09822-7

Lamiell, J. T. (2019). *Psychology's misuse of statistics and persistent dismissal of its critics*. Palgrave Macmillan/Springer International Publishing. https://doi.org/10.1007/978-3-030-12131-0

Luckmann, T. (1963). *Das Problem der Religion in der modernen Gesellschaft. Institution, Person und Weltanschauung*. Rombach.

Luckmann, T. (1991). *Die unsichtbare Religion*. Suhrkamp.

McAdams, D. P. (2013). The psychological self as actor, agent, and author. *Perspectives on Psychological Science*, 8(3), 272–295. https://doi.org/10.1177/1745691612464657

McAdams, D. P. (2015). Three lines of personality development. A conceptual itinerary. *European Psychologist*, 20(4), 252–264. https://doi.org/10.1027/1016-9040/a000236

McLoughlin, N., & Over, H. (2019). Encouraging children to mentalise about a perceived outgroup increases prosocial behaviour towards outgroup members. *Developmental Science*, 22(3), Article e12774. https://doi.org/10.1111/desc.12774

Moritz, S., Ahmed, K., Krott, N. R., Ohls, I., & Reininger, K. M. (2021). How Education and Metacognitive Training May Ameliorate Religious Prejudices: A Randomized Controlled Trial. *International Journal for the Psychology of Religion*, 31(2), 121–137. https://doi.org/10.1080/10508619.2020.1815994

Moritz, S., Lasfar, I., Reininger, K. M., & Ohls, I. (2018). Fostering mutual understanding among Muslims and Non-Muslims through counter-stereotypical information: An educational vs. metacognitive approach. *International Journal for the Psychology of Religion*, 28(2), 103–120. https://doi.org/10.1080/10508619.2018.1431759

Nakamura, Y. (2000). *Xenosophie: Bausteine für eine Theorie der Fremdheit [Xenosophia. Building blocks for a theory of alienness]*. Wissenschaftliche Buchgesellschaft.

Nilsson, A. (2014a). Humanistic and normativistic worldviews: Distinct and hierarchically structured. *Personality and Individual Differences, 64*, 135–140. https://doi.org/10.1016/j.paid.2014.02.037

Nilsson, A. (2014b). A non-reductive science of personality, character, and well being must take the person's worldview into account. *Frontiers in Psychology, 5*, Article 961. https://doi.org/10.3389/fpsyg.2014.00961

Nilsson, A. (2014c). Personality psychology as the integrative study of traits and worldviews. *New Ideas in Psychology, 32*, 18–32. https://doi.org/10.1016/j.newideapsych.2013.04.008

Nilsson, A., & Strupp-Levitsky, M. (2016). Humanistic and normativistic metaphysics, epistemology, and conative orientation: Two fundamental systems of meaning. *Personality and Individual Differences, 100*, 85–94. https://doi.org/10.1016/j.paid.2016.01.050

Osgood, C. E. (1960). Cognitive dynamics in the conduct of human affairs. *Public Opinion Quarterly, 24*(2), 341–365.

Osgood, C. E. (1962). Studies on the generality of affective meaning systems. *American Anthropologist, 17*(1), 10–28.

Osgood, C. E. (1969). The nature and measurement of meaning. In J. G. Snider & C. E. Osgood (Eds.), *Semantic differential techinque: A sourcebook* (pp. 3–41). Aldine, 2nd printing 1972.

Olvia, E., Atherton, M., Brent, Donnellan & Robins, R. W. (2020). Development of personality across the life span. In Corr. P. & Matthews, G. (Eds.) (2020). *The Cambridge handbook of personality psychology*, (2nd. Ed). (pp. 169–182). Cambridge University Press.

Paletz, S. B. F., Bogue, K., Miron-Spektor, E., & Spencer-Rodgers, J. (2018). Dialectical thinking and creativity from many perspectives: Contradiction and tension. In J. Spencer-Rodgers & K. Peng (Eds.), *The Psychological and cultural foundations of East Asian cognition: Contradiction, change, and holism* (pp. 267–308). Oxford University Press. https://doi.org/10.1093/oso/9780199348541.001.0001

Paluck, E. L., Green, S. A., & Green, D. P. (2018). The contact hypothesis re-evaluated. *Behavioural Public Policy*, 1–30. https://doi.org/10.1017/bpp.2018.25

Pasupathi, M., & Adler, J. M. (2021). Narrative, identity, and the life story: Structural and process approaches. In J. F. Rauthmann (Ed.), *The Handbook of Personality Dynamics and Processes* (pp. 387–403). Academic Press. https://doi.org/10.1016/B978-0-12-813995-0.00016-9

Rauthmann, J. F. (Ed.). (2021). *The Handbook of Personality Dynamics and Processes*. Academic Press. https://doi.org/10.1016/C2017-0-00935-7

Reischer, H. N., Roth, L. J., Villarreal, J. A., & McAdams, D. P. (2020). Self-transcendence and life stories of humanistic growth among late-midlife adults. *Journal of Personality, 89*(2), 305–324. https://doi.org/10.1111/jopy.12583

Revelle, W., & Wilt, J. (2021). The history of dynamic approaches to personality. In J. F. Rauthmann (Ed.), *The handbook of personality dynamics and processes* (pp. 3–31). Academic Press. https://doi.org/10.1016/B978-0-12-813995-0.00001-7

Ricoeur, P. (1960). *The symbolism of evil* (E. Buchanan, Trans.). Beacon Press 1969.

Schütz, A. (1932). *The phenomenology of the social world [Der sinnhafte Aufbau der sozialen Welt, Engl.]*. Northwestern University Press 1967.

Schütz, A., & Luckmann, T. (1973). *The structures of the life-world, Vol.1*. Northwestern University Press.

Schütz, A., & Luckmann, T. (1989). *The structures of the life-world, Vol.2*. Northwestern University Press.

Selman, R. L. (1980). The growth of personal understanding: Developmental and clinical aspects. Academic Press.

Smart, N. (1983). *Worldviews: Crosscultural explorations of human beliefs*. Scribner's.

Spencer-Rodgers, J., Anderson, E., Ma-Kellams, C., Wang, C., & Peng, K. (2018). What is dialectical thinking? Conceptualization and measurement. In J. Spencer-Rodgers & K. Peng (Eds.), *The psychological and cultural foundations of east asian cognition: Contradiction, change, and holism* (pp. 1–34). Oxford University Press. https://doi.org/10.1093/oso/9780199348541.001.0001 .

Streib, H. (1991). Hermeneutics of metaphor, symbol and narrative in faith development theory. Peter Lang. https://pub.uni-bielefeld.de/download/1861851/2315007/Streibo1.pdf

Streib, H. (1998). Teilprojekt ‚Biographieverläufe in christlich-fundamentalistischen Milieus und Gruppen'. In Deutscher Bundestag, Enquete-Kommission „Sogenannte Sekten und Psychogruppen" (Ed.), *Endbericht der Enquête-Kommission ‚Sogenannte Sekten und Psychogruppen'. Neue religiöse und ideologische Gemeinschaften und Psychogruppen in der Bundesrepublik Deutschland* (pp. 416–430). Deutscher Bundestag.

Streib, H. (1999). Biographies in Christian Fundamentalist Milieus and Organizations (Part of the research project on "Drop-outs, converts and believers: Contrasting biographical analyses of why individuals join, have a career and stay in, or leave religious/ideological contexts or groups"). In Deutscher Bundestag, Referat Öffentlichkeitsarbeit (Ed.), *Final Report of the Enquête Commission on 'So-called Sects and Psychogroups'. New Religious and Ideological Communities and Psychogroups in the Federal Republic of Germany* (pp. 402–414). Deutscher Bundestag.

Streib, H. (2001). Faith development theory revisited: The religious styles perspective. *International Journal for the Psychology of Religion, 11*(3), 143–158. https://doi.org/10.1207/S15327582IJPR1103_02

Streib, H. (2003a). Religion as a question of style: Revising the structural differentiation of religion from the perspective of the analysis of the contemporary pluralistic-religious situation. *International Journal for Practical Theology, 7*(1), 1–22.

Streib, H. (2003b). Variety and complexity of religious development: Perspectives for the 21st Century. In P. H. M. P. Roelofsma, J. M. T. Corveleyn, & J. W. Van Saane (Eds.), *One hundred years of psychology of religion. Issues and trends in a century long quest* (pp. 123–138). Free University Press.

Streib, H. (2005). Faith development research revisited: Accounting for diversity in structure, content, and narrativity of faith. *International Journal for the Psychology of Religion, 15*(2), 99–121. https://doi.org/10.1207/s15327582ijpr1502_1

Streib, H. (2013). Conceptualisation et mesure du développement religieux en termes de schémas et de styles religieux – Résultats et nouvelles considérations. In P.-Y. Brandt

& J. M. Day (Eds.), *Psychologie du développement religieux: questions classiques et perspectives contemporaines* (pp. 39–76). Labor et Fides.

Streib, H. (2018). What is xenosophia? Philosophical contributions to prejudice research. In H. Streib & C. Klein (Eds.), *Xenosophia and religion: Biographical and statistical paths for a culture of welcome* (pp. 3–21). Springer International Publishing Switzerland. https://doi.org/10.1007/978-3-319-74564-0_1 (post-print at: https://doi.org/10.31234/osf.io/dfx5j)

Streib, H. (2021). Leaving religion: Deconversion. *Current Opinion in Psychology*, 40, 139–144. https://doi.org/10.1016/j.copsyc.2020.09.007 (post-print at: https://doi.org/10.31234/osf.io/r46qt)

Streib, H. (2024). Wisdom and the Other: Responsiveness in development from the egocentric to xenocentric style. *Possibility Studies & Society* 2(2). https://doi.org/10.1177/27538699231205016 (pre-print: https://doi.org/10.31234/osf.io/q5ey2)

Streib, H., & Chen, Z. J. (2021). Evidence for the brief Mysticism Scale: Psychometric properties, and moderation and mediation effects in predicting spiritual self-identification. *International Journal for the Psychology of Religion*, 31(3), 165–175. https://doi.org/10.1080/10508619.2021.1899641 (post-print at: https://doi.org/10.31234/osf.io/6bx2s)

Streib, H., Chen, Z. J., & Hood, R. W. Jr. (2020). Categorizing people by their preference for religious styles: Four types derived from evaluation of faith development interviews. *International Journal for the Psychology of Religion*, 30(2), 112–127. https://doi.org/10.1080/10508619.2019.1664213 (post-print at: https://doi.org/10.31234/osf.io/d3kbr)

Streib, H., Chen, Z. J., & Hood, R. W. Jr. (2023). Faith development as change in religious types: Results from three-wave longitudinal data with faith development interviews. *Psychology of Religion and Spirituality*, 15(2), 298–307. https://doi.org/10.1037/rel0000440 (post-print at: https://doi.org/10.31234/osf.io/qrcb2)

Streib, H., & Hood, R. W. Jr. (2011). "Spirituality" as privatized experience-oriented religion: Empirical and conceptual perspectives. *Implicit Religion*, 14(4), 433–453. https://doi.org/10.1558/imre.v14i4.433

Streib, H., & Hood, R. W. Jr. (2013). Modeling the religious field: Religion, spirituality, mysticism and related world views. *Implicit Religion*, 16(3), 137–155. https://doi.org/10.1558/imre.v16i2.133

Streib, H., & Hood, R. W. Jr. (Eds.). (2016). *Semantics and psychology of spirituality. A cross-cultural analysis.* Springer International Publishing Switzerland. https://doi.org/10.1007/978-3-319-21245-6

Streib, H., Hood, R. W. Jr., Keller, B., Csöff, R.-M., & Silver, C. (2009). *Deconversion. Qualitative and quantitative results from cross-cultural research in Germany and the United States of America.* Vandenhoeck & Ruprecht. https://doi.org/10.13109/9783666604393

Streib, H., Hood, R. W. Jr., & Klein, C. (2010). The religious schema scale: Construction and initial validation of a quantitative measure for religious styles. *International Journal for the Psychology of Religion*, 20(3), 151–172. https://doi.org/10.1080/10508619.2010.481223

Streib, H., & Keller, B. (2018). *Manual for the assessment of religious styles in faith development interviews (Fourth, revised edition of the manual for faith development research).* Bielefeld University/readbox unipress. https://doi.org/10.4119/unibi/2920987

Streib, H., Keller, B., Bullik, R., Steppacher, A., Silver, C. F., Durham, M., Barker, S. B., & Hood, R. W. Jr. (2022). *Deconversion revisited. Biographical studies and psychometric analyses ten years later*. Brill Germany/Vandenhoeck & Ruprecht. https://doi.org/10.13109/9783666568688

Streib, H., & Klein, C. (Eds.). (2018). *Xenosophia and religion: Biographical and statistical paths for a culture of welcome*. Springer International Publishing Switzerland. https://doi.org/10.1007/978-3-319-74564-0

Streib, H., Klein, C., Keller, B., & Hood, R. W. Jr. (2021). The Mysticism Scale as measure for subjective spirituality: New results with Hood's M-scale and the development of a short form. In A. L. Ai, K. A. Harris, R. F. Paloutzian, & P. Wink (Eds.), *Assessing spirituality in a diverse world* (pp. 467–491). Springer Nature Switzerland. https://doi.org/10.1007/978-3-030-52140-0_19 (post-print at: https://doi.org/10.31234/osf.io/gwj2c)

Taves, A. (2018a). Finding and articulating meaning in secular experience. In D. Fleming, E. Leven, & U. Riegel (Eds.), *Religious experience*. Waxmann.

Taves, A. (2018b). What is nonreligion? On the virtues of a meaning systems framework for studying nonreligious and religious worldviews in the context of everyday life. *Secularism & Nonreligion, 7*, Article 9. https://doi.org/10.5334/snr.104

Taves, A. (2020). From religious studies to worldview studies. *Religion, 50*(1), 137–147. https://doi.org/10.1080/0048721x.2019.1681124

Taves, A., & Asprem, E. (2019). Scientific worldview studies: A programmatic proposal. In A. Klostergaard Petersen, I. S. Gilhus, L. H. Martin, J. S. Jensen, & J. Sørensen (Eds.), *Evolution, cognition, and the history of religion: A new synthesis. Festschrift in honour of Armin W. Geertz* (pp. 297–308). Brill.

Taves, A., Asprem, E., & Ihm, E. (2018). Psychology, meaning making, and the study of worldviews: Beyond religion and non-religion. *Psychology of Religion and Spirituality, 10*(3), 207–217. https://doi.org/10.1037/rel0000201

Thurfjell, D., Rubow, C., Remmel, A., & Ohlsson, H. (2019). The relocation of transcendence using Schutz to conceptualize the nature experiences of secular people. *Nature + Culture, 14*(2), 190–214. https://doi.org/10.3167/nc.2019.140205

Tropp, L. R., Mazziotta, A., & Wright, S. C. (2016). Recent developments in intergroup contact research: Affective processes, group status, and contact valence. In C. G. Sibley & F. K. Barlow (Eds.), *The Cambridge handbook of the psychology of prejudice* (pp. 463–480). Cambridge University Press. https://doi.org/10.1017/9781316161579.020

Waldenfels, B. (1990). *Der Stachel des Fremden [The sting of the alien]*. Suhrkamp.

Waldenfels, B. (1997). *Topographie des Fremden [Topography of the alien]*. Suhrkamp.

Waldenfels, B. (1999). Der Anspruch des Fremden [The demand of the alien]. In R. Breuninger (Ed.), *Andersheit – Fremdheit – Toleranz* (pp. 31–51). Humboldt-Studienzentrum.

Waldenfels, B. (2011). *Phenomenology of the alien: Basic concepts [Grundmotive einer Phänomenologie des Fremden, Suhrkamp, 2006, transl. by A. Kozin and T. Stähler]*. Northwestern University Press.

Waldenfels, B. (2012). Responsive ethics. In D. Zahavi (Ed.), *The Oxford handbook of contemporary phenomenology* (pp. 423–441). Oxford University Press. https://doi.org/10.1093/oxfordhb/9780199594900.013.0021

Waldenfels, B. (2016a). Paradoxes of representing the alien in ethnography. In B. Leistle (Ed.), *Anthropology and alterity: Responding to the other* (pp. 45–71). Routledge. https://doi.org/10.4324/9781315616759 (German original published 1999 by Suhrkamp Verlag)

Waldenfels, B. (2016b). The birth of ἦθος out of πάθος. Paths of responsive phenomenology. *Graduate Faculty Philosophy Journal, 37*(1), 133–149. https://doi.org/10.5840/gfpj20163716

Waldenfels, B. (2020). Responsivity and co-responsivity from a phenomenological point of view. *Studia Phänomenologica, 20*, 341–355. https://doi.org/10.5840/studphaen20202015

Chapter 2
A Common Core? Ideographic and Nomothetic Evidence for Mystical Experience in Relationship to Religious Styles & Types

Ralph W. Hood, Jr. & Heinz Streib[1]

Abstract *In this chapter we explore both empirical and conceptual reasons for a dialogue between faith development research and other psychologies. Beginning with the cooperative research on deconversion, two established research programs, one on mysticism in the USA and one on faith development in Germany intermingled. Based upon the first use of the religious-spiritual binary in Germany we found that deconverts were more likely to identify as more spiritual than religious and to be characterized by an openness to experience in contrast to those who remained in tradition. Including mysticism in all of our subsequent research indicated that mysticism was a good predictor of both religious style and was a good measure of spirituality that was developed prior to the binary and independent of faith development research. Mysticism as integral to many psychologies, not simply faith development, reveals its importance in facilitating a dialogue in which faith development research may enrich other psychology programs. However, to do so it must challenge worldviews that in terms of religious styles and types are inadequate to the task. We apply this dilemma of worldview critique to our own work and that of mainstream psychology and the wisdom of mixed methods research that cannot be satisfied with only nomothetic generalization that discount the uniqueness of persons.*

Keywords: *nomothetic; introvertive mysticism; extrovertive mysticism; interpretation; worldview*

---

1   R. W. Hood, Jr., University of Tennessee at Chattanooga, USA, E-mail: ralph-hood@utc.edu; H. Streib, Bielefeld University, Germany. © Heinz Streib, Ralph W. Hood Jr. (eds.): Faith in Development. Mixed-Method Studies on Worldviews and Religious Styles, First published in 2024 by Bielefeld University Press, Bielefeld, https://doi.org/10.14361/9783839471234-004

Part A: Conceptual & Methodological Perspectives

In this chapter the focus is upon the conceptual and empirical claim that worldview, not necessarily Christian, is an appropriate way to provide a conversation that places faith styles research in dialogue with other empirical traditions in psychology, especially mysticism. The focus upon worldviews in the context of advances in Fowler's (1981) stage theory is not to claim that research on faith styles is outside the penumbra of a developmental model that was embedded in what is ultimately a Christian worldview. This chapter will place advances in faith development research in dialogue with results from the study of worldviews many of which seek to include mystical experiences, some in religious, others in secular terms. Fowler's own Christian proclivities are acknowledged but not as a necessary or even to be preferred worldview outcome of faith development (Koltko-Rivera, 2004). Our mixed methods approach since our first book on deconversion (Streib et al., 2009) has consistently employed nomothetic (aggregated) and idiographic (case studies) data, but mysticism has never been an explicit part of the Faith Development Interview, whether in terms of Fowler's stage theory or in terms of Streib's styles theory. However, a fortuitous meeting in Chattanooga resulted in the inclusion of the study of spirituality in faith development research (Streib, 2005), therefore, we have results about the binary spiritual/religion in our first book on deconversion (Streib et al., 2009). We were the first to use the now popular binary in Germany. The binary is variously formed by pairing options for self-identification as "equally religious and spiritual," "neither religious nor spiritual", "more religious than spiritual", or "more spiritual than religious". Differences in wording and minor methodological procedures alter the precise percentage in each classification but the classification is always a binary and it is not without critics (Ammerman, 2013). In our own deconversion research we found the binary empirically useful and have continued its use. This fact led us to a mixed-methods study of the semantics and psychology of religion with extensive focus upon those who identify more closely with more spiritual than religious self-identifications, including vertical (often religiously expressed) and horizontal forms (often expressed in secular terms) of spirituality. This focus led us to include a measure of mysticism (Hood, 1975) as an integral part of subsequent faith development research. It was and is the relationship between mysticism and the binary that is the bridge that links two largely independent research traditions in a synergistic outcome that has produced fruitful empirical and conceptual consequences.

In this chapter we will first document the empirical significance of mysticism as both a predictor of self-rated spirituality and of advanced religious types. Next, we will explore how empirical research on mysticism also links FD research with other mainstream psychologies. Finally, we will note the relevance of FD research to what is an apparent paradox in the way psychological science creates operational measures.

Faith Development in Dialogue

Igor Grossman has cooperated in interacting with our research teams on critically evaluating our methods in terms of how his own team of researchers has approached the study of wisdom (Grossman, et al., 2020). Wisdom research, like mysticism, or faith development is a recognized field of study that has emerged as a relatively isolated field defined by its own conceptualizations, definitions, and procedures. Intuitively, one suspects that wisdom research should not be unrelated to concerns of faith development. Recognizing that clear operational criteria are necessary to empirically delimit the concept of wisdom, one must have a deeper perspective of knowing what something is in order to provide operational criteria. In one initiative, Grossman and his colleagues decided to focus upon colleagues who study wisdom to delimit operational criteria for wisdom. However, such a study should not be confused with the study wisdom in wise persons. Empirical findings cannot escape the fundamental issue that those who study wisdom are not necessarily wise people. Perhaps we may assume that wisdom develops as does faith, as Nashr (2019) has emphasized in his discussion of Quranic psychology. Operational indicators of wisdom depend upon a prior intuition of wisdom in order to judge the empirical fruits that may follow. If the operational definition is unwise, something other than wisdom is being studied. An example from research on mysticism is illustrative of this dilemma. For instance, the Group for the Advancement of Psychiatry (GAP) answered their own question "Mysticism: Spiritual quest or psychic disorder?" in favor of the latter (GAP, 1976). This view is based largely upon well-established similarities between mysticism and madness at the purely experiential level (Boisen 1936/1971). James (1985/1902, pp. 11–29) famously referred to the limits of such operationalization as medical materialism. Medical materialism essentially is dismissal of experience based upon what otherwise can be seen as authoritative and objective operational definitions that permit precision in nomothetic claims that are misconstrued to apply to the individual (Lamiell, 2000). What is medically known about epilepsy is used to dismiss Saul's experience on the road to Damascus as simply another instance of an epileptic seizure or St. Teresa's experiences are simply dismissed as hysteria, etc. (James, 1985/1902, p. 20). James insisted that the nomothetic study of faith development cannot replace faith. "Knowledge about faith is one thing: effective occupation of a place in life, with its dynamic currents passing through your being, is another" (1985/1902, p. 286). Our mixed methods study of deconversion includes placing individual biographies in the context of nomothetic data that remain incomplete without the complementary study of individuals, unique persons with a name (James, 1985/1902, p. 395).

Deconversion Revisited

Our original study of deconversion produced three findings that have proven consistently useful guides, differences in subsequent waves of our research notwithstanding. First, the most surprising finding in the Deconversion Study data (Streib et al., 2009, p. 86) was that the portion of "more spiritual than religious" in the deconverts group has doubled the number of "more spiritual than religious" *traditionalists*. The "more spiritual than religious" were the strongest self-identification in the sample of deconverts. And a strong preference of deconverts, compared to traditionalists, could be documented also on the basis of the two-wave data (Streib et al., 2022, p. 70).

Second, a finding that has been the target of conceptual criticism, is that higher faith stages or religious styles are by individuals who are more spiritual than religious. Compared to traditionalists, deconverts appear to prefer higher stages of faith (Streib et al.,

2009, p. 102)—a trend that could be corroborated also for deconverts who have left their religious tradition between Wave 1 and Wave 2 (Streib et al., 2022, p. 67).

Finally, a predictor of the advancement in faith development is *openness to experience*. In recent analyses using three-wave data that allow bi-directional possibilities of change, we were able to document that *openness to experience* predicts change in religious type (Streib et al, 2023).

However, the apparent paradox for some is that advances in religious style and type are associated with leaving religions and adopting a religious style open to the alien and leaving what for some are the safe haven of more established faiths. Those who stay in tradition are more likely to identify as "equally spiritual and religious" (or eventually "more religious than spiritual" in Germany), seldom are the traditionalists "more spiritual than religious" as are the deconverts. This turned out to be a bridge to anther independently established body of research dealing with the study of mysticism. While no measure of mysticism was involved in our first deconversion study, it was one of the added measures to our cooperative research and that has turned out to be fortuitous.

Mysticism and the Binary

In our second book we explored the binary more fully, focusing upon the semantics and psychology of those who identify as more spiritual than religious (Streib & Hood, 2016). Here we focus not on the details of the more nuanced findings, but upon the more robust findings relevant to our conceptual and theoretical concern in this chapter.

Noting that religion and spirituality are overlapping constructs, it is reasonable to assume that those who stay in tradition find religious beliefs and practices an effective way to express their spirituality, while those who deconvert and identify as more spiritual than religious have in some sense departed from established faith traditions. Religion no longer allows an adequate expression of spirituality. We have argued that many of them may have turned to a privatized or implicit religion. There is thus no compelling conceptual need to assume religion and spirituality are distinct concepts, despite well-established nuances best explored in individual case studies. Further, there is no need to assume that religious views of ultimate reality, often associated with experiences of a connection to God or gods cannot be functionally replaced by a sense of connectedness to nature or humanity. The former we refer to as vertical transcendence, the latter as horizontal transcendence. This conceptualization yielded a wealth of empirical findings in our mixed methods project, documented in almost 700 pages (Streib & Hood, 2016). Here we identify the bridge of the overall sense of these findings to research on mysticism.

Expanding the Binary: Vertical & Horizontal

The foundation was laid for a major advance over our first deconversion book in our inclusion of vertical and horizontal transcendence to the binary in our second book (Hood & Streib, 2016). This produced four additional groupings by adding "atheists or non-theist" to the binary based upon self-identifications. Once again nuanced differences between the eight groups both within cultures and between are ignored here in favor of the bridge that our mixed methods study led to connect with already established research on mysticism.

Because two groups were very small in both Germany and the USA ("equally religious and spiritual atheists/non-theists") and ("more religious than spiritual atheists/non-theists") we studied the remaining six focus groups in detail using mixed methods (see Streib & Hood, 2016, p. 49 for frequency tables & p. 41 for schematic summary of mixed methods used). Explicitly included were two measures of spirituality, one of which was Hood's Mysticism Scale (1975). This provided the bridge needed between two independent research traditions, one associated with Streib and his colleagues on faith development, the other between Hood and his colleagues on mysticism. The result was that two previously independent traditions have evolved to become an ongoing synergetic program that was unanticipated when we began the first deconversion book. However, it was the first deconversion book that suggested that spirituality and faith development were most closely linked among those who are "more spiritual than religious," whether theistic or not. And this link is mysticism. The advantage is that the measure of mysticism developed by Hood and his colleagues was developed independently of faith development research and prior to the emergence of the binary.

Mysticism: Walter Stace & William James

As with the roots of faith development theory and its assessment, the roots of the empirical study of mysticism reach deep into philosophy. In the case of Hood's Mysticism Scale, the influence of the thought of both Stace and James is central (see Hood et al., 2018, Ch. 11; Klein et al., 2016, p. 169–172).

Both Stace and James took experience as their starting point for the study of mysticism. Stace (1960, p. 9) restricted the term "mystic" to a person who has had a mystical experience. He went on to cull primarily from the classic religious and literary writings reports of persons who claimed to have mystical experiences. From these he postulated a universal core to mysticism from which Hood created the measure (M-Scale) which continues to be the most widely used measure of mysticism (Lukoff & Lu, 1988; Papanicolaou, 2021).

The M-Scale consists of 32 items (16 positively worded and 16 negatively worded items), covering all but one (paradoxicality) of the Stace's universal-core thesis. Early studies suggested a simple two factor structure that fits well conceptually providing empirical evidence for the distinction between experience and its interpretation. More recent studies support a three-factor solution in which interpretation remains distinct with Stace's introversive and mysticism emerge as distinct experiences of unity.

An unrealized dialogue remains to be started between faith development research and the renewed interest in the philosophical challenge that Stace's universal core presents to a mainstream psychology, when it remains committed to varieties of positivism (Kelly, Kelly, & Crabtree, 2007; Kelly, Crabtree, & Marshall, 2015; Marshall, 2005, 2019). Mysticism and faith development research both provide means to reconcile science and spirituality. Hence especially biographical data are required to flesh out otherwise anonymous nomothetic claims (see Hood et al., 2018, pp. 384–386; Klein et al., 2016, pp. 170–172; Chen, Qi et al., 2011).

Here we restrict our discussion to empirical studies that use the M-Scale in faith development research. But first we address two conceptual issues that link research on mysticism with research in positive psychology suggesting the additional synergistic breadth of faith development research with mainstream psychology.

Table 2.1: Stace and Hood Models

STACE UNIVERSAL CORE MODEL OF MYSTICAL EXPERIENCE
(PHENOMENOLOGICALLY DERIVED)

Introvertive Mysticism
a. Contentless Unity
b. Timeless/Spaceless

Extrovertive Mysticism
a. Unity in Diversity
b. Inner Subjectivity

Interpretation
a. Noetic
b. Religious
c. Positive Affect
d. Paradoxically (not measured in M Scale)
e. Ineffability (alleged)

HOOD COMMON CORE MODEL OF MYSTICAL EXPERIENCE
(EMPIRICALLY DERIVED)*

Introvertive mysticism (12 items)
a. Contentless Unity items
b. Time/Space items
c. Ineffability items

Extrovertive mysticism (8 items)
a. Unity in Diversity items
b. Inner Subjectivity items

Interpretation (12 items)
a. Noetic items
b. Religious items
c. Positive Affect items

* Several short versions exist, with the same factor structure (e.g., Streib, Klein et. al., 2021)

First, although the distinction between experience and interpretation acknowledges that language is an important interpretative issue, it also forces us to focus upon the experiential basis from which genuine differences in interpretation can arise. Like texts, measurement scales use particular language and thus confound the distinction between interpretation and experience. This confound can partly be addressed by factor analytic methods to show similar factor structures within particular cultures and between cultures as well. For instance, it is clear that the factor structure of the M-scale has strong empirical support, insofar as, regardless of the language used in the M-Scale, the basic structure of the experience remains constant across diverse samples and cultures. We can diagram Stace's claim to a universal core to Hood's empirically derived common core this in Table 2.1.

Positive Psychology and Faith Development

Positive psychology is another area of mainstream psychology for which mysticism provides a bridge to faith development theory. Both areas have a strong interest in transcendence. Positive psychology emerged with strong support from the John Templeton Foundation for its study of virtues (Seligman & Csikszentmihalyi, 2000). Dahlsgaard, Peterson, and Seligman (2005) noted that of seven virtues identified across eight traditions, transcendence of self (mysticism) is explicitly mentioned in the Abrahamic faith traditions of the West (Christianity, Islam, Judaism) and in the two explicit faith traditions of the East (Hinduism, Buddhism). Empirical studies have demonstrated similar factor structures for the M-Scale among adherents of the three Abrahamic faiths for which explicit references to transcendence are well documented: Israeli Jews (Lazar & Kravetz, 2005), Iranian Muslims (Hood et al., 2001), and American Christians (Hood & Williamson, 2000). Similar results have been obtained among adherents of the two Eastern traditions in which such explicit references are well documented: Tibetan Buddhists (Chen, Hood et al., 2011) and Hindus in India (Anthony et al., 2010). Thus, mysticism in faith development research and in positive psychology suggest further synergistic patterns in which faith development research is important for emerging forms of mainstream psychology.

Dahlsgaard et al. (2005) argue that transcendence is also implicit in the two indigenous faith traditions of China, Confucianism and Taoism (as well as Athenian philosophy) traditions not associated with claims to the existence of God or gods. A useful distinction here from the psychology of religion is that transcendence, as Streib and Hood (2016) note, can be "vertical" (and hence religious) or "horizontal" (and hence spiritual). As noted above. Horizontal transcendence need not involve any ontological claims about God, but may include a sense of union with humankind, a oneness with the cosmos, or a sense of oneness with nature (Anthony et al., 2010; Streib & Hood, 2011). Thus, scholars using Stace's common-core thesis have applied it to the remaining traditions identified by Dahlsgaard and colleagues (Chen, Hood et al, 2011; Roth, 1995, 1999). Mysticism is the bridge that connects faith development theory with its value driven model, which identifies an ideal trajectory that moves toward transcendence, or Style 5, as an emerging dialogical style that is open to the alien.

Empirical data in both the semantics book (Streib & Hood, 2016) and studies of mysticism from the three-wave data (Streib & Chen, 2021) reveal nuanced effects of mysticism in the mediating and moderating effects on spiritual self-identification. Our focus here is on our use of William James as a compliment to Walter Stace and to the terminal ideal of faith development explicit in our model of religious styles.

William James and Faith Development Theory

Klein et al. (2016, pp. 169–170) have briefly traced the influence of not only Stace but William James on the development of Hood's mysticism scale. It has also been extensively presented in several publications whose dates both precede and correspond to our co-operative projects that began with the deconversion book. (Hood, 1995, 2006, 2008, 2022).

James' famous text on *The Varieties of Religious Experience* is seldom read as a text on faith development, nor as a rejection of the natural science assumptions of *Principles of Psychology* (1995/1890), but it can and should be (Hood, 1995; 2022). Reflecting on his abbreviation of the *Principles* in the greatly abbreviated Briefer Course (1892) he stated *the natural science assumptions with which we started are provisional and reversible things* (James, 1892, p. 468, emphasis ours). This is the basis both of his appeal to direct experience in his use of documents of *humans* in the *Varieties*, which are subtitled *"A study in human nature."* He asserts personal religious experience has its "root and centre" in mystical states of consciousness (James 1895/1902, p. 301) that are both "noetic" and "ineffable" (p. 302). The experiences are absolutely authoritative for those who experience them, but only sources of hypotheses for those who would study them second hand. In terms of this chapter human nature cannot be understood from nomothetic study alone.

Throughout all of James' massive body of writing, a common theme emerges, that of overbeliefs. It links to our focus upon *worldviews*. Despite the foibles and follies of religions, James asserts that the "best fruits of religious experience are the best things history has to show" (1895/1902, p. 210). He also notes the collective name for these fruits is saintliness and that this ideal terminus of development is the same in all religions (1985/1902, p. 219). This common core can be summarized as (1) connection to a wider reality not merely intellectually but emotionally; (2) a willing self-surrender to this power; (3) immense elation as limited sense of selfhood is lost and (4) a shifting of the emotional center (pp. 219–220). The overbeliefs or worldviews that emerge differ mainly in those who are "both religious and spiritual," the self is merged with what James' simply identified as "MORE of the same quality" (1985/1902, p. 401, emphasis in original)." He also notes that, "It is when we treat of the experience of 'union' with it that their [mystics] differences appear most clearly" 1985/1902 (p. 401). Research based upon free text entries for "spirituality" and "religion" reveal considerable overlap (see Ch. 6). What emerges also are differences in overbeliefs between those who self-identify as "more spiritual than religious" vs. "equally religious and spiritual". The latter interpret their experience in terms of textual or institutional authorities (hence "religion"), while the former and not bound by ontological limits set but external authorities (Klein et al., 2016, pp. 166–167). However, for James the reality of this unseen "more" and he appeals to Plato's theory of forms for his: "brilliant and impressive defense of this common human feeling" (James, 1985/1902, p. 54). Papanicolaou (2021) provides a contemporary defense of the relevance of the Platonic theory of forms for the ontological claims of mystics. Here we simply accept the possibility that the overbeliefs derived from a sense of connectedness to an unseen reality are a bridge connecting mysticism directly and faith development theory indirectly to research in mainstream psychology using mixed methods in the study of noetic claims (Yaden et al., 2016), varieties of transcendent experiences (Yaden et al., 2017) and prejudice (Streib, 2018). Here we focus only on prejudice. We can link faith development research back to James whose views complement Streib's (2018) philosophical contribution to the study of prejudice.

James, Faith Development, and Prejudice

In our operational creating of the four types in our analysis of changes in faith development (Streib et al., 2020), lower faith styles, especially *substantially ethnocentric* and the *predominantly conventional type* are associated with high scores on *truth of texts and teachings (ttt)* of the Religious Schema Scale (Streib, et al., 2010) which in turn predicts prejudice, while the higher types, especially the *emerging dialogical type* is associated with *xenosophia* both conceptually and empirically as indicated by higher scores on the *xenosophia/inter-religious dialog (xenos)* subscale of the Religious Schema Scale (Streib et al., 2020). These contemporary findings mirror a claim made by James:

> The baiting of Jews, the haunting of Albigenses and Waldenses, the stoning of Quakers and ducking of Methodists, the murdering of Mormons and the massacring of Armenians, express much rather that aboriginal neophobia, that pugnacity of which we all share the vestiges, and that inborn hatred of the alien and of eccentricity and non-conforming men as aliens, than they express the positive piety of the various perpetrators. Piety is the mask, the interior force is the tribal instinct. (James, 1985/1902, p. 271).

Here, James provides a rich philosophical frame suggesting that much of "religion" as overbelief can thinly mask bigotry and fear. It is the overcoming of this in terms of further development that allows one to be open to the alien and to the possibilities of transformation that in terms of contemporary religious styles theory permits a "culture of welcome" (see Streib & Klein, 2018). However, James recognizes as an empirical claim, his faith development is an empirical claim to be tested against the realization of its ideal telos that must be empirically evaluated in mundane reality. James notes, "The folly of the cross, so inexplicable by the intellect, has yet its indestructible meaning" (1985/1902, p. 290). Saintliness actually achieved is like all asceticism a tendency to pathology. James's warning is one of the few quotes in the Varieties that is attributed to no source. It actually is the line from Emerson's poem, *Give All to Love*: "Heartily know, when half-gods go, the gods arrive."

We began this chapter with a reflexive evaluation of our own styles typology that we have noted is ordinal and hierarchical but not irreversible. It also helps us understand James' questions about faith development that we hope to empirically provide answers to: (1) should we adapt to the seen or unseen reality? And (2) shall adaptation be aggressive (violent) or not? (James, 1985/1902, p. 297). The answer to both these questions is to focus on mysticism and faith development in dialogue with various psychologies.

Faith Development and Second Naïveté: Style 3 & Style 5

In our model of faith development, Style 5 is the highest and characterized by a dialogical interaction with others, motivated by xenosophia, and facilitated by persons open to experience the alien leaving unanticipated possibilities for personal transformation. Not surprisingly, it is compatible with ourselves as researchers and with those we study. As critiques have noted, we like and study persons like ourselves now associated with the popular acronym WEIRD (Henrich et al., 2010). On the other hand, it has not gone unnoticed that many persons we study, if they are religious, are so in a conventional sense. They are, at least in America, more likely to self-identify as "equally religious and spiritual." They express their spirituality within the confines and constraints of external imposed beliefs, whether from texts or traditions (Williamson et al., 2010). They are distinctively unlike those who study them. Critics of faith development theory have noted that persons committed to conservative traditions fare poorly with both Fowler's stage model and our styles model (Gooren, 2010; Malony, 1990). We place value upon openness and complexity over ethnocentrism and simplicity (cf. Hood & Morris, 1985). Does this suggest a possible cultural and even disciplinary blindness?

Faith Development: Depth vs. Breadth?

We are just beginning to be able to explore possible directionality in changes in religious styles. Considering and including our third wave data confirm the empirical fact that change in religious styles does occur and that faith development is not invariant, person may regress as well as progress. Further we suggest that it is fruitful to hypothesize that there is likely a trajectory based upon our operationalized types created for our three-wave study. The *predominantly individuative type* can be a precursor that mediates change in faith development either to the *emerging dialogical-xenosophia type* or to the *predominantly conventional type*. However, conceptually it may be that the change in each case is an advance in religious commitment. How can this be?

An analogy can be helpful here. With the Olympics on the near horizon, one can consider what often is identified as the "greatest athlete." This title is given the winner of the decathlon, a series of athletic events taking place over two days in which all competitors must compete in all ten events (100-meter dash, long jump, shot put, high jump, 400-meter dash, 110-meter hurdles, discus, pole vault, javelin, and 1,500-meter run). The winner of the decathlon obviously has great skill in a wide range of athletics. This is suggestive of breadth. On the other hand, individuals who compete in decathlon events as isolated, single events and win, always have better performances than the winner of that event in the decathlon. This is suggestive of depth. If you want to be the best 100-meter dash in the Olympics, you cannot do it in the decathlon.

Early on, critics of the psychology of religion have noted a strong bias among those who study others that are conventionally religious (Malony, 1990; Hood & Morris, 1986). Favored are those who are more like the scholars in religious studies themselves who are open and know a lot about transcendent worldviews, whether vertical or horizontal. Complexity and openness, and xenosophia are seen as the proper telos. Simplicity, ethnocentric or mere conventional commitment, and xenophobia are seen as less desirable. Faith development is viewed positively: "Progressive" if one improves from *predominantly conventional* to *emerging dialogical-xenosophic*, and negatively or "regressive" if one moves from a higher type to a lower type.

Our categorization of four distinct types and the possibility to model this on longitudinal, three-wave data suggest putting to the test a new hypothesis. We suggest understanding the *predominantly individuative-reflective type* as phase in a dynamic process, where mystical experience may take place. While certain aspects of Style 4 can feature a kind of relativistic, objectifying, and multi-religious approach that looks at other religions from outside, new experiences may be desirable that allow one to experience the loss of ego or self that is integral in what James and Stace both agree is an essential aspect of religious worldviews. In the *emerging dialogical type* this is marked by an openness to the other, whether idea, or person—to the effect that texts, symbols, and rituals become alive again ("living metaphor" in terms of Ricoeur, 1975), as well as the Unknown or Alien affect the receptive person with the "sting of the alien" (cf. Waldenfels, 2011) and the "demand of the alien" (Waldenfels, 1999). With Ricoeur (1960), we may speak of a second naïveté. On the other hand, the predominantly conventional category allows one to deeply return to and embed in a specific faith tradition, that can only be done by exclusion, whether ideas or persons. This is, in many cases, a return to the first naïveté, which is characterized by the exclusion of critical thought; some people may just not be able to cope with and tolerate the plurality and complexity in modernity. But there may be another developmental avenue: Those committed to an existential view of religion have argued that identity is an inextricable aspect of religion as component aspect of religiosity (Belzen, 2010; Palitsky et al., 2020). Those committed to Sartre's (1957/1963) progressive—regressive method have emphasized that every progression is simultaneously a regression, each choice for entails a rejection. Sartre's dialectical method linking the philosophy of existentialism with Marxism as complementary has not received wide acceptance (See Solif, 1972; Palitsky et. al., 2020). However, Palitsky et al. have wisely noted the value of contrasting progression and regression (2020, p. p.208). Others have used this to suggest trajectories in support of our own where exploration of breadth may precede a reflection can lead to a commitment of depth (Bogaerts, et al. (2018). Rather than simply a regression this may be also a kind of second naiveté.

We expect that this can be identified empirically in either the *predominantly conventional* or the *emerging dialogical-xenosophic* groups by the biographical study of individuals in the process of transition from the *predominantly individuative-reflective type*. It is an error to view worldviews that are rooted in mystical experience as inherently regressive if they exchange self-identification rooted in a commitment of depth for one previously explored in term s of a commitment to breadth (Hood, 1976; Bogaerts et al., 2018, p. 60).

A Closing Dilemma

The likely apocryphal quote attributed to the Buddha in popular expositions of Zen holds true, the finger pointing at the moon is not the moon (Hanh, 1991). We also noted an implicit critique of empirical research that focused too exclusively on those who are distant

Part A: Conceptual & Methodological Perspectives

from the researchers who study them. We now can make that critique explicit. The problem is more precisely that psychological science when exclusively committed to methods dependent on operational definitions is often at risk to be blind for the receptiveness of experiences and intuition that may lead to new avenues for religious identity. The central role of quantification (and the necessity to operationalize in order to measure) are seen as essential for a psychology modeled after the natural sciences. It is often at the heart of "method wars" between qualitative and quantitative research that privilege the latter (Gantt & Melling, 2009). The reduction of human to the natural in the sense of psychological science conceived as committed to naturalism cannot address fully issues that concern worldviews (Platinga, 2011). Operational definitions are at risk of being blind or even avoid the symbolic and bar intuition and all that is intuitive (including mystical experiences and receptive encounter with the alien)—which is obviously very difficult for those who see generalizations based upon nomothetic research as complete. It is not spurring that wisdom research has yet to dialogue with research in faith development. Xenosophia does poorly when confined to statistical truths whose data points are not named.

References

Anthony, F.-V., Hermans, C. A. M., & Sterkens, C. (2010). A comparative study of mystical experience among Christian, Muslim, and Hindu students in Tamil Nadu, India. *Journal for the Scientific Study of Religion*, 49(2), 264–277.

Ammerman, N. (2013). Spiritual but not religious? Beyond binary choices in the study of religion. *Journal for the Scientific Study of Religion*, 52, 258–278.

Belzen, J. A. (2010). Religion and self: Notions from a cultural psychological perspective. *Pastoral Psychology*. 59, 399–409.

Bogartus, A., Claes, L, Verschueren, m., Bastiens, T., Kaufman, E. A., Smits, D. & Luyckx, K. (2018). The Dutch self-concept and identity measure (SCIM): Factor structure and association with identity dimensions and psychopathology. *Personality and Individual Differences*, 121, 56–64.

Boisen, A. T. (1960). *Out of the depths: An autobiographical study of mental disorder and religious experience*. New York, NY: Harper.

Chen, Z., Hood, R. W., Yang, L., & Watson, P. J. (2011). Mystical experience among Tibetan Buddhists: The common core thesis revisited. *Journal for the Scientific Study of Religion*, 50(2), 328–338. https://doi.org/10.1111/j.1468-5906.2011.01570.x

Chen, Z., Qi, W., Hood, R. W., & Watson, P. J. (2011). Common core thesis and qualitative and quantitative analysis of mysticism in Chinese Buddhist monks and nuns. *Journal for the Scientific Study of Religion*, 50(4), 654–670. https://doi.org/10.1111/j.1468-5906.2011.01606.x

Dahlsgaard, K., Peterson, C., & Seligman, M. E. P. (2005). Shared virtue: The convergence of valued human strengths across culture and history. *Review of General Psychology, 9*, 203–213.

Fowler, J. W. (1981). Stages of faith. The psychology of human development and the quest for meaning. Harper & Row.

Gantt, E. E. & Melling, B. S. (2009). Science, psychology, and religion: An invitation to Jameson pluralism. *The Journal of Mind and Behavior*, 30, 149–164.

Gooren, H. (2010). *Religious conversion and disaffiliation: Tracing patterns of change in faith practices*. Palgrave/Macmillan.

Group for the Advancement of Psychiatry (GAP). (1960). Psychiatry and religion (Report No. 48, formulated by the Committee on Psychiatry and Religion). New York, NY

Group for the Advancement of Psychiatry (GAP). (1976, November). Mysticism: Spiritual quest or psychic disorder? (Report No. 97, formulated by the Committee on Psychiatry and Religion). New York, NY.

Grossmann I, Dorfman A, Oakes H. (2020). Wisdom is a social-ecological rather than person-centric phenomenon. *Current Opinion in Psychology*, 32:66–71. https://doi.org/10.1016/j.copsyc.2019.07.010

Grossmann, I. Weststrate, N. M., Ardelt, M., Brienza, J. P., Dong, M. Ferrari, M. Marg. Fournier, M. A., Chao S., Nusbaum, H. C. &, J. (2020) The science of wisdom in a polarized world: Knowns and unknowns, *Psychological Inquiry*, 31:2, 103–133, https://doi.org/10.1080/1047840X.2020.1750917

Han, T, N, (1989). *Dường xua mãy tang old path white clouds: Walking in the footsteps of the Buddha*. (Trans from Vietnamese by Mobi Ho). Berkeley, CA: Parallax Press.

Henrich, J., Heine, S. J. & Norenzayan, A. (2010). The weirdest people in the world? *Behavioral and Brain Science*, pp. 1–75. https://doi.org/10.1017/S0140525X0999152X

Hood, R. W., Jr. (1975). The construction and preliminary validation of a measure of reported mystical experience. *Journal for the Scientific Study of Religion*, 14, 29–41. https://doi.org/10.2307/1384454

Hood, R. W., Jr. (1976). Conceptual criticisms of regressive explanations of mysticism. *Review of Religious Research*, 17, 179–188.

Hood, R. W. Jr. (1995). The soulful self of William James. In D. Capps and J. L. Jacobs (Eds). *The struggle for life: A companion to William James' The Varieties of Religious Experience*. Mennonite Press. pp. 209–219.

Hood, R. W. Jr. (2006). The common core thesis in the study of mysticism. In P. McNamara (Ed.), *Where God and science meet*, Vol. 3, pp. 119–138. Westport, CT: Praeger.

Hood, R. W. Jr. (2008). Theoretical fruits from the empirical study of mysticism: A Jamesian perspective, *Journal für Psychologie*,16, 1–28. https://journal-fuer-psychologie.de/article/view/201

Hood Jr., R. W. (2022). William James and the (non) replication crisis in psychology: Conjectures and controversy in the psychology of religion. In R. W. Hood Jr. & S. Cheruvallil-Contractor (Eds.), Research in the Social Scientific Study of Religion (Vol. 32, pp. 373–398). Brill. https://doi.org/10.1163/9789004505315_021 Hood, R. W. Jr., Ghorbani, N., Watson, P. J., Ghramaleki, A. F., Bing, M. N., Davison, H. K., Morris, R. J., & Williamson, W. P. (2001). Dimensions of the mysticism scale: Confirming the three-factor-structure in the United States and Iran. Journal for the Scientific Study of Religion, 40(4), 691–705. https://doi.org/10.1111/0021-8294.0008

Hood, R. W. Jr., Hill, P. C., & Spilka, B. (2018). The psychology of religion: An empirical approach, 5th ed. Guilford Press.

Hood, R. W., Jr. and Morris, Ronald J. (1985). Conceptualization of quest: A critical rejoinder to Batson. *Review of Religious Research*, 26(4), 391–397. https://doi.org/10.2307/3511052

Hood, R. W. Jr., & Williamson, W. P. (2000). An empirical test of the unity thesis: The structure of mystical descriptors in various faith samples. *Journal of Psychology &Christianity*, 19(3), 222–244.

James, W. (1892). *Psychology: The briefer course*. Henry Holt.

James, W. (1981/1890). *The principles of psychology*. Cambridge, MA: Harvard University Press.

James, W. (1985/1902). *The varieties of religious experience.: A study in human nature*. Harvard.

Kelly, E. F., Crabtree, A., & Marshall, P. (Eds.). (2015). *Beyond physicalism: Toward reconciliation of science and spirituality*. Rowan & Littlefield.

Kelly, E. F., Kelly, E. W., Crabtree, A., Gauld, A., Grosso, M., & Greyson, B. (Eds.). (2007). *Irreducible mind: Toward a psychology for the 21st Century*. Rowan & Littlefield.

Klein, C., Silver, C. F., Hood, R. W. Jr., Streib, H., Hood, R. W. Jr., Coleman, T. III (2016). "Spirituality" and Mysticism. In Streib, H. & Hood, R. W. Jr. (Eds.) *Semantics and Psychology of "Spirituality." A Crosscultural Analysis*. (pp. 165–187). Springer International. https://doi.org/10.1007/978-3-030-52140-0

Koltko-Rivera, M. E. (2004). The psychology of world views. *Review of General Psychology*, 8, 3–58.

Lamiell, J. T. (2000). A periodic table of personality elements? The "Big Five" and trait "psychology" in critical perspective. *Journal of Theoretical Psychology*, 20, 1–24. https://doi.org/10.1037/h0091211

Lazar, A., & Kravetz, S. (2005). Responses to the mystical scale by religious Jewish persons: A comparison of structural models of mystical experience. *International Journal for the Psychology of Religion*, 15(1), 51–61. https://doi.org/10.1207/s15327582ijpr1501_4

Lukoff, D. (1988). Transpersonal perspectives on manic psychosis: Creative, visionary, and mystical states. *Journal of Transpersonal Psychology*, 20, 111–140.

Lukoff, D., & Lu, F. G. (1988). Transpersonal psychology research review topic: Mystical experience. *Journal of Transpersonal Psychology*, 20, 161–184.

Malony, H. N. (1990). The concept of faith in psychology. In J. M. Leed (Ed.)., *Handbook of faith* (pp. 71–95). Religious Education Press.

Marshall, P. (2005). *Mystical encounters and the natural world: Experience and explanations*. Oxford.

Marshall, P. (2019). *The shape of the soul: What mystical experience tells us about ourselves and reality*. Rowan & Littlefield

Nasr, S. H. (2019). Introduction. In Bakhtiar, L, *Quranic psychology of the self: A textbook on Islamic moral psychology (ilm al-nafs)* (pp. xxv–xxix). Kazi Publications, inc.

Palitsky, R., Sullivan, D., Young, I. F., & Schmitt. H. J. (2020). Religion and the construction of identity. In K. E. Vial & C. Routledge (Eds.). *The science of religion, spirituality, and existentialism* (pp. 207–222). Elsevier. https://doi.org/10.1016/B978-0-12-817204-9.00016-0

Papanicolaou, A. C. (2021). *A scientific assessment of the validity of mystical experiences: Understanding altered psychological and neurophysiological states*. Routledge Research in Psychology.

Plantinga, A. (2011). *Where the conflict really lies: Science, religion, and naturalism*. Oxford University Press.

Ricoeur, P. (1960). *The symbolism of evil* (E. Buchanan, Trans.). Beacon Press 1969.

Ricoeur, P. (1975). *La metaphore vive*. Edition du Seuil.

Roth, H. D. (1995). Some issues in the study of early Chinese mysticism: A review essay. *Chinese Review International, 2*, 154–173.

Roth, H. D. (1999). *Original Tao: Inward training (Nei-yeh) and the foundations of Taoist mysticism*. New York, NY: Columbia University Press.

Seligman, M. E. P., & Csikszentmihalyi, M. (2000). Positive psychology: An introduction. *American Psychologist, 55*, 5–14.

Sartre, J. P. (1963). *Search for a method*. (H. E. Barnes, Trans). Alfred A. Knopf. (Original work published 1957).

Soloff, L. (1972). (Review). Search for a method. *Insurgent Sociologists, 2*, 52–53.

Stace, W. T. (1960). *Mysticism and philosophy*. Philadelphia: Lippincott.

Stifler, K., Greer, J., Sneck, W., & Dovenmuehle, R. (1993). An empirical investigation of the discriminability of reported mystical experiences among religious contemplatives, psychotic inpatients, and normal adults. *Journal for the Scientific Study of Religion, 32*, 366–372.

Streib, H. (2005). Research on lifestyle, spirituality and religious orientation of adolescents in Germany. In L. J. Francis, M. Robbins, & J. Astley (Eds). *Religion, education and adolescence: International and empirical perspectives*, (131–163). University of Wales Press.

Streib, H. (2018). What is xenosophia? Philosophical contributions to prejudice research. In Streib, H. & Klein, C. (Eds.), *Xenosophia and religion. Biographical and statistical paths for a culture of welcome*. Springer Nature. https://doi.org/10.1007/978-3-319-74564-0

Streib, H. & Chen, Z. J. (2021). Evidence for the brief mysticism scale: Psychometric properties, and moderation and mediation effects in predicting spiritual self-identification. *International Journal for the Psychology of Religion, 32:3*, 165–175. https://doi.org/10.1080/10508619.2021.1899641

Streib, H., Chen, Z. J., & Hood, R. W. Jr. (2023). Faith development as change in religious types: Results from three-wave longitudinal data with faith development interviews. *Psychology of Religion and Spirituality, 15*(2), 298–307. https://doi.org/10.1037/rel0000440

Streib, H. Chen, Z. H. & Hood, R. W. Jr. (2020) Categorizing people by their preference for religious styles: Four types derived from evaluation of faith development interviews, *International Journal for the Psychology of religion, 30*, 112–127. https://doi.org/10.1080/10508619.1664213

Streib, H., Hood, R. W. Jr., Keller, B., Csöff, R-M, & Silver, C. (2009) *Deconversion: Qualitative and quantitative results from cross-cultural research in Germany and the United States*. (Research in Contemporary Religion, Vol. 5). Vandenhoeck & Ruprecht. https://doi.org/10.13109/9783666604393

Streib, H., Hood, R. W. Jr., & Klein, C. (2010). The religious schema scale: Construction and initial validation of a quantitative measure for religious styles. *International Journal for the Psychology of Religion, 20*(3), 151–172. https://doi.org/10.1080/10508619.2010.481223

Streib, H., & Hood, R. W. Jr. (2011). "Spirituality" as privatized experience-oriented religion: Empirical and conceptual perspectives. *Implicit Religion*, 14(4), 433–453. https://doi.org/10.1558/imre.v14i4.433

Streib, H., & Hood, R. W. Jr. (2016). *Semantics and psychology of spirituality. A cross-cultural analysis.* Springer International Publishing Switzerland. https://doi.org/10.1007/978-3-319-21245-6

Streib, H. & Klein, C. (Eds.), *Xenosophia and religion. Biographical and statistical paths for a culture of welcome.* Springer Nature. https://doi.org/10.1007/978-3-319-74564-0

Streib, H., Klein, C., Keller, B., & Hood, R. W. Jr. (2021). The mysticism scale (M-Scale) as a measure of subjective spirituality: New results with hood's m-scale and the development of a short form. In Ai, A L., Wink, P. M., Paluotzian, R. A. & Harris, K. A. (Eds.), *Assessing spirituality in a diverse world* (pp. 467–491). Springer International Publishing. https://doi.org/10.1007/978-3-030-52140-0_19

Streib, H., Keller, B., Bullik, R., Steppacher, A., Silver, C., Durham, M., & Hood, R. W. Jr. (2022). *Deconversion revisited: Biographical studies & psychometric analyses ten years later.* Brill Germany/Vandenhoeck & Ruprecht. https://doi.org/10.13109/9783666568688

Waldenfels, B. (1999). Der Anspruch des Fremden. In R. Breuninger (Ed.), *Andersheit – Fremdheit – Toleranz* (pp. 31–51). Humboldt-Studienzentrum.

Waldenfels, B. (2011). *Phenomenology of the alien: Basic concepts* [Grundmotive einer Phänomenologie des Fremden, Frankfurt/M.: Suhrkamp, 2006, transl. by A. Kozin and T. Stähler]. Northwestern University Press.

Williamson, W. P. & Hood, R. W. Jr., Ahmad, A., Sadiq, M, & Hill, P. C. (2010). The intratextual fundamentalism scale: Cross-cultural Application, validity evidence, and relationship with religious orientation and the Big 5. *Mental Health, Religion & Culture*, 13, 721–747.

Yaden, D, B, Le Nguyen, K.D., Kem, M. L., Whintering, N. A., Eichstaedt, J. C., Schwartz, E. H., Buffone, A., Smith, L. K., Waldman, M. R., Hood, R. W. Jr., Newberg, A. B. (2016) The noetic quality: A multi-method exploratory study. *Psychology of Consciousness, Theory, Research and Practice*, 4, 54–62.

Yaden, D. B., Haidt, J., Hood, R. W. Jr., Vago, D. T. & Newberg, A. B. (2017). The varieties of self-transcendent experience. *Review of General Psychology*, 21, 143–160.

Chapter 3
Identity and Narrative across the Adult Life-Span – Concepts and Methods for the Study of Worldview and Religion in Consecutive Autobiographical Reconstructions

Barbara Keller, Ramona Bullik & Anika Steppacher[1]

Abstract *Individuals create their identities by reviewing their lives, by autobiographical remembering, narrating, and reasoning. Their worldview or religion is involved in this lifelong process, be it as explicit identification with traditions or ideologies or as implicit commitments expressed in attitudes or in narrated experience, and subject to change as individuals go through their lives in changing times and places. In this chapter, we unfold the concept of the lifelong project of narrative identity with focus on religion and worldview. We show how we capture change in presentations of self and identity, as well as in reflections on such changes, and in subjective narrative constructions of development. Thereby we present the double diachronic perspective of the study of narrative identity presented in a single life review, and of change observed across consecutive autobiographical reconstructions. An outlook on change involving different developmental tasks and social and historical contexts as explored further in the chapters on specific empirical questions and in the case studies concludes the chapter.*

> **Keywords:** *narrative identity; life-span development; worldview; religion; spirituality; autobiographical reconstruction; double diachronicity*

---

1   B. Keller, R. Bullik, A. Steppacher, Bielefeld University, Germany, E-mail: barbara.keller@uni-bielefeld.de. © Heinz Streib, Ralph W. Hood Jr. (eds.): Faith in Development. Mixed-Method Studies on Worldviews and Religious Styles. First published in 2024 by Bielefeld University Press, Bielefeld, https://doi.org/10.14361/9783839471234-005

60   Part A: Conceptual & Methodological Perspectives

Mapping the Development of Faith across the Human Life-Span

How do religiosities and worldviews develop across human lifespans, and how are they involved in how people conceive of their lives and of themselves? A narrative approach, an approach based on narrated experience, seems warranted to complement other methods such as psychometric scales or structural analyses. Moreover, a narrative perspective can shift the focus to complementary ways to study the development of faith. In hindsight, some traces in terms of concepts and methods can already be found in the seminal work of James Fowler, the "Stages of Faith" (Fowler, 1981). For this project, Fowler, theologian and Methodist, used then current developmental psychological concepts and methods and integrated these toward a project designed to study structural change in forms of meaning-making across the human life span (albeit based on cross-sectional data). At the time of his writing life span developmental psychology was still a newly emerging research perspective (Baltes & Schaie, 1973), and neither autobiographical memories nor narratives were in the focus of mainstream developmental or personality psychology. However, there were models of the human life span and its stages[2], such as Erikson's (1950) stages of psychosocial development, and Levinson's eras of the life cycle (Levinson, et al., 1978). Jean Piaget had offered his theory on cognitive development, Lawrence Kohlberg his theory on moral development. As structural theories both focused on the interaction between "an active, innovative subject and a dynamic, changing environment," thus offering a more sophisticated option than the (then still influential) behaviorist or maturationist theories (Fowler, 1981, p. 100). Therefore, Fowler used both approaches when he formulated his "stages of faith." In the following section, his seminal work will be revisited as point of departure for our efforts to conceptualize and empirically study humans' search for meaning as part of their development, with focus on the adult lifespan. From there, we will proceed to introduce revisions and innovations. Drawing on the current study of identity and narrative across the adult lifespan, we then display our research methods.

Religiosity and Worldview in Adult Development:
From "Optimal Parallels" ...

How are religiosity and worldview involved in human development? When James Fowler suggested his inspiring project of "stages of faith" in the 70s of the last century, he relied on "optimal parallels" between eras of the human life span as mapped by Levinson et al., developmental tasks and psychosocial stages (Erikson), and stages of cognitive (Piaget) and moral (Kohlberg) development (Fowler, 1981, p. 52). He aligned Levinson's eras and Erikson's psychosocial stages to his conceptions of structural or faith stages (see Table 3.1, based on table 3.3, Fowler, 1981, p. 113).

---

2   Life stage concepts are not only a subject of developmental psychology. They can be found in many human cultures, and across human history (see Arnett (2016) for recent discussion—and the proposal to include the study of "indigenous life stages" into the study of human development).

Table 3.1: Optimal Parallels (based on Table 3.3 in Stages of Faith)

Levinson's Eras	Erikson's Psychosocial Stages	Piaget's Stages of Cognitive Development + Fowler's Elaborations	Fowler's Faith Stages
Infancy	Trust vs. mistrust	Sensomotoric preoperational	Undifferentiated faith
Childhood (school years)	Autonomy vs. shame and doubt Initiative vs. guilt Industry vs. inferiority	Concrete operations	Intuitive projective faith Mythic literal faith
Adolescence	Identity vs. role confusion	Formal operations Fowler: Early	Synthetic conventional faith
First adult era (young adulthood)	Intimacy vs. isolation	Fowler: Dichotomizing	Individuative reflective faith
Middle adult era (midlife and beyond)	Generativity vs. stagnation	Fowler: Dialectical	Conjunctive faith
Late adult era	Integrity vs. despair	Fowler: Synthetic	Universalizing faith

Levinson's model of the human life span consisted of infancy, childhood and adolescence, early adulthood, middle adulthood, and late adulthood, also specifying transitions between these eras. Erikson's (1950) stages of psychosocial development are structured according to developmental tasks, which are aligned, but not exclusively tied to the life stage in which they emerge. Piaget offered an account of cognitive development that ended with adolescence/young adulthood and the acquisition of formal operations. Since his aim was to map development continuing throughout the adult lifespan, Fowler stretched Piaget's categories to cover middle adulthood as well as old age. Fowler conceptualized his stages of faith thus related to eras and developmental tasks, to an expectable trajectory with age-graded challenges to be mastered in the course of human lives. To these, he saw the development of faith aligned as an invariant upward sequence, in which one stage was followed by the next. For his Piaget-based backbone of structure, *form of logic,* the leading aspect or "window on faith," as Fowler called the different psychological and psychosocial domains of human behavior, where faith development could be discerned, he introduced the additional, dichotomizing, dialogical, and synthetic operations. These elaborations of Piaget's conceptualization characterize individuative-reflective, conjunctive, and universalizing faith, and thus cognitive development across the adult life span (see Table 3.1 and, for more details, chapter 1 of this volume)[3].

---

3   This effort has recently been acknowledged in a discussion of "dialecticism," which captured Fowler's extension of Piaget's model to the adult life span: "For instance, Fowler and Dell (2006) proposed a developmental-stage theory of faith, in which different stages—'synthetic conven-

62   Part A: Conceptual & Methodological Perspectives

... to Complex Trajectories: Stages, Styles and Dynamics

The life stage models Fowler used need to be updated when looking at current trajectories, at least in Western societies: between adolescence and early adulthood we can now place emerging adulthood, we differentiate between young and late midlife, and for the years past 60 and up until 100 gerontologists offer the labels of young and old old age. In addition to mapping a longer life span, we also have to attend to more flexibility in which current individuals live their lives. Sociologists refer to individualization, deinstitutionalization, and destandardization, as we learn from Arnett (2016, p. 305–306) to whose work we will turn again below.

Displayed below in Table 3.2, we align James Fowler's map of faith development to Heinz Streib's model of the religious styles, and to a current conception of the development of self and social cognition, mentalization. The first column displays Fowler's stages 1–6. It has to be kept in mind that Fowler structured faith development across the life span as an invariant and irreversible upward trajectory.

Table 3.2: Exploring parallels of development of faith with development of cognition and emotion—from stages to modes- related to the development of narrative.

Fowler, 1981: Stages of Faith	Streib, 1997: Religious Styles	Fonagy & Target 1996, 2007: Mentalization	Fowler, 1981: Narrative Competences
Intuitive-projective faith	Subjective-undifferentiated	*Teleological mode*: cause and effect, no subjectivity yet	Appreciation of stories told and listened to (129)
Mythic-literal faith	Instrumental-reciprocal or "do-ut-des" religious style	*Psychic equivalence*: inner = outer reality *Pretend mode*: inner life without connection to reality (McAdams: actor)	Begin of narrating of experience (136)
Synthetic-conventional faith	Mutual religious style	Integration toward mentalization (McAdams: agent)	Personal myth (173)
Individuative-reflective faith	Individuative-systemic religious style		Tacit meanings become explicit and reflective (181)
Conjunctive faith	Dialogical religious style	Mentalization: own and others' inner lives (McAdams: author)	Ironic imagination (198)
Universalizing faith			

In the next column, find Heinz Streib's careful revision, the model of religious styles. The styles still describe a hierarchy, here aligned to the stages from which they have

---

tional,' 'individuative-reflective faith,' 'conjunctive faith,' and 'universalizing faith'—map onto stages of development toward dialectical thinking in general" (Grossmann, 2018, p. 15).

evolved, but their developmental trajectories are conceptualized with more flexibility. We assume that the emergence of the styles corresponds to a developmental sequence. However, individual trajectories may differ and may not cover the entire spectrum of styles and may be multi-directional (moving "upwards" or "downwards" in the hierarchy). It is the rule rather than the exception that more than one style is simultaneously available for a person at a certain time, as we show in the case study chapters in this volume. The religious styles perspective describes only five styles, in line with psychological models[4], and discards Fowler's sixth stage of universalizing faith. The conceptual reason for this is that a psychologically plausible model of religious styles does not need, and should not be based on, teleological and theological (eschatological) propositions. Roughly aligned to the religious styles on the other side is the development of mentalization in childhood as studied by Fonagy and his team (Fonagy & Target 1996; 2007; Fonagy, Luyten, Allison & Campbell (2019).

Here, development starts with the teleological mode which is based on the observation of cause and effect. There is barely subjectivity yet, which will emerge out of the interaction with sensitive caretakers who offer marked mirroring of the infant's impulses. This means that they mirror not only the infant's impulses, but do so in a, for example, slightly exaggerating way. This marks the mirroring as such and helps the infant to understand that the parents communicate their perception and understanding of the infant's inner state. Across many interactions the young infant can learn that it has, like the parents, an inner life. Psychic equivalence refers to the discovery that inner processes help to perceive outer reality. However, there is not yet an awareness of inner processes as mediating the perception of outer reality. Rather, reality corresponds to what is perceived and vice versa. With the emergence of pretend mode, inner life can be explored, however, its connection to reality has yet to be established. This is the time of "as if" play. By going back and forth between equivalence mode and pretend mode a child proceeds toward mentalization, which means an awareness of one's own and others' inner states and processes. This awareness can differ in complexity. Similar to the conception of the religious styles, where different styles can be present in different domains, mentalization can be used in complex and differentiated ways in some areas or sometimes in one's life and less so or not at all in others. It can break down in trauma.

In Fowler's conception, differentiation and complexity grow from stage to stage, and are thus built into the invariant upward sequence, structured by cognitive development according to Fowler's extension of Piaget's theory. In the religious styles perspective, and

---

4   There are more models which might have been aligned here, more or less indebted to Piaget's theories: Anna Aragno discussed levels of symbolic organization, from protosensory to intersubjectivity and self-reflection as in the psychoanalytic process (Aragno, 1997), Gisela Labouvie-Vief presented her model of cognitive-emotional integration in adulthood, which assumes growing complexity from concrete/pre-systemic to interpersonal/protosystemic to institutional/intrasystemic to contextual/intersystemic, and, finally, to the dynamic/intersubjective level of emotional development (Labouvie-Vief, 1997). Each level is characterized by aligned levels of, for example, affective, complexity, self-other differentiation, reflectivity. Subic-Wrana and colleagues have introduced a model of levels of emotional awareness, spanning from level 1, bodily sensation, across level 2, action tendency, level 3 single emotion, level 4 blend of emotions to level 5 blend of blends of emotions (Subic-Wrana et al., 2011).

even more in the study of modes developing toward mentalization, there is room for flexibility for the modeling of domain-specific trajectories as well as interactions. The last column contains a rudimentary trajectory of narrative skills taken from Fowler's descriptions of the stages and their means of narrative expression, which will be elaborated in the next section. The table can be read as leading from left to right, from stages to modes—thus, it may illustrate Arnett's observation that toward the end of the 20th century "developmental theorists increasingly questioned the premises and validity of stage theories," however, conceding that life stage concepts continue to be used in developmental psychology to structure fields of research (Arnett, 2016, p. 291).

What other options are there to structure the study of development across the life span? Development has been conceptualized functionally and context-related, as selective age-related change in adaptive capacity (Baltes, Lindenberger & Staudinger, 2006, p. 580). This can be translated to psychoanalytical conceptions of maturity from the relational camp. The late Steven Mitchell quotes Hans Loewald: "maturity ... is not the customary advanced position along a linear developmental scale; ... maturity is the capacity to navigate among and bridge different organizational and developmental levels" (Mitchell, 2000, p. 50, quoting Loewald, 1949, p. 20).

Similar conceptions have been discussed by Klaus Riegel, who was involved in the conceptualization of the life span perspective in psychology. He belonged to those who proposed, in the seventies of the last century, a dialectical psychology (Riegel, 1979). Currently, his work is rediscovered and referred to by those who strive to study wisdom from a psychological viewpoint: "In Riegel's view, mature individuals can often jump between more and less advanced operational stages and are not required to linearly progress from one stage to another" (Grossmann, 2018, pp.8-9).[5]

Parallel to these developments, and attending to discussion in developmental psychology, Heinz Streib designed and elaborated, in critical appreciation of Fowler's work, the perspective of the religious styles (Streib, 2001, see also chapter 1). The conception of the religious styles allows that earlier styles can be re-activated, in line with a person's way of engaging with the challenges in their lives: "Faith development theory and research attend to structural differences in interpreting and communicating experiences of transcendence in terms of ultimate concern. Faith development regards structures (a) in experiencing and interacting with the world, with one's social environment, and with one's own self (perspective-taking; social horizon); (b) structures of being committed to (ultimate) values (morality) and how to relate to, and where to locate, (ultimate) authority (locus of authority); and (c) structures of how to understand symbolic, ritual and narrative representations (world coherence; symbolic function). Structures constitute the differences between styles. The differences in religious styles reflect structural differences between ethnocentric-authoritarian, mutual-conventional, individuative-reflective, or

---

5   Grossmann (2018) reminds us that Klaus Riegel has criticized Piaget's approach already in 1973, when he suggested dialectic approaches to life span psychology. Grossman points out: "For instance, creative scientific thinking often requires intuitive thought, as well as acceptance of contradictions and holistic reasoning, rather than systematic delineation of various issues and calculation of all possible outcomes for a given solution (as would be expected in the formal operational stage of thought)."

dialogical-xenosophic answers to the big questions that human beings face and the FDI questions intend to elicit" (see Streib, chapter 1 of this volume). Thus, religious styles constitute the variations and transformations of subjective religious interpretation of experiences over the life span. This definition is based on a broad concept of "religion," covering diverse subjective conceptions of horizontal and vertical transcendence, sometimes labelled "spiritual," and including nontheist or atheist notions. It stresses variability, subjectivity, and experience. The styles are supposed to appear in a hierarchical order, and older styles retreat, when newer styles appear, but can re-surface. Multidirectionality of faith development has been established empirically by following the recently constructed religious types across three points of measurement: while most observed so far, move upward, some stay, and some move downward respective to the hierarchy the model suggests. This is in line with the more flexible conception of development offered by the mentalization project. In a perhaps similar vein, McAdams has suggested the layers of personality to develop in a sequence: first, self as actor, then as agent, then as author, assuming that, once established, these layers continue to develop (McAdams, 2013; see also Chapter 1, this volume). The challenge seems to be to attend to the emergence of levels, one after the other, across childhood and adolescence, and perhaps stretching into (emerging) adulthood and, when they are there, also to the complex possible interactions between levels. For example, a person who is so reflective that they can even reflect on their lack of felt emotion may, in terms of these hierarchies, go back and revisit something emotional. In the case studies we attend to hierarchical and functional accounts of adult development of religion and worldview, drawing on psychometric profiles and structural evaluation of FDIs, which we combine with the evaluation of content and narrative particularities of the interviews. Thus, while taking Fowler's ideas on narrative development as point of departure, we are already prepared for more complexity.

Narrative and Identity Across the Adult Life Span

Years ago, Heinz Streib has suggested to use, beyond the rating of stages, "the narrative and reflective responses" in Fowler's basic method, the Faith Development Interview as well as the accounts of the life stories that the interviewee offers (Streib, 2005, p. 108–111), thus requesting an "integration of narrative analysis with developmental analysis" (Streib, 2005, p. 113).

The potential for this is discernible in Fowler's references to different narrative styles assigned to different stages of faith (see the last column in Table 3.2 above). In the beginning there is an appreciation of stories told and listened to (Fowler, 1981, p. 129). Mythic-literal faith is characterized by the beginning of narrating of own experiences (p. 136). With synthetic-conventional faith the personal myth is expected to emerge as "the myth of one's own becoming in identity and faith, incorporating one's past and anticipated future in an image of the ultimate environment unified by characteristics of personality" (p. 173). In Fowler's conception the transition to the next stage involves awareness of contradictions between so far valued authority sources (ibid.). With the stage of individuative-reflective faith symbols are recognized as symbols, tacit meanings become explicit and reflective (p. 181). With conjunctive faith ironic imagination emerges, described as "a ca-

66   Part A: Conceptual & Methodological Perspectives

pacity to see and be in one's or one's group's, most powerful meanings, while simultaneously recognizing that they are relative, partial, and inevitably distorting apprehensions of transcendent reality" (p. 198). For stage 6, characterizations of narrative are not given, and there is no interview to illustrate it. Instead, Fowler names as "incarnators and actualizers of an inclusive and fulfilled human community" exceptional human beings like Mother Teresa, Mahatma Gandhi or Martin Luther King (p. 200–201). As already stated above, the religious styles perspective refrains from teleological and theological (eschatological) propositions.

Other assumptions Fowler has made regarding the development of narrating are studied in developmental psychology, in personality psychology and related fields such as the study of autobiographical memory. The recent proliferation of narrative methods in the development of autobiographical narrating and reasoning (Habermas, 2011), in the study of the life story as access to the study of personality (McAdams), or in the exploration of how memories of specific experiences and events are linked to the development of the self or identity (Pasupathi, Mansour, & Brubaker, 2007), opens new vistas. What we can tell about ourselves and our lives involves, in addition to narrative skills, autobiographical memory and remembering: Remembering can be regarded as activity which is involved in the continuous building and revising of what we know about ourselves, or, in the language of this line of research, the memory-self system in long term memory: While memories build on single episodes, they are also organized according to knowledge structures (abstractions, meanings, "semantics"). Memories are seen as transitory mental constructions on different levels: Top down there is on the highest level of autobiographical knowledge the life story, then there are themes, lifetime periods, then general events, and episodic memories, memories of single events or experiences (Conway & Pleydell-Pearce, 2000; Conway, Justice, & D'Argembeau, 2019, p. 29). In this line of research, age-related trends are studied, like the reminiscence bump, the tendency for middle-aged and elderly people to access more personal memories from their adolescence or emerging adulthood (10–30 years of age), or the "semantization" ascribed to memories in old age, suggesting that memories get more abstract and organized according to meaning. For the interpretation of trajectories of consecutively told autobiographical narratives we may look for continuities and change on the different levels of abstractions. For example, can we trace repeatedly told episodes? Abstracted themes and leitmotifs? Can we define areas of re-evaluation and revision? And can we develop hypotheses accounting for stability and change in autobiographical remembering and identity construction?

Identity as development task of adolescence and beyond

In his model of psychosocial development, Erikson portrayed the young person at the threshold of adulthood and confronted with the developmental crisis of identity vs. role confusion (Erikson, 1950). Following Erikson, Fowler has described identity as "an accrued awareness of oneself that maintains continuity with one's past meanings to others and to oneself and that integrates the images of oneself given by significant others with one's own inner feelings of who one is and of what one can do, all in such a way as to enable one to anticipate the future without undue anxiety about 'losing' oneself" (Fowler, 1981, p.

77). Meanwhile, narrative approaches in developmental psychology and personality psychology have empirically studied how, starting in adolescence, life stories, stories which look back on one's life so far, first emerge. Discussed are the cognitive abilities needed to tell a coherent life story which explains how one came to be who one is now, and perhaps, what this means for one's future (Habermas & Bluck, 2000; McAdams, 2001; Negele & Habermas, 2010). The timely acquisition of the necessary skills of storytelling is supported by cultural habits and by the acquisition of knowledge of what belongs into a biography in one's culture, the life script. This is demanded as well as supported by society, for example, when young people in Western industrialized countries learn how to write a curriculum vitae, to form a life story according to specific expectations and to build abstractions from many single episodes by ordering and summarizing them according to their meaning for the purpose of self-presentation. While these formative years pass, the experiences making up the first life stories stay as something to be remembered. A recent meta-study of the reminiscence bump confirms that the narrative/identity account and cultural life script account received the most support for the explanation of its occurrence in adolescence (Munawar, Kuhn, & Haque, 2018).

Since the time of Fowler's writing the concept of emerging adulthood covering the years between the late teens and middle to late twenties has been introduced (Arnett, 2007), suggesting that the developmental tasks of identity and intimacy may have to be negotiated in complex intertwining ways, and take more time—at least in relatively affluent industrial societies. Fivush and colleagues state: "Emerging adulthood is a period of clarifying one's sense of self and standing in the world, as well as growing from past experiences and directing the self toward ongoing goals" (Fivush et al., 2017, p. 137). Drawing on McAdams' model, the self as author emerges (McAdams, 2013).

As we have reported above, differentiations of mapping current adult development across the life span concern young and late midlife and then young and old old age. Accordingly, we can make use of Erikson's "soft" stage conception and expect that identity will remain a developmental task for the adult life span. For example, motivated by the developmental task of midlife, concern for the next generation, i.e., generativity, identity may reflect commitment to others, activities of sharing skills and resources with one's own children or others of the next generation (Fivush et al., 2017, p. 137; McAdams, 2014). This involves a re-evaluation of one's own roles, responsibilities, and, in consequence, oneself. Josselson explored in a longitudinal study "women's search for meaning and identity." She interviewed repeatedly a sample of college-educated women from early adulthood to midlife or from their early twenties to their mid-fifties and notes: "In psychology, adolescence and old age are well-conceptualized, but we understand less about what occurs developmentally in the many decades of adulthood that constitute the middle years. This period reflects continuity as well as growth and change and has its own challenges and possibilities. The women I studied have forged lives very different from one another, yet there are commonalities among them." (Josselson, 2017, p. xiii). Josselson's project demonstrates the merit of the careful comparison of single cases and of attending to complexity. This issue will be taken up below.

McAdams has also studied narrative and identity at midlife. In correspondence with Erikson's model which identifies generativity versus stagnation as the central developmental challenge for midlife adults he formulated the research question: How do life stories help midlife adults solve the problem of generativity? (McAdams, 2014, p. 63). In a retrospective on his own work he portrays redemptive life stories as life stories transporting, by featuring a positively evaluated outcome, the hope that "generative investments will pay off in the long run" (McAdams, 2014, p. 64). He cautions that his research on the life stories of highly generative adults has focused on American adults at midlife and lines out "four canonical versions of redemptive stories" which characterize American culture and history and are taken up in individual redemptive life stories: atonement (from sin to salvation), upward social mobility, emancipation and liberation, and recovery (McAdams, 2014, p. 64–65). These themes, he argues, might function as characteristics of an American master narrative.

For old age and the realization of the finitude of life Erikson saw the developmental task of integrity versus despair, resulting, if resolved, in wisdom. Wisdom, or wisdom-related knowledge, as an area of adult development has been put on the research agenda of life-span psychology (Baltes & Staudinger, 2000, Glück & Staudinger, 2011) and evolved into a currently debated field (Grossmann et al., 2020). One of the starting questions for the study of wisdom in psychology was: How can wisdom be captured? One approach focused on finding exemplars for wisdom, and in this line of research, we meet again (among other exemplars) Fowler's exemplars for stage 6, Mother Teresa, Martin Luther King, Mahatma Gandhi, this time in lists of wisdom prototypes (Weststrate, Ferrari & Ardelt, 2016, p. 666). This strategy focuses on the content of extraordinary lives—not so much on regular development and attitudes toward coping with sickness or the finitude of life. Paul Baltes reminds us that religious traditions have served as repositories of human wisdom across time, when he states, in his unfinished work on wisdom (2004, p. 9) that wisdom "has been at the core of religious and philosophical thinking right from the beginning, when humankind moved toward the creation of an organized form of knowledge." Thus, the reappearance of exemplars of advanced faith development as exemplars of wisdom should not be a surprise, rather illustrate need as well as options for interdisciplinary dialogue.

Another proposal to look at identity in later life concerns a more inwardly turned understanding of self-transcendence and ego-integrity, as proposed by Reischer and colleagues, referring to relevant research:

> "Self-transcendence is often understood to be a natural maturational process most relevant to those in the last stages of life, either due to old age or terminal illness (Erikson, 1997; Levenson et al., 2005; Tornstam, 1997). This developmental understanding of self-transcendence emphasizes a particular wisdom that accompanies approaching death and the accumulation of increasingly difficult life events. [Earlier on the same page:] Like those who exhibit ego integrity, moreover, highly self-transcendent people tend to prioritize questions of life meaning over material possessions (Reed, 1991, 2014), showing what Tornstam (1997) has called 'ego-transcendence' and what Levenson et al. (2005) refer to as 'increased interiority'." (Reischer, et al., 2021, p. 306)

Regarding the extension of mature, or, less euphemistically, old age, the late gerontologist Paul Baltes (2006) has talked of "hope with a black ribbon," alluding to the observation, that the additional years may also come with additional risks of illness and decline, or longer times of suffering. Is this a challenge for the development of wisdom—or rather an additional developmental task, as suggested by Joan Erikson who portrayed it as the ninth stage of development (Erikson, 1997)?

Might the observed "semantization" of autobiographical remembering, the shift from (fewer) episodic to (more) semantic episodes—distilling and preserving abstract meaning from vivid singular episodes—which characterizes remembering in old age, be a narrative characteristic of wisdom? Semantization in old age might be explained by loss of episodic memory ability, but also, alternatively, by an increasing tendency to search for meaning. The authors of a study which found non-inverse development of episodicity and searching for meaning in older age discuss that the semantization effect may not merely be due to an increase in interpretative, that is, increasingly integrative, preferences (Habermas, Diel, & Welzer, 2013).

Thus, identity or identity integration can, as Mitchell and colleagues suggest, be regarded as a lifelong task: "Identity integration describes the process of bringing together various aspects of one's self into a coherent whole, and the sense of self-continuity and wholeness that emerges as a result of these processes" (Mitchell et al., 2021, 1981). This is compared to autobiographical reasoning and applied to narrative:

> "The narrative construct of autobiographical reasoning is closely related to identity integration, reflecting the cognitive processes involved in integrating experiences into one's broader life story (Habermas & Bluck, 2000). Autobiographical reasoning becomes more frequent and sophisticated with age (Pasupathi & Mansour, 2006), and remains an important part of narrative identity development throughout adulthood (Lilgendahl, 2015)." (Mitchell et al, 2021, 1984)

Narrative as life story and layer of personality

The work of Dan McAdams, to which we have already referred, has gained considerable attention. His model suggests regarding life story as one of three developmental layers of psychological individuality, of personality (McAdams & Olson, 2010). According to McAdams' model the self can be seen as actor, characterized by traits, as agent, with personal goals and strivings, and as author of their life story, which is integrating past, present, and future. These layers develop one after the other, starting with self as actor and the emergence of self-attribution and self-regulation in early childhood (age 2–3). Self as agent builds on this, involving exploration of and commitment to life projects and the development of self-esteem in mid to late childhood (age 7–9). The self continuity, and, accordingly, the self as author, that is offered by a life story is available by age 15–25 or adolescence and emerging adulthood (McAdams, 2013, p. 273). Then, autobiographical reasoning skills are available to create a coherent life story looking back on turning points, gaining insight by lessons learned, and perhaps finding redemptive meanings (p. 279).

Thus, narrative became to be regarded as an additional pathway to the study of personality. As stated in a current review of personality across the life span: "Traits are only one component of the personality system, which also includes such elements as needs and motives, attitudes and beliefs, and life narratives." (Costa et al., 2019, p. 2). The authors detail, further below in their review:

> "FFT (five factor theory) conceptualizes dispositional traits as basic, biologically rooted tendencies that are translated into characteristic, culturally contextualized adaptations as basic tendencies interact with external influences. Characteristic adaptations (and maladaptations) may comprise goals, strivings, and attitudes as well as the self-concept, which in turn incorporates self-schemas and the life story." (p. 17)

While the authors appreciate the richer description of the three-layered model, they note the complex developmental interaction on these layers as research desideratum:

> "However, much of the research record remains compartmentalized, focusing on one layer at a time with too little attention to the developmental dynamics of interactions among layers. Five-factor theory (FFT; McCrae & Costa, 2008) can serve as one framework to explore further the processes by which dispositional traits are translated into motivational concepts and narrative constructs, respectively." (ibid.)

Research perspectives from clinical developmental psychology such as mentalization (Fonagy et al., 2019) might help here by offering methods which are tailored toward detecting markers of interindividual difference and of intraindividual change in, for example, reflective functioning (an emerging awareness of inner processes, one's own and others) linked to varyingly complex representations of one's own and others' identities. The growing capacity to reflect and communicate on inner processes may support the development of autobiographical reasoning skills (see Köber et al., 2019). Better self-understanding may support self-regulation and self-esteem. There is need for a framework and methods to study the complex lifelong interactions of the "layers," which perhaps might also be described as functions.

Longitudinal research covering all three layers may help to clarify how traits, personal strivings, and their reflection in life narratives may interact across time or even the human life span. The problem of discrepancies of self-reported and observed change can be addressed by adding observational to self-report data, and by observing "narrative constructs" such as autobiographical narratives across time, looking for indicators of self-reflection. The interdisciplinary range of this kind of narrative work has been outlined in the recent publication of Reischer and others:

> "Spanning cognitive science, personality, social, developmental, and clinical psychology, narrative research recognizes humans to be meaning-making creatures who seek to make sense of their lives by integrating their experiences—past, present, and imagined future—into more-or-less coherent stories." (Reischer et al., 2021, p. 307)

Our longitudinal mixed-methods approach, detailed in chapter 4, looks promising and should support efforts to disentangle different trajectories on different levels of personality description. We would add that it is helpful to also attend to social and historical context and to include knowledge from history, linguistics, sociology, and theology. In the next section we introduce the method we use to elicit rich and autobiographically anchored subjective accounts of meaning making. We go again back to the work of James Fowler.

Research Method: The Faith Development Interview

Here, we present what has been preserved, while carefully adapted during the longitudinal research reported in this volume, the "Faith Development Interview," abbreviated as FDI. Fowler wished to invite research participants to share their attitudes and values in life and the experiences that shaped them. He discusses the problem that introducing the research interview as "Faith Development Interview" might invoke, against his intention, the notions of religion and belief (Fowler, 1981, p. 308). The problem of an inclusive language persists; therefore, we stress, in our introductions of the interview, the broad concept of "faith" that we still use in connection, however, with "religion and worldview" (see, for example, Streib & Keller, 2018). The FDI consists of the four sections of life review, relationships, values and commitments, and religion and world view. Life review still starts with the life chapter question suggested by Fowler. In this part of the interview there is also room for exploring marker events, turning points, changes in relationships and worldviews. Fowler stresses that he makes "the person's own life experiences, responses to challenges and constructions of meanings the subject of the interview" (Fowler, 1981, p. 308). In the second section, the focus is shifted to relationships from parents to groups, institutions, and even causes. Fowler notes that the shift to section 3, values and commitments, may bring a change of the atmosphere. It may feel more like "problem-posing." In the last section, the participant's religious identity is explicitly addressed: How would a person identify themself? To give an example of an adaptation: Since the time of Fowler's writing, the self-identification "spiritual" has gained importance, and we include this in the question 20 of the interview, which now reads as: "Do you consider yourself a religious, spiritual, or faithful person? Or would you prefer another self-description?" and thus paying tribute to growing pluralism. Also explored are existential questions, the finality of human life is addressed, and the interviewee is invited to share their thoughts and feelings. In the last question, options to resolve conflicts around religion and worldview are requested—offering the interviewee to think about options for inter-religious interactions bringing the interview back to a social perspective.

Fowler notes that he asks throughout for examples to see how "beliefs and values relate to action" in participants' lives, and we continue to teach and cultivate this strategy, training interviewers to use prompts and ask for examples. Fowler also reports that respondents often appreciate the opportunity of the experience (1981, p. 310). We can state that the space to reflect on one's life that this research interview offers continues to find appreciation.

"Interfaces" to current (narrative) approaches in Psychology
The Faith Development Interview covers life review, relationships, values and commitments and religion and worldview. Thus, it continues to address, contextualized by per-

sonal experience, a number of issues which are studied in current developmental and personality psychology however, separately, and in different research contexts: The life review section, including the life chapter task, has some similarity with McAdams' life story approach (McAdams et al., 2001, McAdams & Albaugh, 2008, see Keller, 2020, for a detailed comparison). Redemption and contamination are categories we borrow and apply, as people tell us about good things turning bad, and about bad things turning good. They may also tell us about bad things that happen to good people, how good people cope, and what impact this has on them: Adversity may stimulate changes in narrative identity, wisdom, learning, habit formation, stability (Jayawickreme et al., 2020). Thus, the FDI may, by exploring crises and suffering as well as intense joy and experiences of breakthrough, elicit responses comparable to what is studied in the area of posttraumatic growth as change in identity, or what is explored by research on life challenges which may motivate the development of wisdom (for example, in the conception of Glück, 2019).

The section on relationships, especially the question inviting to reflect on the relationship with one's parents, can motivate participants to elaborate responses similar to what is narrated during an Adult Attachment Interview (AAI). The AAI explores how respondents look back on their relationships to their early attachment figures, usually parents.[6] The AAI challenges interviewees to substantiate more general descriptive or evaluative statements on attachment relationships with specific experiences. While such a detailed investigation is not part of the FDI, interviewees may spontaneously reveal comparable experiences when describing their relationships to their parents in the life review or the relationship section of the FDI. This allows interpretations drawing on attachment theory. If what interviewees tell about their relationships to their parents can be related to what they report about changes in their images of God or their world views in the last section, we can offer hypotheses regarding attachment-related trajectories and discuss interpretations involving compensatory or socialization pathways. Thus, we engage in exploratory usage of attachment theory in the case studies in this book, and find encouragement for our efforts: In his recent book, Pehr Granqvist has expanded the classical AAI approach, which is based on identifying a current attachment style based on standardized ratings. He presents case studies (Granqvist, 2020) involving repeated interviewing and an additional format exploring relationships with God as an attachment figure.

Especially the exploration of values and commitments, which includes questions on what is right and wrong, invite the discussion of morals, and allows for the identification of moral foundations as specified by Graham and Haidt (for example Graham et al., 2011), grounded in subjectively constructed autobiographical accounts. The study of how persons construct examples of their own ways of being moral may overlap with the study of moral agency (for example Recchia, Wainryb, Bourne, & Pasupathi, 2015). The last section on religion and worldviews addresses, among other issues, what respondents think and feel about the finitude of life. This resonates with research on terror management (Solomon et al., 2004).

---

6   Attachment is studied in the psychology of religion operationalized by the Adult Attachment Interview (AAI) and by self-report scales (for an overview and discussion see Granqvist's (2020) chapter on individual differences in attachment).

These different "interfaces" are activated during an FDI depending on subjective experience as unfolded in the course of an interview. Throughout the interview, opportunities for autobiographical reasoning arise, and the coherence of autobiographical (re-)constructions (Habermas, 2011) varies. The FDI can thus offer the empirical basis for an integrative perspective which relies on the choices of the participant during a particular interview. For some, the relationship with their parents may be an important issue, for some it may not. Some may discuss morals extensively, others may focus on different issues.

With the FDI we explore several concepts as they are used, integrated in autobiographical accounts, and related to narrative identities. The FDI thus offers access to the study of subjective actualizations and integrations of issues now studied scattered across different research fields, with efforts at integration based on overlap of concepts rather than empirical exploration.

Looking back on looking back: Double diachronicity

We follow reconstructions of individual lives across time, in this volume reporting about three times of interviewing. This means that we have: 1.) the perspective of the single autobiographical review, reported in a single FDI, and 2.) the perspective across three FDIs obtained consecutively over 10–20 years. Thus, we have what we call double diachronicity (see Figure 3.1 which illustrates the concept referring to two points of measurement): Change as reported is based on our respondents' subjective reconstructions of their (religious) lives and accounts of development, resulting in the single diachronicity of individual biographies. We attend, to use McAdams' terminology (McAdams, 2013, McAdams & Olson, 2010), to the self as author with a special interest in "religious identity narratives" (narrated episodes, consisting of orientation, complication, evaluation, resolution, coda, as described by Labov & Waletzky, 1967) giving accounts of one's religious or worldview development (Keller et al., 2016). Change as observed is based on following biographical reconstructions and accounts across time, resulting in the additional diachronic perspective of tracing changes of these accounts and reconstructions (Bullik, 2024; Keller et al., 2021). Thus, we follow the self as author across different subsequent revisions of their autobiography.

When we attend to characteristic adaptations, such as FDI-Profiles or religious types, but also Ryff´s scale of eudaimonic wellbeing (Ryff, 1989; Ryff & Singer 1998a, b, Ryff & Singer, 1996), the Religious Schema Scale (Streib, Hood & Klein 2010), and, as detailed in chapter 1, Hood's M-Scale which explores mystic experience, we follow the self as motivated agent.

When we attend to the basic traits as measured with the Big Five (Costa & McCrae, 1985), we follow the self as actor. As discussed above we need to be aware of interactions: We will act differently, be different agents, as we reflect on our actions and agency—and how we develop as actors and agents is intertwined with the development of our authorship.

Figure 3.1: Double diachronicity

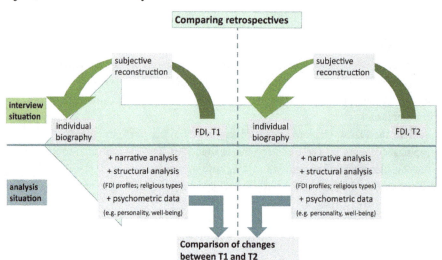

Following Narrative Religious Identities or Worldviews

We follow narrative religious identities and worldviews across three time points, taking together what we can observe when we look across change in all three layers of personality. Do narrative identities differ in stability? Do we find dwellers and seekers? Or can, who has stayed with what they identified, from the first to the second interview, present a new idea of who they are at the third? What kinds of trajectories can we observe? What has brought about change in the view of our respondents, and what do we hypothesize?

The case study section offers examples of stability as well as change and describes different trajectories. There, we attend to narrative identity as displayed in the consecutive FDIs and connect those observations with explicit self-identifications in the interviews. We attend to themes and issues which are introduced by participants and may address questions not yet mapped. This we achieve by a sufficiently open coding strategy (see chapters 4 and 7). Also, we may draw on self-identifications given in the questionnaire, and on the definitions of religion and spirituality given there. Working within a longitudinal perspective, we may get from the micro to the macro-level by making the discovery of trajectories which characterize more than one case and thus work toward typologies of trajectories.

We trace changes in dimensions of personality, in dimensions of psychological well-being and growth, in religious schemata, based on self-report instruments, on quantitative methods. We assess the structure of meaning-making by tracing ratings of Faith Development Interviews from one point of measurement to the next. Rating means to assign a style to each aspect covered by answers to the respective questions of the FDI, resulting in style-aspect profiles (see Streib & Keller, 2018). We also follow the sections of the FDI from one point of measurement to the next, compiling summaries for comparison. And we trace narratives, themes, and leitmotifs (see the case study chapters, and also Bullik, 2024). Thus, we can look at identity as constructed in the FDI, as defined, and as located within current social scientific frameworks as interpreted by the respective interviewee. In this volume, we start with the in-depth analysis of the trajectory of one single case and proceed to comparisons with cases selected according to demographic criteria suggesting differences in identity with view on religion or worldview (for example by gender, age/cohort, nationality).

By careful comparisons of more and more diverse cases, we identify dimensions of descriptions. We proceed from an idiographic approach, focusing on the single case, to an "idiothetic" (Lamiell, 2019, 1981) approach:

> "With the neologism 'idiothetic,' I sought to identify an approach to personality studies whereby the determination of those traits relevant to the description of any given individual's personality would be done idiographically, i.e., case by individual case, 'nomothetic' knowledge would be found, if at all, in what might prove common to all in the domain of personality development." (Lamiell, 2019, p. 32)

Thus, we identify commonalities, based on case-by-case comparison. By ongoing comparison of cases, we identify themes, or narratives that appear in more than one case, and may describe typical configurations. This opens the opportunity to move to case-based lines of comparison and to go from the micro to the macro level and for example create typologies (see chapter 4 for a more detailed discussion of the research design).

The individual trajectories of these specific measures are then linked to change observed in structure and content of the Faith Development Interview. Throughout we apply, as Josselson (2004) has detailed, a hermeneutics of faith, giving our interviewees and their views a voice, but also a hermeneutics of suspicion, which moves beyond their self-presentations and aims at a deeper understanding of their identities.

Changing Narrative Religious Identities in Changing Social and Historical Contexts

Beginning with the Deconversion Study (Streib et al., 2009), continuing with studies on "Spirituality" (Streib & Hood, 2016), recently going longitudinal with "Deconversion revisited" (Streib et al., 2022), we have interviewed people from diverse religious orientations and worldviews in Germany and the US. We have also listened to people from different cohorts. Our oldest participants have survived the 2nd world war, aging "Boomers" can look back on the Vietnam war, on social movements of the seventies, on changes in women's rights and moral standards. For the youngest participants, the German reunification is something they learn about in history books. Current debates on identity politics, antiracism, and anticolonialism offer new challenges to personal identities and how to narrate autobiographies in times already characterized by at least a demand of more flexibility. Figure 3.2 gives an overview of the cases portrayed in this volume.

Figure 3.2: The participants and their interviews in historical context

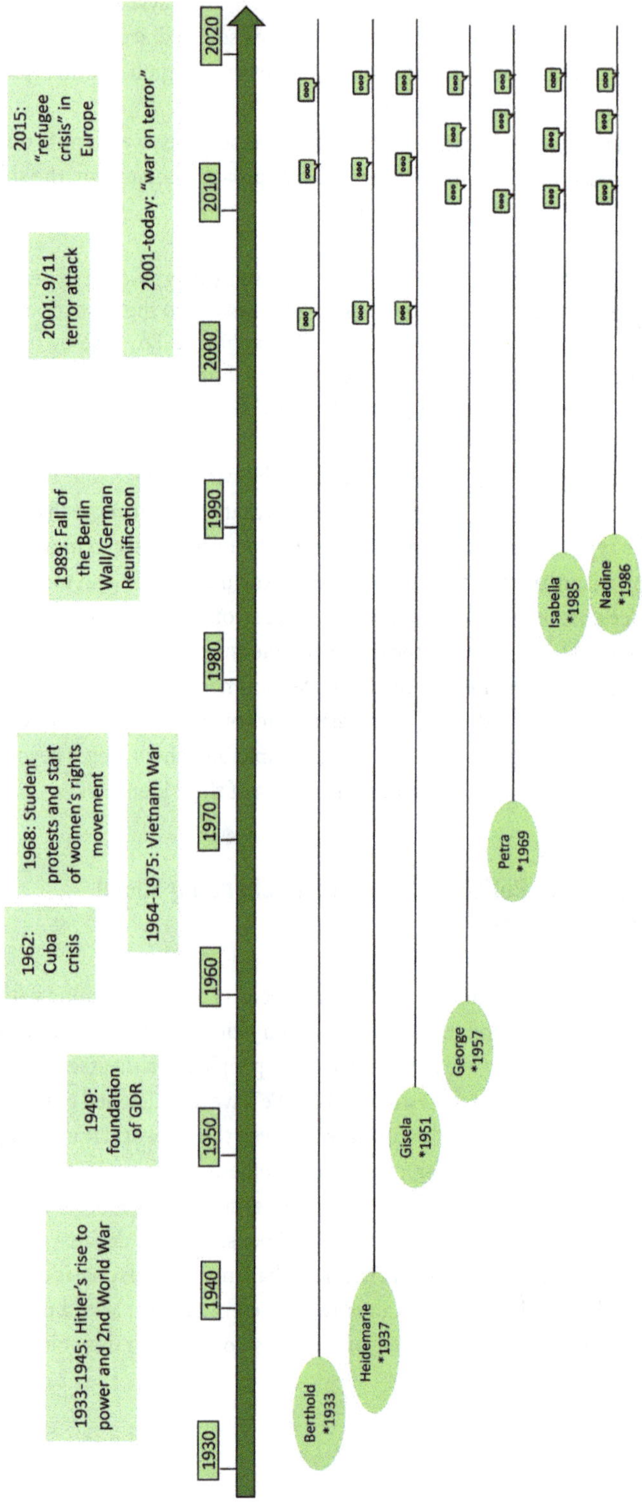

It shows the participants sorted by year of birth and contextualized with (rather broad) historical background information. The figure furthermore indicates the years in which the participants were interviewed, thus giving a first approximation to the historical and social contexts the participants experienced. However, as will become clear in the case study chapters, the individual circumstances are maybe even more relevant for the accounts that we aim to reconstruct. Arnett, in his article on life stage concepts, relates the flexibilization of conceptions of what to expect in a human life to postindustrial societies and individualization:

> "As the industrial economy morphed into the postindustrial economy, institutional-ization was succeeded by deinstitutionalization. Standardization was followed by de-standardization. Chronologization waned and was replaced by individualization, as people were both allowed and required to exercise more individual agency to chart their way through the life course and to determine for themselves the timing of the transitions from one life stage to the next [Heinz, 2002]." (Arnett, 2016, p. 306)

Another recent suggestion concerns the study of different conceptualizations of human life-span as sequence of stages and pertaining developmental tasks. From this perspective, the stages of human life, which are shown to vary with history and culture, offer a master story. This master story tells what is to be expected in a life in a given time or culture. This does not mean that it pictures what most members really live (Arnett, 2016). Normative expectations may impact individual life stories in different ways. Respondents may comment on their perceived version of a master narrative, they may use it, reject it, or offer already available "alternative narratives" (which might be seen as master narratives in their respective (sub-) cultures). In a similar vein, Fivush, Habermas, Waters & Zaman (2011) argued that cultures provide organizational and evaluative frameworks for narrating lives, including canonical cultural biographies, life scripts, and master narratives. Life scripts, cultural conceptions of what a life is supposed to contain and when, what it contains, is supposed to happen (Habermas, 2007) structure individual life stories. Conceptions like "master narratives" ("expected story-lines," cf. Hammack, 2008; Hammack & Toolis, 2015; McLean & Syed, 2015) draw on dominant social norms and expectations. More recently in sociology, the "deep story" or "feels as if it were true story" has been suggested as a concept to explore the "emotional core" of political belief: Different political camps like the conservatives and liberals in the US are supposed to understand and tell their own lives corresponding to different deep stories, stories anchored in feelings, about values one identifies with (Hochschild, 2016, note 135, p. 297). What one identifies with can be challenged, for example by "feeling rules", notions of what one should feel, which are felt to be imposed by those from the "other" camp. This is felt as a threat not just to debatable political opinions, but to something that goes far deeper. A charismatic leader then can appeal to one's deep story and mobilize social and political action (see Hochschild, 2016, p. 15 -16). Conceptual overlap with the concept of the master narrative is in the area of complying with normative expectations, which may deviate from realistic options.

Arnett's discussion of life stages inspires questions for the study of narrative identity in different times and places: This challenges researchers to work toward "languages of

Part A: Conceptual & Methodological Perspectives

translation," to find useful lines of comparison, along which to define differences and demarcations of "common cores" of contents. From there, structures and processes can be explored: Are there different developmental tasks, different timetables? What processes of negotiation do we observe? What developmental trajectories can be identified? On the level of individual autobiographical reconstructions, we hear people endorse as well as criticize, in discussion with perceived larger social or historical context, developments they observe in their immediate social surrounds as well as globally. How is this linked to their ideas of who they are or can aspire to become? Also, what social spaces, what "cultural containers" (Will, 2017) give room as well as vocabulary for the articulation of experience and identity? Do they, for example, draw on psychological vocabulary or refer to therapy as a means of coping with life's challenges? Or do they have religious ties they rely on? We can look at narrative as structure (in a life story, a religious identity narrative) and as process, negotiating identity (during the interview and addressing the interviewer, or discussing perceived larger social or historical phenomena).

Conclusion

Our research on worldviews, religion and the development of narrative identities is itself situated in changing historical and cultural contexts. In need of a more flexible modelling of change across the life span, Fowler's stages have been reconciled ("aufgehoben") through the acknowledgement of more differentiated processes of change which can be studied using different methodological lenses and languages. The revision of Fowler's work which has resulted in Streib's religious styles perspective has been continued here to the study of narrative identity. The narrative integration of identity is conceptualized as an ongoing task, beginning, but not ending in adolescence. Narrative as structure can be seen as life story, as narrative identity at a given time and as such as a layer of personality at a given time. Narrative identity as process can be observed during the interview and reconstructed across time. This may result in a scientific meta-narrative with a specific structure—similar to experience first represented as episode in episodic memory, and later feeding, with other experiences, into abstracted meaning and semantic memory. The rich material offered by the FDI can serve as point of departure for integrative research. Participants raise in their constructions of religious identities and worldviews issues which resonate with concepts and methods currently addressed in segregated research fields. By offering access to how important issues are used (or not used) within autobiographical constructions, the FDI offers a complementary perspective of modelling accounts in development.

We have started to attend to identity beyond narrative, to felt identity. What about mystic experience, and to letting go of self/identity, in mystic experience and as goal of human development in indigenous or "alternative" life stage concepts? With questions like these, we offer yet another venue for interdisciplinary, and, hopefully, intercultural work. The case studies presented in Part C explore these and other questions, proposing an approach to identity development that takes into account individual particularities as well as more general circumstances and data on psychometric scales, thereby arriving at different outlines of adult (religious) development.

References

Aragno, A. (1997). Symbolization. Proposing a developmental paradigm for a new psychoanalytical theory of mind. International Universities Press.

Arnett, J.J. (2007). Emerging adulthood: What is it, and what is it good for? *Child Development Perspectives*, 1(2), 68–73.

Arnett, J.J. (2016). Life stage concepts across history and cultures: Proposal for a new field on indigenous life stages. *Human Development* 59, 290–316. https://doi.org/10.1159/0 00453627

Baltes, P. B. (2004). Wisdom as orchestration of mind and virtue. Max Planck Institute for Human Development, Berlin.

Baltes, P. B. (2006). Hoffnung mit Trauerflor. Lebenslänge contra Lebensqualität – Von der Menschenwürde im hohen Alter. [Hope with a black ribbon. Length of life versus quality of life. Human dignity in advanced age]. Neue Zürcher Zeitung 257 Samstag/ Sonntag 4.5. November.

Baltes, P. B. & Schaie, K. W. (Eds) (1973). *Life-span developmental psychology — Personality and socialization*, Academic Press.

Baltes, P. B., & Staudinger, U. M. (2000). Wisdom: a metaheuristic (pragmatic) to orchestrate mind and virtue toward excellence. *American Psychologist*, 55(1), 122. https://doi. org/10.1037/0003-066X.55.1.122

Baltes, P. B., Lindenberger, U. & Staudinger, U. M. (2006) Lifespan theory in developmental psychology. In R. Lerner & W. Damon (eds), *Handbook of child psychology. Vol. I. Theoretical models of human development*. Wiley.

Bullik, R. (2024). Leitmotifs in life stories. Reconstructing subjective religiosity and narrative identity—developments and stabilities over the adult lifespan. Bielefeld University Press.

Conway, M. A., & Pleydell-Pearce, C. W. (2000). The construction of autobiographical memories in the self-memory system. *Psychological Review*, 107(2), 261–288. https:/ /psycnet.apa.org/doi/10.1037/0033-295X.107.2.261

Conway, M. A., Justice, L. V. and D'Argembeau, A. (2019) The Self-Memory System Revisited In: The organization and structure of autobiographical memory. Edited by: John H. Mace, Oxford University Press. https://doi.org/10.1093/oso/9780198784845.003.0 003

Costa, P. T., & McCrae, R. R. (1985). *Revised NEO Personality Inventory (NEO PI-R) and NEO Five-Factor-Inventory (NEO-FFI). Professional manual*. Odessa.

Costa, P.T., McCrae, R. R. & Löckenhoff, C. E. (2019) Personality across the life span. *Annual Review of Psychology*, https://doi.org/10.1146/annurev-psych-010418-103244

Erikson, E.H. (1950). *Childhood and society*. Norton.

Erikson, E. H. & J.M. (1997). *The life cycle completed. Extended version*. Norton.

Fivush, R., Habermas, T., Waters, T. E. A. & Zaman, W. (2011). The making of autobiographical memory: Intersections of culture, narratives and identity. *International Journal of Psychology*, 46 (5), 321–345. https://doi.org/10.1080/00207594.2011.596541

Fivush, R., Booker, J. A. & Graci, M. E. (2017). Ongoing narrative meaning making within events and across the life span. *Imagination, Cognition and Personality: Consciousness in*

Theory, Research, and Clinical Practic, Vol. 37(2) 127–152. https://doi.org/10.1177/0276236617733824

Fonagy, P., & Target, M. (1996). Playing with reality: I. Theory of mind and the normal development of psychic reality. The International Journal of Psychoanalysis, 77(2), 217–233.

Fonagy, P., & Target, M. (2007). Playing with reality: IV. A theory of external reality rooted in intersubjectivity. *International Journal of Psychoanalysis*, 88(9), 17–37.

Fonagy, P., Luyten, P., Allison, E., & Campbell, C. (2019). Mentalizing, epistemic trust and the phenomenology of psychotherapy. *Psychopathology*, 52(2): 94–103. https://doi.org/10.1159/000501526

Fowler, J. W. (1981). *Stages of Faith*, San Francisco: Harper&Row.

Fowler, J. W., & Dell, M. L. (2006). Stages of faith from infancy through adolescence: Reflections on three decades of faith development theory. In E. C. Roehlkepartain (Ed.), *The handbook of spiritual development in childhood and adolescence* (pp. 34–45). Sage Publications.

Glück, J. (2019). The development of wisdom during adulthood. In R. J. Sternberg & J. Glück (Eds.), *The Cambridge handbook of wisdom* (pp. 323–346). Cambridge University Press. https://doi.org/10.1017/9781108568272.016

Glück, J., & Staudinger, U. M. (2011). Psychological wisdom research: Commonalities and differences in a growing field. *Annual Review of Psychology*, 62(2), 15–41. https://doi.org/10.1146/annurev.psych.121208.131659

Graham, J., Nosek, B. A., Haidt, J., Iyer, R, Koleva, S., & Ditto, P. H. (2011). Mapping the moral domain. *Journal of Personality and Social Psychology*, 101(2), 366–385. https://doi.org/10.1037/a0021847

Granqvist, P. (2020). *Attachment in religion and spirituality: A wider view.* Guilford.

Grossmann, I. (2018) Dialecticism across the lifespan. Toward a deeper understanding of the ontogenetic and cultural factors influencing dialectical thinking and emotional experience. In: J. Spencer-Rodgers & K. Peng (eds). *The psychological and cultural foundations of East Asian cognition: Contradiction, change, and holism.* Oxford Scholarship. https://doi.org/10.1093/oso/9780199348541.003.0005

Grossmann, I., Weststrate, N.M., Ardelt, M, Brienza, J.P., Donge, M., Ferrari, M., Fournier, M. A., Hug, C.S., Nusbaum, H.C. & Vervaeke, J. (2020) The science of wisdom in a polarized world: Knowns and unknowns. *Psychological Inquiry*, 31(2), 103–133.

Habermas, T. (2007). How to tell a life: The development of the cultural concept of biography across the lifespan. *Journal of Cognition and Development*, 8, 1–31. https://doi.org/10.1080/15248370709336991

Habermas, T. (2011). Autobiographical Reasoning: Arguing and Narrating from a Biographical Perspective. *New Directions for Child and Adolescent Development*, 131, 1–17. https://doi.org/10.1002/cd.285

Habermas, T., & Bluck, S. (2000). Getting a life: The development of the life story in adolescence. *Psychological Bulletin*, 126, 748–769. https://doi.org/10.1037%2F%2F0033-2909.126.5.748

Habermas, T., Diel, V. & Welzer, H. (2013) Lifespan trends of autobiographical remembering: Episodicity and search for meaning. *Consciousness and Cognition* 22, 1061–1073. https://doi.org/10.1016/j.concog.2013.07.010

Hammack, P. L. (2008). Narrative and the cultural psychology of identity. *Personality and Social Psychology Review*, 12, 222–247.

Hammack, P. L. & Toolis, E. E. (2015). Putting the social into personal identity: The master narrative as root metaphor for psychological and developmental science. *Human Development 58*, 350–364. https://doi.org/10.1159/000446054

Hochschild, A. R. (2016). *Strangers in their own Land. Anger and mourning on the American Right*. The New Press.

Jayawickreme, E., Infurna, F. J., Alajak, K. et al (2021). Post-traumatic growth as positive personality change: Challenges, opportunities, and recommendations. *Journal of Personality*, 89:145–165. https://doi.org/10.1111/jopy.12591

Josselson. R. (2004). The hermeneutics of faith and the hermeneutics of suspicion. *Narrative Inquiry*, 14(1), 1–28. https://doi.org/10.1075/ni.14.1.01jos

Josselson, R. (2017). *Paths to fulfillment. Women's search for meaning and identity*. Oxford University Press.

Keller, B. (2020). *Toward a binocular vision of religion: Psychoanalytic and psychometric perspectives*. Brill. https://doi.org/10.1163/9789004436343_002

Keller, B., Bullik, R., Steppacher, A., Streib, H., & Silver, C. F. (2021). Following deconverts and traditionalists. Longitudinal case study construction. In H. Streib, B. Keller, R. Bullik, A. Steppacher, C. F. Silver, M. Durham, S. B. Barker, & Hood, Jr., Ralph W. (Eds.), *Deconversion revisited. Biographical studies and psychometric analyses ten years later*. Vandenhoeck & Ruprecht.

Keller, B., Coleman III, T. J., & Silver, C. F. (2016). Narrative reconstruction and content analysis. Content analysis in the interpretation of "spiritual" biographical trajectories for case studies. In H. Streib & Hood, Jr., Ralph W. (Eds.), *Semantics and psychology of spirituality: A cross-cultural analysis* (pp. 251–271). Springer. https://doi.org/10.1007/978-3-319-21245-6_16

Köber, C., Kuhn, M., Peters, I., & Habermas, T. (2019). Mentalizing oneself: Detecting reflective functioning in life narratives. *Attachment & Human Development*, 21, 313–331. https://doi.org/10.1080/14616734.2018.1473886

Labov, W. & Waletzky, J. (1967). Narrative analysis: Oral versions of personal experience. In J. Helms (Ed.), *Essays on the Verbal and Visual Arts* (pp. 12–44). University of Washington Press.

Labouvie-Vief, G. (1997). Cognitive-emotional integration in adulthood. In P.M. Lawton & F. W. Schaie (Eds) Emotions in adult development (pp. 206–236). Springer.

Lamiell, J. T. (1981). Toward an idiothetic psychology of personality. *American Psychologist*, 36(3), 276–289. https://doi.org/10.1037/0003-066X.36.3.276

Lamiell, J. T. (2019). *Psychology's misuse of statistics and persistent dismissal of its critics*. Palgrave McMillan.

Levinson, D., Darrow, C., Klein, E., Levinson, M., & McKee, B. (1978). *The seasons of a man's life*. Knopf.

McAdams, D. P. (2001). The psychology of life stories. *Review of General Psychology*, 5 (2) 100–122.

McAdams, D. P. (2013). The psychological self as actor, agent, and author. *Perspectives on Psychological Science* 8(3) 272–295. https://doi.org/10.1177/1745691612464657

McAdams, D. P. (2014). The life narrative at midlife. In B. Schiff (Ed.), *Rereading personal narrative and the life course*. New Directions for Child and Adolescent Development, 145, 57–69.

McAdams, D. & Albaugh, M. (2008). The redemptive self, generativity, and American Christians at midlife: Explorations of the life stories of evangelical and mainline protestants. In J. A. Belzen & A. Geels (eds.). *Autobiography and the psychological study of religious lives* (pp. 255–286). Rodopi. https://doi.org/10.1163/9789042029125_012

McAdams, D. P., Reynolds, J., Lewis, M., Patten, A. H., & Bowman, P. J. (2001). When bad things turn good and good things turn bad: Sequences of redemption and contamination in life narrative and their relation to psychosocial adaptation in midlife adults and in students. *Personality and Social Psychology Bulletin*, 27(4), 474–485.

McAdams, D. P. & Olson, B. D. (2010). Personality development: Continuity and change over the life course. *Annual Review of Psychology 61*, 517–542. https://doi.org/10.1146/annurev.psych.093008.100507

McLean, K. C., & Syed, M. (2015). Personal, master, and alternative narratives: An integrative framework for understanding identity development in context. *Human Development*, 58, 318–349. https://doi.org/10.1159/000445817

Mitchell, S. A. (2000) *Relationality: From attachment to intersubjectivity*. The Analytic Press.

Mitchell, L., Adler, J. M., Carlsson, J., Eriksson, P., & Syed, M. (2021). A conceptual review of identity integration across adulthood. *Developmental Psychology*, 57(11). https://doi.org/10.1037/dev0001246

Munawar, K., Kuhn, S. K., & Haque, S. (2018) Understanding the reminiscence bump: A systematic review. *PLoS ONE* 13(12): e0208595. https://doi.org/10.1371/journal.pone.0208595

Negele, A., & Habermas, T. (2010). Self-continuity across developmental change in and of repeated life narratives. In K. McLean & M. Pasupathi (Eds.), *Narrative development in adolescence* (pp. 1–22). Springer

Pasupathi, M., Mansour, E., & Brubaker, J.R. (2007). Developing a life story: Constructing relations between self and experience in autobiographical narratives. *Human Development 50*:85–110. https://doi.org/10.1159/000100939

Recchia, H. E, Wainryb, C., Bourne, S. & Pasupathi, M. (2015) Children's and adolescents' accounts of helping and hurting others: Lessons about the development of moral agency, *Child Development 86*(3), 864–876.

Reischer, H. N., Roth, L. J., Villarreal, J. A., & McAdams, D. P. (2021). Self-transcendence and life stories of humanistic growth among late-midlife adults. *Journal of Personality 89*(2), 305–324. https://doi.org/10.1111/jopy.12583

Riegel, K.F. (1979). *Foundations of dialectical psychology*. Academic Press.

Ryff, C. D. (1989). Happiness is everything, or is it? Explorations on the meaning of psychological well-being. *Journal of Personality and Social Psychology*, 57, 1069–1081.

Ryff, C. D., & Singer, B. H. (1996). Psychological well-being: Meaning, measurement, and implications for psychotherapy research. *Psychotherapy and Psychosomatics*, 65, 14–23. https://doi.org/10.1159/000289026

Ryff, C. D., & Singer, B. H. (1998a). The contours of positive human health. *Psychological Inquiry*, 9, 1–28.

Ryff, C. D., & Singer, B. H. (1998b). The role of purpose in life and growth in positive human health. In P.T.P. Wong & P. S. Fry (Eds.), *The human quest for meaning. Handbook of psychological research and clinical applications* (pp. 213–235). Mahwah.

Solomon, S., Greenberg, J. & Pyszczynski, T. (2004). The cultural animal: Twenty years of terror management theory and research. In: J. Greenberg, S. L. Koole, T. Pyszczynski (Eds). *Handbook of experimental existential psychology*. Guilford.

Streib, H. (1997). Religion als Stilfrage. Zur Revision struktureller Differenzierung von Religion im Blick auf die Analyse der pluralistisch-religiösen Lage der Gegenwart [Religion as a question of style. On the revision of structural differentiation of religion in respect to the analysis of contemporary pluralist religion]. In Archive for the Psychology of Religion, 22(1), 48–69. https://doi.org/10.1163/157361297X00054

Streib, H. (2001). Faith development theory revisited: The religious styles perspective. *International Journal for the Psychology of Religion*, 11(3), 143–158. https://doi.org/10.1207/S15327582IJPR1103_02

Streib, H. (2005). Faith development research revisited: Accounting for diversity in structure, content, and narrativity of faith. *International Journal for the Psychology of Religion*, 15, 99–121. https://doi.org/10.1207/s15327582ijpr1502_1

Streib, H., Hood, R. W., Jr., Keller, B., Csöff, R.-M., & Silver, C. F. (2009). Deconversion: Qualitative and quantitative results from cross-cultural research in Germany and the United States of America. Vandenhoeck & Ruprecht. https://doi.org/10.13109/9783666604393

Streib, H., Hood, R. W. Jr., & Klein, C. (2010). The religious schema scale: Construction and initial validation of a quantitative measure for religious styles. International Journal for the Psychology of Religion, 20(3), 151–172. https://doi.org/10.1080/10508619.2010.481223

Streib, H., & Hood, R. W., Jr. (Eds.) (2016). *Semantics and psychology of spirituality: A cross-cultural analysis*. Springer. https://doi.org/10.1007/978-3-319-21245-6

Streib, H., & Keller, B. (2018). *Manual for the assessment of religious styles in faith development interviews* (Fourth, revised edition of the "Manual for faith development research"). Universität Bielefeld. https://doi.org/10.4119/unibi/2920987

Streib, H., Keller, B., Bullik, R., Steppacher, A., Silver, C. F., Durham, M., Barker, S. B., & Hood, R. W., Jr. (Eds.) (2022). *Deconversion revisited. Biographical studies and psychometric analyses ten years later.* Vandenhoeck & Ruprecht. https://doi.org/10.13109/9783666568688

Subic-Wrana, C., Beutel, M. E., Garfield, D. A. S. & Lane, R. D. (2011) Levels of emotional awareness: A model for conceptualizing and measuring emotion-centered structural change. *International Journal of Psychoanalysis*, 92, 289–310. https://doi.org/10.1111/j.1745-8315.2011.00392.x

Weststrate, N. M., Ferrari, M. & Ardelt, M. (2016). The many faces of wisdom: An investigation of cultural-historical wisdom exemplars reveals practical, philosophical, and benevolent prototypes. *Personality and Social Psychology Bulletin* 42(5), 662–676.

Will, H. (2017). Religiöse Erfahrung als Transgression. Ein Gedicht Edith Jacobsons aus nationalsozialistischer Haft als Beispiel (Religious experience as transgression. With reference to a poem written by Edith Jacobson in Nazi detention). *Psyche – Zeitschrift für Psychoanalyse und ihre Anwendungen 71*, 235–259.

Chapter 4
Mixed-Method and Longitudinal. Background and Profile of Our Research Design

Anika Steppacher, Barbara Keller, Ramona Bullik, Christopher Silver, & Heinz Streib[1]

Abstract *In this chapter, we will present the research design of the Bielefeld-Chattanooga longitudinal study of faith development focusing on the methodological discussion about mixed-methods research and the knowledge produced by the qualitative and quantitative strands we employ. First, we will present our research in the light of the pragmatic paradigm that enables us to take multiple perspectives through the triangulation of data as well as research methods and discuss the quality criteria of such an approach. We then will briefly present our qualitative and quantitative methods of data collection with a focus on what kind of information we obtain as well as our methods of data analysis concentrating on the kind of knowledge, we are able to produce. This discussion will demonstrate how we investigate faith development using the nomothetic and the idiographic approach that we regard as complementary. The chapter closes by exemplifying our approach by a longitudinal case study.*

> **Keywords:** *Mixed-Methods; Pragmatic Approach; Idiographic; Nomothetic; research design, methodology*

---

1   A. Steppacher, B. Keller, R. Bullik, H.Streib, Bielefeld University, Germany, E-mail: anika.steppacher@uni-bielefeld.de; C. F. Silver, Sewanee. The University of the South, USA. © Heinz Streib, Ralph W. Hood Jr. (eds.): Faith in Development. Mixed-Method Studies on Worldviews and Religious Styles. First published in 2024 by Bielefeld University Press, Bielefeld, https://doi.org/10.14361/9783839471234-006

Part A: Conceptual & Methodological Perspectives

> In order to get "behind" it, a variety of data had to be collected on any issue under investigation, just as the true position of a distant object can be found only through triangulation, by looking at it from different sides and directions. (*Lazarsfeld, 1971, p. xiv*)

These remarks made by Paul Lazarsfeld in the introduction to the English translation of the Marienthal study, which is famous for being one of the first studies that used a mixed-methods approach, mirrors our own view with regard to how we utilize our data to investigate the phenomenon we want to understand. Over the past two decades, the general interest of our research was to study how faith develops in the lives of individuals and how it helps them to cope with existential questions. In other words, we want to discover and understand the dynamics of developments in religiosities and worldviews on the individual as well as on the group level. By doing so, we want to generate knowledge about the meaning-making processes of people, affiliated to a variety of faith groups as well as the unaffiliated and secular, and how they develop over the lifespan. These questions are best addressed within the fields of psychology and sociology of religion, fields that have long been shaped by the debate on the paradigms accompanying natural as opposed to human science.

In his famous inaugural lecture as Rector of the University of Straßburg, the philosopher Wilhelm Windelband (1894) has called attention to a basic distinction and introduced neologisms for it, when he says that "scientific thought is in the one case nomothetic, in the other idiographic" to immediately conclude that "psychology is by all means to be numbered among the natural sciences" (p. 13). However, already in the next paragraph, Windelband adds that "this methodological opposition classifies only the method and not the content of the knowledge itself," therefore "the same subjects can serve as the object of a nomothetic and at the same time of an idiographic investigation" (ibid.). Thus, in the case of what was at the time the still young science of psychology, Windelband can be interpreted as arguing that psychology may theoretically adopt both kinds of paradigms, but with different epistemic interests: finding general laws for explaining human behavior and phenomena – the nomothetic kind of scientific knowledge most akin to natural science, or understanding the particular, the non-recurring and unique – the idiographic approach of human science (cf. Lamiell, 2019, p. 32; cf. Hopf, 2016, p. 209). However, as Lamiell (2013, p. 65) critically notes, the general trend in psychology came to one-sidedly lean towards the nomothetic form of knowledge by heavily depending on statistical data and methods – a development that he polemically calls 'statisticism,' or a "virtually boundless trust in the aptness of statistical concepts and methods to reveal the 'lawfulness' of human psychological functioning and behavior." The problem, Lamiell argues, lies in the fact that statistical knowledge represents aggregated knowledge about a population and the distribution of certain attributes, and therefore fails to tell us anything about the individuals within this population. By doing so, psychology effectively produces "knowledge of populations and not knowledge of individuals" (ibid.,

p. 18) and thus "knowledge of no one" (ibid., p. 99)[2]. This means that this "psycho-demographic knowledge" (Lamiell, 2019, p. 101) tells us, at best, only part of the story of an individual person that is always more complex than the "laws common to all" (Lamiell, 2013, p. 66).

We have presented the discussion with reference to Windelband, Lamiell and Lazarsfeld in some detail just at the beginning of this chapter, because we claim that our research is a demonstration of the integration of nomothetic and idiographic approaches which we regard as complementary. Investigating the development of religiosities and worldviews requires a perspective that appreciates the complex and multi-faceted nature of individual meaning-making. Therefore, in this chapter we are going to present our mixed-methods research design with particular attention to the kind of knowledge that it is able to produce, and insights we can expect. First, we review the broader methodological discussion around mixed-methods research. We then present our research design and illustrate in detail the quantitative and qualitative strands we employ before offering further insight with a mixed-methods case study example.

Methodological Background

In this first part of the chapter, we discuss the current methodological proposals for mixed-methods research with reference to the pragmatic approach. We discuss essential concepts and terms such as pragmatism and triangulation which inform our research perspective. This will be followed by an elaboration of practical implications of a mixed-methods design. Thereby, a deeper understanding of the underlying assumptions that guide our research will be provided as well as the practical consequences for the research design discussed.

Pragmatism and Triangulation

Since the Mid-20th century, researchers have fallen into two groups and opposed each other's research perspectives arduously with a rift establishing between those who follow a quantitative research paradigm, on the one hand, and those who advocate a qualitative approach, on the other[3]. The incompatibility between the two approaches consists in the supposedly irreconcilable research perspectives, namely an orientation toward objective investigation of social facts that lead quantitative pursuits, and a constructivist perspective that includes the subjective view of the researcher in qualitative investigations (cf. Johnson & Onwuegbuzie, 2004, p. 14). However, some methodologists observe a paradigm shift in social sciences, and thus a shift in "shared belief systems that influence the kinds of knowledge researchers seek and how they interpret the evidence they collect"

---

2   For a more elaborate explanation, see Chapter 3.

3   This dispute began in the 1980s with an increasing appreciation of qualitative methods in social science research, especially visible due to their addition to methodic textbooks that challenged the dominance of quantitative approaches that prevailed since the 1960s (cf. Morgan, 2007, p. 55–56).

(Morgan, 2007, p. 50). Morgan (2007) argues that this shift is the result of a dynamic process originating in an increasing frustration of researchers with the limitations posed by a strict adherence to one paradigmatic approach or the other. At the root of the criticism lies the observation that certain questions cannot be adequately addressed within these paradigms and that new approaches are needed to overcome practical and theoretical obstacles (cf. ibid.).

As a result, a third paradigm has emerged in recent methodological discussions that has been deemed a "way out of the paradigm war" (Flick, 2018, p. 76) and a possible solution for the aforementioned limitations: the pragmatic approach[4]. Pragmatism at its root is a philosophical project that aims at finding middle ground between philosophical dogmas, and, instead of a strict dualism, focuses on how well a philosophy solves a problem. It considers both the physical, objective world as well as the socially constructed, subjective realm and emphasizes the social meaning of human experiences. Knowledge in a pragmatic view is neither completely objective nor subjective but "both constructed and based on the reality of the world we experience and live in" (Johnson & Onwuegbuzie, 2004, p. 18). In this process-oriented perspective, scientifically derived conclusions are not seen as final answers, but as tentative and evolving knowledge ever better suited to solve a problem it sets out to address. This perspective is also grounded in the fact that human reality is constantly changing and therefore our thinking must adapt to that change and our current understanding of the world needs to be improved by new questions and inquiries.

For a pragmatic epistemology, this means that knowledge about the world needs to provide a broader perspective and thus a better possibility to solve the problems in question (cf. Strübing, 2018). This can only be achieved by interaction because "[i]f we want to know the world, we must interact, and as a result, we will know the world only in the way in which it responds to us" (Biesta, 2010, p. 111). Knowledge is thus always the result of interaction with the world and heavily influenced by the way we achieved it, which is of enormous importance with regard to the different approaches we employ to gain scientific knowledge.

One suitable way of gaining knowledge with a pragmatic approach is by abduction which means continuously moving between deductive and inductive logic and thereby achieving tentative conclusions. Abduction relies on logical and methodically controlled conclusions as well as on a creative process that generates new insights (cf. Reichertz, 2017). The abductive form of logic is suited for the pragmatic understanding of gaining knowledge due to an iterative process of interacting with the world and building theories upon these observations (cf. Morgan, 2007). As an example for such a process, Morgan notes: "the inductive results from a qualitative approach can serve as inputs to the deductive goals of quantitative approach, and vice versa" (ibid., p. 71).

Thus, one major development furthered by a pragmatic approach concerns the research design: Instead of ontological or theoretical assumptions, the research question

---

4   Pragmatism is not the only philosophical approach discussed in overcoming these barriers introduced by the aforementioned paradigms. Another focus in this discussion has been set on realism which should be acknowledged but will not be further discussed here (cf. Maxwell & Mittapalli, 2010).

as well as the knowledge the research sets out to produce guide the decision for the actual methods used to investigate the phenomenon in question (cf. Johnson & Onwuegbuzie, 2004, p. 17). This has been poignantly described by Tashakkori and Teddlie as "dictatorship of the research question" (1998, p. 20). In practical terms, the pragmatic approach therefore enables the researcher to choose and mix quantitative and qualitative data and methods that are best suited to address their research questions and most appropriate for the respective phase of research (cf. Morgan, 2007; cf. Johnson & Onwuegbuzie, 2004). In short, the pragmatic approach does not set out to simply replace the former paradigms but to evolve their attainments guided by research interest and in a self-reflective process. One of the most important changes being that there is no a priori limitation restricting researchers in if and how they can cooperate, mix etc. but puts the focus on "shared meaning and joint action" (Morgan, 2007, p. 67). The strict hierarchy of what Morgan calls the "metaphysical paradigm" [5] of ontology, epistemology and methodology is thereby replaced by focusing on the methodological demands.

The ability to fruitfully use these constant changes between different methodical contexts and frameworks requires getting used to different perspectives, or, to borrow Irwin's expression as quoted by Maxwell et al. (2015), 'lenses' through which the data is being viewed. This process is also discussed using the term triangulation, defined as "[t]he combination of different methods, theories, data and/or researchers in the study of one issue" (Flick, 2018). The term implies a profound change in the researchers' perspective, as research methods are not without theoretical baggage. Thus, this combination must be done in a reflective and methodically savvy way as the different elements of the research design produce different kinds of knowledge. Furthermore, triangulation should not be seen as a mere confirmation method (one strand confirming the other) but as a broadening of the research that is to actually grant a greater insight into the phenomenon under study (cf. Flick, 2018). The following section discusses how these requirements can be achieved by implementing a mixed-methods research design.

Mixed Methods

Mixed methods research is currently widely discussed in social scientific research as being an alternative for researchers to overcome established barriers between methodological traditions and being able to investigate research questions in a less dogmatic and restricted way. Mixed-methods methodologists hereby discuss this new development with different emphases, be it concentrating more on philosophical, methodological or practical issues (cf. Creswell, 2015, p. 60). Focusing on the latter, mixed methods approaches can be first and foremost characterized by collecting qualitative as well as quantitative data, integrating the two strands in a way coherent with the overall research design.

---

5   The metaphysical paradigm centers around the hierarchy of ontology, epistemology and methodology with the consequence that "different assumptions about the nature of knowledge and what could be known" (Morgan, 2007, p. 59) in turn restrict the methodological gateways to produce this knowledge. Thus, the researcher's ontological assumptions about reality direct the research possibilities and make certain methodic approaches plausible while precluding others (cf. Morgan, 2007, pp. 58–59).

This includes the rigorous and thoughtful combination of the two methodologies without neglecting epistemological implications and requirements of each strand which can be specified as the "use of both qualitative and quantitative mental models" (Maxwell et al., 2015, p. 227).

Thus, in a mixed methods study both approaches to viewing, collecting and analyzing data are valued in their own right and logic and the reason for combining them should always be to yield greater insights and further knowledge. Therefore, it should, in practice, provide the researcher with more comprehensive results and help to overcome methodological limitations set by either the qualitative or quantitative paradigms (cf. Johnson & Onwuegbuzie, 2004). This combination of methodologies enables at the same time an in-depth as well as general understanding and thereby widens the possible perspectives a researcher is able to take on an issue under study. Thus, a mixed methods approach allows for using the strengths of both strands to look at the phenomenon with different "depths of vision" (Keller, 2020, p. 2) and can capture what each strand separately would have missed in order to better answer the research question (cf. Creswell & Plano Clark, 2018).

A mixed methods design is more than the sum of its parts, and there are certain quality criteria that exceed the ones of separate qualitative or quantitative research (cf. O'Cathain, 2010; cf. Ivankova, 2014; cf. Creswell & Plano Clark, 2018). First, both strands should each be conducted in a rigorous way and according to their respective quality requirements with regard to the methods and data used as well as the conclusions derived from them. In addition, the overall design must be coherent and suitable to answer the research question. In current literature on mixed methods research designs, three basic designs are being proposed: (a) the convergent design that conducts both strands separately in a comparative perspective to converge both results, (b) the explanatory sequential design that collects and analyzes first the quantitative data and uses the qualitative data to explain the results, and (c) the exploratory sequential design that starts with the qualitative strand to create the quantitative strand (cf. Creswell, 2015). Each design has its own logic and particular sorts of results which should be reflected by the researcher. Furthermore, the integration of the results must be rigorously done. Therefore, it is required that conflicting results are discussed and integrated in the final interpretation and a surplus of knowledge needs to be obvious.

In sum, by applying a pragmatic approach we can build on as well as challenge established knowledge on faith development by investigating the phenomenon with different methodic 'lenses.' This combination fosters a research perspective that is more adapted to investigate religiosity and worldview in its complexity as well as finding relevant research questions—in other words, "to generate a more comprehensive (and often more nuanced) appreciation of the issue at hand" (Szostak, 2015, p. 2).

Research Design

Having discussed the methodological background of our research, this next part of the chapter is dedicated to illustrate how we put these considerations into practice in our research design. First, and following a short presentation of the conceptual background and general features of our research design, we will discuss its components and the kind of knowledge they are able to produce. Then the ways in which we combine qualitative and quantitative data and methods are presented and the forms of triangulation characterized. Thereby this part of the chapter is going to discuss how this combination of methods enables us to investigate the complex field of biographical change and development in religion and spirituality by applying a variety of perspectives.

General Features of our Research Design

How do these methodological considerations relate to our investigation of religious, spiritual or secular meaning-making processes? For answering this question, we need to take a look at the theoretical foundations of our research and its practical implications. At the core of our work is James Fowler's Faith Development Theory, introduced in 1981 in his *Stages of Faith*. In it, he presents an inspiring and encompassing conceptualization of 'faith:'

> People's evolved and evolving ways of experiencing self, others and world (as they construct them) as related to and affected by the ultimate conditions of existence (as they construct them) and shaping their lives' purposes and meanings, trusts and loyalties, in the light of the character of being, value and power determining the ultimate conditions of existence (as grasped in their operative images – conscious and unconscious – of them). (Fowler, 1981, p. 92–93)

A few things become apparent in this broad definition of faith: It is a dynamic process that, even though it concentrates and evolves in the mind of individuals, is heavily influenced by their social, cultural, and familial context. In order for people to construct these images of the transcendent, of what they cannot directly experience, they rely on their surroundings, their socialization, cultural norms etc. Second, faith is not merely a separated set of beliefs reserved for the transcendence but deeply affects how a person experiences themselves, other people, and the broader society and world. This influences loyalties "to centers of value and power," as Fowler says, and eventually also to certain groups or individuals as well as moral considerations and images of self. Lastly, this definition is very broad and embraces theistic and non-theistic worldviews, as well as ways of non-religious meaning-making. With this comprehensive concept of faith as a quest for meaning, we are capable of investigating individualized forms of religiosity as well as secular worldviews. Thus, the investigation of religiosity and worldview is a very complex, dynamic and multi-faceted endeavor that requires a multitude of perspectives to be adequately addressed.

Researchers therefore need to adopt an attitude that is open to diverse methodic and theoretical approaches and is not bound to one disciplinary or methodological tradition, but instead appreciates the different kinds of knowledge they respectively are able to provide. First, this is reflected in an interdisciplinary understanding of our research program as well as team composition, which includes theologians and psychologists as well as linguists and sociologists. An interdisciplinary perspective represents a continuation of the origins of our research: In the 1970s, the theologian James Fowler worked with theories derived from psychology such as Piaget's theory of cognitive development or Kohlberg's works on moral judgement. Lifespan development became an important research focus at that time and thus Fowler also put an emphasis on the development of faith within the lifetime of a person. This emerging research focus prompted him to investigate biographic narrations of subjective faith development which demanded terms and methods deriving from a variety of different disciplines.

Each methodical approach represents a different level of analysis and therefore carries distinct epistemological possibilities and thus different answers and interpretations to a variety of questions. Our overall research design consists of quantitative and qualitative components that rely on separately collected data[6]. The quantitative survey data comprises demographic information as well as established psychological instruments whereas the qualitative strand uses the Faith Development Interview (FDI) as basis for the analysis. The qualitative data analysis of the FDI includes three analytical approaches: The most essential and established one is the structural evaluation of the FDI by assigning religious styles, according to the *Manual for the Assessment of Religious Styles in Faith Development Interviews* (cf. Streib & Keller, 2018b). In addition, we broadened the qualitative strand by also analyzing content and narrative particularities, with the qualitative analysis software ATLAS.ti.

The overall design can be characterized as a *convergent mixed methods design*, as each strand is conducted separately and by considering the respective methodic requirements of either qualitative or quantitative research, and both approaches support and inform each other (cf. Creswell & Plano Clark, 2018). In case of the structural evaluation of the FDIs, we can talk of a "data transformation variant" (ibid, p. 73) in which the qualitative and quantitative components are even more thoroughly integrated as the qualitative results are quantified by assigning a religious style ranging from 1 to 5 and analyzed in parallel with the psychometric scales using statistical methods. This will be further elaborated in the part below.

Another essential feature of our study of the development of religiosity and worldview is a longitudinal research design. Therefore, we collected qualitative and quantitative data at three time points over the past 20 years. As a result, we have 75 interviewees from Germany and the United States that participated in the survey as well as the interviews with the FDI three times, with a mean time lag of 6.9 years between the first and second interview, and a mean time lag of about 3.6 years between the second and the third interview.

In the next part of the chapter, we zoom in on these different strands and discuss how the triangulation is realized and what kind of knowledge we are thereby able to gain. To achieve this, we take a step back and discuss how these different perspectives made it possible to look at the phenomenon from different angles, and how the quantitative and qualitative strand could be fruitfully combined to complement, challenge, and broaden each other. Similar to the geological mapping team, from which discipline the term triangulation derives, we pack up our equipment, settle at a different viewpoint, and look at our phenomenon from a whole new perspective in order to get a more precise picture.

---

6 We conduct a qualitative interview and collect questionnaire data from the same participant.

Qualitative, Idiographic Approaches to Triangulation

First, we focus on the qualitative component of our research design and discuss the insights it is granting us. The focus is on *faith* as meaning making process of individuals, which is analyzed (a) for structural differences, and (b) in terms of narrative identity attending to autobiographical reasoning and reconstruction of life stories. Thus, the objective is to get an in-depth understanding of our cases attending to how they construct meaning.

At the basis of this qualitative investigation is the FDI, in which the interviewee is invited to explore his or her own life review and reflect on their past and current relationships, ponder questions of values and morality, and talk about their religion and worldview. The FDI is a semi-structured interview with a fixed set of 25 consecutively asked questions, and the interviewee is given as much time as they need to fully elaborate on these issues. The FDI questions, in particular the very first question, are formulated in a fashion that invites ad-hoc narrations, which the participants are encouraged to unfold. Therefore, an FDI has an average length between 1,5 and 2 hours. All FDIs are audio recorded, fully transcribed, before the evaluation begins.

Structural analysis proceeds according to the latest version of the *Manual* (cf. Streib & Keller, 2018b) by the structural interpretation of each of the answers to the 25 questions, which results in identifying one of five styles for the respective answer and entering a number for that style in the Scoring Sheet. The FDI questions thereby are sorted according to the expected information they may reveal for one of the six aspects of faith (perspective-taking, social horizon, morality, locus of authority, form of world coherence, and symbolic functioning). This method of qualitative data analysis thus consists of identifying "patterns of cognitive and affective operation by which content is understood, appropriated, manipulated, expressed and transformed" (Streib & Keller, 2018b, p. 19) in an interpretative process by assigning the styles that most appropriately describe this pattern. On this structural level of evaluation, we therefore investigate the religious styles as accessible in the interviewee's current responses in the FDI. From re-interviews with the same participant, we identify the processes of their faith development. This provides us with data about the structures of faith that are dominant in the interview and allows conclusions about the process of how participants may have changed in their structure of faith over three times of data collection.

As described in more detail in Chapter 1, there is a necessity to assign an overall score to one FDI, while the variance in style assignments may include two or more styles. The type is the final score for an FDI. Four types are constructed that occur in adult samples: *substantially ethnocentric, predominantly conventional, predominantly individuative-reflective*, and *emerging dialogical-xenosophic*. The construction of types (Streib et al., 2020) is concept-based according to the following algorithm: When most of the 25 FDI answers have been rated style 3, the type is *predominantly conventional*; when style 4 is the most prevalent rating, the type is *predominantly individuative-reflective type*; in cases in which at least 20 % of the ratings are Style two, the type is *substantially ethnocentric;* and when at least 20% of the ratings are Style 5, the type is *emerging dialogical-xenosophic*. The type construction is important especially for statistic modeling, and we have used it for an analysis of faith development over time in our current longitudinal sample (Streib, Chen, et al., 2021); a related analysis is the aspect-specific analysis of faith development that is presented in Chapter 5 in this volume. Thus, we realize the great potential of the type construction for quantitative statistical modeling. Nevertheless, it is important to keep in mind that the type is a summary score for the single FDI that is based on qualitative, idiographic interpretive work.

In a second qualitative approach that is conducted independently from structural analysis, we explore major themes and narrative structures in the interviews as well as their development. Both of these questions of what is being said and what narrative strategies are employed are investigated by applying a coding scheme developed using the qualitative data analysis software ATLAS.ti. This scheme has been developed in a dialogical process involving three researchers with disciplinary backgrounds in psychology, linguistics, and sociology; thus, different perspectives and questions could be fruitfully discussed and integrated. Especially with regard to the inductively derived codes, this process relied on a successive structuring of the code list by directly working with the interview material until a stable coding guideline was established that can be applied across cases. This approach yielded a more tangible understanding of each case as well as an overview of our sample (cf. Friese, 2019, p. 143). As an aid to understand the connection between the relatively large number of content codes, we have begun to explore network analysis,[7] which offers visualizations how content codes relate to each other and thus reflect central themes in an interview as well as changes from interview to interview (more information on the use of Network Analysis of content codes, and a case example, can be found in Chapter 7). To sum up, the aim of the qualitative content analysis is to get a more structured and condensed picture of the themes our interviewees talk about, whereas the narrative analysis explores the strategies the participants use to make their story a coherent one—or how they fail to do so.

What insights do we gain by analyzing our qualitative data in this threefold way and what questions are we therefore able to answer? First, and more akin to qualitative methodology, we focus on the idiographic approach and start with the structural analysis. By an inspection of the style assignments of each case per each question assorted to the six aspects (this is visualized also in what we call style-aspect map, for examples, see Figures 17 and 18 in Keller et al., 2022), we capture what religious styles are prevalent for the specific case and in which aspects the style may differ. Thus, we depict the multidimensionality of meaning making on the individual case level. We evaluate the structural ways in which participants conceive their own inner processes and those of others, in what way they relate to groups and the broader social contexts, how moral questions

---

7   Content codes can be subject to quantitative analysis and visualization using the mathematical tools provided by network analysis. For each interview, content codes form a directed network of adjacent connections among the codes, and the edge weights reflect the frequency of each connection (cf. Pokorny et al., 2018). In the analysis, node and network level statistics of centrality, connectivity, spread, subgroups, and homophily are offered to illustrate the node importance and various network structures (cf. Borgatti et al., 2018; cf. Wasserman & Faust, 1994). Inferential statistics use random graph modeling to test whether any of the network structures significantly differs from randomness such that they convey important information about how different codes connect with each other (cf. Lusher et al., 2013). Visualization of the trimmed networks provide further aid to understand the empirical connections of content codes.

or authorities are reflected and legitimized, how they construct a coherent view of the world and the transcendence, and lastly, how symbols and rituals are understood. More broadly, we answer the question of how the person makes sense of themselves and the world and what meaning making structure or religious style can be identified.

Qualitative content analysis operates on another level of analysis. In respect to a single case, we capture how relationships are characterized and what actual meaning they carry. Are parents presented as perpetrators or supporters? Are the social surroundings or the own partner seen as a source of inspiration or of misery? Furthermore, we learn about the way in which our interviewee wants to present his or her image of self: Do they see themselves as rebellious or anxious, as connected with others or more autonomous? Moreover, the actual content of their moral convictions become visible, and thus if they put a moral emphasis on in-group loyalty and purity of conviction, or if they strive for fairness or authenticity (cf. Haidt & Graham, 2007). The most multi-faceted categories we are able to explore with this methodical approach are the specific contents of the interviewees' beliefs. What are the particular images of God expressed in the interview or what other concepts of the transcendence are shaping their views? What are the practices that surround these beliefs and what role do social aspects of these practices play? Finally, we also investigate the diverse trajectories of faith development the interviewees share with us and are therefore able to capture different conversion and deconversion trajectories that lead away from former religious beliefs or worldviews as well as processes of deepening one's already existing convictions.

Still another level of our qualitative analysis on an idiographic level is the investigation of the narrative structure and identity exhibited in the interviews. Deductively derived codings enable us to investigate how the interviewees give coherence to their own live story by, for example, marking important events as turning points that clearly structure the before and after and emphasize the meaning of this experience (Köber et al., 2015). Thereby the question can be addressed what themes are of particular importance to the interviewee and of what are the reasons for them to tell this story. This approach also includes the interpretation of (small, spontaneous) narratives according to the narrative model presented by Labov and Waletzky (1967) and thus gives us small but dense vignettes demonstrating the meaning of an important life event such as a "religious identity narrative" (see, for example, Keller et al., 2016).

In addition, these several levels are investigated in a longitudinal perspective which includes, for the individual case, the investigation of explanations of their current worldview and religiosity and detailed accounts of the biographical reasoning behind them. We can therefore answer the question of how a participant describes his or her worldview or religiosity at three times of data collection. What has changed in terms of life circumstances in the first, second and third interview? What has changed in the retrospective biographical descriptions? Things become even more complex when the focus is not on a single case, but on the comparison of two or more cases—that may be even from different cultural contexts. Such between-person analysis can address questions of how, for example, the development of a German case compares with one from the United States.

Part Three of this volume will present selected case studies from our three-wave sample. These include analyses about the structures and the processes (Pasupathi & Adler,

2021) of the narrative identity of participants in idiographic perspective. We are, on the one hand, interested to know how the own life stories are constructed and how personal opinions on moral questions, religion and worldview or relationships are explained each single time (structure), but, on the other hand, we are also eager to learn how these retrospectives are changing over the course of several years (process). As the present of the interviewee influences the narration of their past, we can explore how different version of a person's past are being remembered and constructed (Rosenthal, 2006, p. 50). How do current life events shape the memory, reflection and narration of past events? How do these differing stories reflect changes in well-being or image of self? By comparison of these different reconstructions of the past, we aim to circumvent misinterpretation or "hindsight bias" (Helfrich-Hölter, 2006, p. 257) on the part of the interviewees.

To sum up, the analysis of the Faith Development Interview yields results regarding the structural characteristics in terms of religious styles and their development over time, thematic and narrative analyses investigate how the meaning making process develops, what the important themes are, and how they change, as well as how the interviewee talks about them and how these strategies for narrative identity are currently working and how they change over time.

Quantitative, Nomothetic Approaches to Triangulation

The quantitative surveys contain, besides demographics and questions for religious and spiritual self-identification, a selection of psychometric scales that, for the three-wave cases, assesses personality factors, psychological well-being, generativity and religious schemata. Table 4.1 presents all scales that are three-wave, but includes also the scales with data in Wave 2 and Wave 3, thus allow for two-wave analyses.

These quantitative data, of course, clearly suggest statistical analyses using a nomothetic approach. And the longitudinal samples in our data can be used to address many very interesting questions, for some of which we have published results already; these include the following:

- How do the scales in Table 4.1 (or a selection thereof) correlate with or predict faith development in terms of styles and types. Our analysis (Streib, Chen, et al., 2021) will be discussed below in 2.4.
- Is self-rated spirituality predicted by mystical experiences? In an analysis that focused on the newly developed short form of Hood's (1975) Mysticism Scale (Streib, Klein et al., 2021), Streib and Chen (2021) have shown that the M-Scale moderates and mediates the effects of self-rated religiosity on self-rated spirituality.
- What are the outstanding predictors for deconversion? For answering this question, concurrent and cross-wave correlations of all these scales with deconversion reported in Wave 2 and Wave 3 were included. Results are presented in Chapter 9 in this volume.
- How did deconverts and traditionalists change on these scales between Wave 1 and Wave 2 investigation? Quantitative results are presented by Streib and Keller (2022).

Table 4.1: Quantitative Measures in our Longitudinal Faith-in-development Data

Construct	Measure	Wave 1	Wave 2	Wave 3
personality	NEO-FFI (Costa & McCrae, 1985; Borkenau & Ostendorf, 1993)	x	x	x
well-being	Psychological Well-being and Growth Scale (Ryff, 1989; Ryff & Singer, 1996, 1998a, 1998b)	x	x	x
generativity	Loyola Generativity Scale (LGS, McAdams & de St. Aubin, 1992; McAdams et al., 1993; McAdams et al., 1997; McAdams et al., 1998)	x	x	x
religious schemata	Religious Schema Scale (RSS, Streib et al., 2010)	x	x	x
mystical experiences	Mysticism Scale (Hood, 1975; Streib et al., 2021)	x	x	x
intolerance of ambiguity	Intolerance for Ambiguity Scale (Budner, 1962)		x	x
need for cognition	Need for CognitionScale (Cacioppo et al., 1984)		x	x
fundamentalism	items from the Religion Monitor questionnaire (Huber, 2009)		x	x
pluralism	items from the Religion Monitor questionnaire (Huber, 2009)		x	x

Note: The measures listed in this table are described in more detail in the Appendix of this volume, where basic statistics for the scales in the longitudinal data are also presented. All information is also available on the Open Science Framework (osf) at: https://osf.io/3vkw9/.

In the latter analysis, the mixed-method approach of our research is demonstrated. Especially the visualizations of individual profiles on measures from the questionnaire is always connected to the single cases. In our visualizations such as scatter plots (see, for example, Streib & Keller, 2022) and boxplots for the case studies (see Keller et al., 2022), the single cases can be identified, because every dot represents a case which has a name and a biography, but inter-individual differences and the comparison with the general trend of the groups to which the case belongs remains possible. "We can place diverse biographical trajectories in psychometric spaces, and have interpretations of individual trajectories reflect on these placements" (Hood et al., 2022). Thus, we regard this detail of our research as a demonstration of the integration of nomothetic and idiographic approaches, which we view as complementary, and thus responding to Lamiell's (2019) sharp criticism of the exclusive use of nomothetic approaches in personality psychology.

There is still another way by which quantitative and qualitative data relate. The self-report measures from the questionnaire (demographic and scales) allow to present information on our cases which enables us, for example, to identify if cases left a religious group or if changes had occurred between the first, second or third interview in other

Part A: Conceptual & Methodological Perspectives

aspects of their lives. Furthermore, the psychological scales grant us, on an idiographic level, insight into the interviewees' religious schemata, well-being, personality traits and so on as well as their developments. Thus, we can address questions such as: How do the interviewees report on central elements of their well-being? How do they characterize the relationship to religious or authoritative texts or teachings? In addition, we gain valuable contextual information such as age, gender identification, economic and cultural capital, and religious affiliation as well as experiences of deconversion which could shed further light on changes regarding certain developments of the psychometric scales.

Triangulation in our Research Design

After having discussed each strand in detail, we now take a step back and view them in the context of the overall research design, focusing on how they are integrated and interact with each other. Figure 4.1 visualizes the various options of triangulation in our data.[8]

Figure 4.1: Options for Triangulation in our Study Design

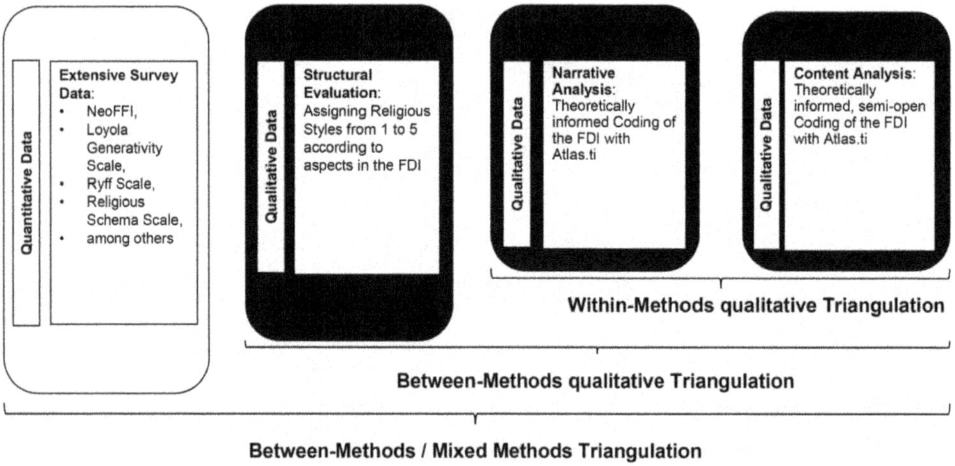

The combination of these methodical approaches can be characterized as follows: First and beginning with the qualitative strand, combining two distinct methodic approaches in one qualitative method, namely the analysis of content as well as narrative particularities, represents a *within-methods qualitative triangulation* (cf. Flick, 2018, p. 144). This method consists of the application of a partly inductively, partly deductively derived coding guideline, and we thus, analyze our qualitative data on two levels with the same method: First with a theoretically informed, semi-open coding on the content level which is primarily inductive and partly deductive. This is followed by a predominantly theoretical narrative coding that is based mainly on models originated in linguistics, developmental psychology (see e.g., Köber et al., 2015) and psychoanalysis that are applied de-

---

8   This figure was produced for our pre-conference workshop at the Conference of the International Association for the Psychology of Religion in Gdansk (Eufinger, Steppacher & Silver, 2019).

ductively on the data. Both levels are systematically integrated, and we move back and forth between induction and discovering new and idiosyncratic findings and deduction with the rediscovery of patterns that are already well established in interdisciplinary research, thus, applying an abductive process as described above.

This can be combined with the structural analysis for religious style and type as part of the current qualitative data analysis, which then can be characterized as a *between-methods qualitative triangulation*. This is the process of combining two distinct qualitative methods that produce different kinds of information. In our case, these are, on the one hand, the structural characteristics of our cases in terms of religious styles and types, which we achieve by conducting a particular rating method (see Chapters 1 and 3 for more details) and, on the other hand, the "essential elements of meaning" (Flick, 2018, p. 39) or content and narrative particularities of our interviews by applying coding schemes. Thus, we analyze the same material, the FDIs, with two distinct perspectives – the structural analysis which is purely deductive, and the content and narrative coding that moves between induction and deduction. This yields a more comprehensive picture of the respective cases: We capture their dominant religious styles and thereby their various ways of meaning making, and furthermore we can explore what these styles carry in terms of content and narrative strategies. Finally, it should be noted that these triangular dynamics in the single cases, multiplies in complexity, when perspectives on the process of development add a within-person differential perspective, and when the simultaneous analysis of multiple cases invites between-person perspectives.

Moving one level further, quantitative and qualitative results are brought together in a *mixed-methods triangulation*. Quantitative and qualitative methods target the same phenomenon, and these two approaches need to be interweaved: Conclusions derived from each strand are integrated to allow for a broader picture as well as better understanding of faith development, but also to uncover conflicts in interpretation, and finally to complement each approach with the information obtained by the other (cf. Streib et al., 2009, p. 66).

Our analysis of faith development over time in our current three-wave longitudinal sample (cf. Streib, Chen, et al., 2021) may serve as an example of triangulation in our data. This study triangulated (a) the *types* resulting from interpretive, structural evaluation of the FDI transcript and (b) the *scales* for personality and religious schemata in longitudinal analysis using methods such as hierarchical linear modeling (HLM) and latent growth modeling (LGM). The full set of our preregistered hypotheses that assumed extensive covariations and predictions was only partially supported by our data. In particular, our hypotheses that faith development would covary with *openness to experience* (openness, NEO-FFI), *truth of texts and teachings (ttt)*, and *xenosophia/inter-religious dialog (xenos)* were not supported by the data, since type slope and the slopes of *openness, ttt,* and *xenos* did not correlate. In regard to results for *openness*, this trangulation demonstrates that faith development is not just a part of personality development; for *ttt* and *xenos*, this may indicate that the Religious Schema Scale does not just measure faith development in terms of types. However, *openness* and *ttt* were confimed in this study as significant predictors for progression in faith development. This analysis is an example of how triangulation can be put to work. But this example also reveals that triangulation may be complex: it does not support each and every hypothesized correspondence or correlation, but results in new knowledge about (non-) relation, thus raising new questions.

However, this study of faith development over time is only part of what can be imagined and expected from triangulatory networking. The results from narrative and content analysis were still not included. Thus, this project of triangulation in our data has just begun and much work is still ahead. An approach to triangulation, from another side as it were, is used in our research quite extensively: the interpretation of single cases (in longitudinal analysis) in light of the psychometric scales and the structural analysis in terms of styles and types. This can be perfectly demostrated by an exemplary case study.

Case Example Carola

In this chapter, we discussed the different methodological assumptions that guide our research as well as the methodic instruments we use and combine to get a more complete picture of the phenomenon of faith development we try to understand. Now, we take a closer look at one case to observe in more detail what we have discussed so far. Thus, by focusing here on the ideographic perspective, we follow a longitudinal case study with qualitative and quantitative data analyzed with diverse methodic approaches and see how a more comprehensive picture of this person emerges. On the case level we really see how the diverse aspects of religious or worldview development unfold in its complexity, inconsistency, and meaning in the person's life. Thus, a mixed-methods approach in this case study helps us understand our findings in a more precise manner as the case provides us with the opportunity to go into the depth of the respective processes (cf. Creswell & Plano Clark, 2018, p. 116). For this illustration, we use a very condensed and shortened version of a case study for which quantitative and qualitative data at three points of data collection are available.

The German case with pseudonym Carola[9] has been interviewed by our research team three times and was 56 years old at her first interview in 2004, 65 years at her second interview in 2013, and at the last interview in 2018 she was 70 years old. Thus, we get an insight into Carola's life in late adulthood, when she was still working as a teacher, all through her entering retirement and old age. She is one of our deconverts, leaving the Protestant church in which she was raised in her early twenties. However, Carola preserved a belief in God for years after that privatizing exit. The struggle with God and other formative relationships such as with her mother, ex-husband and late partner as well as coping with devastating losses are leading themes in her life story.

Results on Psychometric Scales

First, we take a look at Carola's survey data and her results on some selected psychometric scales. In Table 4.2 Carola's scores are presented per wave and listed next to the respective sample means as well as standard deviations.

---

9   The full case study is presented in Ramona Bullik's (2024) dissertation.

Table 4.2: Selected Data from Carola's Survey Answers

	Wave 1		Wave 2		Wave 3	
	Carola	M (SD)	Carola	M (SD)	Carola	M (SD)
Religious Schema Scale						
truth of texts and teachings	1.60	2.53 (1.14)	1.00	2.35 (1.13)	1.00	2.55 (1.12)
fairness, tolerance, and rational choice	4.00	4.38 (0.38)	4.00	4.35 (0.51)	4.20	4.59 (0.40)
xenosophia/ inter-religious dialog	3.40	3.64 (0.82)	3.20	3.58 (0.78)	3.20	3.77 (0.78)
Ryff Scale						
autonomy	3.57	3.69 (0.58)	3.00	3.32 (0.49)	3.29	3.31 (0.53)
environmental mastery	3.43	3.65 (0.75)	3.86	3.67 (0.63)	3.86	3.66 (0.67)
personal growth	4.00	4.31 (0.48)	4.14	4.14 (0.49)	4.14	4.28 (0.52)
positive relations with others	4.29	3.89 (0.67)	4.29	3.91 (0.68)	4.14	3.97 (0.72)
purpose in life	3.86	3.80 (0.68)	4.57	3.78 (0.63)	4.00	3.72 (0.62)
self-acceptance	3.29	3.75 (0.77)	3.71	3.83 (0.69)	3.86	3.87 (0.67)
NEO-FFI						
emotional stability	2.92	3.40 (0.82)	3.58	3.40 (0.74)	3.67	3.41 (0.70)
extraversion	3.17	3.29 (0.62)	3.25	3.28 (0.66)	3.17	3.19 (0.64)
openness to experience	3.92	3.92 (0.89)	3.83	3.89 (0.50)	3.92	3.96 (0.55)
agreeableness	3.58	3.74 (0.46)	4.00	3.75 (0.49)	3.67	3.85 (0.52)
conscientiousness	3.83	3.69 (0.54)	3.75	3.73 (0.53)	3.50	3.79 (0.54)

Note: These calculations are based on a sample size of $n = 75$.

Consulting Carola's scores on the Religious Schema Scale reveals that, while her scores for *ftr* and *xenos* are slightly lower than the means of the sample, her *ttt* score is considerably lower, and even declining to 1.0 between wave one and two. Carola's *xenos* scores, measuring the appreciation of the other or the strange, as well as her *ftr* measuring a neutral and objectifying approach to religious or cultural matters indicate that she does not outrightly reject what or who is different to her and reasonably appreciates a fairness in dealing with them. Her low *ttt* score seems to support this as this subscale measures the extent to which people believe in the texts of their religion in a literal way and points to an absolutistic and exclusivist stance toward the religious teachings. This result emphasizes how much Carola rejects any form of fundamentalist religion (cf. Keller et al., 2016, p. 44).

Consulting her scores on the Ryff scale, we can assess Carola's psychological well-being and how it changed between the three points of data collection. First, the increase on the subscale *purpose in life* between the first and second wave stands out, indicating that she finds meaningful tasks since retiring and interpreting her endeavors as purposeful.

Her scores of *self-acceptance* as well as *environmental mastery* increase slightly over time, however not significantly and within standard deviation. This could indicate that Carola is increasingly accepting the person she has become and feels generally in control of her life and surroundings.

The NEO-FFI scores tell us more about Carola's personality development with *emotional stability* showing an interesting development: her score increasing at each time of data collection, she seemingly steadily recovers from a time of emotional uncertainty as her first score was well below the sample mean. Her *openness to experience* scores are not very remarkable as she fits very well with the overall sample but could lead to the conclusion that she sees herself as somebody rather curious and outgoing.

To sum up this first impression of the case on the basis of her survey results, Carola seems like quite an average case in terms of how she reflects on people or situations that are strange to her and does not seem to take exclusivist stances. We also see some improvements with regard to her well-being and she seems to gain self actualization.

Findings of Structural Analysis

When consulting Carola's style assignments that are summarized in her religious type, we can identify her as a "stayer" over the entire time of investigation. This means that her overall FDI ratings appear not to change much. In general, she shows a consistent tendency toward the mutual style in all three interviews which makes her a "predominantly conventional" religious type. Inspection of the aspect-specific style rating, however, revels a slight variation. In her answers at Wave 1 and two we see much more variation, as nearly half of the answers were rated Style four, whereas in her last interview a clear majority was assigned Style three. Thus, in her earlier interviews she seems to oscillate between a community-oriented view and a desire for consent with her own social group, and the ability for critical examination as well as a more self-selected position, and this is considerably less visible in her last interview. It is particularly interesting to observe her changes in the morality aspect more closely as they are rated between Styles three and four in the first interview and become more unambiguous in the last ratings with an explicit Styles three rating. Overall, it can be stated that her ability to critically reflect and think in abstract ways is displayed least in her last interview. Thus, we can conclude that, while Carola always had the tendency to orient herself towards group consensus and normative stances when it comes to moral, religious or personal matters, this conventional tendency seems to have increased.

Findings Narrative and Content Analysis

With this knowledge about Carola's relation to other religious ideas, her well-being, personality, and the religious styles in her interviews, we now turn to the content and narratives in her interviews. In her life reviews there are certain marker events as well as themes that stand out. First, she describes growing up with a mother that neglected and exploited her, after her father, with whom she felt having a close and loving relationship as a child, died when Carola was still very young. This tragic loss left her with a mother that treated her poorly and preferred her sons over her only daughter. Other adversities and hardships, such as an abusive ex-husband and the death of her beloved partner whom she has met after her divorce, are central themes in all three interviews. However, her life reviews take on a more optimistic tone and much of the bitterness that is very prominent in her first interviews seems to soften, especially in the last one. One reason for this change might be a stable relationship with a new partner as well as a meaningful and supportive relationship to her two adult children. Another aspect in this dynamic might be her becoming a grandmother and thus a new role that gives her purpose and the experience of mutual affection. Nevertheless, while she has found ways of coping with the death of her partner, the relationships to her mother and her former husband remain unresolved and burdensome, as she cannot forgive her abusive ex-partner and is still tied within an unhealthy relationship with her mother.

As mentioned above, Carola deconverted from Protestantism in her early 20s but preserved a privatized belief in God. However, she struggles with a God that did not save her beloved partner and the theodicy problem becomes a turning point in her religious beliefs. She describes a cruel abandonment and disillusionment by God of whose existence she is uncertain and thinks quite a lot about. Although she talks, in all three interviews, about her relationship to God, it becomes clear that she turns her back to this divine figure in disappointment and anger, still preserving the belief in something higher, which also helps her to deal with the uncertainty of death.

Her distance from Protestantism, however, happened much earlier and can be illustrated in a condensed narrative that Carola told at all times of the interview. This story fits the structure presented by Labov and Waletzky (1967). It is the story of the rift between the Protestant Church and Carola that occurred when she was actually meant to have her entrance into the faith community.

104   Part A: Conceptual & Methodological Perspectives

Carola's Narrative: "Confirmation Class"

	Wave 1	Wave 2	Wave 3
Orientation	I remember this experience that really cut to the quick at that time. I was about 13 at the time I guess, quite naïve in general, and I remember	Then I actually experienced the first rift when I was confirmed or rather when I had confirmation classes.	So, I was not brought up in a religious fashion. My mother was Catholic, we kids were Protestant, like my father. We never went to church, but as it was customary at that time, you were confirmed. That's just the way it was.
Complication	we had this church service and us confirmees sat in the first rows, it was a small parish, [...] and I remember I had just gotten new shoes and so I crossed my legs because I was so proud of the shoes [...] and looked at them. [...] And I was all absorbed in my contemplation and then noticed the pastor reprimanded me from the pulpit, in front of the whole parish, saying I should behave properly and how dare I sit like this [...].	Because I was going to school here in [City A], I didn't have the possibility to attend the classes with other confirmees. So, a former classmate from elementary school and I, we were the only ones who had the confirmation classes in the afternoon.	And I had the misfortune that I went [...] to school in [city A] with a former classmate. That meant that confirmation classes for us did not take place in the morning, in the first two lessons, [...] that's why we got extra confirmation classes in the afternoons. [...] When the weather was most beautiful and everybody else was at the swimming pool [...]. Two people, [J.] and I, we sat opposite this pastor, who would regularly lose his false teeth, and who was very languid.
Evaluation	I just remember wishing for the earth to open so I could disappear, afterwards I knew that everybody knew that it was me who had been addressed, [...]	The two of us [...] with this pastor that just languidly told us something about God and the Bible and bullied us with things that we had to learn by heart. From time to time, his false teeth would fall out and it was all very, very awkward for a young girl of 14.	Awful. I have really horrible memories of this man. I don't know, but he was a man of the church and he should have convinced others of his cause. [...] Also with the threat there would be a public hearing in the church, in front of the whole presbytery, the auditorium in the church. [...] And then always the threat, "And if you don't succeed in the test, you fail and will not be confirmed." [...] So, that was a terrible burden and I was glad when it was over.

Resolution	Actually, I wasn't conscious of any guilt, I wasn't aware I had done anything bad, but the pastor suggested that it was bad what happened there.	And it did not bring me any closer to religion. And so, after confirmation, I decided, "You will never go into this church again."	I never went to church after that,
Coda	That was so severe that the church never became dear to my heart anymore, putting it cautiously.[10] (Carola, Narrative Interview, time 1)	And I never did because I thought, "I am not close to the church, the institution 'church' is not close to me, it did nothing for me."[11] (Carola, FDI, time 2)	for me that was a fact, I cannot bear that anymore.[12] (Carola, FDI, time 3)

---

10   Da hab ich auch ein Erlebnis in Erinnerung, das mich damals sehr tief getroffen hat. Ich war, schätze mal, damals 13, eigentlich auch noch sehr unbedarft, und ich erinnere mich, wir hatten also diesen Gottesdienst, wo wir Konfirmanden vorne in den ersten Reihen saßen, es war ne kleine Gemeinde, [...] und ich erinnere mich, dass ich damals neue Schuhe bekommen hatte und hatte dann, weil ich so stolz war auf meine Schuhe, hab ich dann das eine Bein über das andere geschlagen, [...] und habe mir dann meine neuen Schuhe betrachtet. [...] Und ich war also ganz versonnen in meiner Betrachtung und kriegte dann mit, dass also dieser Pastor von seiner Kanzel mich zurechtwies, vor dieser gesamten Gemeinde, ich sollte mich mal anständig benehmen, und wie ich denn da säße [...]. Ich weiß nur, dass ich mir gewünscht habe, der Erdboden möge sich auftun und ich darin verschwinden, ich wusste auch hinterher, alle wussten, dass ich gemeint war, [...]. Ich war mir im Grunde genommen keiner Schuld bewusst, wusste auch nicht, was ich Schlimmes getan habe, aber der Pastor hat mir das ja irgendwo suggeriert, es war was Schlimmes, was da abgelaufen ist. Das war schon so einschneidend, wo mir also die Kirche nicht mehr ans Herz gewachsen ist, sag ich mal vorsichtig so.

11   Dann habe ich den ersten Bruch eigentlich erfahren, als ich konfirmiert wurde oder besser gesagt, als ich meinen Konfirmandenunterricht hatte. Da ich hier in [Stadt A] zur Schule ging, hatte ich nicht die Möglichkeit, mit den anderen Konfirmanden in diesen Unterricht zu gehen. Das heißt, ein früherer Klassenkamerad aus der Volksschule und ich, wir waren die einzigen, die dann nachmittags den Konfirmandenunterricht hatten. Zu zweit [...] mit diesem Pastor, der uns eigentlich nur gelangweilt irgendetwas von Gott erzählte und von der Bibel und uns drangsalierte mit Dingen, die wir auswendig lernen mussten. Ihm fiel dann teilweise immer so ein- sein Gebiss runter und es war alles für so ein junges Mädchen von 14 sehr sehr unangenehm. Und es hat mich eigentlich Religion nicht näher gebracht. Und dann habe ich also beschlossen nach der Konfirmation: „In diese Kirche gehst du nie wieder." Und das habe ich auch wirklich nicht getan, weil ich dachte: „Die Kirche ist mir nicht nahe, die Institution ‚Kirche' ist mir nicht nah, sie hat mir nichts gegeben."

12   Also ich bin nicht sehr religiös erzogen worden. Meine Mutter war katholisch, wir Kinder waren aber evangelisch, mein Vater auch. Wir sind nie in die Kirche gegangen, aber wie das damals war, man wurde konfirmiert. Das war einfach so. Und ich hatte das Pech, dass ich damals [...] mit einem anderen ehemaligen Klassenkameraden in [Stadt A] zum Gymnasium [ging]. Das bedeutete, der Konfirmandenunterricht fand bei uns nicht morgens statt, in den ersten zwei Stunden, [...] deswegen kriegten wir extra Ersatzkonfirmandenunterricht nachmittags. [...] Der war dann bei schöns-

Part A: Conceptual & Methodological Perspectives

It is obvious that Carola did not retell precisely the same story. For one, the first narrative takes place in a different surrounding and has presumably a different antagonist. However, all three narratives are framed as the turning point at which Carola decided that she will leave the Protestant Church – marking this as her deconversion story – and furthermore exhibits the same theme: a young girl, humiliated by an illegitimate, even disgusting male authority figure. It is also noteworthy that she does not talk about her actual beliefs or about God, but about disappointing or even cruel treatment that she had to endure and was not ready to accept. Thus, it was not her convictions that drove her away from the church, but inadequate authority figures that simply did not do a good enough job to convince her to stay.

Carola's moral universe is similarly person-centered. Thus, especially in her first interview, her main focus is on her social surroundings, her family, and caring for their well-being. However, she sees this intimate and wholesome world threatened by the other, or, in her case, by Muslim migrants. It becomes apparent that Carola consumes controversial and one-sided media, which is highly critical of Islam and of the German government's response to an increase in immigration. This ominous danger that seems to surround her immanently threatens her family and all she holds dear; an assumption that is even more convincing to her as there are websites that report on each offence committed by an immigrant, but even more so as she experienced this violence herself: Her abusive ex-partner was a non-German citizen, and this realization gives her an explanation of his abusive behavior. Carola becomes more and more convinced by these explanations and assumptions and illustrates quite openly her frustration with the dominant discourse that does not take her fears and concerns seriously, but challenges and criticizes them. Seemingly disenabled to communicate her observations, Carola gets defensive and very fixed in her views of the contemporary German society. She puts herself in opposition to a more liberal dominant discourse and gets even more convinced of seeing the situation for a threat. Thus, Carola appears to have found an unambiguous answer to much of the hardship she endured and uncertainty she experiences.

Case Discussion and Conclusion

Carola appears to be a person deeply immersed in her personal relationships, and they are what govern her moral judgements and considerations. This interpretation can be

---

tem Wetter, wenn andere im Freibad waren [...]. Zwei Personen, dieser [J.] und ich, wir saßen dann dem Pastor gegenüber, dem immer so das Gebiss gelegentlich runterfiel, der sehr gelangweilt war. Schrecklich. Ich habe ganz furchtbare Erinnerungen an diesen Mann. Ich weiß nicht, der war ja nun ein Kirchenmann und eigentlich sollte er doch die Menschen davon überzeugen. Das Gegenteil ist der Fall gewesen. Ich habe nur meine Konfirmation herbeigesehnt, wo wir dann so im Übrigen noch wahnsinnig unter Druck standen. Wir mussten ganz, ganz viel auswendig lernen. Auch mit der Androhung, es gab eine öffentliche Prüfung in der Kirche, vor dem ganzen Presbyterium, vor dem Auditorium in der Kirche. Also die Kirchenbesucher und dann wurden wir geprüft. Eine Wahnsinns Angst. [...] Und dann immer die Drohung [...]: „Und wenn du die Prüfung nicht schaffst, fällst du durch und wirst nicht konfirmiert." [...] Also das war eine Wahnsinns Belastung und ich war froh, als es vorbei war. Da bin ich nie wieder in die Kirche gegangen, das war für mich Fakt, das ertrage ich nicht mehr.

supported by her predominantly conventional religious type that centers around interpersonal expectations and normative assumptions or group consensus. In Carola's case, this inner circle that is the focal point of her considerations is first and foremost her family. In a life full of hardships, losses, and disappointments it has become her safe haven. This could explain the improvements in her scores on well-being as well as emotional stability: At the time of the first interview, she was likely still in mourning after the death of her partner, whereas by the second interview she had a new relationship and found new meaning through her role as a grandmother and someone who supported her adult daughters.

However, Carola is still deeply embedded in the hurtful experiences of the past and does not seem to forgive or overcome the unjust treatments she had to endure: She talks, in all three interviews, at length about these difficult events and mistreatments by figures of authority or partnership whose roles would have been to guide, protect or nurture her. Accounts concerning her mother, authority figures of the church or her ex-husband are very dominant as if she found solace in clearly identifying the persons who thwarted her personal ambitions and are deserving her anger. God, it seems, is one of these disappointing relationships which fits into her precritical God image of a father figure that should have supported and helped her in times of desperate need but did not answer her pleas.

Carola's world is an antagonistic one with male authority figures that humiliate her, a God that turns his back on people, and a German society full of threats to her and what she holds dearest: her family. The most imminent threat she can identify is the one of the religious other: the Muslim migrant whose daily atrocities she follows on a website and reads about in books that mirror her feelings. These accounts seem quite surprising considering her rather unsuspicious RSS scores. It seems as if Carola answered these items not as a reflection of her attitudes towards the other or strange religion but a as socially desirable image of herself as a woman who is part of a tolerant Western society.

Thus, it can be argued that these theories she refers to more extensively in the second and third interview give a stable frame of reference for the explanations of the unease she seems to have felt for a long time which might explain her improved scores in *environmental mastery* that otherwise seem contradictory considering how she talks about the society she lives in. Furthermore, this could be a second explanation for the development of her scores on the Ryff scale: Carola seems to have a clear idea of a very complex situation colored by her own feelings and anxieties as well an image of herself as a woman who overcame male mistreatment and has now a more valued sense of self, also mirrored in her improved self-acceptance score. She creates an image of a self-sufficient woman who no longer relies on God, the church or other authority figures that guide her.

In conclusion, what have we gained by combining these different methodic approaches on the level of the single case? First, we could observe how some findings derived from different methods supported each other, giving the interpretation more credibility. This was the case when comparing for example Carola's religious type with the role her family and God played in her narratives. Furthermore, they provided context and explanation to one another. This was exhibited when we could frame Carola's development as an improvement of her well-being and of her becoming more self-accepting by consulting her scores and explain these developments with her narrative accounts.

Part A: Conceptual & Methodological Perspectives

This broadened the qualitative interpretation and made it more contextualized as well as gave insights and meaning to the survey data. Finally, we saw how the two strands contradicted each other and lead to a more reasonable interpretation. Had we only looked at Carola's RSS scores we would have missed an important frame to understand her survey answers. Here an important completion of the picture was provided by the qualitative strand which would have been overlooked otherwise.

Conclusion

In the course of nearly twenty years of data collection, we have now access to an extensive body of qualitative as well as quantitative data, allowing us to investigate faith development in considerable depths and breadth. Our research design allows us to triangulate data and methods at various intersection points to provide us with different perspectives on faith development and further our understanding of this complex and multi-faceted phenomenon. This chapter aimed to present our research design not by going into detail with regard to the respective research methods we use, but to show the different angles from which we look at our data and how "something extra is added to both the quantitative and qualitative strand" (Creswell, 2015, p. 60). Furthermore, we illustrated how a longitudinal design enables us to follow our cases over an extended period of time, granting us insights into a significant part of their lifespan development.

Furthermore, the mixed-methods and longitudinal approach also provides us with a surplus of knowledge when investigating the single case, as was illustrated by the case study of Carola. Not only can we attempt a characterization of the single case in context of the whole sample, but the psychometric scales yield information about how this person is positioning him- or herself with regard to certain aspects and we learn what the person thinks "where they fit best" as Keller states (2020, p. 45) referring to Norbert Schwarz. By rigorous qualitative investigation, we then can further understand the biographical reasoning behind the self-report as well as the religious styles typification and get a profound insight into the underlying meaning-making process and structure. It is on this idiographic level we can disentangle the diverse, contradictory, and often confusing aspects and reasonings of a person and make credible interpretations about the individual dynamics of their faith development. In short, the quantitative data give us valuable context information as well as additional information of the case we investigate whereas the qualitative data helps us to understand them more thoroughly. This integration is exemplified by Table 4.2: We visualize the position of our singles cases within the whole sample, and single scores serve as point of reference to compare and contextualize the individual case to the means of the whole sample or subsample (cf. Keller et al., 2021; cf. Streib & Keller, 2018a).

The findings of the in-depth investigation can then feed back to the nomothetic level: The structural analysis of the FDIs aims at identifying the religious style and thereby condensing the qualitative data significantly and making the structures of meaning making tangible. Based on this process of typifying qualitative data the religious types can be constructed, quantifiably assessed as well as further quantitively investigated. This allowed us to identify general developments in our sample as well as finding typical or special trajectories through the longitudinal perspective. We thereby are able to identify cases that provoke interesting questions, address these by our qualitative content and narrative analysis and form new hypotheses, research questions or scales that can be added to the survey. This could also include case comparisons, e.g., in a cross-cultural perspective. Overall, this process improves the credibility of our findings and lead to a better understanding by applying multiple perspectives.

The overall gain of our research design therefore lies in the combination of a comprehensive with a more detail-oriented perspective, giving us both an overview and more general knowledge of as well as a deeper insight into the phenomenon under study. By doing so, we can not only become aware of blind spots or missing information, but also contradictions can be uncovered and generate new research questions which lead us closer to a fuller understanding of intra-individual as well as inter-individual faith development.

We could argue that Lamiell's criticism toward mainstream psychology that introduced this chapter can also be translated to the psychological research on religion and worldview, as the aggregated statistical data is not able to fully capture and adequately address the individual's religious experiences (cf. Keller, 2020, p. 12). Religion encompasses more than the adherence to certain faith traditions as it furthermore represents a relationship to the transcendence. Thus, in order to explore religious development, we follow the individual's reasoning and reconstruction of their lives' story in a longitudinal perspective, in order to understand people's faith and how they construct their worldview in a meaningful way. We are then able to compare cases as well as groups and combine this idiographic knowledge with psychometric scales that represent an equally important part of our research design. By on the one hand utilizing statistical data that help us systemize our findings as well as making them accessible to broader psychological research, and on the other explore the individual's reasoning and narrations, we achieve a more general and contextual understanding as well as "more depth of vision for understanding of religion in its broadest sense in the lives of individuals in their social and historical environment" (ibid., p. 2).

References

Adler, J. M., Lodi-Smith, J., Philippe, F. M., & Houle, I. (2016). The incremental validity of narrative identity in predicting well-being: A review of the field and recommendations for the future. *Personality and Social Psychology Review, 20*(2), 142–175.

Biesta, G. (2010). Pragmatism and the philosophical foundations of mixed methods research. In A. Tashakkori & C. Teddlie (Eds.), *Sage handbook of mixed methods in social & behavioral research* (pp. 95–117). Sage Publications.

Borgatti, S. P., Everett, M. G., & Johnson, J. C. (2018). *Analyzing social networks*. Sage.

Borkenau, P., & Ostendorf, F. (1993). *NEO-Fünf-Faktoren-Inventar (NEO-FFI) nach Costa und McCrae: Handanweisung*. Hogrefe, Verlag für Psychologie.

Budner, S. (1962). Intolerance of ambiguity as a personality variable. *Journal of Personality, 30*(1), 29–50. https://doi.org/10.1111/j.1467-6494.1962.tb02303.x

Bullik, R. (2024). *Leitmotifs in life stories. Reconstructing subjective religiosity and narrative identity—developments and stabilities over the adult lifespan.* Bielefeld University Press.

Cacioppo, J. T./Petty, R. E./Kao, C. F. (1984), The efficient assessment of need for cognition. *Journal of Personality Assessment, 48*, 306–307.

Cho, J. Y., & Lee, E.-H. (2014). Reducing confusion about grounded theory and qualitative content analysis: Similarities and differences. *The Qualitative Report, 19*(32).

Costa, P. T., & McCrae, R. R. (1985). *Revised NEO Personality Inventory (NEO PI-R) and NEO Five-Factor-Inventory (NEO-FFI). Professional manual.* Psychological Assessment Resources 1992.

Creswell, J. W. (2015). Revisiting mixed methods and advancing scientific practices. In S. N. Hesse-Biber & R. B. Johnson (Eds.), *The Oxford handbook of multimethod and mixed methods research inquiry* (pp. 58–71). Oxford University Press.

Creswell, J. W., & Plano Clark, V. L. (2018). *Designing and conducting mixed methods research* (Third edition). SAGE.

Elo, S., & Kyngäs, H. (2008). The qualitative content analysis process. *Journal of Advanced Nursing, 62*(1), 107–115. https://doi.org/10.1111/j.1365-2648.2007.04569.x

Eufinger, V., Silver, C., & Steppacher, A. (2019). Triangulation of qualitative and quantitative results in longitudinal and cross-cultural research. Pre-conference to the Conference of the International Association for the Psychology of Religion, Gdansk.

Flick, U. (2018). *Doing triangulation and mixed methods. The SAGE qualitative research kit: Vol. 9.* SAGE.

Friese, S. (2019). *Qualitative data analysis with ATLAS.ti* (Third edition). SAGE.

Haidt, J., & Graham, J. (2007). When morality opposes justice: Conservatives have moral intuitions that liberals may not recognize. *Social Justice Research, 20*(1), 98–116.

Helfrich-Hölter, H. (2006). Beyond the dilemma of cultural and cross-cultural psychology: Resolving the tension between nomothetic and idiographic approaches. In J. Straub, D. Weidemann, C. Kölbl, & B. Zielke (Eds.), *Kultur- und Medientheorie. Pursuit of meaning: Advances in cultural and cross-cultural psychology* (pp. 253–268). transcript Verlag.

Hood, R. W. (1975). The construction and preliminary validation of a measure of reported mystical experience. *Journal for the Scientific Study of Religion, 14*, 29–41.

Hood, R. W. J., Streib, H., & Keller, B. (2022). What is deconversion? Critiques and current conceptualizations from a faith developmental perspective. In H. Streib, B. Keller, R. Bullik, A. Steppacher, C. F. Silver, M. Durham, S. B. Barker, & R. W. Hood Jr. (Eds.), *Deconversion revisited. Biographical studies and psychometric analyses ten years later* (pp. 17–31). Vandenhoeck & Ruprecht.

Hopf, C. (2016). *Schriften zu Methodologie und Methoden qualitativer Sozialforschung.* Springer VS. http://dx.doi.org/10.1007/978-3-658-11482-4

Hsieh, H.-F., & Shannon, S. E. (2005). Three approaches to qualitative content analysis. *Qualitative Health Research, 15*(9), 1277–1288. https://doi.org/10.1177/1049732305276687

Huber, S. (2009). Religion Monitor 2008: Structuring principles, operational constructs, interpretive strategies. In F. Bertelsmann (Ed.), *What the world believes: Analysis and commentary on the Religion Monitor 2008* (pp. 17–51). Verlag Bertelsmann Stiftung.

Ivankova, N. V. (2014). Implementing quality criteria in designing and conducting a sequential quan -> qual mixed methods study of student engagement with learning applied research methods online. *Journal of Mixed Methods Research, 8*(1), 25–51.

Johnson, R. B., & Onwuegbuzie, A. J. (2004). Mixed methods research: A research paradigm whose time has come. *Educational Researcher, 33*(7), 14–26.

Johnson, R. B., Onwuegbuzie, A. J., & Turner, L. A. (2007). Toward a definition of mixed methods research. *Journal of Mixed Methods Research, 1*(2), 112–133. https://doi.org/10.1177/1558689806298224

Keller, B. (2020). *Taking psychoanalytic and psychometric perspectives toward a binocular vision of religion.* Brill.

Keller, B., & Streib, H. (2013). Faith development, religious styles and biographical narratives: Methodological perspectives. *Journal of Empirical Theology, 26*(1), 1–21. https://doi.org/10.1163/15709256-12341255

Keller, B., Streib, H., Silver, C. F., Klein, C., & Hood, R. W. (2016). Design, methods, and sample characteristics of the Bielefeld-based cross-cultural study of "spirituality." In H. Streib & R. W. Hood (Eds.), *Semantics and psychology of "spirituality." A cross-cultural analysis* (pp. 39–51). Springer International Publishing Switzerland. https://doi.org/10.1007/978-3-319-21245-6_4

Keller, B., Bullik, R., Steppacher, A., Streib, H., & Silver, C. (2022). Following deconverts and traditionalists. Longitudinal case study construction. In H. Streib, B. Keller, R. Bullik, A. Steppacher, C. F. Silver, M. Durham, S. B. Barker, & R. W. Hood Jr (Eds.), *Deconversion revisited. Biographical studies and psychometric analyses ten years later* (pp. 83–106). Vandenhoeck & Ruprecht.

Köber, C., Schmiedek, F., & Habermas, T. (2015). Characterizing lifespan development of three aspects of coherence in life narratives: A cohort-sequential study. *Developmental Psychology, 51*, 260–275.

Kuckartz, U. (2019). Qualitative Content Analysis: From Kracauer's beginnings to today's challenges. *Forum: Qualitative Social Research, 2019, 20, 3, 1.*

Labov, W., & Waletzky, J. (1967). Narrative analysis: Oral versions of personal experience. In J. Helms (Ed.), *Essays on the verbal and visual arts* (pp. 12–44). University of Washington Press.

Lamiell, J. T. (2013). Statisticism in personality psychologists' use of trait constructs: What is it? How was it contracted? Is there a cure? *New Ideas in Psychology, 31*, 65–71.

Lamiell, J. T. (2019). *Psychology's misuse of statistics and persistent dismissal of its critics.* Palgrave Macmillan.

Lazarsfeld, P. (1971). Forty years later. In M. Jahoda, P. F. Lazarsfeld, & H. Zeisel (Eds.), *Marienthal: The sociography of an unemployed community* (pp. vii–xvi). Chicago, IL: Aldine Atherton.

Lusher, D., Koskinen, J., & Robins, G. (2013). *Exponential random graph models for social networks: Theory, methods, and applications.* Cambridge University Press.

McAdams, D. P., & de St Aubin, E. D. (1992). A theory of generativity and its assessment through self-report, behavioral acts, and narrative themes in autobiography. *Journal of Adult Development, 62*, 1003–1015. https://doi.org/10.1037/0022-3514.62.6.1003

McAdams, D. P., Diamond, A., de St Aubin, E. D., & Mansfield, E. (1997). Stories of commitment: The psychosocial construction of generative lives. *Journal of Personality and Social Psychology*, 72(3), 678–694. https://doi.org/10.1037/0022-3514.72.3.678

McAdams, D. P., Hart, H. M., & Maruna, S. (1998). The anatomy of generativity. In D. P. McAdams & E. D. de St Aubin (Eds.), *Generativity and adult development. How and why we care for the next generation* (pp. 7–43). American Psychological Association.

Maxwell, J. A., Chmiel, M., & Rogers, S. E. (2015). Designing integration in multimethod and mixed methods research. In S. N. Hesse-Biber & R. B. Johnson (Eds.), *Oxford library of psychology. The Oxford Handbook of multimethod and mixed methods research inquiry*. Oxford University Press.

Maxwell, J. A., & Mittapalli, K. (2010). Realism as a stance for mixed methods research. In A. Tashakkori & C. Teddlie (Eds.), *Sage handbook of mixed methods in social & behavioral research* (pp. 145–167). Sage Publications.

Morgan, D. L. (2007). Paradigms lost and pragmatism regained: Methodological implications of combining qualitative and quantitative methods. *Journal of Mixed Methods Research*, 1(1), 48–76.

O'Cathain, A. (2010). Assessing the quality of mixed methods research: towards a comprehensive framework. In A. Tashakkori & C. Teddlie (Eds.), *Sage handbook of mixed methods in social & behavioral research* (pp. 531–555). Sage Publications.

Pasupathi, M., & Adler, J. M. (2021). Narrative, identity, and the life story: Structural and process approaches. In J. F. Rauthmann (Ed.), *The handbook of personality dynamics and processes* (pp. 387–403). Academic Press. https://doi.org/10.1016/B978-0-12-813995-0.00016-9

Pokorny, J., Norman, A., Zanesco, A., Bauer-Wu, S., Sahdra, B., & Saron, C. (2018). Network analysis for the visualization and analysis of qualitative data. *Psychological Methods*, 23(1), 169–183.

Reichert, J. (2017). Abduktion, Deduktion und Induktion in der qualitativen Forschung. In U. Flick, E. v. Kardorff, & I. Steinke (Eds.), *Qualitative Forschung: Ein Handbuch* (12th ed., pp. 276–286). Rowohlt Taschenbuch Verlag.

Rosenthal, G. (2006). Biographical research. In C. Seale, D. Silverman, J. F. Gubrium, & G. Gobo (Eds.), *Qualitative research practice* (pp. 48–64). Sage Publications.

Ryff, C. D. (1989). Happiness is everything, or is it? Explorations on the meaning of psychological well-being. *Journal of Personality and Social Psychology*, 57(6), 1069–1081. https://doi.org/10.1037/0022-3514.57.6.1069

Ryff, C. D., & Singer, B. H. (1996). Psychological well-being: Meaning, measurement, and implications for psychotherapy research. *Psychotherapy and Psychosomatics*, 65(1), 14–23. https://doi.org/10.1159/000289026

Ryff, C. D., & Singer, B. H. (1998a). The contours of positive human health. *Psychological Inquiry*, 9(1), 1–28. https://doi.org/10.1207/s15327965pli0901_1

Ryff, C. D., & Singer, B. H. (1998b). The role of purpose in life and growth in positive human health. In P. T. P. Wong & P. S. Fry (Eds.), *The human quest for meaning. Handbook of psychological research and clinical applications* (pp. 213–235). Lawrence Erlbaum Associates.

Saldaña, J. (2016). *The coding manual for qualitative researchers* (3. edition). SAGE.

Schreier, Margrit, Stamann, Christoph, Janssen, T., Dahl, A., & Dahl, W. (2019). Qualitative content analysis: Conceptualizations and challenges in research practice—introduction to the fqs special issue "qualitative content analysis I". *Forum Qualitative Sozialforschung*, 20(3).

Streib, H., & Chen, Z. J. (2021). Evidence for the brief mysticism scale: Psychometric properties, and moderation and mediation effects in predicting spiritual self-identification. *International Journal for the Psychology of Religion*, 31(3), 165–175. https://doi.org/10.1080/10508619.2021.1899641 (post-print at: https://doi.org/10.31234/osf.io/6bx2s)

Streib, H., Chen, Z. J., & Hood, R. W. (2020). Categorizing people by their preference for religious styles: Four types derived from evaluation of Faith Development Interviews. *International Journal for the Psychology of Religion*, 30(2), 112–127. https://doi.org/10.1080/10508619.2019.1664213 (post-print at: https://doi.org/10.31234/osf.io/d3kbr)

Streib, H., Chen, Z. J., & Hood, R. W. (2021). Faith development as change in religious types: Results from three-wave longitudinal data with Faith Development Interviews. *Psychology of Religion and Spirituality*, 15(2), 298–307. https://doi.org/10.1037/rel0000440 (post-print at: https://doi.org/10.31234/osf.io/qrcb2)

Streib, H., Hood, R. W., & Klein, C. (2010). The religious schema scale: Construction and initial validation of a quantitative measure for religious styles. *International Journal for the Psychology of Religion*, 20(3), 151–172. https://doi.org/10.1080/10508619.2010.481223

Streib, H., & Keller, B. (2018a). How faith development interviews reflect biographical paths to xenosophia: Conceptual and methodological considerations. In H. Streib & C. Klein (Eds.), *Xenosophia and religion: Biographical and statistical paths for a culture of welcome* (pp. 85–106). Springer.

Streib, H., & Keller, B. (2018b). *Manual for the assessment of religious styles in faith development interviews* (Fourth, revised edition of the "Manual for faith development research"). Universität Bielefeld.

Streib, H., & Keller, B. (2022). Quantitative perspectives on deconverts and traditionalists revisited. In H. Streib, B. Keller, R. Bullik, A. Steppacher, C. F. Silver, M. Durham, S. B. Barker, & R. W. Hood Jr (Eds.), *Deconversion revisited. Biographical studies and psychometric analyses ten years later.* (pp. 59–82). Brill Germany/Vandenhoeck & Ruprecht. https://doi.org/10.13109/9783666568688.59

Streib, H., Keller, B., Bullik, R., Steppacher, A., Silver, C. F., Durham, M., Barker, S. B., & Hood Jr, R. W. (2022). *Deconversion revisited. Biographical studies and psychometric analyses ten years later.* Brill Germany/Vandenhoeck & Ruprecht. https://doi.org/10.13109/9783666568688

Streib, H., Klein, C., Keller, B., & Hood, R. W. (2021). The Mysticism Scale as measure for subjective spirituality: New results with Hood's M-Scale and the development of a short form. In A. L. Ai, K. A. Harris, R. F. Paloutzian, & P. Wink (Eds.), *Assessing spirituality in a diverse world* (pp. 467–491). Springer Nature Switzerland. https://doi.org/10.1007/978-3-030-52140-0_19 (post-print at: https://doi.org/10.31234/osf.io/gwj2c)

Streib, H., Silver, C. F., Keller, B., Hood, R. W., & Csöff, R.-M. (2009). *Deconversion: Qualitative and quantitative results from cross-cultural research in Germany and the United States of America. Research in Contemporary Religion Vol.5.* Vandenhoeck & Ruprecht. https://doi.org/10.13109/9783666604393

Szostak, R. (2015). Interdisciplinary and transdisciplinary multimethod and mixed methods research. In S. N. Hesse-Biber & R. B. Johnson (Eds.), *Oxford library of psychology. The Oxford handbook of multimethod and mixed methods research inquiry.* Oxford University Press.

Tashakkori, A., & Teddlie, C. (Eds.). (2010). *Sage handbook of mixed methods in social & behavioral research.* Sage Publications.

Wasserman, S., & Faust, K. (1994). *Social network analysis: Methods and applications.* Cambridge University Press.

II. Part B: Results of Quantitative Analyses Including Qualitative Data

Chapter 5
The Six Aspects of Faith Development in Longitudinal Analysis

Zhuo Job Chen, Heinz Streib & Ralph W. Hood, Jr.[1]

Abstract *This chapter examines the meaning and development of the six aspects of faith development, perspective-taking, social horizon, morality, locus of authority, world coherence, and symbolic function. In the existing literature on faith development, the aspects have been used to account for the variety of dimensions that are important for faith, and to warrant equal attention to every aspect when rating the Faith Development Interview and calculating the total FDI score. The aspects have not been given individual treatment. The current study looks into the specific meaning and possible differences among these aspects. We first offer a theoretical overview of what these aspects measure. Then, with data of n = 75 individuals who completed three waves of Faith Development Interviews, hierarchical linear models evidenced upward faith development only in perspective-taking and social horizon, not in the other four aspects. A rigorous outcome-wide analysis explored the possible causes of faith development using self-report personality measures. Most importantly, self-acceptance appeared to be a consistent inhibitor of faith development. There were some associations of neuroticism and the religious schemata of truth of text and teachings and of xenosophia interreligious dialogue with faith development. Overall, the associations of personality measures with faith development aspects were weak and not uniform.*

    Keywords: *faith development; longitudinal; outcome-wide analysis; religious schema*

---

1   Z. J. Chen, School of Nursing, University of North Carolina at Charlotte, USA, E-mail: job.chen@charlotte.edu; H. Streib, Bielefeld University, Germany; R. W. Hood, Jr., University of Tennessee at Chattanooga, USA. © Heinz Streib, Ralph W. Hood Jr. (eds.): Faith in Development. Mixed-Method Studies on Worldviews and Religious Styles. First published in 2024 by Bielefeld University Press, Bielefeld, https://doi.org/10.14361/9783839471234-007

Introduction

Faith as operationalized in faith development research is conceptualized widely and comprehensively. The Faith Development Interview (FDI) with its 25 questions covers life review, relationships with parents and peers, values and commitments, to finally arrive at questions for worldview and religiosity. To account for the width and comprehensiveness of faith in conceptualization and evaluation, Fowler has introduced a number of aspects that deserve equal attention. Fowler has termed these aspects "windows" to a person's faith, assuming that, whatever aspect-window the researcher is looking through, they see one and the same faith stage.

In the evaluation of the FDI each of the 25 FDI questions has been associated to one aspect. One of the reasons for this has been that FDI evaluation should treat all aspects with equal attention. With its special attention to the differences between the aspects of faith as described in the Coding Manual (Streib & Keller, 2018), this study not only continues the differential investigation of faith development but takes this differential analyses further into the longitudinal perspective, that is: into the question of faith *development*.

While it had been observed and noted from the beginning of research with the FDI that style assignments to the answers in one FDI may differ by one (and at times more than one) style, this variance was for a long time systematically explained away by the theoretical assumption that a person can have only one style at a time (the assumption of a "structural whole") and by the corresponding methodical prescription to average all style assignments into a single final FDI score that should be rounded to an integer or half-rounded for "stage transition" (DeNicola & Fowler, 1993; Moseley et al., 1986). In agreement with Kohlberg et al.'s (1983) criteria for structural-developmental stage theories, Fowler (1980, 1981, 2001) has presupposed that faith development proceeds in structurally coherent stages—the assumption of "structural wholes."

The aspects have received greater attention more recently: The third edition of the Coding Manual (Fowler et al., 2004) has laid the groundwork for this study, since it has advanced the aspect-specific rating of the FDI and the visual presentation of the aspect-specific results of the FDI rating. The third edition of the Coding Manual also includes the first discussion of the possibility that, for one and the same FDI, the rater may conclude with not *one*, but *two* final FDI scores, because of a clear difference between aspect-specific style assignment.

Despite this decisive opening for differences in the final FDI score, the difference between aspect-specific ratings has not been systematically researched. Of course, the aspect-specific ratings have on occasion been noted in the case studies and greatly inspired the interpretation of single cases. However, this aspect-specific difference has so far not been explored systematically, and it has not been explored longitudinally. We should begin with giving some detail to the different aspects that we used in this study.

Meaning and Measurement of the Six Aspects in the FDI

Perspective-Taking

This aspect describes the way in which the person constructs the self, the other, and the relationship between them. It looks at how the person is constructing the interiority of another person. It also looks at how the individual is thinking and feeling, and how this relates to the person's knowledge of their own internal states. Thus, this aspect shows a certain "family resemblance" to the concept of mentalization or reflective functioning (Fonagy & Target, 2007).

Regarding the FDI questions, the following were associated with perspective-taking: How persons construct their life's chapters (FDI Question #1), how they describe and reflect on parents (FDI Question #7), past relationships (FDI Question #2), and changes in relationships (FDI Question #3). This information should tell us, how they conceive their own and others' inner processes, how the respondent thinks about other people and their influence on their life, and how the person perceives relationships in general. Within this aspect, we pay particular attention to the respondent's perception of changes in relationships. What made these changes come about – changes in the respondent, changes in the other person, or both?

When focusing on the aspect of Perspective-taking, evaluation of the interview passages involves a decision between the following styles of perspective-taking: *subjective* perspective-taking (Style 1), where the other is taken for granted and their view is not yet differentiated from one's own; *simple* perspective-taking (Style 2), conceding that others have other views, but predominantly focusing on reward/punishment ("do-ut-des") relations and on outer appearance; *mutual interpersonal* perspective-taking (Style 3) where interiority is perceived and related to social roles emerge, often in an implicit way; *third-person* perspective in the form of a system or ideology with explicit reasoning on the construction of possible views (Style 4); or the conceptually mediated *dialogical* perspective of Style 5, which takes into account that all experience is mediated and reflects difference, including the other's perspective on one's own.

Social Horizon

Here, the focus is on the mode of a person's identification in terms of group and family relations. It answers the question of how the person is viewing or constructing the world in which they are embedded, which may be a "small social life world" at first and, in later stages of development, the person's social world may be related to the wider horizon of society in a global perspective. Thus, this aspect attends to the question of how wide or inclusive the social world is to which a person will respond. Who is the person willing to include in his or her thinking and who remains outside? This aspect will also show the differences in how past relations, crises and breakthrough experiences are treated within an individual's structure of meaning making.

The scoring for social horizon includes the following questions, which are likely to provide indicators for this aspect: How does the interviewee narrate breakthrough experiences (FDI Question #5) and experiences of crises in the past (FDI Question #6), how do

Part B: Results of Quantitative Analyses Including Qualitative Data

they characterize current relationships (FDI Question #8) and do they identify with any groups (FDI Question #9)?

Assigning a specific style depends on the answer to the following questions: Is the respondent aware of boundaries (Style 1)? Are the respondent's boundaries best characterized as extended only to "those like us," in familial, ethnic, racial, class and religious terms (Style 2)? Are the respondent's boundaries best characterized as extended to groups and family members to which the subject has emotional bonds and interpersonal relationships (Style 3)? Are the respondent's boundaries best characterized as extended to groups that are ideologically compatible (Style 4)? Are the boundaries open to outgroups and other traditions and their truth claims (Style 5)?

Morality

In assessing the form of morality, we are looking at the patterns of how a person is handling issues of moral significance, including how the person defines what is to be taken as a moral issue and how the person answers the question of why be moral. This aspect answers the question, "What is the nature of the claims that others have on me, and how are these claims to be weighed?"

We expect that the following questions likely provide indicators for this aspect of morality: Are there any beliefs, values, or commitments that seem important to your life right now? (FDI Question #12), Do you think that actions can be right or wrong? (FDI Question #16), Are there certain actions or types of actions that are always right under any circumstances? (FDI Question #17), and the question, What is sin, to your understanding? (FDI Question #23).

Under the aspect of Morality, the FDI evaluator will ask: Would the interview responses be best characterized as motivated by complying with authority and power (Style 1), by reciprocity or do-ut-des (Style 2), by meeting interpersonal expectations (Style 3), by a societal perspective and reflective judgment (Style 4), or by prior-to-society perspective and as dialogical ethic (Style 5)?

Locus of Authority

This aspect looks at three factors: how authorities are selected, how authorities are held in relationship to the individual, and whether the person responds primarily to internal or external authority. This aspect of Fowler's formulation is related to, but transcends the psychological construct of locus of control in that it explicitly addresses powers toward which individual may draw on for orientation. A statement may be coded under Locus of Authority if it answers any of the following questions: Does the person locate authority internally or externally? To whom or what does the person look for guidance or approval? To whom or what does the person hold themselves responsible? How does the person identify authority?

The questions Do you feel that your life has meaning at present? What makes your life meaningful to you? (FDI Question #10), If you could change one thing about yourself or your life, what would you most want to change? (FDI Question #11), the question of how to approach an Important Decision (FDI Question #15), and the question on the Purpose of Human life (FDI Question #18) should provide material on locus of authority.

Style assignment in the aspect of Locus of Authority depends on answers to these questions: Does the respondent rely on external authority which is taken for granted (Style 1)? Is the person relating to an external authority, which is based on orthodoxy and absoluteness, thus on rules (Style 2)? Is authority grounded in tacit interpersonal values consonant with the respondent´s social group (Style 3)? Does the person rely on an internal authority, a self-ratified ideological perspective, an explicit relationship to authority (Style 4)? Is the person relying on an internal authority, which shows reflective engagement with multiple perspectives as well as a disciplined subjectivity (Style 5)?

World Coherence

This aspect describes how a person constructs the object world, including the sense of the ultimate environment. It answers the questions, "How do things make sense?" or, "How do the various elements of my experience fit together?" The form of world coherence is a type of cosmology, whether explicit or tacit. It includes the person's worldview and may include explicitly religious answers. It also includes the principles by which this worldview is constructed, the logical relations by which elements of the world are held together.

The questions on Harmony with the Universe (FDI Question #13), What does death mean to you? What happens to us when we die? (FDI Question #19), How do you explain the presence of evil in our world? (FDI Question #24) and the question of how to deal with religious conflicts (FDI Question #25) may provide data indicating the respondent's form of world coherence.

The rating will attend to the questions: Does the interviewee show an impressionistic picture of the world, a view that seems partial and fragmented (Style 1)? Is world coherence based on cause and effect, based on concrete and empirical evidence and without reflective distance (Style 2)? Is the coherence of the interviewee´s world based on tacit systems, which may also include simple and uncritical pluralism (Style 3)? Does the coherence of the respondent´s world rely on an explicit system, on striving for closure (Style 4)? Is the world coherence characterized by multi-levelled and complex reality, are disparate elements held in tension, displaying a reflective sensitivity toward history and culture (Style 5)?

Symbolic Function

This aspect is concerned with how the person understands, appropriates, and utilizes symbols and other aspects of language in the process of meaning-making and locating their centers of value and images of power. Any passage which reveals how a person interprets symbolic material, particularly those symbols which are important to the individual, can be coded under this aspect.

Material will be provided in particular by the questions regarding the respondent's image of God, conception of the transcendent, or world view and how it has changed over time (FDI Question #4), by the question whether the participant regards themselves as religious, spiritual or faithful person (FDI Question #20), by the way the respondent appropriates symbols (FDI Question #21), and how they understand and use rituals and/or prayer (FDI Question #22), and finally by the question about the person's understanding of mature faith or handling of existential questions (FDI Question #14).

Working on the aspect Symbolic Function the leading questions are: Is there a distinction between the symbol and what it stands for? If not, we see Style 1. Is there an interpretation of symbols, which is literal and perhaps relying on one authoritarian text (Style 2)? Is there a conventional interpretation and pre-critical openness to symbols and their power to evoke feeling and emotion (Style 3)? Does the respondent explicitly translate symbols into concepts or ideas, thus "demythologizing" them (Style 4)? Does the respondent keep the evocative power of a symbol and its ideational content in tension, displaying "second naïveté" (Style 5)?

The Model of Development and the Hierarchy of Types

Streib et al. (2020) explain how the 25 styles can be combined into a final total FDI score using the predominant or substantial frequency of the assignment of a specific style in one interview. This total FDI score is the called the religious type. Here is a brief summary characterization of the four types:

The **Substantially Ethnocentric** Type is characterized by a substantial presence of mythic-literal understanding, substantial ethnocentric, mono-religious claims for the exclusive truth of texts and teachings of one's own tradition, and a substantial support for a system of punishment and reward in regard to justice in heaven and on earth.

The **Predominantly Conventional** Type has a predominant inclination for consent to the conventional beliefs and prescriptions of one's group, religious community or immediate small lifeworld; it has a desire for mutual interpersonal harmony, while rejecting critical questioning.

The **Predominantly Individuative-reflective** Type invites critical and autonomous reflection—featuring multi-religious plurality; in case of conflicting validity claims, models of tolerance are considered.

The **Emerging Dialogical-xenosophic** Type is characterized by an openness for inter-religious dialog and for being challenged and changed by the encounter with the Other/the Alien. On top of the use of critical and autonomous reflection there emerges xenosophia, the wisdom in encountering the Strange/Alien (Waldenfels, 2011; Streib, 2018).

The religious types present a hierarchical order. Progression from the *substantially ethnocentric type* to the *emerging dialogical-xenosophic type* is understood as developmental progress. Thus, we expect to find cases in our three-wave data, who progress to a higher type over the three times of measurement and have arrived at a higher type at Wave 3 (*movers* upward). Further, since we discard the assumption of an exclusively irreversible progressive development, we expect cases who regress on a lower type (*movers* downward). And finally, we expect to find a considerable number of *stayers*, that is participants who have the same religious type consistently over all three times of measurement or at least between at Wave 1 and Wave 3.

Now, for this study, we have constructed the religious types for each aspect. Therefore, a single FDI will receive six different type assignments—which could be identical across all six aspects but could also differ between the aspects. This article will present results from three-wave longitudinal data that include three Faith Development Interviews with the same persons and now six aspect-specific type assignments.

Method

Participants

Analyses are based on a longitudinal sample of $n = 75$ participants who completed three FDIs and answered a comprehensive questionnaire at each time of interviewing. All research projects were simultaneously collecting data in Germany and the USA. In the sample of this study, 16 (21.3%) lived in the USA, 59 (78.7%) in Germany; 35 (46.7%) identified as female, 40 (53.3 %) as male. Mean age at Wave 1 was 45.8 years (range: 18 to 76 years) and 57.0 years (range: 27 to 85 years) at Wave 3. Tertiary education was reported by 72.0 %. Mean annual per-capita income was reported at $38,010.

All $n = 75$ participants had their first interview and survey in either the Deconversion Study (Streib et al., 2009) or the Spirituality Study (Streib & Hood, 2016) with $n = 272$ FDIs and $n = 108$ FDIs, respectively. Both studies used convenience sampling through media such as paper adds, radio, or websites for reaching out to participants. Problems with locating participants at still valid addresses and getting consent for re-interviewing has limited re-participation in Wave 2 to 24.5%, but re-participation rate in Wave 3 was 80.6%. Time lag between the initial FDI at Wave 1 and the second FDI at Wave 2 is 6.9 years—with a subgroup difference: participants with their first FDI in the Deconversion Study ($n = 34$) have a time lag of 10.1 years (range: 6.1 to 13.4), while participants with their first FDI in the Spirituality Study have 4.3 years (range: 3.9 to 5.3) between first and second FDI. Mean time lag between the Wave 2 FDI and Wave 3 FDI is 3.6 years (range: 2.08 to 5.05). The mean time lag between the first interview at Wave 1 and the last interview at Wave 3 is 10.47 years (range: 6.53 to 16.36 years).

Measures

The FDI is a semi-structured interview that may last between 30 minutes to 2 hours. The interview format (for wording of interview questions asked in these FDIs and for evaluation prescription, see Fowler et al., 2004; Streib & Keller, 2018) consists of 25 questions (including associated follow-up questions) that address *life review* (Sample question: *"Reflecting on your life, identify its major chapters"*), relationships (*"Focusing now on the present, how would you describe your parents and your current relationship to them?"*), present values and commitments (*"Are there any beliefs, values, or commitments that seem important to your life right now?"*) and finally *religion and world view* (*"If people disagree about a religious issue, how can such religious conflicts be resolved?"*). Evaluation of the FDI is an interpretative process of identifying, in the responses to the respective FDI question, the structural pattern as described in detail in the *Coding Manual* (Streib & Keller, 2018). This evaluation concludes with the assignment of one of the styles to the respective interacts in the FDI transcript that contain the answers of the interviewees to each of the 25 questions. After entering evaluation results into the quantitative data base, this results in 25 variables with integers for the style assignments. FDI rating checks by a second blind rater in random subsamples of ca. 17% of Wave 1 and Wave 2 FDIs resulted in inter-rater agreement of 80% and 69%, respectively. The inter-rater agreement between three independent raters for the entire Wave 3 FDI sample was 79%.

Our method of constructing the final total FDI score is the religious type (Streib et al., 2020). To construct a summary evaluation of one FDI, the type is constructed according to the following algorithm: Out of the 25 rating variables, if frequency of Style 2 rating is equal to or more than 5 (20%), a person's religious type will be *Substantially Ethnocentric*; if frequency of Style 5 rating is equal to or more than 5 (20%), the type is decided as *Emerging Dialogical-xenosophic Type*; else, the type is *Predominantly Conventional* if frequency of Style 3 rating is greater than that of Style 4 rating, or *Predominantly Individuative-reflective Type* if frequency of Style 4 rating is greater than that of style 3 rating. A specific rule is set in place to break the ties introduced by an identical frequency of Style 3 and Style 4 ratings, and/or both Style 2 and Style 5 ratings exceed 20%. For these situations, the case should be associated with the higher type.

The algorithm used for calculating the religious types as final FDI score for the entire interview (Streib et al., 2020) was used also for the calculation of the aspect-specific types. This made the aspect-specific types considerably more sensitive for ratings of the instrumental-reciprocal style (Style 2) and the dialogical style (Style 5), since the Style 2 or Style 5 rating of one answer can determine the type assignment of the aspect. We think that this weighting procedure is justified, when the aim is to prevent averaging out the still substantial presence of Style 2 or the emerging development of Style 5 in an interview.

Self-rated religiosity and spirituality were assessed on a 5-point scale. The five personality factors were assessed by the NEO-FFI (Costa & McCrae, 1985) that was used in all three waves consistently. For psychological well-being, we used the Ryff-Scales for Psychological Well-being and Growth (Ryff, 1989; Ryff & Singer, 1996). For the assessment of mysticism, Hood's (1975) Mysticism Scale was used. Generativity was measured by the Loyola Generativity Scale (McAdams & de St Aubin, 1992). In Wave 2 and Wave 3 we also used Budner's (1962) Intolerance of Ambiguity Scale, the Need for Cognition Scale (Cacioppo et al., 1984), and the items used in the Religion Monitor (2013) for the assessment of fundamentalism and pluralism. For more detailed information about measures, see the Appendix A in this volume.

Analytic Procedures

In assessing faith development, six separate hierarchical linear models (HLM) were estimated, with each aspect at Wave 1, Wave 2, and Wave 3, as the respective repeated measures. In the HLM, time served as a level 1 variable nested within individuals at level 2, predicting religious type as an ordinal outcome variable. We utilized two approaches. The first approach treated time as continuous random effect (coded as linear increments of 1, 2, and 3) and the model did not include any covariates. The second approach treated time as categorical fixed effect consisting of three categories, with Wave 1 as the baseline reference category. Dummy indicators for Wave 2 and Wave 3 were used to estimate likelihood of change between each later wave and the baseline. Models adjusted for time-variant (i.e., age and income) and time-invariant (i.e., gender and education) demographic characteristics assessed at Wave 1.

In testing predictors of faith development, an outcome-wide analytic approach (VanderWeele et al., 2020) was used to estimate effects, which involved regressing each of the six faith development aspects measured at Wave 3 (i.e., perspective-taking, social horizon, morality, locus of authority, world coherence, symbolic function) on an array of self-report personality measures measured at Wave 2 (i.e., Big Five Personality: openness to experience, extroversion, agreeableness, conscientiousness, neuroticism; Psychological Well-Being: autonomy, environmental mastery, personal growth, positive relations, purpose in life, self-acceptance; Mysticism: introvertive mysticism, extrovertive mysticism, interpretive mysticism. Religious Schemata: truth of text and teachings, fairness tolerance and rational choice, xenosophia; and measures of generativity, intolerance of ambiguity, need for cognition, fundamentalism, pluralism) in separate models. Ordinal logistic regressions were used to estimate the odds ratio of the faith aspect change in exposure to a specific personality variable. All models adjusted for demographic variables of age, gender, education, and income assessed at Wave 1, and prior value of the faith development aspect assessed at Wave 1. We used R package *ordinal* to estimate linear slopes associated with the ordinal variable religious type with cumulative logit link functions.

Results

Differential patterns of faith development

Table 5.1 shows the number and percentage of downward movers (Wave 3 type lower than that at Wave 1), stayers (Wave 3 and Wave 1 at the same type), and upward movers (Wave 3 type higher than that at Wave 1). There were significantly more upward movers than the other two categories in perspective-taking (χ^2 (2) = 19.52, $p < .001$) and social horizon (χ^2 (2) = 8.24, $p = .016$). Percentage of upward movers did not differ significantly in the other four aspects. Comparing across these six aspects, there was no significant difference in the overall proportion of mover types, χ^2 (10) = 13.53, $p = .195$.

To assess faith development, a positive and significant slope would indicate upward development. Odds ratio (OR) could be interpreted as the likelihood for development over stagnancy given one unit increase in time. Under the first approach treating time as a continuous variable, three faith aspects showed an upward development: perspective-taking ($b = 0.99$, OR = 2.69, $p < .001$, slope variability $SD = 1.05$), social horizon ($b = 0.63$, OR = 1.88, $p = .002$, $SD = 0.94$), and world coherence ($b = 0.32$, OR = 1.38, $p = .045$, $SD = 0.16$).

Table 5.1: Distribution of downward movers, stayers, and upward movers in the six aspects.

	Downward Mover	Stayer	Upward Mover
Perspective-taking	15 (20.00%)	17 (22.67%)	43 (57.33%)
Social Horizon	14 (18.67%)	27 (36.00%)	34 (45.33%)
Morality	20 (26.67%)	29 (38.67%)	26 (34.67%)
Locus of Authority	20 (26.67%)	29 (38.67%)	26 (34.67%)
World Coherence	20 (26.67%)	25 (33.33%)	30 (40.00%)
Symbolic Function	22 (29.33%)	25 (33.33%)	28 (37.33%)

Three aspects did not show significant development: morality ($b = 0.17$, $OR = 1.19$, $p = .340$, $SD = 0.64$), locus of authority ($b = 0.19$, $OR = 1.21$, $p = .311$, $SD = 0.81$), and symbolic function ($b = 0.27$, $OR = 1.31$, $p = .114$, $SD = 0.51$). Figure 5.1 displays these trends with a central curve in each of the six aspect-wise plots. There was a negative correlation between intercept and slope suggesting that for people at a lower initial type, they tended to move upward over time, and vice versa.

Figure 5.1: Overall trend of faith development in each aspect over three waves. Locally estimated scatterplot smoothing (loess) is applied for the overall trend, as shown in the center with band of standard errors. Lines in the backgrounds are estimated linear trends for each person.

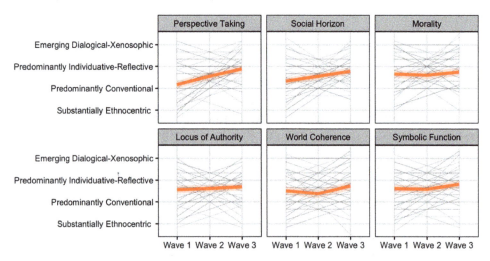

Under the second approach treating time as a discrete variable and controlling for demographic variables, the upward development was only evident for perspective-taking, for which both Wave 2 and Wave 3 were associated with higher types than that of Wave 1, and for social horizon whose Wave 3 type was higher than that of Wave 1. There was no significant association of time with type development for the other four aspects. We even saw some dip at Wave 2, marginally significant at $p = .05$, for world coherence and symbolic function. These trends were evident from Figure 5.1. Demographics showed only limited effects. Low education (up to tertiary) was associated with less likelihood for upward faith development, in perspective-taking (OR = 0.39, p = .030) and morality (OR = 0.37, p = .020). Age was associated with less likelihood for upward faith development in morality (OR = .97, p = .014).

Table 5.2: Effects of time as categorical variable on faith aspects controlling for demographic variables.

Outcomes	Wave 2 vs. Wave 1	Wave 3 vs. Wave 1
	OR [95% CI]	OR [95% CI]
Perspective-taking	5.25 [2.14, 12.92] ***	11.18 [4.27, 29.29] ***
Social Horizon	2.11 [0.95, 4.70]	3.21 [1.37, 7.49] *
Morality	0.56 [0.25, 1.26]	0.84 [0.36, 1.99]
Locus of Authority	0.73 [0.32, 1.66]	0.99 [0.42, 2.37]
World Coherence	0.45 [0.20, 1.00]	1.15 [0.50, 2.66]
Symbolic Function	0.45 [0.20, 1.00]	0.74 [0.32, 1.71]

Note. * p < .05, *** p < .001. All models controlled for time-variant age and income, and time-invariant gender and education.

Combining results from both approaches, there was evident upward faith development in perspective-taking and social horizon. Faith development in the other four aspects was not clearly supported.

Predictors of Faith Development

We ran ordinal logistic regressions with the 6 aspects measured at Wave 3 as outcome variables and 22 self-report personality measures measured at Wave 2 as predictors, one at a time. In each of the 132 (=6*22) regression models, we controlled for age, gender, education, and income measured at Wave 1, and the respective baseline level of faith aspect measured at Wave 1. Table 5.3 reports these results with odds ratio and its 95% confidence interval. An odds ratio greater than 1 indicates that having a higher level of that specific personality attribute can increase the likelihood of an upward faith development. An odds ratio less than 1 indicates having that specific personality attribute would decrease the likelihood of an upward faith development. Since the value of 1 indicates no influence, a confidence interval not including 1 would be equivalent to statistical significance.

Table 5.3: Associations of Personality Variables (Wave 2) With Six Aspects of Faith Development (Wave 3)

	Perspective-taking OR[95% CI]	Social Horizon OR[95% CI]	Morality OR[95% CI]	Locus of Authority OR[95% CI]	World Coherence OR[95% CI]	Symbolic Function OR[95% CI]
Five Factor Personality						
Neuroticism	3.98 [1.29, 16.87]*	1.13 [0.41, 3.36]	2.62 [1.03, 7.09]*	2.34 [0.90, 6.79]	0.79 [0.32, 1.92]	2.28 [0.78, 7.29]
Extroversion	1.04 [0.34, 3.22]	1.33 [0.46, 4.01]	0.70 [0.28, 1.72]	0.48 [0.16, 1.26]	1.62 [0.64, 4.35]	1.05 [0.35, 3.12]
Openness to Experience	1.82 [0.26, 13.62]	3.43 [0.44, 33.81]	1.16 [0.25, 5.50]	0.53 [0.08, 3.27]	0.72 [0.14, 3.50]	3.81 [0.58, 29.31]
Agreeableness	1.51 [0.28, 8.55]	0.95 [0.16, 5.06]	0.35 [0.08, 1.33]	0.41 [0.09, 1.89]	1.91 [0.49, 7.62]	0.82 [0.16, 4.22]
Conscientiousness	0.27 [0.05, 1.26]	0.71 [0.15, 3.90]	0.34 [0.09, 1.22]	0.25 [0.05, 1.00]	2.49 [0.68, 9.91]	0.21 [0.04, 0.96]
Psychological Wellbeing						
Autonomy	0.54 [0.10, 2.84]	0.27 [0.04, 1.56]	0.22 [0.04, 1.04]	0.99 [0.23, 4.24]	0.97 [0.18, 4.97]	0.40 [0.07, 2.11]
Environmental Mastery	0.39 [0.11, 1.31]	0.92 [0.27, 2.93]	0.52 [0.17, 1.55]	0.36 [0.10, 1.11]	1.13 [0.37, 3.47]	0.54 [0.15, 1.87]
Personal Growth	1.28 [0.24, 6.69]	3.11 [0.57, 20.93]	0.52 [0.10, 2.21]	0.23 [0.02, 1.50]	1.05 [0.27, 4.13]	0.57 [0.07, 3.41]
Positive Relations	0.49 [0.13, 1.59]	0.66 [0.18, 2.06]	0.60 [0.23, 1.53]	0.59 [0.20, 1.58]	0.80 [0.29, 2.16]	0.51 [0.15, 1.57]
Purpose in Life	0.77 [0.22, 2.59]	0.50 [0.12, 1.65]	0.47 [0.16, 1.26]	0.54 [0.16, 1.62]	0.71 [0.27, 1.82]	0.40 [0.11, 1.37]
Self-Acceptance	0.18 [0.04, 0.64]*	0.48 [0.12, 1.47]	0.27 [0.09, 0.75]*	0.26 [0.08, 0.78]*	0.79 [0.31, 2.00]	0.26 [0.08, 0.77]*
Mysticism						
Introvertive Mysticism	0.86 [0.40, 1.76]	1.83 [0.85, 4.31]	0.67 [0.34, 1.27]	0.78 [0.38, 1.56]	0.92 [0.50, 1.67]	0.54 [0.19, 1.36]
Extrovertive Mysticism	1.11 [0.56, 2.21]	1.66 [0.77, 3.96]	0.97 [0.55, 1.72]	1.03 [0.54, 1.98]	0.98 [0.56, 1.70]	0.57 [0.22, 1.32]
Interpretive Mysticism	0.77 [0.35, 1.59]	1.23 [0.57, 2.66]	0.56 [0.28, 1.06]	0.68 [0.32, 1.38]	0.95 [0.52, 1.74]	0.35 [0.11, 0.91]*

Religious Schema

Truth of text teachings	0.83 [0.37, 1.86]	1.05 [0.44, 2.72]	0.78 [0.36, 1.70]	0.81 [0.35, 1.87]	1.62 [0.82, 3.26]	0.35 [0.11, 0.83]*
Fairness tolerance ration	2.14 [0.40, 12.41]	0.77 [0.12, 4.76]	1.37 [0.37, 5.19]	0.63 [0.13, 2.90]	7.55 [1.72, 39.45]*	1.00 [0.18, 5.84]
Xenosophia	7.36 [1.88, 44.75]*	0.70 [0.22, 2.08]	1.09 [0.46, 2.63]	0.66 [0.24, 1.81]	1.00 [0.43, 2.36]	1.04 [0.37, 3.02]
Generativity	1.62 [0.20, 13.20]	1.17 [0.16, 8.22]	0.64 [0.12, 3.09]	0.47 [0.07, 2.54]	0.84 [0.17, 4.17]	0.46 [0.05, 3.32]
Intolerance of Ambiguity	0.14 [0.01, 1.66]	0.28 [0.02, 3.18]	0.37 [0.05, 2.73]	0.49 [0.05, 4.33]	0.32 [0.04, 2.04]	0.07 [0.00, 0.86]
Need for Cognition	3.73 [0.57, 26.22]	1.56 [0.30, 10.13]	3.29 [0.8, 15.16]	1.34 [0.30, 6.05]	2.66 [0.64, 11.43]	1.39 [0.25, 7.93]
Fundamentalism	0.63 [0.19, 2.00]	0.37 [0.09, 1.19]	0.50 [0.16, 1.52]	0.99 [0.29, 3.44]	0.73 [0.26, 1.95]	0.45 [0.12, 1.51]
Pluralism	2.77 [1.10, 8.18]*	2.06 [0.79, 6.43]	0.82 [0.42, 1.59]	0.91 [0.44, 1.85]	1.07 [0.55, 2.06]	1.15 [0.52, 2.56]

Note. OR = odds ratio, CI = confidence interval. *$p < .05$. All models controlled for age, gender, education, income and baseline faith aspect measured at Wave 1.

Part B: Results of Quantitative Analyses Including Qualitative Data

To test the robustness of the significant effects, we also performed a sensitivity analysis on the significant effects. The e-values for effect estimates are the minimum strength of association that an unmeasured confounder would need to have with both the predictor and the outcome variable to fully explain away the observed effect, after accounting for the measured covariates (VanderWeele & Ding, 2017). A rough rule of thumb agreed by epidemiologists is that an e-value over 4 would indicate that the effect is robust against alternative explanations.

In predicting perspective-taking, neuroticism (OR = 3.98, e-value = 7.43), xenosophia (OR = 7.36, e-value = 10.31), and pluralism (OR = 2.77, e-value = 4.99) facilitated upward change, whereas self-acceptance (OR = 0.18, e-value = 14.21) inhibited upward change. People that are emotionally unstable, love unknown ideas, seek religious pluralism, and tend to not accept themselves were more likely to increase in perspective-taking over time. In predicting social horizon, none of the variables were significant. In predicting morality, neuroticism (OR = 2.62, e-value = 4.67) facilitated and self-acceptance (OR = 0.27, e-value = 6.74) inhibited upward development. In predicting locus of authority, self-acceptance (OR = 0.26, e-value = 7.04) inhibited upward development. In predicting world coherence, fairness tolerance and rational choice (OR = 7.55, e-value = 14.59) promoted upward development. In predicting symbolic function, self-acceptance (OR = 0.26, e-value = 7.23), interpretive mysticism (OR = 0.35, e-value = 5.09), and truth of text and teachings (OR = 0.35, e-value = 5.24) inhibited upward development. Overall, self-acceptance appeared to be a consistent and strong inhibitor of faith development.

Discussion

Stability and Change in Faith Development – Confirmation of a New Perspective without the "Structural Whole" Assumption

The results presented in this chapter show that faith development in longitudinal assessment does not exhibit a coherent pattern throughout all the aspects. Already the frequency statistics of stayers, downward movers and upward movers (Table 5.1), demonstrate significantly higher portions of upward movers in the aspects of perspective-taking and social horizon, than in the four other aspects. This is reflected in the calculation of slopes that indicate upward faith development, as presented in Figure 5.1: faith development appears to take place only in the aspects of perspective-taking and social horizon (and in the aspect of world coherence, when time was treated as continuous variable, but did not reach significance in the model with time as discrete variable and controlling for demographics). Taken together, these results indicate, first, that upward faith development does not take place simultaneously and coherently across the six aspects, and second, that a slope for faith development is significant only of the two aspects of perspective-taking and social horizon.

Regarding the former, the results of this study contradict the assumption of "structural whole" as a general assumption that is true across all aspects and across individuals. Because Fowler (1980, 1981, 2001) has established the assumption of the "structural whole" as valid for faith development theory throughout, the results of this study contradict his theory at a pivotal point. By demonstrating differential patterns for faith development, the results of this study provide empirical evidence for rejecting the assumption that faith development consistently proceeds in a sequence of "structural wholes." On the contrary, these results indicate that two or more different styles may be operative in one interview. Such synchronous presence of more than one style is clearly acknowledged in the religious styles perspective (Streib, 2001) and the visualization of styles as waves that emerge to the surface and ebb away, but remain available for later revival. Now, the analyses presented in this chapter move on to investigate this variance across aspects and longitudinally with perspective on *development*. Thus, from the religious styles perspective, it is not surprising to find different patterns of styles and aspects in faith development, but the results of this study go into more detail regarding the relation between the aspects and regarding development.

Meaning of the Aspects – Conceptual Implications and Questions

Why is it the aspects of perspective-taking and social horizon that develop upwards over time, while the other aspects rather show stagnation? These results are unexpected, and they are not easily explained. What do perspective-taking and social horizon have in common, and what distinguishes them from the other aspects? What makes perspective-taking and social horizon, in contrast to the other aspects, more open for development? Can they be seen as the motor of development? It is not clear yet whether development in the other four aspects lag behind, and will they experience development later? Is this the empirical documentation of a phenomenon that Piaget has called decalage? These questions call for further investigation, and answers are rather speculative without further empirical evidence. Nevertheless, we note possible interpretations: Social horizon, but especially perspective-taking may be regarded as meta-cognitive preconditions for the cognitive structures of the different styles, whereas morality and locus of authority have a stronger focus on the application of these cognitive structures to questions such as "what makes an action right;" and world coherence and symbolic function have a stronger focus on the application of the cognitive structures to questions of the hermeneutics of world and transcendence. A similar interplay of meta-cognitive preconditions such as perspective-taking or epistemic humility with morality and with worldview is recently presented by Grossmann, Weststrate et al. (2020). They note: "PMC [Perspectival Meta-Cognition] is required to implement wisdom-related moral aspirations. On their own, moral aspirations such as fairness, justice, loyalty, or purity (Graham et al., 2011; Shweder, 1990) are abstract concepts, void of the pragmatic nuances necessary to implement moral concerns in a person's life." (p. 110). Thus, we may interpret our results as confirming the assumption that perspective-taking can be contended as a meta-cognitive precondition for faith development and for the development of wisdom. In addition, social horizon can be understood as the meta-cognitive precondition, by which the social ecological perspective (Grossmann, Dorfman, et al., 2020) is emphasized more strongly.

What Predicts Faith Development?

The comprehensive modeling of predictors in regression analyses could identify a relatively small number of significant effects, but these are remarkable and meaningful for discussion. Self-acceptance, to begin with, emerged as the most consistent predictor across four aspects; but self-acceptance emerged as *negative* predictor—which means that higher report of self-acceptance at Wave 2 counteracts progressing faith development to a higher type at Wave 3. This may appear surprising at first, because it seems to contradict the assumption that faith development should positively correlate with well-being, including self-acceptance; but this result makes sense because the *predicting* effect was analyzed revealing that lower self-acceptance stimulates the readiness to eventually consider and adopt a higher type, thus stimulates progress in faith development. This stimulation of development may remind of the dynamic in cognitive-structural models, which assume that unsuccessful assimilation may elicit the readiness for a new step in accommodation; however, self-acceptance would indicate that there is more than a cognitive misfit, but also emotional factors and questions of meaning-making are at work, when a person is not content or in harmony with their current religious style—thus is ready for something new.

This result for self-acceptance corresponds to the results for neuroticism as predictor of faith development, which has emerged for the aspects of perspective-taking and social horizon. That this effect is significant for perspective-taking and morality means that lower emotional stability may cause a person to search for and adopt higher styles and move to a higher type. Thus, results for neuroticism dovetail with results for self-acceptance.

Interestingly, for symbolic function, which is the aspect that has a strong focus on the interviewees' religiosity (religious person; religious idea, symbols, rituals; pray/meditate; image of god; mature faith), one predictor has emerged that—again negatively—predicts faith development: the religious schema truth of texts and teachings (ttt). This religious schema has a strong focus on the absolute and inerrant validity of one's own religion. Results indicate that high ttt predicts faith development negatively, thus low ttt predicts faith development positively. This confirms our estimation of ttt as predictor of faith development without the differentiation into aspect-specific types, but using the general type for the entire FDI in a cross-lagged panel analysis (Streib, Chen, & Hood, 2021): Scores on ttt at Wave 1 significantly predicted the change in religious type at Wave 2, however negatively. Thus, longitudinal prediction of faith development takes up our own preliminarily analysis that was based on cross-sectional analysis, in which we had demonstrated in an analysis of variance (Streib et al., 2020) that the decreasing scores on ttt correlate with increasing religious types. Taken together, the results of the study presented in this chapter confirm the characterization of faith development—here with special attention to the religiosity-focused aspect of symbolic function—as stepping out from the observance of one's religious tradition to the consideration of alternatives, including the eventual appreciation of previously unknown worldview. The stronger agreement to *ttt*, the stronger the inclination to move down from higher religious types toward the Substantially Ethnocentric Type; and reversely: the lower agreement with *ttt*, the stronger the inclination to progress in faith development toward The Predominantly Individuative-reflective and the Emerging Dialogical-xenosophic types.

Results for the interpretative mysticism, which also emerged as negative predictor of faith development in this study, appear to aim in the same direction, but reveal new and puzzling questions. Of the three factors of Hood's (1975) Mysticism Scale, the factor of interpretative mysticism had a stronger relation to religiosity, in contrast to introvertive and extrovertive mysticism, which did not relate to religion, but rather to self-identified spirituality (Hood, 2003; Klein et al., 2016; Streib et al., 2021; Zinnbauer et al., 1997). Thus, while introvertive and extrovertive mysticism did not emerge as significant predictors of faith development in this study, the interpretation of mysticism in religious, but of course in widely open religious terms did, but *negatively*. Thus, progress in faith development, particularly in its aspect of symbolic function thus with stronger connection to religious ideas, rituals, and practice, appears to be associated with greater distance to religious belief and practice.

Finally, we discuss two significant predictors for faith development: pluralism and xenosophia. As subscale of the Religious Schema Scale, *xenosophia/inter-religious dialog (xenos)* attends to the readiness for dialog, to the appreciation of difference and encounter with the other and unknown, as expressed by the item *"We need to look beyond the denominational and religious differences to find the ultimate reality."* The scale for pluralism with items that were originally taken from the Religion Monitor questionnaire measures very similar beliefs, but has a clearer focus on the openness for other religions and worldviews. Xenosophia and pluralism correlated at $r = .66$ in this sample.

Results of this study confirmed previous preliminary analyses such as the already mentioned the analysis of variance with the newly constructed four faith development types (Streib et al., 2020); there we found not only that agreement with *ttt* is decreasing as the types progress, but also that *xenosophia* is increasing as the types progress from the Substantially Ethnocentric to the Individuative-reflective Type and to the Dialogical-xenosophic Type. These results are reflected in this study, but our current results take the knowledge about faith development a substantial step further into the prediction based on longitudinal data.

Results of this study show that both xenosophia and pluralism assessed in Wave 2 are significant predictors for faith development in the aspect of perspective-taking at Wave 3. This means that the pluralistic and xenosophic beliefs at an earlier time predict their manifestation in, and preference of, the dialogical religious style, and/or motivate development, that is increasing preference for the higher religious style at a later time.

Limitations

Some limitations of this study should be explicated. First, the sample size of $n = 75$ three-wave cases in our data is relatively small. This calls for replications using larger samples. Second, the time lag between FDIs at Wave 1 and FDIs at Wave 2 is not consistent, especially between participants who had their first FDI in the Deconversion Study and participants in the Spirituality Study. To base analyses on a three-wave assessment with more consistent time difference between the FDIs, it is necessary to add another wave of field work. Third, the relatively small sample does not allow for age-cohort modeling. Fourth, part of the movement could be due to ceiling or floor effects that a person who started at either extreme of the scale would only be able to move to the opposite direction if not staying at its starting type. Again, a larger sample size with greater variance in starting faith development type would address this concern. Fifth, our sample is rather highly educated (72.0 % have tertiary education at Wave 3). This needs to be taken into account in the interpretation of the results. Sixth, with only 21% cases from the USA, the sample did not allow for cross-cultural comparison, unfortunately. Seventh, this study could not consider critical life events or world events that may have had an impact on faith development. While we would find this desirable in such a longitudinal study, we regret that we have no quantitative data that document the impact of critical events on our individuals. But the interviews, of course, include a wealth of such information. Thus, we may refer the reader to the case studies that will be published in articles and chapters elsewhere.

Conclusion

In conclusion, this chapter presents three important results that need to be discussed in faith development theory and research: First, aspect-specific rating of the FDI is meaningful and the account for the differences between the aspects may open the possibility to come to terms with FDIs, in which clearly not *one*, but *two* (or more) final FDI scores are suggested. The documentation of the differences between aspect-specific ratings may inspire the interpretation of the single case. Second, the aspects of perspective-taking and social horizon, which can be understood as meta-cognitive preconditions, have emerged as developing upwards, while the other aspects rather show stagnation. These results do not allow for the conclusion that development is excluded in the four other domains since the data base is not large enough. But the question is on the table. Also, the question, what is the motor of development, is opened again. But this invites further investigation based on a larger sample. But, and this is the third point, this study makes a contribution to the identification of predictors for faith development; and it is remarkable that scores on the RSS subscale xenosophia and the scale for pluralism have emerged as the strongest (xenosophia) and still strong (pluralism) predictors for faith development in the (meta-cognitive) aspect of perspective-taking.

References

Borkenau, P., & Ostendorf, F. (1993). *NEO-Fünf-Faktoren-Inventar (NEO-FFI) nach Costa und McCrae: Handanweisung*. Hogrefe, Verlag für Psychologie.

Budner, S. (1962). Intolerance of ambiguity as a personality variable. *Journal of Personality*, 30(1), 29–50. https://doi.org/10.1111/j.1467-6494.1962.tb02303.x

Cacioppo, J. T./Petty, R. E./Kao, C. F. (1984), The efficient asessment of need for cognition, *Journal of Personality Assessment 48*, 306–307.

Costa, P. T., & McCrae, R. R. (1985). *Revised NEO Personality Inventory (NEO PI-R) and NEO Five-Factor-Inventory (NEO-FFI). Professional manual*. Psychological Assessment Resources 1992.

DeNicola, K., & Fowler, J. W. (1993). *Manual for faith development research* (2nd ed.). Center for Research in Faith and Moral Development, Emory University.

Fowler, J. W. (1980). Faith and the structuring of meaning. In C. Brusselmans (Ed.), *Toward moral and religious maturity* (pp. 51–85). Silver Burdett Company.

Fowler, J. W. (1981). *Stages of faith. The psychology of human development and the quest for meaning.* Harper&Row.

Fowler, J. W. (2001). Faith development theory and the postmodern challenges. *International Journal for the Psychology of Religion, 11*(3), 159–172. https://doi.org/10.1207/S15327582IJPR1103_03

Fowler, J. W., Streib, H., & Keller, B. (2004). *Manual for l* (3rd ed.). Research Center for Biographical Studies in Contemporary Religion, Bielefeld; Center for Research in Faith and Moral Development, Emory University. https://doi.org/10.13140/2.1.4232.4804

Grossmann, I., Dorfman, A., & Oakes, H. (2020). Wisdom is a social-ecological rather than person-centric phenomenon. *Current Opinion in Psychology, 32*, 66–71. https://doi.org/10.1016/j.copsyc.2019.07.010

Grossmann, I., Weststrate, N. M., Ardelt, M., Brienza, J. P., Dong, M. X., Ferrari, M., Fournier, M. A., Hu, C. S., Nusbaum, H. C., & Vervaeke, J. (2020). The science of wisdom in a polarized world: Knowns and unknowns. *Psychological Inquiry, 31*(2), 103–133. https://doi.org/10.1080/1047840x.2020.1750917

Hood, R. W. (1975). The construction and preliminary validation of a measure of reported mystical experience. *Journal for the Scientific Study of Religion, 14*, 29–41.

Hood, R. W. (2003). The relationship between religion and spirituality. In A. L. Greil & D. G. Bromley (Eds.), *Defining religion: Investigating the boundaries between the sacred and the secular* (pp. 241–265). Elsevier Science.

Klein, C., Silver, C. F., Coleman, T. J., Streib, H., & Hood, R. W. (2016). "Spirituality" and mysticism. In H. Streib & R. W. Hood (Eds.), *Semantics and psychology of "spirituality". A cross-cultural analysis* (pp. 165–187). Springer International Publishing Switzerland. https://doi.org/10.1007/978-3-319-21245-6_11

Kohlberg, L., Levine, C., & Hewer, A. (1983). The current formulation of the theory. In L. Kohlberg (Ed.), *Essays on l, Vol.II. The psychology of moral development* (pp. 212–319). Harper & Row 1984.

Moseley, R. M., Jarvis, D., & Fowler, J. W. (1986). *Manual for faith development research*. Center for Faith Development, Emory University.

Ryff, C. D. (1989). Happiness is everything, or is it? Explorations on the meaning of psychological well-being. *Journal of Personality and Social Psychology, 57*(6), 1069–1081. https://doi.org/10.1037/0022-3514.57.6.1069

Ryff, C. D., & Singer, B. H. (1996). Psychological well-being: Meaning, measurement, and implications for psychotherapy research. *Psychotherapy and Psychosomatics, 65*(1), 14–23. https://doi.org/10.1159/000289026

Streib, H. (2001). Faith development theory revisited: The religious styles perspective. *International Journal for the Psychology of Religion, 11*(3), 143–158. https://doi.org/10.1207/S15327582IJPR1103_02

Streib, H. (2018). What is xenosophia? Philosophical contributions to prejudice research. In H. Streib & C. Klein (Eds.), *Xenosophia and religion: Biographical and statistical paths for a culture of welcome* (pp. 3–21). Springer International Publishing Switzerland. htt ps://doi.org/10.1007/978-3-319-74564-0_1

Streib, H., Chen, Z. J., & Hood, R. W. (2020). Categorizing people by their preference for religious styles: Four types derived from evaluation of faith development interviews. *International Journal for the Psychology of Religion, 30*(2), 112–127. https://doi.org/10.108 0/10508619.2019.1664213 (https://doi.org/10.31234/osf.io/d3kbr (pre-print))

Streib, H., Chen, Z. J., & Hood, R. W. (2021). Faith development as change in religious types: Results from three-wave longitudinal data with faith development interviews. *Psychology of Religion and Spirituality 15*(2), 298–307. https://doi.org/10.1037/rel000044 0, post-print at: https://doi.org/10.31234/osf.io/qrcb2

Streib, H., & Hood, R. W. (Eds.). (2016). *Semantics and psychology of spirituality. A cross-cultural analysis.* Springer International Publishing Switzerland. https://doi.org/10.100 7/978-3-319-21245-6

Streib, H., Hood, R. W. Jr., Keller, B., Csöff, R-M, & Silver, C. (2009) *Deconversion: Qualitative and quantitative results from cross-cultural research in Germany and the United States.* Vandenhoeck & Ruprecht.

Streib, H., Hood, R. W., & Klein, C. (2010). The religious schema scale: Construction and initial validation of a quantitative measure for religious styles. *International Journal for the Psychology of Religion, 20*(3), 151–172. https://doi.org/10.1080/10508619.2010.481223

Streib, H., & Keller, B. (2018). *Manual for the assessment of religious styles in faith development interviews (Fourth, revised edition of the Manual for faith development research).* Bielefeld University/readbox unipress. https://doi.org/10.4119/unibi/2920987

Streib, H., Klein, C., Keller, B., & Hood, R. W. (2021). The mysticism scale as measure for subjective spirituality: New results with hood's m-scale and the development of a short form. In A. L. Ai, K. A. Harris, R. F. Paloutzian, & P. Wink (Eds.), *Assessing spirituality in a diverse world* (pp. 467–491). Springer Nature Switzerland. https://doi.o rg/10.1007/978-3-030-52140-0_19

Streib, H., Wollert, M. H., & Keller, B. (2016). Faith development, religious styles, and "spirituality". In H. Streib & R. W. Hood (Eds.), *Semantics and psychology of "spirituality". A cross-cultural analysis* (pp. 383–399). Springer International Publishing Switzerland. https://doi.org/10.1007/978-3-319-21245-6_24

Waldenfels, B. (2011). Phenomenology of the alien: Basic concepts [Grundmotive einer Phänomenologie des Fremden, Frankfurt/M.: Suhrkamp, 2006] transl. by A. Kozin and T. Stähler. Northwestern University Press.

VanderWeele T. J. & Ding, P. (2017). Sensitivity analysis in observational research: Introducing the E-value. *Annals of Internal Medicine, 167*(4), 268–275.

VanderWeele, T. J., Mathur, M. B., & Chen, Y. (2020). Outcome-wide longitudinal designs for causal inference: A new template for empirical studies. *Statistical Science, 35,* 437–466.

Zinnbauer, B. J., Pargament, K. I., Cole, B., Rye, M. S., Butter, E. M., Belavich, T. G., Hipp, K. M., Scott, A. B., & Kadar, J. L. (1997). Religion and spirituality: Unfuzzying the fuzzy. *Journal for the Scientific Study of Religion, 36*(4), 549–564.

Chapter 6
Religious or Spiritual? Text Analysis of the Free Entries in Defining Religiosity and Spirituality

Zhuo Job Chen, Anika Steppacher, & Heinz Streib[1]

Abstract *Progress in psychology of religion and spirituality benefits from advancement and enrichment of definitions. Dozens of definitions of religion and spirituality have been offered in the history of the field, however, most of them were generated from a top-down, theory-driven process. This study utilized a bottom-up approach to examine folk definitions of religion and spirituality and, with the help of text analytic tools, offers a complementary from people's (vs. scholarly) perspective. Data were free entries of defining "religion" and "spirituality" collected from English-speaking American individuals. Three waves of data were collected. Wave 1 included n = 1,046 individual definitions, Wave 2 included n = 276 individuals, and Wave 3 included n = 214 individuals. Word frequency approaches showed that religion can be best defined as specific organized beliefs whereas spirituality can be defined as relating to personal world and life. Topic Modeling confirmed the distinctiveness of words that went into defining religion versus spirituality. Finally, a dictionary approach using Linguistic Inquiry and Word Count (LIWC 2015) suggested that the definition of religion involved social connections and power, and a mindset of authority and class. Definition of spirituality involved various human experiences and reflected high level of interest and cognitive complexity. Cohort data suggested a trend that over time definitions of spirituality shifted to focus more on connectedness, personal feelings, and humanity from a previous focus on religious ideas of belief and god.*

> **Keywords:** *spirituality; religion; semantics of spirituality; text analysis; LIWC*

---

1   Z. J. Chen, School of Nursing, University of North Carolina at Charlotte, USA, E-mail: job.chen@charlotte.edu; A. Steppacher, H. Streib, Bielefeld University, Germany. © Heinz Streib, Ralph W. Hood Jr. (eds.): Faith in Development. Mixed-Method Studies on Worldviews and Religious Styles. First published in 2024 by Bielefeld University Press, Bielefeld, https://doi.org/10.14361/9783839471234-008

Existing definitions of religiosity and spirituality are variegated but suggest a key distinction between two approaches, top-down (etic) and bottom-up (emic). Dozens of definitions of religion and spirituality have been offered in the history of the field, however, most of them were generated from, or heavily influenced by, a top-down, theory-driven process. Oman (2013) summarized the variety of past definitions of religion and spirituality in the literature; Harris et al. (2018) using a content-analytical approach to "spirituality" in research reports also documented a broad spectrum of categories included in the term. Thus, spirituality as a concept is not coherent, but has a variety of differing definitions.

But there are also previous studies including an emic approach and using content analysis or other qualitative approaches to make sense of participants' own definitions of "religion" and "spirituality" (Ammerman, 2013; Berghuijs et al., 2013; Demmrich & Huber, 2020; Hyman & Handal, 2006; la Cour et al., 2012; Schlehofer et al., 2008; Steensland et al., 2018; Zinnbauer et al., 1997). Our own research on the semantics of "spirituality" also took a decisive bottom-up approach, as we document below.

In the context of a research program dedicated to the study of change, of the change of religious styles and worldviews across the adult lifespan, special attention to participants' subjective understanding of "spirituality" is most important for several reasons: For many participants in our studies, change and development dovetailed with their preference for a "spiritual" or "more spiritual than religious" self-identification; this was most obvious for deconverts (Keller, Klein, Hood, et al., 2013; Streib, 2014; 2021; Streib, Hood, et al., 2016; Streib et al., 2009). In our Spirituality Study (Streib & Hood, 2016), a very wide spectrum of inter-individual differences in the meaning of "spirituality" has been documented using the Faith Development Interview (Keller et al., 2016), semantic differentials (Keller, Klein, Swhajor-Biesemann, et al., 2013; Streib, Keller, et al., 2016), and free text entries with definitions of "spirituality" and "religion" (Altmeyer & Klein, 2016; Altmeyer et al., 2015; Eisenmann et al., 2016). This semantic variety related differently to psychological and sociological characteristics of participants. The meaning and the subjective importance of "spirituality" may change for a person, and for the culture of which they are part, over time. Therefore, we did the right thing to include the free text entries in the questionnaires of the follow-up studies to aim at longitudinal investigation, or at least in a repeated assessment.

Therefore, this study utilized a bottom-up approach to examine folk definitions of religion and spirituality and, with the help of text analytic tools, offers a complementary from people's (vs. scholarly) perspective. The current project investigated free entries with definitions of "religion" and of "spirituality" that participants entered in three waves of data collection. The aim of this study was to open a perspective on participants' own understanding of "spirituality" and "religion" by using word frequency analysis, topic modeling and a dictionary approach.

Method

Data

Data were free entries of defining "religion" and "spirituality" collected from American individuals. All texts were in English. Three waves of data were collected. Wave 1 included $n = 1046$ individual definitions that are part of the Spirituality Study (data collection: 2009–2011; Streib & Hood, 2016), Wave 2 included $n = 276$ individuals, and Wave 3 included $n = 214$ individuals. A small percentage of individuals remained in the study through multiple waves: $n = 78$ individuals completed both Wave 1 and Wave 2, $n = 36$ individuals completed both Wave 2 and Wave 3, $n = 37$ individuals completed both Wave 1 and Wave 3, and only $n = 22$ individuals completed all three waves. Given that most of the three waves of data were not overlapping, the data was not to be understood as a longitudinal design; instead, differences across waves reflected cohort effects.

Analysis

Text analysis is a family of methods that are specifically designed to process and extract patterns from natural language (Silge & Robinson, 2017). Before analysis, the raw text, sentences defining religion or spirituality, were preprocessed. Preprocessing usually involves removing stop words (articles, prepositions, etc.), and tokenization, that is breaking down the text into individual words or n-grams (e.g., pair of words). Three major text analysis techniques were used in the current study.

The first technique was counting word frequencies, through which we could identify patterns of the frequent words used to define religion and spirituality. The word frequency method could be extended to phrase frequency. When a 2-gram tokenization was employed, we counted the frequency of a pair of words (i.e., phrase), instead of frequency of a single word. This step further contextualized the key words used in distinguishing religion from spirituality.

The second technique was topic modeling. A topic model is a type of statistical model for discovering abstract topics in the text, or in other words, categorizing terms into prespecified topics. A topic model with user specified number of topics would assign a probability value to each term; by examining the most representative term (with highest probability beta) for each topic, one could deduce the meaning of that topic. Among many algorithms used to generate topics, Latent Dirichlet Allocation (LDA) allows sets of observations to be explained by unobserved groups. We used topic modeling mainly to demonstrate that terms used to define religion and terms used to define spirituality were so distinctive that they would naturally fall into two classes that would be detected by topic modeling.

The third technique was the dictionary approach. Dictionary approach comes with a predefined dictionary that puts many words into broad categories. For instance, words such as ugly and bad would be categorized under "negative affect." Numerous dictionaries have existed and in psychology, the Linguistic Inquiry and Word Count (LIWC; Pennebaker et al., 2015) is an established dictionary with over 90 categories. Psychological correlates of some of these categories have been established in psycholinguistic studies (see Tausczik & Pennebaker, 2010 for a review). Different from the word frequency approach which examines the words as data, the dictionary approach uses abstract categories into which words are clustered as data. Not only did this approach offer another perspective into definitions of religion and spirituality, but, since it populated data at an individual level, it enabled statistical comparisons of frequencies of those categories across groups, here between religion and spirituality.

Results

Word Frequency: What Words Define Religion and Spirituality

First set of analyses looked at the most frequently used words in people's definitions of religiosity and spirituality. In addition to tokenization and removal of stop words, we stemmed the words, i.e., removing the suffixes, to combine words such as "belief" and "beliefs." The word "religion" was also removed from the definition for religion, and the word "spirituality" was removed from the definition of spirituality, because many of the definitions started with "religion is" or "spirituality is."

We first examined the frequent words used in defining religion and spirituality, respectively, across three waves or cohorts of data. Comparison across cohorts would reveal which words are stably used across time and which words have changed in their importance of constituting a definition. Figure 6.1 displays words that were mentioned over 1% of time in defining religion (top) and spirituality (bottom) respectively. The number 1% was arbitrary – it was chosen to balance the amount of information to display and their representativeness in defining each of the two concepts.

The most representative words defining religion were belief, god, organ (organized), set, spiritual, people, worship, rule, system, etc. There was little variation in ranking of the words across the three waves. Belief remained the most frequent word in defining religion across all time. Set, practice, rule, and tradition were slightly more important in later waves than in Wave 1. The most representative words defining spirituality included belief, god, person, life, connect, power, feel (feeling), relationship, spirit, believe, live, world, exist, etc. There was some notable variability across time. Belief and god were not as important in later waves than in Wave 1, whereas words such as connect, feel, spirit, world, and human became more important in later waves. The trend suggested that definition of spirituality shifted to focus more on connectedness, personal feelings, and humanity from a previous focus on religious ideas of belief and god. It is interesting to note that definitions of religion and spirituality cross-referenced each other. People used religion in defining spirituality and spirituality in defining religion.

Figure 6.1: The most frequent words (>1%) used in defining religion (top) and spirituality (bottom) across three waves or cohorts of data

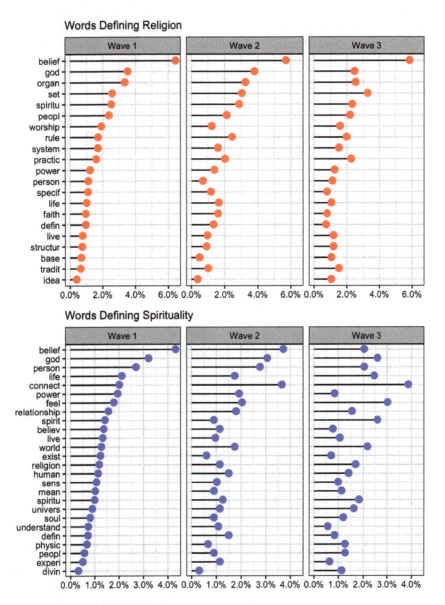

We then compared words defining religion and spirituality. Figure 6.2 plots word frequencies of spirituality against word frequencies of religion. The difference in frequencies was color coded. The red circles represented words that were used more frequently in defining religion than spirituality (difference > 1%; again, the 1% was arbitrarily chosen). The blue circles represented words that were more frequent in defining spirituality than religion. Words that had comparable frequencies in the two definitions were in the green color. The unique words defining religion included belief, organ (organize), people, set, practice, rule, worship, and system. The unique words defining spirituality included person (personal), relationship, connect, feel (feeling), and spirit. Both definitions mentioned, at comparable rate, god, power, life, believe, live, spiritual, faith, human, exist, sense, world, and define. Religion was differentiated from spirituality by an emphasis on social organization and practices. Spirituality, by contrast, emphasized personal experience and connections. Both definitions mentioned belief and god (more in religion than in spirituality), which are also the most frequently used words of all.

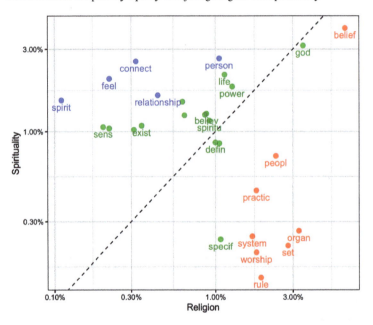

Figure 6.2: The most frequent words (> 1%) used in defining religion and spirituality. Red circles and those well below the diagonal line are words more frequently used in defining religion; blue circles above the diagonal line are words more frequently used in defining spirituality (with difference in frequency > 1%); green circles are used comparably equally in defining religion and spirituality

Aside from comparing raw frequencies, the often-used metric tf-idf (i.e., term frequency times inverse document frequency) was used to identify terms that were selectively important to defining religion or spirituality. To calculate tf-idf, we tokenized the document but did not remove stop words. Figure 6.3 displays the top 10 words based on the value of tf-idf in defining religion and spirituality. Religion mainly consisted of words related to followers' adherence to the established organization and its doctrines, texts, and dogma. Spirituality focused on the immaterial aspects such as soul, inner awareness, energy, and human aspects such as emotion, awareness, and connection.

Taking the word frequency approaches together, it was clear that religion had a well-defined boundary with a focus on specific behaviors and organizational rules, whereas spirituality was less likely to be a monolithic idea but more likely as a collection of immaterial and human aspects centered around the concept of connection.

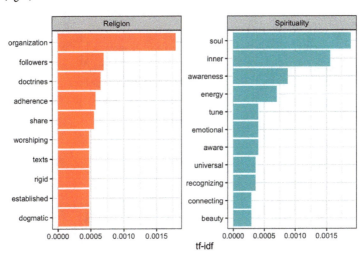

Figure 6.3: *tf-idf for the top 10 words defining religion (left) and spirituality (right)*

2-grams: What phrases define religion and spirituality

The word frequency approach in the previous section tokenized the text into individual words, and by this 1-gram tokenization, it enabled examination of key words individually, irrespective of the other words with which they associated. Similarly, a 2-gram tokenization would identify pairs of words that appeared together in a definition. The 2-gram extended 1-gram by identifying 2-word phrases, instead of single words, that define religion and spirituality. Among the most frequent phrases that defined religion we found belief system(s), organized belief, organized set, organized system, and specific set. The most frequent phrases defining spirituality included personal relationship, daily life, personal connection, physical world, Holy Spirit and Jesus Christ. The mentioning of the latter two Judeo-Christian terms may be due to that many of the participants were evangelical Christians and interpreted spirituality through religious lenses.

Figure 6.4 plots networks of words with edges indicating pairwise connection. Only those connections of frequencies equal to or greater than four times are shown. An arrow points toward the word that appears later in a pair. We removed the word "religion" from the definitions of religion and the word "spirituality" from the definitions of spirituality. For religion, the left network, we observed three major clusters. One cluster revolved around "organized" which emitted many arrows to the words around it, thus forming phrases of organized community, organized worship, etc. Another cluster was observed with the word "specific" as a modifier for dogma, doctrine, etc. One last cluster revolved around "belief(s)" as the receiving word, thus forming phrases such as shared beliefs, spiritual beliefs, etc. For spirituality, the right network, we observed three major clusters. One cluster revolved around "personal," forming phrases of personal connection, personal experience, personal belief, etc. Another cluster revolved around "life," emphasizing daily and everyday life. The last cluster revolved around "world," forming phrases of spiritual, material, and physical world.

The results from 2-grams put the importance or centrality of individual words into context. Words of high frequency indicated that they were popular choices by many people in forming a definition, but these popular words might not affiliate closely with the other less popular words. The network approach defines another type of popularity by counting the number of edges a word receives from other words, the in-degree, and the number of edges a word sends to other words, the out-degree. Without getting into the statistics in these networks, it was already apparent that the central themes for defining religion were *specific organized beliefs* whereas the central themes for defining spirituality were *personal world and life*.

Figure 6.4: Networks, top for religion and bottom for spirituality, of 2-grams depicting pair-wise appearance of words. All connections have appeared four times or more. Thicker edges indicate higher frequency

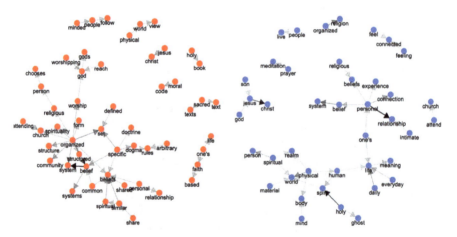

Topic modeling: Hidden factors in the definition

In loose terms, the topic modeling technique categorized terms into clusters based on how closely they tended to affiliate with each other in the document. We created a document term matrix over definitions of both religion and spirituality and extracted 2 topics. Figure 6.5 displays the primary words (probability beta > .01) that belong to each of the two topics. It was obvious that the first topic on the left contained words that defined religion whereas the second topic on the right contained words that defined spirituality. The gamma value, percent of words in a document that belong to a topic, confirmed that. All the words in topic 1 belonged to the document of defining religion and all the words in topic 2 belonged to the document of defining spirituality. These results offered strong evidence for the distinguishability of religion from spirituality.

Figure 6.5: Probability (beta > .01) of words under the two topics

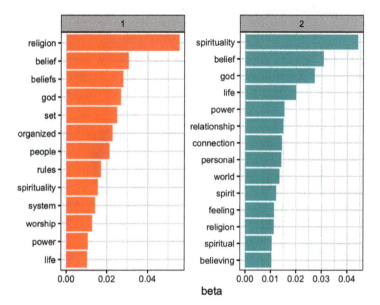

LIWC: Dictionary approach

We applied LIWC 2015's dictionary to transforming texts into categories. Figure 6.6 plots the scores for 25 major categories aggregated over three waves/cohorts of data for the definition of religion (red bar to the left) and for the definition of spirituality (blue bar to the right), respectively. When the standard error bars did not overlap each other, a significant difference could be inferred.

Spirituality scored higher than religion on cognitive processes (e.g., representative words in the LIWC dictionary are cause, know, ought), suggesting cognitive complexity (Tausczik & Pennebaker, 2010); scored higher on perceptual processes (e.g., look, hear, feeling), biological processes (e.g., eat, blood, pain), and relativity (e.g., area, bend, exit). Spirituality also had higher word count indicative of verbal fluency, sounded more authentic, used more words per sentence indicative of cognitive complexity, used more first-person singular pronouns indicative of honesty, more first-person plural pronouns indicative of social connections, more prepositions indicative of education and concern with precision, more auxiliary verbs indicative of informal and passive voice, and more negations indicative of inhibition. Overall, these patterns suggested that definition of spirituality involved various human experiences. When defining spirituality, individuals showed high level of interest and cognitive complexity.

Religion scored higher on negative emotion (e.g., hurt, ugly, nasty), drives (e.g., win, superior, take), affiliation (e.g., ally, friend, social), past focus (e.g., ago, did, talked). Religion also suggested greater level of analytic thinking, clout (speaking of authority), and used more longer words indicative of social class. Overall, these patterns suggested that definition of religion involved social connections and power. Those writing about religion appear to be a bit more scholarly analysis with a focus on history, and perhaps more focus on the church as an institution.

Figure 6.6: The LIWC dimensions of religion and spirituality. The red bar to the left represents definition of religion, whereas the blue bar to the right represents definition of spirituality. In the subtitle for each graph are LIWC categories

Discussion

A synoptic summary of results reported in this chapter revels clear overlap between the definitions of spirituality and religion, but also clear differences. Word frequency analysis, to begin with, indicated (see Figure 6.1 and 6.2) that the definitions of both religion and spirituality included, at a comparable rate, words such as belief, god, power, life, believe, live, spiritual, faith, human, exist, sense, world, and define. If in the definitions of religion *and* spirituality the same vocabulary is used, we may conclude that there is a clear overlap in the understanding, the commonality may outweigh the difference for many participants. But there are also clear differences indicated: Religion was differentiated from spirituality by an emphasis on social organization and practices as indicated by words such as people, practice, system, organization, set, worship, or rule; spirituality, by contrast, emphasized personal experience and connections, indicated by word such as person, relationship, connectedness, feeling. Taken together, word frequency analysis revealed that the definitions of religion mainly consisted of words related to followers' adherence to the established organization, and its doctrines, texts, and dogma, while definitions of spirituality focused on the immaterial aspects such as soul, inner awareness, energy, and human aspects such as emotion, awareness, and connection.

These results from our present study highly concur with previous analyses of the same data using corpus analysis, which compared the corpus of words used in the free text definitions of religions and spirituality with the American National Corpus, a very large reference dictionary of written English (Altmeyer & Klein, 2016; cf. Altmeyer et al., 2015). Such high convergence between results should be expected, when using the same data and rather similar word frequency analyses that attend to the single words.

There is an advantage in the study presented in this chapter, however: While previous analyses could use only the data from Wave 1 and could not account for change over time, the results presented in this study indicate changes that are visible from comparing Wave 1, Wave 2 and Wave 3 data: In the definitions of religion, belief remained the most frequent word, but results indicate that words such as set, practice or tradition increased in frequency and importance over time. In the definitions of spirituality, words such as connect, feel, spirit, world, and human became more important in later waves, while words such as god and belief have declined in importance in the definition of spirituality. This may indicate that spirituality became more clearly separated from connotations of religion, and more clearly profiled in human experience and a sense of connectedness. While this result is rather a trend, it is noteworthy that this study is the first to investigate the semantics in people's definitions of religion and spirituality over time.

The results presented in this chapter also moved beyond the previous analyses by taking the connection between words into account. Using a 2-gram tokenization that identifies pairs of words that appeared together in a definition, the analysis moved toward identifying phrases, instead of single words. This allowed to focus the analysis on the frequency of links (edges) between the words, and identifying the words with high numbers of in-coming and out-going edges, which, in turn, can be visualized using network analysis as visualized in Figure 6.4; also topic modeling could be used to rank the probability of words to connect with others, as visualized in Figure 6.5. Topic modeling (Figure 6.5) shows, again, that words such as belief and god are top-connected words in definitions of both religion and spiritualty, but also highlights the highly connected words that are specific for religion (organized people, rules system, worship, etc..) and spirituality (relationship, connection, personal feeling, etc.).

The results from network analysis (Figure 6.4) open new perspectives on the nodes with highest number of in-going and out-going edges. This way, centers that are specific for spirituality (personal, life, world, etc.) and religion (organized, beliefs, specific, god, etc.) are indicated. These results corroborate the single-word analyses of this study and the previous corpus analyses (Altmeyer & Klein, 2016; cf. Altmeyer et al., 2015), but clearly move toward an interpretation of phrases and their meaning. Since this is to our knowledge the first time that a 2-gram and network approach has been used for an analysis of participants free-text definitions of religion and spirituality, we cannot discuss it in direct comparison with previous results. But these results correspond to the results from the interpretation-based factor analysis presented by Eisenmann et al. (2016), which, with focus on the definitions of spirituality in Wave 1, revealed participants' understanding of spirituality included semantic dimensions such as a sense of connectedness, inner search for higher self, or relation to others and humanity. And interestingly, other dimensions that have emerged in Eisenmann et al.'s (2016) factor analysis such as spirituality as part of religion and belief in higher powers or individual religious praxis are reflected in the network analysis in Figure 6.4 by little *separate*, but less dense network clusters including nodes such as Jesus, prayer, church. This, again, indicates that spirituality can include connotations to lived religion and a traditional Christian theology. Our methodological conclusion is that network analysis is a very promising approach for the analysis of free text entries.

The last analysis reported in this chapter is the dictionary approach using Pennebaker et al.'s (2015) LIWC dictionary. To our knowledge LIWC was not used in previous studies about peoples' definitions of religion and spirituality. Results of this study (Figure 6.6) show the differences between the definitions of religion and spirituality over all three waves of our research in some most important categories of the LIWC dictionary. Definitions of spirituality scored higher than definitions of religion on words that are indicative of cognitive complexity, relativity, perceptual processes such as feelings, and authenticity. The definitions of religion, in contrast, scored higher on negative emotion, drives, affiliation, the past, and clout; they are associated with authority and membership. Thus, despite some proviso regarding the interpretative openness with the LIWC categories, the definitions of religion and spirituality appear to differ along the polarity of institutional affiliation vs. subjectivity, negative vs. positive evaluation, authoritative certainty vs. cognitive complexity and relativity. This reflects previous results on the, compared to religion, much more positive evaluation of spirituality using Osgood's (1962; 1969; Snider & Osgood, 1969) semantic differential (Streib, Keller, et al., 2016). The interpretation using the LIWC categories also have parallels to the results of word frequency analysis presented in this study and in previous analyses (Altmeyer & Klein, 2016; Altmeyer et al., 2015) with their polarity between social organization and practices (religion) and human aspects such as emotion, awareness, and connection (spirituality).

Conclusion

This study took a bottom-up approach to examine folk definitions of religion and spirituality as entered in free text space in the questionnaire, and, with the help of text analytic tools, attends to people's perspective. Of the methodic approaches used in this study, it appears that the most promising and most inspiring interpretation of the definitions of religion and spirituality emerge from the attention of the *connection* between the words and the visualization of these connections in a network. Results from network analysis are most suitable for triangulation with other methods that used more open interpretative approaches such as used by Eisenmann et al. (2016). The distinct clusters in the networks clearly reflect the variety of different definitions for both religion and spirituality that the participants have entered in the questionnaire. And the variety of different definitions indicated in this study correspond to and corroborate pervious results that, based on people's texts, resulted in a variety of dimensions for spirituality, such as the studies by Zinnbauer et al. (1997), Schlehofer et al. (2008), La Cour et al. (2012), Ammermann (2013), Berghuijs et al. (2013) Eisenmann et al. (2016), or Steensland et al. (2018). A cohort analysis by comparing changes across the three waves of data suggested certain level of sematic shift in defining spirituality with a greater focus on connectedness.

In their literature review, Wixwat & Saucier (2021, p. 124) conclude that there are "multiple meanings for spirituality" and spirituality is "heterogeneous," while spiritual tendencies can, at least in Western populations, "be differentiated from conventionally religious tendencies." With the indication of the variety in the polarized semantic field, the results from this study, especially from the network analysis, are a contribution to the literature on ordinary people's understanding of religion and spirituality.

References

Altmeyer, S., & Klein, C. (2016). "Spirituality" and "religion" – Corpus analysis of subjective definition in the questionnaire. In H. Streib & R. W. Hood (Eds.), *Semantics and psychology of "spirituality". A cross-cultural analysis* (pp. 105–123). Springer International Publishing Switzerland.

Altmeyer, S., Klein, C., Keller, B., Silver, C. F., Hood, R. W., & Streib, H. (2015). Subjective definitions of spirituality and religion. An explorative study in Germany and the USA. *International Journal of Corpus Linguistics, 20*(4), 526–552. https://doi.org/10.1075/ijcl.2 0.4.05alt

Ammerman, N. T. (2013). Spiritual but not religious? Beyond binary choices in the study of religion. *Journal for the Scientific Study of Religion, 52*(2), 258–278. http://dx.doi.org/1 0.1111/jssr.12024

Berghuijs, J., Pieper, J., & Bakker, C. (2013). Conceptions of spirituality among the dutch population. *Archive for the Psychology of Religion, 35*(3), 369–397. https://doi.org/10.1163 /15736121-12341272

Demmrich, S., & Huber, S. (2020). What do seculars understand as 'spiritual'? A replication of eisenmann et al.'s semantics of spirituality. *Journal of Religion in Europe, 13*, 67–95. https://doi.org/10.1163/18748929-13010008

Eisenmann, C., Klein, C., Swhajor-Biesemann, A., Drexelius, U., Streib, H., & Keller, B. (2016). Dimensions of "spirituality: The semantics of subjective definitions. In H. Streib & R. W. Hood (Eds.), *Semantics and psychology of "spirituality". A cross-cultural analysis* (pp. 125–151). Springer International Publishing Switzerland.

Harris, K. A., Howell, D. S., & Spurgeon, D. W. (2018). Faith concepts in psychology: Three 30-year definitional content analyses. *Psychology of Religion and Spirituality, 10*(1), 1–29.

Hyman, C., & Handal, P. J. (2006). Definitions and evaluation of religion and spirituality items by religious professionals: A pilot study. *Journal of Religion and Health, 45*(2), 264–282. https://doi.org/10.1007/s10943-006-9015-z

Keller, B., Klein, C., Hood, R. W., & Streib, H. (2013). Deconversion and religious or spiritual transformation. In H. Westerink (Ed.), *Constructs of meaning and religious transfor-*

mation. Current issues in the psychology of religion (pp. 119–139). Vienna University Press; V&R unipress.

Keller, B., Klein, C., Swhajor-Biesemann, A., Silver, C. F., Hood, R. W., & Streib, H. (2013). The semantics of "spirituality" and related self-identifications: A comparative study in germany and the usa. *Archive for the Psychology of Religion, 35*(1), 71–100. https://doi.org/10.1163/15736121-12341254

Keller, B., Klein, C., Swhajor-Biesemann, A., & Streib, H. (2016). Mapping the varieties of "spiritual" biographies. In H. Streib & R. W. Hood (Eds.), *Semantics and psychology of "spirituality". A cross-cultural analysis* (pp. 275–280). Springer International Publishing Switzerland.

la Cour, P., Ausker, N. H., & Hvidt, N. C. (2012). Six understandings of the word spirituality in a secular country. *Archive for the Psychology of Religion, 34*(1), 63–81. https://doi.org/10.1163/157361212X649634

Oman, D. (2013). Defining religion and spirituality. In R. F. Paloutzian & C. L. Park (Eds.), *Handbook of the psychology of religion and spirituality, 2nd ed.* (pp. 23–47). The Guilford Press.

Osgood, C. E. (1962). Studies on the generality of affective meaning systems. *American Anthropologist, 17*(1), 10–28.

Osgood, C. E. (1969). The nature and measurement of meaning. In J. G. Snider & C. E. Osgood (Eds.), *Semantic differential techinque: A sourcebook* (pp. 3–41). Aldine (2nd printing 1972).

Pennebaker, J. W., Boyd, R. L., Jordan, K., & Blackburn, K. (2015). *The development and psychometric properties of LIWC2015*. University of Texas at Austin.

Schlehofer, M. M., Omoto, A. M., & Adelman, J. R. (2008). How do "religion" and "spirituality" differ? Lay definitions among older adults. *Journal for the Scientific Study of Religion, 47*(3), 411–425. http://www3.interscience.wiley.com/cgi-bin/fulltext/1213907 79/PDFSTART

Silge, J., & Robinson, D. (2017). Text mining with R: A tidy approach. O'Reilly Media, Inc.

Snider, J. G., & Osgood, C. E. (1969). *Semantic differential techinque: A sourcebook.* Aldine, 2nd printing 1972.

Steensland, B., Wang, X., & Schmidt, L. C. (2018). Spirituality: What does it mean and to whom? *Journal for the Scientific Study of Religion, 57*(3), 450–472. https://doi.org/10.1111/jssr.12534

Stifoss-Hanssen, H. (1999). Religion and spirituality: What a European ear hears. *International Journal for the Psychology of Religion, 9*(1), 151–166. https://doi.org/10.1080/0161 2840601096552

Streib, H. (2014). Deconversion. In L. R. Rambo & C. E. Farhadian (Eds.), *Oxford handbook on religious conversion* (pp. 271–296). Oxford University Press.

Streib, H. (2021). Leaving religion: Deconversion. *Current Opinion in Psychology, 40*, 139–144. https://doi.org/10.1016/j.copsyc.2020.09.007

Streib, H., & Hood, R. W. (Eds.). (2016). *Semantics and psychology of spirituality. A cross-cultural analysis.* Springer International Publishing Switzerland.

Streib, H., Hood, R. W., & Keller, B. (2016). Deconversion and "spirituality:" — Migrations in the religious field. In H. Streib & R. W. Hood (Eds.), *Semantics and psychology* of "spirituality". A cross-cultural analysis (pp. 19–26). Springer International Publishing Switzerland.

Streib, H., Hood, R. W., Keller, B., Csöff, R.-M., & Silver, C. (2009). Deconversion. Qualitative and quantitative results from cross-cultural research in Germany and the United States of America. Vandenhoeck & Ruprecht.

Streib, H., Keller, B., Klein, C., & Hood, R. W. (2016). Semantic differentials open new perspectives on the semantic field of "spirituality" and "religion". In H. Streib & R. W. Hood (Eds.), Semantics and psychology of "spirituality". A cross-cultural analysis (pp. 87–103). Springer International Publishing Switzerland.

Tausczik, Y. R., & Pennebaker, J. W. (2010). The psychological meaning of words: LIWC and computerized analysis methods. Journal of Language and Social Psychology, 29, 24–54. https://doi.org/10.1177/0261927X09351676

Wixwat, M., & Saucier, G. (2021). Being spiritual but not religious. Current Opinion in Psychology, 40, 121–125. https://doi.org/10.1016/j.copsyc.2020.09.003

Zinnbauer, B. J., Pargament, K. I., Cole, B., Rye, M. S., Butter, E. M., Belavich, T. G., . . . Kadar, J. L. (1997). Religion and spirituality: Unfuzzying the fuzzy. Journal for the Scientific Study of Religion, 36(4), 549–564.

Chapter 7
Network Analysis of Case Study Petra S.:
A Mixed-Methods Approach

Zhuo Job Chen, Anika Steppacher, & Heinz Streib[1]

Abstract *Three waves of Petra's interviews (her case study appears in Chapter 11) have been coded with the recently developed content coding scheme that applies over 150 prominent codes to describe each interview. These content codes are subject to quantitative analysis and visualization using the mathematical tools provided by network analysis. For each interview, content codes form a directed network of adjacent connections among the codes, and the edge weights reflect the frequency of each connection. In the analysis, node and network level statistics of centrality, connectivity, spread, sub-groups, and homophily are offered to illustrate the node importance and various network structures. Inferential statistics use random graph modeling to test whether any of the network structures significantly differs from randomness such that they convey important information about how different codes connect with each other. Visualization of the trimmed networks provide further aid to understand the empirical connections of content codes. These quantitative analyses are enriched with interpretations of Petra's life stories, thus providing both a panoramic view of the structure of her interviews, and a high-resolution view of some of their details. The use of network analysis to understand the structure of a qualitative interview opens doors to an array of mixed-methods research possibilities with the Faith Development Interview data and qualitative data alike.*

Keywords: *social network analysis; ATLAS.ti; content analysis; case study; mixed method*

---

1   Z. J. Chen, School of Nursing, University of North Carolina at Charlotte, USA, E-mail: job.chen@charlotte.edu; A. Steppacher, H. Streib, Bielefeld University, Germany. © Heinz Streib, Ralph W. Hood Jr. (eds.): Faith in Development. Mixed-Method Studies on Worldviews and Religious Styles. First published in 2024 by Bielefeld University Press, Bielefeld, https://doi.org/1 0.14361/9783839471234-009

Part B: Results of Quantitative Analyses Including Qualitative Data

In this chapter we are going to examine the networks emerging from the Faith Development Interviews (FDIs) with a case to whom we gave the pseudonym Petra. Petra is a woman from Germany we interviewed three times during a period of eight years: The first interview took place in 2011 when Petra was 41 years old, the second one in 2017 with her being 47 years old, and we interviewed her last in 2019 when she was 50 years old. We were therefore able to accompany her over an extended period of her midlife and learned about the key elements of her life story and how they evolved over time. Petra grew up in the former German Democratic Republic (GDR) in a Christian surrounding, which was very unusual in this strictly secular state. She fled the GDR in the very last days of its existence in her late adolescence in search for freedom and a better life in the West. There she lived and worked in one of Germany's biggest cities before moving, somewhat disillusioned from the capitalist society she had been living in for many years, back to her hometown in East Germany by the time of her last interview.

The main themes of Petra's interviews center around the significance and development of her worldview that can be described as *spiritual atheism*. This means that although she rejects and indeed harshly criticizes religious teachings and instead wants to base her worldview on evidence-based and rational inquiry, she still preserves an openness for what cannot be explained by scientific investigation – for the spiritual realm (for the complete analysis, see Chapter 11). However, her way of exploring and presenting her beliefs, and what has been termed her "personal enlightenment" changes over time which will be the focus of the analysis below.

By analyzing Petra's interviews using network analysis, we will be able to present a compact and interconnected picture of her complex and multi-faceted reasoning. Thereby, prominent elements of content can be identified, and their connections described, enabling the exploration of essential thematic patterns. While the case study approach considers the entire biographical context in a thorough in-depth investigation of the case, the network analysis enables us to concentrate on themes and how they connect back to the biographical accounts. We therefore move from a case level to a thematic level of analysis which offers a more concise picture that invites comparisons and discussions beyond the single case.

Method

Coding Scheme

The content coding scheme describes the tool we developed for the Qualitative Content Analysis (QCA) of our FDIs. This approach serves to facilitate the subjective interpretation of the content of our vast body of qualitative material and to describe its meaning by systematic coding. Thus, QCA uses a set of codes to organize the material and provides an intersubjective understanding of the phenomenon under study by identifying themes and patterns. By assigning large amounts of qualitative material to precisely defined categories that have been derived from inductive inquiry, the meaning of the text becomes tangible (for further discussion on qualitative content analysis please read Hsieh & Shannon, 2005; Cho & Lee, 2014; Elo and Kyngäs, 2008), and researchers attain a "condensed and broad description of the phenomenon" (Elo & Kyngäs, 2008, p. 108).

The process of coding is an interpretative act, or a "judgment call" that means translating interview text into more abstract concepts (Saldaña, 2016, p. 4). This is achieved by applying a coding scheme that guides coders as an initial step with the goal to organize the qualitative material into fewer information, and to find patterns or themes derived from the data (Hsieh & Shannon, 2005). In practical terms this means that every segment in the interview text that transports meaningful statements will be coded, or in other words will be assigned a code of the coding guideline. This excludes, for instance, conversations with the interviewer or utterances that are overly descriptive or for which no meaningful content can be identified. It can be a short sentence or a whole paragraph, but it is important that the coded segment is long enough to "understand its meaning without context" (Friese, 2019, p. 116).

The coding scheme has been developed by a team of three researchers with differing disciplinary backgrounds in psychology, linguistics and sociology. The development began with an open and unstructured process of searching through eight FDIs of cases with varying religious affiliations and faith trajectories, while capturing interesting or surprising aspects. This open collection of observations, accompanied by regular team discussions was then the basis for the creation of a coding guideline: Successively and by including more interviews, the vague categories were specified and their characteristics identified. According to Friese we therefore "push[ed] codes from a descriptive to a conceptual, more abstract level" (Friese, 2019, p. 113). This process resulted in a system of categories and sub-categories that mainly derived inductively from the qualitative material, and which can now be applied deductively to new interviews. Two categories of the content coding guideline were identified in former research and investigated further in a top-down fashion. The first was from our own research and contained the elements of Trajectories of Faith Development such as exit trajectories and deconversion criteria (Streib et al., 2009), the second concerned Moral Orientation that derived from established concepts like Graham and Haidt's model of moral intuition (Graham & Haidt, 2011).

Figure 7.1: Part of the Content Coding Scheme focusing on Relationship to Parents

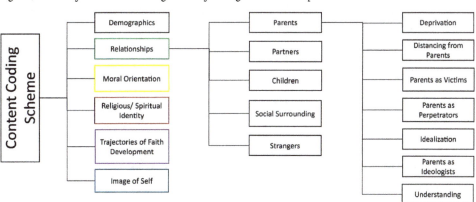

This system is to be understood as a hierarchy as can be seen in Figure 7.1 with the broadest categories of *Demographics* (a purely descriptive category, capturing demographic data that might have been missed by the questionnaire), *Relationships*, *Moral Orientation*, *Religious/Spiritual/Worldview Identity*, *Trajectories of Faith Development* and *Image of Self* structuring the whole scheme. These categories contain sub-categories that specify the category further. To take one example: There is the category "Relationships" with one of the sub-categories being "Relationship to parents." Codes are the finest tool of the coding guideline, describing the meaning of the text segment they were assigned to. One example for a code of the sub-category "Relationship to Parents" could be the code "Relationship to Parents Distancing" which mirrors the coders interpretation that the interviewee described his or her relationship to the parents as not very close and searching for independence and distance from them. Although the coding scheme is still under development and may be subject to change, it is sufficiently saturated to be applied across several interviews and cases.

Network Data

Data are three directed networks of content codes that have been assigned to three waves of interviews. The basic unit of data consists of content codes (i.e., nodes in the network) and their connections (i.e., edges in the network). Two codes are connected in the network if and only if they have been assigned to the same or to two adjacent narratives (Pokorny et al., 2018). If two codes have been assigned to the same narrative, then there are arrows both coming in and going out of each of the two codes. If two codes have been assigned to two adjacent narratives, then an arrow will come out of the code that appears first and go into the code that comes next. As an example, consider a situation with three consecutive narratives A, B, and C. Codes 'a1' and 'a2' have been assigned to narrative A, code 'b' has been assigned to narrative B, and codes 'c1' and 'c2' have been assigned to narrative C. With the five codes, eight edges are constructed: a1 → a2, a2 → a1, a1 → b, a2 → b, b → c1, b → c2, c1 → c2, and c2 → c1.

This process, starting from the code(s) assigned to the first narrative and ending at the code(s) assigned to the last narrative in the interview, results in a list of edges (i.e., an edge list). Since a code may appear multiple times to describe different narrative in the interview, there are edges that connect a code to itself, and there are edges that appear more than once. The self-referential edges are removed; the duplicate edges are combined with a weight variable created to record the frequency of appearance. Thereby, the final network is directed and weighted.

The raw network can be too dense to visualize, containing numerous ties and nodes that appear only once or lie at the periphery of the narrative. By contrast, essential nodes can appear multiple times throughout the narrative and/or are well connected to the other nodes in the network. Pruning a network by edge weights and node characteristics has been an effective approach to reveal the core structure of the network (Borgatti et al., 2018). Depending on the network complexity, we may trim the network by retaining edges greater than a certain weight (e.g., > 1, appeared twice or more) or retaining the nodes of certain importance (e.g., high hub score).

Network Analysis

While the traditional statistical method only examines attributes of the codes isolated from other codes, network analysis enables examining the properties and patterns of connections among the codes. Various packages in R (i.e., *igraph, ggraph, tidygraph*, and *statnet*) were used to analyze and visualize the data (Kolaczyk & Csárdi, 2020). Among the many components in a network to examine, we focus on two levels of analyses that offer both an overview of network structure and provide information about the importance of specific nodes in the network (Wasserman & Faust, 1994).

Network Level

At the network level, we will present statistics on the number of nodes and edges, and the number of edges of specific weights (i.e., frequency). In addition, the following statistics, indicating connectivity, spread, subgroups, and homophily, will offer various insights to network structure.

Edge density. As a global measure of connectivity, density is the proportion of present edges to all possible edges in the network.

Reciprocity. As a measure of dyadic relationship, reciprocity is the proportion of mutual connections between a pair of nodes. Since our network is directed, some edges have double arrows (i.e., mutual), whereas others only go in one direction (i.e., asymmetrical). Nodes connected by reciprocated edges indicate high level of network connectivity.

Transitivity. As a measure of triadic relationship, transitivity assesses the probability that the adjacent nodes of a node are connected. It is the ratio of triangles (direction disregarded) to connected triples. Among 16 possible types of triads for a directed network, the completely connected triangle includes three nodes that share reciprocated edges.

Centralization. Various centrality measures – degree, closeness, eigenvector, and betweenness – document the importance of nodes (described below). Centralization is the network level summary of node-level centralities.

Diameter. Being a measure of network dispersion, diameter records the longest geodesic distance (length of the shortest path between two nodes) in the network.

Distance. As the paths that connect different pairs of nodes vary by length, distance indicates the average distance between each pair of nodes in the directed network.

Cliques. Indicating existence of subgroups in the network, cliques are completely connected subgraphs. Cliques can vary by size: a c-clique is a clique with c connected nodes. In a network, numerous c-cliques exist; we will present the mean value of c for all cliques to indicate average clique sizes.

Community detection. Various algorithms detect hidden communities beyond observation of existing cliques. The *Newman-Girvan* algorithm detects community based on edge betweenness. High-betweenness edges are removed sequentially to divide the network and the best partitioning of network is selected. Another technique is based on *propagating labels*. This process assigns node labels and replaces each label with the label that appears most frequently among its neighbors. The steps are repeated until each node has the most common label of its neighbors. Finally, a computation driven method, greedy optimization of modularity, finds the communities by optimizing modularity.

Modularity. As a measure of partitioning quality, modularity compares the number of internal links in a community to random. High modularity for a partitioning reflects dense connections within communities and sparse connections across communities.

Assortativity. As a measure of homophily, assortativity is the tendency of nodes to connect to others who are similar on some variable. Since the current network do not include external node attributes other than the internal ones described above, the use of this coefficient is limited.

Node Level

At the node level, several indices of centrality record the importance of each node in connection with other nodes.

Hub. The hub scores of nodes are defined as the principal eigenvector of $A^*t(A)$, where A is the adjacency matrix of the graph and $t(A)$ is its transpose. Given this definition, hubs lie at the center of a network in charge of information distribution and contain large number of outgoing edges.

Authority. In contrast to hub, the authority scores are defined as the principal eigenvector of $t(A)^*A$. Authorities also assume a central rule but would get many incoming links from hubs.

Degree. In-degree centrality records the number of edges coming into a node whereas out-degree is the number of edges coming out of a node. The in-degree can be seen as an indicator of popularity and the out-degree and indicator of activity.

Closeness. Based on distance to others in the graph, closeness is inverse of the node's average geodesic distance to others in the network.

Eigenvector. Proportional to the sum of connection centralities, eigenvector centralities are values of the first eigenvector of the graph matrix. Nodes of high eigenvector centrality are connected to the more influential nodes.

Betweenness. Betweenness is a centrality measure based on a broker position connecting other nodes; nodes of high betweenness controls the flow of information.

Coreness. As a measure of node-level subgrouping, the k-core is the maximal subgraph in which every node has degree of at least 'k.' Nodes of high coreness connect with other nodes to form cliques of large size.

Network Visualization

In addition to statistical information, visualization of networks offers direct insight to how content codes are connected to each other. We plotted the full networks for all three waves, and trimmed networks based on edge weights and nodes' hub scores. The Fruchterman-Reingold algorithm was used to configure network layout that places high-centrality nodes in the center of the graph and highly connected nodes close to each other. Interpretation of the network visualization is empowered by subjective knowledge of the qualitative data – the meaning of the qualitative codes, the coding rules, and the overall content of an interview from which the codes were derived.

Statistical Testing

The abovementioned statistics are mainly descriptive. Exponential random graph model (ERGM) enables simulation-based inferential statistics that test the structural configuration of the network (Lusher et al., 2013; Cranmer et al., 2021). By maximizing the likelihood of the observed network, the model solves for parameters offering insight into the unique features of network configuration compared to a randomly generated network. The following set of parameters are suggested for ERGM configuration (Lusher et al., 2013). Parameter names used in the *statnet* package and illustrations appear in the parentheses.

Arc (edges). Similar to the intercept of a regression model, arc counts the number of edges and is the baseline propensity for network formation.

Reciprocity (mutual, a → b, b → a). A positive value indicates that reciprocated edges are likely to be observed.

Popularity spread (idegree1.5, a1 → b, a2 → b, a3 → b, etc.). Testing hypothesis about the in-degree centrality, a positive popularity spread parameter indicates that nodes differ on their levels of popularity, such that the network is centralized on in-degree.

Activity spread (odegree1.5, a → b1, a → b2, a → b3, etc.). Testing hypothesis about the out-degree centrality, a positive activity spread parameter indicates that some nodes have much higher activity than others, such that the network is centralized on out-degree.

Simple connectivity (twopath, a → b, b → c). A two path measures the extent to which nodes who send out edges also receive edges from other nodes, controlling for the correlation between in- and out-degree.

Multiple connectivity (gwdsp, a1 → b, b → c1, a2 → b, b → c2, etc.). Generalized from a two path, a negative value in conjunction with positive transitivity indicates that 2-paths tend to be closed.

Transitivity/triangulation (gwesp, a → b, b → c, and a → c). A positive effect indicates there is a high degree of closure or multiple clusters of triangles.

Cyclic closure (ctriple, a → b, b → c, c → a). A negative effect indicates tendencies against cyclic triads or a tendency against generalized exchange or reciprocity.

Parameter estimation quality is suggested by well-mixed, stationary Monte Carlo Markov Chains (MCMC), such that the chains thoroughly explore the parameter space and do not get stuck in local maximum. Measures of goodness-of-fit check the statistics included in the model against observed data. Indicating the difference between the observed networks and simulations from the model, a p-value closer to one is better.

Results

Three waves had roughly the same number of nodes (i.e., distinct codes), but Wave 3 data had more edges, and more edges with weighs greater than 1, than did data of the other waves. Figure 7.2 shows the full networks for all three waves of data. Wave 3 network was more densely connected than the other two waves.

Network Level Analysis

Table 7.1 lists all the network-level descriptive statistics for both full and trimmed (weights > 1) networks. Compared to Waves 1 and 2, the full network of Wave 3 had higher density, higher reciprocity with a greater number of mutually reciprocated ties and was more internally connected. However, Wave 1 had higher levels of centralization suggesting that the network was centered on important nodes. The three waves had comparable spread measures, with Wave 2 slightly more dispersed (also visible from Figure 7.2). In terms of subgroups, Wave 3 included cliques of greater size. Three community detection algorithms showed differential performance, with the greedy optimization method yielding the highest modularity score. For all waves, 4 to 5 groups were suggested. Overall, Wave 2 network could be better subdivided with the highest modularity score. Homophily was not apparent for the networks as assortativity scores were all negative.

Trimmed networks showed similar results on connectivity but were reasonably more spread out as many weak links had been removed. Subgroups were more apparent with overall high modularity scores. These results would be described in the following section.

Figure 7.2: Illustration of full networks for three waves of data.

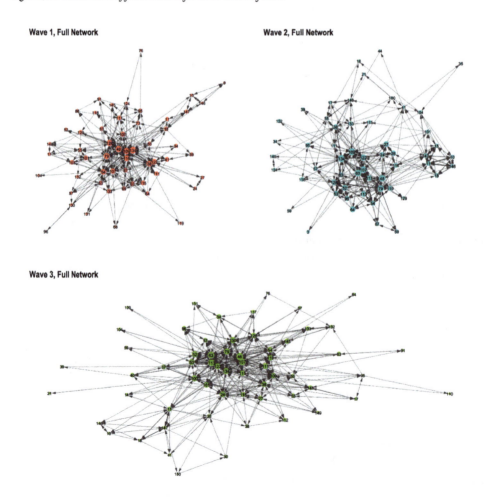

Table 7.1: Network statistics of full and trimmed network (weights > 1) of three waves.

	Wave 1		Wave 2		Wave 3	
	Full	W >1	Full	W >1	Full	W >1
Nodes	56	32	55	34	61	46
Edges	356	69	351	78	524	178
Weights = 1	287	-	273	-	346	-
Weights = 2	45	-	54	-	99	-
Weights = 3	12	-	14	-	48	-
Weights > 3	12	-	10	-	31	-
Connectivity Measures						
Density	.116	.070	.118	.070	.143	.086
Reciprocity	.590	.580	.524	.513	.637	.663
Mutual	105	20	92	20	167	59
Asymmetrical	146	29	167	38	190	60
Transitivity	.367	.331	.378	.368	.457	.411
Complete Connected	83	7	45	2	223	39
Centralization						
Degree	.364	.228	.229	.147	.303	.264
Closeness	.422	.131	.342	.040	.375	.044
Eigenvector	.723	.784	.641	.909	.664	.769
Betweenness	.195	.162	.162	.134	.106	.101
Spread Measures						
Diameter	6	14	6	15	5	18
Distance	2.36	2.54	2.44	2.69	2.30	2.56
Subgroups						
Cliques	3.34	2.13	3.19	2.07	4.54	3.04
Community Detection						
Newman-Girvan	11	19	33	6	15	8
Propagating Labels	2	11	2	7	2	11
Greedy Optimization	4	5	5	5	5	8
Modularity						
Newman-Girvan	.045	.175	.068	.528	.051	.197
Propagating Labels	.063	.145	.225	.465	.105	.187
Greedy Optimization	.266	.357	.392	.617	.295	.377
Homophily						
Assortativity	-.173	-.038	-.080	-.228	-.006	.085

Node Level Analysis

Table 7.2 displays the node labels and the explanation of each node. These labels will be used throughout the analysis for ease of display. Table 7.3 lists the top influential nodes for the networks in the three waves. Although the rank was based on hub score, the top nodes also scored high on other centrality metrics. Common to all three waves were codes "Personal Enlightenment" and "Intellectual Doubt", both belonging to the sub-category Motives for Faith Trajectory, as well as "Scientific Reasoning" describing the sub-category Beliefs as part of Petra's Spiritual Identity, the Moral Orientation of "Authenticity/ Honesty/Integrity" and finally her description of Image of Self centered around "Humility." Common to two waves were the Moral Orientation of "Harm/Care" and the Image of Self as "Well-Read" (Wave 1 & Wave 3), the Moral Orientations of "Social Criticism" and "Fairness/Reciprocity" with a focus on "Social Fairness" (Wave 2 & Wave 3), and Petra's Image of Self described as "Know Oneself, Reflective" (Wave 1 & Wave 2).

Table 7.2: Meanings of major nodes.

Node Label	Node Explanation
10	Relationships_Parents_Deprivation
11	Relationships_Parents_Distancing from Parents
15	Relationships_Parents_Parents as Victims
18	Relationships_Parents_Understanding ones Parents
27	Relationships_Partner_Opportunity to reflect, widen horizon, mirroring
28	Relationships_Partner_Shared religion/ worldview
38	Relationships_Social surroundings_Opportunity to reflect, widen horizon, mirroring
41	Relationships_Social surroundings_Support, consolation, stability
48	Moral Orientation_authenticity/honesty/ integrity
50	Moral Orientation_fairness/reciprocity
52	Moral Orientation_Fairness/reciprocity_Pluralism, debate, freedom of speech
53	Moral Orientation_fairness/reciprocity_Social fairness
54	Moral Orientation_harm/care
55	Moral Orientation_harm/care_Christian charity
57	Moral Orientation_harm/care_Engagement for the poor and underprivileged
63	Moral Orientation_Social Criticism
64	Moral Orientation_struggle with moral questions
67	Religious/Spiritual/Worldview Identity_Beliefs_All-connectedness
69	Religious/Spiritual/Worldview Identity_Beliefs_concepts regarding death

73	Religious/Spiritual/Worldview Identity _Beliefs_Image of god_Being at odds with god
79	Religious/Spiritual/Worldview Identity _Beliefs_Scientific Reasoning
83	Religious/Spiritual/Worldview Identity _Faith experience_Inner harmony
96	Religious/Spiritual/Worldview Identity _Social embeddedness_Emphazsing the need for Secularism
100	Image of Self_Autonomy
101	Image of Self _Being shaped by upbringing
107	Image of Self _Humility
109	Image of Self _Know oneself, reflective
111	Image of Self _Open
113	Image of Self _Political, Socially aware, critical
115	Image of Self _Professional life, job
116	Image of Self _Rebellious, nonconformist
117	Image of Self _Religiously unmusical
119	Image of Self _Serenity, self-satisfaction
122	Image of Self _Well-read
128	Trajectories of Faith Development _ Motives _intellectual doubt
130	Trajectories of Faith Development _ Motives _Moral criticism
131	Trajectories of Faith Development _ Motives _Moral criticism_(emotional) manipulation
132	Trajectories of Faith Development _ Motives _Moral criticism_Hierarchy, suppression
134	Trajectories of Faith Development _ Motives _Personal Enlightenment
146	CONTEXT_Relationships _Only father
147	CONTEXT_Relationships_ Only mother

Table 7.3: Top codes (ranked by hub) based on hub and authority scores for three waves of data.

Top Codes ID	Hub	Authority	In-Degree	Out-Degree	Closeness	Eigenvector	Betweenness	Coreness
Top 10 Wave 1 Codes. All other codes have hub < .185, authority < .315								
134	1.000	0.942	26	26	0.011	1.000	535	11
109	0.905	1.000	21	21	0.011	0.995	467	11
54	0.617	0.440	17	15	0.009	0.496	290	11
48	0.615	0.808	18	20	0.009	0.819	225	11
38	0.504	0.560	15	15	0.010	0.565	276	11
79	0.430	0.523	14	18	0.010	0.530	313	11

164   Part B: Results of Quantitative Analyses Including Qualitative Data

Top Codes ID	Hub	Au-thori-ty	In-De-gree	Out-De-gree	Close-ness	Eigen-vector	Bet-ween-ness	Core-ness
107	0.381	0.264	11	10	0.010	0.302	155	11
116	0.365	0.274	15	13	0.010	0.280	245	11
128	0.357	0.429	19	21	0.010	0.472	472	11
122	0.317	0.409	10	14	0.009	0.423	167	11

Top 11 Wave 2 Codes. All other codes have hub < .558, authority < .504

134	1.000	1.000	16	20	0.011	0.729	402	11
63	0.921	0.522	13	14	0.010	0.482	246	11
109	0.886	0.787	17	20	0.011	0.605	527	11
107	0.851	0.402	11	15	0.011	0.377	312	11
11	0.787	0.725	10	8	0.009	0.929	69	10
79	0.775	0.935	16	17	0.010	0.843	275	11
147	0.671	0.789	11	10	0.009	1.000	118	10
128	0.591	0.574	14	10	0.010	0.553	265	11
48	0.587	0.411	11	14	0.010	0.396	142	11
117	0.410	0.623	9	9	0.009	0.511	73	11
53	0.287	0.613	8	8	0.009	0.458	58	11

Top 11 Wave 3 Codes. All other codes have hub < .341, authority < .345

134	1.000	1.000	20	23	0.009	1.000	203	17
130	0.968	0.931	24	26	0.009	0.945	342	17
128	0.848	0.884	23	22	0.007	0.915	171	17
79	0.728	0.632	20	16	0.008	0.664	178	17
54	0.592	0.806	24	29	0.009	0.809	411	17
53	0.573	0.710	12	16	0.008	0.703	218	17
48	0.565	0.494	18	18	0.009	0.527	158	17
63	0.559	0.449	15	16	0.008	0.474	94	17
113	0.544	0.461	15	10	0.007	0.517	70	17
122	0.498	0.620	20	14	0.008	0.625	125	17
107	0.440	0.492	15	14	0.008	0.489	66	17

Note: Meanings of the nodes with numeric labels can be found in Table 7.2.

ERGM

Excepting the model with transitivity, all models converged properly. A visual examination of diagnostic plots suggested that MCMC routines behaved well – thoroughly explored the parameter space and did not wander over the course of the simulation –evidencing that parameter estimates were likely good approximations. Table 7.4 shows all the parameter estimates, standard errors, and goodness-of-fit (GOF) p-values. Positive and significant estimates of reciprocity, popularity, and activity suggested that influential nodes in the networks tended to connect with each other, and the networks were centralized on these influential nodes. This offered some evidence for the existence of a strong core of content codes that would define the narratives. Negative and significant estimates of connectivity and cyclic closure suggested that many nodes were lying on the periphery of the network as "end nodes," such that an edge was sent and ended at them, or they sent an edge without receiving one. This result dovetailed with the positive centrality estimates, showing that the networks were concentrated on a core of several important nodes that connected well with each other and reached out to other less central nodes like revolving satellites.

Table 7.4: ERGM parameter estimates (standard errors) and goodness-of-fit measures (GOF) for network of three waves.

Network Effect	Wave 1		Wave 2		Wave 3	
	Estimate (SE)	GOF	Estimate (SE)	GOF	Estimate (SE)	GOF
Arc	-2.03 (.06)	1.00	-2.01 (.06)	.92	-1.79 (.05)	.94
Reciprocity[a]	3.24 (.20)	.96	2.79 (.19)	.88	3.31 (.16)	.86
Popularity Spread[a]	0.48 (.03)	.76	0.40 (.04)	.76	0.45 (.02)	.96
Activity Spread[a]	0.49 (.02)	.94	0.44 (.03)	.82	0.46 (.01)	.98
Simple Connectivity[b]	-0.10 (.00)	.94	-0.12 (.01)	.94	-0.07 (.00)	.82
Multiple Connectivity[b]	-0.15 (.01)	.84	-0.16 (.01)	.92	-0.16 (.01)	.94
Cyclic Closure[b]	-0.47 (.03)	1.00	-0.55 (.03)	.64	-0.30 (.02)	.98

Note. a. models controlled for arc; b. models with the variable only. All estimates are statistically significant at $p < .001$.

Interpretation of Network Connections

As the hubs show the central concentrations of content codes in an interview, they enable the researcher to focus on particular coding and serve as practical starting point for interpretation. In order to illustrate the value of this mixed-methods approach, the next paragraphs yield insight into the case of Petra by exploring a selection of hubs as shown in Figure 7.3 (for a full analysis of the case, see Chapter 11). Furthermore, by comparing

166   Part B: Results of Quantitative Analyses Including Qualitative Data

the three waves we not only can reconstruct central themes from Petra's narrative but also follow their development.

First, we turn to the pattern emerging around the code "personal enlightenment" that was assigned numerous times in Petra's interviews. As can be illustrated by the fact that this hub is highly weighted throughout all three waves, this code is central in Petra's narratives and captures how she describes the development of her worldview by emphasizing personal growth through gaining knowledge. In her biographical accounts, she states that this development started when she began to critically examine Christian teachings which were part of her upbringing. Consulting the Wave 1 network at the top panel of Figure 7.3, this is illustrated by the asymmetric edge leading away from the node "distancing from parents." This indicates that Petra followed up the accounts on her family's religion with this central developmental theme. Personal development through increasing knowledge is an essential theme for her life reviews and is accompanied by her strong identification with enlightenment ideals such as evidence-based inquiry and rational reasoning. This can be further illustrated in the network at Wave 1, with the connection between the hubs "personal enlightenment" and her belief in "scientific reasoning" with a mutual edge indicating that both elements are part of the same narratives. Another important and similarly closely connected aspect of how she presents her personal development is that it demands critical self-reflection and honesty when confronted with new and challenging arguments, on the one hand, and how this in turn enables her to learn more about her own limitations and biases, on the other hand. This is why we can observe mutual edges between the subjective description of her development as "personal enlightenment" and both her image of self as someone "reflective" which is also highly weighted as well as her moral orientation towards "authenticity/ honesty/integrity." Thus, integrity and humility are important elements characterizing her story of personal growth which is fueled by philosophical and scientific literature as well as honest and sometimes difficult discussions with her social surroundings. Here we can see mutual edges between this central hub and her self-presentation as someone who is "well-read" as well as how she describes her social surroundings as an "opportunity to reflect and widen her horizon."

In Wave 2 as illustrated in the central panel of Figure 7.3, another pattern around "personal enlightenment" can be focused: Her personal development which aims at better understanding the world around her is no longer directly connected to her beliefs in "scientific reasoning." However, her trust in science and evidence-based thinking is in all three waves closely related to "intellectual doubt" which, in Petra's case, is exclusively expressed when talking about organized religion. This connection is not only mutual but also highly weighted, indicating its closeness as she uses both codes frequently for the same argumentations. In her narratives, she criticizes the logical fallacies that she encounters in religious reasoning going so far as to allege that people are purposefully mislead making this criticism not only an epistemological but also a moral one. We see in the Wave 2 network the sequential coding leading from "intellectual doubt" to moral orientation towards "harm/care," suggesting that Petra follows up her criticism with these moral considerations. On the contrary, Petra puts her trust in humanist organizations as well as scientific solutions, when it comes to improving the lives of people instead of religion, which she interprets as manipulative and power-hungry. This is why we can observe in the network at Wave 2 the asymmetric edge pointing from "harm/care" back to "scientific reasoning." In her interviews, the general tone toward the church but also religion as a whole becomes much harsher from the first to the second one. This can also be exemplified by the fact that, turning back to Wave 1, she does accompany her doubts in religious teachings with the admission that she still struggles with the image of God formed in her childhood whereas in Wave 2 she seems to no longer have any remaining belief in a personal God, emphasizing the need for secularism instead. In Wave 1 we see the mutual edge between "intellectual doubt" and her image of God as "being at odds with God", a node that disappears in the central panel for Wave 2. Instead, another mutual edge appears between her intellectual criticism and her plea for "secularism." Thus, whereas an intellectual humble way of engaging in discussions and thinking about complex issues still is an important part of her subjective development, other elements emerge and disappear which present this theme in a slightly different light.

Petra's third interview is much denser and lengthier than the former ones, which can be illustrated by the complex network in the bottom panel of Figure 7.3. In Wave 3 the way of framing her life story as pursuing a deeper understanding of the world by rigorous investigation and study continues to be an essential theme and is still framed in harsh opposite to religious teachings. Her main point of criticism is that religion prevents the pursuit of knowledge by presenting answers and dogmatic assumptions without any means to prove them and thereby closing any possibility of debate or new ways of thinking about these questions. This, once again being the opposite of "scientific reasoning," which demands not only prove for claims made, but also obliges to adjust them when they are no longer supported by the evidence. Here we observe again the mutual edge between "scientific reasoning" and "intellectual doubt" mirroring this juxtaposition. This rigorous inquiry is connected with Petra's appreciation for "humility" as one must admit that all knowledge is temporary and needs to be challenged which is closely linked to her moral plea for honesty and integrity. This can be illustrated by the asymmetric edge leading from "scientific reasoning" to "humility" which is in turn linked by a mutual edge to her moral orientation of "authenticity/ honesty/integrity." In sum, by consulting the networks and following the changes in pattern, we are able to reconstruct how the structures in Petra's subjective developmental story changed and how elements disappeared, and new ones emerged.

Furthermore, there is another essential pattern closely linked to the one described above that gained importance over the past 8 years we interviewed Petra which is her increasingly decisive criticism toward the social circumstances she observes. This development is represented in the networks by the increasingly highly weighted code "social criticism" which is in Wave 1 a node and evolves to a hub in Wave 2 and 3. At Wave 1, she mentions her discontent regarding social inequality mostly with an emphasis on a moral obligation to care for those that are disenfranchised. As can be seen in the top panel of Figure 7.3, this is illustrated by a mutual edge between her moral orientation "harm/care" and "social criticism." Petra is a health care worker in a large German city, witnessing living conditions and health problems of homeless people firsthand, which, although not being a central topic in her first interview, still is a point of concern. Advocating for those that are at the fringes of society seems to be an aspect of Petra's self-presentation as non-conforming and rebellious, which becomes visible when following up her narratives coded with the code for image of self as "nonconformist/rebellious" with the mentioned grievances.

In her second interview, Petra expresses her social criticism more frequently and explicitly as can be seen in the increasing weight as well as the denser connection to other nodes making the code "social criticism" a hub. It is accompanied by more explicit demands toward larger society with regard to a minimum of social welfare and care that must be granted to the members of any given society. Thus, in the network in the central panel of Figure 7.3 we see that her criticism toward social circumstances is followed up with a plea for "social fairness." Besides this call for fairness and reciprocity Petra still emphasizes the moral obligation to care for the disenfranchised, treating them with dignity and kindness as these narratives also precede "harm/care" coding. Her criticism that the current social circumstances force individuals to compete and struggle for their survival instead of fulfilling their full potential is now accompanied by mentioning schools of philosophical thought as these elaborations are followed by her presentation of self as someone who is "well read." In this context she admits that religion offers solace to those who have to live in these circumstances which does, however, not convince her. Petra, in this regard can be described as "religiously unmusical" which is a Weberian term describing someone who is concerned with religion, acknowledging some values of being faithful, but who cannot bring themself to believe. Here we see the edge pointing from "social criticism" to seeing oneself as "religiously unmusical" as she mentions them in order to arrive at her conclusion that "scientific reasoning" is a much better solution for the problems she describes. Thus, religion, this is Petra's credo, cannot help better these precarious developments, but only concrete action and political change.

By the time of her last interview, this connection between social criticism and her self-presentation as a political person becomes even more explicit and central to her elaborations. Not only that her self-image as someone being "socially and politically aware" becomes a hub, but the mutual edge between this hub and "social criticism" is highly weighted. She still uses similar examples, most often encountered during her work as can be illustrated by the fact that the node "professional life/job" is relevant in all three interviews. This time, however, it is more focused on her own situation. This cannot be directly observed from the networks and needs some biographical context: At Wave 3 Petra was forced to move away from the city in which she had been living in for years as she could no longer afford to pay the increasingly high rent price. Petra, now in her 50s, moved back to her childhood hometown in East Germany and is confronted with the prospect of a small pension after a long working history. This anxiety in combination with the fact that she now earns even less than before, as wages in East Germany are lower than in West Germany, fuels her criticism even more. This also prompts a change in the focus of her life review in which growing up in the former German Democratic Republic (GDR) becomes a much more central topic. In Wave 1 she did mention this fact only once, whereas in Wave 2 and especially in Wave 3 it seems to be an important part of how she frames her current worldview. Here the node "being shaped by upbringing" means something different at the respective waves: Whereas in her first interview it illustrates her accounts when talking about her religious socialization, it is almost exclusively reserved for her upbringing in the GDR in her last two interviews. At Wave 3, she explicitly states that she turns back to the materialist and socialist teachings she experienced as a child finding terms and explanations that help her understand her own as well as the societal situation she criticizes. This complex pattern emerges as a completely connected triangle in the bottom panel of Figure 7.3 between the three hubs "social criticism," standing for her criticism of social inequality which is connected to her moral plea for "social fairness" that she explicitly connects to socialist ideals and her self-image of being "politically/socially aware," or in Petra's case her identification as a leftist.

Figure 7.3: Trimmed Wave 1 (top), Wave 2 (center), and Wave 3 (bottom) networks. Note. Left network includes only nodes with edges > 2. Right network includes the network involved with the top hubs in Table 7.3 and nodes with edges > 1. Size of nodes represent hub scores. Top hubs are colored gold in the right graph. See Table 7.2 for meanings of nodes.

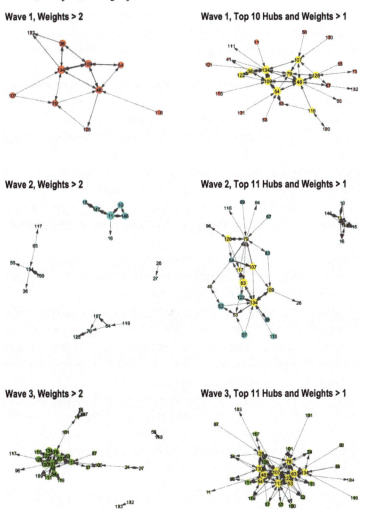

Discussion

This chapter presented some insight into the development of Petra's worldview and the development of her worldview over the past 8 years. Thereby, our interpretation has focused on selected aspects such as Petra's "personal enlightenment," her relation to religion and her church, and how this related to questions of morality and, increasingly over time, with a radical social and political identity. Trimming the networks greatly helps to identify most important and central themes (top hubs) in an interview and to visualize how they change over time. As the complexity of the network visualizations suggests, there is, of course, much more information about how relationships, biographical particularities and beliefs interrelate to portray Petra's complex reasoning and how it develops over time. However, we hope that this chapter could demonstrate how network analysis, as an approach that uses mathematical tools to assess and visualize the relations between content codes, facilitates a structured, focused, and synoptic view on the themes in an interview and their internal logic. Network Analysis allows the identification of essential themes by following the patterns consisting of diverse elements and their connections with other patterns.

As mentioned above, this illustration also shows that this complex web is not an objective portrayal of the interview text but must be understood as the result of interpretative work not only on the level of coding but also when describing the meaning of their connections and identifying major themes. Thus, knowledge about and familiarity with the interview text, on the one hand, and network visualizations, on the other hand, interact to draw meaningful conclusions about the case. The networks offer a structured view of qualitative and often-times "messy" data that could not be achieved in such a rigorous way otherwise. Nevertheless, these analyses and interpretation are part of the idiographic approach, even though highly sophisticated mathematics are used to assist the interpretation.

This demonstration of the effectivity of network analysis was limited to one case, the case of Petra. It remained on the level of case-specific top hubs and in longitudinal perspective of within-person differences. What is not demonstrated in this chapter, but is also a considerable potential of network visualization, is its aid for determining between-person differences. This indicates the enormous potential that we can expect from including network analysis in the evaluation of interviews. Combining case studies and network analysis to evaluate longitudinal cases will enable us not only to assess change in content but also to reveal change in structure.

Therefore, as noted in Chapter 4, we understand network analyses as a quantitative complement to the mixed-methods approach of studying faith development. Network analysis could become an integral tool in a mixed-method research design that works with a triangulation of content analysis, narrative analysis, structural evaluation for style and type, and results from psychometric scales.

References

Borgatti, S. P., Everett, M. G., & Johnson, J. C. (2018). *Analyzing social networks*. Sage.

Cho, J. Y.; Lee, E.-H. (2014): Reducing confusion about grounded theory and qualitative content analysis: Similarities and differences. *The Qualitative Report 19* (32).

Cranmer, S. J., Desmarais, B. A., & Morgan, J. W. (2021). *Inferential network analysis*. Cambridge.

Elo, S.; Kyngäs, H. (2008): The qualitative content analysis process. *Journal of Advanced Nursing 62* (1), 107–115. https://doi.org/10.1111/j.1365-2648.2007.04569.x

Friese, S. (2018). *Qualitative data analysis with ATLAS.ti*. Third edition. Sage.

Graham, J., Nosek, B. A., Haidt, J., Iyer, R., Koleva, S., & Ditto, P. H. (2011). Mapping the moral domain. *Journal of Personality and Social Psychology, 101*(2), 366–385.

Hsieh, H.-F.; Shannon, S. E. (2005): Three approaches to qualitative content analysis. *Qualitative health research 15* (9), 1277–1288. https://doi.org/10.1177/1049732305276687

Kolaczyk, E. D., & Csárdi, G. (2020). *Statistical analysis of network data with R* (2e). Springer.

Lusher, D., Koskinen, J., & Robins, G. (2013). *Exponential random graph models for social networks: Theory, methods, and applications*. Cambridge University Press.

Pokorny, J., Norman, A., Zanesco, A., Bauer-Wu, S., Sahdra, B., & Saron, C. (2018). Network analysis for the visualization and analysis of qualitative data. *Psychological Methods, 23*(1), 169–183.

Saldaña, J. (2016): *The coding manual for qualitative researchers*. 3. edition. Sage.

Streib, H., Hood, R. W., Keller, B., Csöff, R.-M., & Silver, C. (2009). *Deconversion. Qualitative and quantitative results from cross-cultural research in Germany and the United States of America*. Vandenhoeck & Ruprecht. https://doi.org/10.13109/9783666604393

Wasserman, S., & Faust, K. (1994). *Social network analysis: Methods and applications*. Cambridge University Press.

Chapter 8
Predicting Deconversion. Concurrent and Cross-Time Correlations in Three Samples

Heinz Streib & Zhuo Job Chen[1]

Abstract *This chapter presents results about one of the questions that our research has focused from the beginning: religious change and deconversion. While in the Deconversion Study (2001–2005) we could use only cross-sectional data to estimate characteristics of deconverts in the U.S.A. and Germany, the analyses reported in this chapter are based on repeated surveys in three waves that allow the identification of concurrent and cross-time correlations—thus, open perspectives on the prediction of deconversion. Results indicate that, with difference between the three waves, deconversion concurrently may correlate positively with openness to experience and negatively with consciousness, it may correlate also with mysticism and show concurrent correlations with truth of texts and teachings and self-rated religiosity. Cross-time correlations indicated as (negative) predictors of deconversion: self-rated religiosity, extraversion, agreeableness, environmental mastery, positive relations with others, purpose in life, self-acceptance, interpretive mysticism, and truth of texts and teachings. We conclude that low scores on variables for religiosity and religious cognition, but also personality and well-being variable that call for emotional compensation are predictors of deconversion.*

Keywords: *deconversion; disaffiliation; leaving religion; religious change*

---

1   H. Streib, Bielefeld University, Germany, E-mail: heinz.streib@uni-bielefeld.de; Z. J. Chen, School of Nursing, University of North Carolina at Charlotte, USA. © Heinz Streib, Ralph W. Hood Jr. (eds.): Faith in Development. Mixed-Method Studies on Worldviews and Religious Styles. First published in 2024 by Bielefeld University Press, Bielefeld, https://doi.org/10.14361/9783839471234-010

174 Part B: Results of Quantitative Analyses Including Qualitative Data

Introduction

Our Bielefeld-Chattanooga research has focused from the beginning on religious change. A great beginning was the Deconversion Study (2001–2005; Streib et al., 2009) with a mixed-methods design combining narrative and Faith Development Interviews with a comprehensive questionnaire to investigate characteristics of deconverts in the U.S.A. and Germany. In the meantime, we could collect more data and this chapter is based on three additional samples: the Spirituality Study (Streib & Hood, 2016) and two more waves for the longitudinal study of faith development. Now, these new three-wave data can be used to analyze concurrent and cross-wave correlations that open perspectives on the prediction of deconversion.

As summarized by Streib (2021) and by Steppacher et al. (2022), the study of deconversion is an emerging field in psychology, and the contributions to the literature gradually increased in the recent years. Most interesting for this chapter are results about the prediction of deconversion.

From a psychological perspective it would be impressive, when deconversion could be explained by personality traits such as the five-factor model (Costa & McCrae, 1985). Some contributions have explored the predicting role of the five personality factors on deconversion. Saroglou et al. (2020) report results from their study in Belgium that investigated religiosity, spirituality, personality, and values of deconverts in comparison with non-religious and socialized religious respondents. Their findings include that higher *neuroticism*, opposition to the value of conservation, and search for autonomy are characteristics for exiters. These results are reflected in Hui et al.'s (2018) longitudinal study of Christians in China who deconverted within a 3-year time frame. Their results indicate that low *emotional stability* (*neuroticism*, reversed) predicted deconversion, while the other five personality factors did not. Stronge et al. (2020) have used a representative national sample of New Zealand adults (2009–2017) to analyze, using piecewise latent growth models, longitudinal change in the five personality traits and in honesty-humility before and after conversion or deconversion ($n = 540$ converts, $n = 886$ deconverts). The researchers observed no personality changes before conversion or after deconversion; but their result regarding *deconverts* demonstrate an increase in honesty-humility and a decrease in *agreeableness* preceding deconversion. Our report from the Bielefeld-Chattanooga Study on Deconversion (Streib et al., 2009) presented, for deconverts, considerably higher *openness to experience*, and, for German deconverts, lower scores on *extraversion*, *agreeableness*, and *conscientiousness*; and, also for the German deconverts, lower ratings on the Ryff-Scale factors of *environmental mastery, positive relations with others, purpose in life*, and *self-acceptance* were indicated. We may conclude that deconversion research so far, including our own previous results from the Deconversion Study (Streib et al., 2009), has produced no convergent results regarding the prediction of deconversion using the five personality factors.

Values are another set of potential predictors that were taken into consideration. Schwartz's (Bilsky et al., 2011) Portrait Values Questionnaire (PVQ) has been included in studies about deconverts (Hui et al., 2018; Hui et al., 2015; Saroglou et al., 2020). From their longitudinal research with Chinese deconverts, Hui et al. (2018, p. 115) conclude that "faith exit is predicted by the values of self-direction, stimulation, hedonism, achievement, and power." Correspondingly, Saroglou et al. (2020) report that deconverts have lower scores on conservation values such as security, conformity, tradition.

Finally, attachment has been recently included as lens for understanding conversion and deconversion. Greenwald et al.'s (2018) study demonstrates the benefits of including attachment theory in the study of deconversion. Attachment-related variations (attachment anxiety; avoidance) and their relation to religious change themes (compensation, exploration, socialization) open perspectives on individual differences: attachment anxiety is associated with emotional compensation, and compensation themes are associated with lower well-being at present and a heightened link between attachment anxiety and distress, while attachment security is less related to compensation themes, but rather open for the exploration of new ideas.

This study takes up the thread of this previous research, including our own findings from the Deconversion Project (Streib et al., 2009), to add to the literature another contribution that is based on three samples which allow the analysis of concurrent and cross-time correlations—and, with the latter, yield new perspectives on the prediction of deconversion. Thereby, this study will engage in an open exploration of all possible variables in our data.

Method

Participants

While in the Deconversion Study (Streib et al., 2009) we could use only cross-sectional data to estimate characteristics of deconverts in the U.S.A. and Germany, the analyses reported in this chapter are based on in three additional samples: the sample of the Spirituality Study (Streib & Hood, 2016) that are the Wave 1 data in this study, and two more waves for the longitudinal study of faith development. Table 8.1 presents the basic information about these three samples. For more detailed description of these samples, see the Appendix in this book; in addition, there is most detailed information in the key publications (Streib & Hood, 2016; Streib et al., 2022).

Table 8.1: Brief Description of the Three Samples Used in This Study

	Name	Sample size for concurrent analyses	Core time of questionnaire participations	Key publications
Wave 1	Spirituality Study	$n = 1806$	2010 – 2011	(Streib & Hood, 2016)
Wave 2	Longitudinal I	$n = 310$	2015 – 2016	(Streib et al., 2022)
Wave 3	Longitudinal II	$n = 176$	2019 – 2020	-

Not all participants in Wave 2 and Wave 3 are longitudinal cases, which is due to the fact that Waves 2 and 3 are primarily limited to the participants who also agreed to a Faith Development Interview, and we could of course not successfully invite 100% of the interviewees from the previous wave; also, we have a number of new participants in each new wave. Therefore, cases included in Wave 1 – Wave 2 cross-wave analyses are $n = 264$, cases included in Wave 1 – Wave 3 cross-wave analyses are $n = 155$, and cases included in Wave 2 – Wave 3 cross-wave analyses are $n = 142$.

Measures

Deconversion was assessed by the answers to the item in the questionnaire "Have you left a religious tradition or worldview in the recent or more distant past?" Demographics included age, gender, country, and education that was calculated according to ISCED (Unesco Institute for Statistics, 2006) standards and then dichotomized in non-tertiary and tertiary education. Self-rated religiosity and spirituality were assessed on a 5-point scale. The five personality factors were assessed by the NEO-FFI (Costa & McCrae, 1985) that was used in all three waves consistently. For psychological well-being, we used the Ryff-Scales for Psychological Well-being and Growth (Ryff, 1989; Ryff & Singer, 1996). For the assessment of mysticism, Hood's (1975) Mysticism Scale was used. Generativity was measured by the Loyola Generativity Scale (McAdams & de St Aubin, 1992). In Wave 2 and Wave 3 we also used Budner's (1962) Intolerance of Ambiguity Scale, the Need for Cognition Scale (Cacioppo et al., 1984), and the items used in the Religion Monitor (2013) for the assessment of fundamentalism and pluralism. For more detailed information about measures, see the Appendix in this book.

Results

Concurrent Correlations with Deconversion

In a first step, the concurrent correlations within the data of each wave were analyzed using logistic regression with self-reported deconversion in the same wave as the outcome variable. Table 8.2 presents results from three logistic regression models (Wave1, Wave 2, and Wave 3) using all independent variables that could possibly predict self-reported deconversion at the same wave. Thus, the table shows the concurrent correlations between personality variables and deconversion within the three waves.

Attending generally to the significant results, we begin with the basic demographics: Table 8.2 shows that *age* correlates with deconversion in Wave 1 ($OR = 1.02$, 95%CI: 1.01-1.03) and Wave 3 ($OR = 1.04$, 95%CI: 1.00-1.08) with a relatively small effect, however. This may indicate that the older the participants, the more time they had to experience a deconversion, but it could also indicate that the older generation is more inclined to deconversion. Also, being *male* clearly correlates with deconversion at Wave 1 ($OR = 1.27$, 95%CI: 1.01-1.60) and Wave 3 ($OR = 3.12$, 95%CI: 1.20-8.84).

Table 8.2: Concurrent correlations of self-reported deconversion and personality variables in three waves

| | Wave 1 (n = 1807) | Wave 2 (n = 310) | Wave 3 (n = 176) |
	OR [95% CI]	OR [95% CI]	OR [95% CI]
Demographics			
Age	1.02*** [1.01, 1.03]	1.01 [0.98, 1.03]	1.04* [1.00, 1.08]
Gender (Male)	1.27* [1.01, 1.60]	1.27 [0.70, 2.34]	3.12* [1.20, 8.84]
Country (Germany)	1.84*** [1.44, 2.37]	0.56 [0.22, 1.40]	0.17* [0.03, 0.89]
Education (Tertiary)	0.93 [0.75, 1.16]	1.42 [0.79, 2.59]	1.62 [0.64, 4.27]
Self-Rated Religious	0.88* [0.80, 0.97]	0.62*** [0.47, 0.82]	0.40*** [0.25, 0.62]
Self-Rated Spiritual	0.93 [0.84, 1.04]	1.14 [0.87, 1.51]	0.98 [0.62, 1.59]
Five Factor Personality			
neuroticism	0.90 [0.70, 1.15]	1.28 [0.66, 2.50]	1.46 [0.56, 3.92]
extraversion	0.77 [0.60, 1.00]	0.59 [0.29, 1.19]	0.75 [0.25, 2.19]
openness to experience	1.54** [1.18, 2.02]	1.37 [0.62, 3.06]	2.40 [0.60, 10.07]
agreeableness	1.21 [0.92, 1.60]	2.62** [1.29, 5.47]	3.83* [1.19, 13.36]
conscientiousness	0.65*** [0.51, 0.82]	0.71 [0.38, 1.32]	0.92 [0.38, 2.21]
Psychological Wellbeing			
autonomy	1.08 [0.86, 1.37]	1.10 [0.53, 2.31]	0.76 [0.24, 2.34]
environmental mastery	0.84 [0.62, 1.12]	1.69 [0.74, 3.90]	1.13 [0.38, 3.51]
personal growth	1.33 [0.98, 1.80]	1.64 [0.78, 3.50]	2.02 [0.54, 7.87]
positive relations	0.84 [0.65, 1.09]	0.62 [0.28, 1.34]	0.62 [0.18, 2.06]
purpose in life	1.14 [0.89, 1.47]	1.18 [0.62, 2.27]	0.72 [0.28, 1.79]
self-acceptance	1.17 [0.89, 1.55]	0.66 [0.31, 1.38]	0.85 [0.28, 2.49]
Mysticism			
introvertive mysticism	1.21* [1.01, 1.46]	1.11 [0.70, 1.76]	1.53 [0.90, 2.71]
extrovertive mysticism	0.77** [0.65, 0.92]	1.04 [0.69, 1.56]	0.86 [0.51, 1.45]
interpretive mysticism	1.30* [1.03, 1.63]	1.16 [0.68, 1.98]	1.50 [0.76, 3.02]
Religious Schemata			
truth of text teachings	0.74*** [0.65, 0.85]	0.70 [0.44, 1.10]	1.00 [0.53, 1.89]
fairness tolerance	1.27* [1.01, 1.59]	0.81 [0.42, 1.55]	0.45 [0.11, 1.72]
xenosophia	0.97 [0.83, 1.13]	0.93 [0.57, 1.51]	0.85 [0.40, 1.80]

	Wave 1 (n = 1807)	Wave 2 (n = 310)	Wave 3 (n = 176)
	OR [95% CI]	OR [95% CI]	OR [95% CI]
Generativity	1.10 [0.79, 1.53]	1.24 [0.55, 2.84]	1.04 [0.26, 4.38]
Intolerance of Ambiguity		1.38 [0.54, 3.55]	0.17* [0.04, 0.73]
Need for Cognition		0.56 [0.22, 1.41]	0.17* [0.03, 0.80]
Fundamentalism		0.78 [0.49, 1.23]	0.90 [0.47, 1.68]
Pluralism		0.82 [0.56, 1.18]	0.78 [0.42, 1.44]

Note. Each column represents a model. Logistic regressions entered all predictor variables simultaneously in the same model. Each regression had the predictor variables and outcome variable measured at the same wave. Reference group of the outcome variable deconversion is non-deconvert. OR = odds ratio. An OR > 1 indicates that the variable is associated with a higher chance of deconversion. An OR < 1 indicates that the variable is associated with a lower chance of deconversion. * $p < .05$, ** $p < .01$, *** $p < .001$.

Finally, *country* correlates with self-reported deconversion, but with mixed effect in Wave 1 and Wave 3: Germans in the Wave 1 sample have a considerably higher chance of reporting deconversion ($OR = 1.84$, 95%CI: 1.44-2.37), while Germans in the Wave 3 sample appear to have considerably lower chance ($OR = 0.17$, 95%CI: 0.03-0.89).

Also, the concurrent correlations of the big five personality factors with deconversion show mixed results: At Wave 1 deconversion related positively to *openness to experience* ($OR = 1.54$ (95%CI: 1.18-2.02), and negatively to *conscientiousness* ($OR = 0.65$ (95%CI: 0.51-0.82). However, at Wave 2 and Wave 3 it is only *agreeableness* that, *positively*, correlates with deconversion ($OR = 2.62$, 95%CI: 1.29-5.47 and $OR = 3.83$, 95%CI: 1.19-13.36, respectively). Both *intolerance of ambiguity* and *need for cognition* have *negative* relation with deconversion at Wave 3, which is counter-intuitive for *need for cognition*. Closer inspection of the model revealed that *agreeableness* and *need for cognition* flipped the sign due to the inclusion of gender and education as control variables. This could possibly be due to the tendency that women are more agreeable, and the more educated people are, the higher their need for cognition.

For mystical experiences concurrent effects with deconversion were indicated only for Wave 1. Here, all three M-Scale factors were significant, with *introvertive mysticism* positively ($OR = 1.21$, 95%CI: 1.01-1.46), *extrovertive mysticism* negatively ($OR = 0.77$, 95%CI: 0.65-0.92), and *interpretation of mysticism* positively ($OR = 1.30$, 95%CI: 1.03-1.63) relating to self-reported deconversion.

Finally, we attend to the variables with specific information about religiosity and religious cognition. The self-rating of being religious is the single variable that negatively correlated with deconversion: in Wave 1 ($OR = 0.88$, 95%CI: 0.80-0.97), Wave 2 ($OR = 0.62$, 95%CI: 0.47-0.82), and Wave 3 ($OR = 0.40$, 95%CI: 0.25-0.62). From the subscales of the RSS, *truth of texts and teachings* concurrently correlated with deconversion in Wave 1, which was negative as expected ($OR = 0.74$, 95%CI: 0.65-0.85). *Fairness, tolerance and rational choice* had a positive concurrent correlation with deconversion in Wave 1 ($OR = 1.27$, 95%CI: 1.01-1.59).

Cross-wave Predictions of Deconversion

Analyzing the cross-wave correlations opens the perspective on predicting self-reported deconversion. Results are presented in Table 8.3, where each row represents a separate logistic regression model. In the first two columns, each regression included the predictor variables measured at Wave 1, controlled for age, gender, country, education, and for baseline deconversion. Outcome variable was either deconversion at Wave 2 (first column), or deconversion at Wave 3 (second column). In the third column, each regression included the predictors measured at Wave 2 and outcome deconversion at Wave 3, and controlled for baseline predictor at Wave 1, in addition to all other covariates in the models presented in the first two columns.

Starting with the big five personality factors, only *extraversion* and *agreeableness* measured in Wave 1 show a predicting effect on deconversion reported at a later wave; other factors of the big five such as *openness to experience* or *neuroticism* were not significant. *Extraversion* at Wave 1 negatively predicts deconversion at Wave 2 ($OR = 0.56$, 95%CI: 0.34-0.89) and at Wave 3 ($OR = 0.51$, 95%CI: 0.25-0.98). And agreeableness at Wave 1 negatively predicts deconversion at Wave 3 ($OR = 0.38$, 95%CI: 0.16-0.88).

Table 8.3: Cross-wave predictions of Wave 1 personality on self-reported deconversion at Wave 2 (column 1), deconversion at Wave 3 (column 2), and predictions of Wave 2 personality on deconversion at Wave 3.

Predictors	Wave 1 predicting Wave 2 deconversion ($n = 264$) OR [95% CI]	Wave 1 predicting Wave 3 deconversion ($n = 155$) OR [95% CI]	Wave 2 predicting Wave 3 deconversion ($n = 142$) OR [95% CI]
Self-Rated Religious	0.65*** [0.53, 0.78]	0.58*** [0.44, 0.75]	0.43** [0.25, 0.72]
Self-Rated Spiritual	1.03 [0.86, 1.23]	0.91 [0.69, 1.17]	1.08 [0.70, 1.67]
Five Factor Personality			
neuroticism	1.15 [0.80, 1.67]	1.71 [1.01, 3.02]	2.04 [0.89, 4.91]
extraversion	0.56* [0.34, 0.89]	0.51* [0.25, 0.98]	0.50 [0.16, 1.53]
openness to experience	1.21 [0.68, 2.15]	1.07 [0.48, 2.32]	1.68 [0.45, 6.29]
agreeableness	1.03 [0.58, 1.84]	0.38* [0.16, 0.88]	1.78 [0.58, 5.47]
conscientious-ness	1.11 [0.7, 1.77]	0.57 [0.28, 1.12]	1.06 [0.36, 3.01]
Psychological Wellbeing			
autonomy	1.14 [0.69, 1.87]	1.09 [0.56, 2.12]	0.65 [0.23, 1.84]
Environmental mastery	0.82 [0.55, 1.22]	0.51* [0.28, 0.89]	0.61 [0.26, 1.38]

Predictors	Wave 1 predicting Wave 2 deconversion (n = 264) OR [95% CI]	Wave 1 predicting Wave 3 deconversion (n = 155) OR [95% CI]	Wave 2 predicting Wave 3 deconversion (n = 142) OR [95% CI]
personal growth	0.93 [0.54, 1.60]	0.97 [0.43, 2.12]	0.70 [0.25, 1.90]
Positive *relations*	0.68 [0.44, 1.06]	0.38** [0.18, 0.74]	0.86 [0.33, 2.16]
purpose in life	0.74 [0.48, 1.12]	0.48* [0.25, 0.88]	0.59 [0.23, 1.43]
self-acceptance	0.79 [0.54, 1.15]	0.60 [0.33, 1.04]	0.41* [0.18, 0.89]
Mysticism			
introvertive mysticism	0.84 [0.65, 1.09]	0.75 [0.52, 1.08]	0.81 [0.44, 1.47]
extrovertive mysticism	0.84 [0.67, 1.05]	0.76 [0.54, 1.04]	0.95 [0.49, 1.79]
interpretive mysticism	0.74* [0.54, 0.99]	0.56** [0.35, 0.86]	0.87 [0.38, 1.99]
Religious Schema			
truth of text teachings	0.62*** [0.48, 0.80]	0.63** [0.45, 0.88]	0.80 [0.45, 1.39]
fairness tolerance...	0.87 [0.46, 1.65]	0.53 [0.20, 1.34]	0.96 [0.40, 2.30]
xenosophia	0.94 [0.69, 1.28]	0.87 [0.56, 1.32]	0.75 [0.36, 1.53]
Generativity	0.72 [0.37, 1.39]	0.48 [0.18, 1.24]	0.90 [0.21, 3.82]
Intolerance of Ambiguity			0.74 [0.28, 1.97]
Need for Cognition			0.56 [0.20, 1.54]
Fundamentalism			0.64 [0.40, 1.01]
Pluralism			0.81 [0.57, 1.14]

Note: Each row represents a separate logistic regression model. In the first two columns, each regression included the predictor measured at Wave 1, controlled for age, gender, country, and education measured at Wave 1, and controlled for baseline deconversion measured at Wave 1. Outcome variable was either deconversion at Wave 2 (first column), or deconversion at Wave 3 (second column). In the third column, each regression included the predictor measured at Wave 2 and outcome deconversion at Wave 3, and controlled for baseline predictor at Wave 1, in addition to all other covariates in the first two column models. The baseline Wave 1 predictor was not controlled for the last 4 variables due to unavailability. Reference group of the outcome variable deconversion is non-deconvert. * $p < .05$, ** $p < .01$, *** $p < .001$.

All variables in Ryff's Psychological Well-being and Growth Scale (1989; Ryff & Singer, 1996) that reached significance are *negative* predictors for deconversion. And interestingly, the well-being factors at Wave 1 unfold their effect on deconversion at Wave 3: Self-reported deconversion at Wave 3 is predicted by lower *environmental mastery* (OR = 0.51, 95%CI: 0.28-0.89), lower *positive relations with others* (OR = 0.38, 95%CI: 0.18-0.74), and lower *purpose in life* (OR = 0.48, 95%CI: 0.25-0.88). Also, deconversion at Wave 3 is predicted by lower *self-acceptance* at Wave 2 (OR = 0.41, 95%CI: 0.18-0.89).

From the Mysticism-Scale (Hood, 1975), neither *introvertive mysticism* nor *extrovertive mysticism* were significant, but only the third factor, *interpretive mysticism* at Wave 1 predicted, however negatively, deconversion at Wave 2 (OR = 0.74, 95%CI: 0.54-0.99) and Wave 3 (OR = 0.56, 95%CI: 0.35-0.86).

From the Religious Schemata Scale (Streib et al., 2010), the subscale *truth of texts and teachings* negatively predicted deconversion at Wave 2 (OR = 0.62, 95%CI: 0.48-0.80) and deconversion at Wave 3 (OR = 0.63, 95%CI: 0.45-0.88). The two other subscales, *fairness, tolerance and rational choice* and *xenosophia/inter-religious dialog* were not significant in predicting deconversion.

Finally, self-rated religiosity was the only, again *negative*, predictor for deconversion in all three waves: low self-rating as religious at Wave 1 predicted deconversion at Wave 2 (OR = 0.65, 95%CI: 0.53-0.78) and at Wave 3 (OR = 0.58, 95%CI: 0.44-0.75); low self-rating as religious at Wave 2 predicted deconversion at Wave 3 (OR = 0.43, 95%CI: 0.25-0.72).

To test the robustness of the significant effects, we also performed a sensitivity analysis on the significant effects. The e-values for effect estimates are the minimum strength of association that an unmeasured confounder would need to have with both the predictor and the outcome variable to fully explain away the observed effect, after accounting for the measured covariates (VanderWeele & Ding, 2017). A rough rule of thumb agreed by epidemiologists is that a e-value over 4 would indicate that the effect is robust against alternative explanations. The significant predictors including the odds ratio and the e-value is summarized in Table 8.4.

In predicting Wave 2 deconversion, people of high self-rated religiousness (OR = 0.65, e-value = 2.46), *extraversion* (OR = 0.56, e-value = 2.99), *interpretive mysticism* (OR = 0.74, e-value = 2.06), and *truth of text and teachings* (OR = 0.62, e-value = 2.59) were less likely to deconvert.

In predicting Wave 3 deconversion, people of high self-rated religiosity (OR = 0.58, e-value = 2.83), *extraversion* (OR = 0.51, e-value = 3.35), *agreeableness* (OR = 0.38, e-value = 4.69), *environmental mastery* (OR = 0.51, e-value = 3.35), *positive relations with others* (OR = 0.38, e-value = 4.75), *purpose in life* (OR = 0.48, e-value = 3.56), *interpretive mysticism* (OR = 0.56, e-value = 2.97), and *truth of text and teachings* (OR = 0.63, e-value = 2.53) were less likely to deconvert.

Part B: Results of Quantitative Analyses Including Qualitative Data

Table 8.4: Summary of Predictors of Self-rated Deconversion

Predictors for Deconversion	OR	e-value
Predictors for deconversion at Wave 2		
self-rating as religious (Wave 1)	0.65***	2.46
extraversion (Wave 1)	0.56*	2.99
interpretive mysticism (Wave 1)	0.74*	2.06
truth of texts and teachings (Wave 1)	0.62***	2.59
Predictors for deconversion at Wave 3		
self-rating as religious (Wave 1)	0.58***	2.83
extraversion (Wave 1)	0.51*	3.35
agreeableness (Wave 1)	0.38*	4.69
environmental mastery (Wave 1)	0.51*	3.35
positive relations with others (Wave 1)	0.38**	4.75
purpose in life (Wave 1)	0.48*	3.56
interpretive mysticism (Wave 1)	0.56**	2.97
truth of texts and teachings (Wave 1)	0.63**	2.53
Predictors for deconversion at Wave 3		
self-rating as religious (Wave 2)	0.43**	4.07
self-acceptance (Wave 2)	0.41*	4.35

Note: OR = odds ratio. All OR values are taken from Table 8.3. The e-values for effect estimates are the minimum strength of association that an unmeasured confounder would need to have with both the predictor and the outcome variable to fully explain away the observed effect, after accounting for the measured covariates (VanderWeele & Ding, 2017). A rough rule of thumb agreed by epidemiologists is that an e-value over 4 would indicate that the effect is robust against alternative explanations. * $p <$ .05, ** $p <$ .01, *** $p <$ .001.

The most rigorous test of prediction is presented in the third column of Table 8.3 and third block in Table 8.4. Those predictions not only controlled for the baseline deconversion but controlled for the baseline predictors. This rigorous design added another layer of protection: any unmeasured confound can only influence the results by having association with the predictor above and beyond the baseline exposure. People of high self-rated religiousness (OR = 0.43, e-value = 4.07) and *self-acceptance* (OR = 0.41, e-value = 4.35) were less likely to deconvert.

The predictors for self-reported deconversion in our three-wave data that are summarized in Table 8.4 can be divided into two groups: a) predictors of personality and personal well-being, and b) self-reported religiosity and religious cognition. Further, as Table 8.4 shows, all predictors are *negative*. This means that a) lower *extraversion*, lower *agreeableness*, and/or lower ratings on various *well-being factors*, and b) lower self-rated religiosity, lower agreement to the *truth of text and teachings*, and lower *interpretive mysticism* are among the predictors for deconversion at a subsequent time of measurement.

Discussion

The summarized results of this study confirm, but also refute, findings from our own previous Deconversion Study (Streib et al., 2009) and findings from other contributions to the study of deconversion that were noted in the Introduction of this chapter.

Comparison of Results with the Deconversion Study

The report from the Bielefeld-Chattanooga Study on Deconversion (Streib et al., 2009) noted, for deconverts, considerably higher *openness to experience*, and, for German deconverts, lower scores on *extraversion, agreeableness*, and *conscientiousness*; and, also for the German deconverts, lower ratings on the Ryff-Scale factors of *environmental mastery, positive relations with others, purpose in life*, and *self-acceptance* were noted. Further, deconverts were characterized by higher self-identification as "more spiritual than religious."

The clearly higher concurrent *openness to experience* has continued also in the Wave 1 data collected in the Bielefeld-Chattanooga Study on the Semantics of Spirituality (Streib & Hood, 2016), as documented in this study (see Table 8.1). However, what has emerged as significant concurrent correlation, does not necessarily become successful as predictor for deconversion reported at a later time. This is true for *openness to experience*, which, according to the results of this study, did not predict deconversion at all. This calls the assumption into question that deconversion is a function of the personality trait of *openness to experience*. However, (lower) *extraversion* did emerge as significant predictor for deconversion at Wave2 and Wave 3, and (lower) *agreeableness* for deconversion at Wave 3. This finding may support the assumption that personality has had an influence on deconversion: A highly extraverted person with eventually high agreeableness may have a considerably lower chance for deconversion at a later time.

The clearly lower well-being scores that were reported for the (German) deconverts in the Deconversion Study (Streib et al., 2009) were not continued in the later waves of our research: None of the Ryff-Scale factors did concurrently correlate with deconversion (see Table 8.2). Thus, the Deconversion Study findings may be unique to the sample gathered 2002–2005 and included a substantial portion of deconverts from high tension groups. Anyway, looking at the prediction of deconversion, it is surprising that certain factors of the well-being scale were significant. This changes the basic assumption that well-being is only to be regarded as outcome; This study documents predicting effects of well-being factors, since (low) *environmental mastery, positive relations with others*, and *purpose in life* at Wave 1 predict deconversion at Wave 3, and (low) *self-acceptance* at Wave 2 predicts deconversion at Wave 3.

Finally, deconverts in the Deconversion Study were characterized by higher self-identification as "more spiritual than religious." In this study, however, self-rated spirituality did not have any effect, neither concurrently, nor cross-wave. Instead, only self-rated religiosity has emerged as the variable with most consistent and powerful concurrent and cross-wave correlations with deconversion. The difference can partly be explained with the selection of variables: while the four-option item including "more spiritual than religious" was used in the Deconversion Study, the two self-ratings for religiosity and spirituality were used in this study. Thus, results from this study would translate in the prime role of the "neither religious nor spiritual" self-identification. The results from this study thus account for, and point to, the most effective correlate and predictor for deconversion—which is (low) religiosity.

Discussion of Results in Relation to Other Previous Research

One of the consensual results in the deconversion research literature regarding the prediction of deconversion is the effect of *neuroticism* (or reversed: *emotional stability*). This is reported in the studies of Saroglou et al. (2020) and in the longitudinal study of Hui et al. (2018), but not confirmed by the study of Stronge et al. (2020). The study reported in this chapter confirms Stronge et al.'s (2020) findings regarding the insignificance of *emotional stability*—which was not significant, neither concurrently, nor cross-wave.

Regarding *openness to experience* the Deconversion Study appears even more unique with its findings of strong correlations with deconversion, since not only this study, but also a series of other studies show no effect of *openness to experience* on deconversion (see Streib, 2021). This is different for *agreeableness*, however: Our finding that *agreeableness* at Wave 1 has strong ($OR = 0.38$) and powerful (e-value = 4.69) predicting effect on deconversion at Wave 3, clearly corresponds with Stronge et al.'s (2020) findings that lower scores for agreeableness were a significant predictor of deconversion in their longitudinal New Zealand sample.

Regarding well-being, the findings from extant research are rather incoherent and in part contradictory. While our findings of lower well-being scores for (German) deconverts in the Deconversion Study (Streib et al., 2009) could be interpreted as signs of a crisis, other research such as Nica's (2019) study of exiters from Christian fundamentalist groups indicate improved well-being after deconversion. Also, Hui et al.'s (2018, p. 116) study of Chinese deconverts concludes that "changes in psychological well-being are not identical for all faith exiters," but "for some, leaving the religion is psychologically beneficial; for others, leaving the religion has just the opposite consequence."

An explanation is offered by the study of Greenwald et al. (2018) who were the first to systematically study deconversion and reconversion with an attachment perspective. Especially their distinction between two developmental pathways, "emotional compensation" and "exploration," can be related to the results in this study: By the strong role of (low ratings on) the personality factor of *extraversion* and the strong role of various well-being factors (such as *environmental mastery, positive religions with others, purpose in life*, and *self-acceptance*), the findings in this study would suggest a central role of the *compensation pathway*, while the exploration pathway was stronger in the foreground in the original Deconversion Study (Streib et al., 2009). Thus, an explanation for the less favorable well-being is offered by Greenwald et al. (2018): lower well-being may be associated with attachment anxiety, and this association is stronger in deconversions on the compensation pathway.

Conclusion

It is one of the main findings of this study that deconversion dovetails with low self-rating for religiosity, (the interpretation of) mystical experience, and low scores on the religious schemata, especially on the subscale *truth of text and teachings*. Before these findings are dismissed as self-evident and uninteresting, it should be taken into account that the predictive, cross-wave correlations document that rejection or low appraisal for aspects of religiosity were there *five or ten years before* the deconversion has taken place. This is confirmation for the criteria that Streib & Keller (2004) have established for deconversion: loss of religious experiences, intellectual doubt, moral criticism, emotional suffering, and disaffiliation from the community. The results of this study suggest that four of these five criteria, or eventually only part of them, had been characteristics of people *years before* they actually experience the religious change that they will report as deconversion in the questionnaire. Our results are thus generally well understood in light of Hui et al.' (2018) conclusions, which suggest that changes in beliefs and values might have begun long before the actual faith exit, whereas personality change, if any, might take a long time after the transition.

An unexpected finding in this study was that lower well-being may contribute to the disposition for later deconversion. In predicting deconversion, certain factors of the well-being scale were significant. Thus, this study documents that (low) *environmental mastery, positive relations with others*, and *purpose in life* at Wave 1 predict deconversion at Wave 3, and (low) *self-acceptance* at Wave 2 predicts deconversion at Wave 3. Further, (low) *extraversion* has emerged as predictor for deconversion at Wave 2 and Wave 3. This not only calls into question the basic assumption that well-being is only to be regarded as outcome, but may reflect the predicting effect of low *emotional stability* as documented in previous research (Hui et al., 2018; Saroglou et al., 2020). In conclusion, this may suggest that, in our three waves after the initial Deconversion Study, there was a kind a paradigm change from the exploration model to the compensation model (according to Greenwald et al., 2018).

References

Bilsky, W., Janik, M., & Schwartz, S. H. (2011). The Structural organization of human values-evidence from three rounds of the European Social Survey (ESS). *Journal of Cross-Cultural Psychology, 42*(5), 759–776. https://doi.org/10.1177/0022022110362757

Budner, S. (1962). Intolerance of ambiguity as a personality variable. *Journal of Personality, 30*(1), 29–50. https://doi.org/10.1111/j.1467-6494.1962.tb02303.x

Cacioppo, J. T., Petty, R. E., & Kao, C. F. (1984). The efficient asessment of need for cognition. *Journal of Personality Assessment, 48*(3), 306–307.

Costa, P. T., & McCrae, R. R. (1985). *Revised NEO Personality Inventory (NEO PI-R) and NEO Five-Factor-Inventory (NEO-FFI). Professional Manual.* Psychological Assessment Resources 1992.

Greenwald, Y., Mikulincer, M., Granqvist, P., & Shaver, P. R. (2018). Apostasy and conversion: Attachment orientations and individual differences in the process of religious change. *Psychology of Religion and Spirituality*, https://doi.org/10.1037/rel0000239

Hood, R. W. Jr. (1975). The Construction and preliminary validation of a measure of reported mystical experience. *Journal for the Scientific Study of Religion*, 14, 29–41.

Hui, C. H., Cheung, S.-H., Lam, J., Lau, E. Y. Y., Cheung, S.-F., & Yuliawati, L. (2018). Psychological changes during faith exit: A three-year prospective study. *Psychology of Religion and Spirituality*, 10(2), 103–118. https://doi.org/10.1037/rel0000157

Hui, C. H., Lau, E. Y. Y., Lam, J., Cheung, S. F., & Lau, W. W. F. (2015). Psychological predictors of Chinese Christians' church attendance and religious steadfastness: A three-wave prospective study. *Psychology of Religion and Spirituality*, 7(3), 250–264. https://doi.org/10.1037/a0039216

McAdams, D. P., & de St Aubin, E. D. (1992). A theory of generativity and its assessment through self-report, behavioral acts, and narrative themes in autobiography. *Journal of Adult Development*, 62, 1003–1015. https://doi.org/10.1037/0022-3514.62.6.1003

Nica, A. (2019). Exiters of religious fundamentalism: Reconstruction of social support and relationships related to well-being. *Mental Health, Religion & Culture*, 22(5), 543–556. https://doi.org/10.1080/13674676.2019.1636015

Religion Monitor (2013). Religion Monitor 2012 [machine-readable data file] Bertelsmann Foundation.

Ryff, C. D. (1989). Happiness is everything, or is it? Explorations on the meaning of psychological well-being. *Journal of Personality and Social Psychology*, 57(6), 1069–1081. https://doi.org/10.1037/0022-3514.57.6.1069

Ryff, C. D., & Singer, B. H. (1996). Psychological well-being: Meaning, measurement, and implications for psychotherapy research. *Psychotherapy and Psychosomatics*, 65(1), 14–23. https://doi.org/10.1159/000289026

Saroglou, V., Karim, M., & Day, J. M. (2020). Personality and values of deconverts: A function of current on-belief or prior religious socialisation? *Mental Health, Religion & Culture*, 23(2), 139–152. https://doi.org/10.1080/13674676.2020.1737922

Steppacher, A., Streib, H., Bullik, R., & Keller, B. (2022). Recent research on deconversion. In H. Streib, B. Keller, R. Bullik, A. Steppacher, C. F. Silver, M. Durham, S. B. Barker, & R. W. Hood Jr. (Eds.), *Deconversion revisited. Biographical studies and psychometric analyses ten years later*. Vandenhoeck & Ruprecht. https://doi.org/10.13109/9783666568688.33

Streib, H. (2021). Leaving religion: Deconversion. *Current Opinion in Psychology*, 40, 139–144. https://doi.org/10.1016/j.copsyc.2020.09.007 (post-print: https://doi.org/10.31234/osf.io/r46qt)

Streib, H., & Hood, R. W. Jr. (Eds.). (2016). *Semantics and psychology of spirituality. A cross-cultural analysis*. Springer International Publishing Switzerland. https://doi.org/10.1007/978-3-319-21245-6

Streib, H., Hood, R. W. Jr., Keller, B., Csöff, R.-M., & Silver, C. (2009). *Deconversion. Qualitative and quantitative results from cross-cultural research in Germany and the United States of America*. Vandenhoeck & Ruprecht. https://doi.org/10.13109/9783666604393

Streib, H., Hood, R. W. Jr., & Klein, C. (2010). The Religious Schema Scale: Construction and initial validation of a quantitative measure for religious styles. *International Jour-*

nal for the Psychology of Religion, 20(3), 151–172. https://doi.org/10.1080/10508619.2010.481223

Streib, H., & Keller, B. (2004). The variety of deconversion experiences: Contours of a concept in respect to empirical research. *Archive for the Psychology of Religion*, 26(1), 181–200. https://doi.org/10.1163/0084672053598030

Streib, H., Keller, B., Bullik, R., Steppacher, A., Silver, C. F., Durham, M., Barker, S. B., & Hood, R. W. Jr. (2022). *Deconversion revisited. Biographical studies and psychometric analyses ten years later*. Vandenhoeck & Ruprecht. https://doi.org/10.13109/97836665 68688

Stronge, S., Bulbulia, J., Davis, D. E., & Sibley, C. G. (2020). Religion and the development of character: Personality changes before and after religious conversion and deconversion. *Social Psychological and Personality Science*, Article 1948550620942381. https://doi.org/10.1177/1948550620942381

Unesco Institute for Statistics. (2006). *International standard classification of education (ISCED 1997)*. UNESCO Institute for Statistics. http://www.uis.unesco.org/TEMPLATE/pdf/isced/ISCED_A.pdf

VanderWeele, T. J., & Ding, P. (2017). Sensitivity analysis in observational research: Introducing the E-Value. *Annals of Internal Medicine*, 167(4), 268–274. https://doi.org/10.7326/m16-2607

III. Part C: Longitudinal Case Studies—Qualitative Analyses Including Quantitative Data

Chapter 9
Reconstructing Individual Trajectories across Time:
A Short History and a Guide to Understanding
the Case Studies

Barbara Keller & Ramona Bullik[1]

Abstract *This chapter presents a brief history of the development of the methods on which we build our case studies, which we adapted to the longitudinal research design. Our current methods of triangulation of different types of data on the level of the single case and to work toward scientific accounts of situated individual faith development have evolved with the development of the research program, and with methodological discussion and innovation in psychology. We argue for a pragmatic approach, for formulating and using research questions to structure the choice of methods and their combinations for the study of single cases. We explain how research questions direct choice of cases and of methods for working toward a reconstruction of development based on individual trajectories for which we combine different types of methods and of data. We regard this as contribution to an ongoing dialogical engagement with qualitative and quantitative methods and nomothetic and idiographic scientific reasoning in our longitudinal mixed methods approach. To expand toward a longitudinal perspective means adding complexity, which grows with each additional point of measurement. We now follow change in individual reconstructions, in individual psychometrics, and personal definitions, obtained in three waves of data collection, and are preparing a fourth wave.*

Keywords: *individual development; faith development; narrative; longitudinal; mixed-method*

---

1   B. Keller, R. Bullik, Bielefeld University, Germany, E-mail: barbara.keller@uni-bielefeld.de. © Heinz Streib, Ralph W. Hood Jr. (eds.): Faith in Development. Mixed-Method Studies on Worldviews and Religious Styles. First published in 2024 by Bielefeld University Press, Bielefeld, https://doi.org/10.14361/9783839471234-011

Development of the Case Studies

Case studies based on James Fowler's Faith Development Interview (FDI, Fowler, 1981) have been part of our study of contemporary religiosities and worldviews from its beginning: Streib's (1999; 2000) earlier research on Christian fundamentalist biographies in Germany and his careful revisions of Fowler's work (see Streib, 2001; 2005) have fed into the conceptualizations of the case studies of German and US-American deconverts (Streib et al., 2009), which, in turn, inspired the consecutive study on the semantics of spirituality (Streib & Hood, 2016). Case studies combining qualitative with structural analyses of the FDI and with individual profiles on relevant psychometric scales proved to be a useful way of presenting results from a research design which includes a narrative method inviting people to share their experience of their faith or worldview as they understand it: The questions of the FDI elicit narratives, they open opportunities for participants to dive into the depths of their own biographies. Narrating and reviewing how their religiosity or worldview developed results in rich data. Working with these gets richer, but also more complex with longitudinal designs and consecutive interviews. Then, we also study the stability and change in how interviewees look back on their own development at different points in their lives. First efforts have been presented in the study on *Deconversion Revisited* (Streib, et al., 2022, see also Keller et al., 2022). For the case studies presented in this volume, this means tailoring qualitative analyses for each subject under study. This means attending to different perspectives: In a single FDI, participants explore their faith and their understanding of its development, and we, as researchers, take up these individual constructions to craft our interpretations. To our understanding of what people tell us in the interviews we add data from other sources: how they describe themselves on the psychometric scales we offer, and how they use the spaces in our surveys where they are invited to give their own definitions of central concepts of our research, such as "religion" or "spirituality." Thus, we gain individual psychometric profiles of variables which are connected to faith development, such as personality characteristics, markers of positive adult development, or religious schemata.

The interpretation of qualitative data together with individual scores on relevant scales has been part of this interdisciplinary research program from its beginning 20 years ago. While what started with the project on deconversion in Germany and the USA evolved into a longitudinal mixed-methods project, qualitative work has (re-)gained scientific acknowledgement in psychology. This is exemplified in a recent publication on the defining criteria and standards for qualitative work and their rationale:

> The term qualitative research is used to describe a set of approaches that analyze data in the form of natural language (i.e., words) and expressions of experiences (e.g., social interactions and artistic presentations). Researchers tend to centralize the examination of meanings within an iterative process of evolving findings—typically viewing this process as driven by induction (cf. Wertz, 2010)—and viewing subjective descriptions of experiences as legitimate data for analyses. (Levitt et al., 2018, p. 27).

From a cultural psychological perspective on the study of religion, Pak argues, in her recent monography (2020), for using narrative inquiry for the exploration of complexity as well as change. She discusses the familiar dualistic conceptions: paradigmatic vs. narrative thought (Bruner, 1986), quantitative vs. qualitative data, inductive vs. deductive reasoning, and the basic distinction of idiographic vs. nomothetic research (as derived from Windelband, and adapted by Lamiell, discussed in detail in Chapter 4, this volume). We agree with her call for methodological pluralism and her criticism of what she labels "misuse of mixed methods," referring to using qualitative methods as "handmaiden" (Pak, 2020, p. 7) to quantitative designs. This happens, as per Pak's criticism, when qualitative methods are restricted to exploratory purposes or qualitative data as input to be quantified for nomothetic research. Consequently, we suggest methodological pragmatism as option beyond asymmetrical dualisms. That means that we regard our scientific inquiry as ongoing process in a specific context which is guided by research questions and continuous reflections on methods. From the beginning with the deconversion study, this research combined deductive and inductive strategies (Streib et al., 2009, p. 50), making use of the "abductive" logic of moving between logical and methodically controlled conclusions and creative processes for the generation of new insights (see Chapter 4), qualitative methods being used as central part of a mixed-methods design.

Case Studies in Mixed-Methods Designs of the Research Program

We have, in the past, worked with mixed research designs when creating "maps" for the explorations of research landscapes. We started with outlines of what we already knew about the territory, about its landmarks, and with tools for the identification and documentation of new findings—for example, collecting data on deconversions, attending to surveys as well as interview studies (see Streib et al., 2009, Chapter 2). The detailed study of deconversions was based on a sample of deconverts with diverse (former) religious affiliations in Germany and the US, and included, for thorough comparison, interviews with current members of the respective groups as well as a larger diverse sample of questionnaires. Thus, it was possible to study single cases against the background of general trends in psychometric variables characterizing specific subsamples or the whole sample, and in results from the structural analysis of the FDI (according to the latest version of the Manual for Faith Development Research; see Fowler et al., 2004; Streib & Keller, 2018).

We looked for general trends and for options of "zooming in" on special areas of interest for more detailed analysis of single trajectories and subjective reconstruction. Group-based statistics were used to create individual profiles based on single scores on relevant scales. In our case studies, our efforts to chart single trajectories, we have included those profiles in joint discussion of data from other sources such as structural analyses of the FDI and narrative analyses of what people told in their interviews. The research design also allowed for comparisons between the individual profiles of specific deconverts with average profiles of current members of the communities they had left in an additional effort to explore gains and losses involved in deconversion. Thus, we have adapted and redrawn maps to document deconversion in Germany and the US, joining quantitative and qualitative data on different levels of analysis.

Beginning with the Deconversion Study, an important step was to derive markers from then available literature, like the five deconversion criteria and the six exit trajectories, and to apply these in a top-down process (Streib et al., 2009 p. 107). This helped us structure the complete set of quantitative data, and, for example, state that half of the deconverts in our sample had left the field of organized religion. While this method of group-based analyses informs about general trends, it stays silent on biographical particularities and culturally as well as historically situated individual trajectories as well as subjective perspectives on one's development. Therefore, we relied on interpretative bottom-up strategies for the analysis of single autobiographical interviews. Thus, we attended to deconversion processes portrayed in the context of individual autobiographical reconstructions. Carving out specific themes and dynamics and comparing our findings across different interviews, we came to suggest four clusters organized around four ideal types which we named *Pursuit of Autonomy*, Debarred from Paradise, *Finding a New Frame of Reference*, and *Lifelong Quests—Late Revisions* (Streib, et al., 2009, p. 109–110).

Why is this retrospective on the beginning of our research important? In our first effort at a longitudinal perspective on *Deconversion Revisited*, we also revisited this typology (Streib, et al., 2022, p. 293–297). The general map based on the mixed-methods research design and the roadmaps for zooming in on subjective individual reconstructions and processes, the methods for the case studies, have been adapted. We also adapted the efforts to deepen understanding of general trends by zooming in on individual cases, as well as efforts to better understand individual trajectories by comparing them with relevant results from group-based analyses and surveys. Together with new entries of markers of the development of religion and worldview, such as the religious types (see Chapter 1) this has informed the development of the research enterprise from which we now, in this volume, report the results of a third wave of data collection. Thus, in our research we have, from the start, worked within as well as between paradigms and research perspectives in a pragmatic way. We have combined, in our designs, the "paradigmatic mode" of "formal mathematical systems of description and explanation" with the "narrative mode" of "meaning that is ascribed to experiences through stories" (Pak, 2020, p. 5), when we used psychometric measures, structural analysis of the FDI, and narrative analyses of subjective reconstructions of faith development. We reported statistical analysis, in line with the claim that "good paradigmatic explanations should accurately predict observable phenomena," and case studies and typologies of cases, in line with the claim that "good narratives should meaningfully capture the shifting contours of lived experience" (ibid.).

Capturing Complex Longitudinal Individual Trajectories

For further differentiation and illustration of the complexity of the development of our designs we may consider Pak's discussion of the distinction of "small q" and "Big Q," suggested by Kidder & Fine (1987): Small q refers to the question set in qualitative paradigm (e.g. open-ended questions in surveys) and the incorporation of non-numerical data in hypothetico-deductive designs using predetermined categories. Big Q refers to open-ended inductive methodologies to generate theory and new insights. Pak cautions to gloss over differences in "purpose, logic, and assumptions" which characterize qualitative versus quantitative methods: The goal of qualitative research is not generalization in terms of probabilistic generalizable explanations (Pak, 2020, p. 8), while quantitative research is not meant to apply to every individual in a given population but to capture trends (ibid., p. 9). A model longitudinal "Big Q" study might be Josselson's (2017) research that followed the development of women's identities.

However, for mixed methods designs things are more complex. Therefore, we see here a call for further differentiation and suggest to distinguish between the contexts of data collection and the contexts of data processing and data analysis and to focus on the different scientific perspectives involved. For example, we might speak of "Big Q" for qualitative data or idiographic data collection or rather data generation as in an interview, which is then followed by inductive analyses, and of "small q," if such data is processed via procedures of counting or rating according to predefined "nomothetic" categories, such as FDI ratings according to the current manual. Vice versa we might speak of "small n" (for quantitative or nomothetic) when referring to individual profiles on psychometric scales, which are used in narrative as well as qualitative case studies, and of "Big N" when referring to psychometric scales used for group based quantitative analyses.

We work between deduction and induction, drawing on data of qualitative and data of quantitative origin, submitting these data to quantitative or qualitative steps of further evaluation. Finally, we proceed to integrate the insights gained toward a portrayal of the trajectory of a single case, which can be compared to trajectories of other cases. How does this affect how we conceive of our data?

Types of Data, Types of Analysis: Working from Individual toward Typical Trajectories

What happens, for example, when we include single scores on psychometric scales in case studies? We might regard this as a "small q" strategy of using data from research based on a quantitative paradigm, which is then transferred to the qualitative context of exploring single cases. However, the aim is not to submit quantitative data to qualitative logic. Rather, including single scores on scales in case studies gives these "quantitative" data a qualitative or narrative turn. This is achieved by taking what supposedly measures—according to nomothetic logic—the calculated differences in degree of a specific common psychological marker, a variable, between persons to the idiographic context of the reconstruction of an individual life at a specific point in time and a specific period of individual development. Responses to questionnaires can, from a narrative perspective, be regarded as drastically restricted answers to questions offered in a highly standardized language. The restriction to marking a point on a scale (usually ordinal, but treated as interval or even ratio) is intended to allow comparison across individuals who are supposedly using the same scale of evaluation. From a narrative perspective, we can understand concordant or contradictory patterns in single profiles as concordant or contradictory self-presentation. We follow individual patterns of change or stability when looking at individual responses to psychometric scales across time. Thereby we take individual response patterns on the respective scales as, albeit restricted, patterns of answers to questions, which we have asked with each survey. We use the single profiles of psychometric scores as summary of individually meaningful answers to questions. Thus, we translate and transfer quantitative data to a qualitative as well as narrative interpretation. Taking up Pak's discussion and expanding on Kidder and Fine's terminology, we might label this transfer as "small n."

To this interpretation of single trajectories, we add other information on the respective single case, such as structural analyses of the FDI (see below for a brief description of this method), which could be characterized as "Big Q" regarding data collection by interview, and "small q" regarding the rating, to be followed by the "Big Q" step of interpretation in the context of the single trajectory. Narrative analyses of what a single person has told across consecutive interviews might qualify for straight "Big Q". Thus, in our case studies, we look at individual trajectories across time:

a. based on data of *qualitative* origin when we follow answers to the same questions, trace narratives or leitmotifs (Big Q),
b. drawing on data with *qualitative origin* and *quantitative processing* such as structural analyses of the FDI resulting in religious styles and further calculation to religious types (Big Q at data collection, small q at next step of data processing, and Big Q at interpretation in case study),
c. using data of *quantitative origin*, and qualitative processing, when we look for individual change and stability in psychometric measures (small n).

Thus, we use data of qualitative and quantitative origin, some of which have been submitted to further qualitative or quantitative processing, and work them into the narrative of a case study. When we look for individual configurations of psychometric measures, and then compare these configurations to summary configurations such as aggregated psychometric data of groups or subgroups, we stay within the boundaries of the quantitative methods – and might speak of "Big N" for "nomothetic."

What we do when attending to single cases, and what has been described as triangulation on the level of the single case (see Chapter 4, this volume) can, in turn, be used to reflect back on group-based quantitative analyses. We can locate single scores within distributions of scores within our sample or subsamples. Thus, we can "zoom in" and see how well specific as well as complex individual profiles are captured by observed general trends and thus give observations of general trends more depth. This gets more complex in longitudinal perspective, when we include comparisons of trajectories.

From a qualitative and narrative perspective, we strive to work toward describing typical trajectories. Typical is different from "representative" in the sense of likely occurrence in a specific population. For further differentiation of typicality, we use the concept of "theoretical representativeness"—a term suggested in German sociology:

> Rather, according to their claim, qualitative studies are representative of the spectrum of empirically founded theoretical concepts in which the empirical conditions can be adequately depicted. One could therefore sensibly speak of theoretical representativeness. (Hermanns, 1992, p. 116)

Qualitative studies are not representative in a statistical sense. They do not state how frequently facts can be found in a defined population. Qualitative studies claim representativity in terms of empirically grounded theoretical concepts, in which empirical facts can be adequately represented. In our research we are interested in this criterion, and have, for example, in earlier research looked for persons with deconversion experiences or people interested enough in questions of religion and spirituality to accept our interview invitation. However, we strive for more and therefore include basic demographic characteristics and psychometric data which allow to contextualize and situate our complex case-based research results.

A longitudinal perspective of religious development has first been the focus of the studies in *Deconversion Revisited* covering two waves (see Streib et al., 2022). The contributions in this volume here now cover three waves of data collection. Therefore, the format of the case studies had to be adapted first to the longitudinal designs, and, second, to specific research questions arising from previous research und interpretations as well as findings emerging from the new material (for a more thorough description, see Keller et al., 2022; also Bullik, 2024). In all cases, combining data from the surveys and findings grants, "on an idiographic level, insight into the interviewees' religious schemata, well-being, personality traits and so on as well as their developments" (Chapter 4, this volume), while, at the same time, we are able to follow cases in their changing socio-historical contexts (see Chapter 3). This allows us to widen the perspective, to compare cases inter-individually and to find new lines of comparison for structuring the cases under study.

Therefore, we chose cases of maximal difference in terms of demographics, and included, where possible, a comparative perspective. The next paragraph will detail what kind of data and analyses exactly we put into the case studies, followed by the research questions that were leading in writing each chapter and an introduction to the cases.

What Goes into Longitudinal Case Studies?

The different maps that are layered above one another to create a case study have already been introduced in Chapter 4, illustrated with the basic framework of a case study, emphasizing the mixed-methods character of our approach. Thus, it shall suffice here to summarize rather briefly how different data are presented in our case studies:

The chapters start with short *biographical outlines*, summarizing basic demographics (partly derived from the questionnaire data) and important markers of the individual biography (as they are reported by the individual in their interviews). Note that already in this first step we use data based on quantitative and qualitative methods.

Next follows a look into the *psychometric profile* derived from the survey data, showcasing scores from the NEO-FFI (Costa & McCrae, 1985; for basic personality traits), the Ryff Scale on Psychological Well-Being (Ryff, 1989; understood here as adaptations in specific dimensions of adult development), the Religious Schema Scale (Streib et al., 2010; which assesses religious/worldview schemata), and the Mysticism Scale (Hood, 1975; as indicator of experienced-based religiosity, spirituality, or relation to the transcendent). When used in an individual profile, psychometric scores are seen as "parts of the story," in longitudinal perspective as changing parts of a changing story. We take landmarks from the map of the whole area (i.e. the whole sample) to map longitudinal individual development by offering a comparison of single case scores with the means and the standard deviations of the sample.

The *structural analysis* captures religious styles which account for the way a person deals with questions of ultimate concern, how they reconstruct their relationships and the way they engage with others (for a comprehensive introduction to this topic, see Streib & Keller, 2018; Bullik, 2024). Quantifying those ratings, religious types are computed (Streib et al., 2020), which give an overall estimation of the style predominant in one interview. Longitudinally, those types offer insights into developments and trajectories over the life span and allow to zoom in on change in specific aspects (Bullik, 2024). This structural analysis strives to work toward patterns underlying the actual content of the interviews offering a more abstract depiction which is based on developmental concepts, on faith development theory and the religious styles perspective, and not attending to the variety of the contents of autobiographical reconstructions that we find in the interviews.

Accordingly, we view the *content and narrative analysis* as the key instruments used for the case studies. The *content analysis* offers the option to find themes and topics in a top-down fashion as well as attend to particularities that are not captured by the other methods mentioned above and which are found in a bottom-up process (see Chapter 4; Bullik, 2024, 2021). The *narrative analysis* captures linguistic particularities like argumentation strategies and pays special attention to little narratives (Labov & Waletzky, 1967) that are often interwoven in the participants' accounts; a special form of those narratives, we have, in an earlier project, identified as religious identity narratives (Keller, Coleman III, & Silver, 2016). Moreover, this analysis attends to the negotiation that happens between biographical accounts and prevalent master narratives (see Chapter 3). Both the content and the narrative characteristics are assessed using two distinct coding guidelines that are still under development to be made available in manualized form (see Appendix B for an excerpt of the current form). In longitudinal perspective, we follow narratives and leitmotifs across different points of measurement as well as different developmental periods, thus documenting and studying change as well as stability on the level of individual autobiographical (re-)construction.

In other words: we start with a rudimentary map structured by age and related developmental tasks, gender, nationality, religious or worldview orientation, and info on trajectories. Then, by careful case-based analyses drawing on psychometric and interview data, we explore further options to map individual trajectories and define lines of case-by-case comparison. Self-report measures like those used in our surveys, and, similarly, self-presentations in the FDI, may be affected by social desirability, impression management depending on the agenda a person has in mind when describing themself according to the options offered by a scale. We also conduct interviews because we are interested in how respondents reconstruct and understand their religiosities or worldviews as embedded in their own lives, while being aware that this need not necessarily be closer to any "objective" truth. Different degrees of accuracy of self-observation, different degrees of willingness to self-disclose, may challenge any method aiming at understanding people. Thus, with the combination of these different approaches, we aim at balancing possible biases and achieve a more holistic picture of the portrayed person. The structure laid out here, though, is an idealized one and does not appear in its full form in all of the case studies presented here. This will be explained by the different research questions and approaches that the author teams adopted with the respective case study. With growing complexity due to more points of measurement, it felt necessary, while maintaining a common framework, to set special foci, either guided by research questions, or by the special features offered by one case or the perspective of comparison. Demographic markers, for example, already stimulated first formulations of research questions. These were further refined, and additional research questions were formulated during the process of triangulating data from different sources on the level of the individual case and in longitudinal and in most chapters, also inter-individually comparative perspective. Summed up, the approach we took here can be labeled as pragmatic approach (see Chapter 4; also: Bullik, 2024), choosing "the combination or mixture of methods and procedures that works best for answering [our] research questions" (Johnson & Onwuegbuzie, 2004, p. 17).

How Research Questions Structure Case Studies: Introducing the Cases

The cases for the chapters in Part C of this volume were chosen (a) to cover the adult life span from emerging/young adulthood to young old age. The aim also was (b) to present cases from the two different research contexts, USA and Germany. And (c) we selected the cases to cover religious as well as non-religious trajectories. Thus, we aim at teasing out lines of comparison, based on single case-by-case comparisons, which follows an idiothetic approach as introduced in Chapter 3. For an overview, we refer the reader to the figure in Chapter 3 in which we illustrate the age distribution of the cases and, moreover, emphasize the socio-historic contextualization that will play a role in the reconstruction of the individual biographies. Here, starting with the research questions on which the choice of the cases has been based, we give a brief introduction to the cases and their specifics.

Thus, we explore in the following chapters:

- *How are non-religious trajectories from emerging to young adulthood narrated and accounted for in different cultural contexts?* Chapter 9 will portray Isabella from the USA and Nadine from Germany, who are young adults in their 20s in Wave 1, thus constituting a minimal contrast regarding age and life phase, gender, and religion/worldview, offering the possibility for cross-cultural comparison. Both cases deal with the question of what comes after death, yet with strikingly different answers. Similarly, they discuss the question what it means to not believe in a higher power and to not have a rulebook to follow.
- *How can a spiritual as well as atheist perspective develop in different political systems?* In Chapter 10, we introduce Petra who serves, in a single case study, to illustrate the type of a spiritual atheist, while at the same time giving a thorough insight into what it was/is like to be living in three different Germanies (childhood/adolescence in the GDR; shortly before the Reunification, she fled to what then still was West-

Germany and has, by Wave 3, moved to the Eastern part of meanwhile re-unified Germany—back in terms of geography, but not in terms of political development). Petra, whom we followed across earlier middle age, cultivates science as a form of faith while struggling with a society that does not seem to live up to her standards. With these special characteristics, she proved to be such a unique case that the we decided for a single case study.

- *How do Protestants, interviewed across transitioning from later middle to early old age, look at their involvement with and development within, their respective affiliations?* Chapter 11 presents a cross-cultural comparison focusing on two middle-aged people with a Protestant background. Gisela (Germany) and George (USA) have both, more or less constantly, been members of their Protestant communities, yet the chapter will carve out the quite different developments that are possible, regarding for example the subjective religiosity or their approach to moral questions. Gisela and George are, in contrast to the other case studies portraying two cases, presented separately to pay tribute to the very different Protestant developments within the respective cultural context.

- *How do people in the later phases of their lives rely on their traditional Christian affiliations as they are coping with the challenges of late life?* "The impact of exclusivist faith in old age" is shown in Chapter 12, illustrated by the two German cases of Heidemarie and Berthold, who were chosen due to their rather conservative approach to questions of faith and the certainty with which they present their beliefs. They have lived their lives in times of war and conflict, which they reconstruct very differently. Therefore, we decided to start their case study with a focus on the reconstructions of their consecutive life reviews instead of a biographical outline. They constitute interesting examples of a *Substantially Ethnocentric Type* that may, in Heidemarie's case, still develop into a higher type in old age; in Berthold's case, this type is found in his last interview, regressing to the *Substantially Ethnocentric Type* from the *Predominantly Conventional Type* in his previous interviews. However, as the case studies show, religious change and development can mean more than advancing in the hierarchies of religious types, and movement downward can be subjectively functional.

While the research questions address core areas of religious development, we expect the case studies to not only offer answers. We also expect new lines of comparison and perspectives for new research questions to emerge since case studies involve explorative work, which allows to find new insights—both into single cases, but also across cases by identifying typical cases, cases best representing access to the questions under study. In our mixed-methods design, we analyze different types of data with different methods of data analysis and interpretation: Predominantly qualitative "Big Q" might mean to condense interpretations of qualitative data based on accumulating case studies and systematic comparisons of interpretations. This allows, building on the revision presented in *Deconversion Revisited*, to suggest a more comprehensive update of our typologies of religious and worldview development elaborated so far. This "Big Q" would, however, contain the "small ns" of individual psychometrics which were included in the case studies.

Narrative methods may also inspire transfer of new content or connections found in a single case to the level of the study of aggregated data, for example following trajectories of representative groups of young atheists in different cultures. This would, however, mean more than "small q" or, in Pak's words, qualitative research as handmaiden. Rather, it would imply careful translation of constructs from "q" to "n," for example, from creative as well as theory-guided interpretation to formulating and validating coding instructions. This would also open options to explore how well single cases can be captured with a common method or by a general concept. Do we get a plausible distribution of cases if we, as we did in the *Spirituality Study*, align the cases along *openness for experience* and *mysticism*? How does this comprehensive view relate to an open comparative exploration of the cases regarding "depth" and "breadth" of their faiths and worldviews? We offer some suggestions in our concluding chapter.

References

Bullik, R. (2024). Leitmotifs in life stories. Reconstructing subjective religiosity and narrative identity—developments and stabilities over the adult lifespan. Bielefeld University Press.

Costa, P. T., & McCrae, R. R. (1985). Revised NEO Personality Inventory (NEO PI-R) and NEO Five-Factor-Inventory (NEO-FFI). Professional manual. Psychological Assessment Resources 1992.

Fowler, J. W. (1981). Stages of Faith, San Francisco: Harper&Row

Fowler, J. W., Streib, H., & Keller, B. (2004). *Manual for faith development research*. Research Center for Biographical Studies in Contemporary Religion.

Hermanns, H. (1992). Die Auswertung narrativer Interviews. Ein Beispiel für qualitative Verfahren. In J. H. P. Hoffmeyer-Zlotnik (Ed.), *Analyse verbaler Daten. Über den Umgang mit qualitativen Daten* (pp. 111–137). Westdeutscher Verlag.

Hood, R. W. (1975). The construction and preliminary validation of a measure of reported mystical experience. *Journal for the Scientific Study of Religion*, 14(1), 29. https://doi.org/10.2307/1384454

Johnson, R. B., & Onwuegbuzie, A. J. (2004). Mixed methods research: A research paradigm whose time has come. *Educational Researcher*, 33(7), 14–26. https://doi.org/10.3102/0013189X033007014

Josselson, R. (2017). *Paths to fulfillment. Women's search for meaning and identity*. Oxford University Press.

Keller, B., Bullik, R., Klein, C., & Swanson, S. B. (2018). Profiling atheist world views in different cultural contexts: Developmental trajectories and accounts. *Psychology of Religion and Spirituality*, 10(3), 229–243. https://doi.org/10.1037/rel0000212

Keller, B., Bullik, R., Steppacher, A., Streib, H., & Silver, C. F. (2022). Following deconverts and traditionalists. Longitudinal case study construction. In H. Streib, B. Keller, R. Bullik, A. Steppacher, C. F. Silver, M. Durham, S. B. Barker, & Hood, Jr., Ralph W. (Eds.), *Deconversion revisited. Biographical studies and psychometric analyses ten years later* (pp. 83–108). Vandenhoeck & Ruprecht. https://doi.org/10.13109/9783666568688.83

Keller, B., Coleman III, T. J., & Silver, C. F. (2016). Narrative reconstruction and content analysis. Content analysis in the interpretation of "spiritual" biographical trajectories for case studies. In H. Streib & Hood, Jr., Ralph W. (Eds.), *Semantics and psychology of spirituality: A cross-cultural analysis* (pp. 251–271). Springer. https://doi.org/10.1007/97 8-3-319-21245-6_16

Keller, B., Streib, H., Silver, C. F., Klein, C., & Hood, R. W. (2016). Design, methods, and sample characteristics of the bielefeld-based cross-cultural study of "spirituality". In H. Streib & J. R. W. Hood (Eds.), *Semantics and psychology of spirituality: A cross-cultural analysis* (pp. 39–51). Springer. https://doi.org/10.1007/978-3-319-21245-6_4

Kidder, L. & Fine, M. (1987). Qualitative and quantitative methods: When stories converge. New Directions for Program Evaluation; volume 1987, issue 35, page 57–75; ISSN 0164–7989 1551-2371. https://doi.org/10.1002/ev.1459

Labov, W., & Waletzky, J. (1967). Narrative analysis: Oral versions of personal experience. *Journal of Narrative and Life History*, 7(1–4), 3–38. https://doi.org/10.1075/jnlh.7.02nar

Levitt, H. M., Bamberg, M., Creswell, J.W., Frost, D.M., Josselson, R. & Suarez-Orozco, C. (2018). Journal article reporting standards for qualitative primary, qualitative meta-analytic, and mixed methods research in psychology. *American Psychologist* 73(1), 26–46. http://dx.doi.org/10.1037/amp0000151.

Pak, J. H. (2020). Integrating psychology, religion, and culture. The promise of qualitative inquiry. *Psychology and Religion.* Brill.

Ryff, C. D. (1989). Happiness is everything, or is it? Explorations on the meaning of psychological well-being. *Journal of Personality and Social Psychology*, 57(6), 1069–1081. https://doi.org/10.1037/0022-3514.57.61069

Streib, H. (1999). Sub-project on 'biographies in christian fundamentalist milieus and organizations.' In Deutscher Bundestag, Referat Öffentlichkeitsarbeit (Ed.), *Final report of the Enquête Commission on 'So-called Sects and Psychogroups'* (pp. 402–414). Bonn.

Streib, H. (2000). Biographies in christian fundamentalist milieus and organizations. Report to the Enquete Commission of the 13th German Parliament on "So-called Sects and Psychogroups". translated by Ella Brehm, Center for the Interdisciplinary Study of Religion and Society, Bielefeld.

Streib, H. (2001). Faith development theory revisited: The religious styles perspective. *International Journal for the Psychology of Religion*, 11(3), 143–158. https://doi.org/10.1207/S 15327582IJPR1103_02.

Streib, H. (2005). Faith development research revisited: Accounting for diversity in structure, content, and narrativity of faith. *International Journal for the Psychology of Religion*, 15, 99–121. https://doi.org/10.1207/s15327582ijpr1502_1

Streib, H., Hood, R. W., & Klein, C. (2010). The religious schema scale: Construction and initial validation of a quantitative measure for religious styles. *International Journal for the Psychology of Religion*, 20(3), 151–172. https://doi.org/10.1080/10508619.2010.48122 3

Streib, H., Chen, Z. J., & Hood, R. W. (2020). Categorizing people by their preference for religious styles: Four types derived from evaluation of faith development interviews. *International Journal for the Psychology of Religion*, 30(2), 112–127. https://doi.org/10.108 0/10508619.2019.1664213

Streib, H., Chen, Z. J., & Hood, Jr., Ralph W. (2021). Faith development as change in religious types: Results from three-wave longitudinal data with faith development interviews. *Psychology of Religion and Spirituality.* https://doi.org/10.1037/rel0000440

Streib, H., & Hood, J. R. W. (Eds.). (2016). Semantics and psychology of spirituality: A cross-cultural analysis. Springer. https://doi.org/10.1007/978-3-319-21245-6

Streib, H., Hood, R. W., Keller, B., Csöff, R.-M., & Silver, C. F. (2009). *Deconversion: Qualitative and quantitative results from cross-cultural research in Germany and the United States of America*. Vandenhoeck & Ruprecht. https://doi.org/10.13109/9783666604393

Streib, H., & Keller, B. (2018). Manual for the assessment of religious styles in faith development interviews (Fourth, revised edition of the "Manual for faith development research"). Universität Bielefeld.

Streib, H., Keller, B., Bullik, R., Steppacher, A., Silver, C. F., Durham, M., Barker, S. B., & Hood, Jr., Ralph W. (Eds.). (2022). *Deconversion revisited. Biographical studies and psychometric analyses ten years later*. Vandenhoeck & Ruprecht. https://doi.org/10.13109/9783666568688

Chapter 10
Varieties of Non-Belief in Young Adulthood.
A Cross-Cultural Comparison of Nadine and Isabella

Ramona Bullik, Martin Hornshaw, & Daimi Shirck[1]

Abstract *This chapter compares the trajectories of two young women: one from the US and one from Germany. While Isabella from the US defines herself as atheist and neither religious nor spiritual, Nadine (Germany) rejects the attribution as atheist; however, she self-identifies as more spiritual, yet at the same time does not report being affiliated with any religion[2]. Both share the self-assessment of being rather non-sociable and not within the mainstream of their generation. They also report having been in contact with religion in their childhood. Childhood religious exposure did not seem to have any significant effect on Nadine, but Isabella describes her experiences in Christian summer camps and Sunday schools as unpleasant. This may contribute to her complete rejection of religiosity later, which is much stronger and more pronounced than is the case with Nadine, who has dealt, on an intellectual level, with a variety of religions in her adolescence when she was exploring her identity. This chapter will therefore give an interesting insight into the varieties of non-belief in young adulthood as well as into cultural differences regarding the necessity to have a label for one's (non-)belief. It is argued that in the US being religious in any form still is the norm, and being an "outed" atheist means deviating from that norm, while any form of non-belief is no big deal in Germany. The chapter will also shed some light on the question how an atheist worldview may develop over time, exemplified with the question of what happens after death.*

Keywords: *atheism; non-belief; religious development; death; meaning-making*

---

1   R. Bullik, M. Hornshaw, Bielefeld University, Germany, E-mail: barbara.keller@uni-bielefeld.de; D. Shirck, University of Tennessee at Chattanooga, USA. © Heinz Streib, Ralph W. Hood Jr. (eds.): Faith in Development. Mixed-Method Studies on Worldviews and Religious Styles. First published in 2024 by Bielefeld University Press, Bielefeld, https://doi.org/10.14361/9783839471234-012

2   Nadine has been portrayed as well in Bullik (2024). Parts of the analysis for this case have been taken from this work and carefully adapted to fit the format of this chapter. Isabella was first portrayed in Coleman et al. (2016) with a focus on carving out how a worldview is constructed without a religious or spiritual framework.

Part C: Longitudinal Case Studies—Qualitative Analyses Including Quantitative Data

People studying the psychology of religion have a soft spot for those who claim to believe in nothing—atheists and non-believers have been intensively studied in the past 10–15 years (cf. Cragun, 2016, for an overview). Silver and colleagues (2014), for example, have found six different types of non-belief, ranging from Academic Atheists over Seeker Agnostics to Non-Theists. A publication from our research group has identified differences in non-belief depending on the overall religious landscape, comparing atheists and other non-believers from Germany and the USA (Keller et al., 2018). However, longitudinal research on how those who do not believe in a God and do not follow any denomination is widely missing. Therefore, this chapter will, in an exemplary fashion, outline the trajectories of two young women, from the US and from Germany, following the question how meaning-making happens in non-religious people and how they approach questions of ultimate concern. The choice of cases will moreover allow for tentative comparisons of the German and the US religious landscape, even though we are well aware of the fact that this landscape is multi-faceted and highly dependent on one's actual environment. However, the two cases seem comparable to a certain degree as they are both college-educated and living in an urban area. Both of them were first interviewed in the course of our study investigating subjective meanings of spirituality (Streib, 2016) and have been interviewed twice since; additionally, both of them have, at each timepoint, filled out our surveys, allowing us to add their quantitative results to our primarily qualitative narrative analysis of their interviews.

Nadine, from Germany, is 25 years old at the time of the first interview and 34 at the third timepoint. During her first and second interview, she was studying in a social science program at university, while at time 3 she states that she is "working." Nadine reports having had a difficult time during her adolescence, even considering suicide at some point. She seems, in the interviews, rather introvert, her answers being often short and abstract. Isabella from the US, on the other hand, even though she directly describes herself as an introvert, seems much more eloquent when talking about her life. She is 26 at the time of her first interview and 35 when she was last interviewed. She had just finished college at time 1 and has by time 3 moved back in the area where she originally came from and where her parents still live. Both women do not report any denomination, yet otherwise they are pretty different in their approaches to the questions we want to investigate here. The chapter will start with a look into their respective survey data and their religious styles and types derived from the structural analysis of their interviews. The major part, though, will be taken up by an in-depth analysis of selected answers of the interviews, with the aim to carve out the individual changes and stabilities.

Selected Results from Survey Data

Taking seriously the idea of data triangulation, we first look separately at the different kinds of data that were aggregated in the course of the studies. That way, each kind of data can be assessed isolated from each other and then, in a next step, synergized and interpreted in their interplay. Starting with selected scales from the extensive surveys that have always been part of the study design, we get a first impression of religious schemata, well-being, personality traits and mystical experiences as they are assessed by the participants themselves. Looking first at Nadine's survey data, we see that her scores on the Religious Schema Scale (RSS, Streib et al., 2010) do not deviate too much from the means of the total sample (*n*=75).

Table 10.1: Nadine's Scores on Selected Scales from the Surveys

	Wave 1		Wave 2		Wave 3	
	Nadine	*M (SD)*	Nadine	*M (SD)*	Nadine	*M (SD)*
Religious Schema Scale						
truth of texts and teachings	2.00	2.53 (1.14)	1.40	2.35 (1.13)	1.40	2.55 (1.12)
fairness, tolerance...	4.40	4.38 (0.38)	5.00	4.35 (0.51)	4.80	4.59 (0.40)
xenosophia	4.60	3.64 (0.82)	3.40	3.58 (0.78)	4.00	3.77 (0.78)
Ryff Scale						
autonomy	4.00	3.69 (0.58)	3.86	3.32 (0.49)	3.43	3.31 (0.53)
environmental mastery	3.14	3.65 (0.75)	2.43	3.67 (0.63)	2.14	3.66 (0.67)
personal growth	4.71	4.31 (0.48)	4.29	4.14 (0.49)	4.14	4.28 (0.52)
positive relations	3.29	3.89 (0.67)	2.71	3.91 (0.68)	2.57	3.97 (0.72)
purpose in life	3.43	3.80 (0.68)	3.14	3.78 (0.63)	3.29	3.72 (0.62)
self-acceptance	3.14	3.75 (0.77)	3.14	3.83 (0.69)	2.86	3.87 (0.67)
NEO-FFI						
emotional stability	3.08	3.40 (0.82)	2.67	3.40 (0.74)	2.50	3.41 (0.70)
extraversion	2.92	3.29 (0.62)	2.42	3.28 (0.66)	2.08	3.19 (0.64)
openness to experience	3.50	3.92 (0.49)	3.92	3.89 (0.5)	3.75	3.96 (0.55)
agreeableness	3.17	3.74 (0.46)	3.33	3.75 (0.49)	3.17	3.85 (0.52)
conscientiousness	3.92	3.69 (0.54)	3.92	3.73 (0.53)	3.92	3.79 (0.54)
M-Scale						
introvertive mysticism	4.92	3.52 (1.16)	4.00	3.60 (1.00)	5.00	3.40 (1.00)
extrovertive mysticism	4.25	3.45 (1.19)	4.25	3.46 (1.10)	4.50	3.29 (1.23)
interpretation	4.00	3.65 (1.11)	3.42	3.72 (1.00)	4.17	3.63 (1.00)

Nadine's scores on *truth of texts and teachings (ttt)* are low, indicating that she rejects the notion of gathering unambiguous truths from a (religious) text. Seeing that her score declines between times 1 and 2, it may be argued that this conviction manifests even further. Especially interesting to see is that her score for *xenosophia (xenos)*, the subscale measuring the extent to which a person is willing to engage with the strange and to appreciate the encounter with the unknown, is not stable: starting with a high score at time 1 which is well above the average of the sample, this score drops significantly at time 2 (albeit within the standard deviation of the sample mean), only to rise again, but not as high as it used to be, at time 3. Taken together, these observations might indicate that Nadine is a woman who rejects a fundamentalist approach to religion and, in tendency, appreciates the encounter with new and diverse views, but with constraints that may be attributed to other meaningful results from the survey.

In her answers on the Scale for Psychological Well-Being (Ryff Scale; Ryff, 1989; Ryff & Keyes, 1995), we see that she is, more than the average of the sample, struggling to find purpose in life, to establish and maintain positive relations with others, and to "choose or create environments suitable to [...] her psychic conditions" (Ryff, 1989, p. 1071), to a varying, yet in tendency even declining degree. Similar tendencies can be found on the NEO-FFI subscales *emotional stability* (which is neuroticism reversed) and *extraversion*, low scores on which might possibly point to a personality prone to depression (cf. Costa & McCrae, 1985/1992). Combining these results with her scores on *xenos*, we might have a character here that is willing to engage with the strange, yet is inhibited at times by other personality traits.

Interesting, and to be further investigated in the content analysis, is the fact that Nadine scores high on all subscales of the Mysticism Scale (M-Scale; Hood, 1975; Hood et al., 2001; Streib, Klein et al., 2021). On the subscale *introvertive mysticism*, which focuses on experiences related to the internal world of the individual, Nadine shows, at times 1 and 3, very high scores, indicating that she, despite not calling herself religious, experiences mystical experiences in forms of, for example, dreams, visions, etc. *Extrovertive mysticism* is also high, pointing to a feeling of the "outward merging with the wholeness of all existence" (Keller et al., 2016, p. 43). Lowest of the subscales is *interpretation*, which, with its aspect of positive affect, sacredness and noetic quality, might not seem as fitting to Nadine.

Overall, we have the first impression of Nadine as a person who rejects an orthodox approach to questions of faith, who seems to be struggling in some places of her life and personality, and who has, even though she does not identify with any form of religion, a high affinity to what we call mystical experiences.

Turning now to Isabella, we see an even lower score on *ttt*, but, and that is an interesting difference, also rather low scores, yet rising, for *xenos*. It seems as if, despite displaying a high appreciation for fairness, tolerance, and rational choice (*ftr*), that Isabella is, at time 1, hesitant to engage with the alien and only when proceeding further in young adulthood is she able to appreciate more the benefits that emerge from those encounters.

Table 10.2: *Isabella's Scores on Selected Scales from the Surveys*

	Wave 1		Wave 2		Wave 3	
	Isabella	M (SD)	Isabella	M (SD)	Isabella	M (SD)
Religious Schema Scale						
truth of texts & teachings	1.20	2.53 (1.14)	1.00	2.35 (1.13)	1.00	2.55 (1.12)
fairness, tolerance…	4.80	4.38 (0.38)	4.60	4.35 (0.51)	5.00	4.59 (0.40)
xenosophia	2.60	3.64 (0.82)	3.20	3.58 (0.78)	3.60	3.77 (0.78)
Ryff Scale						
autonomy	3.43	3.69 (0.58)	4.00	3.32 (0.49)	4.00	3.31 (0.53)
environmental mastery	4.57	3.65 (0.75)	3.86	3.67 (0.63)	4.14	3.66 (0.67)
personal growth	3.71	4.31 (0.48)	4.29	4.14 (0.49)	4.86	4.28 (0.52)
positive relations with others	4.71	3.89 (0.67)	4.86	3.91 (0.68)	5.00	3.97 (0.72)
purpose in life	4.43	3.80 (0.68)	4.43	3.78 (0.63)	4.29	3.72 (0.62)
self-acceptance	4.71	3.75 (0.77)	4.86	3.83 (0.69)	4.57	3.87 (0.67)
NEO-FFI						
emotional stability	3.92	3.40 (0.82)	3.92	3.40 (0.74)	3.67	3.41 (0.70)
extraversion	3.08	3.29 (0.62)	3.33	3.28 (0.66)	2.92	3.19 (0.64)
openness to experience	4.25	3.92 (0.49)	4.42	3.89 (0.50)	3.83	3.96 (0.55)
agreeableness	3.92	3.74 (0.46)	4.25	3.75 (0.49)	4.67	3.85 (0.52)
conscientiousness	4.25	3.69 (0.54)	4.00	3.73 (0.53)	4.08	3.79 (0.54)
M-Scale						
introvertive mysticism	1.42	3.52 (1.16)	1.33	3.60 (1.00)	1.67	3.40 (1.00)
extrovertive mysticism	1.63	3.45 (1.19)	1.38	3.46 (1.10)	1.13	3.29 (1.23)
interpretation	2.25	3.65 (1.11)	2.17	3.72 (1.00)	1.92	3.63 (1.00)

Isabella shows increasing scores on the subscale *personal growth*, indicating that, after having finished her studies and having started her career, she is focused on achieving goals of personal enhancement and promotion. At the same time, her scores for *self-acceptance* are comparably high, which points to a personality that is self-assured and content with their place in life, which is a stark contrast to what we have seen in Nadine's data. Isabella obviously also is a person who strives to get along well with others, as mirrored in her high scores on *positive relations with others* and *agreeableness*. As for her scores on the M-Scale, we see that the items offered to her here were at no timepoint very appealing. It appears that she does not identify at all with any form of mystic experience.

So, as a short interim comparison we have the data of two young women with different types of personality. While Nadine appears to be insecure with regard to herself as well as others, yet with an appreciation for the mystical and unexplainable, Isabella

Summary of Their Religious Styles and Types

Turning now to the interviews of our two cases, we first take a look at the structural evaluation of their Faith Development Interviews (FDI) which is done, in the last wave at least, based on the instructions in the *Manual for the Assessment of Religious Styles* (Streib & Keller, 2018), coming up with, ideally, 25 ratings of a person's religious styles. In the earlier waves of this longitudinal project, an earlier version of the *Manual* was used (Fowler et al., 2004). Some of these older ratings did not seem plausible to us anymore when looking at them from today's perspective, so they were redone with careful consideration of both the former rater's argumentation as well as the coding criteria as formulated in the most recent version of the *Manual*. This form of structural analysis gives a very good insight into the way a person thinks about questions of faith and morality and the way they structure their world and 'make meaning.' Sorting the 25 questions of the interview into six aspects, we get a comprehensive and multi-faceted look at people's 'faith,' thereby, of course, applying Fowler's encompassing definition that has been presented in Chapter 4. The respective single ratings are, in a next step, transformed into more general religious types (Streib et al., 2020; Streib, Chen et al., 2021). These types serve as a means to follow trajectories regarding the religious development of our participants.

As for her religious type, Nadine is classified as a mover upward. While, at time 1, her interview has the exact same number of Style 3 and 4 assignments and is therefore sorted into the *predominantly individuative-reflective type*, her second interview is characterized with the *predominantly conventional type*, indicating a predominantly conventional approach to our questions. At time 3, however, she has moved on to the *predominantly individuative-reflective type*. At time 3, most of Nadine's answers were rated Style 4, indicating an increase of explicit reasoning, the explicit reference to the larger society and the ability to critically reflect on one's own viewpoints. Most striking are the ratings for her answers to the questions "What does death mean to you?," and "How do you explain the presence of evil in our world?," both of which were rated Style 5 in the third interview.

Isabella, on the other hand, is classified as a stayer after carefully re-rating both her time 1 and time 2 interview which resulted in a different type estimation of her time 1 interview, while the type assigned to her time 2 interview stayed the same. Her answers were rated, with varying frequency, mostly to be Style 4, individuative-reflective, meaning that Isabella is mostly able to think systematically and take into consideration different viewpoints, without, however, letting her stance be truly challenged by those different from her own. Her overall religious type is therefore determined to be the *predominantly individuative-reflective type*.

So, taken together, both women show a tendency toward the *predominantly individuative-reflective type*, even though there seems to be more movement in Nadine's structural evaluation than in Isabella's and the former is even tentatively showing some Style 5 ratings in her last interviews. In order to see what these ratings mean content-wise and how these styles flesh out differently in two persons who have been estimated, in a first interpretation of the quantitative data, to be rather different, we now turn to key aspects in the interviews.

Early Religious Socialization and Search for Meaning

3.1 Nadine

Nadine's interviews are comparably short, and especially the answers to the first, more biography-oriented questions suggest that she is reluctant to share too much personal information or does not know how to talk about her life and her relationships in an adequate way. We learn, looking closely at her interviews, that she in general is rather shy and, more or less implicitly, and that she feels she does not fit into social groups.

She talks, rather in by-passing, about her socialization, being brought up by a single mother and taken care of by her maternal grandmother as well. This grandmother obviously has been an important person for Nadine; however, we do not get to know details about her or the relationship. What is mentioned, though, is that her grandmother was Catholic and Nadine went to a Catholic kindergarten:

> I went to a Catholic kindergarten, where we made nice things around Easter, like the Easter story and stuff like that, but I did not relate to that. As a child, I guess, you usually just don't. Like, of course, you just participate and there was this Jesus and this God, as you teach this to children, I knew all of that. But I never had any personal relationship. Like, I did not grow up super faithful or anything, not at all. My mom totally left it up to me what I do with that. I went to that kindergarten by chance because it was close, [...]. Like, sure, granny says stuff like, the good God will cry because you've been naughty, that's what they tell you as a child. But I couldn't relate to this, like, this didn't scare me as a child or something, it was just neutral.[3] (Nadine, FDI, time 1)

Nadine talks about a childhood which she spent partially with her Catholic grandmother and in a Catholic kindergarten. However, this did not seem to have any effect on her and she talks about that in a distanced way. She characterizes those experiences as being a norm, obviously not realizing that what her grandmother told her may not have actually been the norm. But Nadine states that none of these experiences affected her in any emotional way, neither scaring nor impressing her, implying that she has never been suscep-

---

3   Ich war auf einem katholischen Kindergarten, da hat man ja immer was gemacht ganz nett zu Ostern, Ostergeschichte und dies und das, aber da hatte ich kein Bezug dazu. Als Kind, glaube ich, hat man das auch nicht so richtig. Also klar, man hat das alles mitgemacht und da war der Jesus und das war der Gott, wie man das halt so den Kindern beibringt, das kannte ich alles. Aber so ein persönliches Verhältnis dazu hatte ich nicht. Also ich bin auch nicht streng gläubig oder so aufgewachsen, gar nicht. Meine Mama hat mir das völlig freigestellt, was ich da mache. Ich war dann zufällig auf dem Kindergarten, weil der in der Nähe war, [...]. Also klar, die Oma sagt dann, der liebe Gott weint, weil du böse warst und so, das kriegt man ja zu hören als Kind. Da konnte ich aber nichts mit anfangen, also das hat mich als Kind nicht verängstigt oder irgendwie, es war einfach neutral.

Part C: Longitudinal Case Studies—Qualitative Analyses Including Quantitative Data

tible for any form of religious proselytization. In her other interviews, this first contact with religion is only mentioned in a half-sentence (time 2) or not at all (time 3).

In Nadine's interviews, we can detect a journey, a search for hope, support, and meaning. And even though Nadine arrives at a worldview which is not decidedly religious (see paragraph below), on this journey she engages with religion:

> I have relatively early, at the age of 10, 11, started to deal with religion. When I was 13, I read the Bible. [...] Yeah, I just wanted, I was in search of... Like, I wanted to see what benefits do people gain from that? Does it make sense? Does it not make sense? How do I position myself? I wanted to experience all of this. [...] So, I was always in search of how other people do that [...] and processed a lot, thought a lot, read a lot.[4] (Nadine, FDI, time 1)

Here, she portrays herself as a person who is well-read; having read the Bible completely by the age of 13 may be seen as a rebellious act because by doing so, she seems to deviate a lot from what would normally be expected from a teenager. The reason why she did that, though, seems to have to do less with wanting to be different, but because she wanted to understand the benefits people gain from being religious. It seems that she was hoping for support and to find meaning, maybe not only in the religious area, but as a means to better understand people in general.

At time 2, this search is framed as follows:

> I was always searching for my worldview and really engaged with a lot of things, with religion, philosophy, I read the Bible from the beginning to the end, I engaged with Buddhism a lot, like, the things you do [...]. During a period when I felt really bad, I was kind of searching again in some form, I guess, but yes, actually, I've not been searching actively for anything for years now because, for me, it's okay as it is. [...] I'm rather flexible in my mind and perhaps I'm not really able to assemble a fixed worldview, which is something to get to grips with of course.[5] (Nadine, FDI, time 2)

Her answer takes up very similar topics: she talks about her searching movements and the ways she engaged with different approaches to answering her questions, to perhaps

---

4   Ich habe mich dann relativ früh, so mit 10, 11 ging es langsam los, angefangen mit Religion zu beschäftigen. Ich habe, als ich 13 war, die Bibel gelesen. [...] Ja, ich wollte einfach, ne, ich war quasi auf der Suche ne. Also wollte einfach gucken, was haben die Leute davon. Macht das Sinn? Macht das keinen Sinn? Wie stehe ich dazu? Ich wollte das alles erfahren. [...] Also ich war eigentlich da immer sehr viel auf der Suche zu gucken, wie machen das andere Menschen [...] und habe da auch ganz viel verarbeitet, drüber nachgedacht, viel gelesen. [...].

5   [Ich] war erst einmal eigentlich immer auf der Suche nach meinem Weltbild und habe mich wirklich auch viel mit allem Möglichen beschäftigt, mit Religion, Philosophie, ich hab die Bibel von vorne bis hinten gelesen, ich habe mich mit Buddhismus viel beschäftigt, also, was man dann so tut [...]. Ich hab es dann auch nochmal in der Phase, wo es mir recht schlecht ging, war ich glaube ich auch noch irgendwie am Suchen in irgendeiner Form, aber ja, also ich suche schon seit vielen Jahren eigentlich nicht mehr aktiv nach irgendwas, weil das so für mich in Ordnung ist, wie es ist. [...] Ich bin da eher sehr flexibel im Kopf und bin vielleicht auch nicht so richtig in der Lage, mir ein Weltbild fest zusammen zu bauen, womit man natürlich dann auch erst einmal klar kommen muss..

finding support and stability, emphasizing, again, the intellectual way she deals with these topics, this time, however, marking it as an expected behavior ("like, the things you do"). More emphasis is put on herself being at peace with the fact that she could not come up with a fixed worldview. Having to deal with an unstable worldview is described as hard work ("which is something to get to grips with of course"), but she can accept it now just as it is, implicitly characterizing herself as strong and autonomous, as a person who can live without easy and unambiguous answers. Another way to interpret this, though, may be that she, at some point, gives up the attempt to find answers to very difficult questions.

At time 3, this search is brought up again, however, this time, the topic is not named to be religion, but instead, more general, worldview:

> Since I was eight, I think, I slowly started to ponder, do I have a worldview? And if so, what does it look like? [...] And since then I've usually been looking at multiple different worldviews. So, in the end, for me it is difficult because every person has a view of the world, and so do I. But I could not assert that I have a fixed worldview. There are just too many variables that I cannot take into account objectively because I am a subjective being, [...]. For my life, I just try to figure out what is important in the respective situation or relevant or what is useful. [...] So, I have engaged with that a lot, met people accordingly and questioned them about their faith. [...] At least, for me, that widened my horizon concerning other people, and therefore contributed to my basal understanding of the world, so, in the end, to my worldview, which I can't really grasp because it is not fixed.[6] (Nadine, FDI, time 3)

We can still see the search for meaning ("try to figure out what is important in the respective situation"), but it seems like Nadine has, by time 3, changed the way she approaches those different worldviews: while at time 1 and time 2, she talks about reading a lot, here she explains how she has met different people with different backgrounds (and it is implied that she maybe even sought those encounters deliberately) and thereby widened her own horizon. These encounters also help her get a better understanding of the world and of her own stance towards it, even though she still arrives at the conclusion that her worldview cannot be fixed because there are too many unknown variables. This indicates a certain tendency to hold her own worldview higher than that of others, since she does

---

6   Ich habe dann irgendwann so ab acht, glaube ich, habe ich langsam angefangen, mir zu überlegen, habe ich ein Weltbild? Und wenn ja, wie sieht es aus? [...] Und seitdem schaue ich mir in der Regel recht viele Weltbilder an. Also letztendlich ist es für mich schwer, weil sich natürlich jeder Mensch ein Bild von der Welt macht, also auch ich. Aber ich könnte jetzt nicht von mir behaupten, dass ich ein festes Weltbild hätte. Es sind einfach zu viele Variablen, die ich nicht alle objektiv berücksichtigen kann, weil ich ein subjektives Wesen bin, [...]. Ich versuche eben, für mein Leben dementsprechend mir das rauszusuchen, was gerade in der Situation wichtig ist oder relevant ist oder mir grad nützt. [...] Also ich habe mich da viel mit beschäftigt, habe auch entsprechend Menschen kennengelernt und die befragt zu ihrem Glauben. [...] Das hat zumindest, glaube ich, auch meinen Horizont, was andere Menschen betrifft, erweitert, ja, und dementsprechend ja auch zu meinem basalen Verständnis der Welt beigetragen, also letztendlich auch zu meinem Weltbild, was ich schlecht greifen kann, weil es nicht fix ist.

Part C: Longitudinal Case Studies—Qualitative Analyses Including Quantitative Data

not deem it very plausible to hold firm beliefs. In the end, she concludes that those encounters have helped her understand people as a whole better.

Turning to Isabella, we will see how she talks about her religious socialization and how she came to be an atheist.

3.2 Isabella

Like Nadine, Isabella has experienced religion as a child. Her mother being a "staunch" Lutheran (as Isabella puts it), she made Isabella go to church every Sunday which she was not very fond of, even though, in hindsight, she admits that it was not that awful. However, she recalls, at time 1, an experience in a Christian summer camp which is marked as important by the way Isabella talks about it, framing it in a little narrative which can be divided according to the schema introduced by Labov and Waletzky (1967), adapted by Habermas and Berger (2011) and introduced into the research on religious identity by Keller et al. (2016):

Table 10.3: Isabella's Narrative: "Christian Summer Camp"

Orientation	So, I did have a Christian background, but it never, kind of like, caught on.
Complication	[...] And I even remember, specifically, one summer they had this like summer of camp for kids [...] and my mom made me attend some year and I really didn't want to, 'cause you know summer was the time for like not doing stupid church things. One craft they had us do was make these suns with, like, tissue paper in the middle so you could, like, hang them up in a window or something and [...] construction paper cutouts and they'd have you write "I love Jesus" in the middle. And I don't remember how old I was at the time, maybe around like eight to ten and I refused to write "I love Jesus."
Evaluation	And I don't know if I was just at this point, I honestly can't say because I was just bitter about having to go or because at that point I knew it was a lie and I didn't want to put that down. But I wrote "I love myself" on mine and I brought it home and hung it
Resolution	'cause, you know you can't argue with a kid that says, "I love myself" and you can't say, (exaggerated voice) "No, you're not allowed to love yourself!"
Coda	Um, so I think even back then, I kind of had this idea of like, this just doesn't make sense to me. (Isabella, FDI, time 1)

Here, Isabella brings up a criticism toward her mother who made her attend that church camp, so the pretext for this episode might as well be read as an (early) adolescent rebellion. Reconstructing her motivation for refusing to fulfill the task as it was intended, Isabella muses that it may just have been an act of bitterness "about having to go," but then resolves to interpret this episode as an early indicator for having intellectual doubts toward the church and for detecting a form of hypocrisy within that context. Interestingly, she omits the reactions she received from the adults (which might be due to the fact that it was not such a big thing for them in the first place), but it becomes clear that she expects her behavior to be rated as deviant. This episode for her symbolizes her early distancing from the church and from the faith her mother wanted to acquaint her with.

At time 2, this episode is only brought up again when the interviewer asks for it specifically, the act itself not taking up much space, yet preluded with a framing that shows a more abstract way of thinking about the situation:

> I was still pretty young, so I don't know how much I can trust my memories [...]. I do remember the incident as, at least I interpret it now as an early instance of non-belief. Um, but, again, I don't know if that is just how I'm interpreting it now, because I did eventually become an atheist, uh, versus I don't know if I was just angry that day and being stubborn. [...] At the time I must have been somewhere between 8 and 12. Um, so I don't think children really can understand religious concepts, a child's religion is just parroting back whatever they're taught. And they are just starting to really think about it in context and be able to evaluate the truth behind these things. So I interpret it now as being an early sign of saying, "No, I don't accept your religion." (Isabella, FDI, time 2)

Her developmental status is emphasized more here, serving as an autobiographical argument (Köber & Habermas, 2017) to emphasize that she was just a child and she cannot reliably reconstruct her motives from back then. That may be the reason why she did not bring up this episode of her own accord since she is not sure whether the gravity of this situation is over-estimated from her current atheist standpoint. But even though she states that she may not have been fully able to understand what she was doing and why, she evaluates this scene to be a first sign for her upcoming atheism and her rejection of her mother's faith. At time 3, she is very brief regarding her upbringing, mainly she just repeats that her mother made her go to church on Sundays. Since that interview as a whole is rather short, it can only be suspected that she has continued her way of integrating that experience into her narrative identity and that the story of how she became an atheist is not as relevant for her current positioning.

While Nadine explicitly speaks about a search for meaning, it is not that clear how Isabella came to be an atheist. Mainly, we have to stick to her statement that the Christian faith "never, kind of like, caught on" (time 1). However, her Christian roots become apparent from time to time as can be illustrated in this quote when she talks about making important decisions and the time when she decided to propose to her boyfriend:

> And specifically related to atheism, I also had to think to decipher what does being married mean for me. Because like I said earlier, as an atheist you don't have a book that says: The Meaning of Life, you don't have a book that is The Meaning of Marriage. [...] It can't just be like, "What does marriage mean to the Catholic church?" [...] Why would I want to get married? What does a commitment mean? So that was a big decision for all of those factors. (Isabella, FDI, time 1)

As she states on various occasions throughout her first two interviews, being an atheist means you have to figure out things for yourself, suggesting that there is no universal guideline that gives advice on how to handle things. When she thinks about getting mar-

216 Part C: Longitudinal Case Studies—Qualitative Analyses Including Quantitative Data

ried, she feels like she has to find an answer to the question what that would mean for her all on her own, in opposition to a Catholic who would be able to hold on to a set of traditional values and answers. It seems that she feels left alone and that this decision is bigger for her than it would be for someone with a strict religious background. To make up for this, she is a member of a local atheist group which she cherishes because she shares a lot of interests with the people she meets there, atheism being but one topic among others during their meetings. This feeling of being part of a community is something, according to Isabella, a lot of people seem to miss when they leave the church because it is hard to come up with an alternative since "atheists kind of lack that pillar to gather around. Because it's hard to gather around something that you don't believe in" (time 1).

At time 2, when she is asked directly to talk about how she came to her non-belief, she describes a search for meaning and how she participated in various religious and spiritual groups while she was in high school and college, concluding, however:

> Actually I took a class on Buddhism in college, because it seemed interesting. Um, and also in college, um, one of roommates was actually a Hare Krishna, so I heard about their faith. Not that she was like trying to convert me in anyway, but just through discussions with her because it was interesting. [...] Um, so I certainly had exposure to different faiths and I was never drawn towards any of them, and never took anything specific as the one truth. Um, so I did firm up on the atheism idea, um, but just as a course of self-understanding overtime, not necessarily as any specific epiphany or specific incident. (Isabella, FDI, time 2)

Isabella lists here in detail the occasions in which she got in contact with different faiths, sometimes actively seeking those encounters, sometimes by chance. She emphasizes that she valued all those encounters and the opportunities to discuss matters of religion and morality with different people. However, and that is the reason why Isabella's interviews have an overall estimation of being a the *predominantly individuative-reflective type* (and not an *emerging dialogical type*), Isabella does not really let herself be changed by those "strange" opinions. For her, these discussions affirm her non-belief, a process which is, as she says herself, not going along with any sudden realization or epiphany, but rather by being confirmed over and over again. At time 3, she basically affirms this by describing that it was a process of realizing that what she had been believing (or, rather, not believing) actually had a label.

Besides identifying as an atheist, she also calls herself a humanist (see below); but she has another label for herself that she strongly promotes especially at time 1: moderate hedonism. This term is defined as "just try and have a good time" (time 1), which she, at another point in the interview, elaborates as "just do fun stuff that wouldn't ever be lucrative," in opposite to doing work to earn a living. By time 3, these statements that reflect on her rather young age at that time, have grown into a more abstract statement when asked about whether her life has meaning at present:

> Yes, definitely. So, I don't necessarily believe that life has an outside or inherent or imposed meaning. I definitely think it's what you make of it. Everyone here is given a life, and have to do the best they can with it. And so it's a very self-guided system.

> So, for me personally, I think it's really just, I don't know, a lot of things. So, like the search for self-improvement. I'm always trying to be the best person I can. (Isabella, FDI, time 3)

This statement encompasses her lack of guidance as well as her plea for authenticity and individualism. She has developed the thought of missing a set of principles into a "self-guided system" which is, in her notion, driven by the idea to do the best you can. It remains unclear here what that means exactly, but, at least in this answer, Isabella is mostly focused on her own self-improvement and not that much invested in caring for the welfare of others. This finding, however, goes along with her increasing score on *personal growth* of the Well-Being Scale.

Having now presented the reconstructions of their religious socialization, we now turn to the content of Nadine's and Isabella's worldview. How do they define what they believe and how does that translate into values and morality?

Worldviews without a God

In order to get access to the way Nadine and Isabella define their worldview, we take a look at different kinds of data: first, the free entries from the survey which asked the participants to define both religion and spirituality. Additionally, also from the survey, we provide the self-assessment of whether they define themselves as "more religious than spiritual," "either religious and spiritual," "more spiritual than religious," or "neither religious nor spiritual." These rather short definitions and assessments are then compared with the answer to question 20 of the FDI: Do you consider yourself a religious, spiritual, or faithful person? That way, we hope to have a multi-faceted impression of the way each of the two cases assesses the thematic complex of religion/spirituality.

4.1 Nadine's Worldview

Nadine, throughout all waves, self-identified as "more spiritual than religious." And even though, according to her interviews, she does not identify with any form of religion, she also rejects the label "atheist." As will be seen in Table 10.4, Nadine's belief system obviously cannot be assessed with conventional categories.

218   Part C: Longitudinal Case Studies–Qualitative Analyses Including Quantitative Data

Table 10.4: Data on Nadine's Worldview

Nadine	Wave 1	Wave 2	Wave 3
Free entries	*spirituality*: There is nothing that's not spiritual, I view everything that is as spiritual. Terminologies are a matter of interpretation and I see a definition of something not as the only, but as one possibility among others.	*spirituality*: "Geistigkeit, Geistliches" (which both, in English, translate to the term spiritual(ity), with the connotation of mental, intellectual)	*spirituality*: "Geistig-keit," inner life
	religion: For me personally, religion means: religiare – reconnection (to God). In my common parlance for me it means, though: a human construct, created to hold on to and produce meaningfulness	*religion*: belief system with metaphysical or transcendental content	*religion*: literally: reconnection
Self-assessment	more spiritual than religious	more spiritual than religious	more spiritual than religious
Answer to Q20: Do you consider yourself a religious, spiritual, or faithful person?	Umm, spiritual. But like I said, spiritual, what does that mean? [...] For me, it's not connected with a community or with a little group that I hang out with or with a denomination. [...] I think to be spiritual, for me that's just trying to live consciously and to the best of my knowledge and to be mindful and to try to look behind things and just be open for everything [...], because the other person is a part of the creation just like me, why should they be wrong and I am right? No, that's not plausible and that's why spirituality for me is an awareness of this level on which there is no valuation. On my lower human level, I evaluate just like any other person does.	Definitely not faithful. Religious in the sense it is connotated in our society today—neither. Most likely I would probably say I have a spiritual element, at least due to my experiences and because I engaged with that a lot, like during adolescence, when I was still searching. I engaged myself a lot with faith, religion, and spirituality and from this, spirituality—as the term is used—is what's closest to me. Like, actually I would describe myself as a latently spiritual person. [...] I used to wish sometimes that I could [be religious], because it's nice to have a system you can hold on to,	Umm, of these three, maximally spiritual, but this with caution since, like I said, I just don't feel belonging to a group, no faith community. I don't follow a special worldview or a model or something. I'm just interested in those things, I'm interested in religion, spirituality, what others believe, what kind of experiences they have made, what kind of realizations they had in this area, that's what I'm interested in, and that's what I engage with, now and then.

Right, you can't avoid that. [...] But often, I'm on this level where there is no valuation.[7]

that's really helpful, you know, but, since I cannot do this, I could not fit into this or just accept that for myself, things like, that's true, that's false, that's good, that's bad, that's right, these are the laws, these are the commandments, that's how you're supposed to live, God is this and that, you have to follow what God says, like, this is... nay.[8]

[...] And I don't associate spirituality with a rigid system or something, [...]. Like, I'm not a person who'd say, "So, this guy can see angels, has he lost all his marbles or something?" I can just accept that and be like, okay, well, why not. Like, I do not necessarily judge this.[9]

---

7   Mhm, spirituell. Aber wie gesagt spirituell was heißt das? [...] Das ist für mich nicht mit einer Gemeinschaft verbunden oder mit kleinem Grüppchen mit dem ich zusammenglucke oder mit einer Glaubensrichtung. [...] Ich glaube zum spirituell sein, ist für mich eigentlich nur, dass man versucht bewusst zu leben und nach bestem Wissen und Gewissen zu leben und achtsam zu sein und auch mal versuchen hinter die Sachen zu gucken und einfach offen zu sein für alles [...], weil der andere Mensch ist ja genauso ein Teil der Schöpfung wie ich, warum soll der Unrecht haben und ich Recht? Nee, das kann ja eigentlich gar nicht sein und darum ist Spiritualität viel für mich ein Bewusstsein dieser Ebene, auf der es keine Bewertung gibt. Auf meiner unteren menschlichen Ebene werte ich genauso wie jeder andere Mensch auch. Ne, lässt sich ja nicht vermeiden. [...] Aber ich bin oft auf dieser Ebene, wo es keine Wertung gibt.

8   Gläubig schon mal gar nicht. Religiös in dem Sinne, wie es konnotiert ist in unserer Gesellschaft auch nicht, am ehesten würde ich aber wahrscheinlich schon sagen, so einen spirituellen Einschlag habe ich allein aufgrund dieser Erlebnisse und aufgrund dessen, dass ich mich damit auch viel auseinandergesetzt hab, also in meiner Jugend und so, wo ich noch auf der Suche war. Ich habe mich viel mit Glaube, Religion und Spiritualität beschäftigt und da ist mir die Spiritualität – so wie der Begriff verwendet wird – am nähesten. Also, ich würde mich schon tatsächlich als latent spirituellen Menschen beschreiben. [...] Manchmal hab ich mir schon früher gewünscht, ich könnte [religiös sein], weil, es ist schön, wenn man so ein System hat, das einem Halt gibt, das ist total hilfebringend ja, so, aber, da ich das nicht kann, ich könnte mich da nie einfügen oder das nie für mich annehmen, so zu sagen: Das ist wahr, das ist falsch, das ist gut, das ist schlecht, das ist richtig, das sind die Gesetze, das sind die Gebote, so sollst du leben, Gott ist das und das, du sollst dich so nach Gott verhalten, also das ist... nee.

9   Hm, von den drei Wörtern maximal spirituell, aber das auch mit Vorsicht, weil, ich fühle mich eben, wie gesagt, keiner Gruppe zugehörig, keiner Glaubensgemeinschaft. Ich verfolge kein spezielles Weltbild oder Modell oder irgendwas. Ich interessiere mich aber für solche Sachen, ich interessiere mich für Religion, Spiritualität, dafür, was andere Menschen glauben, welche Erfahrungen sie gemacht haben, welche Erkenntnisse sie auf dem Gebiet haben, dafür interessiere ich mich, und da beschäftige ich mich auch mit, hin und wieder. [...] Und ich verbinde mit Spiritualität jetzt eben kein festes System oder irgendwie, [...]. Also ich bin jetzt auch niemand, der irgendwie sagt: „Ja und wenn der Typ da Engel sehen kann, hat er einen an der Waffel oder so?" Ich nehme das so hin und gucke mal, also, ne, kann so sein. Also so, ich werte das jetzt nicht unbedingt.

Wave 1

Her concept of spirituality, as she provides it in the survey, is an encompassing one, and she states that everything is spiritual. At the same time, she emphasizes her openness to different interpretations, thereby rejecting narrow-mindedness. On the other hand, religion, besides the literal translation of re-connection (a detail that she gives at every timepoint, it is interesting to note here that her translation seems to imply returning to something that someone was once already connected to in the past), is something man-made, something created to give support and provide meaning. These two definitions show the contrast she sees between those two concepts and imply that religion, for her, is something that is connotated slightly negatively, rather by omission than by actually saying it, since the openness that is emphasized in her definition of spirituality is missing when she defines religion, which is characterized as a more concluded concept. This is in accordance with her choice for "more spiritual than religious" and is further supported by her answer in the interview in which she chooses "spiritual" for characterizing herself. Again, there is a clear distinction between spiritual and religious, the latter obviously being connected to a community (implying, again, a certain rigidness). On the other hand, being spiritual is described as being open, aware, and mindful, a condition that seems desirable to her (and probably also desirable for society as a whole), since, in addition, she distinguishes between a "spiritual level" and a "human level." The human level, on which she finds herself sometimes as well, is judgmental and probably not very tolerant, while a person on the spiritual level does not valuate others, showing a great sense of tolerance, with the presupposition that there is no reason to believe that the person in front of her should be wrong while she is right. Here, Nadine shows, at a relatively young age, traces of a xenosophic approach by emphasizing an equality between all humans, even though she does not go as far as letting herself be actually changed by the other.

Wave 2

This time, her definitions are really short, for "spirituality" she gives merely two words which in the German language are associated with intellect or the mind. Her definition of "religion" may be seen as in opposition to this "Geist," by naming "belief" as first association. Interestingly, a transcendental reference is brought up here which does not appear in the other data in this table. In her interview answer, she chooses to characterize herself as spiritual again, this time, however, not so much with reference to an open mind, even though she indirectly names her open mind as a reason for her spirituality. But her statement sounds less deterministic than at time 1, which may be an indicator for a development, Nadine maybe having integrated this stance and feeling less compelled to declare this as a prerequisite for everyone. Her own "supernatural" experiences are named as an additional factor for her own spirituality, hereby giving a biographical background information which serves as an autobiographical argument, since, as a logical consequence of having actually experienced something supernatural, it can be assumed that this would not leave a person without effect. Moreover, she portrays herself here as an intellectual person who has, despite not being faithful herself, engaged with religious and spiritual people and literature, describing a thorough searching movement, implying that she was not looking for easy answers. However, she admits, when turning to the term "religion" in her answer, to sometimes flirting with the idea of following a religion with its strict and unambiguous system of rules. But obviously she cannot bring herself to believe in something like that, implying a certain rebelliousness which prevents her from actually "fitting in." This might be, on the one hand, described as just not being able to get to the core of a belief. On the other hand, we have a very strong self-characterization of Nadine as an autonomously thinking person who, despite admitting to certain "weaknesses" now and then, prefers making decisions for herself and not following blindly any kind of rule-book. This is also in accordance with what has been said about her approach to religion at time 1.

Wave 3

Her definitions in the survey are, again, very short. In addition to the term "Geistigkeit" (which is, by the way, not a very common word in German), she makes a reference to the "inner life," without elaborating on that further, which may be taking into account her answers from the earlier interviews, be understood as an inner attitude. Interestingly, in contrast to her other interview answers, being spiritual is not embraced as unconditionally as before, rather appearing as the best, but not correct approximation to a self-characterization. Again, she rejects the idea of belonging to a community and emphasizes her individual, intellectual approach of engaging with religious and spiritual topics. An intellectual curiosity can be inferred from her statement, which was there already at time 2, but not with the same emphasis. While at time 2 this engagement was justified with her searching for something at time 3 it seems as if she does that with the aim of gathering knowledge and of a better understanding of people in general. In this statement, she is also demanding tolerance, or rather: describes lived tolerance, also for people who are obviously outside a norm. Her last sentence infers a certain openness and acceptance of approaches that obviously seem improbable to her, however, this does not seem to go further than just letting the other be, in a "live and let live" manner.

Taking together all the findings from the data assembled here, Nadine's worldview can probably best be described as agnostic. She does not want to be associated with any form of organized religion, yet she has no fixed opinion regarding the existence of God, which is mirrored also in her answers regarding her image of God. Her self-characterization of being spiritual gets less convinced over time and the meaning it has for her becomes less abstract and less life-defining. However, it becomes clear that this whole topic has some relevance for her life; she names it directly when talking about her searching movements in her youth. It is striking that she takes a very rational and intellectual approach when investigating other worldviews and that there obviously is not much that she can fall back onto, and there seems to be a strong desire to engage with this topic, albeit with a critical stance. But, unlike you would expect it from someone who does not have any special form of religiosity or spirituality, Nadine defines herself consistently as "more spiritual than religious." There is a prevailing uncertainty, or, more positively, an openness for something that may be beyond her otherwise rational approach. Looking at her answers regarding her worldview, we see a development insofar as there is less critical engagement with organized religion. While, in the first two interviews, she noticeably contrasts her own stance with that of faithful people, she seems more self-assured in her third interview, obviously more settled in her not-fixed worldview. Interestingly, while at times 1 and 2, she mainly talks about reading a lot, at time 3, her focus is on engage-

Part C: Longitudinal Case Studies—Qualitative Analyses Including Quantitative Data

ment and dialog with people with diverse backgrounds. And even though it cannot be said for certain how much Nadine internalizes from these conversations, how much she lets herself be actually changed, it can be stated that Nadine is moving toward a more xenosophic worldview over the years.

4.2 Isabella's Worldview

Turning now to the data assembled for Isabella, the most obvious difference is that Isabella constantly defines herself as "neither religious nor spiritual," a self-assessment that is, however, to be expected from someone who furtively calls herself atheist.

Wave 1
As in all her other surveys, Isabella here defines herself as neither religious nor spiritual. When asked in the interview, she states that she does not really know the difference between the concepts. The way she then defines spirituality ("religion-lite") makes it clear that she is not convinced of that concept and she rejects the idea of believing in something without reflecting about it first. Here, we have a moral criticism directed toward people who will stop thinking for themselves and will name God as the reason for it. Isabella portrays herself in contrast to those people by calling herself a "pretty strict rationalist" and emphasizing that she usually tries to understand things.

Wave 2
In her definition for "spirituality," she takes up the thought again that the term is not really defined and rather fuzzy, adding the experience that there are many subjective definitions which have to be known in order to understand what a person means when they call themself spiritual. Religion, on the other hand, is rather unambiguously defined as a belief in and worship of one or more higher being(s). In her interview answer, she starts with the same observation she made in her survey definition, namely that spirituality is understood quite differently. Then, she explains what being an atheist means for her, a form of scientific reasoning being constituent for her understanding. Going beyond that, she also talks about the other side of the term atheism, that is, the "lack of belief in a God." She emphasizes, though, that there is, theoretically, the possibility to be convinced otherwise should there be enough evidence. So, for Isabella at time 2, it seems that a scientific, rational view on the world is what most defines her, and she calls this atheism.

Table 10.5: Data on Isabella's Worldview

Isabella	Wave 1	Wave 2	Wave 3
Free entries	*spirituality*: not answered	*spirituality*: I do not believe this term has a specific definition. Whenever it comes up in discussion, I always ask the other party to define what they mean by it, as everybody has different uses for this word.	*spirituality*: A general feeling of divine/supernatural existence in the world.
	religion: not answered	*religion*: Religion is the belief in and possibly worship of a specific higher entity(/ies).	*religion*: An organized structure with specific dogma and cohesiveness between members.
Self-assessment	neither religious nor spiritual	neither religious nor spiritual	neither religious nor spiritual
Answer to FDI Q20: Do you consider yourself a religious, spiritual, or faithful person?	I don't even understand what the difference in spirituality is. I think spirituality is just people who say I want to believe in something, but I don't know what. I just want to believe that there is something. [...] It's like I see that as religion-lite. So, no, I think of myself as a pretty strict rationalist. I try and really understand what's going on and not use just a blind belief to say, "Oh it's something spiritual." 'Cause I think that's a failing in thinking through things and analyzing them. You just say, "Oh, it's religion," and then stop. "Oh God did it. The end."	I'm an atheist. Some people use words like spiritual, but I don't really know what that means, because everyone uses it differently. [...] I believe that the world is best understood through rationality and investigation. So, I do identify as an atheist, which is a label with a lot of controversy and misunderstanding. I go by the specific literal meaning, lack of belief in a God, atheism. It's not belief that there definitely are no Gods. It is that a lack of belief is the null hypothesis, which I don't believe that anyone has mounted enough evidence to cause me to reject the null hypothesis.	Cold-hearted rationalist (laughing). So that means that I don't turn to any sort of supernatural force. I believe that the universe can be explained and understood as a set of physical laws. Now certainly we haven't fully explored them, and we don't know everything about what they are yet. Humanity might someday, but certainly at this point we spend a heck of a lot of time researching those, and they are very, very complex. But they are for us to discover and understand, and you don't need to appeal to any sort of supernatural entity or entities to have that understanding.

Wave 3

Interestingly, at this time point, the "fuzziness" of the concept that was noted at the other time points is here taken as the main characteristic, spirituality for her being the "general feeling" of something higher existing (note, however, that she does not speak of "belief" here). The main characteristic of religion, on the other hand, is its level of organization and its uniformity. When she is asked in the interview how she would define herself, she calls herself a "cold-hearted rationalist" which she further elaborates to be someone who believes in science and who does not need any higher entity to explain questions of ultimate concern. And even though she admits that humans do not yet know the answer to everything, she still does not feel like this should be a reason to turn to something supernatural for guidance.

Comparing her answers, we see that Isabella consistently asserts that she is a rational person who prefers scientific reasoning over beliefs in something higher. Interestingly, while at time 2 she leaves open the possibility, at least theoretically, that she might be convinced otherwise, this door seems to have closed at time 3. Religion and spirituality both seem strange to her, but the moral criticism that accompanied her answers in the interviews 1 and 2 has softened. It seems that her self-understanding as an atheist, and, going along with that, the rejection of anything religious, is not in the focus of her life and her thoughts anymore. Isabella is, while calling herself a hedonist, also a strong advocate for humanism, being certain that people can be good or bad out of their own accord without needing a mediating force for that. She also states that all lives are valuable without any preconditions. Along with that, she speaks in favor of social fairness, most often at time 3, arguing that being a nice person basically is "one of the foundational ideas that an entire system revolves around." With those values at the core of her (non-)belief system, it becomes clear that Isabella really does not need any higher being to structure her world. She puts her entire trust, without being deluded or overly optimistic about it, in a horizontal transcendence that relies on her fellow humans to help make the world a better place.

Having laid out the basics of both of their worldviews, we now turn to a specific question which is often difficult for people who do not have a concept of an afterlife per se, taking them to the limits of their worldview: What happens to us when we die? We will see how both Nadine and Isabella integrate their thoughts on this question into their worldview, thereby getting interesting insights into meaning-making processes.

The Meaning of Life and Death

Both women talk, of course, about what they think about death. But aside from the actual question that is asked within the interview, both of them report incidents related to death that seem to be meaningful to them, which is not necessarily to be expected at such a young age. Therefore, the next section will take a closer look at their theoretical conceptions and personal experiences regarding death and dying.

5.1 Nadine—Rational Considerations and Emotional Experiences

When looking at her FDI ratings, it became clear that the question "What does death mean to you? What happens to us when we die?" might serve as an example to trace how Nadine's religious style has developed over the years, so looking at this question specifically makes sense in more than one way. She takes a seemingly pragmatic approach at time 1:

> Yeah, it happens. (laughs) I believe [...] I'm not afraid of it, though I wouldn't cheer it either. It's just a process, like going to the loo, so, everything that lives in a biological sense, dies at one point [...]. Even though I adored my grandma, it was not upsetting when she died, like, it was not upsetting for me. With that, I am pretty out of the ordinary.[10] (Nadine, FDI, time 1)

She states that death itself for her is a normal process and just a part of human existence. She even underlines that opinion by mentioning how unaffected she was by the death of her grandmother. She is, of course, aware of the fact that this is something that sets her apart from the majority of people, making her special, or the "odd one out." However, despite this very rational approach, Nadine also has had experiences beyond that rationality. She talks about the nature of those memories and experiences a bit when asked for breakthrough experiences. Nadine has had, in her youth, a time when she was depressed and even considered suicide. Getting out of this state is achieved by an experience that could be called spiritual. For Nadine, this is something she has to argue strongly:

> You have to be careful how you talk about all this, but I was quite depressive and was feeling poorly. I sometimes thought about suicide, never seriously tried, but thought about it, and then I once had this very intense dream and after that, I was finished with that... I knew the score. That was very interesting. Like, I had stuff like this from time to time, wherever this comes from, and I don't mean to judge, whether I was on a different level or in heaven or something like that. Well, heaven is wrong as well since I don't believe in that Christian heaven. [...] Whether this comes out of my brain or wherever that comes from, I don't know. Well, I'm not crazy (laughs), but those

---

10   Ja passiert. (Lachen) Ich glaube, [...] ich habe da keine Angst vor, ich würde ihn auch nicht bejubeln. Es ist einfach nur ein Prozess, wie aufs Klo gehen also, ne, alles was biologisch lebt, stirbt irgendwann [...]. Obwohl ich meine Oma über alles geliebt habe, war es auch nicht schlimm für mich, dass sie gestorben ist also, das ist für mich nicht schlimm. Damit falle ich schon ziemlich aus dem Rahmen.

were partly helpful things. [...] The terms are difficult because a lot of esoterics are going into that direction, with whom I don't want to be stuck into a box, but there is something like a higher consciousness, which is always there but which you can't always reach and in this night I just could reach it. And looking back it's like, the knowledge has always been there but could not be reached and so this was such an enlightenment.[11] (Nadine, FDI, time 1)

The answer is initiated with a cautious statement indicating that Nadine is well aware of the fact that the things she is going to say might be controversial, knowing that the narrative identity she displayed throughout the interview is one that is oriented toward science and not at all religious. So, the spiritual experience she describes then is formative in more than one way: not only does it end her suicidal thoughts, but it also makes her realize that, despite being a rational person, there is a "higher consciousness" that is usually out of reach. She is obviously struggling for the right words here, coming to the conclusion that both the Christian framework ("heaven") and the esoteric one ("higher consciousness") do not suit her well, even though she does not succeed in describing her experience without referring to either of those. Obviously, being associated with both Christians and esoteric people is connotated negatively for her. Interestingly though, these efforts of justification are mainly with the outside world, she does not seem to struggle with integrating these experiences in her self-perceived identity.

In her second interview, she basically affirms what she said in her first interview regarding her attitude toward death, stating that it does not frighten her and making it sound as if she sees that as a kind of game which she is excited to play at one point. Again, it seems as if she is observing what her brain is doing with a mild curiosity or an intellectual interest, but still without the need to religiously frame those experiences. Again, Nadine talks about her spiritual experience which made her abandon her suicide plans, again when asked for breakthrough experiences:

That's probably a bit difficult to describe, I mean, other people would probably file that under spiritual experience—I know that, and I just accept it—but from time to time I had very enlightening experiences, inspirations, that helped me on. Like, for example, in my youth I was really depressive and often thought about suicide and

---

11   Muss man natürlich immer vorsichtig sein, wie man das alles erzählt, aber ich war relativ depressiv und es ging mir schlecht. Ich habe manchmal über Selbstmord nachgedacht, nie ernsthaft versucht, aber nachgedacht und habe dann einmal einen sehr intensiven Traum gehabt und danach war das gegessen also mit dem... da wusste ich Bescheid. Das war sehr interessant. Also solche Sachen habe ich auch öfter gehabt, dass ich irgendwo, wo auch immer das herkommt, ich erlaube mir halt auch kein Urteil darüber, ob ich auf anderen Ebenen unterwegs war und im Himmel war und solche Sachen. Also Himmel ist auch verkehrt. Ich glaube ja nicht an diesen christlichen Himmel. [...] Ob das jetzt aus meinem Gehirn, sonst woher kommt, wo das herkommt, das weiß ich nicht. Also verrückt bin ich nicht (Lachen) aber das waren auch teilweise hilfreiche Sachen. [...] Die Begriffe sind schwierig, weil viele Esoteriker sind da dann auch so in die Richtung, mit denen ich auch nicht in einer Schublade stecke, aber es gibt so was wie ein höheres Bewusstsein, was eigentlich immer da ist, wo man aber nicht immer dran kommt und in dieser Nacht, da bin ich da einfach drangekommen. [...] Und im Nachhinein ist das so, das Wissen ist eigentlich immer da gewesen, aber man kam nicht dran und deshalb war das so eine Erleuchtung.

how I just don't want to anymore and so on, but then I just… it was shown to me or I made the experience, don't know, doesn't matter at all what my brain did there, but since then I could never again seriously consider this […]. Like, that was quite interesting, I don't know exactly how to call it, like, if you should call it a vision or something, yes, but since then, the topic was done, and it's always like this: I've never known in my life how it would go on, I don't have any goal, which is probably related to my lack of self-image or worldview or something like that. […] I just have things like that sometimes. Basically, they are also somehow parts of me that are obviously doing something, but this may also go against my actual opinion.[12] (Nadine, FDI, time 2)

The way she starts her answer appears defensive, as if she expects some form of judgment from the interviewer, probably because she has faced criticism when telling her story before. The nature of her experience remains vague in this account as well, but it becomes clear that it was a life-changing experience which cannot be put into words, maybe best described with "directly experiencing a form of transcendence." Again, by mentioning her brain and the way it functions, she implies that this experience might be a neurological phenomenon, but she obviously does not feel the necessity to resolve this fully. She then says that she does not have a real direction in her life and attributes this to a "lack of self-image or worldview"; and, obviously, this gap in her life plan is filled with those experiences that push her life in a certain direction, whether she likes that direction or not. This remark is interesting because it serves the purpose to render her inspirations more believable: they work, even if she does not want them to work, making them "real magic," since they work against her own intuition and will at times. This overall makes her statement at time 2 more defensive than at time 1, though, as if the need for justification has grown over the years, maybe also due to age.

Turning now to her time 3 interview, we have this answer, which was rated a Style 5:

I guess what I think about death is connected to what I think about life. For me, this whole concept is so crazy, to somehow come into being and then be no more. That can't be understood easily, I believe. [I: And what happens to us when we die?] We rot. (smiles) No, I don't know, like, on a spiritual level I don't know that and otherwise,

---

12 Das ist nur wahrscheinlich ein bisschen schwierig zu beschreiben, ich meine, andere Leute würden es wahrscheinlich – ich weiß, ich nehme das so hin – unter spirituelle Erlebnisse verbuchen, aber ich hatte doch mal immer mal wieder sehr erhellende Erlebnisse, Erfahrungen, Eingebungen so, die mich eben dann weitergebracht haben. Also, zum Beispiel war ich sehr viel in meiner Jugend und so depressiv und habe auch öfter über Selbstmord nachgedacht und mir das überlegt, dass ich kein Bock mehr habe und überhaupt, aber ich habe dann eben doch… mir wurde gezeigt oder ich habe eine Erfahrung gemacht, keine Ahnung, ist ja auch völlig egal, was mein Gehirn dann gemacht hat, aber seitdem konnte ich nie wieder ernsthaft darüber nachdenken, […]. Also, das war ganz, ganz interessant, ich weiß aber nicht genau, wie man das nennen soll, also, ob man das jetzt Vision nennen soll oder irgendwas, ja, seitdem ist das Thema eben vom Tisch und es ist irgendwie immer so: Ich weiß in meinem Leben eigentlich nie, wie es weitergeht, ich habe überhaupt gar kein Ziel, hängt wahrscheinlich auch mit meinem mangelnden Selbstbild und Weltbild und überhaupt allen Bildern zusammen. […] Solche Sachen habe ich manchmal. Das sind ja letztendlich zwar schon auch irgendwie Teile von mir, die da anscheinend irgendwas machen, aber das kann eben auch gegen meine eigentliche Meinung gehen.

of course, the body decays into its components, in one way or another. And perhaps you passed on your genes and you can wonder whether this leads anywhere. And everything else, if there is such a thing like a soul beyond the brain and so on, I just can't tell, the same with the question of a higher power or something else. I have experienced stuff that could be called spiritual experiences. I can't say whether my brain fired and mixed something together or not. [...] But I just let it stand as it is. And therefore, I can leave open the question as to what happens after death. I cannot answer this and I will surely find out.[13] (Nadine, FDI, time 3)

This answer takes into consideration aspects that were not mentioned in her first two interviews: a more holistic view on life and death as a whole. The biological side is described and there is even the notion of generativity, i.e. passing on one's genes, a virtue that is otherwise not very present in Nadine's interviews. All these aspects are considered with a certain curiosity and in the end again enriched with her spiritual experiences, which add a different perspective on the whole topic which is, as she admits, not to be answered easily. Nadine seems more certain and more self-assured in this answer than she was in her first two interviews. The challenge to not ultimately know everything and to deal with uncertainties seems something she is even more at peace with. She also talks again about the spiritual experiences she has at times when she is asked for breakthrough experiences:

Sometimes there are those intuitions, like suddenly I know I have to do that. They come out of the blue or like I know why I should not do a certain thing or [...] I get a certain dream somehow, which is quite different from this usual dream nonsense. And then I just know... I'm basically a different person in the morning because I'm like, oh, okay, this has to be different from now on. And I don't always like that, but it always turned out to be the right thing. [...] I believe the most remarkable situation was that at one point, basically from one night to the other, by having this sort of experience, I knew that I would not kill myself, I would not want to do that. [...] Since this night, I never seriously considered it. [...] Which I find stupid at times, (smiles)

---

13   Ich glaube, alles, was ich über den Tod denke, ist auch verknüpft mit dem, was ich über das Leben denke. Ich finde überhaupt dieses ganze Konzept so abgefahren, irgendwie zu entstehen und dann nicht mehr zu sein. Das ist nichts, was man so einfach begreifen kann, glaube ich. [I: Und was passiert mit uns, wenn wir sterben?] Wir verrotten. (lächelt) Nein, ich weiß nicht, also auf einer spirituellen Ebene weiß ich es nicht und ansonsten, klar, der Körper zersetzt sich wieder in seine Bestandteile, auf die eine oder andere Art. Und man hat dann vielleicht seine Gene weitergetragen und kann sich überlegen, ob das jetzt irgendwie noch weiterführend ist. Und alles andere, ob es so etwas wie eine Seele jenseits des Gehirns gibt und so weiter und so fort, kann ich genauso wenig sagen, wie die Frage nach der höheren Macht oder irgendwas anderem. Ich habe ja nun durchaus einige Sachen erlebt, die man als spirituelle Erlebnisse bezeichnen würde. Ich kann ja jetzt auch nicht sagen, ob mein Gehirn das sich zusammengefeuert hat oder nicht. [...] Also ich lasse das so stehen. Und dementsprechend lasse ich es für mich auch so stehen, was passiert nach dem Tod? Das kann ich nicht beantworten und ich werde es rausfinden, ne.

but, yeah, that's why I would say: yes, there are such experiences.[14] (Nadine, FDI, time 3)

Her line of argumentation is interesting here: those "intuitions" come out of the blue, are unwanted and inconvenient at times. Obviously, they appear on such a regular basis that she cannot ignore them and so instead she decides to make them part of her life narrative, albeit with a skeptical undertone that shows a certain distance from her own experience and at the same time makes it harder to argue against it, since even though she does not embrace them, and is a reflective and rational person, those dreams and intuitions are still there. This is a similar line of argumentation like at time 2, however, this time it comes across in a less defensive way, and it becomes clear that Nadine is at peace with the way those dreams and spiritual experiences "haunt" her.

5.2 Isabella—The Beauty of the Universe and Questions of Ultimate Concern

In her first two interviews, Isabella makes frequent reference to pop culture, talking about movies and quoting from them. At time 3, there is little evidence of that, which might be due to the fact that the last interview is rather short. Often, these quotes and references seem, for her, to sum up her own thoughts and feelings better, or more pointedly. In her first interview, she talks about a key scene in the movie *American Beauty* and ties this back to her own experience:

[I: Have you had any moments of intense joy or a break though experiences that have changed your sense of life's meaning?] Well, this is going to sound kind of copy cat, I think, but you know that scene in- What movie was it? I think it was American Beauty where, like, the kid is like filming this bag floating through the air. [I: Yeah.] Okay, and so, I think I've had a lot of small moments like that and even like a bag floating through the air, I've seen the same thing and thought, "That is beautiful." Not 'cause the bag is inherently beautiful, but just like the basic underlying physics of the universe and how it expresses itself in even everyday motion of bags through the air being a visible sign of air vectors and turbulency is beautiful. And so I kind of find that life-affirming to me because when you're an atheist, you have this problem of, like, "Oh shit, what happens when you die? Nothing has meaning." Well, nothing has to have meaning. It can just be the universe is just inherently beautiful on its own. And it doesn't need to care a shit about humans ultimately, but if the universe is beautiful, we're part of that beauty. (Isabella, FDI, time 1)

---

14 Es gibt da manchmal so Eingebungen, wo ich weiß, ich muss das jetzt tun. Die kommen aus dem Nichts oder ich weiß, warum ich irgendetwas nicht tun sollte oder [...] ich kriege dann irgendwie einen bestimmten Traum, der sich von dem normalen Traumblödsinn, den man träumt, unterscheidet. Und dann weiß ich eben... bin ich quasi morgens dann jemand anderes, weil ich dann, oh, okay, das muss jetzt anders sein. Und das gefällt mir nicht immer, das hat sich aber eigentlich immer als richtig erwiesen so. [...] Ich glaube, das Markanteste ist einfach, dass ich irgendwann mal, irgendwie quasi von einer Nacht auf die andere, durch eben so ein bestimmtes Erlebnis wusste, dass ich mich nicht umbringen werde oder will. [...] Seit dieser Nacht habe ich da halt nie mehr ernsthaft drüber nachgedacht. [...] Was ich auch teilweise ein bisschen blöd finde, (lächelt) aber, genau, deswegen würde ich sagen: Ja, sowas gibt es.

The movie scene she refers to here is a bit odd, yet at the same time rather touching: the (nerdy) boy who films this plastic bag floating through the air and later shows that film to the girl he loves, telling her that he feels like in this small and meaningless plastic bag dancing in the air all the beauty in the world is accumulating. Isabella has had similar experiences, one actually pretty similar to that in the movie, and the feelings she has in these little moments are comparable: seeing a small, at first glance unimportant item and suddenly realizing the immense power behind and the beauty beyond that. For her, as an atheist, these moments of all-connectedness are what constitutes a greater, life-affirming meaning. Not having a perspective of what happens after death is seen as a problem and is resolved by becoming aware of the little things connecting and adding up to a beautiful universe that she is part of.

The prospect of dying, however, is still terrifying for Isabella, as she admits when asked for crises, by telling a little story in the classic form of the narrative:

Table 10.6: Isabella's Narrative: "Realizing I am Mortal"

Orientation	Actually, when I realized I was going to die, like, really, deeply realized, "Oh no, that applies to me too." [...] I remember the actual moment when it struck me, 'cause I was sleeping in bed with my then boyfriend. Like about to fall asleep
Complication	and I realized I was going to die, like, it was total non sequitur. And of course, the first thought was, "But I don't want to."
Evaluation	And I actually, like, stayed up and cried for a few minutes because it was the realization of my own mortality. And I was, like, twenty-two at the time. And I realized I'm going to die and that's really going to suck.
Resolution	Since then I really haven't found any real way to deal with that. Mostly I just try to not think about it.
Coda	Because that really ties into, everyone is going to die, and no one is going to remember me. [...] Like once I'm dead it won't matter if people remember me or not, because I'll be dead and I won't be able to experience being remembered. (Isabella, FDI, time 1)

Isabella recalls a specific situation from when she was in her early 20s when, out of nowhere obviously, the thought of her own mortality struck her. Despite her earlier statements of commitment to scientific reasoning, here she describes a moment in which science does not help her. She has struggled with that question ever since, not really finding a solution or a good way to deal with that. She does not mention, however, what specific ways she may or may not have tried, but, as her resolution suggests, none of them convinced her. The narrative is left open, the coda is not resolving the actual problem, it just makes clear that Isabella is able to formulate the core of her problem here: She will not be remembered, and not even experience not being remembered. Isabella may be thinking about the concept of generativity here (cf. Erikson & Erikson, 1998) without being aware of that concept, of course. The feeling that she has, so far, not contributed anything worth being remembered for is still troubling her, combined with the assumption that death means nothingness, yet, with another quote (the source of which, however, is not given) she tries to reassure herself:

> The quote is, "Can you remember what it was like before you were born? Death is a lot like that." And I actually find that comforting because like I said, I'm frankly scared about dying. I don't want it to happen. And I really hope they get this whole immortality thing down before I die, but that's not really looking very good, so I just have to remember: It's not even oblivion. (Isabella, FDI, time 1)

Meeting her fears with humour and sarcasm, Isabella tries to comfort herself with the thought that she will not actually experience what it is like to be dead.

"A cessation of existence" is how Isabella defines death in her second interview. And then she talks about the instant again in which she realized that she, ultimately, was going to die:

> Actually, there was a specific incident in my understanding of death where it was actually after a completely normal day, I was in bed, um next to my then boyfriend, now husband, going to sleep, and all of a sudden I realized that I was going to die, like, I had always known it in general, yes, all humans die. But at that point... there was nothing about that moment that would have caused that. It was just random that it happened at that time that my train of thought applied it to me specifically. And I was like early 20's at the time. And I really, really realized, no, I'm going to die. I mean, I'm perfectly healthy, so not necessarily yet, any nearby point, but just eventually, it's inevitable. And I'm not very happy about that because obviously existence is all that I know. I find some comfort... There is a quote that goes, "Death is nonexistence. Do you remember what it was like before you were born? Death is like that." And so death isn't an experience of nonexistence, it is not having experiences, and there's no way to understand that. [...] No one ever knows that they die because to know that you die, you have to have the experience of knowing that you are dead. And death is the lack of experience of any further experiences. (Isabella, FDI, time 2)

The way the story is told is more distanced, less episodic, which may be due to the longer time period elapsed since the event. There is neither direct speech nor the mention of her crying when the realization struck her. So, in sum, the experience is still constituent, yet has lost some of its eventful character. Added here are thoughts attempting to rationalize her fears (concerning her health, for example) and the statement that "existence" is all that she knows. The explanation of death being a state of nonexistence and of nonawareness is comforting to her, the quote from the first interview being taken up again, but explained and interpreted more elaborately. So, compared to her first interview, Isabella shows more abstract thinking here, a rationalized way to cope with the (irrational) fear of her own death, yet still has kept the concepts she already held at time 1.

We still find the concept of the universe's inherent beauty at time 2, when she is asked when she finds herself most in harmony with the universe:

Part C: Longitudinal Case Studies—Qualitative Analyses Including Quantitative Data

> All the time, which is kind of weird answer, because I said that like I haven't had any like huge experiences of joy or ecstasy, I just- it's a very low baseline of like, wow, the world is amazing. I mean you can look at anything, and if you'll think about it, it's pretty damn cool. Just based on how atoms interact and that physics of the universe. [...] I'm just trying to like think of anything specific and I mean it's not like I go around my whole day being, whoa, that's so cool (dramatic), but I mean it's there if you think about it, but it's something you have to kind of like concentrate on and specifically look at, because it's so easy to get caught up in the day-to-day and then when you're driving into work if you take a moment to realize, [...] I'm just an average person and society allows me to be in control of a thousand tons of metal at any time that I want. And that's pretty amazing. And it's just, so it could be a daydream like that that you've like just realized, you like look around the corner and realize the awesomeness, or even the absurdity of the universe. (Isabella, FDI, time 2)

Isabella displays here, again, her ability to experience joy and amazement in the little things. You may call what she describes here a very direct experience of transcendence, but it very definitely is a horizontal transcendence that does not need any higher being. The amazement described here is within the framework of scientific reasoning and the discovery of mechanisms that she had not thought about before. The way she talks about this emphasizes the wonder she actually seems to feel. In very lively speech, she describes an instant in which she realized the weirdness/greatness of the fact that she is allowed to drive a car even though this might become a dangerous weapon. Isabella shows here that she is able to "see behind" things and may understand the underlying logic, but can, at the same time, be impressed by both the realization and the mechanism. She describes all this with reference to society, and to science, but without even having to think of a vertical transcendence.

In her third interview, the instance when she realized she was mortal is not mentioned again, her answer regarding the meaning of death is rather short:

> [I: What does death mean to you?] Death is an ending of your self-experience. Basically everything that our brain does... When it doesn't do that, that's it. [I: What happens to us when we die?] I mean, it's not a specific happening to us. It's the lack of ongoing processes. (Isabella, FDI, time 3)

The basics of her earlier answers are there, the scientific explanation as well as the assumption that with death, all forms of self-experience end with all other processes. What is missing here is the experience dimension that was present in her other interviews. It is but a mere guess that maybe Isabella did not show as much enthusiasm for the interview than before, maybe just punctually due to any current circumstances unknown to the researchers, or maybe because these questions do not play such a prominent role in her life at the moment. Adding to this, her answer regarding a feeling of harmony with the universe is rather short and more prosaic as well:

> [I: Okay. When or where do you find yourself most in communion or harmony with the universe?] I don't necessarily really have the touchy feel like that. [...] Yeah, I don't necessarily feel that especially. I mean I certainly marvel at the universe and feel

awed at it sometimes, but not [it's not as if?] there's just a specific place or state. (Isabella, FDI, time 3)

Here she seems to have lost some of the "beauty" that she originally saw in the universe. While in her other interviews, she tells little episodes illustrating her "marveling," here she rejects the "touchy feel" dimension that was certainly palpable before.

Comparison—Variations of Non-Belief in Isabella and Nadine

The analysis above has shown that Nadine and Isabella are quite different kinds of non-believers. Isabella can probably best be sorted into the category of the Intellectual Atheist, since she enjoys educating herself about various topics and likes engaging in conversations with others and, furthermore, has a community of fellow atheists she meets with on a regular basis (Silver et al., 2014, pp. 4–5). While she sympathizes with certain movements and mindsets (such as humanism and the Democratic Party), she could not be called very active in this regard. Nadine, on the other hand, fits pretty well into the description of the Seeker Agnostic who will actively search for answers and keep an open mind regarding the existence of God (ibid.). Even though she does not choose the label "agnostic" for herself, the analysis made clear that she is aware of the boundaries of scientific reasoning and has come to a point where she just accepts her somehow spiritual experiences. Those spiritual experiences are one of the major differences that could be detected when analyzing the women's answers, especially those dealing with ultimate questions like death (and the occuring wish to die, in Nadine's case), accounting also for the difference in self-assessment found in the questionnaire. While Isabella's statement that she is neither religious nor spiritual seems in line with her atheism, Nadine stating that she sees herself as spiritual is somewhat puzzling. Her case might contribute to the discussion about the "spiritual but not religious" (SBNR), which is favored by an increasing number of people (for a recent overview, see Wixwat & Saucier, 2021). For her, those spiritual experiences are a way of coping with feelings of uncertainty, she claims those dreams or visions often occur when she is at a point where she does not know how to continue and she accepts the decisions these visions purport, even though she is not always happy with them at first. This trust in or acceptance of something higher is remarkable and therefore can serve as an illustration of how a spiritual agnostic worldview might look like. Isabella cannot fall back on coping meachnisms like that, her worldview seems strictly rational and oriented toward scientific reasoning, without room for anything mystic, as is reflected also in her low scores on the M-Scale. Interestingly, the prospect of her own death is something that terrifies Isabella and we see her, at all timepoints, struggling with that as well as with the question how a meaningful life would look like.

Isabella is a self-proclaimed atheist who absolutely identifies with this label, to the point that she attends meetings of the atheist community. And even though this strong self-identification seems to become weaker over time, it may still point to an important intercultural difference. It seems that in the US society it is more important to have a label for one's mindset, life style, or worldview, than it is in Germany. Moreover, being

Part C: Longitudinal Case Studies—Qualitative Analyses Including Quantitative Data

an atheist still seems more out of the norm in the US (Keller et al., 2018). This hypothesis might be illustrated by a little story that Isabella tells in her first interview:

Table 10.7: Isabella's Narrative: "Coming out as an Atheist"

Orientation	I guess around here, it's definitely majority Christian, but I don't think it's ever like, I don't ever feel like I would be in like physical danger if people found out I was atheist. [...] I've never had like any sort of bad or extreme reaction and I'm fairly out. I remember, this is actually an amusing anecdote. I was speaking to one of the people in my prior job and we were just sitting around and lunch talking about like somehow like what denomination are you and it came up because she's Greek Orthodox [...] and it got around me and I was like, "Oh, I'm an atheist. I'm not actually Christian."
Complication	And she was like, "Oh, what does that mean?" Like she had not heard the term "atheist." And so I said, "Oh, it means I don't believe in God." She said, "You-you wha-you-you don't believe in God?" like this was mind boggling, like the very idea had not crossed her mind that there might be people who actually don't believe in God. [...] And so she says, "Well, what do you believe in?" and that actually would have been a really interesting discussion, but another co-worker answered for me saying like, "Oh, it means she believes in like evolution and stuff."
Evaluation	And I try to say [...], "Well, evolution isn't really need to believe in. It's there whether you believe it or not." But then she was like, "What's evolution?" (laughing)
Resolution	Like I wasn't even going to like touch that. So. [...]
Coda	And like that was the weirdest reaction I got when I came out to someone, and it wasn't even like malicious or angry or anything, it was just like complete flabbergastedness that this option even existed. (Isabella, FDI, time 1)

This narrative hints at the struggles that might go along with being openly atheist, especially in some regions of the country. The danger of being beaten up or shunned for one's non-belief is obviously real (the interviewer confirms that). The rather funny story that follows this rather gloomy orientation serves to illustrate several things: First, one's denomination is a topic that may be talked about in a group of acquaintances. Second, it is obviously more normal to actually have a denomination than not to have one. The way Isabella recounts her co-workers' reaction to her outing makes it clear that being an atheist is something out of the ordinary. This is supported by the fact that another co-worker jumps in to explain what being an atheist means. This explanation for Isabella is maybe as "mind-boggling" as was her self-identification for her co-worker, since this explanation basically states that atheism is just a different form of believing, neglecting the fact that phenomena like evolution may not actually be subject to belief, but to evidence. She rates this as the "weirdest reaction" to her open atheism, which calls for caution when deducting intercultural differences. But experiencing a situation like that, and fearing to face threats because of one's non-belief, is something that would rather not be expected to happen in Germany.

Summed up, these two cases serve as illustrations of various kinds of non-belief. Both women stick to their basic worldviews they held in emerging adulthood, yet it seems that they have more come to terms with the way they are, appearing both more reassured and less defensive in their last interviews. This change partially shows in their type assignments: the development Nadine goes through is captured by her upward trajectory in the religious types, moving to a solid *predominantly individuative-reflective type* in her last interview; Isabella's development is subtler and not causing an upward movement in type. Her case study has shown how a constant *predominantly individuative-reflective type* may yet develop and how this type assignment shows in an atheist worldview. Viewing these two cases side by side has shown a glimpse of differing perspectives, in two different cultures, that offer us intriguing insight into the lives of these non-believers and how they have developed over time.

References

Bullik, R. (2024). Leitmotifs in life stories. Developments and stabilities of religiosity and narrative identity. Bielefeld University Press.

Coleman III, T. J., Silver, C. F., & Hood, R. W. (2016). "...if the universe is beautiful, we're part of that beauty."—A "neither religious nor spiritual" biography as horizontal transcendence. In H. Streib (Ed.), *Semantics and psychology of spirituality: A cross-cultural analysis* (pp. 355–372). Springer. https://doi.org/10.1007/978-3-319-21245-6_22

Costa, P. T. & McCrae, R. R. (1985/1992). *Revised NEO Personality Inventory (NEO PI-R) and NEO Five-Factor-Inventory (NEO-FFI). Professional manual.* Psychological Assessment Resources.

Cragun, R. T. (2016). Nonreligion and atheism. In D. Yamane (Ed.), *Handbooks of sociology and social research. Handbook of religion and society* (pp. 301–320). Springer International Publishing. https://doi.org/10.1007/978-3-319-31395-5_16

Erikson, E. H., & Erikson, J. M. (1998). *The life cycle completed* (Extended version). W.W. Norton.

Fowler, J. W., Streib, H., & Keller, B. (2004). *Manual for faith development research*. Research Center for Biographical Studies in Contemporary Religion.

Habermas, T., & Berger, N. (2011). Retelling everyday emotional events: Condensation, distancing, and closure. *Cognition & Emotion, 25*(2), 206–219. https://doi.org/10.1080/02699931003783568

Hood, J. R. W., Ghorbani, N., Watson, P. J., Ghramaleki, A. F., Bing, M. N., Davison, H. K., . . . Williamson, W. P. (2001). Dimensions of the Mysticism Scale: Confirming the three-factor structure in the United States and Iran. *Journal for the Scientific Study of Religion, 40*(4), 691–705. https://doi.org/10.1111/0021-8294.00085

Hood, R. W. (1975). The construction and preliminary validation of a measure of reported mystical experience. *Journal for the Scientific Study of Religion, 14*(1), 29. https://doi.org/10.2307/1384454

Keller, B., Bullik, R., Klein, C., & Swanson, S. B. (2018). Profiling atheist world views in different cultural contexts: Developmental trajectories and accounts. *Psychology of Religion and Spirituality, 10*(3), 229–243. https://doi.org/10.1037/rel0000212

Keller, B., Streib, H., Silver, C. F., Klein, C., & Hood, R. W. (2016). Design, methods, and sample characteristics of the Bielefeld-based cross-cultural study of "spirituality." In H. Streib (Ed.), *Semantics and psychology of spirituality: A cross-cultural analysis* (pp. 39–51). Springer. https://doi.org/10.1007/978-3-319-21245-6_4

Köber, C., & Habermas, T. (2017). How stable is the personal past? Stability of most important autobiographical memories and life narratives across eight years in a life span sample. *Journal of Personality and Social Psychology*, 113(4), 608–626.

Labov, W., & Waletzky, J. (1967). Narrative analysis: Oral versions of personal experience. *Journal of Narrative and Life History*, 7(1-4), 3–38. https://doi.org/10.1075/jnlh.7.02nar

Ryff, C. D. (1989). Happiness is everything, or is it? Explorations on the meaning of psychological well-being. *Journal of Personality and Social Psychology*, 57(6), 1069–1081. https://doi.org/10.1037/0022-3514.57.6.1069

Ryff, C. D., & Keyes, C. L. M. (1995). The structure of psychological well-being revisited. *Journal of Personality and Social Psychology*, 69(4), 719–727. https://doi.org/10.1037/0022-3514.69.4.719

Silver, C. F., Coleman, T. J., Hood, R. W., & Holcombe, J. M. (2014). The six types of nonbelief: a qualitative and quantitative study of type and narrative. *Mental Health, Religion & Culture*, 17(10), 990–1001. https://doi.org/10.1080/13674676.2014.987743

Streib, H. & Hood, R. W. (Eds.) (2016). *Semantics and psychology of spirituality: A cross-cultural analysis*. Springer. https://doi.org/10.1007/978-3-319-21245-6

Streib, H., Chen, Z. J., & Hood, R. W. (2020). Categorizing people by their preference for religious styles: Four types derived from evaluation of Faith Development Interviews. *International Journal for the Psychology of Religion*, 30(2), 112–127. https://doi.org/10.1080/10508619.2019.1664213

Streib, H., Chen, Z. J., & Hood, Jr., Ralph W. (2021). Faith development as change in religious types: Results from three-wave longitudinal data with faith development interviews. *Psychology of Religion and Spirituality*. https://doi.org/10.1037/rel0000440

Streib, H., Hood, R. W., & Klein, C. (2010). The religious schema scale: Construction and initial validation of a quantitative measure for religious styles. *International Journal for the Psychology of Religion*, 20(3), 151–172. https://doi.org/10.1080/10508619.2010.481223

Streib, H., & Keller, B. (2018). *Manual for the assessment of religious styles in faith development interviews (Fourth, revised edition of the "Manual for faith development research")*. Universität Bielefeld.

Streib, H., Klein, C., Keller, B., & Hood, R. (2021). The mysticism scale as a measure for subjective spirituality: New results with Hood's M-Scale and the development of a short form. In A. L. Ai, P. Wink, R. F. Paloutzian, & K. A. Harris (Eds.), *Assessing spirituality in a diverse world* (pp. 467–491). Springer International Publishing. https://doi.org/10.1007/978-3-030-52140-0_19

Chapter 11
"The Personal is always Connected to Society."
The Pro-Social Values of a Spiritual Atheist. The Case of Petra

Anika Steppacher, Ramona Bullik, & Barbara Keller[1]

Abstract *At the time of her first interview, Petra was a 41-year-old woman and is in her 50s by the time of her third one, thus giving us insights into an extended period of her midlife. She can be characterized as upward mover during this time as she moves from the predominantly conventional type in the first interview to the emerging dialogical-xenosophic type in the last two interviews, making her a rather consistent "emerging xenosophic type." Petra grew up in the strictly secular German Democratic Republic (GDR) in a family that was part of a Christian community. In her youth, she fled the GDR and left behind her religious upbringing as well, cultivating a worldview that can be described as spiritual atheism. Petra thereby preserves, despite her focus and appreciation of evidence-based reasoning, a remarkable openness to the spiritual realm. In her elaborations about moral and social questions she demonstrates a multitude of perspectives with a high degree of intellectual humility and honesty as well as concerns for others and society in general. In this chapter, we explore what it can mean to be spiritual while appreciating scientific reasoning and how this can affect moral reasoning.*

Keywords: *case study; narrative analysis; lifespan development; spiritual atheism; intellectual humility*

---

1   A. Steppacher, R. Bullik, B. Keller, Bielefeld University, Germany, E-mail: anika.steppacher@uni-bielefeld.de. © Heinz Streib, Ralph W. Hood Jr. (eds.): Faith in Development. Mixed-Method Studies on Worldviews and Religious Styles. First published in 2024 by Bielefeld University Press, Bielefeld, https://doi.org/10.14361/9783839471234-013

Part C: Longitudinal Case Studies—Qualitative Analyses Including Quantitative Data

For decades now, researchers in sociology and psychology of religion have been interested in the growing number of people self-identifying as *spiritual but not religious*. Spirituality has thereafter been widely characterized as an individualized and experience-oriented path (Streib & Hood, 2011) to connect to the transcendent vertically and horizontally inside and outside religious institutions (see Chapters 1 and 2 in this volume). However, for a better understanding of this phenomenon, we began investigating the subjective meaning of spirituality in order to learn what people actually mean by this self-description (Streib & Hood, 2016). Further, a great number of studies found that a large part of participants associated the term with their individual lifeworld, did so however especially with reference to their personal values, directing them in their everyday lives and connecting them with the world around them (Altmeyer et al., 2015; Ammerman, 2013; Berghuijs et al., 2013; Demmrich & Huber, 2019; Eisenmann et al., 2016; la Cour et al., 2012; Steensland et al., 2018; Zinnbauer et al., 1997). In this way, the moral dimension became an essential aspect in the understanding of contemporary spirituality which is supported by empirical evidence uncovering a correspondence of pro-social values and spirituality (Saroglou & Munoz-Garcia, 2008). However, especially with a focus on spiritual movements such as the New Age Movement, the significance of moral or social issues for self-identifying spiritual people has been put into question. Rather, this group is widely viewed as self-centered, and exclusively interested in self-improvement or therapeutic gains as well as purely secular motivations without any consideration of what is outside themselves like the people or society around them (Bellah et al., 1996; Bruce, 2017; Partridge, 2007). Based on their longitudinal study, Dillon, Wink, and Fay (2003) have cautioned that it is necessary to distinguish between different – more self-expanding versus more community-oriented – varieties of lived spirituality.

However, the conclusions within the research landscape on spirituality still seem divided. But is this really the case, or might a more reasonable assumption be that spirituality is used as such a broad term that it allows very different personal approaches to what surpasses the individual life? In order to better understand the meaning of spirituality in the life of a person, a case study approach, focusing on the biographical as well as moral reasoning of a single case offers a promising pathway. Therefore, we address this question with a longitudinal mixed-methods case study, combining results of survey answers with the findings derived from Faith Developments Interviews (FDIs). More precisely, this chapter will investigate with an in-depth perspective the narrative accounts as well as self-reporting statements of one of our three-wave cases with the pseudonym Petra.

At the time of her latest interview, Petra[2] is a 50-year-old health care worker who we interviewed three times over the course of eight years (interviews took place in 2011, 2017, and 2019) which gave us insight into a considerable period of her midlife. Growing up with a presumably Protestant background, she developed a stable atheist worldview

---

2   We discussed Petra in Keller et al. (2018) focusing on different varieties of atheism, as well as in Bullik et al. (2020). when discussing her non-religious journey in a cross-cultural perspective. Petra's interviews are also analyzed using network analysis in Chapter 7 in this volume.

in her young adult life[3]. Unsurprisingly, Petra states that she views herself as "not at all religious," does however self-identify as spiritual at all three times of data collection. Thus, from her survey answers we can conclude that Petra not only belongs to those who identify as *spiritual but not religious*, but also can be grouped to the *spiritual atheists* in our sample. The juxtaposition with the label "atheist" that at first glance seems to deny interest for the transcendent with the appreciation of spirituality is intriguing and raises interesting questions. Thus, in this chapter we explore Petra's non-religious meaning making as well as her moral reasoning and concerns for social and ethical questions with particular attention to her understanding of spirituality.

Changes in Survey Results

In this first part of the chapter, we are going to take a closer look at Petra's survey answers with regard to selected psychometric scales[4]. Thus, we examine how over the past eight years she has been relating to other religions, describing mystical experiences, and what personality traits can be observed according to her self-reports. In the table below, Petra's survey results are listed per wave, accompanied by the respective sample means as well as standard deviation (see Table 11.1).

The focus of the Religious Schema Scale is on how one views religions other than one's own on a "spectrum between a more fundamentalist orientation on the one hand and tolerance, fairness, and openness for dialog on the other" (Streib et al., 2010, p. 155). First, her scores on the RSS subscale *truth of texts and teaching*, measuring a literal and fundamentalist understanding of one's own faith tradition, is considerably lower than the sample mean for two out of three times of measurement. This indicates that Petra disagrees strongly throughout all three waves with a view of religion that makes absolute claims to the truth while rejecting dialog with other faith traditions. Petra's scores on *fairness, tolerance, and rational choice* are well within the sample mean and also stay rather stable and thus, we can assume that Petra has moderately tolerant views on religious pluralism. Her scores on *xenosophia/inter-religious dialog* on the other hand are more interesting: This scale measures the openness to be inspired by the strange, or how someone appreciates "the wisdom in encounter with the alien" (ibid., p. 155) and engage in dialog. Petra seems to be rather reserved toward an encounter with the unknown and toward a dialog with other worldviews, particular with religious beliefs, since her scores are substantially lower than the sample mean in the last two waves. This indicates that she increasingly rejects worldviews other than her own and becomes less open to learn and be moved by others. In sum, Petra seems to reject fundamentalist views while at the same time not being interested in interreligious dialog.

---

3   In her FDIs at time 1 and 2 she states explicitly her identification as an atheist whereas she does not use this label in her last interview. However, her survey answers show that she also identifies as an atheist "quite a bit" at time 3.

4   In this case study we chose to exclude Petra's scores on the Ryff-Scale as these results would not substantially further the broader research question of this chapter.

240　Part C: Longitudinal Case Studies—Qualitative Analyses Including Quantitative Data

Table 11.1: Selected Data from Petra's Survey Answers

	Wave 1		Wave 2		Wave 3	
	Petra	*M (SD)*	Petra	*M (SD)*	Petra	*M (SD)*
Religious Schema Scale						
truth of texts and teachings	1.00	2.53 (1.14)	1.40	2.35 (1.13)	1.20	2.55 (1.12)
fairness, tolerance..	4.20	4.38 (0.38)	4.20	4.35 (0.51)	4.40	4.59 (0.40)
xenosophia	3.20	3.64 (0.82)	2.60	3.58 (0.78)	2.80	3.77 (0.78)
M-Scale						
introvertive mysticism	2.75	3.52 (1.16)	2.17	3.60 (1.00)	2.50	3.40 (1.00)
extrovertive mysticism	2.50	3.45 (1.19)	3.00	3.46 (1.10)	2.88	3.29 (1.23)
interpretation	2.42	3.65 (1.11)	2.08	3.72 (1.00)	2.42	3.63 (1.00)
NEO-FFI						
emotional stability	3.00	3.40 (0.82)	3.25	3.40 (0.74)	2.75	3.41 (0.7)
extraversion	2.75	3.29 (0.62)	2.75	3.28 (0.66)	2.75	3.19 (0.64)
openness to experience	4.42	3.92 (0.49)	4.08	3.89 (0.5)	4.67	3.96 (0.55)
agreeableness	3.58	3.74 (0.46)	3.50	3.75 (0.49)	3.42	3.85 (0.52)
conscientiousness	3.17	3.69 (0.54)	3.17	3.73 (0.53)	3.25	3.79 (0.54)

Note: These calculations are based on a sample size of N = 75.

With the Mysticism Scale we gain insight into how our participants report on mystical experiences which can be both made within or outside faith traditions. Individuals might even characterize them as being the opposite of religion which further emphasizes the essential core characteristic of mysticism: experience as opposed to belief (Hood, 2006). This experience as reported by the participants and assessed by the *M-Scale* is, as Hood referred to it by citing Matilal, an experience "that is at once unitive and nondiscursive, at once self-fulfilling and self-effacing" (Matilal, 1992, p. 143). First, we see that Petra's score on *introvertive mysticism* is lower than the sample mean throughout all waves, but most remarkably so at the second one. Thus, we can assume that Petra has rather not had experiences of timelessness and spacelessness, ego loss, or ineffability (Streib et al., 2021). Her scores on *extrovertive mysticism* and thus on mystical experiences relating to the external world are similarly low and increase slightly in the last two waves. This means that experiences involving feeling unity with the universe seem rather foreign to her (ibid). Petra's scores on *interpretation* are throughout all three waves considerably lower than the sample mean. Thus, she does not seem to have had experiences she would classify as altering her sense of reality or that she would call sacred (ibid). We therefore can conclude that Petra seems to be someone who does not report on unexplainable or mind-altering experiences which seems most explicit at wave two.

Lastly, the NEO-FFI characterizes Petra's personality traits and how they changed over time. First, we notice that her *emotional stability* scores increase slightly from wave one to two, before decreasing somewhat in the last wave, while still being within the sample mean. This indicates that she sees herself as reasonably content with her emotional state, even if less so at the last wave. Petra's *extraversion* scores are well within the sample mean and do not change throughout the three waves. This means that she considers herself a moderately sociable person, not extensively seeking contact to others but not minding it either. Her *openness to experience* scores are more interesting because they are, at Wave one and three, very much above the sample mean and increase between the first and last wave, while decreasing slightly in between. Thus, for Petra it is important to see herself as someone who is interested in experiencing new situations and sensations and does appreciate other perspectives. This trait seems to be one Petra shares with other people that self-identify as spiritual (Saroglou & Munoz-Garcia, 2008). Her *agreeableness* scores are slightly below the mean, however, not substantially and they remain rather stable over time, suggesting that she sees herself neither overly accommodating nor dismissive. Generally, we can assume from Petra's NEO-FFI scores that at the time of her last interview she feels less emotionally stable and that she generally is a person interested in the exchange with others without being overly accommodating or outgoing.

Petra's scores give us a first impression on her attitudes regarding certain issues and how she views herself. We can conclude that she does not seem appreciative of religious teachings, no matter if they are fundamentalist or dialogical and similarly that a religious understanding of transcendent experience does not resonate with her. On the other hand, she exhibits a considerable openness for experiences and does not seem to be uninterested in the encounter with others. For a more in-depth understanding of Petra's trajectory, we turn from self-report measures to the structural as well as content analysis of her interviews.

Changes in Religious Styles

The religious style perspective offers characterizations of our participants' meaning-making processes. The religious styles assignments according to the *Manual* (Streib & Keller, 2018) grant us insight into the structures of *how* Petra reflects on her life and relationships, matters of religion and morality as well as how she constructs her worldview, understands symbols, and considers the perspectives of others[5]. Furthermore, the longitudinal design with three points of data collection broadens our understanding of how these structures developed.

In Petra's first interviews her religious style could be described as predominantly mutual (Style 3), with a tendency toward an individuative-systemic style (Style 4). A Style 3 perspective is mostly exhibited in Petra's moral reasoning and form of world coherence. Thus, it can be assumed that she tends to answer moral questions with reference to her

---

5   Especially between the time of the first and second interview, there have been revisions to the *Manual*. At the time of the first interview, the answers were evaluated according to seven aspects: *form of logic, social perspective-taking, form of moral judgment, bounds of social awareness, locus of authority, forms of world coherence*, and *level of symbolic functioning*, which were later shortened by *form of logic* and slightly renamed (see also chapters 1 and 3 for a brief history of the development of the method).

own social group and offers a rather tacit understanding of how her worldview is constructed. On the other hand, we see that Petra's form of logic and symbolic functioning tend toward Style 4 and can thus be characterized as being more reflective and relying on explicit considerations.

At Petra's second interview, the image has changed significantly. Her religious style can now be depicted as individuative-systemic (Style 4) with elements of a dialogical religious style (Style 5). *Perspective-taking, social horizon* and *locus of authority* are entirely considered being Style 4 which means that Petra has a systemic and conceptually mediated view of others and the world around her, influenced by self-selected and self-ratified assumptions. Her answers regarding *morality* on the other hand seem to exhibit a more complex reasoning, surpassing ideological assumptions and striving for a prior-to-society reasoning oriented towards universal principles. A similar tendency can be observed in Petra's *form of world coherence*, where she can appreciate the complexity of reality with an openness to aspects she cannot explain.

In Petra's third rating this trend seems to continue as her religious style can still be characterized as primarily oscillating between individuative-systemic (Style 4) and dialogical (Style 5). Thus, we can conclude that Petra's views are still filtered through an ideological lens when thinking about others and when choosing her social surroundings. However, her reasoning when it comes to moral questions and symbols seem to occasionally surpass ideological boundaries. Thus, although she still tends to interpret moral issues and symbols as reflected by her self-chosen principles, she can also appreciate the multi-layered nature of these issues. The same is true when looking at Petra's *form of world coherence* and *locus of authority*: She is more appreciative of complexity, can critically reflect on her own views and takes multiple perspectives.

In sum, there seems to be a significant development in Petra's reasoning which tended toward normative assumptions and in-group orientation in her first and a more complex thinking about these issues in the last interview. We now turn to the content of Petra's interviews which might help us see her survey answers and religious style in a different light.

Life Review: Secular Seeking

Petra grew up in the former German Democratic Republic (GDR) and thus in a society committed to a socialist political order as well as materialist and atheist educational principles. Until this day, East Germany is considered a predominantly secular region which is mostly attributed to a highly successful and lasting campaign by the former socialist state. However, in this strictly secular society religious communities persisted even though they did so in rather precarious conditions and in tension with the socialist state (Wohlrab-Sahr et al., 2009). Petra's family was one of those families that held on to their Christian tradition, and thus she experienced both a religious as well as atheist education. However, although the religious environment she was brought up in can be characterized as opposing to the secular societal norms, Petra does not mention any major conflicts or disadvantages in terms of her education or career which research suggests would have been quite common for children from religious families (ibid, p. 24). Interestingly, this autonomous space outside the state's control that is maybe best exemplified by Petra attending a Christian kindergarten and therefore receiving a religious preschool education, was not challenged by the state. Instead of facing obstacles due to this deviation from the state's atheist principles, the affiliation to the Christian community is presented as an advantageous situation as it provided employment to her mother and an enjoyable family tradition passed on by her devout grandmother. Petra is well aware of the special situation she grew up in, presents it, however, as a merely practical and normative practice.

> And that was more a kind [...] of rite, actually a kind of ritual praying, that you do in the evening, because I learned it that way. And to nicely state your wishes and so on. (Petra, FDI, time 3)[6]

There is futhermore an interesting shift that can be observed in Petra's life reviews over the years: Whereas in her first interview she talks more about her upbringing in a religious context and the following disengagement from it, growing up in the GDR becomes a much more central topic in the consecutive interviews. This might be illustrated by the fact that in her first interview she only talks about the GDR once but it becomes an increasingly important theme in her life reviews during the second and particularly in her last interview. When talking about her socialization and childhood beliefs, she seems to have a growing appreciation for the secular teachings as opposed to the religious ones furthered by her family. She even goes so far as to state that she "returned to the wordview of her childhood"[7] (Petra, FDI, time 3) referencing the materialist education she received in the GDR. In another quote, she opposes the two views in more detail.

> [...] I did not question my religious attitude because it was associated with positive things, as I said, in the first phase, I was not pushed. Although I was always reminded to think of the good Lord and pray and so on, [...] but in school, of course in the GDR I was confronted with absolutely atheistic attitudes, but the scientific ... this was also not simply presented, but they tried to theoretically and logically and with means of knowledge, which yes ... God is not tangible, so this had a certain basis, this had a certain methodology. And you could accept them or you couldn't. And that at least taught me to question things.[8] (Petra, FDI, time 2)

---

6   Und das war aber eher so eine Art [...], so ein Ritus, so eine Art rituelles Beten war das eigentlich, abends zu sagen, weil ich das auch so gelernt habe. Und dann mal schön noch Bitten zu formulieren und so weiter.

7   ich im Prinzip zurückgekommen bin zur Weltanschauung meiner Kindheit.

8   [...] meine religiöse Einstellung, die habe ich nicht hinterfragt, weil sie eben mit positiven Sachen verbunden war, wie gesagt, in der 1. Phase, man mich auch nicht gedrängt hat. Man zwar immer mal den Finger gehoben hat und denk an den lieben Gott und schön beten und so weiter, [...] aber auf der anderen in der Schule, mit natürlich in der DDR absolut atheistischen Einstellungen konfrontiert war, aber die wissenschaftlich ... die auch nicht einfach dahingestellt waren, sondern man hat schon versucht, das Ganze theoretisch und logisch und mit Mitteln der Erkenntnis, die ja ... Gott ist ja nicht erkennbar, also das hatte eine gewisse Grundlage, das hatte eine gewisse Methodik. Und die konnte man nun annehmen oder konnte man nicht. Und das hat mich zumindest gelehrt, Dinge zu hinterfragen.

244 Part C: Longitudinal Case Studies—Qualitative Analyses Including Quantitative Data

The religious practices, although being experienced as pleasant by her childhood self, today seem hollow and meaningless as compared to the secular teachings she received as child and now returns to in later adulthood. Petra seems to share this lasting appreciation for a scientifically grounded education system dedicated to rational principles with many other former GDR citizens as it is a popular theme in biographical research in Eastern Germany (Wohlrab-Sahr et al., 2009, p. 350).

This is part of an interesting development in her life review as it is a reencounter with a worldview she distanced herself from very radically in young adulthood. When Petra was approximately 20 years old, she fled the GDR before the official reunification of East and West Germany and as soon as the borders were partially opened between the Federal Republic of Germany and the Czechoslovak Socialist Republic. This decision is presented as adventurous and spontaneous as she had no way of knowing if the borders would close again, making her move to the West a possibly permanent separation from her family and former social surroundings.

> Yes, of course, this flight was significant for me, like, these concrete life changes, concrete life circumstances that have changed. This complete overturning of a worldview that you had up to a certain point.[9] (Petra, FDI, time 2)

> But, just the thought that you go away at such a young age. And there was also the question of not returning back. The borders were still closed at that time. The borders could have been closed again, after I fled across the border, although it was relatively late in '89. And then the thread to my family here would have been torn off, so to speak.[10] (Petra, FDI, time 3)

Petra stresses that the reason for her decision to leave the GDR in such a risky and consequential way were not any tangible disadvantages, suffering or conflicts with the socialist state, but her striving for freedom. She wanted to travel freely and enjoy the seemingly glamourous consumer society she imagined in the West. In her accounts she presents herself as a rebellious, maybe even carefree young woman hungry for experiences and adventures with happiness, autonomy and enjoyment at the center of her decision to leave everything she had known behind.

> [I: And you went to the West for professional reasons?] No, that was actually … it was really a flight and […] the reason was basically rather worldly, respectively to be subsumed under the broad term freedom. […] So more precisely, I actually wanted to travel and of course I wanted to have certain material advantages. They seemed

---

9   Ja, bedeutsam war natürlich für mich diese Flucht, also diese konkreten Lebensänderungen, konkrete Lebensumstände, die sich geändert haben. Dieses komplette Umwerfen eines Weltbildes, was man bis zu einem gewissen Zeitpunkt hatte.

10 Aber, allein schon der Gedanke vielleicht, dass man abhaut in so einem jugendlichen Alter. Und da war ja auch die Frage des nicht Wiederkehrens, ja, zurück. Die Grenzen waren ja damals noch zu. Es hätte ja auch sein können, dass die Grenzen jetzt nun wieder zugingen, nachdem ich da über die Grenze geflüchtet bin, wobei es relativ spät war da, 89 war das. Und dann wäre ja auch sozusagen der Faden abgerissen zu meiner Familie hier.

more tangible to me in the West and not in the East. That was the reason why I left [...].[11] (Petra, FDI, time 2)

Similarly to the focus on her socialization in the GDR, she only talks about this episode in the second and third interviews and it illustrates a coherent image of herself as someone who takes risky decisions seemingly on a whim and even though they could be considered reckless or at least highly consequential and unusual by normative standards. Rather casually she mentions for example that she married and presumably divorced someone without any further elaboration which is only one circumstance in which she calls herself and her actions "unconventional," or as doing "things everybody would say, you cannot do that, and I do it anyway"[12] (Petra, FDI, time 3).

Petra's self-image as outside the norm can also be illustrated by how she presents her beliefs as opposed to the greater society she is living in: In the secular GDR, she grows up in a religious context, which she recognized as unusual, whereas in West Germany where it is considered much more common to belong to the Protestant or Catholic church she identifies as an atheist. In both cases she does not emphasize alienation or even discrimination she could have experienced. On the contrary, as mentioned above, being part of a religious community even came with certain advantages such as her mother's employment but also little privileges such as religious festivities which meant special gifts and consumer items not readily accessible to other children in the GDR. Furthermore, in the Federal German Republic, atheism is nothing foreign and has its place in a society that upholds the ideal of religious or non-religious pluralism (Silver et al., 2014). However, as we are going to see in her first interview, she puts herself in the position of the outsider when she argues in favor of religion in her atheist surroundings, as well as against the churches within the religious context of her work for a health care facility operated by a Christian institution. In both cases, she takes the unusual, uncomfortable position which, ironically, would have been completely aligned with the norm the other way around.

So, for me, the only time I defended God or even religion was because of my teacher. That was the civics teacher and he was an atheist, most of the teachers were, actually, and it was about causalities etc. and then we talked about whether you would come to the conclusion that it was God when you talk about creation and [...] he then said, yes and who created God or Adam or Eve, [...] but I tried to defend that and he in

---

11 [I: Und das waren dann berufliche Gründe, dass Sie in den Westen gegangen sind?] Nein, das war tatsächlich eine Flucht [...], der Grund war eigentlich ein eher materieller beziehungsweise unter dem groben Begriff Freiheit zu fassen. [...] Also um es konkret zu machen, also ich wollte eigentlich reisen und wollte natürlich auch gewisse materielle Vorteile haben. Die schienen mir nun im Westen greifbar zu sein und nicht im Osten. Das war der Grund, warum ich gegangen bin [...]

12 Sachen, von denen jeder sagen würde, nee, das kann man nicht so machen und das mache ich aber dann trotzdem.

Part C: Longitudinal Case Studies—Qualitative Analyses Including Quantitative Data

> turn went along with it and, so I actually only took a counterposition.[13] (Petra, FDI, time 1)

> [I] try to influence my personal surroundings, my work colleagues, etc., not to influence them, but at least to talk to them and collect counterarguments. So, [...] I always try take the opposite position, in order to ultimately come to a sort of thesis, antithesis perhaps, and then to a solution and I do that, but rather in my personal environment and as I said at work.[14](Petra, FDI, time 1)

Furthermore, Petra's criticism toward her religious employer becomes an increasingly important topic, and especially the circumstance that she cannot formally terminate membership with the church because of the right to her employer to fire her if she decides to do so. However, by the time of her third interview we see Petra's risk taking once again when she decides to disaffiliate anyway without certainty that this decision might cost her employment.

> So [leaving the church] was almost a mandatory step that I should have taken a long time ago. But, as I said, I couldn't. And that, I have to say, does not speak (laughs) in favor of the Church. I can't because that's grounds for dismissal. But if you look at it, who pays for the hospitals, who pays for everything? That's what the state does and in principle I myself now pay for the whole hospital. [...] But why I did it now, it was the mandatory step at some point. [...] So I'm very curious and I'm really interested, it's like a small experiment, so there is constant talk of how bad the situation is in the hospitals. That there is no staff. And I am now interested in the extent to which the mission, the concrete mandate to help people, is met, so to speak, by dismissing a [health care professional].[15] (Petra, FDI, time 3)

---

13 Also für mich hat das einzige Mal, dass ich Gott verteidigt habe oder überhaupt die Religion war gegenüber meinem Lehrer. Das war der Staatsbürgerkundelehrer und der war Atheist, waren die meisten Lehrer eigentlich und da ging es um Kausalitäten usw. und wir haben dann darüber geredet, ob man nicht zum Schluss wer hat was erschaffen auf Gott kommt und [...] er sagte dann, ja und wer hat Gott erschaffen oder Adam oder Eva, [...] aber das habe ich da versucht zu verteidigen und er wiederum hat das mitgemacht und hat, also ich habe im Prinzip nur eine Kontrastellung eingenommen.

14 [Ich] versuche dann eben aber eher mein persönliches Umfeld, meine Arbeitskollegen usw. zu beeinflussen, nicht beeinflussen, sondern zumindest mit ihnen zu reden und Gegenargumente zu sammeln. Also [...] ich versuche mich auch immer auf den Gegenstandpunkt zu stellen, um letztlich zu einer, also These, Antithese vielleicht, und dann zu einer Lösung zu kommen und das mache ich aber eher in so einem persönlichen Umfeld und wie gesagt in der Arbeit.

15 Also [der Kirchenaustritt] ist ja quasi zwingender Schritt gewesen, den ich schon lange hätte machen sollen. Aber, wie gesagt, ich konnte es ja nicht. Und das, muss man sagen, das spricht nun auch nicht (lächelt) für die Kirche. Ich kann es nicht, weil es ein Kündigungsgrund ist. Wenn man sich jetzt aber betrachtet, wer bezahlt die Krankenhäuser, wer bezahlt alles? Das macht ja der Staat und ich im Prinzip ja nun selber bezahle ja nun die ganzen Krankenhäuser. [...] Aber warum ich es jetzt gemacht habe, es war ja irgendwann der zwingende Schritt. [...] Also ich bin sehr gespannt, was mich auch ausgesprochen interessiert, wie so ein kleines Experiment, also wird hier auch ständig kolportiert, wie schlecht es in den Krankenhäusern aussieht. Dass es kein Personal gibt. Und mich interessiert jetzt, inwieweit man sozusagen dem Inhalt, dem konkreten Auftrag, Menschen

The way she talks about this presumably consequential step is interesting: She presents this decision as an experiment seemingly removed from her actual life world and as if it did not have severe personal consequences for her, implicitly presenting herself, again, as a person who is ready to take risks and is not afraid to face the consequences of her actions. However, the grievances she has with her work are major themes especially in her last two interviews: Besides the religious background being an essential point of concern, she equally criticizes the compensation she considers too low, especially considering the workload and responsibilities she has as a health care worker. In the last interview, this criticism becomes even more explicit as she had to move back to her small town of origin because she could no longer afford the rent in the big city she had been living in for years[16]. According to her survey answers, Petra can be considered to be in a comparatively low-income group as she earns considerably less than 30,000 € a year, and even less after moving to the Eastern part of Germany at the time of her last interview. However, aside from the criticism of lower wages in East Germany, one additional aspect that contributes to her economic situation is that Petra has during almost all her employment history worked part-time. This was a decision she made consciously as she wanted more time for her personal development which she reflects quite positively on in her second interview:

> So, I've always worked part-time, and I have to say, again and again I have a permanent feeling of freedom. Freedom in the sense of being able to dispose of my time. [...] Although I don't have as much in the material sense as I did when I was working full-time, because of traveling and so on, I still have a sense of freedom by having time for myself or [...] for reflections and so on. [...] This is really a very positive feeling, I have to say again and again, especially when I am always confronted with it, yes. And also the joy to say: Well, I'm going to plan my day on my own terms.[17] (Petra, FDI, time 2)

However, the tone changes considerably by the time of her last interview: Besides her now being forced to leave a city she actually would have preferred to continue living in, she is also confronted with the prospect of a small pension after a long working history which adds to her anxiety as well as her social criticism. She is afraid of poverty in old age despite having worked all her life in a demanding and socially important position

---

zu helfen, dahingehend nachkommt, indem man eine [Fachperson im Gesundheitswesen] entlässt.

16 According to Statista, a German company providing statistics on market developments, rent prizes in Germany have increased by 8% nationwide from 2015 to 2018. The economic pressure caused by housing costs has been most severe in urban areas with the city Petra used to live in being one of the most expensive places to live in terms or rent prizes (Statista, 2021).

17 Also ich hatte immer nur eine Teilzeitstelle und ich muss sagen, immer wieder habe ich ein permanentes Gefühl von Freiheit. Freiheit im Sinne, über meine Zeit verfügen zu können. [...] Ich habe zwar materiell jetzt nicht mehr so viel zur Verfügung wie früher als ich voll arbeitete, wegen der Reisen und so weiter, aber ich habe trotzdem wirklich ein Freiheitsgefühl dadurch, dass Zeit für mich beziehungsweise [...] für das Nachdenken und so weiter habe. [...] Das ist wirklich ein sehr positives Gefühl, muss ich immer wieder sagen, grade wenn ich immer wieder drauf gestoßen werde. Ja. Und auch Freude zu sagen: Hach, ich teile mir einen Tag jetzt heute mal selber ein.

Part C: Longitudinal Case Studies—Qualitative Analyses Including Quantitative Data

and now feels that her capabilities for personal fulfillment are unfairly narrowed which makes her decision to risk her employment by the disaffiliation from the church even more surprising.

> So, as I said, right now I'm in a crisis and I have to say, damn it, at my age you have to... I'm going to get a small pension, how am I going to live? At the current state in my life, I have to deal with it, so to speak, and I have to be afraid of what my future will look like. And if, as I said, I have to make a living and that I have enough income and that I do not disadvantage others, I have to deal with that. And this is so pathetic to our world that in general I really have a very pessimistic worldview.[18] (Petra, FDI, time 3)

Nevertheless, the central theme in Petra's life review does not center so much on her life circumstances, although she gives extensive accounts on them, but on the development of herself by honest reflection and rigorous inquiry. This is a developmental trajectory one might characterize as a form of personal enlightenment in the sense of widening her capabilities to understand the world by the means of personal study. In her first interview, she points to the start of this journey by critically reviewing religious teachings and the image of God in particular which is prompted by the deeper involvement in the Catholic church of a close friend of hers.

> [...] a friend of mine [...] wanted to study theology and then I started to engage in these questions [...] and I started to research it and engage as best I could and then of course my awakening began, so to speak, that I actually rationally thought about it and also listened to my inner voice and tried to define this word God etc. for me: what does it actually mean, how do I understand it and how do others understand it etc. and I investigated this issue very thoroughly and that ultimately led to the rift with him [...] and then in the end I developed my attitude which I also somehow refined and changed over the years because I always read and listen to new things and [....] I would call myself an atheist.[19] (Petra, FDI, time 1)

---

18 Also wie gesagt, im Moment bin ich so, dass ich in einer Krise bin und sagen muss, verdammt nochmal, in meinem Alter muss man- ich werde wenig Rente bekommen, wie werde ich leben? Ich muss mich sozusagen jetzt in meinem Leben damit beschäftigen und muss Angst haben, wie sieht meine Zukunft aus. Und muss mich, wie gesagt, mit Geld und dass ich genügend Auskommen habe und das ich andere auch nicht benachteilige, damit muss ich mich beschäftigen. Und das ist dermaßen erbärmlich für unsere Welt, dass ich im Prinzip wirklich eine sehr pessimistische Weltanschauung habe.

19 [...]ein Freund von mir [...] wollte Theologie studieren und dann habe ich mich damit beschäftigt [...] und dann fing ich aber an darüber zu recherchieren und mich damit auseinanderzusetzen so gut ich das konnte und da fing natürlich dann so mein Erwachen an sozusagen, dass ich tatsächlich damit, also rational mir überlegt habe und auch in mich hineingehorcht habe und das versucht habe, dieses Wort Gott oder usw. für mich erstmal zu definieren, was ist das überhaupt, was versteht man darunter und was verstehen andere darunter usw. und da habe ich mich wirklich sehr massiv damit beschäftigt und das führte dann letztlich auch zum Bruch mit demjenigen [...] und dann habe ich eben letztlich meine Einstellung entwickelt, die sich immer irgendwie auch ein bisschen verfeinert und verändert so im Laufe der Jahre, weil ich immer wieder neue Sachen lese und höre und [....] ich würde mich schon als Atheist bezeichnen.

The examination of religious teachings she had received in her childhood and had not critically scrutinized before led not only to a rupture in this friendship but to the "awakening" of a new worldview she is at that time comfortable in calling atheism. This disengagement from Christian beliefs is presented as the central turning point in her first and second interview which preceded her current secular worldview and way of thinking about questions with existential meaning. Thus, criticism of religion can be interpreted as the corner stone of current worldview. Although she did not follow Christian teachings or integrated them in her life, she talks about a certain anxiety when denouncing God and religion openly as if there still were some residues of her religious socialization which she has to thoroughly remove. In her first interview, this process seems to be ongoing, and she even still follows certain religious practices:

> As I said, this detachment from religion was also a bit fearful. Well, as I said, I was actually socialized like that, but had not really noticed it, until later and I still have concerns, like will the good God punish me. So, I still have that, but it's getting less and less and the detachment process, as I said, was already intense and now it is getting less and less and that's why I pray occasionally.[20] (Petra, FDI, time 1)

Whereas in the second interview she talks about this episode initiated by the friend's turn to faith as well but very briefly and without further elaboration, this turning point seems to be caused by the personal encounter with a philosopher in the third one. Criticism of religion still is the central cause of these new reflections, however, the disengagement from religion seems to be completed without any emotional consequences for Petra.

> And that's when I became concerned with criticism of religion. And that's where I met this philosopher [...] and that's when I started to read about the matter as far as I could. And [...] that's when my studies began to engage more deeply with such things and to see, oh God, it's not that simple. And then I read specifically about criticism of religion and at that moment I also realized how influenced I am, although I would not have thought so, and there I really have to say how indoctrinated I have been, religiously.[21] (Petra, FDI, time 3)

---

20 Wie gesagt, ist ja auch noch so ein bisschen angstbesetzt diese Loslösung von der Religion. Also ich hatte ja dann nun gesagt, dass ich da eigentlich sozialisiert bin, das aber gar nicht so richtig wahrgenommen hatte, sondern eher dann später und dass ich immer trotzdem noch so Bedenken habe, dafür wird mich der liebe Gott bestrafen. Also das habe ich durchaus noch, aber das wird eben immer weniger und der Ablösungsprozess, wie gesagt, der war schon heftig und jetzt wird es immer weniger und deswegen bete ich gelegentlich noch.

21 Und da habe ich mich dann mit Religionskritik beschäftigt. Und da bin ich auch auf diesen Philosophen [...] getroffen und da habe ich mich in die Materie eingelesen, soweit mir das möglich war. Und [...] da fing auch mein Studium an, mich eben tiefergehend mit solchen Dingen zu beschäftigen und zu sehen, oh Gott, so einfach ist das aber alles nicht. Und da habe ich mich dann konkret mit Religionskritik beschäftigt und habe in dem Moment auch festgestellt, wie geprägt ich doch bin, obwohl ich das gar nicht gedacht hätte, wie also und da muss ich wirklich sagen, wie indoktriniert ich auch gewesen bin, also religiös.

Part C: Longitudinal Case Studies—Qualitative Analyses Including Quantitative Data

In all three interviews, criticism toward religion is presented as a turning point and a central component of her life review which led her to the current chapter in her life which is characterized by studying, reflecting, growth in her understanding of the world and open discussion. The complexity and seriousness of this process can be illustrated in the following quotes:

> The third or even the more interesting is, the discovery of knowledge itself, in other words, understanding. So, I was always very interested in that, to try to understand the world. Before, I actually was in fixed tracks and there was no window and I think I've overcome that a bit after a time.[22] (Petra, FDI, time 1)

> And further experiences of liberation, yes, this mental freedom, I have to say that, which basically is an illusion. But nevertheless, I feel that (laughs) just quantitatively, the more information you absorb, the more variables you have, the freer you feel at least. And that never stops, there is always something to add. [...] Just the thought that you are able to. I have to say that when I look back now, this is one of the greatest experiences for me.[23] (Petra, FDI, time 3)

When reviewing Petra's life reviews, a broad spectrum of themes emerges accompanied by meaningful turning points which are retrospectively evaluated. Her life story centers around extraordinary experiences as well as a constant pursuit of knowledge and personal growth. In the following parts of this chapter, we learn how this biographical background interacts with Petra's relationships as well as religious and moral stances.

Relationships: Autonomy and the Struggle with Trust

Petra grew up in a single parent household with her mother and brother as her parents separated when she was still a very young child. In all three interviews she describes this upbringing as a precarious situation with an unreliable caregiver.

> My parents, or the father, was rather absent and I would describe my mother as a bit unstable. But, on the other hand very combative and very committed and very protective in a positive sense, so basically a bit unpredictable for me, or ambivalent actually, and yes as I said, the father was rather absent. He wasn't there, but I did

---

22 Das Dritte ist oder noch weitere interessante, ja das Entdecken auch von Wissen an sich, also von Erkenntnis. Also das hat mich immer sehr interessiert, dass man versuchen kann die Welt zu verstehen. Das war vorher für mich eigentlich in festen Bahnen und es gab kein Fenster und das meine ich ein bisschen überwunden zu haben in der Zeit.

23 Und weitere Befreiungserlebnisse, ja, diese gedankliche Freiheit, das muss ich auch sagen, die ich, im Grunde ist es ja eine Illusion. Aber trotzdem empfinde ich das (lächelt) einfach auch quantitativ, je mehr Information man aufnimmt, je mehr Variablen, je freier kommt man sich zumindest vor. Und das hört aber ja nie auf, es kommt ja immer wieder was hinzu. [...] Überhaupt den Gedanken zu reflektieren auch. Das das muss ich sagen, wenn ich jetzt zurückblicke, das ist für mich eines der größten Erlebnisse.

know him, he is rather, almost insignificant. So I'm a child of divorce, and this happened when I was two years old and that's why I probably don't have any conscious emotional attachments.[24] (Petra, FDI, time 1)

In contrast to her father with whom she does not seem to have any deeper emotional connection, the relationship to her mother is difficult and "ambivalent" as she describes her as rather unsecure and emotionally not available. Petra's attachment to her mother might therefore be characterized as an insecure one, failing to provide her childhood self with security and support (Granqvist et al., 2020). However, although the image of the emotionally distant mother in her childhood is stable throughout all three interviews, she offers a seemingly contradictory picture of her: on the one hand unstable and overwhelmed, on the other hand protective and strong when faced with adverse circumstances. This is especially visible when she reflects on her mother's behavior from the standpoint of her adult self in the first and second interview, oscillating between reproach and understanding but seeing their formerly distanced relationship improved.

[...] yes, ambivalent for me, or unclear for me. What does she actually want, my mother for example, what does she want from me, but that has improved, because I just see that she had difficulties in a certain way at that time and I understood that [...], it just doesn't help me, because many things went wrong, and I have to deal with them later. But I see her now as a woman who had to go her way somehow with the many difficulties that she had.[25] (Petra, FDI, time 1)

Although Petra still recognizes her mother's struggles and difficult living situation in which she had to bring up her and her brother, her tone gets less apologetic and more frustrated when she talks about her upbringing in the last interview. To understand this change, it is worth reviewing the relational history between Petra and her mother. Following a conflict-ridden and, as she states, "bad" relationship in childhood and especially in her youth, Petra decided to leave not only the GDR but also her mother to flee to West Germany without, as mentioned above, knowing whether or not she might see her again. After this abrupt break followed a period of three years with little contact and therefore little fights. Petra describes this time as calming for both herself and her mother, giving them time to reflect on their relationship, with her mother acknowledging mistakes

---

24 Meine Eltern, also der Vater war eher abwesend und meine Mutter würde ich eher so ein bisschen als labil bezeichnen. Aber auch auf der anderen Seite sehr kämpferisch und sehr engagiert und sehr beschützend im positiven Sinne, also im Grunde so ein bisschen für mich uneinschätzbar, so ambivalent eigentlich, und ja gut wie gesagt, der Vater war eher abwesend. Der war ja nicht da, aber ich habe ihn auch erlebt, ist eher, fast schon unbedeutend. Ja. Also ich bin ein Scheidungskind, deswegen wahrscheinlich und das war im 2. Lebensjahr und deshalb habe ich wahrscheinlich auch keine bewussten emotionalen Bindungen.

25 ja ambivalent für mich, also unklar für mich. Was möchte sie eigentlich meine Mutter z. B., was will sie von mir und wie, das hat sich aber verbessert, weil ich eben einfach sehe, dass sie eben damals Schwierigkeiten in gewisser Weise hatte und das habe ich verstanden [...], es nutzt mir nur im Grunde nichts, weil eben dann, wenn viele Dinge schief gelaufen sind, ich muss später damit zurecht kommen. Aber ich sehe sie jetzt als als Frau, die ihren Weg da irgendwie gehen musste mit vielen Schwierigkeiten, die sie eben gehabt hat.

Part C: Longitudinal Case Studies—Qualitative Analyses Including Quantitative Data

and Petra having time to miss and appreciate her from the far. Thus, the geographical distance may have facilitated emotional distance and reflection. This may have led to a time of reconciliation, still not entirely harmonious and with occasional conflicts, but enjoyable and considerably warmer than before. However, this changes when Petra moves back to the small town where she grew up in and where her mother is much closer to her, with old conflicts now ever more present. It seems as if the conflict was bearable for Petra as long as it was more abstract and distant and not actually experienced giving her the opportunity to theorize about it and making it less emotionally challenging. Now, old unresolved conflicts come to the surface again "that lay dormant because of the local separation" (Petra, FDI, time 3)[26] and she presents her mother as an adult she could have expected more of legitimating her original criticism instead of relativizing it:

> And that changed now, I have to say, well, I pitied her as well. But that has changed in such a way that I think to myself, well, she knew what she wanted. And she was a sophisticated person and the resistance is still right, [...] because even if many things are not her fault, I cannot forgive her everything, so to speak, and bend to her will, so to speak, or her ideas of how to be. So that has changed.[27] (Petra, FDI, time 3)

Her distant mother is contrasted by a warm and loving grandmother that is presented as an essential and important attachment figure. When talking about her, this is one of the rare cases in which Petra talks unambiguously describing her as a virtuous, caring and affectionate person she could rely on:

> Otherwise in terms of relatives I definitely need to mention my grandmother to whom I had a very close relationship, who did not live in the same town, a few kilometers away, but to whom I could always go, who was always positive. She was rather pious [...] a practical piety rather. That is, she embodied what is ideally understood with Christianity, i.e. piety, pious behavior, willingness to help. Willingness to help strangers [...]. So in that way, my grandmother was an example for me [...].[28] (Petra, FDI, time 2)

---

26 die hat nur mal geschlummert eben aufgrund der örtlichen Auseinanderseins.

27 Und dann hat sich das jetzt im Jetzt verändert, dass ich sagen muss, naja, das war zwar dieses mitleidige Bild, war das auch. Aber das hat sich dahingehend verändert, dass ich mir denke, naja, die wusste schon auch, was sie wollte. Und das ist eben eine differenzierte Person gewesen und der Widerstand ist schon immer noch richtig, [...] weil sie für viele Dinge nichts konnte, dass ich ihr dann sozusagen alles durchgehen lasse und mich sozusagen ihre Sache sozusagen oder ihren Vorstellungen, wie ich zu sein habe, beuge. Also das hat sich verändert.

28 Ansonsten zu Verwandtschaft auf jeden Fall noch meine Großmutter wäre da noch zu nennen, zu der ich eine sehr inniges Verhältnis hatte, die nicht am selben Ort wohnte, ein paar Kilometer weiter, aber zu der ich eigentlich immer kommen konnte, die immer positiv eingestellt war. Die war relativ fromm und aber [...] also eine praktische Frömmigkeit eher. Das heißt, sie hat das, was im Idealfall unter Christentum, also unter Frömmigkeit, frommen Verhalten, versteht, also Hilfsbereitschaft. Hilfsbereitschaft Fremden auch gegenüber [...] Also das hat meine Oma mir vorgelebt, [...].

Petra describes her grandmother as a devout Christian and sees the close relationship she had with her as the reason why she experienced Christianity as something positive as a child. Despite her personal aversion towards the church and Christian dogma nowadays—which will be explored in more detail below—, she sees her as a moral ideal because of her charity and altruism she interprets as general virtues.

Petra seems to have been a very sociable person, or maybe she still is. However, it is striking that she mostly talks about numerous relationships in the past that broke away over time. In all three interviews, she talks about a group of friends she met as a young adult and with whom she had an impressionable time, feeling accepted and at home in what she deems a counter-culture milieu, which she elaborates for example in her last interview:

> And the other relationships were like, just these loose relationships with friends. They have shaped me in a way that they have made my life easier. That I immersed myself in that life, so to speak, which was completely different. And they somehow took me as I am. Even if I was or still am a bit weird. [...] Even though, as I said, not everything has always been so rosy, but due to the many people, and also in the subculture, where you are generally always more accepted if you are a little different, this may have saved me in a way from a not so beautiful life or phase of life.[29] (Petra, FDI, time 3)

However, when talking about her social surroundings, the focus seems to rely more on groups than on individual friendships. Apparently, there has been a variety of friendships that were of great importance to her at some point but that did not hold until the present. We learn, in each interview, from different relationships to people she felt close to but does not anymore. For example, in her first interview she talks about her friend who wanted to become a priest and because of the incompatibility of their worldviews this friendship broke apart, as further described above. In her second interview she talks about a very close friend she knew since school who suddenly died several years ago which meant a great loss for her. In her third interview she mentions a gay couple she had an affectionate relationship with over several years and with whom she shared a big part of her life until the relationship inexplicably ended when the couple moved away. All these accounts share a common coda: You cannot trust relationships to last forever, most explicitly expressed in her second interview when talking about the death of her friend:

> Well, I won't get emotionally involved in friendships anymore if they suddenly break off and with all the consequences this entails, that you miss them, that you question

---

29   Und die anderen Beziehungen sind so gewesen, das waren eben diese lockeren Beziehungen zu den Freunden. Die haben mich dahingehend geprägt, als dass sie mir das Leben erleichtert haben in gewisser Weise. Dass ich sozusagen in ein Leben eingetaucht bin, was ganz anders gewesen ist. Und die haben mich irgendwie so genommen, wie ich bin. Auch, wenn ich ein bisschen komisch war oder bin auch vielleicht immer noch. [...] Wobei, wie gesagt, nicht immer alles so rosig gewesen ist, aber durch die vielen Leute, und auch in der Subkultur, wo man generell ja immer eher angenommen wird, wenn man ein bisschen anders ist, hat mich das in gewisser Weise vielleicht vor einem nicht so schönen Leben oder Lebensabschnitt eigentlich gerettet.

eternities in general. And, as I said, you should ask this question because there are consequences, that you may change in this regard and no longer enter into such close friendships or trust in eternity, in connections.[30] (Petra, FDI, time 2)

She talks considerably less about current meaningful relationships with one important exception which is the relationship to her life partner who becomes ever more important in her accounts. They have been a couple throughout all the years we interviewed Petra, and we learn the great appreciation Petra has for this relationship as well as how it evolved as illustrated by these accounts in her last interview.

And of course, the [relationship] brings with it a lot, from responsibility to compromise, many compromises and so on. That was also a rather difficult chapter for me at the beginning [...]. However, it has stood the test of time and has also become very stable. And is also such an anchor for me. So, I have also changed a bit, as far as my personality is concerned, I have changed in such a way that for me it also has to do with trust, what I have learned, which perhaps I didn't before, [....] not to the same extent. That has changed me. So, the partnership has changed me. I would say primarily on terms of trust [...].[31] (Petra, FDI, time 3)

She mentions her trust issues in this context again, stating also in another part of the interview that she was not able or willing to maintain romantic relationships before because she did not want to be bound to someone else. However, now her partner seems to have become an attachment figure over the past years she can turn to for support and safety (Granqvist, Mikulincer, & Shaver, 2020, p. 176). It appears that she found someone worthy of her trust, after a lengthy period of trials and work on their relationship that is characterized by open discussion, emotional stability, and intellectual exchange. From an attachment perspective, Petra may have "earned" an internal model of secure attachment, that can go along with a forgiving attitude toward shortcomings of attachment figures like partners or caretakers. Persons with earned secure attachment "tend to value attachment and yet be relatively autonomous and objective in their descriptions" (Granqvist, 2020, p. 111).

---

30 Naja, ich werde mich emotional nicht mehr so auf Freundschaften einlassen, wenn die dann plötzlich abbrechen und mit all den Folgen, die man hat, dass man denjenigen vermisst, dass man eben Ewigkeiten generell in Frage stellt. Und die Frage sollte man sich, wie gesagt, auch darauf einlassen, das hat ja dann Folgen, dass man sich vielleicht auch diesbezüglich dann verändert und gar nicht mehr so engere Freundschaften eingeht oder vertrauen mag auf Ewigkeiten, auf Verbundenheiten.

31 Und die [Beziehung] bringt natürlich nochmal einiges mit sich, von Verantwortung über Kompromisse, viele Kompromisse zu schließen und so weiter. Das war für mich auch ein recht schwerer Abschnitt am Anfang, [...]. Und das hat sich aber jetzt bis zum heutigen Tage also bewährt und auch gefestigt. Und ist auch für mich so ein Anker. Also auch, ich habe auch so ein bisschen, was meine Persönlichkeit angeht, habe ich mich dahingehend verändert, dass das für mich auch mit Vertrauen zu tun hat, was ich gelernt habe, was vielleicht auch vorher, [....] nicht in dem Maße gehabt habe. Das hat mich schon verändert. Also die Partnerschaft hat mich verändert. Ich würde sagen, primär so auf der Vertrauensbasis [...].

However, mostly when Petra talks about current relationships, she talks about her difficulties finding connections in her new surroundings and the mistrust she encounters. Instead, Petra turns to the Internet and specific online groups which is something she already appreciated in her second interview, but which becomes increasingly explicit and important in her last one. She seeks out groups with similar interests to hers in order to exchange ideas and broaden her views on issues of interest such as religion or politics.

> And then you can join any groups, including political ones, discussion groups or maybe even groups critical of religion. And then you can simply experience it on a discussion level, simply by participating in such forums on the internet, for example. And that's where you can go and that makes it easier.[32] (Petra, FDI, time 3)

Apparently, for Petra, the appreciation of those online groups lies in their fluid character and the anonymity they provide. This makes it possible for her to engage in discussions about topics she wants to learn more about, having an intellectual exchange with people without having to enter into a relationship with them. That way she can have what she seems to value very much: exchange of ideas and the opportunity to widen her horizon without giving up her autonomy and having to dare trusting the people she engages with. This might also have become more relevant to her as she appears rather isolated in the small town she is currently living in. In sum, when reviewing how Petra talks about friendships and relations to peers, there is an emphasis on the anxiety to be hurt and a reluctance to trust others on the one hand and a desire to engage and exchange ideas on the other.

Religion and Worldview: Science as Form of Faith

As stated above, Petra's current worldview centers around her criticism of religion as it can be interpreted as the starting point in her engagement with existential questions by means of critical investigation. Thus, over the years Petra established a stable and unapologetically negative view of religion with an explicit focus on religious institutions. In all three interviews, she elaborates extensively on her criticism which can be summarized in moral failings of the church and intellectual inconsistencies of religious teachings but are worth exploring in more detail. For that, we first turn to Petra's subjective definition she gave for the word "religion" in her survey, and then to parts of the answer she gave in her first interview when asked whether she considers herself to be religious, spiritual, or faithful:

---

32   Und dazu kann man sich dann irgendwelche Gruppen anschließen, auch irgendwelchen politischen vielleicht, Diskussionsgruppen oder vielleicht auch religionskritischen Gruppen. Und dann kann man einfach das auf einer Diskussionsebene leben, einfach indem man im Internet sich eben an solchen Foren beteiligt zum Beispiel. Und da kann man eben auch gehen und das macht es einfacher.

> [How would you define the term "religion"?] superstition, storytellers, models of world explanation, man-made, moral guide without legitimation, discrepancies.[33] (Petra, survey, time 1)

> [Religion] is partly deceiving itself, because acknowledging is evidence, [...] I think there is a contradiction between the religious and the other, [...] I think in religion you have a contradiction in yourself and you try to resolve it somehow by patching together your worldview just like that, I have experienced that with many religious people. Because if you then asked them, what does that actually look like: "Oh no, I don't believe that, but that I do and that I don't, but hell no longer exists, it is abolished or something." [...] That's all incorrect and I mean, there is a contradiction somewhere and that may be because you are not honest with yourself.[34] (Petra, FDI, time 1)

We can interpret Petra's view on religious teachings as a convenient lie people tell themselves when they cannot or will not engage in complex questions. It can even be seen as deceiving or dishonest, not sincerely dealing with contradictions and the true complexities of reality, but blindly and irrationally trusting religious authorities that are not even consistent in what they preach as they can apparently remove essential parts of their teachings such as "cancelling hell." Thus, her main criticism of religion in the first interview, and as well in her definition in the survey, is its perceived deception of people dealing with existential questions. In her second interview the criticism remains the same with a slightly different focus:

> [How would you define the term "religion"?] primarily organized exercise of power over the promise to give true answers to supposedly (last) questions. Sense of community.[35] (Petra, survey, time 2)

> But there is no such thing as faith, i.e. religious faith. So, I'm always ready to argue (laughs), but only because I'm ultimately affected by it. If I wasn't affected by it, if it was a private matter, I wouldn't mind. But as I said, this has an effect on our society and is in the worst case really rigid and as I said, when I see evangelicals and so on, otherwise I wouldn't care, but I'm affected.[36] (Petra, FDI, time 2)

---

33   aberglaube, geschichtenerzähler, welterklärungsmodelle, menschengemacht, moralischer wegweiser ohne legitimation, widerspüche.

34   Die [Religion] macht sich da was vor teilweise, weil dieses Erkennen sind ja so Evidenzen, [...] ich glaube da gibt es einen Widerspruch zwischen dem Religiösen und zwischen dem anderen, [...] ich denke, religiös hat man einen Widerspruch in sich und man versucht den irgendwie aufzulösen, indem man sich sein Weltbild eben dann so schustert und das hat man, habe ich bei vielen erlebt, die religiös sind. Denn wenn man sie dann gefragt hat, ja wie sieht das aus: „Ach nee, das glaube ich dann doch nicht und das schon und das jene nicht, aber Hölle gibt es ja gar nicht mehr, ist abgeschafft oder also." [...] Das stimmt dann alles nicht und das meine ich eben, da gibt es irgendwo einen Widerspruch und weil man vielleicht nicht ehrlich zu sich ist.

35   primär organisierte machtausübung über das versprechen wahre antworten zu geben auf vermeintliche (letzte) fragen. gemeinschaftsgefühl.

36   Aber Glauben, also religiösen Glauben gibt es auf gar keinen Fall. Also da bin ich auch immer bereit, mich zu streiten sozusagen (lacht), aber nur, weil ich letztlich davon betroffen bin. Wenn ich

Instead of the intellectual doubt, Petra now focusses more on the moral criticism of what she understands as religion, emphasizing the risk religious teachings could pose to society. It seems as if Petra feels personally threatened by religious groups such as the evangelical movement she views as a fundamentalist or highly conservative force menacing her way of life. It is interesting that she does not give any examples here of what these threats would actually be and how the evangelicals or their religious convictions could further these developments. It can be assumed that she is informed about this religious community but seems to interpret it as one homogenous school of thought with a singular socially regressive leaning. In her last interview, her views on religion have become even more explicit with a renewed focus on their intellectual inconsistency and logical fallacies:

> [How would you define the term "religion"?] humbug that evolved in the desire to explain life, to find meaning, to control fears, to answer last questions, supported by so-called revelation experiences, alleged miracles, the inability of science to answer last questions.[37] (Petra, survey, time 3)

> The conversation ends between religious and non-religious [...]. If someone is against abortion, he cannot tolerate the other, that is not possible. That doesn't work. That's a lie. [...] Someone who is convinced that this is a sin, or wrong, cannot tolerate it in the other. That's why it doesn't work. This is all a waste of time.[38] (Petra, FDI, time 3)

> And as I said, if you argue with the greatness of God and the spirit and the influence of God, then there is no more debate if you say: But I am influenced by God or something like that. These are entities that are no longer measurable. And then it doesn't work anymore anyway.[39] (Petra, FDI, time 3)

Her main criticism at this point is that religion not only gives false answers to existential questions but thwarts any possibility of thinking about them. As they introduce concepts

---

    davon nicht betroffen wäre, das eine Privatsache wäre, hätte ich nichts dagegen. Aber wie gesagt, das wirkt in unsere Gesellschaft hinein und im schlimmsten Falle richtig rigide und wie gesagt, wenn ich Evangelikale sehe und so weiter, sonst würde das mich nicht weiter kümmern, aber ich bin betroffen.

37   humbug entstanden im wunsch das leben zu erklären, sinn zu finden, ängste in den griff zu bekommen, letzte fragen zu beantworten, gestützt durch sog. offenbarungserlebnisse, angebliche wunder, dem nichtvermögen von wissenschaft, letzte fragen beantworten.

38   Das Gespräch endet da zwischen religiös und nicht Religiösen. [...] Wenn jemand gegen Abtreibung ist, der kann den anderen nicht tolerieren, das geht nicht. Das funktioniert nicht. Das ist eine Lüge. [...] Jemand, der überzeugt ist, dass das eine Sünde ist, oder falsch ist, der kann doch das beim anderen nicht tolerieren. Deswegen funktioniert das nicht. Das ist alles Makulatur.

39   Und wie gesagt, wenn man die Größe Gott und den Geist und den Einfluss Gottes da noch mit reinnimmt, dann ist man sowieso raus, wenn man sagt: Da hat ich aber der liebe Gott jetzt beeinflusst oder sowas. Das sind ja Größen, die dann eben nicht mehr messbar sind. Und dann funktioniert das sowieso nicht mehr.

258 Part C: Longitudinal Case Studies—Qualitative Analyses Including Quantitative Data

such as God that have no means to be measured or proven, the discussion of them becomes impossible. She illustrates this with a religiously legitimated rejection of abortion that cannot be discussed or changed when the underlying religious rule is absolute and cannot be changed either.

Thus, in sum Petra seems to have a quite firm and homogenous understanding of religion in form of institutionalized and dogmatic teachings. She explains at lengths her grievances with religious institutions and beliefs in all three interviews, but they become most explicit in her third one. However, Petra does emphasize in several parts of her interviews that she tolerates religion as a private practice and "would not take it away from anybody"[40] (Petra, FDI, time 3), even appreciating its function in form of support and consolation it offers to believers. However, these statements are always followed by the caveat that religion is only a distraction from really engaging in existential questions and should not have any social or political influence. Thus, on the one hand, her criticism consists of the moral failings of the churches in terms of the misuse of power, dishonesty when dealing with existential questions and the consequential deception of people who follow their teachings. On the other hand, she views religion as a misleading epistemic system as answers are presumed and fixed instead of investigated and explored. Although Petra's elaborations are consistent and reasonably founded, it becomes clear that her definition of religion itself is very narrow and unreflective of the internal differences, discussions and rifts. Thus, Petra's views on religion might be influenced by a prejudiced view of this realm she currently has no affiliation to and whose convictions she sees as foreign to her own which might restrict her otherwise passionate pursuit of knowledge (Colombo et al., 2020).

Petra juxtaposes this naïve or even misleading form of religious belief with what she states has good reasons for putting her faith in: Science. She expresses this belief "that surpasses the need for a God"[41] in all three interviews, does it, however, in her second one most poignantly.

> And faith [...] basically science is just faith. I've always seen it the other way around. I think science is faith and religion is conviction. And that's how I actually see it and that's why (laughs) I would have to say: I believe [...] at the moment in a certainty that I have, but which can be dissolved at any time. And that's not the case with religion, because there it's the end of it. Yes, there is nothing to question. And that's why I believe more in science and its method.[42] (Petra, FDI, time 2)

Once again, Petra exhibits her understanding of religion as firm, dogmatic convictions or answers given from religious authorities instead of, for example, a symbolic realm giving

---

40   Ich würde natürlich niemanden den so wegnehmen wollen.

41   dass man Gott gar nicht mehr braucht letztlich.

42   Und Glauben [...] im Grunde ist Wissenschaft ja auch nur Glaube. Ich habe es immer anders gesehen. Ich finde, Wissenschaft ist Glauben und Religion ist Überzeugung. Und so rum sehe ich das eigentlich und deswegen müsste ((lächelt)) ich sagen: Ich glaube [...] im Moment an eine Gewissheit die ich hab, aber jederzeit umgeschmissen werden kann. Und das ist eben bei Religion ja nun nicht der Fall, da ist ja Schluss. Ja, da gibt es nichts zu hinterfragen. Und deswegen glaube ich schon eher an die Wissenschaft und an ihre Methode.

space for evoke reflections on questions of ultimate concern. Her appreciation of science on the other hand is more nuanced in comparison, viewing it not as a set of answers but as a method of how to explore these questions. The evidence-based nature of this method as well as its duty to adapt to new evidence instead of insisting in fixed answers convinces her to the point that she accepts science as a worthy framework guiding her view of the world. However, Petra's worldview is not limited to what can be proven or measured. On the contrary, she acknowledges the realm of the unexplainable and mystical by meaningfully incorporating the term spirituality in her worldview. Thus, to better understand the depth of her characterization of science of faith, we need to turn to Petra's understanding of spirituality and how it influences the way in which she understands the world. Therefore, we first turn to her subjective definition of spirituality in her first survey answer and interview.

> [How would you define the term "spirituality"?] asking existential questions, immersion, tracing feelings, concepts such as infinity, wanting to experience transcendence, wanting to go beyond the everyday, learn right and good life, solve moral problems, interconnectedness.[43] (Petra, survey, time 1)

> Spirituality as another form of knowledge, so to speak, there is a rational one and that is rather a direct knowledge, like when the religious person meditates, that he then has the experience of infinity or of all these things, I can do that without including God, I can also experience that as an atheist, and this also aims at knowledge, to recognize, but not like science through empirical research, but through direct access to it and you can certainly do that, I think.[44] (Petra, FDI, time 1)

By the means of spirituality, Petra can access the realm of the unexplainable which is not accessible by employing logical thought or rational investigation, but by contemplation. It is a way of gaining knowledge separate from scientific inquiry leading beyond the mundane. It is an experience-based form of knowledge seeking and in her interviews, she gives examples like listening to the music of Bach and being immersed in the sound for when she comes close to a spiritual state. She mentions this example in all three interviews and states that she appreciates this experience especially in churches which, as she emphasizes, does not conflict with her atheist belief as it is the experience and not the religious frame making it meaningful. In the second Wave of data collection, she decided on using a quote by the philosopher Ludwig Wittgenstein to define spirituality,

---

43 sich existenziellen fragen stellen versenkung gefühlen nachspüren begriffe, wie unendlichkeit , transzendenz erfahren wollen über das alltägliche hinausgehen wollen richtiges, gutes leben lernen, moralische probleme lösen verschränkung.

44 Spiritualität als andere Form der Erkenntnis sozusagen, eine rationale und das ist eher so eine direkte Erkenntnis eben, wie wenn der Religiöse meditiert, dass er dann die Erfahrung hat von Unendlichkeit oder von all diesen Dingen, das kann ich eben auch, ohne dass ich eben Gott da reinnehmen, kann ich das auch erleben als Atheist, und das ist auch auf Kenntnis ausgelegt auf erkennen aber nicht wie die Wissenschaft eben durch empirische Forschungen, sondern durch den direkten Zugang dazu und das kann man durchaus auch, meine ich.

Part C: Longitudinal Case Studies—Qualitative Analyses Including Quantitative Data

seemingly exhibiting her understanding of spirituality at the same time as her rigorous reading of philosophical literature.

> [How would you define the term "spirituality"?] Quote: We feel that even if all sorts of scientific questions have been answered, our life problems are not even touched. Of course, then there is no longer any question; and that is the answer. Ludwig Wittgenstein.[45] (Petra, survey, time 2)

> And try, as I said, to explore my inner attitudes in this way, towards things like infinity, to the existential questions that arise, and I try to do that as honestly as possible. That is already such a [...] to cultivate inwardness, so to speak. [...] So maybe to get in touch, to absorb that, to feel that, to perceive that, [...] you do have the feeling that there is something incomprehensible, [...] what you can't know, [...] that there must be something there, yes and you just try to cultivate that or not to think about it calmly, but to feel it, so to speak. It is not simply deal with all this, as I said, either through science or concrete life, but to try to integrate it into certain rituals, to sit or look into the night sky full of stars or just to be somewhere in peace.[46] (Petra, FDI, time 2)

Here, the insights she is able to gain through spiritual experiences is stated once again, giving her a vehicle to explore questions of ultimate concern not accessible by scientific reasoning. She now focuses some more on the actual experience, going into further detail of what it is she feels and experiences. This can be characterized as mystical experience which is at the core of all religious traditions but not bound to religious affiliations, cultural definitions or mediations. Hood (2006) called this *spiritual mysticism* which he views as typical for people identifying as *spiritual but not religious*. These are states of closeness to the transcendence that cannot be put into words and which refer to "the 'experience' of unity with something greater" (Klein et al., 2016). As mentioned above, Petra explores this experience-based seeking in moments of awe when listening to music. In her last survey answer and interview, however, she gives a deeper insight into these practices and the feelings they evoke:

---

45 Wir fühlen, dass, selbst wenn alle möglichen wissenschaftlichen Fragen beantwortet sind, unsere Lebensprobleme noch gar nicht berührt sind. Freilich bleibt dann eben keine Frage mehr; und eben dies ist die Antwort. Ludwig Wittgenstein.

46 Und versuche, wie gesagt, meine inneren Einstellungen so zu erforschen, zu Dingen wie Unendlichkeit, zu den existenziellen Fragen, die sich auftun und das versuche ich eben so redlich wie möglich. Das ist schon auch so eine [...] also Innerlichkeit zu kultivieren sozusagen. [...] Also in Kontakt auch vielleicht zu treten, das aufzunehmen, das zu spüren, das wahrzunehmen, [...] man hat ja schon das Gefühl, dass da irgendwie was Unfassbares, [...] was man nicht wissen kann, [...] dass da irgendwas sein muss, ja und das versucht man aber eben zu kultivieren oder darüber in Muße nicht zu denken, aber das zu erspüren sozusagen. Das schon, dass ich, wenn ich so einfach das alles, wie gesagt, entweder über Wissenschaft oder über das konkrete Leben so abhandle, sondern schon versuchen, das eben auch in gewisse Rituale zu kleiden, mal zu sitzen oder mal in den Sternenhimmel zu schauen oder einfach irgendwo in der Ruhe zu sein.

[How would you define the term "spirituality"?] a feeling of coherence, reflected through experiences also with the help of attention techniques, body techniques, prosocial action perpetual reflection.[47] (Petra, survey, time 3)

[I] can only describe it as a feeling, in the stomach, it is a very pleasant, a relaxed feeling to look up there. And I think if I try to reflect on that, it's probably the vastness. It is the vastness, it is certainly also the unknown, to know that the universe goes on and on perhaps, that it is infinite. And there are dots of light and otherwise it is a nice homogeneous background and there are beautiful dots of light that change. We don't know what's there. There is still a lot to see. And I can – but regarding the feeling it is just nice and warm in the stomach – it is really as they say, a feeling of happiness.[48] (Petra, FDI, time 3)

Looking at the night sky is when she comes close to experiencing the infinity of the universe and consequently the width that surrounds human existence. She tries to explain what it is that evokes this feeling, contents herself in the end, however, with the appreciation of the sense of harmony and happiness it enables.

In all three accounts, her reasoning with regard to spirituality as well as the interpretation of what it means to her are similar and coherent with her worldview committed to honest and rigorous inquiry. The seeming contradiction of being an atheist focusing on evidence-based knowledge seeking and identifying as spiritual in all three interviews is resolved by her openness for what she cannot explain or access through science. It is exactly this honesty that leads her to the acknowledgment of this meaningful scientific residue she can only marvel and wonder about. This attitude leans on the concept of *intellectual honesty* which Petra explicitly refers to in all three interviews. It is elaborated in an essay by the German philosopher Thomas Metzinger (2013) who characterized spirituality as an "epistemic system" stating that "[s]piritual persons do not want to believe, but to know" (ibid., p. 6). Spiritual experiences, he argues, are the vehicles for this knowledge seeking in the same way that rational arguments are: "Here, we have the dissolution of the phenomenal self, there, the ideal of continually and repeatedly letting one's own theories fail through their contact with reality" (ibid., p. 26). Both are methods of knowledge seeking fueled by "the unconditional desire for truth" (ibid., p. 28) beyond the bond of previous assumptions or dogmatic limitations.

Another interesting example for this are her imaginations of what happens after death that are also consistent throughout all interviews but expressed most clearly in her last one:

---

47 ein gefühl der stimmigkeit, reflektiert über erfahrungen auch mit hilfe von aufmerksamkeitstechniken, körpertechniken, prosoziales handeln immerwährende reflektion.

48 [I]ch kann es nur als Gefühl beschreiben, so im Bauch, ist es ein ganz angenehmes, ein gelöstes Gefühl, da hochzuschauen. Und ich denke mal, wenn ich dann versuche, das zu reflektieren, ist es die Weite vermutlich. Es ist die Weite, es ist sicherlich auch das Unbekannte, zu wissen, es geht immer weiter vielleicht, das ist ja unendlich, das Universum sozusagen. Und es gibt Lichtpunkte und ansonsten ist es schön ein homogener Hintergrund und es gibt wunderschöne Lichtpunkte, die sich verändern. Wir wissen nicht, was da ist. Es gibt noch viel zu sehen. Und ich kann- aber vom Gefühl her ist es einfach nur im Bauch ein schönes warmes- es ist wirklich wie man sagt, ein Glücksgefühl.

Well, dust to dust, ashes to ashes, I believe that, for example. But in a way that at some point we will be reborn in others as atoms, we will be atomized, so to speak, at some point after decay. Then it just goes into the cycle. I think that's beautiful. And then it goes into the cycle and then you become a tree [...] and then you become a fruit. And someone eats the fruit again and [...] then I am born again in part in someone else. Of course, not as far as my consciousness is concerned, but an atom is part of consciousness. But, this is a beautiful thought, that in me there is something of Shakespeare, even of some killers perhaps.[49] (Petra, FDI, time 3)

In this death conception Petra constructs the image of an afterlife that does not betray her scientific reasoning. It is based on a reasonable observation—human bodies disintegrate in ever smaller pieces after death—and combined with a rather romantic imagination of those pieces becoming part of something new and therefore remaining within a connected cycle.

Finally, to understand Petra's worldview, it seems fruitful to take a closer look at her self-identification as atheist as she states it in her first and second, but not explicitly in her last interview. In her first two interviews, however, she shortly describes her understanding of atheism and why it is a label she chooses for herself.

I would call myself an atheist. So, something else is too dishonest for me, e.g., agnostic. So, I wouldn't say that and that's why, out of pragmatic considerations anyway and because of theoretical reflections [...].[50] (Petra, FDI, time 1)

And science will... doesn't help me either, so to speak, but is still a, as I said, practical atheist, so that still helps me. In practical life, however, I would act on the basis of scientific knowledge and not on the basis of religious beliefs, yes, in practical terms.[51] (Petra, FDI, time 2)

It seems as if Petra chose the self-description atheist because it would most honestly depict her reliance on scientific thought and her rejection of religious answers when confronted with worldly questions. It is more a "pragmatic" reason than a firm identification as the non-existence of God is for her a currently convincing fact. Calling herself

---

49   Gut, Staub zu Staub, Asche zu Asche, das glaube ich zum Beispiel. Aber dahingehend, dass wir irgendwann mal in anderen wiedergeboren werden so als Atome, wir werden ja atomisiert sozusagen irgendwann mal dann nach der Verwesung, atomisiert. Dann geht das eben in den Kreislauf über. Das finde ich doch wunderschön. Und dann geht es in den Kreislauf und dann wird man zum Baum [...] und dann wird man eine Frucht. Und die Frucht isst wieder jemand und [...] dann werde ich in einem anderen wiedergeboren zum Teil. Natürlich nicht, was mein Bewusstsein angeht, aber als ein Atom, ist ja Teil des Bewusstseins. Aber sozusagen, das ist für mich ein wunderschöner Gedanke, dass in mir was von Shakespeare ist, auch von irgendwelchen Schlächtern vielleicht.

50   ich würde mich schon als Atheist bezeichnen. Also, das andere ist mir auch zu unredlich so, also diese Agnostiker. Also ich würde sagen nicht und deswegen habe ich noch überlegt, aus pragmatischen Erwägungen heraus sowieso und aus Erkenntnissen theoretisch [...].

51   Und wird mir Wissenschaft ... hilft mir sozusagen auch nicht weiter, aber ist immer noch eine, wie gesagt, praktischer Atheist bin, also das hilft mir immer noch. Im praktischen Leben würde ich dennoch aufgrund von wissenschaftlichen Erkenntnissen handeln und nicht aufgrund von religiösen Überzeugungen, ja, praktisch gesehen.

an agnostic as she states for example in her first interview would be a dishonest label presumably because it would cast doubt on her conviction.

In her last interview she maintains the same principles and openness for mystical experiences while rejecting religious interpretations, does so, however, with a much more political focus. Thus, atheism and the rejection of religious dogma are self-evident at that point and need no further emphasis by calling herself an atheist. However, as mentioned above, her life circumstances have become more difficult which arguably also led her to intensify her social criticism as she interprets her personal crisis as being part of a larger societal development and a general criticism and disappointment by the promises of a capitalist society. Although she has expressed her opinions on social inequality in all three interviews, in her last one she talks more openly about her political identification as a leftist and her interest and appreciation of Marxist political theory. She does reflect on this development and states it explicitly when she says she has "become political[52]" (Petra, FDI, time 2) and avocates for radical social changes.

> I am convinced that you have to really change the roots, you have to change and these tiny reforms and so on, they accomplish nothing at all, they only bring new problems. So, I, as I said, rather go in the direction of (smiles) Marxism. I hope the BND [federal intelligence agency in Germany] doesn't listen.[53] (Petra, FDI, time 3)

Petra is not involved in any political movement, although she is politically engaged by participating in protests. For her, standing up for one's convictions at protests is nothing she is particularly proud of as to her it is the least one could do and an obvious commitment. It is the theoretical investigation and the discussion of these issues that is most important to her. Coherent with her worldview, Marxism convinces her in this regard because it examines these issues while relying on scientific reasoning and promoting strict secularism which for her is the most honest way to organize society. And, again, she emphasizes that her political views deviate from the norm when she jokingly mentions the fear of being surveilled by federal intelligence. In terms of existential questions, however, she adds a new self-description as existentialist in her last interview when reflecting on meaning in her life:

> But, if you don't believe all that anymore, then I'm with the existentialists and they say: Well, I'm just thrown in there and then I want to see what I make of it. Also, with certain ethical requirements. And that's basically how I see it. So, I think I'm an existentialist who says to herself, I think all this is rather bad, but just try to find something for me and try not to harm anyone, like that. [...] That's the meaning I personally give to my life, I would say.[54] (Petra, FDI, time 3)

---

52 [...] bin ich politisch geworden.

53 Ich bin der Überzeugung, man muss also richtig die Basis, muss man verändern und diese kleinen Reförmchen und so weiter, die bringen gar nichts, die bringen nur neue Probleme auf. Also da bin ich schon, wie gesagt, eher dann, gehe ich in Richtung (lächelt) Marxismus. Ich hoffe, der BND hört nicht mit.

54 Aber, wenn man das eben alles nicht mehr glaubt, dann bin ich so bei den Existenzialisten und die sagen: Naja, ich bin da nur reingeworfen und dann will ich mal gucken, was ich draus mache. Auch mit bestimmten ethischen Vorgaben. Und so sehe ich das im Grunde auch. Also ich glaube, da bin

Petra states in several parts of the interviews one of her core beliefs that humans are not capable of realizing the all-encompassing truth and thus she can only position herself temporarily with the arguments that are most convincing to her at the moment. Existentialism seems to give her a suitable concept to make this existence, that has no firm or objective meaning, meaningful nonetheless: Living in a way that is ethical and good is meaning enough and does not need a cosmological order.

When Petra describes her conceptualization of spirituality and how it shapes her worldview the complexity of her reasoning is most visible. While her views on religion seem narrow, or even prejudiced at times, portraying religion as homogeneously dogmatic and institutionalized, her understanding of spirituality preserves her an openness to the unexplainable that does not betray her dedication to scientific investigation. It furthermore leads her to unapologetically criticize social pathologies she observes in the world around her which is an important part of her moral orientation further explored in the part below.

Values and Commitments: The Impossibility and Striving for the Good Life

It can be assumed from her elaborations so far that honesty is an important virtue for Petra which she explicitly mentions when reflecting on religious or moral questions. Here, Petra does not talk about the honesty towards other people and thus being more socially compatible and predictable for her surroundings which would be a fitting argument for a Style three reasoning. Her emphasis lies, however, on the honesty toward oneself when being faced with complex questions that require rigorous investigation and reflection even if one's own convictions are being painfully challenged. In accordance with Metzinger, it is about "the 'principle of self-respect'—about how not to lose one's dignity and mental autonomy" (Metzinger, 2013, p. 15). Thus, autonomy, authenticity and integrity are the cornerstones for Petra's moral orientation: What you tell about your beliefs should reflect your actual convictions, but these convictions must be subject to change if you get moved by a better argument or if they did not hold up to reality. The first point can be illustrated by a quote from her third interview:

> That I also take a stand and that I defend people in a certain way, although it can be dangerous. So that [...] I actually demonstrate my convictions to the outside world and stand by them.[55] (Petra, FDI, time 3)

Petra emphasizes the difficulties and effort that she expects when engaging in difficult discussions, probably facing adversities and losing sympathies. Authenticity seems to

---

ich Existenzialistin, die sich sagt, ich finde das hier alles zwar eher schlimm, aber versuche eben, für mich was zu finden und versuche keinem zu schaden, so. [...] Das ist der Sinn, den ich meinem Leben persönlich gebe, würde ich sagen.

55 Dass ich da eben auch Stellung beziehe und das ich in gewisser Weise also Leute verteidige, obwohl das in gewisser Weise auch gefährlich ist. Also das [...] ich meine Anschauungen tatsächlich auch konkret nach außen trage und dazu stehe, zu den Überzeugungen.

be a virtue in need of commitment and defense even if painful consequences are to be feared, making the honesty when facing the world more important than being liked or socially accepted. However, this painful honesty needs to be extended to inner considerations as well:

> So, I wouldn't say that I'm constantly honest with myself, for heaven's sake, that's an illusion. You would make a fool of yourself. But you should at least try, and I think that's spiritual, to somehow try to get to the truth or to an understanding without lying to yourself.[56] (Petra, FDI, time 1)

> Yes, knowing that you don't know anything. That one should rather let a conviction die than let people die for a conviction. [...] I read that somewhere, it's certainly not originally from me, but that convinced me in a way. [...] And perhaps we should also present our convictions with a certain modesty and always make a certain offer to the other. And also explain why we came to this conclusion. [...] There is no final answer, but that is what drives me at the moment. And, if I am provided with good arguments or whatever, that I would then of course also change my mind probably. But that you yourself are also fallible and of course can misunderstand things. Maybe you simply don't understand a better argument.[57] (Petra, FDI, time 3)

In her quest for knowledge and understanding, honesty also with regard to one's own limitations and the request to change one's convictions if they do not stand the test of reality is essential. Petra explicitly argues for a humble approach when dealing with complex questions which is exhibited in the quote above from her last interview. However, throughout her interviews she offers numerous examples for this attitude when she emphasizes that her own reasoning should not be taken as the final answer but as a consideration that—for the time—makes the most sense to her. This mindset might be characterized as *intellectual humility* which encompasses the capability of not only recognizing the confines of one's understanding but furthermore an inoffensive and honest dedication to the pursuit of truth (Bak, 2021). This also includes letting one's mind be changed by convincing evidence and thus leads to a greater openness and appreciation of differing opinions and argumentations of others (Colombo et al., 2021). This commitment is

---

56   Also ich würde ja auch nicht sagen, das ich ständig ehrlich zu mir bin, um Himmelswillen, das ist ja eine Einbildung. Dann macht man sich ja lächerlich. Aber man sollte es zumindest versuchen und ich glaube, das ist so das Spirituelle, irgendwie das zu versuchen eben zu der Wahrheit oder zu der Erkenntnis zu kommen ohne sich in die Tasche dabei zu lügen.

57   Ja, zu wissen, dass man nichts weiß. Dass man lieber eine Überzeugung sterben lassen sollte, als Leute für Überzeugungen sterben zu lassen. [...] Das habe ich mal irgendwo gelesen, das ist sicherlich nicht originär von mir, aber das hat mich in gewisser Weise überzeugt. [...] Und seine Überzeugung aber mit einer gewissen Bescheidenheit auch vielleicht vortragen sollte und dem anderen immer so ein gewisses Angebot machen sollte. Und auch erklären sollte, warum man zu dieser Sache gekommen ist. [...] Es gibt ja keine Letztbegründung dafür, aber das ist das, was mich im Moment umtreibt. Und ich das aber jederzeit, wenn mir gute Argumente oder was auch immer, geliefert wird, dass ich dann natürlich auch umschwenken würde vermutlich. Aber das man selber auch fehlbar ist und Dinge natürlich auch nicht verstehen kann. Vielleicht versteht man ein besseres Argument auch schlicht nicht.

Part C: Longitudinal Case Studies—Qualitative Analyses Including Quantitative Data

visible throughout all of Petra's interviews with longwinded answers that tend to oscillate between different arguments and include numerous admissions of her own blind spots or possible knowledge gaps and as illustrated by her admission that maybe she would underappreciate a better argument because she is not able to understand it. This can be interpreted as the cognitive aspect of intellectual humility which is "associated with a particular sensitivity to the purity and clarity of reasoning, its logical correctness and the ability to recognize the limitations of knowledge resulting from an individual's insufficient cognitive skills" (Bac, 2021, p. 3). However, usually Petra ends these elaborations by taking a position and thus closes her complex argumentation without fully engaging in other perspectives. She rather uses them to acknowledge the difficulty of the problem and to contrast them with her standpoint which can be interpreted as consistent with her high Style four ratings.

As stated above, Petra found a suitable theoretical framework for her moral commitment to openly reflect on difficult religious or moral issues in *intellectual honesty*, a concept she takes from Metzinger. It is part of how Petra understands spirituality which requires a commitment to the principle that there will always be a realm that is unknowable and nonetheless not getting discouraged in the quest for knowledge (Metzinger, 2013). This concept has been convincing to her for at least the last eight years in which we were able to interview her, as illustrated in her last interview:

> And spiritual, I understand it that way, [...] as a certain honesty that I'm in harmony with myself, that I have examined things for myself and at least thought about things before I have somehow accepted them. And that because of my humanity I can only come to a certain conclusion, to a certain conviction or to a certain view, but that I have at least reflected on it. [...] And that's just for me to look at the sky and look at nature and say: Oh, how beautiful. And to be quite satisfied with the explanatory models of evolution and also to be quite satisfied, also to know that there are gaps and [...], because it is just a belief and a theory, this is more honest for me than a conviction. [...] This is spirituality for me, I would say [...] To have feelings, corresponding feelings, exactly. So, one thing is the intellectual debate, this attempt at honesty.[58] (Petra, FDI, time 3)

With this concept, Petra unites several of her convictions in a coherent manner, giving her accounts and complex reasoning a stable framework. For her, honesty relies on the

---

58 Und spirituell dahingehend, als dass ich das so verstehe, [...] so eine gewisse Redlichkeit, dass ich mit mir im Einklang bin, dass ich Dinge für mich geprüft habe und mir zumindest mal Gedanken über die Dinge gemacht habe, bevor ich sie irgendwie angenommen habe. Und dass ich dann aufgrund meines Menschseins auch nur zu einer bestimmten Sache kommen kann, zu einer bestimmten Überzeugung oder zu einer gewissen Anschauung, aber dass ich es wenigstens mal reflektiert habe. [...] Und das ist für mich eben in den Himmel zu schauen und mir die Natur zu betrachten und zu sagen: Ach, wie wunderschön. Und mit den Erklärungsmodellen auch vielleicht der Evolution und auch durchaus zufrieden zu sein, auch zu wissen, dass es da Lücken gibt und [...], weil es eben ja nur ein Glauben und eine Theorie ist, für mich redlicher ist, als von der Überzeugung. [...] Das ist für mich so eine Spiritualität, würde ich sagen [...] Gefühle zu haben, mit entsprechenden Gefühlen auch, genau. Also das eine ist das intellektuelle Auseinandersetzen, dieser Versuch der Redlichkeit.

acknowledgement that human reasoning by its nature is fallible as it is not able to realize the objective truth entirely. To commit to this honesty means refuting certainties be it communicated by others or presented by convictions one arrived at one's own. One does have to form an opinion, but only after rigorous reflection and research and with the acknowledgement that the world encompasses more than is comprehensible by observation. One might rely on empirical models to understand aspects of the world, but there will always be a residue inaccessible to explanations and only available through experience and feelings. However, although Petra explicitly states that she engages in discussions to "refute my own convictions[59]" (Petra, FDI, time 2) it is noticeable that they remain remarkably stable even if somewhat more political at least over the past eight years.

One of those general moral orientations Petra explicitly states in all interviews is the prevention of suffering. This can be illustrated by numerous statements in her interviews when she talks for example about caring for the sick in her work or when reflecting on an action that is always right:

> A [...] supposedly good action, I can save a child that drowns, now this is a stupid example. This child can then get cancer two months later and can go through a path of suffering that is horrible. So, but [...] I ignored that possibility. I have to act and in the moment, I try to do the right thing in the sense of my core convictions, yes.[60] (Petra, FDI, time 3)

The prevention or at least minimization of suffering is at the core of her moral reasoning and, thus, the starting point for her social criticism which is fueled by the observation that there is avoidable suffering in the world preventing people from realizing the highest good: a good life. This turns her into an "idealistic pessimist" (Bullik et al., 2020), as she wishes for a better world but cannot see a convincing way out of current societal status quo:

> So, a concern for me is that everyone has a good life. [...] I can't really live a good life for myself. I can't do that if I know that others are doing badly, because I'm here in [city in West Germany], maybe it really has practical reasons, I'm always confronted with a lot of suffering here in [city in West Germany], maybe because of my profession [...].[61] (Petra, FDI, time 1)

---

59 meine eigenen Überzeugungen zu widerlegen.

60 Eine [...] vermeintlich gute Handlung, ich kann ein Kind retten, was ertrinkt, jetzt als blödes Beispiel. Das kann dann zwei Monate später an Krebs erkranken und kann einen Leidensweg hinter sich legen, der grauenhaft ist. Also, aber [...] das habe ich verdrängt, diese Möglichkeiten. Ich muss handeln und in dem Moment versuche ich das Richtige zu tun im Sinne meiner Grundüberzeugungen, ja.

61 Also ein Anliegen ist schon für mich, dass jeder ein gutes Leben führt. [...] Ich kann für mich eigentlich kein gutes Leben führen. Ich kann das nicht, wenn ich weiß, dass es anderen schlecht geht, weil ich auch gerade hier in [Großstadt in Westdeutschland], vielleicht hat es auch wirklich praktische Gründe, ich bin hier in [Großstadt in Westdeutschland],immer auch mit viel Leid konfrontiert, vielleicht auch in meinem Beruf [...].

> [I]n the present world I am not happy. So, I do have happy moments, definitely, but that I accept this world as it is in some way [...] not at all. [...] The here and now is basically lost. [...] There is nothing, concretely, no, that makes no sense, [...] ... as I said, because I think the personal is always connected to society.[62] (Petra, FDI, time 2)

> And as I said, not to harm anyone, rather perhaps to bring joy and for myself, of course. But, this is dishonest and in the end I know exactly, [...] it's actually not appropriate for the world [...] I don't understand how you can be happy when confronted with the world. [...] Honestly, we shouldn't, in view of the suffering in the world. But if I, I have read this once, I found that quite sensible, if I'm unhappy, so to speak, then I add my suffering, my unhappiness, to the suffering that prevails. (smiles) That saved me a bit.[63] (Petra, FDI, time 3)

Thus, Petra is faced with the question how to act morally in a society she deems immoral. A good and happy life is denied to many people in the society she observes, and she is confronted with the misery of those who cannot keep up and suffer. Petra seems to find an answer preventing her to succumb to nihilism. Her way out of this dilemma is not to add to the existing suffering she witnesses, by treating others kindly and not adding to their burden on the one hand, as well as not becoming herself part of this misery on the other and preserving her personal happiness where she can. Thus, she finds an interpretation enabling her to experience happiness without denying the shortcomings she criticizes. This expectation of how to treat others is part of an attitude she calls "reciprocal altruism," or the opinion that she cannot be happy when being confronted by the despair of others, and thus caring for others must be honestly interpreted as a self-serving act. This is close to Erich Fromm's reasoning as discussed by Endler, arguing that actions that help people to life a virtuous life in an imperfect world should orient toward the good of others as well as one's own in order to achieve societal changes: On the one hand, the individual must find a salutary way to deal with the tension between themselves and society, e.g., by spiritual practices, and on the other hand, the society the individual is confronted with must change as well in order to accommodate the fulfillment of their full potential (Endler, 2019). Or, in Petra's words:

---

62   [I]n der jetzigen Welt bin ich nicht glücklich. Also ich habe konkrete glückliche Momente, auf jeden Fall, aber dass ich diese Welt hier so wie sie ist in irgendeiner Weise [...] akzeptiere oder, also überhaupt nicht, ne. [...] Das Hier und Jetzt ist verloren im Grunde. [...] Da gibt es nichts, bei mir konkret, ne, das macht alles keinen Sinn, [...] ... wie gesagt, weil ich denke, das Persönliche hängt immer mit dem Gesellschaftlichen zusammen.

63   Und wie gesagt, keinem zu schaden, eher vielleicht Freude zu bringen und für mich und mir selber natürlich auch. Aber, das ist unredlich und am Ende weiß ich genau, [...] es ist im Grunde der Welt nicht angemessen, [...] Ich verstehe es nicht, wie man angesichts der Welt fröhlich sein kann. [...] Redlich betrachtet, dürfte man es nicht, angesichts des Leides auf der Welt. Aber wenn ich, das habe ich mal gelesen, das fand ich ganz sinnig, wenn ich sozusagen dann darüber selber noch unglücklich bin, dann würde ich ja quasi dem Leid, das herrscht, noch mein Leid hinzufügen, mein Unglücklichsein. (lächelt) Das hat mich dann so ein bisschen gerettet.

Because I think that if everyone is doing well, I'm fine. So that's my core belief. And you are nothing without the other. And anyone who thinks that you don't need the other and that you can do everything through, for example, organizations or through concrete conditions ..., so to have a good relationship with the other, that's what I'm trying to do. So that's reciprocal altruism, I think it's called. So [...] my altruism is certainly also an egoism. Just because I know [...] that the other person is doing well, that I'm also doing well. I am- we are always dependent on the other.[64] (Petra, FDI, time 3)

We have seen that Petra's understanding of spirituality and her moral orientation are closely connected. An honest reflection of society—which her moral orientation towards *intellectual honesty* requires—can only end in the conclusion that social inequality threatens the capabilities of living a happy and fulfilling life of many people, including her own. As grant societal changes are out of her control, the only way to act morally in this immoral society is not to add to the burden of others, show them compassion and kindness as well as seek happiness where she can find it.

Conclusion

In this chapter we explored the worldview and biography of someone who identifies as a spiritual atheist who exhibited apart from this intriguing self-description an interesting (non-)religious journey. We followed the middle-aged Petra's biographical accounts in a longitudinal perspective and encountered besides a remarkable life story a complex way of dealing with moral and existential questions. Petra's life story is one of challenging relationships, adventurous decisions and an intentional and honest seeking for knowledge and understanding. In this context, reflecting on religion has a particular significance and changes across her narratives: the religious life in Petra's childhood is narrowly connected to the warmth of her grandmother who supports her in a difficult relationship with her overwhelmed single mother. However, religious teachings do not seem particularly meaningful to her until she centers her current worldview on an explicit criticism toward everything religious. From this point on, she primarily focusses on her intellectual development and her capability to better understand the world around her by the means of evidence-based reasoning. She seems to have incorporated the ideals of the enlightenment tradition of rejecting religious feelings in favor of rational thought. All three interviews center around this personal enlightenment in form of "a systemic enhancement of one's own mental autonomy" (Metzinger, 2013, p. 29) which is fueled by extensive

---

64 Denn ich denke immer, wenn es allen gut geht, geht es mir auch gut. Also das ist meine Grundüberzeugung. Und man ist ohne den anderen nichts. Und jeder der meint, man bräuchte den anderen nicht und man könne alles über zum Beispiel über Organisation oder über die konkreten Verhältnisse ..., also mit den anderen im guten Verhältnis stehen, das versuche ich eben. Also das ist so ein reziproker Altruismus, glaube ich, nennt sich das. Also [...] mein Altruismus ist sicherlich auch ein Egoismus. Nur weil ich weiß, [...] dass es dem anderen gut geht, mir auch gut geht. Ich bin- wir sind immer auf den anderen angewiesen.

study of a broad array of philosophical and scientific literature as well as a vivid exchange with colleagues and online communities.

When Petra reflects on problems regarding morality, meaning or society, she exhibits and argues for what was identified above as an *intellectually humble* way in dealing with these questions. Her acknowledgement of the complexity of the issues is visible in Petra's answers that tend to go back and forth between different arguments accompanied by numerous caveats. Suitable to her predominantly Style 5 reasoning she considers multiple perspectives and arguments. However, she closes her considerations with a clear positioning and while not exhibiting overconfidence in her beliefs she can state them firmly (Bac et al., 2021, p. 5). This cognitive flexibility is also mirrored in her NEO-FFI scores that show at two points of measurement a significantly higher score on *openness to experience* than the sample mean which is also consistent with what would be expected of an intellectually humble person (Colombo et al. 2021, p. 356). Furthermore, a similar picture in her religious style assignments emerges at Wave two and three in which a dialogical style (Style 5) in her *form of world coherence* suggests an openness and appreciation for the depths and multidimensionality of reality.

However, as her aspect specific style assignment also showed, this openness is not exhibited in all areas of her interviews which is consistent with the characterization of *intellectual humility* as a character trait that can be demonstrated in certain domains while being absent in others (Colombo et al. 2021, p. 365). Thus, paradoxically, intellectual humble people can be prejudiced in some domains, whereas they exhibit great considerations in others which research suggests is especially visible towards groups that are not considered similar to one's own (ibid, p. 353). In Petra's case this might be most obvious when she thinks about religious or theological arguments. What changes in Petra's elaborations in this regard is a noteworthy shift in tone: In her first interview, she focuses on her disengagement from her religious upbringing, admitting that there is still a part of her that could not quite get rid of her childhood belief in god. In the second and third interview, however, her elaborations get markedly more critical, and she talks more openly about her political convictions that return to the materialist worldview of her childhood education in the GDR, including a harsh and more unforgiving denigration of religion. This reappreciation of her upbringing and the socialist teachings might also be heightened by her economic struggles which lead to her moving back to her small town of origin which is experienced as a crisis. Whatever the case may be, god and religion do not seem worthy of any consideration for Petra and religion is viewed as something deceptive that should not be taken seriously. This unwillingness to engage with religious or conservative groups has been reported for people advocating for intellectual humility, with a socially progressive leaning as they might expect intellectual humility also from others and see this expectation disappointed by those groups (Colombo et al., 2021, p. 366). Such an attitude might also be connected to Petra's identification with intellectual honesty. It might be mirrored in her low *xenos scores* that assess the willingness to be inspired by the (religious) other as Petra seems convinced that religion cannot teach her anything new because in her view it closes instead of widens the possibilities of knowledge seeking.

However, Petra cannot be characterized as a positivist who only considers logical arguments or measurable evidence either, but as an honest secular seeker with a special appreciation for the spiritual. As illustrated by the quote of Wittgenstein she uses for her definition of spirituality in Wave two: Science cannot solve our lives' problems and instead she preserves openness to this residue with a conceptualization of spirituality as *intellectual honesty*. It is part of a constant seeking and challenging of ideas, arguments, and views which she fosters in sincere and arduous discussions, markedly with people she does not have to form relationships with and can preserve her autonomy. Thus, Petra views spiritualty as surpassing but not threatening her scientific worldview and as part of her knowledge seeking enabling her to "confront existential questions" (Petra, survey, time 1). She not only acknowledges this spiritual realm inaccessible by logical arguments, but also actively seeks out these experiences and appreciates them. This is illustrated in sublime feelings she experiences when listening to music or when becoming aware of the infinity of existence when looking at the night sky. This observation is somewhat surprising when revisiting her low scores on the *M-scale* and leads to the assumption that although Petra reports these experiences and the feelings they evoke, she seems to focus in general more on the logical challenges that arise when confronted with existential questions.

Finally, her conceptualization of spirituality as *intellectual honesty* according to Metzinger also has strong implications for Petra's moral orientation. It implies a radical honesty towards others and oneself by sincere reflection and acknowledgement of the confines of one's reasoning. This constant reevaluation of the viewpoints one might hold dear implies an openness for the better argument. This openness is in turn what enables Petra to respect the realities of others and an honest and virtuous view on the world forces her to acknowledge that the society and world around her does not meet with the standards of fairness and care she would consider essential for human happiness. This well-being of all people is what Petra explicitly presents as the highest good and whose nonfulfillment for many she extensively and reasonably criticizes. Thus, the dedication to honest reflection of worldly as well as spiritual questions which is inspired by her conceptualization of spirituality seemingly make it impossible for her to ignore the suffering of others. Spirituality understood in this way enables her to focus on criticizing the societal shortcomings she encounters as well as granting inspirations for living a good and virtuous life.

Turning back to our initial question about the connection of morality and spirituality, we could see Petra as a case that illustrates the research findings on the association between a spiritual as well as non-religious identification and a life-affirming as well as value-based attitude that exhibit a "prosocial tendency" as well as "universalistic values" (Saroglou & Munoz-Garcia, 2008, p. 93). However, we have seen that this is only a reasonable conclusion keeping Petra's definition of spirituality in mind that she adopted from Metzinger. Therefore, this case study could further a discussion on how an intellectual humble and honest spirituality could foster prosocial values and the engagement with social issues.

References

Altmeyer, S., Klein, C., Keller, B., Silver, C. F., Hood, R. W., & Streib, H. (2015). Subjective definitions of spirituality and religion. An explorative study in Germany and the USA. *International Journal of Corpus Linguistics, 20*(4), 526–552. https://doi.org/10.1075/ijcl.20.4.05alt

Ammerman, N. T. (2013). Spiritual but not religious? Beyond binary choices in the study of religion. *Journal for the Scientific Study of Religion, 52*(2), 258–278. http://dx.doi.org/10.1111/jssr.12024

Bak, W. K., Jan; Wójtowicz, Bartosz. (2021). Intellectual humility: An old problem in a new psychological perspective. *Current Issues in Personality Psychology.* https://doi.org/10.5114/cipp.2021.106999

Bellah, R. N., Madsen, R., Sullivan, W. M., Swidler, A., & Tipton, S. M. (Eds.). (1996). *Habits of the heart* (revised ed.). University of California Press.

Berghuijs, J., Pieper, J., & Bakker, C. (2013). Conceptions of spirituality among the Dutch population. *Archive for the Psychology of Religion, 35*(3), 369–397. https://doi.org/10.1163/15736121-12341272

Bruce, S. (2017). *Secular beats spiritual. The westernization of the easternization of the West.* Oxford University Press.

Bullik, R., Özisik, S., & Steppacher, A. (2020). Development in religious and non-religious biographies from a cross-cultural perspective. *Journal of Empirical Theology, 33*, 65–82. https://doi.org/10.1163/15709256-12341398

Colombo, M., Strangmann, K., Houkes, L., Kostadinova, Z., & Brandt, M. J. (2020). Intellectually humble, but prejudiced people. A paradox of intellectual virtue. *Review of Philosophy and Psychology.* https://doi.org/10.1007/s13164-020-00496-4

Demmrich, S., & Huber, S. (2019). Multidimensionality of spirituality: A qualitative study among secular individuals. *Religions, 10*(11). https://doi.org/10.3390/rel10110613

Dillon, M., Wink, P., & Fay, K. (2003). Is spirituality detrimental to generativity? *Journal for the Scientific Study of Religion, 42*(3), 427–442.

Eisenmann, C., Klein, C., Swhajor-Biesemann, A., Drexelius, U., Streib, H., & Keller, B. (2016). Dimensions of "spirituality:" The semantics of subjective definitions. In H. Streib & R. W. Hood (Eds.), *Semantics and psychology of "spirituality." A cross-cultural analysis* (pp. 125–151). Springer International Publishing Switzerland.

Granqvist, P., Mikulincer, M., & Shaver, P. R. (2020). An attachment theory perspective on religion and spirituality. In K. E. Vail & C. Routledge (Eds.), *The science of religion, spirituality, and existentialism* (pp. 175–186). Academic Press.

Hood, R. W. (2006). The common core thesis in the study of mysticism. In P. McNamara (Ed.), *Where God and science meet: How brain and evolutionary studies alter our understanding of religion*, Vol 3 (pp. 119–138). Praeger Publishers.

Keller, B., Bullik, R., Klein, C., & Swanson, S. B. (2018). Profiling atheist world views in different cultural contexts: Developmental trajectories and accounts. *Psychology of Religion and Spirituality, 10*(3), 229–243. https://doi.org/10.1037/rel0000212

Klein, C., Silver, C. F., Coleman, T. J., Streib, H., & Hood, R. W. (2016). "Spirituality" and mysticism. In H. Streib & R. W. Hood (Eds.), *Semantics and psychology of "Spirituality." A cross-cultural analysis* (pp. 165–187). Springer International Publishing Switzerland.

la Cour, P., Ausker, N. H., & Hvidt, N. C. (2012). Six understandings of the word spirituality in a secular country. *Archive for the Psychology of Religion*, 34(1), 63–81. https://doi.org/10.1163/157361212X649634

Matilal, B. K. (1992). Mysticism and ineffability: Some issues of logic and language. In S. T. Katz (Ed.), *Mysticm and language.* (pp. 143–157). Oxford University Press.

Metzinger, T. (2013). Spirituality and Intellectual Honesty. Self-Published.

Partridge, C. (2007). Truth, authority and epistemological individualism in New Age thought. In D. L. Kemp, James R. (Ed.), *Handbook of New Age* (Vol. 1, pp. 231–254). Brill.

Saroglou, V., & Munoz-Garcia, A. (2008). Individual differences in religion and spirituality: An issue of personality traits and/or values. *Journal for the Scientific Study of Religion*, 47(1), 83–101. https://doi.org/10.1111/j.1468-5906.2008.00393.x

Silver, C. F., Coleman, T. J., Hood, J., & Holcombe, J. M. (2014). The six types of nonbelief: a qualitative and quantitative study of type and narrative. *Mental Health, Religion & Culture*, 17(10), 990–1001. https://doi.org/10.1080/13674676.2014.987743

Steensland, B., Wang, X., & Schmidt, L. C. (2018). Spirituality: What does it mean and to whom? *Journal for the Scientific Study of Religion*, 57(3), 450–472. https://doi.org/10.1111/jssr.12534

Streib, H., & Hood, R. W. (2011). "Spirituality" as privatized experience-oriented religion: Empirical and conceptual perspectives. *Implicit Religion*, 14(4), 433–453. https://doi.org/10.1558/imre.v14i4.433

Streib, H., Hood, R. W., & Klein, C. (2010). The Religious Schema Scale: Construction and initial validation of a quantitative measure for religious styles. *International Journal for the Psychology of Religion*, 20(3), 151–172. https://doi.org/10.1080/10508619.2010.481223

Streib, H., & Hood, R. W. (Eds.). (2016). *Semantics and psychology of spirituality. A cross-cultural analysis.* Springer International Publishing Switzerland. https://doi.org/10.1007/978-3-319-21245-6.

Streib, H., & Keller, B. (2018). *Manual for the assessment of religious styles in Faith Development Interviews (Fourth, revised edition of the Manual for Faith Development Research).* Bielefeld University/readbox unipress.

Streib, H., Klein, C., Keller, B., & Hood, R. W. (2021). The Mysticism Scale as measure for subjective spirituality: New results with Hood's M-Scale and the development of a short form. In A. L. Ai, K. A. Harris, R. F. Paloutzian, & P. Wink (Eds.), *Assessing spirituality in a diverse world* (pp. 467–491). Springer Nature Switzerland.

Wohlrab-Sahr, M., Karstein, U., & Schmidt-Lux, T. (2009). *Forcierte Säkularität. Religiöser Wandel und Generationendynamik im Osten Deutschlands.* Campus Verlag.

Zinnbauer, B. J., Pargament, K. I., Cole, B., Rye, M. S., Butter, E. M., Belavich, T. G., . . . Kadar, J. L. (1997). Religion and spirituality: Unfuzzying the fuzzy. *Journal for the Scientific Study of Religion*, 36(4), 549–564.

Chapter 12
Varieties of Being Protestant in the USA and Germany—The Cases of Gisela and George

Ramona Bullik, Matthew Durham, & Barbara Keller[1]

Abstract *Both cases presented here are Protestant and moving upward in religious type, yet from very different starting points: George (from the US) is a member of the Lutheran church, but it is not clear whether he is a believer, and his focus tends to be more on a philosophy-based (rather than religious) worldview combined with a deep appreciation of his Lutheran community. While George leans toward a the emerging dialogical-xenosophic type in his later interviews, Gisela (Germany) is a representative of the predominantly conventional type moving toward the predominantly individuative-reflective type; so this chapter will cover varieties of Protestant beliefs. Moreover, different possible upward movements regarding the religious types will be traced, showing how religious development may look like while formally staying within one's faith community; in other words: how much development is possible or even promoted within a community? Therefore, the case studies will focus on the development of the participants' subjective religiosities and, additionally, their approach to moral questions.*

Keywords: *protestantism; religious experience; religious development; morality; qualitative analysis; longitudinal*

---

1   R. Bullik, B. Keller, Bielefeld University, Germany, E-mail: ramona.bullik@uni-bielefeld.de; M. Durham, University of Tennessee at Chattanooga. USA. © Heinz Streib, Ralph W. Hood Jr. (eds.): Faith in Development. Mixed-Method Studies on Worldviews and Religious Styles. First published in 2024 by Bielefeld University Press, Bielefeld, https://doi.org/10.14361/9783839471234-014

How do people's lives develop who, on the surface at least, seem to be classical "stayers," i.e. people who never formally leave a religious community and who seem to be rather constant in their societal circumstances? The chapter will trace the trajectories of two cases, one from Germany and one from the US, who have both, over the course of our study, remained with their Protestant denomination. We will first present the German case, Gisela, giving an insight into selected results from her survey data, and then summarizing her faith development as seen in the structural analysis according to the Manual for the Assessment of Faith Development (Streib & Keller, 2018). The major part of the case study is taken up by the content analysis which was done with the help of our newly created coding guideline using the qualitative analysis software ATLAS.ti. This way, we are able to assess key aspects of her interviews and show in detail how her subjective religiosity and morality have developed and changed over the years. Concluding the case study of Gisela, we triangulate the different data to arrive at the most comprehensive picture of Gisela. The chapter will then proceed likewise with the case of George. In the end, the two cases will be compared.

Gisela

Biographical Outline

Gisela is a Protestant woman from Germany who was first interviewed during the second part of the Deconversion project in 2004 when she was 53 years old. Her second interview took place in 2013 and her third in 2018 when she was 67 years old. Gisela grew up in the post-war era, that is, the 1950s and 1960s in West-Germany, describing her childhood as "not easy" and the relationship with her parents as strained, feeling she was unloved and not well taken care of. Going to Sunday school, she made her first positive experiences with the Protestant church. Gisela got pregnant and married when she was 16 years old, and despite critique and skepticism from her family, she has stayed married with her husband until the present. She went through difficult times with her son, who was a drug addict for many years, and has found strength in her faith during that time. However, there were doubts as well, and for a very short period, she even formally terminated her church membership, an episode that is, however, not captured by her survey answers, yet is constituent for her religious identity as becomes apparent in the analysis of her interviews.

Selected Survey Results

As our research aims to triangulate the various data aggregated in each project, we first take a look at selected results from the extensive surveys (Table 12.1) that were always part of the research design, focusing on the different religious schemata (Religious Schema Scale (RSS), see Streib, Hood, & Klein, 2010), well-being (assessed by the Scale for Psychological Well-Being, Ryff & Keyes, 1995; Ryff, 1989), personality traits as assessed by the NEO-FFI (Costa & McCrae, 1985/1992, 2008), and mysticism (M-Scale; Hood et al., 2001;

Hood, 1975). In the analysis to follow, not all results will be discussed in detail, instead, we focus on those that stand out or seem remarkable in a certain way.

Gisela has not filled out major parts of the survey in Wave 2, so some of the observations made here refer to Wave 1 and 3 only. As for Gisela's results on the RSS, we see that she has high scores on the subscale *truth of texts and teachings (ttt)*, both scores more than one standard deviation higher than the rest of the sample. This points to a form of faith that is rather orthodox, orienting itself by the holy texts of one's religion. Remarkable is this high score especially in combination with her high scores on the subscale xenosophia (xenos), which mark her as a person who is willing to engage with the strange and appreciates the "sting of the alien" (Streib, 2018; Waldenfels, 1998). So, Gisela appears to be both very strict regarding her belief and very open to the strange which is a rather rare mixture.

Table 12.1: Selected Survey Results for Gisela

	Wave 1		Wave 2		Wave 3	
	Gisela	*M (SD)*	Gisela	*M (SD)*	Gisela	*M (SD)*
Religious Schema Scale						
truth of texts and teachings	4.20	2.53 (1.14)	-	2.35 (1.13)	4.00	2.55 (1.12)
fairness, tolerance, ...	4.20	4.38 (0.38)	-	4.35 (0.51)	4.80	4.59 (0.40)
xenosophia/inter-religious dialog	4.40	3.64 (0.82)	-	3.58 (0.78)	4.80	3.77 (0.78)
Ryff Scale						
Autonomy	3.71	3.69 (0.58)	-	3.32 (0.49)	3.29	3.31 (0.53)
environmental mastery	4.00	3.65 (0.75)	-	3.67 (0.63)	3.29	3.66 (0.67)
personal growth	4.71	4.31 (0.48)	-	4.14 (0.49)	4.29	4.28 (0.52)
positive relations with others	4.29	3.89 (0.67)	-	3.91 (0.68)	4.00	3.97 (0.72)
purpose in life	3.29	3.80 (0.68)	-	3.78 (0.63)	3.71	3.72 (0.62)
self-acceptance	4.29	3.75 (0.77)	-	3.83 (0.69)	3.43	3.87 (0.67)
NEO-FFI						
emotional stability	3.25	3.40 (0.82)	2.83	3.4 (0.74)	3.58	3.41 (0.70)
Extraversion	3.42	3.29 (0.62)	3.58	3.28 (0.66)	3.17	3.19 (0.64)
openness to experience	4.08	3.92 (0.49)	4.33	3.89 (0.50)	4.00	3.96 (0.55)
agreeableness	4.17	3.74 (0.46)	3.92	3.75 (0.49)	4.00	3.85 (0.52)
conscientiousness	3.83	3.69 (0.54)	4.17	3.73 (0.53)	3.42	3.79 (0.54)
M-Scale						
introvertive mysticism	-	3.52 (1.16)	5.00	3.60 (1.00)	4.17	3.40 (1.00)
extrovertive mysticism	-	3.45 (1.19)	5.00	3.46 (1.10)	4.50	3.29 (1.23)
interpretation	-	3.65 (1.11)	5.00	3.72 (1.00)	5.00	3.63 (1.00)

Her scores for well-being and on the NEO-FFI all being more or less within the range of the whole sample, we turn to the other remarkable finding in Gisela's survey data: her scores on the M-Scale. This was not yet part of the survey when Gisela first participated, but in the other two waves, her scores are among the highest of the whole sample. Scoring the highest ratings possible in Wave 2 on all subscales, her answers in Wave 3 show more nuances, yet less deviation from the sample mean. *Introvertive mysticism* indicates mystical experiences that are related to the internal world of the individual, while *extrovertive mysticism* rather focuses on feelings/experiences coming from the outside which are then merged with the "wholeness of all existence" (Keller, Streib et al., 2016, p. 43). *Interpretation*, for which Gisela scores highest in both surveys, refers to sacredness, positive affect and noetic quality of experiences, and it can be hypothesized that Gisela has visions, dreams, or other mystical experiences that she perceives as holy and eye-opening. The following content analysis will shed light on this part of her religiosity as well as try to find proof or rejection for our interpretation of her scores on the Religious Schema Scale.

Summary of Gisela's Faith Development

Gisela has been classified, in the typology of religious types as introduced by Streib et al. (2020), as a mover upward, shifting from the *predominantly conventional type* in Wave 1 and 2 to the *predominantly individuative-reflective type* in her third interview. For her first two interviews, it can be stated that Gisela takes a rather conventional approach to questions of *morality*, her *social horizon* showing a clear focus on a rather limited group of people with, in general, a similar mindset, striving for harmony in her relationships. There is limited evidence of critical and systemic thinking. This changes when we look at her ratings in the third interview: Here, the rater acknowledged that Gisela was able to take into account perspectives that are different from her own and detects abstract thinking that is not focused on harmony that much but explicitly defends her own standpoint. When she talks about groups, those seem to be chosen more actively, and her perspective in tendency appears self-ratified and based on consciously approved values. However, the aspects *morality* and *form of world coherence*, both of which contain questions that may easily be answered with reference to religion, remain, in majority, in a Style 3 structure. This is an interesting observation since it appears that Gisela prefers the more dogmatic, more conventional approach to moral and religious questions when the opportunity arises (which aligns with her rather high scores on *ttt*), yet is able to think in a more individual, abstract way when it comes to *perspective-taking*, *social horizon*, and *locus of authority*. This indicates that Gisela may be on a path to a more individualized thinking and it will be interesting to see whether she follows this path further.

When we look at her interviews in more detail now, we first focus on her religiosity as it is assessed and described by herself, and then go on to look at her approach to moral questions. It is an analysis which may flesh out what being a mover upward in the mentioned typology means on an idiographic level.

Gisela's Religiosity and Worldview—A Self-Chosen Belief in the Love of God

Gisela, at all timepoints, emphasizes the important role her faith plays in her life. It helped her overcome the big life crisis she had when her son was a drug addict for several years. She is engaged in voluntary work for her parish, even sometimes appearing as a lay preacher, and, for her personal education, studies theology at university. In order to approximate the core of this faith, we assemble, in the table below (Table 12.2), different kinds of data from her surveys and her interviews.

Table 12.2: Data on Gisela's Subjective Religiosity

	Wave 1	**Wave 2**	**Wave 3**
free entries	spirituality: no data	spirituality: belief in an INCONCEIVABLE LOVE from which we came to be. Then the path of life begins with a yearning inside us for this origin of love. I call this GOD and this term encompasses religion, psychology, philosophy and more.	spirituality: Spirituality for me means to see everything that happens within a big context. A view from above, integrated in one LOVE which is inconceivable and in which I feel sheltered. Not to doubt this LOVE and to recognize it in everyday life
	religion: no data	religion: Religion for me is one possibility to get to this origin of LOVE. In Christianity, for me it's JESUS CHRIST who has become my guide to this love. The reconnection to the inconceivable LOVE by the book of all books – the Bible.	religion: Religion for me means the reconnection to the history of mankind. Recognize different cultures and learn from each other, For me, GOD equals LOVE – to explain further questions.
self-assessment	equally religious and spiritual	equally religious and spiritual	equally religious and spiritual

	Wave 1	Wave 2	Wave 3
Answer to Q20: Do you consider yourself a religious, spiritual, or faithful person?	I consider myself religious. For me, this means, […] religio also means reconnection, […] and that's exciting and interesting […] today, when I read a word in the Bible, I don't read it, it connects itself to myself, it goes through me. […] Never mind if it's Buddhism, Hinduism, when the word is alive in a way that it serves peace and love, then for me it's a good religion, but not if it destroys or when it takes this image of God as a reason for war, I don't see it this way.[2]	So, I consider myself religious, because I always have this religio, this reconnection to our ancestors, a connection to the Bible. For me, the Bible has become the book of all books. […] That's where I find what I don't find elsewhere. Right? Spiritual for me means that I believe in something that I cannot comprehend. I find that in the Bible, but also with the mystics. And faithful, well, I have a faith. I am faithful.[3]	I am faithful, right? Really, I have a very strong faith. […] But I'm also very spiritual, I have to say that. I can see something in everything. And if it's just a water lily with its roots floating upside down, which makes me have an epiphany. My husband will say, "This one has to go, that does not look pretty." And I say, "Fine, I had my epiphany." And then we remove it, like that. […] And religious for me means, I lean onto it. And I try to make everybody understand that, religion means reconnection. so, where we come from. And as long as humanity exists, we always asked, where are we coming from and where are we going? That's the question of life. So, in the end, religion is one way to find an answer to that.[4]

---

2   Ich halte mich für religiös. Für mich heißt das, […] religio heißt ja auch Rückverbindung, […] und deswegen finde ich es ganz spannend und auch interessant, […], immer wenn ich heute n Wort lese in der Bibel, das lese ich nicht mehr, das bindet sich an mich, das geht durch mich durch. […] Egal ob jetzt Buddhismus, Hinduismus, wenn das Wort lebt und zwar so lebt, dass es dem Frieden und der Liebe dient, dann ist es für mich ne gute Religion, aber nicht, wenn es zerstört oder wenn es dieses Gottesbild als Ursache noch dafür nimmt Krieg zu führen, ja, das sehe ich nicht so.

3   Also ich halte mich für religiös, weil ich immer diese Religio, diese Rückbindung an unsere Vorfahren, auch in Anbindung an die Bibel. Für mich ist die Bibel wirklich das Buch der Bücher geworden. […] Da finde ich das, was ich woanders nicht finde. Ja? Spirituell heißt für mich, dass ich an etwas glaube, was ich nicht fassen kann. Was ich auch in der Bibel finde, was ich bei den Mystikern finde. Ja? Und gläubig nja, ich habe einen Glauben. Ich glaube.

4   Ich bin gläubig, ja? Wirklich, ich habe einen ganz starken Glauben. […] Ich bin aber auch sehr spirituell, muss ich sagen. In allem kann ich was sehen. Und wenn es eine Seerose ist, deren Wurzeln oben schwimmen, wo ich dann eine Erkenntnis habe. Mein Mann sagt denn: „Die muss da weg, das sieht doch nicht aus." Ich sage: „Gut, ich hatte ja meine Erkenntnis." Dann machen wir sie wieder weg da, so, ne. […] Und religiös heißt für mich, da lehne ich mich an. Und das versuche ich auch immer allen klar zu machen, Religion heißt ja Rückbindung. Also das, wo wir herkommen. Und solange es Menschen gibt, haben sie sich immer die Frage gestellt, woher kommen wir und wohin gehen wir? Das ist die Frage des Lebens. Also und Religion ist letztendlich ein Weg, wo man Antworten finden kann.

We have the free entries from the surveys in which people were asked to describe how they define religion and spirituality; then, the self-assessment from the survey with the forced-choice item asking the participants whether they identify as a) more religious than spiritual, b) more spiritual than religious, c) equally religious and spiritual, or d) neither religious nor spiritual. Additionally, we take into account Gisela's answers from the interview to the question, "Do you consider yourself a religious, spiritual, or faithful person? Or would you prefer another description?" This way, we can compare these different approaches to the topic and note change and development in the course of the three waves.

Wave 1

The free entries category did not yet exist in this project phase, so there is no data regarding her definitions there. Like at all other timepoints, she self-identifies as "equally religious and spiritual" in the survey. However, in the interview, she explicitly calls herself religious. This choice is explained firstly with reference to its Latin origin. The literal meaning speaks to her since she feels connected to the words of the Bible on a seemingly emotional, maybe spiritual, level, hinting here to a direct experience of faith. Going into a different, more abstract direction, she then talks about religions in general, marking the core of all religions as serving peace and love, a demand for tolerance, contrasted with those who, in the name of their religion, start wars. This answer indicates that, while Gisela can certainly be called religious, she draws a clear line between what is an acceptable religion for her and what is not.

Wave 2

In her free entries, it can be assumed that the topic of religion/spirituality is an emotional one for Gisela, indicated by the capitalization of key terms. The two definitions seem to complement each other, both having "love" in their center. Religion here seems to be the more specialized way, or one way among others, to get to this core of love and to God, while spirituality seems to be the more general form. Her answer in the interview sounds a bit as if she was giving definitions for the terms offered to her in the question; however, reading those, we get the impression that those definitions all apply to Gisela. The answer encompasses a favor for dogma, or at least tradition ("connection to the Bible") as well as an openness for mystical experience, however, it is shorter and less vivid than her free entries.

Wave 3

Again, she capitalizes the words LOVE and GOD in the free entries section, underlining their importance for herself (and she states that God and love for her are the same). Spirituality, here, explicitly takes into account the "bigger picture." The absence of doubt is part of her definition as well as the integration of that spirituality in everyday life. The definition of religion here has a more historical ring to it, which is consonant with her elaborations in all her interview answers regarding the Latin origin of the word. Interestingly, her definition also contains a plead for tolerance and the willingness to be open and learn from others. Her answer in the interview again stresses her faithfulness and the fact that being spiritual for her means to "see something in everything," again emphasizing that this is part of her everyday life, which is supported by a little episode she tells. This episode also suggests that she is not too dogmatic and reliant on symbols, since she can easily let go of things. When she talks about religion, she explicitly mentions the questions that religion may give an answer to, underlining the search for meaning that is important for her, and connecting this to a greater context again.

Taken together, it becomes clear that Gisela is religious in different facets, even though, while she does consider historical backgrounds and religious tradition, her focus seems to be the emotional dimension. The changes over the years are rather gradual. It is interesting to note, especially regarding the next paragraph which will deal with her stance toward tolerance and moral questions, is that at Wave 1 and 3, she makes rather explicit references to the uniting character of religion. The integration of spirituality in her everyday life comes more into focus in her last interview, something that was not mentioned that much in her first interview.

The importance of the experience dimension, which is also supported by her high scores on all subscales of the M-Scales as detailed above, is stressed as well by the observation that Gisela tends to tell narratives frequently, two of which appear in all her interviews and deal with her deconverting and then reconverting. The way she tells those narratives, using present tense and direct speech a lot, suggests that Gisela is reliving these experiences as she tells them, stressing the importance of the moments she talks about. However, the narratives change gradually over time.

Narratives: Experiences of Enlightenment

Gisela's life was at a low point when she was in her thirties (she is not precise about the exact time). Her son being a drug addict, she went through hard times for several years. When things settled down a bit, she decided to go to a psychosomatic clinic to take care of herself. This is the back story for her personal experience of enlightenment, which gave her life and her faith a new direction. This story is told in all three interviews, yet it is interesting to see how it changes gradually. The narratives are formatted according to the narrative schema as developed by Labov and Waletzky (1967), and adapted by Habermas and Berger (2011). Keller, Coleman III, and Silver (2016) have found out that religious identity narratives, that is, stories that are important for the narrator's subjective religiosity, often marking a crucial turning point, can often be segmented according to this format.

At time 1, Gisela tells the story as follows (Table 12.3).

Table 12.3: Gisela's Narrative: "Seeing a New Sky" [5]

Orientation	But I have another experience [...] And that was [...] I went to a psychosomatic convalescent care for seven weeks, [...] and then I came back home and everything was as it had been and I got physically sick again.
Complication	And then I woke up one morning, [...] and I noticed something had changed with me, and I woke up at the crack of dawn at four or five, this divine hour, and had this feeling that someone is filling me up. I lay in bed and felt nothing but warmth and love. I lay there thinking, what is that?
Evaluation	And this feeling, this warmth, this feeling of security that I never had experienced in life [...], and I thought that's how it must be like to be on drugs. Suddenly I had this connection with our son who was heavily addicted to drugs at that time [...]. I woke up my husband and explained him everything and that this was my second birthday [...],
Resolution	and then I got up in the morning and saw, as it is said in Revelation, I saw a new sky and I saw a new earth and [...] I thought, "If I had to die now, I'd have lived." [...] And this made a new image of God accessible, I said, "There is only one I can say thank you to."
Coda	That was in January, and in February, I left the church, with this image of God who let me feel love, who let me be free, yes, and that's how my new path in faith started. (Gisela, FDI, time 1)

The narrative has the tension arc of a redemption story (McAdams et al., 2001), starting at a low-point after her stay in psychosomatic care when she realized that the situation at home as well as her own had basically not changed. The experience she then describes is very oriented toward her feelings at that time, there is little attempt at interpreting it or speculating what might have happened. For Gisela, this experience makes her feel closer to her son since she wondered during the experience that the state she was in was comparable to being high. This experience of directly feeling the transcendence obviously completely changed the way Gisela looked at the world, making her content

---

5   Aber ich hab auch noch ein anderes Erlebnis, [...] und zwar war das, ich [...] habe ne psychosomatische Kur gemacht sieben Wochen, [...] und dann kam ich nach Hause und das Alte war wieder da, ich wurde wieder körperlich krank. Und dann wurde ich eines Morgens wach, [...] und ich merkte schon, mit mir war was verändert, und ich bin dann morgens wach geworden in aller Herrgottsfrühe um vier oder fünf zu dieser göttlichen Stunde, und hatte dieses Gefühl, dass mich einer auffüllt. Ich lag im Bett und spürte nur Wärme und Liebe. Ich hab da gelegen, ich denke, was ist das, und in diesem Gefühl, dieser Wärme, diese Geborgenheit, was ich nie im Leben so erfahren hab [...], da habe ich gedacht, so muss das sein, wenn man Drogen nimmt. Auf einmal hatte ich diese Verbindung zu unserem Sohn, der härteste Drogen-Abhängigkeit hatte in der Zeit auch [...]. Ich habe meinen Mann noch wach gemacht, hab ihm das erklärt und das ist mein zweiter Geburtstag [...], und da bin ich morgens aufgestanden, und ich sah, wie in der Offenbarung steht, und ich sah einen neuen Himmel und ich sah eine neue Erde und [...] ich habe gedacht: „Wenn ich jetzt sterben müsste, ich hätte gelebt." [...] Und da hat sich das Gottesbild neu erschlossen, da habe ich gesagt: „Es gibt nur einen, dem ich danken kann." Das war im Januar und im Februar bin aus der Kirche ausgetreten, mit diesem Gottesbild, der mich Liebe spüren ließ, der mich frei werden ließ, ja, und so fing dann mein neuer Glaubensweg an.

Part C: Longitudinal Case Studies—Qualitative Analyses Including Quantitative Data

and firmer in her faith. Yet, the path she obviously chose after that conversion experience was one of individuation, a more personal relationship with God making her skeptical toward the Protestant church she used to attend, which is the end of that narrative, the coda. The story of how she actually came to formally terminate her membership and then rejoined the church only a few weeks after is also told in this interview (Table 12.4).

Table 12.4: Gisela's Narrative: "Leaving and Rejoining Church"

Orientation	And then there was this situation, during the Gulf War, '91, that was a time when I had to demonstrate, pretty late, but then was just the time for me, I couldn't bear it, when I sat in front of the TV, tears would flow. So I got dressed and went to demonstrations. [...] Yes, and then I was demonstrating with my friend and her brother and she said, "Should we go to church?" There was this prayer for peace, [...] and I was like, "Nope, I'll go home, I'm not that much into the church thing." [...] then we were in front of the church and the bells started to toll and I said, "You know, I guess I'll have to go into the church anyway." [...]
Complication	Well, and then those Christians would stand up and step forward and were supposed to speak prayers of peace and all I can remember are tons of condemnations against the warmongers, against all kinds of people and I sat there in the church and I had something great to say, you know (laughs). I had the feeling I have to step forward and give courage to the parents whose kids are in the military, [...] and say to all parents, "Encourage your kids to say, I'm not going there. We did not bring our children into this world for this war. This is not God's will." And I found that really great, but I didn't dare to say it, I listened to the others' speeches and thought, "How can they judge, do they know what's good and right?" And then I didn't dare, my heart was pounding, I broke into sweat,
Evaluation	and then I sat in this church and thought, "If there is a God that I believe in, then He cannot wish for me to be afraid in His house. I have to leave the church." And then I went home and said to my husband, "I'm leaving the church." And he was like, "I wanted this for a while, I'll go with you." [...] So we both formally left.
Resolution	Next Sunday, my godchild was presented to the church, they went to confirmation, so I went to the service, as godmother, and suddenly felt this freedom, [...] and I knew I'll have to rejoin at some point. [...] On the fourth Sunday, there were four baptisms, and I experienced them as my own, I wanted to go up front and get a baptism candle, but I didn't. I called the priest and I said, I have to rejoin, I wasn't able to explain it, and so I rejoined after four weeks.
Coda	That was like, I knew I couldn't explain it, this changed my image of God, I noticed within myself that there is someone who pulls me, who says, you have to do that, when the intellect has not caught up yet.[6] (Gisela, FDI, time 1)

---

6   Und dann gab es eine Situation, dass ich, da war der Golfkrieg, '91, und das war ne Zeit, wo ich demonstrieren musste, ziemlich spät, aber das war für mich halt dran, ich hielt das nicht aus, wenn ich vorm Fernseher saß, kullerten die Tränen. Also angezogen und dann demonstrieren [...]. Ja und dann war ich mit meiner Freundin demonstrieren und mit deren Bruder noch, und dann sagt sie: „Wollen wir noch in die Kirche?" Da gab es ein Friedensgebet, [...] und dann sag ich: „Nee, ich fahre nach Hause, mit Kirche habe ich es nicht so." [...] Dann standen wir da am Parkplatz und dann fingen die Glocken an zu läuten und dann sag ich: „Du, ich muss wohl doch in die Kirche." [...] Naja und dann standen die Christen auf, gingen dann nach vorne und sollten eben Friedensgebete

In this narrative, it becomes clear how Gisela is torn between rejecting the church and feeling drawn to it. Following the urge to step into the church, the experience is disappointing, even humiliating for her. She feels a great insecurity, but, having had the enlightenment described above, she does not really doubt her faith. What she does doubt is her connection with the church since she cannot accept that the God she believes in so fiercely would want her to suffer in His house. The motif of emotional suffering was found to be one of the major motifs for people to leave their church and/or their faith (see Streib et al., 2009) and it seems that this was the main reason for Gisela, too, to make the decision to terminate her membership. The criticism at this point is clearly directed toward the church or the parish, while she does not actually doubt her own faith anymore. However, only a few weeks after that incident, and after having directly put into practice her plan to formally leave the church, Gisela experiences yet another epiphany, which is the actual and more important resolution of her narrative. The sacred rituals of confirmations and baptism appeal to her, touch her in a spiritual way. It becomes clear here that her decision is driven by these spiritual experiences and not by rational considerations, and she even puts this in her coda explicitly, "the intellect has not caught up yet."

In her second interview, both of these stories are told again. For the sake of brevity, we will concentrate here on those passages that differ significantly. The way the experience is retold is very similar to what Gisela tells at time 1, which suggests that it is a story that she has told/thought about many times and which therefore may be labeled as constituent for her (religious) identity, or a pertaining personal myth (cf. McAdams, 1993, Conway & Pleydell-Pearce, 2000, Vaughn & Rawson, 2011). Yet, resolution and coda are somewhat different:

---

sprechen und dann kann ich mich nur erinnern, dass da lauter Verurteilungen dran waren gegen die Kriegstreiber, gegen alle möglichen Leute und ich saß da in der Kirche und ich hatte was ganz Tolles zu sagen ne (lacht). Ich hatte das Gefühl, du musst jetzt nach vorne gehen und den Eltern Mut machen, deren Kinder bei der Bundeswehr sind, [...] und allen Eltern [sagen]: „Macht euren Kindern Mut zu sagen, da gehe ich nicht hin. Wir haben unsere Kinder nicht für diesen Krieg in die Welt gesetzt. Das ist nicht Gottes Wille." Und das fand ich so super und ich traute mich nicht, ich hörte mir die Reden der Leute vorne an und hab gedacht: „Wie können sie urteilen, wissen sie, was gut und richtig ist?" Und dann habe ich mich nicht getraut, ich kriegte Herzklopfen, ich kriegte Schweißausbrüche, und dann saß ich in dieser [Kirche], und hab gedacht: „Wenn es 'n Gott gibt, an den ich glaube, dann kann er nicht wollen, dass ich in seinem Hause Angst habe. Ich muss aus der Kirche austreten." Und dann bin ich nach Hause gegangen und habe zu meinem Mann gesagt: „Ich trete aus der Kirche aus." Da sagt er: „Ja, hatte ich schon immer vor, ich komme mit." [...] Sind wir beide ausgetreten. Und sonntags wurde mein Patenkind in unserer Kirche vorgestellt, die gingen zur Konfirmation, dann gehe ich sonntags in den Gottesdienst, als Pate, und spüre auf einmal in mir diese Freiheit, [...] da merkte ich schon, dass ich irgendwann wieder eintreten muss. [...] Am vierten Sonntag waren vier Taufen, ja und die habe ich als meine erlebt, ich wär am liebsten nach vorne gegangen, hätte mir die Taufkerze geholt und habe aber das nicht gemacht. Hab den Pfarrer dann angerufen, hab gesagt, ich müsste wieder eintreten, ich könnte es nicht erklären, und dann bin ich vier Wochen später wieder eingetreten. Das war wieder so, wo ich dann merkte, ja, das kann man nicht erklären, da hat sich auch mein Gottesbild verändert, da habe ich eben in mir gespürt, dass da jemand ist, der mich zieht, der sagt, das musst du jetzt tun, wo der Verstand noch gar nicht nach-kommt, ne.

286 Part C: Longitudinal Case Studies—Qualitative Analyses Including Quantitative Data

> Then I thought, Martin Luther said this once, I think, if I had but one day left to live, I would still go and plant an apple tree. And while I hung the washing, I thought, "If I had to die today, I would have lived." That was the most drastic experience. [...] So, I can only thank God for this. [...] And then this sentence came to me, "God is love. Who stays within love, stays within God and God within you." So I took this sentence and thought, "That's how it is. I want to stay on this path," I made a conscious decision for this path of love.[7] (Gisela, FDI, time 2)

Quoting Martin Luther's famous saying, she stresses the importance and validity of her own thought, which is repeated almost literally, compared to time 1. The changed image of God is made more explicit here than it was at time 1, again explained with a quote, this time from the Bible. Her coda in this second interview is more focused on her conscious decision to follow the path of love the epiphany has shown her. The story of how she sat in church after the demonstration follows straight after that (at time 1, the chronology is less clear) and is, again, told in a strikingly similar fashion. Looking at resolution and coda of that narrative, however, reveals that the overall evaluation of this experience is slightly different:

> So I called the priest on Monday morning. I say, "I experienced this and that. I almost went up front and took a baptism candle." And he says, "Yes, Mrs. P., you should have done that." – "Really?" – "The custodian had laid out an additional one." And then I say, "Yes, I would like to have that." And so I got the baptism candle, [...]. Well, and I am in the church now. I knew at one point there will be the call for the parish council, and that happened in '92, and I said "yes" immediately, even though I didn't know what to expect. And then I became part of the parish council and I've been there for 22 years now. And so my way within-, with the church continued.[8] (Gisela, FDI, time 2)

This part of the narrative takes up a lot more room than at time 1; parts of it are told in present tense, and the dialog between herself and the priest is quoted, allowing the assumption that Gisela is basically reliving this experience. The fact that there was indeed an additional candle underlines the fatefulness of the whole scene, a decision was made,

---

7   Da habe ich gedacht, Martin Luther hat das glaube ich mal gesagt, wenn ich nur einen Tag zu leben hätte noch, dann würde ich ein Apfelbäumchen pflanzen. Und ich habe dann beim Wäscheaufhängen gedacht: „Und wenn ich heute sterben müsste, ich hätte gelebt." Das war das einschneidende Erlebnis. [...] Also da kann ich mich nur bei Gott bedanken. [...] Und dann kam mir der Satz entgegen: „Gott ist die Liebe. Wer in der Liebe bleibt, bleibt in Gott und Gott in dir." Also habe ich mir diesen Satz genommen und habe gedacht: „So ist das. Auf dem Weg will ich bleiben", habe ich mich ganz bewusst für diesen Weg der Liebe entschieden.

8   Also habe ich den Pastor angerufen Montagmorgen. Ich sage: „Das und das habe ich erlebt. Ich wäre am liebsten nach vorne gegangen und hätte mir eine Taufkerze geholt." Da sagt er: „Ja, Frau P., das hätten Sie mal machen sollen." – „Ja?" – „Der Küster hatte eine mehr hingelegt." Und dann sage ich: „Ja, die hätte ich gerne." Also habe ich die Taufkerze gekriegt, [...]. Ja, und so bin ich jetzt in der Kirche. Ich wusste dann auch, dass irgendwann der Ruf kommt zum Kirchenvorstand und das war dann auch in '92, habe ich auch gleich „Ja" gesagt, obwohl ich gar nicht wusste, was mich erwartet. Und dann bin ich in den Kirchenvorstand gegangen und bin da 22 Jahre drin jetzt. Und so ging mein Weg in-, mit der Kirche weiter.

but it was predestined. Interestingly, her coda this time focuses on the path she then took within the church, the formal organization she had left for a short period of time, even though she had already been part of that parish council at the time of her first interview.

At time 3, the experience Gisela has in her sleep is told again as well, and, again, it is mainly the resolution and the coda that have changed:

> When I got up, I thought: you're healthy now. [...] It was like a new life. So, this is my second birthday. [...] But since then I have the feeling of being healthy, a holistic health. Doesn't mean I'm always healthy. But I have this feeling of health and this feeling that nothing can happen to me anymore. And I didn't know who to tie this to. In '91, I started writing, I filled ten books, got everything off my chest what came to the surface. And it was like, I was thinking, whom do you want to thank? [...] And that's what we call God, within religion. And then I needed a guide, of course. And that's what Jesus Christ became for me.[9] (Gisela, FDI, time 3)

The implication "you're healthy now" is brought up here for the first time. Consequently, she elaborates on that thought in the following sentences, amplifying the ways she is feeling healthy, implying that this experience for her was beneficial on more than one level; this may be an indicator for the way she perceives her faith: as something that is working holistically, not just for one part of her, but for her overall well-being. Faith, for her, seems to have a healing function. Interestingly, the image of God she hints at here, as well as her commitment to Jesus, seem to be in unquestioned accordance with the general stance of the Protestant church. While in the other interviews, especially in the first, she emphasizes the effect of individuation this experience has had, this is not her coda anymore. Her experience during the prayer for peace is not mentioned in the interview directly; however, when, after having answered all of the FDI questions, she is asked whether she wanted to add something, Gisela brings up that story, embedded in a general, albeit kind of unorganized, display of her faith biography.

Overall, it can be said that Gisela's faith has different facets: she is an active member of a Protestant parish, and therefore a lot of faith content she describes is in accordance with the Protestant church. Moreover, Gisela has, for many years, taken university courses in theology, engaging with the scientific discourse on religion. However, Gisela also puts a lot of emphasis on the experiential dimension of her faith. The conversion experiences or epiphanies she describes are mostly free of any attempt of rationalization. The facet that has not yet been looked at more closely is the community aspect. The next

---

9   Als ich dann aufstand, habe ich gedacht, du bist gesund. [...] Es war wie so ein neues Leben. Also das ist mein zweiter Geburtstag. [...] Aber seitdem habe ich das Gefühl der Gesundheit, der ganzheitlichen Gesundheit. Das heißt nicht, dass ich immer gesund bin. Aber ich habe dieses Gefühl der Gesundheit und so dies Gefühl, dir kann eigentlich gar nix mehr passieren. Und jetzt wusste ich aber nicht, an wem mache ich das fest. Ich habe '91 angefangen zu schreiben, ich habe zehn Bücher oben vollgeschrieben, mir alles von der Seele geschrieben, was so hochkam. Und da war das halt so, dass ich gedacht habe, wem willst du danken? [...] Und das ist, was wir Gott nennen, in der Religion. Und dann brauchte ich natürlich einen Wegweiser. Das ist für mich Jesus Christus geworden.

288   Part C: Longitudinal Case Studies—Qualitative Analyses Including Quantitative Data

paragraph will sketch out the changing way in which Gisela talks about the importance of community.

What Does Community Mean for Gisela?

As an active member of her church parish, Gisela designs and actively shapes the community she chose to be a part of. In university, on the other hand, she learns to view the topic of religion from a more scientific point of view and appreciates the group of people she meets there as well. When in the interviews she is asked for important groups and causes, the focus she chooses each time is different. At time 1, she states the following:

> Yes, I am in the church, I am in the parish council, [...] like, church-wise, I am connected, parish-wise. [...] At uni too, the theological courses and also the community, it's like a family, like, we've known each other for so many years, [...] I feel comfortable there, basically in all groups in which I perceive this foundation of faith, I really feel at home there, those can be total strangers, I'm at home there. [I: And why are these groups important for you?] Because of the community, and because of the exchange of course, because I think there needs to be a flow. I went to women's groups a few times [...], so, I feel comfortable there, when I can share some of what I had to live through and endure, what I could and did endure, then I see that it is fruitful.[10] (Gisela, FDI, time 1)

Gisela here describes the way she feels embedded in communities of people that, however different they may be otherwise, share a mindset: that of the (mainly Lutheran) Protestant faith. It seems that she values the positive effects these groups have, implicitly also stating that she appreciates the homogeneity of these groups, since she does not mention any stress or discussions. The communities also offer a form of support and stability since she is, in those circles, able to share her experiences and to pass on some of her knowledge and coping strategies.

At time 2, her emphasis is a different one:

> Church. Of course, I'm fully immersed there, I'm in the synod, parish council. Causes... to really proceed on this path of love and share it with the people who want that. [...] And I say, "I have to be able to think aloud in my family or my relationship. And if I can't do that, I'm wrong here, never mind how much my husband groans." [...] And in other circles, in church, I always see the facts and try to say that in the parish

---

10   Ja, einmal bin ich in der Kirche, ich bin im Kirchenvorstand, [...] also kirchenmäßig bin ich angebunden, gemeindemäßig. [...] Uni natürlich auch, die theologischen Seminare und auch diese Gruppe, das ist auch wie so ne Familie, also man kennt sich ja schon so viele Jahre, [...] da ich fühle mich da sofort wohl und eigentlich in allen Gruppen, wo ich dieses Fundament des Glaubens auch so wahrnehme, also da fühle ich mich richtig zu Hause, die können mir noch so fremd sein, also da bin ich zu Hause. [I: Und warum sind Ihnen diese Gruppen so wichtig?] Wegen der Gemeinschaft, und wegen des Austausches natürlich auch, weil ich denke, es muss ja fließen. Ich war jetzt ein paar Mal in Frauenkreisen [...], also da fühle ich mich wohl, wenn ich auch von dem, was ich durchleben und durchleiden durfte, konnte, musste, abgeben kann, dann sehe ich, dass das Frucht bringt.

council, "It's about the facts. When I mention something, it's not against you as a person, [...]."[11] (Gisela, FDI, time 2)

While at first she mentions her embeddedness in the parish again, she then goes on to talk on a more abstract level about what she needs in a relationship (and relationship here not only refers to marriage, but is meant on a more general level): she needs to be able to think aloud. This displays a form of autonomy, self-reflectiveness, and individuation that we did not see at time 1. It appears that Gisela is not that focused on the harmony within a group but instead wants to be able to address problems on the basis of facts rather than ad personam attacks; in other words, she is standing up for herself more.

This standpoint is elaborated further at time 3:

I always tell my husband, "I have to be able to think aloud in a relationship." That's important in any kind of relationship, what I call relationship. If this is not the case, I'm wrong here. And that's what I also see in the relations with the parish, the relations within the Christian family [...] and I hold true to that. Even if sometimes people don't understand that, but for me, it's about the facts, about what constitutes being human, you know. [...] In this Christian family, of course I feel sheltered, sheltered in the community. Because that's like a family. Yes, and I see parallels to the Biblical stories. Who is my mother, who is my father? Who are my siblings? Those who are on the same level with me and are happy when I'm happy and argue without degrading the other. So, that's important, respecting each other.[12] (Gisela, FDI, time 3)

She brings up her guiding principle again, again stressing her autonomy and the claim to think for herself. This time, though, it sounds more like desirable norms; authenticity and integrity, even though not named explicitly, are principles that should apply to everybody and might even be constituent for a society. After a short digression in which she talks about groups that she left because they did not live up to her standards, she then returns to her so-called "Christian family," here, like at time 1, emphasizing the importance of

---

11   Kirche. Natürlich bin ich voll drin, bin in der Synode, Kirchenvorstand. Meine Anliegen... wirklich diesen Weg der Liebe weiterzugehen und davon abzugeben. Den Menschen, die es möchten. [...] Und ich sage: „Ich muss in meiner Familie oder in meiner Beziehung laut denken können. Und wenn ich das nicht kann, bin ich hier verkehrt, und wenn mein Mann noch so schwer atmet." [...] Und in anderen Kreisen wie Kirche, ich sehe immer die Sachen und versuche auch bei uns im Kirchenvorstand zu sagen: „Es geht um eine Sache. Wenn ich etwas anspreche, das geht nicht gegen dich persönlich, [...]."

12   Ich sage zu meinem Mann immer: „Ich muss in einer Beziehung laut denken können." Das ist für mich in jeder Beziehung wichtig, was ich Beziehung nenne. Wenn das nicht der Fall ist, dann bin ich verkehrt. Und so sehe ich in den Beziehungen auch zu der Kirchengemeinde, die Beziehungen in der christlichen Familie natürlich [...] und das halte ich bis heute durch. Also auch, wenn manchmal dann vielleicht nicht so ein Verständnis ist, aber mir geht es einfach um diese Sache, um das, was Mensch sein ausmacht, ne. [...] Es ist jetzt so, dass ich in der christlichen Familie natürlich mich geborgen, in der Gemeinschaft geborgen fühle. Weil, das ist wie eine Familie. Ja und da finde ich halt immer Parallelen zur biblischen Geschichte. Wer ist meine Mutter, wer ist mein Vater? Wer sind meine Geschwister? Das sind die, die mit mir auf einer Ebene sind und sich mit mir freuen oder mit mir streiten, ohne sich klein zu machen. Also das ist für mich ganz wichtig, dieses schon sich gegenseitig so achten.

Part C: Longitudinal Case Studies—Qualitative Analyses Including Quantitative Data

shared values and the support she receives from this group. Interesting here is that this feeling of community is argued with reference to "Biblical stories," an attempt to give her arguments more credibility and to further underline her rootedness in the words of the Bible, which goes along well with the finding from above that her scores on *ttt* were high in her survey results.

Summed up, we see here that Gisela values community highly. But, while she focuses on the positive effects only at time 1, her answers become more critical and nuanced in the other interviews. At time 3, she even rudimentarily sketches out a societal ideal in which critique can be addressed without degrading one another and which otherwise is supportive and understanding. This moral claim provides a bridge to the next paragraph in which we will discuss Gisela's stance toward questions of morality and tolerance.

Morality and Tolerance—Finding the Core and Focusing on Fairness

Love and fairness seem to be the themes that thread through Gisela's interviews at all timepoints. At time 1, she says that an action for her is right when it serves humankind, everything that is done out of love is good and right. When asked for moral opinions that everyone should agree on, she names loyalty, both to God the Creator and to oneself. This is, as she puts it, the basis for everything else. So, her answers regarding these questions oscillate between harm/care regarding her fellow humans and ingroup/loyalty when it comes to her relationship with God (Graham et al., 2011), and it is not quite clear whether she means this on an interpersonal level or also on a more general, societal level. Being loyal to oneself, or, in other words, being upright and with integrity, is an addition that may rather go beyond the pure interpersonal focus. When asked how religious conflicts can be resolved, she states the following:

> By looking at the core of it. If I have the core of something, it is God's love. There was this nice talk by the ecumenical church [...], there are different bridges, [...] and we walk on the bridge of Christianity, over there, there's Judaism, and there are the other religions [...]. And if we concentrate on the core, that we are just on different paths, we should not have any problems, and the aim is the same, we all walk to the same mark, I guess, and basically, there should not be any problems, but of course there are plenty.[13] (Gisela, FDI, time 1)

Gisela borrows a metaphor from a speech she has heard, different bridges (religions) all leading to the same point, a common core which is, in her eyes, God's love. She vaguely, rather implicitly, appreciates that other religions might have different paths, yet, as long as everybody agrees on that common core, there should not be any conflicts. This is a very basic form of tolerance and the assumption of God's love being at the core of every

---

13 Indem man auf den Kern der Sache guckt. Wenn ich den Kern der Sache hier habe, das ist die Liebe Gottes. Dann gab's immer so'n schönes Referat an der ökumenischen Kirche [...], da gibt es dann die verschiedenen Brücken, [...], wir gehen die vom Christentum, da ist das Judentum, da die anderen Religionen [...]. Und wenn wir uns auf die Mitte konzentrieren, dass wir alle nur auf einem anderen Weg sind, dürften wir keine Probleme haben, und das Ziel ist das gleiche, wir gehen alle auf ein Ziel hin, denke ich und eigentlich dürfte es da keine Probleme geben, aber gibt es ja, reichlich.

religion might sound naïve, but Gisela knows that, obviously, the picture she paints is abstract and that, in reality, there are plenty of problems.

Interestingly, the metaphor of different bridges is brought up again in her second interview when she is asked what constitutes a mature faith:

> A mature faith for me is to know about my roots which I locate within Christianity. Even though I have engeaged with other religions. [...] And still I feel rooted in Christianity, in this love that I attach to God; that I attach to Jesus Christ as a person. [...] I think it was Dorothee Sölle who once said, "At the core, I see love. And we go over the bridges up to this core." And each time I say something like that I also speak to myself, to my core. And I walk over the bridge of Christianity, [other] over that of Islam, Buddhism, Hinduism, And the further we are apart, the more alienated we become. And the more we get to know each other, the more we know how similar we are. And then there are no more religious wars. But there are a lot of fundamentalist Christians who say, "But they don't have Jesus in Islam," there's a lack of tolerance there. Currently, I'm visiting [a course on] "Interreligious dialog" because that's the theme of our time.[14] (Gisela, FDI, time 2)

This time attributing the bridge metaphor to German feminist theologian and poet Dorothee Sölle, Gisela unfolds her thoughts on tolerance here a lot more explicitly than at time 1. While firmly stating that she herself is rooted within the Christian faith, we learn that she has studied other religions as well and pleads for interreligious dialog in order to find similarities. This is a different picture than at time 1 in which it rather seemed that the people walking on the different bridges could/would not actually see and acknowledge each other. Asked for a solution for religious conflicts later in the interview, Gisela states that it is important to work on a small scale and see what every individual can do for others and/or for society, advocating social fairness, albeit on a more or less interpersonal level.

Her answer to the question of mature faith is again a good example for how Gisela defines tolerance at time 3:

> Mature faith for me means to believe in something that you cannot capture. [...] And that's for me, if I can believe in this unfathomable, incomprehensible, then I'll have a different point of view. And then fundamentalism is a foreign concept. Like, I say, I

---

14 Ein reifer Glauben ist für mich, dass ich um meine Wurzeln weiß, die ich jetzt im Christentum festmache. Obwohl ich mich mit allen Religionen auseinandergesetzt habe. [...] Und trotzdem fühle ich mich im Christentum verwurzelt, in dieser Liebe, die ich jetzt an Gott festmache; die ich an Jesus Christus als Person festmache. [...] Ich meine, hier das hat Dorothee Sölle sicher mal gesagt: „In der Mitte sehe ich die Liebe. Und wir gehen über die Brücken zu dieser Mitte hin." Und immer, wenn ich sowas sage, spreche ich auch zu mir, zu meiner Mitte. Und ich gehe über die Brücke des Christentums, [andere] über die des Islams und Buddhismus, Hinduismus. Und, je weiter wir entfernt sind, umso fremder sind wir uns. Und je mehr wir uns kennenlernen, umso mehr wissen wir, wie ähnlich wir uns sind. Und dann gibt es keine Religionskriege mehr. Aber es gibt sehr viele fundamentalistische Christen, die sagen: „Nur Jesus, das hat der Islam nicht und die Toleranz fehlt da. Und jetzt besuche ich ja noch mal [das Seminar] „Interreligiösen Dialog, weil das das Thema dieser Zeit ist.

Part C: Longitudinal Case Studies—Qualitative Analyses Including Quantitative Data

> do live in Christianity, and I'm rooted there, but the biggest part of humanity is not. And this freedom in faith, that's important for me, mature faith must be liberating. [...] If I believe that, then I try, of course, to see each human, each being differently. As a gift, as part of the big picture. And then I'm inclined to act as not to hurt anybody, at least not consciously. And that way, I can reach inner peace.[15] (Gisela, FDI, time 3)

Gisela is staying closer to her own faith here than in the answer she gives at time 2. But she argues that this specifically is what gives her the freedom to be tolerant, to recognize that Christianity is not the answer to everything for everybody. This realization is liberating for her and enables her to appreciate the individuality of everyone and everything. As an example for the mature faith that she proclaims, we have this part of her answer on religious conflicts:

> Yes, to find a common denominator. To discuss and find a common point. For example, the Catholic church, and the Protestants even more, how much they stick to the topic of not having the Holy Communion together. That is just part of their faith. I need not pinpoint the whole faith onto this. [...] And then I think when you say something like this, when at the core there is God's love in Jesus Christ, then I don't have to burden myself with something like that, you know.[16] (Gisela, FDI, time 3)

Gisela does not support discussions about details, it seems. She rather advocates to see the bigger picture, or, rather, the common core that is God's love. Concentrating on this, she feels, would eliminate side issues and petty conflicts like the question whether Protestants and Catholics can go to Communion together.

Summed up, Gisela proclaims tolerance from a decidedly Christian perspective at all timepoints. Her moral foundation can best be described as focusing on fairness/reciprocity, even though there are notions as well of authenticity and integrity, which, however, is not yet captured by the theoretical model of moral intuitions (cf. Graham et al., 2011). Her considerations, in general, become more abstract, while, at the same time, she seems to stand firmer on the Christian foundation with each interview.

---

15   Reifer Glauben bedeutet für mich, an etwas glauben, was wir nicht fassen können. [...] Und das ist für mich, wenn ich an dieses Unfassbare, Unbegreifliche glauben kann, dann bekomme ich eine andere Sichtweise. Und Fundamentalismus ist dann ein Fremdwort. Also dass ich dann sage: Ja, ich lebe zwar im Christentum, bin auch da verwurzelt, aber der größte Teil der Menschheit eben nicht. Diese Freiheit im Glauben, das ist für mich ganz wichtig so, reifer Glauben muss frei machen. [...] Wenn ich daran glaube, dann bin ich natürlich bemüht, oder dann ergibt sich das, dass ich jeden Menschen, jedes Geschöpf anders sehe. Als Geschenk, als Teil des Ganzen. Und ich natürlich geneigt bin, mich so zu verhalten, dass ich dem anderen nicht weh tue, jedenfalls nicht bewusst. Und dass ich dadurch auch einen inneren Frieden bekomme.

16   Ja, dass man einen gemeinsamen Nenner findet. Dass man darüber diskutiert und einen gemeinsamen Punkt findet. Wie jetzt die katholische Kirche sich daran aufhält, nur so ein Beispiel, oder die Evangelen halten sich da noch mehr dran auf, dass man nicht gemeinsam Abendmahl feiern kann. Das ist ein Teil des Glaubens. Da muss ich doch den Glauben nicht dran aufhängen. [...] Und dann denke ich auch, wenn man solche Aussagen macht, wenn das Zentrum die Liebe Gottes in Jesus Christus ist, dann brauche ich doch nicht mich damit aufhalten, ja.

General Interpretation of Gisela's Religious Development —Triangulating the Data

Gisela is a woman who has consciously made the decision to live her faith in the Protestant church. Her survey results indicating that she favors a literal understanding of the Holy Script, the interpretation of key aspects of her interview has shown that she indeed emphasizes the original Latin meaning of the word "religio," meaning a link back to the past, and values the words of the Bible highly, and even shows dogmatic tendencies at some points in her interviews. This stays rather constant over the years and is in accordance with the results of the structural analysis of her FDIs which have been rated Style 3 in those aspects that focus on questions of faith and world coherence. However, we also see a development in Gisela's elaboration, especially in the segment of personal relationships, but also regarding moral questions. Here, her answers become more differentiated and abstract over time, maybe a result of her ongoing studies at university, in any case also displayed in the Style 4 ratings she received at time 3 and, to a lower extent, also already at time 2. Quite obvious is the connection between her high scores on the M-Scale and the fact that Gisela's faith is very oriented by experiences. The experiences of enlightenment that have been described above are constituent for the way she lives her religiosity and defining for her overall life, as can be seen at time 3 when she names said experience as the reason for why she has been healthy since then. The way Gisela approaches these experiences is not critical, she seems more or less caught up in reliving them, an observation that adds to their mystical quality.

So, Gisela obviously combines different forms of lived religion in one person: On the one hand, her starting point is experience-based, rather uncritical and favoring the mystic; on the other hand, we see her engaging in a more abstract way with questions of morality, seeking dialog and pleading for tolerance. She does all of this within her clearly defined group of like-minded people. So, the tolerance that Gisela advocates, most strongly and in a generalizable way at time 3, comes from a clearly Christian perspective, and it seems that, from this very secure place Gisela sees herself in, she is able to look at others in a more tolerant way, without, however, truly aiming at understanding them. This only partially explains her high scores on xenos, since a xenosophic person would more actively seek the encounter with the strange than does Gisela who seems to be staying in the (however wide) realms of her parish and her university community, so it can be assumed that there may be a theoretically higher appreciation for the strange than is actually displayed and put into praxis. Yet, and this is mirrored in the observation that Gisela moves from a *predominantly conventional type* to a *predominantly individuative-reflective type* in her last interview, we can see a development from a more conservative, more conventional standpoint to a view that shows ability for reflective, sometimes critical thinking.

Turning now to the case of George, we will see how his form of Protestantism plays out in his interviews.

George

Biographical Outline

George, from the United States, was 54 years old at the time of his first interview, which took place in 2011 and 63 years old in 2018 when his third interview took place. George grew up on a farm in the American mid-west as the son of a Roman Catholic mother and a "kind of an agnostic" (time 1) or "probably, more or less, atheist" father (times 2 & 3) as well as various secular Jewish extended family members (time 1). He describes his mother as a German "war bride" who came to the United States when she was 15 years old after marrying his father who had served as a soldier in World War II, and that he himself grew up speaking exclusively German on his family farm before going to school. This experience might have been a first encounter with the feeling of being "the stranger" or the odd one out.

After high school, George left home for college and completed his undergraduate and graduate degrees at a pair of mid-western universities, after which he took various research and post-doctoral positions locally and internationally, eventually returning to the American mid-west to begin his work as a professor. In addition to his psychology specialty, he is an avid reader of philosophy and theology. In his interviews, he identifies himself as "spiritual" at Wave 1, "faithful" at Wave 2, and "humanist" at Wave 3.

George's wife was an Irish Catholic when the two married. After having to opt for a late-term abortion due to medical reasons, her church's views on abortion became "too much" for George's wife, and she left to join George's Lutheran church. At the time of the third interview, George continues to attend a Lutheran church with his wife. They have two children, one of which he and his wife adopted from a foreign country.

Selected Survey Results

Table 12.5 presents George's selected results on the scales that were included in the questionnaire.

George's scores on *ttt* are low in Wave 1, more than one standard deviation lower than the sample mean. Interestingly, though, this score increases, albeit on a low level to almost reach the sample mean in Wave 3. As a working hypothesis, we may suppose that George has, over the years, developed a more positive stance toward religion and its holy texts. At the same time, we see high scores on *xenos* which suggests that his appreciation for the strange is strong and that he is open for new experiences, which is also mirrored in his fairly high scores for *openness* on the NEO-FFI.

Turning to the Ryff Scale, we see remarkably low scores on all subscales except *autonomy*. Those scores are, at all timepoints, mostly well below the average of the sample. Taken together with his exceptionally low scores on *emotional stability* of the NEO-FFI, these findings might point to a personality which is not stable, a person who has faced a lot of hardships in his life, has possibly been disappointed by others, and has maybe not found a good way to cope with them. However, we do see a slight increase in *purpose in life* which may indicate that George has found a new goal in his life.

Table 12.5: Selected Survey Results for George

	Wave 1		Wave 2		Wave 3	
	George	M (SD)	George	M (SD)	George	M (SD)
Religious Schema Scale						
truth of texts and teachings	1.20	2.53 (1.14)	1.60	2.35 (1.13)	2.20	2.55 (1.12)
fairness, tolerance, ...	5.00	4.38 (0.38)	5.00	4.35 (0.51)	5.00	4.59 (0.40)
xenosophia/inter-religious d.	4.80	3.64 (0.82)	4.00	3.58 (0.78)	4.60	3.77 (0.78)
Ryff Scale						
autonomy	4.14	3.69 (0.58)	3.71	3.32 (0.49)	3.57	3.31 (0.53)
environmental mastery	1.86	3.65 (0.75)	2.00	3.67 (0.63)	1.43	3.66 (0.67)
personal growth	3.00	4.31 (0.48)	3.71	4.14 (0.49)	3.86	4.28 (0.52)
positive relations with others	2.57	3.89 (0.67)	2.57	3.91 (0.68)	2.14	3.97 (0.72)
purpose in life	1.86	3.80 (0.68)	1.86	3.78 (0.63)	2.43	3.72 (0.62)
self-acceptance	1.14	3.75 (0.77)	1.29	3.83 (0.69)	1.83	3.87 (0.67)
NEO-FFI						
emotional stability	1.67	3.40 (0.82)	1.75	3.40 (0.74)	1.75	3.41 (0.70)
extraversion	2.42	3.29 (0.62)	1.75	3.28 (0.66)	2.17	3.19 (0.64)
openness to experience	4.08	3.92 (0.49)	4.08	3.89 (0.50)	4.08	3.96 (0.55)
agreeableness	3.25	3.74 (0.46)	3.75	3.75 (0.49)	3.75	3.85 (0.52)
conscientiousness	3.00	3.69 (0.54)	3.33	3.73 (0.53)	3.00	3.79 (0.54)
M-Scale						
introvertive mysticism	3.00	3.52 (1.16)	1.42	3.60 (1.00)	3.25	3.40 (1.00)
extrovertive mysticism	2.38	3.45 (1.19)	3.13	3.46 (1.10)	3.50	3.29 (1.23)
interpretation	1.25	3.65 (1.11)	1.33	3.72 (1.00)	1.92	3.63 (1.00)

His scores on the M-Scale are moderate to low; especially low are his scores on *interpretation*. This indicates that George either has never had experiences that he would describe as religious/mystical or that at least he did not interpret them as religious/mystical.

Summary of George's Faith Development

George's faith development, according to the typology proposed by Streib, Chen, and Hood (2020), follows the pattern of the mover upward. In Wave 1, George aligns most with the *predominantly individuative-reflective type*. This type is characterized by an autonomously reflective and critical approach to assessing the accuracy of religious ideas, as well as the use of tolerance when religious claims come into conflict. In Waves 2 and 3, George shifts towards the *emerging dialogical-xenosophic type*. This reflects movement towards pragmatic universal principles and an intentional pursuit of dialog with and

Part C: Longitudinal Case Studies—Qualitative Analyses Including Quantitative Data

learning from the other or "the strange." This deliberate engagement with the other opens up the possibility of emergent wisdom and creativity. The most substantial changes in the aspects that make up these types are in George's *social horizon* and *locus of authority*, wherein he is categorized as a *predominantly individuative-reflective type* for both at Wave 1 and then shifts towards a mix of the *individuative-reflective* and the *dialogical-xenosophic* types at Waves 2 and 3. His consistent increase in *locus of authority* suggests that he has moved from implicit values stemming from his social context towards an internally validated perspective that explicitly and humbly seeks out other perspectives for the purpose of comparison and growth.

George's Religiosity and Worldview—Fostering Connections to Others

As with Gisela, we have below provided George's answers to the "free entries" on religion and spirituality, together with his self-assessment of being spiritual and/or religious and his answer to question 20 ("Do you consider yourself a religious, spiritual, or faithful person?") of the Faith Development Interview below (Table 12.6).

Table 12.6: Data on George's Religiosity and Worldview

	Wave 1	Wave 2	Wave 3
Free Entries	*spirituality:* Someone is spiritual who appreciates the intrinsic morality of the broader human experience and helps other humans.	*spirituality:* That which promotes the welfare of planet earth and all life as well as the interests of humanity.	*spirituality:* Spirituality is the way that we connect to other humans and the world in which we live. It also deals with our connection to nature and other life on the planet. I've always had the feeling that spirituality is certain, universal, necessary and timeless.
	religion: That person is religious who affirms that some Deity exists and has some moral imperative for humanity.	*religion:* Religion involves some commitment to metaphysical notions such as an afterlife or the existence of a personal divinity and is frequently organized within the context of an institutional hierarchy.	*religion:* Religion is a set of metaphysical assumptions used to make sense of the world. unfortunately it also keeps existing power structures in place and hierarchies which are often unjust. At its best it represents the best collective knowledge that a culture h[as to offer?]
Self-Assessment	more spiritual than religious	more spiritual than religious	more religious than spiritual

	Wave 1	Wave 2	Wave 3
Answer to Question 20 (Religious, Spiritual, Or Faithful Person)	I would say I'm probably spiritual. I would stand very committed to other people, I think it's wonderful that religions exist and that they help people get through life, people adjust to the loss and also how to organize their lives. I'm probably you know personally totally aware, I can tend to tell what other people are thinking, I can take other people's perspectives and I think it is that compassion that kind of steers my life.	Faithful sounds good. That's kind of a "stand up and deliver" type person. Uh, I mean, if there are extra human intelligences out there, I would think that I'm acting to the best of my knowledge with those, I mean, I have not had an experience of what that would be like. I mean those who have had them seemed to have enjoyed them, although they are inexpressible, um, you know, and I'm favorably disposed to them, to those people to the extent that they can inform my worldview.	I am a faithful person if by faithful, you mean honestly inquiring, and honestly trying to build relationships, and honestly trying to help other people. If by religious, you mean participating in church services, I do that. [...] But do I necessarily subscribe to everything that a particular denomination, or religion thinks I should, well, no, I'm not religious in that way. Spiritual, I mean people often talk about feeling connected, or feeling their soul drift up from their body, or having out of death experiences, I'd say that's never happened to me. Uh, I wouldn't be upset if it did, but it just hasn't happened. To each of those things, you could say, you know, yes and no.

Wave 1

George identifies himself as being more spiritual than religious at Wave 1. He describes spirituality in terms of a recognition of the "intrinsic morality of the broader human experience" as well as action that "helps other humans." It is not clear what he means here by "intrinsic morality" and he does not elaborate in his interview on this notion. George distinguishes "spiritual" from "religious" by noting that religion has to do with a Deity and that Deity's moral commands. He admires religions for how they can give meaning and organization to peoples' lives. George opts to describe himself in the interview as spiritual, and he ultimately focuses on compassion as the driving value for his life, which is in accordance with his free entry.

Wave 2

Here, George maintains being more spiritual than religious. He again relates spirituality to being about the welfare of others, but additionally now includes the welfare of the earth itself and all living beings. When offering his definition of religion, he again relates it to a belief/commitment to the existence of a deity, but now also includes "an afterlife" as an additional qualifying alternative. Interestingly, he also speaks to how religion often includes an organizational hierarchy component. However, when George is asked in the interview whether he considers himself to be religious, spiritual, or faithful, this time he chooses faithful. Here he focuses on a notion of faithful that relates to "acting to the best" of his knowledge with regards to "extra human intelligences" (plausibly a more technical description of a Deity or supernatural being). George acknowledges that he has not had

Part C: Longitudinal Case Studies—Qualitative Analyses Including Quantitative Data

any experiences of encounters with such beings but notes that he is open to such experiences and welcomes the perspectives of those who do speak of having such experiences and even considers the possibility of broadening his own horizon by their experiences.

Wave 3

At Wave 3, George again expands upon his notion of spirituality. He continues to describe it as being about to how humans relate to each other and the world around them. He also associates it with feelings of connectedness and "out of body experiences" in his interview, again, similar like at Wave 2, emphasizing that he has never had such experiences himself; however, he seems not to exclude the possibility of experiencing them in general. In the free entries, he describes spirituality as being "certain, universal, necessary and timeless." He does not elaborate on this point here, but it is perhaps interesting to note that he uses nearly identical phrasing in his interview when describing how conflicts between worldviews or religions should be resolved:

> So, science- you know, I know sociologists don't like to hear this, but, you know, there is no science of history, there is no science of sociology, or there is no real science of psychology apart from- how we identify problems that are there, and propose solutions, and then weed out solutions, and we will never arrive at a single correct answer that will stand for all time that would be **certain, unconditional, necessary, and timeless**, we'll arrive at answers that are conditional, uncertain, and to some extent, particular, but that's all that humans can do. (George, FDI, time 3) (emphasis by authors)

This is a curious way to frame things as it may suggest that George does not think that humans are capable of spirituality (e.g., we can only arrive at answers that are "conditional, uncertain, or particular"). It may well be that George sees spirituality as filling the place of science in this case, as spirituality seeks to be certain, universal, necessary, and timeless. But how this works in practice is left unexplained.

At Wave 3, George again positively identifies as faithful—though he caveats this with the assumption that being faithful means something akin to being a genuinely honest person in life's endeavors. He also identifies as spiritual and religious, though in these cases as well he acknowledges that there are multiple ways of understanding these terms—only some of which apply to him. With respect to religion, he retains elaborated elements from previous waves (e.g., "metaphysical assumptions," "power structures" and "hierarchies which are often unjust"). But he also adds an additional piece at Wave 3, which is that he also sees the potential for religion to be a kind of repository for humanity's collective wisdom.

Summed up, it seems that George may well be experiencing an increasing appreciation for conceptual depth and multiple perspectives at Wave 3. This shift may also be reflected in the consistent increase of George's scores in the Religious Schema Scale's *truths of texts and teachings (ttt)* subscale amongst the three waves as well as his shift from a *predominantly individuative-reflective* religious type at Waves 1 and 2 to an *emerging dialogical-xenosophic type* at Wave 3.

One of George's major inspirations for his approach to religious commitment and intellectual inquiry was the minister who performed the marriage ceremony for him and his wife.

Table 12.7: George's Narrative: "Learning from a Minister with a Dark Past"

Orientation	The gentleman who married us was a minister originally from [a country in Northeastern Europe].
Complication	During the wars, he served- I mean I asked him once why he did this, but he served in the, uh, Nazi army in [that country]. And I said, well, why did you do that?
Evaluation	And he says, "Well, if it wasn't an option to pick America, you either had- you were either going to fight for Stalin, or you'd fight for Hitler," and he thought Hitler was a short-term phenomenon, whereas Stalin was more dangerous.
Resolution	So, uh, he had kind of a complicated history, because basically he hid out, and as he said- put his uniform up for a while in [country in Central Europe], and eventually enrolled in theology school in [a Central European city], and got his degree, and became a clergyman in America.
Coda	But, I had a- it was really a model for religious commitment, and intellectual inquiry with respect to religion. (George, FDI, time 3)

George does not elaborate on how this minister's background served him as a model for religious commitment and intellectual inquiry. It may be that this minister serves as an example of someone who can come out of a very morally questionable situation (something that maybe resonates with experiences of the German part of George's family?) and still choose to pursue a virtuous path. This passage also seems to reflect a pattern in George's interviews. When he is asked about people and past events in his life, he occasionally presents narratives like the above. But when he is asked about abstract ideas like spirituality or morality, he tends to avoid narratives and shifts towards more strictly philosophical approaches. Part of this may be accounted for by his admission that he has not had spiritual experiences, and so he has little to draw upon beyond philosophical abstraction. George also works in academia, which can encourage a tendency towards detached analysis. Or it may simply be an artifact of George's personality or disposition. It may also constitute a perceived unspoken expectation from George's interviewers (or from the questions themselves) that he responds in this manner.

However, George in some ways engages not only with theories, but also in groups, and, given that he identifies as a Lutheran and attends services, there may be something in these groups for George that keep him there, despite he himself obviously being rather skeptical about organized religion as well as spiritual experiences.

Part C: Longitudinal Case Studies—Qualitative Analyses Including Quantitative Data

What Does Community Mean for George?

To investigate this question, we reviewed George's responses to the interview question which asked "What groups, institutions, or causes do you identify with?" At time 1, George provided the following response:

> I would say philosophy and some theology books because they talk about what a moral life could be and what the goals of a good life are and how to go through life and cope with the suffering that is kind of inherent in existence. [...] I guess another thing to mention is [...] we had to make a decision to terminate that pregnancy late so the other thing that I do is to testify, the uh, senate state legislatures, the need for late term abortion, and so Planned Parent[hood] is something that I identify with. You tend to list in church um there are many nice people there. Uh, I'm a freemason, and it's kind of an interesting organization dedicated to doing the right thing. (George, FDI, time 1)

George's response draws not only from the groups, institutions, and causes with which he identifies, but initially also focuses on the literature from which he draws moral inspiration. Even though he is being asked about specific groups or causes, his initial inclination is to address how he investigates the moral ideals that drive his affiliation with these groups or causes. For George, his affiliation with these groups is directly informed by his moral ideals rather than by historical happenstance. On the other hand, there seems to be the need to somehow identify with a group or a cause on a personal level. Drawing on his experience with having to make a decision about a late-term abortion, he justifies his identification with Planned Parenthood, an organization that is engaged in reproductive health care in the US. The other groups he names (church, freemasons) are rather vaguely described as the possibility to meet "nice people" or "doing the right thing." So, beside an intellectual entitlement, there also seems to be a side in George which has a more basic need for community.

At time 2, George includes analysis of some of the challenges involved with being in his church:

> A lot of the older members, who do nothing but watch Fox News are very hard being along with. Some of the lifelong denominational Lutherans are hard to get along with, because they don't- they basically, you know, want the church to be a country club for Swedish people. And it's hard to say you know, well, here's my kid from [Asia] and here's things I want to do in the community, here's things- you know, ways to reach out to the Hispanic community and so forth. They're not- they're only about that. Um, so those are hard. Uh, and similarly people my own age, and younger couples- I mean, you will encounter a diversity of viewpoints, but bring it around to how can you help people, how can, you know, what will be the right thing to do, what are the things that are good about life, I can have a pretty much, a pretty agreeable conversation with everybody and get along with them. Uh, one disaster happened when one of the- we have two ministers in our church and one of them just decided to put me in charge of the worship committee. I found out that that's the place where everybody who has an awful lot of time on their hands comes to complain (laugh-

ing). And I saw some very unbeautiful behaviors on the part of a lot of old people. (George, FDI, time 2)

George takes issue here with the political and moral stance of many of the older members of his church. He would rather they focus on community outreach rather than being a "country club for Swedish people." His reference to older church members who "do nothing but watch Fox News," and who come to "complain" and demonstrate "unbeautiful behaviors" also suggests some degree of frustration with these church members. Overall, this response suggests a shift to a focus on praxis rather than necessarily aligned moral values, although, along with his criticism, we have an implicit positioning of himself in a superior position. George remains a member of his church even though the older members do not align with his desire to focus on community outreach. As for whether George remains a member of the freemasons, he does not mention it at time 2 or time 3. Consequently, we are left curious as to whether he remains affiliated or, if not, why he no longer associates with the freemasons.

At time 3, George does not mention his relationship with his church in response to this question, providing the following response:

I'd say I'm a humanist. To me, that involves trying to be an activist for people who don't have a fair shot at life. Uh, I think some of that deals with promoting women's reproductive health care, and health care for poor people. I don't know if I'm, you know, closing the door after the horse is out of the barn, but, you know, it would have been nice if my sister could have had access to health care when she was without a job, uh, you know, testing for STDs, and giving health care to people who can't afford it is an important thing. I try to train professionals in my department. I teach psychology. I try to model what a gracious, and beneficent professional in the area does. I try to be kind to people, and to encourage them very often. (George, FDI, time 3)

Here George is exclusively focused on praxis and comes back to the topics that he named as important at time 1. His identification as a humanist suggests a pursuit of universalizing principles. He is not so much concerned with specific groups or organizations, but rather orients his response towards the abstract principles (e.g., being gracious, beneficent, kind, encouraging, and supporting of "those who don't have a fair shot at life) that he is trying to exhibit in his daily and professional life. Yet, again, he draws on autobiographical arguments (Habermas & Köber, 2015) when explaining why these causes are important for him: obviously having made the second-hand experience what it is like to be without health care, George, from his privileged position takes this as a starting point to campaign against this injustice.

Overall, George seems to view the groups and institutions with which he associates himself in a pragmatic fashion. Pursuing relationships with others in these groups does not appear to be the primary goal. Rather, George is most concerned with the praxis of his moral values regardless of the context within which he is operating.

George's Moral Perspective and his Approach to Tolerance

At the time of interview 1, George approaches moral issues as involving a combination of values and processes. He advocates for a morality which "promotes the care of human beings while preserving their dignity [...]." When asked whether there are certain moral opinions that he thinks everyone should agree on, he notes that common moral values do not necessarily lead to a uniform application of those values:

> If by moral opinion you mean a general life principle like now valuing human dignity or caring for other people, yeah. I believe many of us would say that we do. There are very few people who advocate hurting other people just for the heck of it. Uh, but if by moral opinion you mean is abortion always wrong, or is divorce always wrong, I don't think that those particular applications have answers that everyone should necessarily agree on. (George, FDI, time 1)

Yet George also acknowledges that people can make mistakes in applying their values in a manner that comes at the cost of others. To address this potential failure, he takes an approach very similar to Rawls' (1971/2009) "Veil of Ignorance" when he notes that:

> If you are all sitting around the table that you all make a decision and at the end, your role would be assigned to you. So, you might be the patient, you might be the doctor, you might be something else, and just so long as you're comfortable saying for all the players involved everyone should be happy with the decision not knowing what role they will have that's what I would say is [the] morally right answer. (George, FDI, time 1)

Here, George is aligning with Rawls' idea that, if we were to design a maximally just society, we should design it without knowing which place in society each person (including ourselves) might occupy. If any given position in society is acceptable to all of us, then our society is just.

When asked "What is sin, to your understanding?" George describes it very straightforwardly as a "failure or unwillingness to understand or do what would help other people." The brevity of his response to this question is uncharacteristic for George, both in this interview and compared to his later interviews. Whether this reflects a lack of interest in the idea of sin is not clear. It might be an attempt to translate the refusal of the idea of "being one's brother's keeper" (or even a spin on "treat your neighbor as yourself") into humanist language, however, without further elaboration, this cannot be said for sure. Taken together, these responses from George at time 1 suggest that he is focused both on the ideal common moral values that undergird society as well as the process by which those values are applied. He recognizes that there will be variation in how these ideas are applied, but that if we adopt something like a Rawlsian approach, we can more closely approach a more ideal application of our shared values.

In his time 2 interview, George again focuses both on common moral values as well as process. When asked whether he thinks that actions can be right or wrong, he responds by noting that "yes, I do believe opinions can be right or wrong." He expands upon this by describing how someone should go about "being a knower," which is that they must be able to "reason across contexts" and disciplines in order to "come to a position that seems to you to be most reasonable in light of the available evidence." He gives as an example a person with a Ph.D. in psychology learning how to perform a regression analysis both within their own field as well as in neuroscience. Given the nature of his example, it is not clear whether George is speaking of opinions about morals or opinions about facts or processes. Is this George's commentary on morality or epistemology here? Or both, if he considers the search for reliable methods a moral project?

His response to whether there are certain moral opinions that he thinks everyone should agree on is as follows:

> Yeah, I'd say the answer is no, because I can always think of an extenuating circumstance. The value and dignity of the other humans that one encounters, I think, everyone should adopt that as a value, and a respect for the life of the planet. I think people should be very concerned about dangers to this little blue dot in the middle of the cosmos. (George, FDI, time 2)

Here, George initially answers that there are no moral opinions everyone should hold, but then he advocates for everyone adopting a respect for the value and dignity of all humans and life on the planet. Whether this is George working through his ideas in the moment, or whether he is trying to maintain elements of both moral relativism and ideal common moral values, is not clear as he does not elaborate further.

When George is asked to describe sin in his second interview, he provides an example using the case of his son (who, like George, grows up being a "stranger" in his environment) experiencing racism to analogize sin as "ignorance, [...] lack of understanding, lack of compassion, and lack of the necessary information." This answer portrays sin as either a moral or epistemic failure and aligns closely with his answer at interview one and can also be seen as a tentative approach to George's understanding of tolerance.

At time 3, when he is again asked whether there are certain moral opinions that everyone should agree upon, George responds thus:

> Well, as a thought experiment, none come to mind. However, it's more of a probabilistic continuum. I mean there are some things that are so far along the continuum of probably right that I am comfortable treating them as right. [...] I think they should agree in- the dignity, and innate worth of humans under a larger roof. (George, FDI, time 3)

This response seems less tentative than his interview 2 response. This orientation towards probabilistic thinking may reflect a shift away from his earlier possible use of moral relativism. In effect, George suggests that some moral positions may be so likely to be correct that he is comfortable acting as though they are. Sadly, George did not expand upon this thought by providing any illustrative examples. On the question of whether actions can be right or wrong, George distinguishes between correct versus incorrect facts and right versus wrong actions:

Actions cannot be deduced from facts, although actions have a great deal to do with facts. Uh, yes, I mean- I think anyone judges actions as right or wrong. Uh, we may wrongly judge them to be wrong or right based on our incomplete knowledge of the motivations and what somebody else is trying to accomplish. (George, FDI, time 3)

This response may constitute an evolution of his interview 2 response, in which it was not clear whether he was speaking of correct facts or correct moral opinions. George seems to see moral judgements as depending upon having a grasp of the relevant facts (e.g., the motivations of involved individuals). If a person does not possess this grasp, their moral judgments may be in error.

A right action, for George:

[...] promotes the dignity of humans, and to some lesser extent animals, and the rest of the world around us. Uh, a wrong action exploits short-term gain in exchange for valuations or the worth of other people, or the worth of other things around us. (George, FDI, time 3)

Here, George has begun to include the dignity of non-human animals in his moral calculus, a seeming enlargement of those he includes in his realm of moral concern. His thoughts about exploitation and the focus on short-term gains are expanded when he is asked about sin:

Well, to my understanding, or what I would consider sin is existing in a fraudulent way in any relationship, adultery, pretending to care about someone when you don't, saying that you love the sinner and hate the sin when you really just hate the sinner, or abusing the world around us for short-term gain, and not realizing the sacredness of the world around us, and of other people. (George, FDI, time 3)

This response is initially suggestive of a shift in George's notion of sin. In a departure from his previous two interviews, which described sin as being either a moral or epistemic failure, George now thinks of sin as a form of fraud or deception. Yet at the end of his response, he also alludes to the epistemic failure of "not realizing the sacredness of the world around us, and of other people." Though he does not explicitly announce this as a separate way of being sinful, its inclusion suggests that his idea of sin likely remains relatively unchanged throughout all three interviews.

Throughout all three interviews, George remains consistent in advocating for a recognition of the value of human dignity and worth, though he does also include dignity for non-human animals in interview 3. He also shows minimal variation in his notion of sin. Where George does appear to show change is in both his clarity and his orientation towards values over explicit processes. He more clearly addresses some of the distinctions he alluded to in his second interview, and he seems less focused on (Rawlsian) ideas of justice or interdisciplinary reasoning.

When asked how religious or worldview conflicts can be resolved in his first interview, George responds with:

> I think first by stepping back and considering the context of those worldviews or religions [...]. I think that once you appreciate that context you have to acknowledge the incomplete and conflicting nature of that information and solutions would involve maybe even re-conceiving the problem across those contexts and acknowledging the multiple [...] through which you can think about a problem and I believe that. We have a way to come together on the basis of a reasonable argument. (George, FDI, time 1)

Here he is suggesting a two-stage approach, in which we should step back from the conflict and try to understand the context within which the other person sees it. He acknowledges that this is a difficult process, replete with "incomplete" or "conflicting" information, and he ultimately settles on "reasonable argument" as how we may "come together." In his second interview he responds as follows:

> Through a critical argument and refutation, and a decision about how resources can be best allocated to alleviate suffering. I don't think it's possible to promote happiness, mainly because what would make me happy is different than what would make you happy, but there is so much suffering in the world, I see one could come closer to agreeing on what the greatest suffering is, and the decision as to what to do in those situations must be done on the basis of rational discussion and not magical thinking. (George, FDI, time 2)

Here George closes the door to what he describes as "magical thinking" in favor of rational discussion. Gone is the explicit focus on understanding the context within which the other is operating, replaced instead with a concern for alleviating suffering. George sees suffering as having a more universal, or perhaps more basic, quality to it than happiness which he seems to see as wholly subjective and varying based on individual differences. In other words, George puts (inter)personal concerns aside in favor of a principle that is oriented by the general welfare of society as a whole, which might even condone constraints for the individual.

In his third interview, George presents us with a more detailed clarification of the process through which conflicts should be resolved:

> When people disagree about issues that don't have a single correct answer as worldviews do, I think that what's going on there is striving of a better understanding, or a different understanding as to what the problem at hand is, and a difference in the relative valuing of parts of that problem, and what the solution should look like. [...] People should realize the limitations, the conditional properties of the various perspectives, but also be willing to consider an alternative argument, maybe even strengthen it beyond what's originally proposed as a way of producing a good dialogue, and maybe even deciding that the problem at hand is not the problem that either side considers. So, it's in fact a different problem that's larger than the current size you're considering. (George, FDI, time 3)

Reflecting his shift towards the *emerging dialogical-xenosophic type*, George advocates here for both an openness to multiple perspectives as well as a kind of intellectual humility which recognizes we may discover that the problems which we think underlie conflicts may be different or larger than we suppose. And he recommends that "strengthening" opposing arguments in order to produce a "good dialog" is how these discoveries can be made.

Across all three interviews, George draws consistently upon both the care/harm and fairness/reciprocity moral foundations (Graham et al., 2011). He is also plausibly drawing upon the purity/sanctity foundations insofar as he advocates for a universal respect for human dignity and a value for all life on earth. Across these interviews, we also see several changes in how George approaches moral questions. George expands the boundaries of his moral concern from humans towards all life on the earth. He shifts away from a Rawlsian-style approach to justice, instead focusing more on moral virtues. He also demonstrates some variation in how he approaches understanding the other, with time 3 reflecting a return to George showing explicit concern for this. Further, he even advocates for strengthening opposing perspectives as a means of resolving conflict. Lastly, George seems to have arrived at a place of greater clarity in his ideas by time 3, perhaps demonstrating that he has engaged in substantial reflection on his moral perspective in the intervening time.

General Interpretation of George's Moral and Spiritual Journey —Triangulating the Data

Overall, our impression of George is of someone who is reflective, analytical, process-oriented, practical, praxis-focused, and increasingly seeking the perspective of the other, which is in consonance with his high score on *xenos*. He is more and more drawing upon a self-ratified *locus of authority*. He demonstrates a close personal connection with his family; but when it comes to groups or institutions, he seems oriented more towards practical outcomes and the collaborative pursuit of his moral commitments. Religion, insofar as it is a set of metaphysical commitments, can be useful to others. But for George, it instead serves the practical purpose of a repository for collected human wisdom. Both of these observations, however, may account for the slight increase of his score on the *truth of texts and teachings* subscale. Rather than being about experiences with the supernatural, spirituality for George seems to reflect his broadening social horizon as it is increasingly about connection to and concern for life as broadly construed as possible. And he sees the primary mechanism for resolving conflict as the intentional seeking and strengthening of opposing perspectives towards the goal of uncovering hidden barriers to progress.

George's scores on the scale for well-being were remarkably low (except for *autonomy*) and we hypothesized that this may have to do with the hardships that he had to endure in his life. Having analyzed his interviews on a content level now, we see a discrepancy here: George is quite elaborate when it comes to theoretical solutions; yet, it may be that on a more practical level, he is not satisfied with what he has actually achieved. He might be an introvert who joins with others when it is about projects or ideas but who is less engaged in sharing emotions. However, as has been pointed out in the analysis above, his overall approach to questions of faith and morality has become more abstract, yet is still at times tied back to the individual, reflecting his assignment to the *emerging dialogical type*.

Conclusion—Comparing Gisela and George

Gisela and George both identify as Protestants in their survey answers, yet the way they "live" that faith is strikingly different: while Gisela's faith constitutes itself on decidedly mystical experiences, George's approach is more rational. Gisela asserts that she is "equally religious and spiritual" which seems in accordance with what she tells in the interviews. George's self-assessment is more puzzling, it changes from being "more spiritual" in Waves 1 and 2 to "more religious" at Wave 3. It seems that being spiritual for George means something different than it does for Gisela. While his take on that term seems to be oriented toward humanism, sustainability and the welfare of others, when Gisela talks about being spiritual, she alludes to a belief in something incomprehensible. Her belief in God and his unconditional love is at the center of her belief system, making it plausible that her scores on *truth of texts and teachings* are high continuously. George does not seem to believe in a Deity, which makes his self-assessment as "more religious" a bit counter-intuitive. Yet it seems that George values the general benefits religions can have, even though he himself sees things from a more distanced perspective and therefore also does not draw on any form of mystical experience, even though he indicates an openness for those in his interviews.

Gisela and George both are active members of their respective parishes and other groups, but while Gisela clearly names the community itself as important and values the opportunity to spend time with people who have a similar mindset, George seems to focus more on possible societal goals that can be achieved through these engagements. This observation may serve as an illustration between the assigned types: The *predominantly conventional type* which can be found in Gisela's first two interviews is more community-oriented on an interpersonal basis; the *predominantly individuative-reflective type*, from which George starts his journey and which is the type assigned to Gisela's third interview, is characterized as more individualized, more reflective. This reflectiveness can be seen in George's general stance as has been described above. It can also be seen in Gisela's last interview when she talks in a more abstract and more critical way about the groups she participates in and in the way she emphasizes her autonomy and integrity. The *emerging dialogical-xenosophic type* shows in George's later interviews when he talks about being enriched by others' opinions; the Style 5 assignments, which are the basis for the *emerging dialogical-xenosophic type* classification, indicate that, while he has a differentiated view on society and how living together should be structured, he can still keep in mind the welfare of a single person.

The case studies have carved out characteristics of two single cases and can serve as good examples for different trajectories of religious development over the years. Yet the extent to which those findings can be generalized is limited. It can be assumed, drawing on findings of gender differences regarding religiosity in Western societies with a Christian tradition (Klein et al., 2017), that the differences between Gisela's and George's approach that were lined out here can at least be partly attributed to their respective gender, or, more precisely, to their gendered upbringing. And while Gisela may be a good representative of a woman having grown up in post-war Germany who has found consolation and meaning in faith and a religious community, the case of George does not appear prototypical enough to draw conclusions regarding a cultural difference between

Germany and the US. However, these cases may serve as a good starting point for further investigation on varieties of Protestantism in both countries. Seeing that there are already meaningful differences comparing two cases, it can be assumed that the analysis of further cases and their individual trajectories will shed light on the question of what happens with beliefs and values in the course of a lifetime while formally staying within the same faith tradition, thereby arriving at a description of religious development within a tradition or community.

References

Costa, P. T., & McCrae, R. R. (1985/1992). Revised NEO Personality Inventory (NEO PI-R) and NEO Five-Factor-Inventory (NEO-FFI). Professional Manual. Psychological Assessment Resources.

Costa, P. T., & McCrae, R. R. (2008). The Revised NEO Personality Inventory (NEO-PI-R). In The SAGE handbook of personality theory and assessment: Volume 2 — Personality measurement and testing (pp. 179–198). Sage. https://doi.org/10.4135/97818 49200479.n9

Graham, J., Nosek, B. A., Haidt, J., Iyer, R., Koleva, S., & Ditto, P. H. (2011). Mapping the moral domain. Journal of Personality and Social Psychology, 101(2), 366–385. https://doi.org/10.1037/a0021847

Habermas, T., & Berger, N. (2011). Retelling everyday emotional events: Condensation, distancing, and closure. Cognition & Emotion, 25(2), 206–219. https://doi.org/10.10 80/02699931003783568

Habermas, T., & Köber, C. (2015). Autobiographical reasoning is constitutive for narrative identity: The role of the life story for personal continuity. In K. C. McLean & M. Syed (Eds.), The Oxford Handbook of identity development. Oxford University Press.

Hood, R. W. (1975). The construction and preliminary validation of a measure of reported mystical experience. Journal for the Scientific Study of Religion, 14(1), 29. https://doi.org/10.2307/1384454

Hood, J. R. W., Ghorbani, N., Watson, P. J., Ghramaleki, A. F., Bing, M. N., Davison, H. K., . . . Williamson, W. P. (2001). Dimensions of the Mysticism Scale: Confirming the three-factor structure in the United States and Iran. Journal for the Scientific Study of Religion, 40(4), 691–705. https://doi.org/10.1111/0021-8294.00085

Keller, B., Coleman, T. J., & Silver, C. F. (2016). Narrative reconstruction and content analysis. Content analysis in the interpretation of "spiritual" biographical trajectories for case studies. In H. Streib & Hood, Jr., Ralph W. (Eds.), Semantics and psychology of spirituality: A cross-cultural analysis (pp. 251–271). Springer. https://doi.org/10.1007/978-3-319-21245-6_16

Keller, B., Streib, H., Silver, C. F., Klein, C., & Hood, R. W. (2016). Design, methods, and sample characteristics of the Bielefeld-based cross-cultural study of "Spirituality." In H. Streib & Hood, Jr., Ralph W. (Ed.), Semantics and psychology of spirituality: A cross-cultural analysis (pp. 39–51). Springer. https://doi.org/10.1007/978-3-319-2124 5-6_4

Klein, C., Keller, B., & Traunmüller, R. (2017). Sind Frauen tatsächlich grundsätzlich religiöser als Männer? Internationale und interreligiöse Befunde auf Basis des Religionsmonitors 2008. In K. Sammet, F. Benthaus-Apel, & C. Gärtner (Eds.), Veröffentlichungen der Sektion Religionssoziologie der Deutschen Gesellschaft für Soziologie. Religion und Geschlechterordnungen (pp. 99–131). Springer VS. https://doi.org/10.1007/978-3-658-17391-3_5

Labov, W., & Waletzky, J. (1967). Narrative analysis: Oral versions of personal experience. Journal of Narrative and Life History, 7(1–4), 3–38. https://doi.org/10.1075/jnlh.7.02nar

McAdams, D. P., Reynolds, J., Lewis, M., Patten, A. H., & Bowman, P. J. (2001). When bad things turn good and good things turn bad: Sequences of redemption and contamination in life narrative and their relation to psychosocial adaptation in midlife adults and in students. Personality and Social Psychology Bulletin, 27(4), 474–485. https://doi.org/10.1177/0146167201274008

Rawls, J. (1971/2009). A theory of justice. Harvard University Press. https://doi.org/10.2307/j.ctvjf9z6v

Ryff, C. D. (1989). Happiness is everything, or is it? Explorations on the meaning of psychological well-being. Journal of Personality and Social Psychology, 57(6), 1069–1081. https://doi.org/10.1037/0022-3514.57.6.1069

Ryff, C. D., & Keyes, C. L. M. (1995). The structure of psychological well-being revisited. Journal of Personality and Social Psychology, 69(4), 719–727. https://doi.org/10.1037/0022-3514.69.4.719

Streib, H. (2018). What is xenosophia? Philosophical contributions to prejudice research. In H. Streib & C. Klein (Eds.), Xenosophia and religion. Biographical and statistical paths for a culture of welcome (pp. 3–21). Springer International Publishing.

Streib, H., Chen, Z. J., & Hood, R. W. (2020). Categorizing people by their preference for religious styles: Four types derived from evaluation of Faith Development Interviews. International Journal for the Psychology of Religion, 30(2), 112–127. https://doi.org/10.1080/10508619.2019.1664213

Streib, H., Hood, R. W., Keller, B., Csöff, R.-M., & Silver, C. F. (2009). Deconversion: Qualitative and quantitative results from cross-cultural research in Germany and the United States of America. Vandenhoeck & Ruprecht. https://doi.org/10.13109/9783666604393

Streib, H., Hood, R. W., & Klein, C. (2010). The Religious Schema Scale: Construction and initial validation of a quantitative measure for religious styles. International Journal for the Psychology of Religion, 20(3), 151–172. https://doi.org/10.1080/10508619.2010.481223

Streib, H., & Keller, B. (2018). Manual for the assessment of religious styles in faith development interviews (Fourth, revised edition of the "Manual for faith development research"). Universität Bielefeld.

Waldenfels, B. (1998). Der Stachel des Fremden. Suhrkamp.

Chapter 13
"It's the certainty that my faith reflects a reality that I can't see at the moment, but this is where I'm going" – The Impact of an Exclusivist Faith in Old Age. Comparison of Berthold and Heidemarie

Anika Steppacher, Ramona Bullik, Barbara Keller, & Daimi Shirck[1]

Abstract *Both Heidemarie and Berthold are elderly people we interviewed in a time when they passed from young old age to old old age, and thus are in their 80s at the time of the third interviews. They have different religious affiliations, Berthold is Catholic and Heidemarie Protestant, but both have stayed with their respective faith communities for all their lives. They take opposite directions in their type development/trajectory, though: Berthold moves down from the predominantly conventional type to the substantially ethnocentric type, while Heidemarie moves up from the substantially ethnocentric type to the predominantly conventional type. A glimpse into their questionnaire responses reveals a rather interesting picture regarding the understanding of their respective beliefs: Whereas Berthold scores, throughout all three waves, the highest on the fundamentalism scale, Heidemarie did not fill out a large part of the questionnaire because she does not trust it to adequately portray her faith. So, it seems reasonable to assume that both take their faith very seriously and give an impression of being very certain, authoritative and traditionalist when it comes to addressing religious questions, although they do this in somewhat different ways. This chapter will therefore aim to reconstruct their biographical reasoning behind this certainty in faith, addressing the questions: What makes them so certain about their beliefs? How does this affect their moral reasoning? Can we observe commonalities and differences?*

Keywords: *faith development; old age; exclusivist faith; fundamentalism*

---

1   A. Steppacher, B. Keller, R. Bullik, Bielefeld University, Germany, E-mail: anika.steppacher@uni-bielefeld.de; D. Shirck, University of Tennessee at Chattanooga, USA. © Heinz Streib, Ralph W. Hood Jr. (eds.): Faith in Development. Mixed-Method Studies on Worldviews and Religious Styles. First published in 2024 by Bielefeld University Press, Bielefeld, https://doi.org/10.14361/97838394 71234-015

Introduction

In contemporary Western societies, old age is widely viewed as a rather undesirable state in favor of a more active young and middle age, which reduces the value of aging and depicts the elderly as primarily vulnerable and passive (Coleman, 2013). They are, however, a very interesting and uneven social group confronted with particular life circumstances: They comprise a great and growing part of the population, especially in modern societies, and vary significantly in milieu affiliation, economic status, and other relevant social classes, which impacts the life experiences of individuals immensely. However, despite this variety older people are faced with similar challenges due to their advanced life stage. Existential questions of loss, death but also legacy and generativity tend to become more relevant and concrete which may lead to a heightened importance of religion for people of old age. This assumption can be corroborated by study results from different countries stating that older people are generally more involved in religious communities and practices (PEW, 2018). Although this strong adherence to faith traditions might also be due to a more rigorous religious socialization of this generation (Shaw, Gullifer, & Wood, 2016), studies also found numerous tangible benefits of a religious life for the elderly in different cultural contexts, such as better physical health (Braam et al., 2008), psychological resilience (Butenaite, 2020; Coleman, 2013), security and community (Shaw, Gullifer, & Wood, 2016) as well as orientation, consolation and meaning when faced with pressing existential questions (Oliveira & Menezes, 2018; Fortuin, Schilderman, & Venbrux, 2019). Thus, the elderly are a diverse group faced with a universal existential challenge which is widely addressed with religious teachings.

Therefore, it would be naïve to assume that people in their late stages of life address these questions in a homogenous way or with the same benefits in mind. Consequently, this chapter is going to explore the religiosity of two cases that exhibit a particular approach to religious texts and communities: Berthold and Heidemarie are two cases from Germany and are mostly in their early and late eighties during the three times of data collection that stretched over 14 years[2]. They value the truth they expect to be communicated by religious texts and authorities as well as their religious communities to a very high degree as they both have been typed as "ethnocentric religious type" at certain times. Thus, we can assume that both cases generally approach religious matters in an exclusivist and rigid way and exhibit a more orthodox and literal understanding of their respective faith traditions. Berthold identifies as a Catholic and Heidemarie mentions in her first survey that she belongs to an evangelical/Pentecostal[3] denomination. Our cases, therefore, belong to different Christian faith tradition to which they converted at a young age and adhered to ever since. However, does staying with the same religion and entering late

---

2   The first interview and questionnaire were conducted in 2004, the second in 2013, and the last one in 2018.

3   Pentecostals are part of the free churches in Germany which are Christian communities that position themselves explicitly in opposition to the established Protestant and Catholic churches, and can thus be interpreted as oppositional religious group in tension with wider society (Streib et al., 2009, p. 26). They put much emphasis on active membership and are comparatively restrictive in their religious practices (Krech et al., 2013).

stage of life mean that there is no more development in a person's faith? We would argue that this is unlikely and agree with Rizzuto's assessment of an image of God that maintains its dynamic until old age and beyond (Rizzuto, 1979, p. 203). Therefore, this chapter compares two cases with not only a similar religious journey and generational background but also a comparably literal and exclusivist approach to religious meaning making and examines its functions when faced with the existential questions that are imposed by old age. How do they maintain this certainty and undoubting trust in their religious convictions? How do they construct their image of God and how does it help them to cope with questions of loss and death? What differences can be observed due to their distinct religious groups and what commonalities prevail?

By addressing these questions, we will offer an insight into the dynamics of meaning making processes in old age that heavily rely on religious dogma and orthodoxy. Although it could be assumed that such a religiosity is rather unchanging and stable, it in fact needs to be continuously negotiated and reconciled with personal experiences, moral assumptions, and religious teachings. Thus, in order to adequately answer these questions, a developmental perspective is required which can be addressed with longitudinal data. Furthermore, in this mixed methods case study, we are going to address these questions with different methodic approaches and material, offering insights into the biography and religious reasoning of our cases from different angles. First, we consult their survey results and discuss some selected psychometric scales, before moving on to the analysis of their Faith Development Interviews (FDIs) which will be first analyzed in terms of structure and then of content.

Changes in Survey Results

First, we turn to the survey results and thus to psychometric scales that assess our participants' attitudes towards other religions and fundamentalist stances, their self-reported well-being as well as personality traits. It should be noted, however, that we will only be able to present Berthold's survey answers as Heidemarie consistently refused to fill out the questionnaire. She justified her refusal with the explanation that these questions wouldn't adequately capture her faith (as she told a member of the research team when she was reminded to fill out the survey). Berthold, on the other hand participated in the questionnaire at all three timepoints and therefore we see in the table below his survey results per time of data collection aside the sample mean and standard deviation (see Table 13.1).

314 Part C: Longitudinal Case Studies—Qualitative Analyses Including Quantitative Data

Table 13.1: Berthold's Survey Results on Selected Scales

	Wave 1		Wave 2		Wave 3	
	Berthold	*M (SD)*	Berthold	*M (SD)*	Berthold	*M (SD)*
Religious Schema Scale						
truth of texts & teachings	4.60	2.53 (1.14)	4.60	2.35 (1.13)	4.00	2.55 (1.12)
fairness, tolerance, ..	4.20	4.38 (0.38)	3.60	4.35 (0.51)	4.60	4.59 (0.40)
Xenosophia	2.80	3.64 (0.82)	2.20	3.58 (0.78)	3.8	3.77 (0.78)
Fundamentalism	4.40	2.60 (0.91)	4.46	2.40 (0.85)	4.44	2.53 (0.85)
Ryff Scale						
environmental mastery	4.43	3.65 (0.75)	4.29	3.67 (0.63)	3.57	3.66 (0.67)
personal growth	4.43	4.31 (0.48)	4.00	4.14 (0.49)	3.57	4.28 (0.52)
positive relations ...	4.00	3.89 (0.67)	3.14	3.91 (0.68)	3.29	3.97 (0.72)
purpose in life	4.29	3.80 (0.68)	4.43	3.78 (0.63)	3.00	3.72 (0.62)
self-acceptance	3.86	3.75 (0.77)	4.14	3.83 (0.69)	3.57	3.87 (0.67)
NEO-FFI						
emotional stability	4.25	3.40 (0.82)	4.25	3.40 (0.74)	3.58	3.41 (0.70)
openness to experience	3.50	3.92 (0.49)	3.33	3.89 (0.50)	3.08	3.96 (0.55)
conscientiousness	4.25	3.69 (0.54)	4.67	3.73 (0.53)	4.55	3.79 (0.54)

Note: These calculations are based on a sample size of $n = 75$.

By examining Berthold's results on the Religious Schema Scale, we learn whether his religiosity can be described as authoritative and exclusivist or oriented towards interreligious dialogue and an openness to learn and be inspired by the other (Streib et al., 2010, p. 155). The sub-scale *truth of texts and teachings* (*ttt*) assesses the exclusivity and totality of one's own faith that is viewed as being the one true religious teaching, and which denies validity to other religions or worldviews in contrast. Berthold's scores are considerably above the sample mean at all times of data collection on this subscale, indicating that he firmly believes in the absolute truth propagated by the religious teachings he follows. His results on the *fairness, tolerance, and rational choice* subscale (*ftr*) on the other hand do not deviate substantially from the sample mean except at Wave 2. This can be interpreted as Berthold being able to weigh different claims against each other to a reasonable degree, which seems less possible for him at Wave 2. However, this sub-score is relatively high for the entire sample and may not capture a differentiated picture. Berthold's results on the *xenosophia* subscale (*xenos*) mirror this trend as he is within the sample mean at Wave 1 and 3, however significantly below at Wave 2. This means that he is able to appreciate the wisdom of other religions to some extent, however, considerably less so at Wave 2. There might be some context gained by consulting Berthold's results on the fundamentalism scales[4]: Comparable to his *ttt*-scores, he is consistently and significantly above the sample mean with regard to the intransigency and totality with which he views the claims to truth of his religion. Thus, we can conclude that while he is able to appreciate viewpoints and claims of different worldviews and religions to a certain extent, Berthold's faith can be primarily characterized as exclusivist, and authoritative while viewing the own religious teachings as in possession of the truth.

With the results of Berthold's answers on selected scales from Ryff's scale of positive adult development or eudaimonic wellbeing, we get further insight into how he interprets his own psychological well-being. In terms of *environmental mastery*, his scores at Wave 1 and 2 are slightly higher than the sample mean, do, however, decrease considerably with each point of data collection. Therefore, it is probable that he finds it increasingly difficult to get a sense of control of his external world. The same trend can be observed regarding *personal growth* which falls substantially below the sample mean at Wave 3, indicating that he feels more and more unable to find challenges and inspirations. A similar pattern emerges in how Berthold views (positive) *relations with others*, a score that decreases below the sample mean at Wave 2 indicating that he is experiencing a lack of close relationships and a sense of isolation. When consulting the results on *purpose in life* we see this trend repeated again: While at Wave 1 and 2 he is still within the sample mean, his scores decrease at Wave 3 and are considerably below the rest of the sample. Berthold thus seems to have lost a sense for direction and purpose and does no longer appear to strive for a meaningful future. Only his *self-acceptance* scores seem comparatively stable over time, indicating that he does preserve a reasonably positive view of himself. With Berthold's results on the Ryff Scale we can conclude that he appears to find himself in an increasingly difficult period of his life characterized by a loss of meaningful goals, a lack of control as well as close relationships.

Finally, we take a closer look at Berthold's personality traits as assessed by the NEO-FFI. On the sub-scale *emotional stability* (neuroticism reversed) we can see that he views himself as capable of dealing with difficult life circumstances with scores that are consistently above the sample mean and deviate at Wave 2 even from standard deviation. His *openness to experiences* decreases however and is, at Wave 2 and 3, substantially below the rest of the sample which means that Berthold does not seem to be interested in new experiences or stimulations. Finally, his considerably higher scores on the sub-scale *conscientiousness* at all times of data collection indicate that Berthold appreciates order, performance, and sense of duty to a very high degree.

Taking Berthold's survey results together it emerges an image of a person with a fundamentalist religious leaning who does not seem to be especially willing to challenge his own views, and who, on the contrary, seems rather isolated and convinced of his worldview. This isolation, lack of control and exchange appears to be increasingly burdensome to him, and we will examine in the remainder of this chapter how these first impressions of Berthold can be further illuminated.

---

4   At wave 1, these correspond to Altemeyer and Hunsberger's Religious Fundamentalism Scale (2004), whereas at wave 2 and 3 the Religious and Worldview Fundamentalism Scale by the Religionsmonitor was used (Pickel, 2013).

Changes in FDI Profiles

After having gained a first impression of the self-reported attitudes and traits of one of the cases discussed in this chapter, we now turn to the structural analysis of Berthold's and Heidemarie's FDIs. By analyzing the interviews according to the *Manual* (Streib & Keller, 2018) we are able to examine patterns that emerge when our interviewees review their lives, evaluate their relationships, and negotiate questions of religion and personal values. The analysis focuses on different aspects such as *Perspective-taking*, *Social Horizon*, *Morality*, *Locus of Authority*, *Form of World Coherence*, and *Symbolic Functioning*[5], enabling the researcher to discuss the multi-faceted nature of the meaning making processes of the interviewees. Thus, in this part of the chapter we discuss the religious styles Heidemarie and Berthold present in their interviews, and how they change over the course of 14 years.

In Heidemarie's first interview she can be characterized as an "substantially ethnocentric type," oscillating quite evenly between an *Instrumental-Reciprocal or Do-Ut-Des Religious Style* (Style two) and a *Mutual Religious Style* (Style three). When she talks about the inner lives of others, she exhibits a Style three perspective emphasizing uncritical interpersonal concordance and the wish for harmonious relationships. Her *Form of World Coherence* follows the same Style three pattern, and thus she seems content with conventional and uncritical interpretations of abstract issues such as meaning in life or concepts of death. Her moral considerations, understanding of symbols or the awareness of her social horizon on the other hand tend toward a Style two reasoning which focusses on instrumental reciprocity. This means that Heidemarie has a rather taken-for-granted understanding of her social environment and does not think abstractly about moral issues or symbols but in terms of concrete consequences and by considering the expectations she anticipates by authority figures.

At Wave 2, Heidemarie's religious style assignments evolve noticeably, making her an "predominantly conventional type" which means that in her interview she was primarily assigned style three ratings. Thus, while her perspective-taking can still be described as oriented towards mutual understanding and meeting the expectations of others as well as interpersonal harmony, and her beliefs are based on implicit and normative understandings of concepts or teachings, the other aspects have changed: Her moral considerations and understanding of symbols have become somewhat more complex, not focusing on concrete consequences for her but on normative expectations or interpretations she strives to uphold. Furthermore, her social environment now seems to be opened to a wider social network and now includes people outside for example the immediate family.

At Wave 3, we see a quite fragmented picture emerging as only 15 out of 25 questions could be assigned a religious style. Heidemarie can still be classified as a "predominantly conventional type," with, however, more deviations toward Style four. In terms of *Perspective-taking* for example, we see that she becomes more systematic and conceptual when thinking about others' perspectives. Similarly, her approach to authorities is characterized by a Style four reasoning which means that they are self-selected and ideologically

---

5   It should be noted here that the structural evaluation of the FDI changed slightly between wave 1 and 2: The aspect *Form of Logic* has been removed, some questions have been assigned to different aspects, and some aspects have been renamed.

legitimated instead of uncritically trusted. However, her dealing with moral issues still seems heavily influenced by normative assumptions and the considerations of her social group.

Our second case, Berthold can at Wave 1 be characterized as a "predominantly conventional type" with only two deviations towards Style four. Thus, at that time he is aware of the inner lives of others, however, not in a systematic or conceptual way but with an emphasis on interpersonal understanding and concordance. His moral reasoning, approach to authorities, and understanding of symbols are similarly not mediated through abstraction or conceptual considerations but are based on normative assumptions and in-group expectations. He exhibits an uncritical approach to complex issues that relies not on explicit or abstract considerations but rather on normative assumptions and expectations. Only in terms of social horizon, Berthold seems to be capable of including people beyond his peer group and on the grounds of ideological compatibility.

At point 2 of data collection Berthold's religious type changes from "predominantly conventional type" to "substantially ethnocentric type," taking thus the opposite trajectory compared to Heidemarie. This means that aside of a still prevalent *Mutual Religious Style* (Style three) there now emerges a considerable *Instrumental-Reciprocal or Do-Ut-Des Religious Style* (Style two). This is visible in his way of perspective-taking: He no longer considers inner thought processes or feelings of others but exhibits a limited understanding of their internal reasonings which leads to an objectifying and even judgmental way of seeing the motivations or inner worlds of others. Similarly dominated by Style two reasoning he now relates to authorities in an absolute and orthodox way, being more concerned with meeting their expectations than evaluating their arguments and claims over him.

Finally, this pattern is repeated at Wave 3 with these two aspects dominated by Style two and the rest of the aspects by Style three reasoning. Thus, at both times of data collection Berthold has only a limited understanding or willingness to engage in the perspective of others and values authority for its own sake and without critical examinations. On the other hand, he still answers moral questions with normative interpretations and assumptions, most likely deriving from his in-group which is also what guides his understanding of symbols.

In sum, although taking opposite trajectories we can assume that Berthold and Heidemarie have a lot in common in terms of how they make sense of the world and the way they think about issues regarding relationships, morality, or religion. In general, both seem to value the interpretations of their in-groups more than conceptual considerations—although Heidemarie seems more capable of abstract reasoning in her later interviews—and they tend, at different times, towards a literal and instrumental understanding of these issues. In the next section, we examine what lies behind this reasoning by illuminating their biographical accounts.

Life Review: Finding Meaning and Healing through God

In this part of the chapter, we turn to the content of Heidemarie's and Berthold's FDIs and examine their life stories. Their respective upbringing and essential turning points

318　Part C: Longitudinal Case Studies—Qualitative Analyses Including Quantitative Data

in their biographies are discussed as well as their images of self and ways of narrating their biographies reconstructed. Thereby, we gain a first insight into the biographical contexts of their religious reasoning as well as an impression of how they portray themselves. Berthold and Heidemarie both grew up in Germany and belong to the same generation born in the 1930s, and we first examine how they present their upbringing and childhood.

Heidemarie: Turn to God to Find Community and Meaning

Heidemarie does not go into a lot of detail when talking about her past, but at time 2, we learn that she grew up on a farm with parents she talks very affectionately about. She portrays them in all three interviews as commendable and devoted parents, even as role models and describes her relationship with them as "shaped by gratitude[6]" (Heidemarie, FDI, time 1). At Wave 2, this attitude toward her parents becomes visible in the following quote:

> No, the image I had of my parents changed completely. So, I learnt, the same way I got to know myself in my relationship to God, I learnt to respect them, [...] how was the relationship? Well, my relationship was just shaped by gratitude. My parents they ... [...] I'm from a farm and my parents worked for us three kids. They kept this farm running.[7] (Heidemarie, FDI, time 2)

Apparently, Heidemarie's relationship to her parents has also been influenced by her religious journey, and although she does not talk about how she felt about her parents before this transformation, we see a religious commandment integrated here: Honor your parents. This interpretation can furthermore be strengthened by the fact that she uses the same expression "shaped by gratitude" in both interviews, giving the impression of a sacred commandment, or more precisely the following of the fourth commandment "Honor thy Father and thy Mother". Thus, while we could suspect that she idealizes the relationship to her parents and possibly omits more difficult aspects of her upbringing, she gives numerous accounts of the support and understanding she receives from them, e.g., as she explains at time 3 having the opportunity to openly talk to them and having "a base on which we could come together[8]" (Heidemarie, FDI, time 3). Heidemarie's attachment style, that she developed in childhood toward her parents, can therefore be characterized as secure attachment as they seem to have offered her comfort and security in these young years while supporting her to explore options. As a result, it is likely that she was able to establish a stable sense of self and a secure and reciprocal way of relating to others in her adult life (Bartholomew & Horowitz, 1991). This can be further

---

6　von Dankbarkeit geprägt.

7　Nein, mein Bild hat sich völlig verändert von den Eltern. Also ich habe gelernt, so wie ich mich kennengelernt habe in meiner Beziehung zu Gott, da habe ich gelernt, sie zu achten, [...] wie war die Beziehung? Also meine Beziehung, die war einfach von Dankbarkeit geprägt. Meine Eltern, die haben uns ... [...] ich stamme von einem Bauernhof und meine Eltern, die haben für uns drei Kinder gearbeitet. Sie haben diesen Hof gehalten.

8　eine Basis, auf der man sich begegnet.

corroborated by the recollections of her early life, when Heidemarie exhibits an image of her younger self as autonomous and independent. In her second interview she also emphasizes how extraordinary this was for a girl at that time, stating: "I got a job training and went as a _girl_ (laughs) to the city, so young and (laughs) nobody _understood_ that at the time[9]" (FDI, Heidemarie, time 2). Heidemarie apparently attributes becoming that way to the fact that she was well protected and supported by her parents, as exemplified by the following quote from her second interview:

> [...] they didn't say: „No, you have to stay here, you have to help your mother on the farm" – no, no. They recognized even then somehow that I wanted to (laughs) make my mark in some way, (laughs) one way or the other. Well, I remember these times as more chaotic (laughs) but I just felt loved and sheltered with my parents. And somehow understood. [...] So, this hasn't changed until today.[10] (FDI, Heidemarie, time 2)

This view of herself as self-determined is also reflected in her more current accounts. She emphasizes in all interviews her role as a professional which also entailed making a significant career change in the midst of her professional life, from the care to the scientific field. She goes into considerable detail when talking about her work as a technical research assistant in the medical field and does apparently not only take a lot of pride in her professional role but also states at time 1 that she

> "had identified [...] with my profession"[11] (Heidemarie, FDI, time 1).

However, although Heidemarie mentions these biographical details in her interviews, accounts regarding her relationships and upbringing remain rather vague, and the focus of her life story centers instead around one pivotal turning point: Finding faith and living a life with God. This can be exhibited in the way she explicitly divides her life chapters into a life "without and with God" (Heidemarie, FDI, time 1), or as she put it at time 2:

> Yes, I would like to divide my life into two basic chapters which are a time when I did not believe in God and did not have trust in God and the time after.[12] (Heidemarie, FDI, time 2)

In her twenties, Heidemarie came to her current beliefs when she worked as a childcare worker and began rediscovering elements of her Christian upbringing. She was not re-

---

9   ich habe eine Ausbildung bekommen und ging als Mädchen (lachend) in die Stadt, so früh schon und (lachend) kein Mensch verstand das dann.

10   sie haben nicht gesagt: „Nein, du musst hier bleiben, musst mit der Mutter helfen auf dem Bauernhof – nein, nein. Sie haben da schon irgendwie erkannt, dass ich da mich irgendwo (schmunzelnd) profilieren wollte, (lachend) in welcher Richtung auch immer. Also ich habe diese Zeiten mehr als chaotisch in (lachend) Erinnerung aber doch ich fühlte mich einfach geliebt und geborgen bei den Eltern. Und irgendwie verstanden. [...] Also und das hat sich bis heute nicht geändert.

11   [...] hab mich [....] mit meinem Beruf identifiziert.

12   Ja, ich möchte mein Leben in zwei grundlegende Abschnitte einteilen und zwar in die Zeit, als ich nicht Gott glaubte und kein Gottvertrauen hatte und die Zeit danach.

Part C: Longitudinal Case Studies—Qualitative Analyses Including Quantitative Data

ligiously socialized but grew up as a member of the Protestant church. In this period of her life, she went through a crisis of meaning and was open and looking for answers in religion that until then did not play a major role in her life or worldview. This turn to religion intensified when she met a couple who she worked for and found, especially with the husband, a common interest in questions of faith and the quest for meaning. In him she found an interesting partner, with whom she read the Bible and invited other young people to join them and discuss matters of faith, meaning in life, and religious teachings. This encounter helped her finding answers for the existential questions she had at the time, and which prevailed until today. It laid the groundwork for her current faith which centers around the realization that God is not imaginary but a real presence in her life she "could count on," communicate with and expect support from. Accordingly, when Heidemarie talks about the process of becoming a believer, she frames this change in her life as a *redemption story*, and thus as a story evolving from bad to good (McAdams et al., 2001): From a life devoid of meaning and direction she is now living with the certainty of following God's plan for her, as she explains at time 1 and 2:

> It really was, well, a realization or an acknowledgement of the lack of meaning in my life. [...] That there was no motivation, no satisfaction in [...] that there were no friends for example. Or there could be no relationships to other people. [...] A paralysis for example. [...] Even if I didn't think about this at that time or I didn't realize it that I was, um, in a depression, I realized later [...] this was what faith actually is, yes.[13] (Heidemarie, FDI, time 1)

> That I just realized that I didn't live according to his plan, not at all. I wasn't interested in that. And yes, and this had consequences for me. Well, I had a life until then that was rather joyless.[14] (Heidemarie, FDI, time 2)

This story mirrors the evangelical conversion narrative which requests the believer to take an active decision for God and Jesus which is often framed as a conscious breach with one's former life and a willingness to fully submit to God's plan. Thereby, adherents evolve from sinners to redeemed believers who can follow God's guidance which assures them a happy and fulfilled life (Hoberg, 2017).

Although her religious journey still is essential in her autobiographical accounts at Wave 3, she then talks in a much more abstract way about how she found her faith and what it means to her. She seems to have changed the way she constructs her life review: from a unique turning point to a development process. For example, she does not divide the chapters of her life in the same way but recalls worldly experiences that are, however,

---

13   Es war durchaus ja, eine Erkenntnis oder ein Feststellen der Sinnlosigkeit in meinem Leben. [...] Dass man ähm keine Motivation, keine Zufriedenheit in [...] dass keine Freunde da waren, zum Beispiel. Oder keine Beziehung zu anderen Menschen sein konnte. [...] Eine Lähmung, zum Beispiel. [...] Wenn ich auch damals nicht darüber nachgedacht habe oder mir nicht darüber klar war, dass es äh depressiv war, das hab ich nachher eben mir gedacht [...] was eigentlich Glauben ist, ne.

14   Dass ich eben gemerkt habe, ich habe nicht nach seinem Plan gelebt, gar nicht. Ich habe mich das nicht interessiert. Und ja, und das hatte aber auch Folgen für mich. Also ich habe das war eben in meinem Leben bis dahin, was sehr ziemlich freudlos war.

not explicitly remembered but presented as abstract lessons learnt, and which outline a vague developmental process centering around a deepening of her faith. However, these elaborations are presented in such a fuzzy way that they are not easy to follow which can be exemplified by how she, at Wave 3, talks about finding her current faith:

> Well, my worldview changed insofar, changed completely [...]. So that I could see, well this one, this is all still very even but when you work on it then you see, then there has been a force at work that caused something to change. And it was this way for me that I actually can pinpoint it to an event when this realization came to me that, I'd say, an effect could happen. So, now we talk about the active spirit, namely God when I talk about that, yes. And this was an interesting turn in my life which I embraced.[15] (Heidemarie, FDI, time 3)

The meaning of her turn to God—which she now sometimes refers to as 'Spirit'—is still apparent; however, she now seems to concentrate more on the inner process than on the actual experiences. Generally, Heidemarie presents her faith at time 3 more as knowledge of an absolute truth than as quest for meaning and communal support which will be further explored below.

After having gained a deeper insight into Heidemarie's biography, we now briefly turn to the way in which she constructs her life story. Generally, Heidemarie's way of narrating is striking as her answers are rather unstructured and convoluted, and she seemingly has difficulty generating a coherent narrative. This differs slightly from interview to interview, as at Wave 2, Heidemarie gives much more detailed information about her faith and how it is connected to her biography whereas her first interview lacks these elaborations, and she contents herself with a strong emphasis on her absolute faith without explanation. In the third interview, it becomes particularly difficult to follow her elaborations: It seems as if she wants to present something very abstract, for which she apparently cannot find the right words. One might hypothesize that she puts her thoughts and convictions in such an abstract way because she wants to give her faith more weight or academic credibility instead of talking about her personal experience that may not seem generalizable. Whatever the case may be, what we learn about Heidemarie in all three interviews is how unambiguously she positions and identifies herself with her faith and thus, the dominant information about her as a person is that she is an uncompromising believer.

---

15   Also das Weltbild hat sich insofern verändert, so verändert wie umgegraben [...]. Dass ich also sehen konnte, also diese eine, das ist alles ganz gleichmäßig noch, aber wenn das bearbeitet wird, dann sieht man da, dann ist da eine Kraft am Werk gewesen, die hat da was bewirkt, was anders geworden ist. Und so war das auch bei mir, dass ich da ein Ereignis auch festmachen kann durchaus, wo ich auf den Gedanken gekommen bin, dass ein, ich sage mal, dass da eine Wirkung passieren konnte. Also jetzt [...] geht es mir um den wirksamen Geist, nämlich Gott, wenn ich da bin, ne. Und das war dann schon eine interessante Wendung in meinem Leben, auf die ich mich eingelassen habe.

Berthold: Turn to God as Rescue from a Difficult Childhood

For Berthold, on the other hand, talking about his upbringing and childhood in Germany during the Second World War makes up a significant part of his narrative especially in his first and second interview. His accounts differ significantly from Heidemarie as he describes growing up during active war time in an extremely instable and dangerous situation. With his father gone to war, he was evacuated together with his siblings and mother from the region of his childhood as it was under attack by the allied forces:

> Yes, so logically I am a human child damaged by the war (laughs). Because I had – changes – many schools, well different and always went to the easiest. I began in [region in Eastern Europe formally occupied by the Nazis], well, to be exact I began in [city in Western Germany] but I was only there for six or ten months or something like that at this school. Then [...] I was sent to my aunt. By that time the war was of course well underway and [...] it had to be around that time because we were already bombed or something. [...] I think, this had a lot to do with the evacuation of children in Germany during World War II because we were four kids and we were – father was at war of course and they maybe preferred that we survived. (laughs) And they sent us away numerous times. The first time was in [region in Eastern Europe formally occupied by the Nazis] this must have been a private effort to my aunt and when the war with Russia started it was high time that we (siffles) went as soon as possible – and we caught the last train my brother and I, [...] so we went with the last train and were already warned that we could be fired at. We had to lie down and between the seats and yes (laughs). Luckily nothing bad happened or at least not to my knowledge.[16] (Berthold, FDI, time 2)

While his accounts in the first interview are concise and reported in a more neutral tone, the laughing and sarcastic remarks in the quote provided above are in harsh contrast to the terrifying situations his childhood self must have experienced. Remarkably, he talks about this period in his life only very briefly and almost casually in his interview at Wave 3. However, in his first two interviews it becomes apparent that being forced to relocate

---

16 Ja, bin logischerweise ein kriegsgeschädigtes (lacht) Menschenkind. Weil ich habe- Wechsel- viel Schulen also verschiedene und immer nur die einfachsten gehabt habe. Ich fing in [Region in Osteuropa, die von den Nazis besetzt war] an, also das heißt genau gesagt fing in [Stadt in Westdeutschland] an, aber da war ich auch nur ein halbes, dreiviertel Jahr oder irgend so etwas Ähnliches auf der Schule. Dann [...] wurde ich zu meiner Tante geschickt. Da war der Krieg natürlich schon angefangen und [...] irgendwann um den Dreh rum gewesen sein, weil wir eben schon hier bombardiert wurden auch schon oder was. [...] Das war es hatte viel auch mit der Kinderlandverschickung, glaube ich, zu tun, weil wir waren vier Kinder und wir waren dann- Vater war im Krieg natürlich und da wollten sie wohl, dass wir vielleicht besser übrig bleiben. (lacht) Und wir sind dann also mehrfach verschickt worden. Das erste, [Region in Osteuropa, die von den Nazis besetzt war], das muss wohl noch privat gewesen sein zu meiner Tante dahin und als dann der Krieg mit Russland anfing, da wurde es natürlich höchste Zeit, dass wir (pfeift) so schnell wie möglich- und wir sind noch mit dem letzten Zug, der durch den Korridor gefahren ist, mein Bruder und ich, [...] wir sind also mit dem letzten Zug und wurden da schon gewarnt, wir könnten beschossen werden. Mussten uns da hinlegen und so, eben die zwischen die Sitze und so. (lacht) Ist aber zum Glück wohl nichts passiert, also zumindest nicht, dass ich es mitgekriegt hätte.

numerous times during war time seemed to have destabilized is childhood even further. He describes this experience as burdensome and suggests by describing the schools he attended as "easiest" that his education might have suffered because of these instable conditions. This situation becomes even more difficult for Berthold as he was separated from his family several times. When he was reunited with his mother and siblings shortly after the war ended, his mother became seriously ill and had to spend an extended period in the hospital while his father was still absent. During this time, he and his siblings moved to an orphanage run by a Catholic convent for two years, which seems to have been a less tumultuous time for him. Although moving to the convent and attending classes in Catholicism was a practical choice made by his mother in the beginning, so he and his siblings could be cared for and educated while she was in the hospital, this time is presented by Berthold as an essential turning point in his first and second interview. With this rather practically intended introduction to Catholicism initiated by his irreligious mother, he found his faith as a child that prevailed and remained stable all his life. He can point this conversion to a concrete moment during this time in the convent, when he comes across a book about the legends of saints:

> Well, then this actually from that day on developed when I read the first book in the orphanage, it was a story about saints. A book with many life stories and this must have captured me from the beginning (laughs) [And your worldview, did it change?] No, so that remained unchanged in my case. And it rather became more stable.[17] (Berthold, FDI, time 3)

Apparently, Berthold found solace and some much-needed stability in his faith that he could not get from his parents. Besides the physical separation from his caregivers, Berthold describes a childhood devoid of reliable attachment figures, and it seems as if in this vulnerable position he was not adequately sheltered or protected. He talks about the lack of care from his parents and even episodes of neglect and deprivation. The description of his upbringing is dominated by instability, precarity and the lack of his parents who, even when they were around, are characterized as cold and loveless. His father went to war when Berthold was five years old and died a few years after the war ended, and thus, he "didn't have much to do with him[18]" (Berthold, FDI, time 1) as Berthold puts it in all three interviews. However, even in the short time they spent together, his father is portrayed as antagonistic and actively standing between Berthold and his self-selected faith as a Catholic:

> Well, this was not very pleasant because, well, as I said, he was against my religion.[19] (Berthold, FDI, time 1)

---

17   Naja, dann hat sich das eigentlich von Anfang an so entwickelt, als ich das erste Buch, was ich gelesen habe im Kinderheim, ist eine Heiligengeschichte. Ein Buch mit vielen Lebensläufen da und das muss mich irgendwie schon, von Anfang an so, naja, in Besitz genommen haben. (lächelt) [I: Und Ihr Weltbild, hat sich das verändert?] Nee, also das ist mir in der Hinsicht immer unverändert geblieben. Und wurde eher noch gefestigt immer.

18   habe ich nicht viel mit ihm zu tun gehabt.

19   Um, das war noch nicht sehr erfreulich, weil er ja, wie gesagt, gegen meine Religion was hatte.

> Well, regarding my faith it was granted to me from the beginning let's say to be allowed to remain in my Catholic faith. My father was very much against it, he deregistered me. And, when I turned 18, I registered myself again when he had no say in the matter anymore.[20] (Berthold, FDI, time 3)

In his second interview we also learn that Berthold's irreligious father was not only forbidding him to remain in the Catholic church but put him—also for pragmatic reasons—into another American Christian group as he expected care packages from them. However, Berthold remained commited to his faith and defies his father's wishes as soon as he can decide for himself. He characterizes his mother as overwhelmed by the difficult circumstances but also as neglecting and careless.

> My mother was very strict and commanding, you could say. Um, this is of course why I didn't have a very loving relationship maybe. And I just did what got me through this life.[21] (Berthold, FDI, time 1)

> Then, I came back to [city in Western Germany] because my mother didn't like something. After a few months we were here again and then I was sent back to the respective school where I was initially enrolled. But then she already wanted to get rid of us and my sister was just born.[22] (Berthold, FDI, time 2)

It seems as if—in his view—she did not want to care for him and sent him away because she took care of her other children, prompting him to stress his early independence. Berthold's attachment can be typed *dismissive* or *avoidant* as he clearly seeks distance from his parents while understating the impact this lack of security must have meant to him (Bartholomew & Horowitz, 1991). However, at the time of his first interview he is caring for his elderly mother with whom he still has a distanced relationship, but which gains a redemptive turn, as he sees himself appreciated by her. This is exemplified by small episodes in which he makes her laugh which noticeably pleases him. Nonetheless, this pattern of neglect and lack of a reliable caregivers is repeated in his childhood accounts when he recollects staying for a certain time with his aunt. The description of her remains rather shallow, what becomes clear, however, is that she does not fulfill her role as a caregiver either, even in such a substantial way that he experiences hunger. Ultimately,

---

20 Naja, glaubensmäßig ist das von mir von Anfang an, sagen wir mal, vergönnt gewesen, in meinem katholischen Glauben bleiben zu dürfen. Mein Vater hatte schwer was dagegen, hat mich auch abgemeldet. Und als ich dann 18 war, da habe ich mich halt wieder angemeldet, als er nichts mehr zu sagen hatte.

21 Mutter war sehr streng und beherrschend, kann man schon sagen. Ähm, insofern hatte ich da natürlich auch nicht unbedingt nen allzu liebevolles Verhältnis vielleicht. Und ich hab eben gemacht, dass ich mich selbst durch's Leben brachte.

22 Dann kam ich wieder hier nach [Stadt in Westdeutschland], weil meiner Mutter da irgendetwas nicht passte. Nach ein paar Monaten waren wir wieder hier und dann kam ich wieder hier auf die zuständige Schule, wo ich eingeschult wurde. Und dann wollten die uns aber schon wieder loswerden und meine Schwester war da gerade geboren.

she, too, sends him away as soon as she meets her husband, which Berthold describes as being viewed as "redundant"[23] (Berthold, FDI, time 1).

> I lived with her then. But rather badly I have to say. This is when I really experienced hunger and hardship. Um, I had to for example, um, look more after getting something to eat. With these meal vouchers that we had back then. So, I had to stand in line more than study. Just to survive. Well, it was hard. Not a pleasant time to be honest.[24] (Berthold, FDI, time 1)

> And then I came to [city in Eastern Germany] and went to gymnasium [academic high schools in Germany] and had the questionable (laughs) pleasure that I had to, instead of learning my Latin vocabulary and things like that, arrange for something to eat. My aunt was always away, had a chemical factory in the meantime and didn't look after me at all at that time [...] so, I stood in line for hours to be able to buy what was still available with meal vouchers (laughs) somewhere, well, [...].[25] (Berthold, FDI, time 2)

Not only the theme of abandonment and neglect is taken up again but also the disadvantage this meant for his education. Berthold creates a narrative of his former self as someone who had to take care of himself and who had to endure abandonment, instability and a generally burdensome upbringing. However, the way he talks about these events changes noticeably. This can be exemplified by the two quotes above: In his first interview he does not omit the fact that he experienced this time as difficult and arduous. He does not laugh or trivializes his experience in any way but explicitly qualifies them as "hard" and "not a good time." In his second interview this portrait changes: It is remarkable that instead of talking about the understandable suffering this time must have caused him, he laughs every time he talks about dangerous scenes like being threatened by bomb fire. This seemingly nonchalant portray emphasizes his past image of self as a very capable person who had to conquer numerous and life-threatening circumstances and leads to the assumption that he is increasingly unwilling to admit weaknesses or moments of suffering.

This also mirrors his current image of self as he focuses at all three interviews on his performance, creativity, autonomy, and particularity which is made apparent by emphasizing his independence from his father in his first interview as exemplified above when

---

23 dann war ich dann sowieso dann über.

24 Hab dann bei ihr gelebt. Aber allerdings recht schlecht, muss ich sagen. Da habe ich wirklich Hunger und Not kennengelernt. Ähm ich hatte zum Beispiel äh mich mehr drum zu kümmern, dass man überhaupt irgendwas essbares kriegte. Auf die Marken, die es damals ja noch gab. Da habe ich also mehr angestanden als gelernt. Eben um überhaupt zu überleben. Na ja, es war hart. Keine schöne Zeit, ehrlich gesagt.

25 Und dann kam ich in [Stadt in Ostdeutschland] aufs Gymnasium und hatte dann schon mal das (lacht) zweifelhafte Vergnügen, dass ich da, statt dann meine Vokabeln im Latein und sowas zu lernen, sehen musste, wo wir was zu essen herkriegten. Meine Tante war ständig unterwegs, hat inzwischen auch noch eine chemische Fabrik da und kümmerte sich also überhaupt nicht um mich [...] also stand ich stundenlang Schlange, um das, was auf Lebensmittelmarken (lacht) noch zu kaufen gab irgendwo naja, [...].

326   Part C: Longitudinal Case Studies—Qualitative Analyses Including Quantitative Data

he decided to not honor his father's decision and reaffiliates with the Catholic church. However, at time 2 and 3 he is even more explicit, answering the question if he could name relationships that influenced or shaped him by stating:

> Well, it's rather that I surely have influenced <u>many people</u> with my different way of thinking. I know that. But I would rather negate, um, that someone influenced me, I have to say honestly.[26] (Berthold, FDI, time 2)

> All in all I just think that I also, when I go back, that it was in fact the case that many people were rather impressed by me than I was impressed by others, yes.[27] (Berthold, FDI, time 3)

Thus, in line with his dismissive attachment style, Berthold seems to be highly reluctant to get too close to other people and strives to establish "a sense of independence and invulnerability" (Bartholomew & Horowitz, 1991). However, it seems that this self-perception is not as independent and self-sufficient as Berthold would like to present it. All throughout his three interviews it is apparent how important it is to him to have his creativity and talent endorsed and approved by authorities which further serves to establish his excellence in numerous fields. This becomes particularly obvious when he talks about his artwork, be it for example a painting that gets special attention by being exhibited in the local townhall in his first interview. In another episode at Wave 2, he talks about a lecturer who offered a course in writing and who was impressed by his religious poems to such an extent that he traveled to Berthold's public readings as an amateur writer years after the course ended. In the same interview he also mentions the encounter with a nun he had the possibility to talk to during a guided visit to a pilgrimage destination, and which serves as example for how he perceives himself as especially interesting and pleasing to religious or academic authorities who he always describes as being "not just anybody:"

> Yes, in any case it <u>happened</u> that while we were discussing that that I said that I write such prayers and then she of course was curious (laughs). I knew many of them by heart of course and could recite some of them to her and she, I might add, was <u>very</u> impressed by them, [...] you have to know that this is not some ordinary nun but a younger [...] nun who is trained to manage the whole Germany-wide operation. So, not just anybody."[28] (Berthold, FDI, time 2)

---

26   Also eher ich habe mit Sicherheit einige beeinflusst durch mein anderes Denken. Das weiß ich. Aber dass mich da irgendjemand mh würde ich eher verneinen, muss ich echt sagen.

27   Im Großen und Ganzen meine ich eben, dass ich schon auch, wenn ich das so rückwärts so ablaufen lasse, dass das schon so war, dass da viele eher von mir beeindruckt waren, als dass ich von anderen, ja.

28   Ja, jedenfalls kam es dann dazu, während wir dann uns darüber unterhalten haben, dass ich dann gesagt habe, dass ich solche Gebete schreibe und da war sie natürlich schon neugierig, (lacht). Ich kannte natürlich auch eine ganze Reihe auswendig, dann konnte ich der dann so einige vorgetragen und die sie ich darf jetzt sagen so beeindruckt haben, [...] man muss jetzt noch dazu wissen, dass das nicht irgendeine Schwester ist, sondern das ist eine jüngere [...] Schwester, die ausgebil-

In this context it can be noticed that Berthold's *narrative identity*—a term which, citing McAdams (2011, p. 100) can be defined as the "internalized and evolving story of the self that provides a person's life with some semblance of unity, purpose, and meaning"—but also his way of talking about others changes noticeably: In his first interview, as already mentioned above, he does not omit the insecurities he had to endure and feelings of powerlessness which caused him a great deal of suffering. His art and creativity are proudly presented, and it becomes clear that this is a way for him to express much of what concerns him. In the first interview, a positive self-description prevails which does not require harsh devaluation of others and allows to admit mistakes which can be exemplified by the following quote:

> It was, let's say, a positive fact that I was very well respected by my [business partners]. They of course gave me a lot of goods, so I could continue. Back then, I made the mistake of not accepting help. I know that today. But I thought, well, you manage that as well with God's help. But then it went, well, [...] for 13 years altogether rather badly.[29] (Berthold, FDI, time 1)

In the consecutive interviews he abandons this humility and wants to establish instead an identity characterized by success and creative power, which in turn makes him become much more defensive, pejorative and unforgiving. His high self-assessment is now achieved by the devaluation of numerous others, like students who cannot spell correctly, or artists whose work he does not appreciate. In his third interview for example, he does not start by giving his biographical accounts following the question for his life chapters but begins with a longwinded answer in which he presents himself in contrast to other creatives, presenting himself as the more gifted artist due to his "natural talent" with which he seemingly also wants to argue for his superiority.

Comparison of Heidemarie and Berthold

In this part of the chapter, we have so far taken a closer look at Berthold's and Heidemarie's life reviews separately and are now turning to a short comparison of our cases. Both can be considered to be part of the same generation, growing up during German fascism as well as the Second World War and post-war era. However, they speak very differently about this time: Berthold remembers the war very vividly and his life review centers around stories characterized by danger, precariousness and deprivation, even a struggle for survival as a child. Heidemarie, on the other hand, reports a sheltered and secure upbringing on the farm without mentioning the war or the regime that provoked it at all. Of course, this may be due to age as Heidemarie is four years younger than

---

det wurde, um den ganzen Betrieb sagen wir mal, den deutschlandweit zu leiten später. Also nicht irgendwer.

29   Es hatte sich, sagen wir mal, positiv gezeigt, dass ich bei meinen [Geschäftspartner] sehr angesehen war. Die haben mir natürlich jede Menge Ware gegeben, damit ich weitermachen konnte. Ich habe damals den Fehler gemacht, dass ich keine Hilfe angenommen habe. Dass weiß ich heute auch. Aber ich dachte, na ja, dass schaffste dann auch noch, mit Gottes Hilfe. Es ging aber dann, na ja, [...] 13 Jahre insgesamt ging recht und schlecht gut.

Berthold, but she must also have been enrolled in school during the Nazi regime and at least experienced the post-war period as a child. It seems their respective experiences, or at least how they recollect them, shed a light on how they present their respective narrative identities: Berthold seems to view himself as someone who overcame incredibly hard circumstances on his own and without any help from those who should have supported him; a self-made man constantly struggling with the injustices he is faced with. Heidemarie also wants to be seen as independent and self-sufficient but sees the origin of this self-image in her sheltered and supportive upbringing that gave her the strength to go out into the world as a young woman and face challenges head-on. Others are not seen as threats but as possible communities for deepening her faith in a like-minded surrounding. Thus, obviously the self-portrayals of both are very dissimilar and also develop differently: Berthold is increasingly defensive, and would like to be understood as successful, and creative, while Heidemarie emphasizes the value of community in the first two interviews and becomes more abstract and theoretical in the last one. Furthermore, it is obvious that for both their respective faith is a central part of their identities to which they both were introduced in times of crisis: Heidemarie had as she states a crisis of meaning as a young adult and Berthold faced existential threat as a child. For both this initiated an enduring and stable religious commitment which they never doubted, but further stabilized and deepened.

Relationships: God as Reliable Support and Divine Inspiration

Although the meaning of relationships for Berthold and Heidemarie has already been mentioned as structuring part of their life reviews, and especially in the context of their primary socialization and relationships to their parents, we now examine how they relate to others further. By doing so, we not only get further insights into their social surroundings as well as their ties to friends and families, but also gain an understanding of their relationship to God.

Heidemarie: Security in an Evangelical Identity

Heidemarie rarely talks about individual people but rather in a more abstract sense about the value of community and interpersonal connections especially regarding the development of her faith. There is, apart from the recollections regarding her parents, one rare exception when she actually presents concrete people, namely when she talks about the man who introduced her to Bible study and the group of like-minded believers she found as a result of this encounter:

> And then I met this family and that was the point when, this man who, as I learnt then, that he was also interested in questions of faith, on the search for meaning, but he was in a way, he researched these questions as a scientist. [...] But he was interested, and we discovered our shared interest in our discussions and then we read the Bible together. He then invited, there were also some other young people and then, we were maybe three or four, we met at his house. And this was a very interesting

community with discussions about biblical texts and the question of their meaning for our lives, what they meant. [...] It just was this encounter with those other people, [...] that had a similar interest, namely the meaning of life and were ready to respect God; to investigate those thoughts, [...]. This was meaningful.[30] (Heidemarie, FDI, time 2)

In her first interview, Heidemarie remains vague about the group of people she is talking about and the impact they had on her. In her second interview, however, she tells this episode in a more experience-oriented way, which might explain her dominant Style three rating at that time. We not only learn about the people involved in this meaningful experience but can also understand what this exchange meant to her and her religious journey. This is also when we learn more about Heidemarie's social surroundings and family life. For example, she explains that she has never been married or had children, mentions her siblings and also that she cared for her sick sister-in-law. In her last interview she does not talk about this episode but gives this rather abstract explanation for the meaning of relationships which illustrates the general tone of her narrations at time 3:

Well, I would say every relationship is very meaningful. And it's (laughs), [...] that satisfies me very deeply. [...] There is no relationship that isn't meaningful. Yes, this is also related to values. [...] Yes, with the knowledge of [...] who you are as a person, this is what I mean, it's related to that.[31] (Heidemarie, FDI, time 3)

As she did in the quote above, Heidemarie emphasizes in all three interviews the importance of relationships and connections to others. However, it is likely that she prefers to establish such a connection with people who share the same faith which can be illustrated by quotes from her second and third interview:

A very smart man said: "Either we return to God, or we are lost," or something like that he said. [...] I'm in good company with that when I say: „Return to God." But I still have the Good News which we didn't receive for no reason that we are encouraged to

---

30   Und da habe ich diese Familie kennengelernt und das war also der Punkt, dass dieser Mann, der, wie sich nachher herausstellte, dass der auch Interesse hatte an Glaubensfragen, auf der Suche war nach dem Sinn, aber er war in dem Sinne, dass er als Wissenschaftler hat er da recherchiert [...]. Aber dass er da ein Interesse hatte und da haben wir in Gesprächen das gemeinsame Interesse herausgefunden und dann haben wir zusammen in der Bibel gelesen. Da hat der eingeladen, da waren noch ein paar andere junge Leute, und dann haben wir also vielleicht zu dritt oder viert uns bei ihm dann getroffen. Und dann gab es eine sehr interessantes Miteinander beim Gespräch über die biblischen Texte und die Frage nach ihrer Bedeutung für unser Leben, was das sagt. [...] Es war eben die Begegnung mit diesen anderen Menschen, [...] die ihr Interesse in die gleiche Richtung gewandt haben, nämlich nach dem Sinn des Lebens und bereit waren, Gott zu respektieren; sich auseinanderzusetzen mit diesem Gedanken, [...]. Das war schon besonders.

31   Also ich würde sagen, jede Beziehung total bedeutsam. Und das ist (lächelt) so, [...] das befriedigt mich zutiefst. [...] Das ist keine Beziehung, die nicht bedeutsam ist. Ja, aber das hängt auch mit dem Wert. [...] Ja, mit der Erkenntnis, [...] wer man ist als Mensch, das meine ich, damit hängt es zusammen.

330   Part C: Longitudinal Case Studies—Qualitative Analyses Including Quantitative Data

encourage each other. And we need each other, this is why there are relationships.[32] (Heidemarie, FDI, time 2)

I know, I realize, [the belief in the Spirit] is also a symbol of recognition for the relationship to other people. It doesn't mean, I still can, well, without disrespecting them or judge them or something. This is not what it means. But it is a sign of recognition which is way more comprehensive as if someone just says something.[33] (Heidemarie, FDI, time 3)

Heidemarie seems compelled to share the gospel and convince others to follow the same path which is one of the pillars of evangelical faith (Geldbach, 2001). Thus, fulfilling the duty of missionary work and deepening her faith by the exchange with like-minded groups seems more important than friendships to individual people. In her third interview she seems less determined to convince others, but in both instances, we can see how closely relationships and her faith are connected. This connection is especially visible when we examine how she copes with difficult choices or decisions in her three interviews:

Um, then I sit down and talk. With God. With Jesus. With God's Spirit and ask him for guidance. And ask him for clarity, so I present my plan to him, what I intend to do and say [...] I have this plan what would be best [...] first I ask if that is according to God's will. And then I decide. [...] I submit this to God, God's Spirit, and him. And I asked for an answer, for example, I have three questions at the moment, or four. And I said, I ask for your wisdom what would be the right thing to do, to say, to act.[34] (Heidemarie, FDI, time 1)

[...] when I didn't feel particularly well, that I searched the closeness to God, [...] this really concerns life with him, with the knowledge that he is there, that he has an interest in me, and this knowledge that he has an interest in me, not only knowledge but also the experience that I realized that he takes the burden of my worries, and of course desperate situations didn't suddenly disappear but this confrontation, well,

---

32   Da hat ein kluger Mann gesagt, hat gesagt: „Entweder wir kehren um zu Gott oder wir sind verloren", oder so etwas hat er gesprochen. [...] ich bin in guter Gesellschaft damit, wenn ich sage: „Kehr um zu Gott." Aber ich habe eben noch die frohe Botschaft, die man nicht umsonst ist das so, dass wir aufgerufen sind, uns gegenseitig zu ermuntern und zu ermutigen. Und wir brauchen uns, dafür sind unsere Beziehungen da.

33   Ich weiß, ich erkenne da, das ist auch ein Erkennungszeichen für die Beziehung zum anderen Menschen. Bedeutet nicht, deswegen kann ich trotzdem, also ihnen zu nahetreten oder ihn beurteilen oder irgendwas. Das hat das nicht zu bedeuten, ne. Aber es ist ein Erkennungszeichen, was viel umfassender ist als wenn jemand etwas sagt nur, ne.

34   Ähm dann setze ich mich hin und rede. Mit Gott. Mit Jesus. Mit Gottes Geist und bitte ihn um Weisung. Und bitte ihn um Klarheit, lege ihm also meinen Plan vor, was ich vorhabe, und sage, [...] ich hab dieses Vorhaben, was wäre das das Beste [...] erst mal frage ich, ob das nach Gottes Willen ist. Ne. Und dann entscheide ich darüber. [...] Das unterstelle ich Gott, Gottes Geist, und ihm. Und bitte dann um Antwort, zum Beispiel, ich hab da drei Fragen, im Moment, oder vier. Und habe gesagt, ich bitte dich um Weisheit, was hier das Richtige zu tun, zu sagen, zu handeln ist.

that I learnt that I'm allowed to confront myself with that. I [...] don't have to be afraid to disappear from his view.[35] (Heidemarie, FDI, time 2)

I pray, so I <u>speak</u> (laughs) to – I contact the Spirit that lives insight me and say: I want – I make use of this relationship, this is what I say, yes, to explain it. It's nothing else, right. I engage in conversation. And I also expect an answer.[36] (Heidemarie, FDI, time 3)

These quotes grant us insight into Heidemarie's image of God. For her, God seems to be a wise and benevolent advisor who is always available and accessible through prayer or a kind of inner process. This also mirrors the evangelical understanding of a personal and intimate relationship to God "who not only cares about your welfare but worries with you about whether to paint the kitchen table" (Luhrmann, 2021, p. XV, cited in Hoberg, 2017, p. 211). At the same time, he is a force inside her and an external entity, as he is something separate from her own self but "residing" inside her. She expects guidance and permission in form of concrete answers to concrete questions, but she also trusts to be cared for by him. Interestingly, not only in the quotes above but throughout her interviews, Heidemarie finds different names for this guiding presence: In her first interview she puts more emphasis on Jesus, in her second on God, and in her last on the Spirit. The function of this internalized force for which she uses different names, that are all part of the Holy Trinity and therefore are all God, remain the same . Therefore, her relationship to God is the one in Heidemarie's narratives that stays the most visible, stable, and central: he is for her "a lifelong companion" (Rizzuto, 1979). Thus, we see both an emotional and cognitive component to Heidemarie's construction of her image of God: The former seems similar to her childhood experience of being cared for and advised by wise caregivers, whereas the latter corresponds to the image presented by the religious group she is influenced by (Braam et al., 2008).

In her second and third interview, we also learn how she views the concrete connection and communication with this invisible force, and how this close relationship is realized through her faith:

And then I also learnt that I'm face-to-face with God – I now refer to spiritual truths (laughs), let's say why? Because it now concerns faith because I don't <u>see</u> God, right? I communicate, I know his spirit influences <u>me</u>. This spirit, that made heaven and earth and has a plan for us humans <u>who</u> has an influence. [...] Well, I've known him

---

35   [...] wenn es mir nicht besonders gut ging, dass ich dann Gottes Nähe gesucht habe, [...] das trifft jetzt wirklich das Leben mit ihm, mit dem Wissen um seine Gegenwart, um sein Interesse an mir, und dieses Wissen um sein Interesse an mir, nicht nur das Wissen, sondern auch die Erfahrung, dass ich dabei gemerkt habe, er nimmt mir die Last der Sorge ab, um aussichtslose Situationen die waren natürlich nicht <u>weg</u> sofort, aber das dieses sich stellen, also gelernt habe ich dabei, dass ich mich stellen darf. Ich [...] brauche keine Befürchtungen zu haben, dass ich aus diesem Blickfeld Gottes hinausgerate.

36   Ich bete, also ich <u>spreche</u>, (lächelt) mit- ich nehme Kontakt mit dem Geist, der in mir lebt und sage: Ich will hier- ich nehme diese Beziehung in Anspruch, sage ich so, ja, um das zu erklären. Es ist nichts anderes, ne. Ich suche das Gespräch. Und das ist ja auch, dass ich- und erwarte eine Antwort.

Part C: Longitudinal Case Studies—Qualitative Analyses Including Quantitative Data

> in such a way that I said: "From now on I want to live my life within this spirit". So, I know to whose spirit I belong to.[37] (Heidemarie, FDI, time 2)

> Well, for me the most important thig is to talk to the Spirit I cannot see as if it were another person, like with a person, like with you. And this is of [...] greatest importance because this is what we live for. If this does not happen, we die. We know that that people cannot live without this relationship.[38] (Heidemarie, FDI, time 3)

Heidemarie compares the relationship to God with the relationship to other people in that she states that she can communicate with God as if he would be a person sitting in front of her, while recognizing that connections to others are a vital human need. This, in turn, gives her the certainty of belonging and a clear distinction for her identity. Her image of God can therefore be characterized as an "active" one who is able to directly impact her life and alleviate her from doubts or worldly difficulties (Butenaite, 2020, p. 38). Heidemarie's relationship to God can hence be seen as an example of how people form attachment relations to invisible entities and entertain an "interactive relationship" to an "exalted attachment figure" (Granqvist, 2016, p. 918).

Berthold: Relationship to God Provides Security and Divine Inspiration

Now turning to Berthold, we can first of all note that he is more explicit when talking about important relationships in his life and clearly expresses the wish for stimulating exchange and a sense of loneliness and lack of meaningful friendships and connections. In his first and last interview he reflects on this sense of deprivation thusly:

> Yes, other people, I actually was always only involved in family life and then I traveled for work as a salesperson later. You just don't have much time to spend with others.[39] (Berthold, FDI, time 1)

> It's strange but I didn't have much longer relationships in this regard. I of course became aware of this. I always wonder why? I obviously can have very good conversations with other people, but when I really had something, it ended a few years later because of death. Well, this is something that, let's say, I miss a little bit. I would like

---

37 Und dann habe ich dabei auch noch gelernt, dass ich Gottes Gegenüber bin- jetzt spreche ich geistliche Wahrheiten (schmunzelnd) aus, sagen wir mal warum? Weil das jetzt um den Glauben geht, denn ich sehe ja Gott, nicht? Ich kommuniziere, ich weiß sein Geist beeinflusst mich. Dieser Geist, der Himmel und Erde gemacht hat und einen Plan mit uns Menschen hat, der beeinflusst. [...] Also dass ich ihn so kennengelernt habe, dass ich gesagt habe: „Ich will in Zukunft mein Leben in diesem Geiste leben. Weiß also, wes Geistes Kind ich bin.

38 Also für mich ist das Wichtige, dass ich also mit dem Geist, den ich nicht sehe, rede, wie mit meinen Nächsten, wie mit einem Menschen, mit Ihnen, ne. Und das ist also von [...] größter Bedeutung, weil davon leben wir. Wenn das nicht passiert, sterben wir. Wir wissen das, dass der Mensch nicht leben kann, ohne dass dieses Miteinander, [...].

39 Ja Menschen, da hab ich eigentlich in erster Linie immer nur Familie dann gekannt und da ja nun viel im Außendienst, als selbständiger Kaufmann später. Da hat man ja nicht viel Zeit, noch sich, sonst mit vielen anderen abzugeben.

to have witty conversations with really competent people, but this rarely happens.[40] (Berthold, FDI, time 3)

Berthold explicitly expresses his wish for companionship and intellectual exchange while wondering why he does not seem capable of establishing such a relationship. Whereas in his first interview he explains the lack of friendships with the familial focus of his life, he hints at a friendship in his last one that he lost due to death. He might be talking here about a very close and important friend he had already lost shortly before the first interview and of whom he talks even 14 years later in an equally fond and admiring way. He was friends with this man for approximately eight years, and Berthold met him when the friend recited poems in public. He portrays him as a very intelligent, energetic and talented person with whom he clearly had a meaningful connection and inspiring exchange about topics that were important to him. Interestingly, his friend was an atheist that later found, through his own considerations, an alternative concept of God. Surprisingly, this is not criticized or belittled by Berthold, but he clearly values his friend's considerations in religious matters and probably attributes some of his newly found ideas to their exchange. The memories of his friend are reported in a noteworthily unchanging way in all three interviews and thus this quote at time 1 illustrates how he talks about him and what details he uses to describe him at all three interviews:

Back then, he was actually godless. And uh, we spent half nights discussing this religious topic with each other. He remarkably stated once that I was the only Catholic he could ever accept. (Laughs) He was a very strong guy. A very dynamic guy. [...] He also wrote, poetry and so forth. Uh, just like me. [...] To what extent I helped him to find God, I can't say. I only know that in the course of the years he came more and more to the conclusion that there must be something else. Uh, he always assumed that everything has two sides. So there had to be for him logically to this world also a beyond. And, he has there [...], he didn't become religious per se. But he has, let's say, found a special way. [...] And despite our discussions, which were quite controversial, but always friendly. So, we never quarreled. Uh, he had his opinion, I had mine, of course.[41] (Berthold, FDI, time 1)

---

40 Ich habe merkwürdigerweise auch fast nie längere Beziehungen gehabt, in der Hinsicht. Das ist mir auch natürlich aufgefallen. Ich frage mich immer noch warum? Ich kann mich offensichtlich sehr gut mit anderen Menschen unterhalten, ne, aber wenn ich dann mal wirklich was hatte, dann ist das nach ein paar Jahren wieder, durch Tod, war es wieder zu Ende. Naja, das ist etwas, was mir, sagen wir mal, schon ein bisschen fehlt. Ich würde gerne mal geistreiche Gespräche mit wirklich kompetenten Menschen führen, aber dazu kommt es selten.

41 Er war seiner Zeit ja, eigentlich gottlos. Und äh, wir haben also da halbe Nächte dann über also dieses religiöse Thema diskutiert miteinander. Bemerkenswert war einmal seine Aussage, dass ich der einzigste Katholik sei, den er jemals akzeptieren konnte. (Lacht) Er war ein sehr starker Typ. Ein sehr dynamischer Typ. [...] Der sprach wirklich mit den Händen. Er schrieb auch, Gedichte und so weiter. Äh, genau wie ich. [...] Inwieweit ich ihm da nun zu seiner Gottfindung verholfen habe, kann ich nicht beurteilen. Ich weiß nur, dass er im Laufe der Jahre immer mehr doch dazu kam, dass es doch noch irgendetwas anderes geben müsste. Äh, er ging immer davon aus, jedes Ding hat zwei Seiten. Also musste es für ihn logischerweise zu dem Diesseits auch ein Jenseits geben. Und, er hat da [...], nicht, dass er direkt dann nun religiös geworden wäre. Aber er hat, sagen wir mal, einen besonderen Weg gefunden. [...] Und trotz unserer Diskussionen, die recht konträr,

Part C: Longitudinal Case Studies—Qualitative Analyses Including Quantitative Data

This is the only relationship Berthold reports on, and the only one which seemed meaningful to him. On the contrary, most people he talks about are either portrayed as adversaries or his feelings for them remain unclear. This is especially visible when he talks about his ex-wife from whom he is in the process of separating in the first interview. Then, it still seems difficult for him to talk about the separation, and he states that although it is not probable, he would prefer saving the marriage. In his second interview, however, his tone becomes harsh and leaves no doubt about who is to blame for the marriage falling apart. He portrays her as an intolerable partner with a mental illness who left him, although he would have taken on the burden of marriage due to his Catholic convictions. He tries to define her mental disorder, does, however, not remember the name of the illness and, although there is no formal diagnosis, he bases the disorder he ascribes to her on his own research. It seems likely that he wants to pathologize his ex-wife who he clearly resents for leaving him after 40 years of marriage, describing her as "illogical," "dependent," and a pathological "liar." His feelings towards her can be exemplified by his answer to the question of times of crisis: "Of course there were times of suffering, yes, 40 years of marriage with a lunatic (laughs)[42]". (Berthold, FDI, time 2) His accounts become more reconciling at time 3. This could be due to the fact that he has a new romantic relationship, and his ex-wife is seriously ill. Thus, he seems to have lost the reason for the resentment somewhat. Little is learned about the new partner as she appears more as an accessory to his stories.

Similar to Heidemarie, Berthold has one stable relationship that never disappoints him: his relationship to God. This seems, however, based on different conditions and dynamics. Berthold is sure to serve the right and only God in such a successful way that he rewards him with special inspirations. Thus, his creative achievements, which he emphasizes more than anything else, are almost divine, given by "the spirit of Mary," or "the Holy Spirit" (Berthold, FDI, time 2). Instead of support or orientation, his relationship to God—which he establishes through the 'right' religious practices—enhances his natural talent and creates the image of a divinely gifted artist. This can be illustrated by these quotes of his three interviews:

> Um, my faith, of course, is worth everything. That's obvious. And that is what guides everything what I think and do. Through this, of course, my many, very meaningful poems have also come to me. They did not come from me. I know that.[43] (Berthold, FDI, time 1)

> [...] which proves quite clearly, you could say, that it can't come from me. Because I just said how I grew up as a child, right. You can imagine that I didn't get the slightest instructions or anything from school that could have led me to these literary, well,

---

aber immer freundschaftlich waren. Wir haben uns also nie gestritten. Äh, er hatte seine Meinung vertreten, ich meine natürlich.

42 Zeiten des Leidens gab es natürlich ja, 40 Jahre Ehe mit so einer Geisteskranken (lacht) auf jeden Fall.

43 Ähm, mein Glaube natürlich alles wert. Das ist ganz klar. Und danach richte ich mich, in allem was ich denke und tue. Dadurch sind natürlich mir auch sicherlich meine vielen, sehr sinnvollen Gedichte auch zugeflogen. Die sind nicht von mir aus sind die nicht gekommen. Das weiß ich auch.

I can say "achievements", because I've indeed written fitting short stories and everything like that, you know?[44] (Berthold, FDI, time 2)

I've painted the Holy Trinity in absolutely unique colors, and I think almost, you could say, that could not be improved. [...] That they are unchangeably connected with each other. So, yes and then the Holy Spirit has told me or shown me, let's say.[45] (Berthold, FDI, time 3)

Following Berthold's elaborations on his relationship with God and also having the situation of his conversion as a child in mind, this development can be described as a *compensation pathway* in which God replaces not only the lacking reassurance by his parents but also the relationships to other people (Granqvist, 2020). It seems as if Berthold replaced his antagonistic father as well as his unavailable mother with God as a secure attachment figure representing a "safe haven," (ibid., p. 919) and support for his personal and artistic development that was otherwise thwarted by circumstances and caregivers.

Comparison of Heidemarie and Berthold

When comparing Heidemarie and Berthold on the basis of how they view and present their relationships there are some meaningful commonalities and differences that can be observed. First, both express their desire for social engagement and exchange. Heidemarie seems to be looking for community and encounter with like-minded people which stabilizes her faith and religious identity. Berthold, on the other hand, is looking for stimulation and intellectual exchange, and seems rather unfulfilled and lonely in this regard. He only once talks with an unambiguous admiration and warmth when remembering the conversations with his late friend. Otherwise, he expresses numerous times disapproval or even contempt towards people with whom he had a relationship, like his ex-wife, or only passingly mentions them without any further elaboration, like in the case of his children and new romantic partner. For both, the only infallible relationship it seems is the one they have with God. For Heidemarie this interpretation is not as clear as she does not give any details about meaningful relationships, and thus one might assume that this too points to a lack that is filled with a benevolent and supporting attachment to God. However, and this might be explained by the different religious traditions they adhere to, the conditions for these relationships differ: Heidemarie merely needs to declare her will to follow God and can than directly be in contact with him. Berthold, on the other hand, achieves divine inspiration and has a less direct relationship with God but one facilitated by Catholic teachings.

---

44   [...] was ganz eindeutig, man kann schon sagen, beweist, dass das nicht aus mir kommen kann. Denn ich sagte ja eben, wie ich aufgewachsen bin als Kind, nicht. Sie können sich ja vorstellen, dass ich da nicht die geringsten Anleitungen oder was aus der Schule gekriegt habe, die mich zu diesen schriftstellerischen nun ja, kann schon sagen „Leistungen", denn ich habe ja auch passende Kurzgeschichten schon geschrieben und alles so, ne?

45   Ich habe die Heilige Dreifaltigkeit in einer absolut einmaligen und ich glaube fast auch sagen zu können, nicht verbesserbaren Farbe gemalt mal. [...] Dass die unveränderlich miteinander verbunden sind. So, ja und dann hat der Heilige Geist jetzt mir gesagt oder da gezeigt, sagen wir mal.

Part C: Longitudinal Case Studies—Qualitative Analyses Including Quantitative Data

Religion and Values: Finding Certainty in Following Religious Teachings

So far, we have learnt what important and redemptive role the turn to religion meant in the lives of Berthold and Heidemarie and how they connect to their image of God. In this last part of the narrative analysis, we now examine their personal values and commitments to gain an understanding of how they navigate moral questions and how their religious beliefs play into these considerations.

Heidemarie: The Word of God as Moral Certainty

In Heidemarie's interviews it becomes obvious that her moral universe is governed by religious convictions and images and that other considerations do not play a role when she thinks about these issues. To exemplify this point, Heidemarie states in her first interview that she believes that religious conflicts cannot be resolved by conciliation, dialogue or any other means of mediation but only by "the Spirit of God and [...] by his intervention,[46]" (Heidemarie, FDI, time 1) and that the meaning of life is to "recognize God[47]" (Heidemarie, FDI, time 1) and to "remind ourselves of God's existence, that we remind ourselves of God's love, and thereby honoring him in the way he deserves[48]" (Heidemarie, FDI, time 2). When Heidemarie discusses moral issues, she does so with an explicit and unambiguous focus on the religious teachings she abides by, or more specifically to the word of God. She expresses in no uncertain terms that one must obey God's commandments in order to act morally which also implies that any worldly considerations do in her view not have the same value or demand the same commitment. This interpretation can be corroborated by the following quote from her second interview answering the question what causes she identifies with:

> First of all, I could imagine that you realized that I want to make God's cause my own. That is central for me. And that I look, that I think about it, about God's plan for us humans; also, what he says in terms of behavior. His yes, suggestions that he makes to us; to consider his commandments and to look at <u>how</u> they can be realized.[49] (Heidemarie, FDI, time 2)

Thus, for Heidemarie religious commandments are not of theoretical or symbolic meaning but inform the way she behaves and judges the behavior of others. To act morally in this understanding means exclusively acting in accordance with the word of God and,

---

46   durch Gottes Geist und [...] durch sein Eingreifen.

47   Gott erkennen.

48   dass wir einander an Gottes Existenz erinnern, dass wir einander an Gottes Liebe erinnern zu uns, und damit Gott die Ehre geben, die ihm gebührt.

49   Also erst einmal könnte ich mir vorstellen, dass Sie gemerkt haben, dass ich mir Gottesanliegen zu meinen machen möchte. Das ist für mich zentral. Und dass ich gucke, dass ich mir Gedanken darüber mache, über Gottes Plan mit uns Menschen; auch, was er zum Verhalten sagt. Seine ja, Vorschläge, die er uns macht; seine Gebote zu bedenken und nachzugucken, wie sie realisiert werden können.

therefore, following the religious commandments without further elaboration or interpretation. This can be exemplified by Heidemarie's admission that she does rely completely on the religious teachings when engaging in moral considerations and even explicitly rejects the idea of reflecting on these questions herself. The quote from her interview at time 3 when she thinks about actions that are right or wrong, also show that this conviction is a very stable one:

> So basically they are right, if they are in accordance with the will of God. Otherwise [...] I abstain – so uh I am convinced that I have no way of judging without the will of God, and without the spirit of God, that is behind it. That is clear, yes [...] On this principle that the will of God is uh the right thing, we should (emphatically) all agree.[50] (Heidemarie, FDI, time 1)

> I do not presume to know it from my own authority or from my own knowledge. [...] I cannot judge it. [...] Yes, when I don't have to ask anything anymore, when I have this expectation, that really my life has a goal, when that is achieved and when I experience that, and then realize, [...] then I will see, [...] I will also recognize that, (smiles) whether that was right or not. [...] Because I can only think like a human being.[51] (Heidemarie, FDI, time 3)

Heidemarie's quotes exhibit, besides her exclusive orientation towards religious teachings when confronted with moral considerations, also a forgiving attitude towards the fallibility of human beings such as herself as well as a pious humility toward these questions she refuses to answer for herself. However, this humble assessment does not translate to Heidemarie's beliefs which she presents with utmost certainty and rigor. This can be further exemplified by a rather baffling scene in her second interview in which she abruptly changes her tone in a surprising way by answering the question if she would like to explain why she rejects the terms spiritual or religious and what it means to her to consider herself faithful instead with "I'm annoyed. This pisses me off [long pause of 30 seconds]. My life has meaning because of it. To the rest I can simply say 'no'"[52] (Heidemarie, FDI, time 2). This unwillingness to even consider or explain different elements of faith than the conviction to obey God is repeated when she shortly after explains, in a calmer tone, that she rejects rituals because they could "develop a claim of their own[53]" (Heidemarie, FDI, time 2), seemingly rivaling the pure obedience to God. Similarly, she rejects

---

50 Also grundsätzlich sind sie richtig, wenn sie nach dem Willen Gottes sind. Sonst [...] enthalte mich – also äh bin der Überzeugung, dass ich kein Urteilsvermögen ohne den Willen Gottes, und ohne den Geist Gottes habe, das steckt dahinter, ne. Dass das klar ist, ja [...] Über diesen Grundsatz, dass der Wille Gottes äh das Richtige ist, sollten wir uns (nachdrücklich) alle einig sein.

51 Ich maße mir nicht an, es aus eigener Machtvollkommenheit oder aus eigenem Wissen zu wissen. [...] Ich kann das nicht beurteilen. [...] Ja, wenn ich nichts mehr fragen muss, wenn ich diese Erwartung, das wirklich mein Leben ein Ziel hat, wenn das erreicht ist und wenn ich das erlebe, und dann erkenne, [...] dann werde ich sehen, [...] werde ich auch das erkennen, (lächelt) ob das richtig war oder nicht, ne. [...] Denn ich kann ja nicht anders denken als Mensch.

52 Ich bin gereizt. Mich kotzt sowas (lacht) [...] (sehr lange Pause, ca. 30 Sek.) Dadurch hat mein Leben einen Sinn. Alles andere hier da kann ich einfach „Nein" sagen.

53 einen Eigenanspruch entwickelt.

338 Part C: Longitudinal Case Studies—Qualitative Analyses Including Quantitative Data

the concept of cosmos, by addressing it saying "Don't you have any claims towards me. Because you don't have any. Because God has claims on me and this is my testament"[54] (Heidemarie, FDI, time 2), or when she rejects the notion of higher powers thusly:

> The thing with the powers, I don't like that. Well, because [...], I don't want to leave it like that [...]. Because I don't want to answer this question. [...] Actually, I'm only bothered by the fact that it's in plural.[55] (Heidemarie, FDI, time 3)

We could furthermore interpret this passage as Heidemarie's firm declaration of loyalty to the one God she believes in as it is required of her as per the first commandment further suggesting a strictness with which she follows religious beliefs. The absoluteness and exclusivity with which Heidemarie constructs her faith as well as the consequences of not following the same path is furthermore most poignantly exhibited when she talks about death:

> God is the Lord over death and my life is buried in God and when we die we are with Him. Unless we don't want it. [...] Then, – it would be a great pity. So we have testimonies about it, also God's word tells us something about it. [...] But I can't give a sermon here about the death of the godless. But I can say one thing: God is not pleased with the death of the godless. This is what his word says.[56] (Heidemarie, FDI, time 2)

One might hypothesize if the strictness she exhibits in her elaborations about the afterlife is connected to her own aging and the dealing with death that become more important in her last two interviews. In her second interview she talks about her fears of aging and not being cared for, the sacrifices it demands like giving up driving but also about her wish to enjoy and cherish the time she has left. In her last interview, however, she becomes much more explicit when talking about death as if it feels much closer to her now:

> So I need to sort out my life. I'm 81 now, I will be this year, and now it's time to put my life in order, because I have to die. Because, I mean, life is designed to be finite. Yes, we had a beginning and it will come to an end. And, to prepare that, there are steps necessary. For one, in the housekeeping. I have to put my estate in order, I have to put the household in order, and that's connected with that. [...] Yes, and then it's also

---

54   Habe du keine Ansprüche an mich. Die hast du nämlich nicht. Denn Gott hat Ansprüche auf mich und das ist mein mein Zeugnis.

55   Dieses mit den Mächten, das gefällt mir nicht. Also, weil [...], das möchte ich auch so nicht stehenlassen [...]. Weil, ich möchte diese Frage nicht beantworten. [...] Eigentlich störe ich mich nur da dran, dass das hier im Plural steht.

56   Gott ist der Herr über den Tod und mein Leben ist verborgen in Gott und wenn wir sterben, sind wir bei ihm. Es sei denn, wir wollen es nicht, ne. [...] Dann, – es wäre sehr schade. Also wir haben darüber Zeugnisse auch Gottes Wort sagt uns da einiges drüber. [...] Aber ich sage es ich kann jetzt hier nicht eine Predigt halten über das Sterben der Gottlosen. Aber eins kann ich sagen: Gott hat keinen Gefallen am Tod der Gottlosen. So spricht sein Wort.

about the agreement to let go of my life. That's also what it's about. So to consent to mortality.[57] (Heidemarie, FDI, time 3)

It seems as if Heidemarie approaches this chapter calmly and with a clear plan that relies on worldly tasks on the one hand, and on her conviction to go somewhere on the other. Thus, we can conclude that Heidemarie's faith is the exclusive basis for her interpreting various facets of her life and provides her with answers when confronted with difficult moral questions as well as comfort when thinking about her own mortality.

To examine how she establishes such certainty that seemingly excludes any doubt or justification further we first turn to how Heidemarie talks generally in all three interviews about herself, her biography, and most importantly her faith. As mentioned above, it is striking how little we learn, especially in her first and last interview, about her and her life. Instead, she firmly states again and again her beliefs, giving the impression that her interviews are testimonies and not explanations to her faith. This is reminiscent of the evangelical practice of testifying to one's conversion brought about by a personal decision that is grounded on the free will granted by God and which must be continuously confirmed (Geldbach, 2001, p. 266; Hoberg, 2017, p. 211). We learn of Heidemarie that she sees herself as a "person who believes in Jesus Christ, in God, the God of the Bible[58]" (Heidemarie, FDI, time 2) and little more. She does not tell what teachings she is referring to, what she has read – not even what parts of the Bible-, or with whom she has spoken. Her faith seems not to be explicitly stabilized by her religious community, which she does not mention, but by her personal and continuous decision for God. Therefore, it is not the ties to other believers or the adherence to dogma or tradition that grounds her faith, but she as a believer herself. This mirrors the teachings in evangelical and free church environments: It is not mere membership that makes you a believer but a continuous and rigorous devotion to your faith in daily life (Hoberg, 2017, p. 214). Part of this seeming freedom from religious authorities is the belief that God is not an external figure, but the "Spirit that resides, that lives"[59] (Heidemarie, FDI, time 3) in her and thus she is and will always be "connected [with God and with Jesus] [...] without end"[60] (Heidemarie, FDI, time 1) and does not need authoritative figures to establish this connection. She explains this in the following quotes from her second and third interviews:

Nobody has seen God, but I mean, when I look at myself and when it's written there, then I also understand what this has to do with the independence which God has given me, that is, has imagined me, that I'm free in my will, in my ways of acting,

---

57   Also mein Leben ist zu ordnen, ne. Ich bin jetzt 81, werde ich dieses Jahr und jetzt ist es dran, mein Leben zu ordnen, weil ich sterben muss. Weil, ich meine, das Leben ist so konzipiert, dass es endlich ist. Ja, wir haben einen Anfang genommen und es wird zu einem Ende kommen. Und da, um das vorzubereiten, sind Schritte nötig. Einmal in der Haushaltsführung, ne. Ich muss meinen Nachlass ordnen, muss den Haushalt ordnen und da hängt das dann zusammen mit. [...] Ja und dann, geht es auch um das Einverständnis, also mein Leben loszulassen. Da geht es auch drum. Also einzuwilligen in die Endlichkeit.

58   ein Mensch, der an Jesus Christus glaubt, an Gott, dem also dem Gott der Bibel.

59   Geist, der in mir lebt, in mir wohnt.

60   mit Gott und mit Jesus verbunden bin und sein werde, ohne Ende.

Part C: Longitudinal Case Studies—Qualitative Analyses Including Quantitative Data

> [...] what this has to do with freedom. With the freedom of will. So that comes to my mind, [...] then that means that God has created me in such a way that I can say "yes" or "no" to what he has imagined. So I can say: "Not with me, " but I can also say: (vehemently) "Yes! With me, this is my identity". And I identify myself, what I just said, with God's mind. I can do that. And that's my freedom that I have. I say "yes" or "no" to that possibility.[61] (Heidemarie, FDI, time 2)

Thus, instead of concentrating on the community she adheres to she focusses on explicit declarations of her faith which she frames as conviction and certainty:

> And that convinces me, it convinces me more and more how God loves us. I say, follow this example and do the same (laughing) things . That's the only way I can say it. Yeah yeah, that's really good.[62] (Heidemarie, FDI, time 2)

The focus with which she presents her faith changes, however, between the interviews: From the focus of how her relationship to God gave meaning and direction to her life in the first and second interview to an insistence of knowing the absolute truth in her last one. Both elements are present in all interviews, however, not equally focused at each time of data collection. For example, in her first interview she shortly explains that in her view scientific knowledge must be inspiration introduced by God thereby implying that God is in possession of the truth and through him there will be "very different perspectives for us to see, to see what He sees because this is His will"[63] (Heidemarie, FDI, time 1). However, she does not go further into detail here, whereas she presents her beliefs explicitly as certainty and deeper knowledge in her last interview:

> It's the certainty that my faith reflects a reality that I can't see at the moment but this is where I'm going.[64] (Heidemarie, FDI, time 3)

> I thought it was an ignorance or a question of knowledge. Because that's where the knowledge already comes into play and yes.[...] So it's a knowledge, knowledge or something that I encountered and with which I couldn't do anything, let's put it like

---

61 Niemand hat Gott gesehen, aber ich meine, wenn ich mich anschaue und wenn das dann da steht, dann verstehe ich aber auch, was das mit der Unabhängigkeit, zu der mich Gott gemacht hat, also sich vorgestellt hat, dass ich frei bin in meinem Willen, in meinen Handlungsweisen, [...] was das mit der Freiheit auf sich hat. Mit der Willensfreiheit. Also das geht mir dabei auf, [...] dann bedeutet das ja, Gott hat mich so geschaffen, dass ich „Ja oder „Nein sagen kann zu dem, was er sich gedacht hat. Das kann ich also ich kann sagen: „Nicht mit mir. Aber ich kann eben auch sagen: (inbrünstig) „Ja! Mit mir, das ist meine Identität. Und ich identifiziere mich, was ich eben sagte, mit Gottes Geist. Das kann ich tun. Und das ist meine Freiheit, die ich habe. Ich sage „Ja" oder „Nein" zu dieser Möglichkeit.

62 Und das überzeugt mich, es ist überzeugt mich immer mehr, wie Gott uns liebt. Sage ich. Nehmen Sie sich ein Beispiel und machen Sie die gleichen (lachend) Sachen. So kann ich das nur sagen. Jaja, das ist wirklich gut.

63 ganz andere Perspektiven hätte er uns eröffnet, zu sehen, zu sehen, was er sieht, weil das sein Wille ist.

64 Dass ich Gewissheit habe, dass dieser Glaube eine Realität, auf eine Realität gerichtet ist, die ich im Moment nicht sehe, aber die da ist und wohin ich gehe.

that. And that is the question about God and this knowledge about him.[65] (Heidemarie, FDI, time 3)

Thus, over the course of her interviews, Heidemarie does not seem to understand her faith as a trust in God that could be objected to doubt, challenge, or change but as a certainty of knowing the truth. Fittingly, a desired development for her in this regard is a deepening and stabilizing of her existing convictions which is what she interprets as growth:

> [...] that is related to life and to growth. So I can grow, I can become stable. That's to say, from the- I can therefore my faith, it can attain a position where it's, yes, I must say, where it's stable, where it's insurmountable, where it's not- yes, that is a criterion of faith.[66] (Heidemarie, FDI, time 3)

Berthold: The Catholic Church as Infallible Moral Guide

In Berthold's case we can get a first insight into his understanding of religion by consulting his subjective definitions of religion as he filled out the questionnaire and answered the question "How would you define religion" at Wave 2 and 3 (the question was not included in the Wave 1 survey). He gives concise descriptions of the term 'religion,' defining it as "firmly believing in the truth that has been revealed to us (RC)[67]" (Berthold, survey, Wave 2), and "I obey God's commandments[68]" (Berthold, survey, Wave 3). Therefore, we can assume that for him faith is narrowly connected to a firm and dogmatic belief in one God as well as an understanding of the Bible as, in his case, communicated by the authority of the Catholic church. At one point in his first interview he affirms this assumption explicitly when stating that for him a mature faith is "living in accordance with the will of the Creator,[69]" which is communicated by the pope who is "a point of orientation for a Catholic[70]" (Bertold, FDI, time 1), or by answering the question in which case an action is always right in his first interview with "as a Catholic, when I act in a way the church wants me to[71]" (Berthold, FDI, time 1). Berthold's moral reasoning can thus be characterized as being oriented towards *authority/respect*: The rules are clearly laid out by authorities legitimated by the respective institutions and must be followed by the adherent who is expected to fulfill his or her duties within this faith tradition (Graham & Haidt, 2010).

---

65 Ich dachte, das ist eine Unwissenheit oder eine Wissensfrage. Da kommt nämlich die Erkenntnis schon ins Spiel und ja. [...] Also es ist eine Erkenntnis, Wissen oder etwas, was mir begegnet ist und womit ich nichts anfangen konnte, sagen wir so. Und das ist nämlich die Frage nach Gott und dieses Wissen über ihn.

66 [...] das hängt mit dem Leben zusammen und mit dem Wachstum. Also ich kann wachsen, ich kann fest werden. Das heißt, von den- ich kann also meinen Glauben, der kann eine Position erlangen, wo er, ja, ich muss sagen, wo er stabil ist, wo er unüberwindlich, also wo er nicht- ja, das ein Kriterium des Glaubens.

67 Fest glauben an die uns geoffenbarten Wahrheiten (r. kath)

68 Ich befolge immer Gottes Gebote

69 Einklang mit dem Willen des Schöpfers zu leben

70 als Orientierungspunkt für nen Katholiken

71 Als Katholik, wenn ich so handle, wie die *Kirche das will

342   Part C: Longitudinal Case Studies—Qualitative Analyses Including Quantitative Data

For Berthold, acting morally involves following the religious rules he abides by in the best way he can and expecting this impeccable behavior to be rewarded which can be further illustrated by Berthold's reflections on death in his second and third interview:

> Yes, let's say, the knowledge, the absolute confidence that for me as a child of God there was also always a guideline and an, what I already hinted at earlier, unconditional, firm confidence that I will have lived my life well, let's say, and well, let's say, (grinning) will be welcome up there.[72] (Berthold, FDI, time 2)

> And I think that I've been rewarded (smiles) quite well, yes. So this life of faith, which I'm allowed to live, I think that's not given to many. Always in the absolute certainty, already [...] since that time I'm absolutely sure that I would have no ambition at all even remotely towards hell. I am absolutely sure.[73] (Berthold, FDI, time 3)

> Yes, I'm going to heaven. (smiles) I wish to see you there again, but (smiles) you'll have to cooperate a bit.[74] (Berthold, FDI, time 3)

Thus, these quotes show that Berthold's moral behavior is grounded entirely on his religious beliefs without any considerations that exceed pure obedience or following the commandments which he believes to be the word of God. He does not explain why these commandments are important to him, or why they foster a better life, or a better society. These rules seem only important because they are clearly communicated by religious authorities and can be rewarded or punished. Therefore, acting morally becomes manageable as it comprises following the rules as narrowly as possible not because of considerations regarding decency or compassion but in order to get the anticipated reward. In one anecdote this becomes obvious when he tells the story of buying something to eat for a homeless person only to be rewarded afterwards with coin he finds on the ground. However, Berthold surprisingly is not as exclusive when it comes to religious practices. For example, in his last interview he talks about watching services on television of a religious group that despises Catholicism and whose teachings he clearly does not appreciate, calling them "idiocy," and finding their teachings for example of vegetarianism unconvincing and incoherent. However, he enjoys the meditation they show on their program accompanied by "music and most importantly by magnificent images" (Berthold, FDI, time 3). He turns down the volume and prays to these images he clearly finds inspiring despite being offered by a group he does not want to belong to. Thus,

---

72   Ja, sagen wir mal so, das Wissen, das absolute Vertrauen darauf, dass es für mich als Geschöpf Gottes auch immer einen Leitfaden gab und eine, was ich vorhin schon mal anklingen ließ, unbedingte, feste Zuversicht, dass ich also mein Leben sagen wir gut gelebt haben werde und na, sagen wir mal, (grinsend) willkommen sein werde da oben.

73   Und ich glaube, das ist mir (lächelt) ganz gut honoriert worden, ja. Also dieses Glaubensleben, was ich leben darf, ich glaube, das ist nicht vielen gegeben. Wirklich immer in der absoluten Sicherheit, schon [...] seit der Zeit bin ich absolut sicher, dass ich überhaupt keine Ambition auch nur im entferntesten Richtung Hölle hätte. Ich bin absolut sicher.

74   Ja, ich komme in den Himmel. (lächelt) Ich wünsche, dass wir uns da wiedersehen, aber (lächelt) da müssen Sie auch ein bisschen mitarbeiten

Berthold is not quite as restrictive and traditionalist with his religious practices as he is with his beliefs, but rather experience oriented.

We can therefore conclude that Berthold's certainty in faith derives from the Catholic church. He puts absolute trust into the Catholic authorities, and, as examined above, his moral ideals are strictly aligned with Catholic dogma and the Vatican's teachings. In contrast to Heidemarie, for him the religious community he belongs to is of utmost importance when considering questions of faith, values or commitments. In his interviews this becomes especially visible when he reflects on moral issues by stating that this is important to "us Catholics," or on meaningful symbols for which he chooses the cross because "it is our symbol as Christians[75]" (Berthold, FDI, time 2). This clear in-group orientation is contrasted with a harshly criticized and strictly separated out-group. When he talks about people with different beliefs or groups that do not behave in the way his religious teachings would demand his tone becomes openly prejudiced and derogatory.

> Which ideas are central for me? Let's say first and foremost, of course, anything that might go against our faith, that's (laughs) rather important to me, yes. I have no understanding whatsoever that we have gays as foreign ministers and adulterers as federal presidents. So that is, to be honest, completely impossible for me to be enthusiastic about it.[76] (Berthold, FDI, time 2)

> [...] and now the Muslim brothers are there. The only bad thing is that they are now dragging our churches into this, too. Of course, I don't like that at all. They should bash eachothers heads in for all I care. The fewer of them there are, the better for the world, (laughs) I would say casually. But they should at least leave our fellow believers out of it.[77] (Berthold, FDI, time 2)

Here, he clearly states that the rules of his religious group are more important than any other moral consideration. There seems to be little room for Christian compassion or forgiveness: not for people with a sexual orientation that would be sanctioned by his church, nor for believers of religions different from his own. It remains unclear in his second quote if it is the religious extremists he condemns or the whole religious group of Muslims. What is emphasized, however, is that he does not care about the suffering this conflict causes for the people of a different faith who are confronted with it, but about

---

75 unser Zeichen halt als Christen

76 Welche Ideen für mich zentral sind? Sagen wir natürlich in erster Linie alles, was eventuell gegen unseren Glauben geht, das ist (lacht) für mich schon wichtig, ja. Ich habe keinerlei Verständnis dafür, dass wir Schwule als Außenminister haben und Ehebrecher als Bundespräsidenten. Also das ist mir, ehrlich gesagt, völlig unmöglich davon begeistert zu sein

77 [...] und jetzt sind da die Moslembrüder da, nicht, ne. Das Schlimme ist nur, dass sie jetzt unsere Kirchen da auch noch mit reinziehen, ne. Das gefällt mir natürlich gar nicht. Die sollen sich von mir aus selber die Köpfe einschlagen, ne. Umso weniger es davon gibt, umso besser für die Welt, (lacht) würde ich mal so (lacht) ganz salopp sa But I also influence, for example, my partner somewhat in that respect[...]. She also still sees that, although she (smiles) was a religion teacher. You have to think about that, but she knows that I am the better Christian. (smiles) She would be 100, but I'm 150-percent. (laughs) And that means somethinggen. Aber die sollten wenigstens unsere Glaubensbrüder dabei aus dem Spiel lassen.

whether or not his own religious group is implicated. Thus, for Berthold answering to moral questions is remarkably easy and characterized by a strong identification with his religious community and *in-group loyalty* (Graham & Haidt, 2010, p. 145). In his view, he can be certain to follow the "right path of faith" (Berthold, FDI, time 3) while others can be clearly identified and their moral actions condemned.

Another important element of Berthold's understanding of religiously legitimated morality is the blending of faith and achievement: He portrays himself as a particularly successful believer who writes the poems in the 'right way,' whose art can express God's will and grace exceptionally well, and who even manages to meditate for a particularly long time. Here we see Berthold's idea of his own grandiosity rather poorly disguised as religious virtues. In his presentation, he is not only a believer but a successful one who can be certain of his reward and favoritism by God. This unfitting juxtaposition of the good Christian whose main virtues can be seen in serving and modesty, becomes visible for example when he explains that he is very good in helping others out of his Catholic conviction, following this declaration with the explanation that he fulfills this religious duty better than others. He presents following religious rules and fulfilling Christian duties as a competition which is especially poignant when he compares himself to his partner in time 3:

> But I also influence, for example, my partner somewhat in that respect[...]. She also sees that, although she (smiles) was a teacher for religion. You've to think about that, but she knows that I am the better Christian. (smiles) She would be 100, but I'm 150-percent. (laughs) And that means something.[78] (Berthold, FDI, time 3)

Comparison of Heidemarie and Berthold

When comparing both cases, their shared certainty in their respective faith as well as a comparable link between morality and religious teachings become apparent. However, although their accounts are very similar in some parts, we can carve out some meaningful differences. Heidemarie's as well as Berthold's moral universe center around what they perceive to be the word of God which for them goes well beyond any human moral considerations. Thus, for both, morality can be characterized as following the teachings they abide by as best and narrowly as possible in order to act morally correct. They both—and Heidemarie more explicitly—even refuse to make any moral considerations on their own, referring, however, to different authorities: Heidemarie only considers God who she views as being inside her and whose will she can detect by studying his word or by reflecting inward which mirrors the expectations of her religious group. Berthold, on the other hand, relies on religious authorities from his faith tradition who legitimate or sanction actions and thus interpret God's word for him, offering clear rules and rewards. For him, God is external but closely connected in a relationship that

---

78   Aber ich beeinflusse auch, zum Beispiel meine Lebensgefährtin in der Hinsicht etwas[...]. Sie sieht das auch noch, obwohl sie (lächelt) Religionslehrerin war. Das müssen Sie sich mal überlegen, aber sie weiß, dass ich der bessere Christ bin. (lächelt) Sie wäre zwar 100, aber ich bin 150- prozentig. (lacht) Und das will doch schon was heißen, ne.

favors him for his impeccable and religiously legitimated behavior. However, although Heidemarie does not elaborate on the importance of her religious group explicitly, we can assume that she does follow their rules closely as her convictions are well aligned with evangelical teachings. Thus, although the interpretation of God's word might be differently facilitated, their moral orientations are governed by very similar principles.

This points to another similarity between the both of them: Their image of God is one of a personal relationship with a guiding God who accompanies them, supports them, cares for them, similar to a parental figure. They have an unrestricted and unquestionable certainty in the existence and guidance of God, who they can contact through prayer and communicate with. They also receive answers: Berthold receives inspiration for his art, and Heidemarie has the idea that the "spirit influences her." We see that both view themselves close to God who gives them implicit support and certainty in their religious journey, but also an unquestionable and unambiguous moral orientation and – in Berthold's case explicitly – a sense of superiority. This certainty can be exemplified by the fact that both have no doubt of where they are going after death which as we saw above is of increasing importance to the two elderly participants: They trust that they made the right decision to follow God's commandments and thus there is nothing to fear but instead to look forward to.

Conclusion

In this chapter we examined the life stories and religious reasoning of two elderly participants by investigating their accounts from different perspectives and with longitudinal data. We were therefore able to reconstruct meaning making processes that are exclusively relying on religious teachings and understand it in its developing biographical context. By comparing two cases with different Christian religious affiliations and life experiences we furthermore gained a greater understanding of commonalities and differences regarding morality, relationships and their images of God. Berthold and Heidemarie both belong to the generation that grew up during German fascism and the Second World War and, while recollecting their upbringing very differently, both turned to their religious traditions in times of crisis and state to never have doubted their faith again.

Their approach to religious matters was particularly characterized by an exclusive and unambiguous interpretation of their respective religious texts and teachings. Berthold's survey results on the *ttt* subscale as well as the fundamentalism scale strengthen this interpretation. Furthermore, the development in his religious styles corroborates this finding further as it regressed from predominantly conventional to ethnocentric in Wave 2 and 3 when his portrayal of people who do not share his convictions or with whom he is in disagreement became increasingly condescending and prejudiced. Berthold therefore also mirrors research findings indicating that highly religious people tend to dislike change – with which he is especially confronted in an increasingly liberal society – in favor of more conservative values (Saroglou, 2008) which is reflected in his decreasing NEO-FFI scores on the subscale for *openness to experiences*. Unfortunately, we don't have any survey results for Heidemarie but can observe the opposite trend in her religious styles development as they evolve from ethnocentric to conventional. First and foremost, we could see how her accounts at Wave 1 that were not very elaborated became more community oriented in Wave 2 and more abstract but also more incoherent in Wave 3. However, when it came to questions of morality or religion, she at all times tended towards a Style two reasoning which can also be exhibited in her quotes on these matters. Thus, while Heidemarie is in certain questions able to take a more community-oriented perspective, she keeps an exclusivist view in religious and moral matters. In both cases we could observe a fundamentalist dealing with these questions as they put their sacred rules above any other, e.g., societal considerations (Shupe, 2009, p. 481) and view their religious teachings as revelation of an objective and absolute truth one cannot deviate from (Hood et al., 2005, p. 22). Heidemarie and Berthold justify their convictions by a strict orientation toward what is called in the literature *binding moral foundations*: This characterizes a moral orientation that is not focused on the individual and its freedoms but on binding people to an exclusive group or social entity (Graham et al., 2011, p. 368). This could be observed in the moral reasoning of the two cases, constructing an impenetrable bond and identity with their respective religious teachings and faith traditions, strengthened by the conviction that the absolute truth was communicated by them.

Fostering this worldview makes it impossible to accept other realities than the one they interpret as the objective truth revealed to them by their religious texts which also affects relationships with people that don't adhere to the same principles (Hood et al., 2011, p. 23). This can result in a strict isolation from a modern society that predominantly follows a more individualistic morality. Berthold exhibited an interesting exception with his atheist friend but does in general seem to live a rather secluded life from an outside world with the values of which he widely disagrees. The overall turn in his life review which increasingly contains *contamination stories* accompany a declining sense of well-being which could be seen in his decreasing scores on the Ryff Scale, and which fits other research results (McAdams et al. 2001, p. 480). While he is able to form relationships with others such as his late friend or his partner, his primary goal seems to be to convince people of his way, and he harshly judges people with differing opinions while pertaining a defensive self-image which makes fostering new relationships very difficult and mirrors his dismissive attachment style. Heidemarie on the other hand does not give any detailed accounts of currently meaningful relationships and we do not learn how she views her well-being either. She does elaborate in her interviews on the importance of certain relationships in the past, though, and seems to view other people primarily as a part of a like-minded community which fits with her secure attachment style. However, Heidemarie, too, seems to be less involved in relationships to others which could be observed in her interview at wave 3 when she seems more concerned with herself and her abstract convictions than with relationships or even missionary work. Thus, both cases seem to retrieve more from the world and social life and have only one stable relationship which is the one they have with their God. Graham and Haidt argue that it is not primarily the religiosity that brings about an increase in happiness but the communal aspects of faith, which they explain in this fitting metaphor: "If God is a maypole, then health and happiness benefits of religion come from participating in the maypole dance, not from sitting at home thinking about the pole" (Graham & Haidt, 2010, p. 146).

Thus, we can assume that Berthold and Heidemarie do not benefit from this communal aspect of faith and isolate themselves from those who they do not share the same convictions with. They do gain, however, a certainty in another area in their lives that becomes more important as they grow older: Dealing with the uncertainty of death. As could be shown above, both exhibit an understanding of religious rules as secure guideline in that following the teachings will grant them access to the promised afterlife. This certainty helps them managing the uncertainty of death and reliefs them from fear which can be characterized as a form of "terror-management" (Graham & Haidt, 2010, p. 146). The positive effect of high religiosity in dealing with aging and death have been well documented in recent research (Fortuin et al., 2019; Coleman, 2013; Quinodoz, 2014; Shaw, Gullifer, Wood, 2016; Butenaite, 2020). However, Berthold and Heidemarie achieve this certainty in where they will go after they die by denying any other interpretation and by isolating themselves from worldviews and people that differ from these convictions. Thus, this undoubting certainty in their faith seems, although alleviating some of the pain of aging and being confronted with death, to be an exchange for the benefits of aging in the community with others. Berthold put his feelings regarding death into a poem which serves as a fitting illustration for his comfort with death and readiness to leave the worldly realm behind:

I am looking forward to death
may he still be far,
he is the gateway through which one goes
into eternal glory[79] (Berthold, FDI, time 2).

References

Altemeyer, B., & Hunsberger, B. (2004). A revised religious fundamentalism scale: The short and sweet of it. *International Journal for the Psychology of Religion*, 14(1), 47–54. http://www.leaonline.com/loi/ijpr

Bartholomew, K., & Horowitz, L. (1991). Attachment styles among yound adults: A test of a four-category model. *Journal of Personality and Social Psychology*, 61, 226–244.

Braam, A. W., Schaap-Jonker, H., Mooi, B., de Ritter, D., Beekman, A. T. F., & Deeg, D. J. H. (2008). God image and mood in old age: Results from a community-based pilot study in the Netherlands. *Mental Health, Religion & Culture*, 11(2), 221–237. http://www.informaworld.com/10.1080/13674670701245274

Butėnaitė, J. (2020). Roman Catholic faith of older people as a source of psychological resilience. *Contemporary Research on Organization Management and Administration*, 8(2), 32–46.

Coleman, P. G. (2013). Religion and age. In D. P. Dannefer, Chris (Ed.), *The SAGE handbook of social gerontology* (pp. 164–176). Sage.

---

79 Ich freue mich schon auf meinen Tod, ist er auch wohl noch weit, ist er doch das Tor, durch das man geht in die ewige Herrlichkeit.

de Oliveira, A. L. B., & de Oliva Menezes, T. M. (2018). The meaning of religion/religiosity for the elderly. *Revista Brasileira de Enfermagem*, 71(2), 770–776.

Fortuin, N. P. M., Schilderman, J. B. A. M., & Venbrux, E. (2019). Religion and fear of death among older Dutch adults. *Journal of Religion, Spirituality & Aging*, 31(3), 236–254.

Geldbach, E. (2001). Evangelikale Bewegung. In H. Gasper, J. Müller, & F. Valentin (Eds.), *Lexikon der Sekten, Sondergruppen und Weltanschauungen. Fakten, Hintergründe, Klärungen* (7 ed., pp. 263–271). Herder.

Graham, J., & Haidt, J. (2010). Beyond beliefs: Religions bind individuals into moral communities. *Personality and Social Psychology Review*, 14(1), 140–150. http://psr.sagepub.com/content/14/1/140

Graham, J., Nosek, B. A., Haidt, J., Iyer, R., Koleva, S., & Ditto, P. H. (2011). Mapping the moral domain. *Journal of Personality and Social Psychology*, 101(2), 366–385.

Granqvist, P. (2020). *Attachment in religion and spirituality: A wider view*. Guilford Press.

Hoberg, V. (2017). Evangelikale Lebensführung und Alltagsfrömmigkeit. In F. Elwert, J. Schlamelcher, & M. Radermacher (Eds.), *Handbuch Evangelikalismus* (pp. 209–226). Transcript Verlag.

Hood, R. W., Hill, P. C., & Williamson, W. P. (2005). *The psychology of religious fundamentalism*. Guilford Press.

Krech, V., Schlamelcher, J., & Hero, M. (2013). Typen religiöser Sozialformen und ihre Bedeutung für die Analyse religiösen Wandels in Deutschland. *Kölner Zeitschrift für Soziologie und Sozialpsychologie*, 65(S1), 51–71. https://doi,org/10.1007/s11577-013-0218-5

McAdams, D. P., Reynolds, J., Lewis, M., Patten, A. H., & Bowman, P. J. (2001). When bad things turn good and good things turn bad: Sequences of redemption and contamination in life narrative and their relation to psychosocial adaption in midlife adults and in students. *Personality and Social Psychology Bulletin*, 27(4), 474–485.

Pew Research Center. (2018). *The age gap in religion around the world*.

Pickel, G. (2013). *Religion Monitor – Understanding common ground*. Bertelsmann Foundation.

Rizzuto, A. M. (1979). *The birth of the living God. A psychoanalytic study*. University of Chicago Press.

Saroglou, V., & Munoz-Garcia, A. (2008). Individual differences in religion and spirituality: An issue of personality traits and/or values. *Journal for the Scientific Study of Religion*, 47(1), 83–101. https://doi.org/10.1111/j.1468-5906.2008.00393.x

Shaw, R., Gullifer, J., & Wood, K. (2016). Religion and spirituality: A qualitative study of older adults. *Ageing International*, 41(3), 311–330.

Shupe, A. (2009). Religious fundamentalism. In P. B. Clarke (Ed.), *The Oxford handbook of the sociology of religion* (pp. 478–490). Oxford University Press.

Streib, H., Hood, R. W., & Klein, C. (2010). The Religious Schema Scale: Construction and initial validation of a quantitative measure for religious styles. *International Journal for the Psychology of Religion*, 20(3), 151–172. https://doi.org/10.1080/10508619.2010.481223

Streib, H., Hood, R. W., Keller, B., Csöff, R.-M., & Silver, C. (2009). *Deconversion. Qualitative and quantitative results from cross-cultural research in Germany and the United States of America*. Vandenhoeck & Ruprecht. https://doi.org/10.13109/9783666604393

Streib, H., & Keller, B. (2018). *Manual for the assessment of religious styles in Faith Development Interviews (Fourth, revised edition of the Manual for Faith Development Research)*. Bielefeld University/readbox unipress.

IV. Part D: Conclusion

Chapter 14
Longitudinal Mixed-method Study of Worldviews and Religious Styles in the Adult Lifespan – Current Conclusions and Future Directions

Ramona Bullik, Zhuo Job Chen, Matthew Durham, Ralph W. Hood, Jr., Martin Hornshaw, Barbara Keller, Daimi Shirck, Christopher F. Silver, Anika Steppacher, & Heinz Streib[1]

Abstract *This concluding chapter presents a synopsis of the case studies that were described in the previous chapters of this volume in greatest possible detail. Thus, with this synopsis we move forward from the idiographic to explore idiothetic perspectives and consider typological patterns of the cases. Then, drawing on our mixed-methods design, the chapter presents summary perspectives and conclusions about the results from analyses that used the quantitative three-wave data and relates them to the case studies. The chapter concludes with notes on future perspectives for research on faith development and with suggestions for interdisciplinary networking—whereby narrative identity research and wisdom research stand out.*

Keywords: *faith development, religion, worldview, wisdom, narrative identity, case study, mixed methods*

---

1   R. Bullik, ;. Hornshaw, B. Keller, A. Steppacher, H.Streib, Bielefeld University, Germany, E-mail: ramona.bullik@uni-bielefeld.de; Z. J. Chen, School of Nursing, University of North Carolina at Charlotte, USA; M. Durham, R. W. Hood, Jr, D. Shirck, University of Tennessee at Chattanooga, USA; C. F. Silver, Sewanee. The University of the South, USA. © Heinz Streib, Ralph W. Hood Jr. (eds.): Faith in Development. Mixed-Method Studies on Worldviews and Religious Styles. First published in 2024 by Bielefeld University Press, Bielefeld, https://doi.org/10.14361/9783839471234-016

354   Part D: Conclusion

This book presents the current state of conceptual and methodological considerations, quantitative analyses, and typical case studies based on three waves of data. It is the first presentation of current results from our three-wave longitudinal research in faith development. In this concluding chapter, the case studies presented in chapters 10 through 13 receive priority. This reflects our central—idiographic—commitment to demonstrating faith development in the context of individual biographical trajectories, which extends to an idiothetic approach by case comparison and considering a typological structure for the cases[2]. Then, we will turn to a summary perspective and conclusion on the results on faith development based on quantitative analyses of the three-wave data—some of which are included in Part B of this book. And finally, we conclude with some notes on future perspectives for research on faith development.

Updating the Typology of Trajectories in Faith

The Cases—Selection and Overview

Turning to case studies means focusing on qualitative data and exploring options of discovering lines of comparison. This has inspired us to reorganize the cases chosen according to demographics and psychometric data by describing and discussing how they could be mapped in more complex ways when including findings from narrative analyses (Keller, Streib & Hood, 2016). By mapping, we mean laying out the cases and finding connections on different levels (see also Chapter 9 for a more elaborate description of this process).

The cases that were selected for the elaboration of case studies in Part C represented variations according to gender, age (and associated with age: developmental tasks), religion/worldview, and, according to their developmental trajectories, as movers up, movers down, or stayers in the hierarchy of religious styles and types. But they can also be mapped according to psychological variables, as in our previous study on Spirituality. We have shown in earlier research that groups organized according to basic variables show plausible patterns when plotted in the two-dimensional space of *openness to experience* and *mysticism* (Streib & Hood, 2016c; Keller et al., 2016). Now we use *openness to experience* and *mysticism* as two axes to plot the cases and highlight those cases that were selected for longitudinal case studies in this book. This is the option that we use in Figure 14.1 below. First, we present a summary overview of the cases using most important basic characteristics. Table 14.1 gives an overview of the cases in Chapters 10 through 13.

As Table 14.1 shows, the selection of the cases aspires to reflect the variety of the 3-wave sample and how we are, with this variety, able to answer different research questions. For those chapters containing a comparison of cases, the aim was to present subjective reconstructions of faith developments of people who were similar in age and reli-

---

2   Whereas an idiographic approach focuses on individual, unique portrayal of a case, the idiothetic perspective looks for options to aggregate data starting from case by case between-person comparisons and conclusions about commonalities and differences in a wider sample (see also Chapter 3).

gious denomination, and/or non-belief. Thus, we could line out how, for example, a common category like "Protestant" can mean something different for people identifying with the label as in the case studies for Gisela and George. However, in this chapter we strive for a more general overview. Based on overarching lines of comparisons and themes, we offer an overview on how our respondents handle certainty and doubt, how they deal with death and dying and what community means to them.

These analyses are based on group discussions among the case study authors and on the thorough content and narrative analyses displayed in chapters 10 to 13. In addition, we dedicate space to the aspect of morality and its development in the context of individual trajectories of subjective constructions of religious and worldview development.

The cases in Chapters 10 through 13 represent age, starting in emerging/young adulthood (Isabella and Nadine), and proceeding to old age (Heidemarie and Berthold). This structure pays tribute to the fact that, with our longitudinal research, we wish to explore changes happening throughout the entire adult lifespan. While following individual trajectories over a certain age span, we are also able to portray different life phases and discuss their particularities and developmental tasks, taking into account the different social and historical contexts. This we do by attending to how respondents themselves take up or elaborate on the social or historical conditions of their lives, thus offering a complementary view to data analyzed at the group level.

Thus, these different participants told us how they dealt with specific developmental tasks in and across different times and places: Identity and search for autonomy (atheist and/or spiritual) emerged as developmental tasks for Nadine and Isabella. The "midlifers," Petra, George, and Gisela, were concerned with issues of identity and autonomy as well, but also, in addition, with different versions of generativity, including social issues, religion as tradition preserving wisdom across generations, and exchange with younger people. Berthold and Heidemarie, finally, are portrayed as holding onto their religious tradition as a "secure base" in light of advancing age and being confronted with the end of life coming closer. Thus, we could reconstruct how these participants dealt with their developmental tasks.

Table 14.1: *Overview of the Cases*

	Life phase	Religious affiliation, worldview	Country	Religious Types + Movement Wave 1; 2; 3	Openness to experience Wave 1, 2, 3	Mysticism Introvertive Wave 1, 2, 3	Extrovertive	Interpretive	Deconversion/ Developmental Trajectory
Isabella	Young Adult	atheist	USA	Type 3 staying	3.50, 3.92, 3.75	1.42, 1.33, 1.67	1.63, 1.38, 1.13	2.25, 2.17, 1.92	Pursuit of Autonomy, with scientific worldview
Nadine		agnostic	Germany	Type 3; 2; 3 downward; upward	4.25, 4.42, 3.83	4.92, 4.00, 5.00	4.25, 4.25, 4.50	4.00, 3.42, 4.17	Pursuit of Autonomy, with experience-based horizontal transcendence
Petra	Midlife	spiritual atheist	Germany	Type 2; 4; 4 upward; staying	4.42, 4.08, 4.67	2.75, 2.17, 2.50	2.50, 3.00, 2.88	2.42, 2.08, 2.42	Life-long quest for meaning
George	Midlife to Young old	Lutheran	USA	Type 3; 4; 4 upward; staying	4.08, 4.08, 4.08	3.00, 1.42, 3.25	2.38, 3.13, 3.50	1.25, 1.33, 1.92	Pursuit of Autonomy based on reflective faith
Gisela		Protestant	Germany	Type 2; 2; 3 staying; upward	4.08, 4.33, 4.00	--, 5.00, 4.17	--, 5.00, 4.50	--, 5.00, 5.00	Overcoming doubt and rediscovering faith
Heidemarie	Young to old	Evangelical	Germany	Type 1; 2; 2 upward; staying				Not available	Holding on to faith
Berthold		Catholic	Germany	Type 2; 1; 1 downward; staying	3.50, 3.33, 3.08	--, 3.58, 3.27	--, 3.13, 3.25	--, 4.83, 4.33	Holding on to faith

Note. Type 1 = The Substantially Ethnocentric Type; Type 2 = The Predominantly Conventional Type; Type 3 = The Predominantly Individuative-reflective Type; Type 4 = The Emerging Dialogical-xenosophic Type.

In addition to the examination of age and cohort, we also looked at different forms of religiosity and worldviews, thereby focusing on individual trajectories of development, and, from there, also drawing lines of comparisons between single cases, sometimes with an eye toward cross-cultural differences as well. As a short reminder, we briefly sum up here basic characteristics of each case portrayed. Note that we draw on earlier typologies to locate their trajectories in a changing religious field:

- *Isabella* (USA) is a self-proclaimed atheist who attends atheist meetings and reports no spiritual experiences. She finds beauty in the experiences of horizontal transcendence (e.g., illustrated by the story of a plastic bag floating in the air) and has, in her first two interviews, shared to be scared by the prospect of her own mortality. Drawing on our earlier typology of deconversion trajectories (Streib et al., 2009), her trajectory can be described as an ongoing pursuit of autonomy, including moving away from organized humanism;
- *Nadine* (Germany) can best be defined as secular/agnostic who also describes herself as spiritual; she has engaged with many different religions in adolescence and early adulthood and reports spiritual experiences which influence her life decisions. Key terms for her might be 'mystic experience' and 'transcendence.' Her calm and self-reliant way of handling "special" experiences, experiences transcending everyday life, can be seen as an agnostic variety of experience-based receptivity toward messages which can be labelled as religious or spiritual (discussed in Keller, Streib, & Hood, 2016). As she herself is, in her interviews, rejects these labels, we might see her on an autonomous trajectory outside religious or spiritual organizations, scenes, or interpretations;
- *Petra* (Germany) is characterized as a spiritual atheist; she was brought up in the secular GDR but within a religious community; after she left the GDR, she adopted a more hedonistic lifestyle but after a while became disillusioned with the capitalist society; her interviews contain harsh criticism of religion while she upholds pro-social values, and they also suggest that so far she may be on a life-long quest for meaning (cf. Streib et al., 2009; Keller, Bullik, Streib, et al., 2022), as Nadine outside of organizations or scenes, but more explicitly drawing on literature and current intellectual discourse;
- *George* (USA) is a Lutheran Christian; he can be described as philosophically oriented as he values religion as a repository for humanity's wisdom and also cherishes his religious community both for its rituals as well as its capacity to support the broader community; he can be characterized as displaying a reflected and autonomous faith, thus perhaps representing a trajectory toward a reflective variety of faith, located in scientific discussion and participation in his religious community;
- *Gisela* (Germany) is a Protestant Christian with an experience-oriented approach and spiritual experiences, often related to difficult times in her life; these experiences seem to have great influence on her life decisions; she is well integrated into her religious community as well as a group of theology students; the "leitmotif" of her trajectory so far can be described as overcoming doubt and rediscovering faith (cf. Keller, Bullik, Streib, et al., 2022); community for her serves as a means for personal encoun-

ters, and thus she participates in an established and integrated religious community as well as in scientific reflection;

- *Heidemarie* (Germany) is an Evangelical Christian; she gives little personal information and mainly focuses on describing her faith which is characterized as exclusivist/undoubting. She can be described as holding on to faith, also resonating with "Relying on God, Scripture and Community" as described in Keller, Streib, and Hood (2016). Her affiliation, however, can, in Germany, be regarded as oppositional (Streib et al., 2009, p. 26);
- *Berthold* (Germany) is a Catholic who reports vivid WWII memories; having grown up with non-religious parents, he converted against their wish in childhood; his faith can be described as exclusivist/undoubting, and his trajectory as growing into (or rather holding on to?) faith. He relies on the teachings of the Catholic Church, which in Germany is well-integrated into the larger society.

In the earlier research referred to above, *openness to experience* and *mysticism* have proved useful as variables assessing a personality characteristic and a characteristic adaptation, thus two variables are different from, but relevant to, the development of religiosity (Streib & Hood, 2016c; Keller et al., 2016). *Openness to experience* as one dimension/subscale of the Big 5 personality traits (Costa & McCrae, 1985) can be defined as being open to and enjoying new situations, including a curiosity for the strange. Mysticism is measured with different subscales focusing on *introvertive* and *extrovertive mysticism* and on *interpretation*: The subscale *introvertive mysticism* strives to capture experiences that are primarily related to the internal world of the individual. Experiences that have a focus on the relation to the external world are addressed by the subscale *extrovertive mysticism*. Experiences that the individual associates with symbolic language and calls them holy, sacred, divine, wonder, or revelation are in the focus of the subscale *interpretation*. The Mysticism Scale (M-scale) proved useful for the assessment of the subjective experience-based religiosities and spiritualities of diverse participants who affiliate with various religious traditions and worldviews, including non-religious, atheists, and non-theist options (Streib et al., 2021). Data on general openness toward new experiences in combination with data on subjective religiosities with roots in inner or outer experience or in connections to what is symbolized as transcendent, may inspire conceptualizing "depth" and "breadth" (see chapter 2, this volume) as related to the development of faith and of religious types.

Therefore, we feel encouraged to explore mapping the trajectories of the cases according to these variables:

Gisela shows high scores in *openness* as well as *mysticism*. In her case study we learn about her open negotiations of religiosity, including doubt, leaving, and returning to her protestant community. Her trajectory from later midlife to early old age leads from the *predominantly conventional type* to the *predominantly individuative-reflective type*.

Higher scores in *mysticism* also characterize the profiles of Nadine and Berthold. In Nadine's case, the scores for the subscales of *introvertive* and *extrovertive mysticism* are rather high. This resonates with the unusual experiences which in her interviews she is reluctant to label as "spiritual." However, her confident way of handling these experiences may be described as experience-based receptivity of something special which occurs spontaneously. Her scores on *openness* are moderate which is, in the case study, explained with her general rather cautious, introvert personality, even though she claims to seek dialog with others who have opinions different from her own. In terms of types, we see her, in young adulthood, move from the *predominantly individuative-reflective type* to the *predominantly conventional* and, again, to the *predominantly individuative-reflective type*. Berthold's high scores in *mysticism* in the last two waves are to be found on the subscale *interpretation*, which refers to the sacredness and noetic quality of one's own religion. This is something that is definitely important for Berthold, while he is hesitant to hostile regarding other religions. He displays the lowest scores on *openness* of the cases portrayed in this book. We see him, from "young" to "old" old age, move from the *predominantly conventional* to the *substantially ethnocentric type*. The apparent contradiction between growing in faith while regressing in faith development can be resolved: Berthold's almost childlike trust in the truth of the teachings of his chosen tradition may help him cope with the challenges of his advanced age, and the pertaining growth in subjective functionality is distinct from progress in terms of the hierarchical model of the religious styles.

Thus, we may see here perhaps varieties of depth: Nadine's high scores, in particular on *introvertive mysticism*, can be read as deep reliance on her "strange" transcendent experiences, which she does not wish to label "spiritual." Berthold's mysticism may refer to deep and exclusive reliance on his Catholic tradition. Neither Nadine nor Berthold seem to endorse "breadth," if we take their—for this sample—moderate scores in *openness to experience* for a proxy. Rather, both display remarkable "depth," however, in very different ways: Nadine relies, sometimes reluctantly, on her own inner experience, which she understands in a non-religious way, while Berthold dwells in his faith, structured by the tradition which helps him to come to terms with life's challenges.

Isabella, Petra, and George have in common rather high scores for *openness*, while being low on all *Mysticism* subscales. Here, a look, in addition to their data in Table 14.1, at their different profiles on the Religious Schema Scale offers helpful information on what may structure openness for them: With regard to their high scores on the subscale *fairness, tolerance, and rational choice (ftr)* and low scores on *xenosophia (xenos,* i.e. the explicit appreciation of the strange, and the advocation of dialog), Isabella and Petra display an openness that is, at the same time, rejecting anything that sounds "too religious," even though they claim to be open to the new and strange in general. This may point out what they have in common: a focus on horizontal transcendence that is rather abstract and, in contrast to Nadine and Gisela, not based on personal, special experiences. Rather, they draw more on scientific reasoning and philosophical discussions. Isabella was continuously seen as the *predominantly individuative-reflective type*, as we followed her through young adulthood. Petra progressed from *predominantly conventional* to *emerging dialogical-xenosophic* while moving from younger to later middle age. Thus, we may see here how similar "breadth" in terms of individual scores on *openness* may be qualified by difference in religious schemata.

Nadine, on the other hand, shows higher-than-average scores on *xenos*, despite its religious framing. As for the RSS subscale *truth of texts and teachings (ttt,* assessing an exclusivist understanding of sacred texts), all "non-believers," unsurprisingly, show very low scores. Gisela and Berthold, though, display high scores, both also show high scores on the *interpretation* subscale of the M-scale, indicating that, despite their obvious differences in their openness for other religions, they practice their own religion with a considerable depth. Heidemarie, whom we followed from young to later old age, and who moved from the *substantially ethnocentric* to the *predominantly conventional type*, has continuously rejected to answer psychometric scales. Perhaps this may be regarded here as a statement of insisting on displaying her view on her religion in her own words?

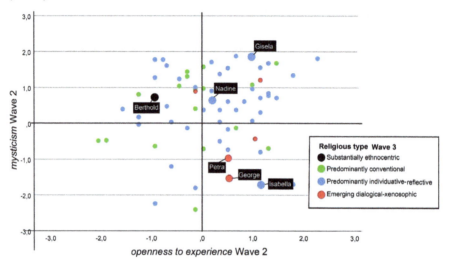

Figure 14.1: *Three-wave Cases (Wave 3) in the Space of Mysticism and Openness to Experience (Wave 2)*

In Figure 14.1, we look at *openness* and *mysticism* across the sample and the religious types documented, and offer a longitudinal exploration: We plot in the two-dimensional space described by *openness* and *mysticism* at Wave 2 and the religious types assessed at Wave 3. This way, we get a distribution of our cases in which Gisela and Nadine (albeit with scores closer to the midlines) appear in the upper right quadrant with high scores in both variables and with an assigned *predominantly individuative-reflective type* at Wave 3. In the right lower quadrant (high *openness* with low *Mysticism*), we find Isabella, also assigned *predominantly individuative-reflective* at Wave 3, and George and Petra, assigned the *emerging dialogical type*. Berthold can be found in the left upper quadrant, with high *Mysticism* and low *openness*. Heidemarie refused our questionnaire, and thus is missing. According to the hierarchy of religious styles and types, "higher" types seem to be associated with higher scores in *Mysticism* and perhaps more so *openness*. This looks like a plausible involvement of *openness* and *Mysticism* in faith development in longitudinal perspective—and is a promising point of departure for explorations beyond the single case (see more below in the second part of the chapter).

The case studies, allowing the inspection of individual configurations, suggest to attend to different ways of handling overarching themes, as will be outlined in the next section.

Emerging Overarching Themes and Ways to Present One's Worldviews —An Idiothetic[3] Approach

When looking for new lines of comparison starting from the study of the single case, and for common characteristics of the cases, we add individual psychometric data to a narrative and biographical perspective. When we use such measures and compile them to individual profiles of a single person, we regard them as part of what a single person tells us about themself, thus making them part of the portrait of a person. This allows us to see not only how open a person is according to their individual score, for example, but also how a person is open as exemplified by experiences offered in narratives. When individual scores are seen in longitudinal perspective, they are supposed to measure change or stability in the degree of expression across time. Included in our case studies, they become part of the reconstructed biography. The focus on the individual case and its specific context also allows the identification of characteristics not or not yet captured by established psychometric variables. From a narrative perspective, this implies not only new lines of comparison, but also openness to emerging "alternative narratives," complementing as well as challenging the "master narratives" or narrative templates, which are regarded normative in a given historical and cultural context (McLean et al., 2018).

When looking at the cases presented in the chapters 10–13, it becomes clear that they vary already regarding characteristic ways of presenting themselves which shape the autobiographies and subjective accounts of development and are thus worth exploring. People differ greatly in terms of how much/what kind of information they are willing to share. This has an impact on psychometric as well as narrative data. For example, Heidemarie refused to answer any questionnaire. Then, there is variety in the ways participants respond to the questions in the FDI. Some people, like Nadine or Heidemarie, are rather reluctant when asked to talk about their life and their relationships; they do not seem to feel comfortable sharing that much personal information with a stranger. Interestingly, though, they are more willing to open up when asked for elaborations regarding their faith or their spiritual experience. Most of the others seize the chance the FDI offers and reflect openly and comprehensively about how what they believe in is grounded in their experience and weave little narratives into their accounts. This can be regarded as an interesting observation: what elicits narratives (in our case, identified by the schema introduced by Labov & Waletzky, 1967)? When do our participants refer to personal stories or use autobiographical arguments (Habermas & Köber, 2015; Köber et al., 2018) to make their point and to create coherence in their life story? And while these are questions worth exploring systematically across participants and/or across questions in the future, we observe here, for example, that Nadine and Gisela tell lively narratives about their spiritual experiences, while other accounts remain more abstract and refer to other means of argumentation strategies to justify their opinion. We noted that Gisela quotes Dorothee Sölle, a German feminist theologian and poet, when she strives to lay out her

---

3   We suggest to use Lamiell's (1981; 2019) neologism as bridging concept for the exploration starting from single cases and looking for what might describe a single case, and then work toward what could be generalized beyond the single case; see Chapter 3 for a more comprehensive discussion.

model of mature faith, Petra has read and quotes Ludwig Wittgenstein and Thomas Metzinger, a contemporary German philosopher, and Heidemarie and Berthold refer to the Bible—the common principle of argumentation here is a topos of authority (a term going back to Aristotle): a renowned person or text is quoted to strengthen one's own argumentation and to encounter assumed criticism (for more details, see Bullik, 2024; Kindt, 1992; also note the negotiation of ideas and master narratives as has been described in Chapter 3, this volume). The choice of authority, of course, is also meaningful for the overall self-presentation, suitable to create the image of a person who is scientifically minded and well-read, or devout and relying on the sacred texts of their tradition, or interested in popular culture (in Isabella's case: she likes to quote from various movies, popular TV shows and books). These observations were made based on the analysis of narrative particularities using the narrative coding list (for a description of the coding system and procedure, see Chapters 4 and 7; also, Bullik, 2024); however, the main focus of the case studies was on content, the chapters each concentrating on one or more topics. When trying to get to a synopsis of the cases, some themes emerged that were important in more than one chapter and that allowed for comparisons across cases. The following sections will detail those themes and suggest interindividual comparisons of trajectories that will find interesting similarities as well as a broad variety of approaches.

The themes that will be presented in the following sections are the result of a bottom-up oriented process of analyzing the interviews, i.e. the themes are derived directly from the interview material, meaning that careful case-based inductive work was followed by case-by-case comparison as demonstrated in the respective chapters, then followed by group discussions within the team of the case study authors. The selection of themes is based on what impressed as important in most or all single cases, thus hinting to important topics that appear to be universal when thinking about one's life and worldview. From our perspective, it is a merit of this procedure that it is able to come up with themes that are not apparent from any pre-set category (even though those themes do, of course, not appear out of the blue but are created in response to questions asked in the interview).

Trust in Certainty and Doubt

Interesting observations can be made when looking at the way the respective 'faith' manifests in each of the cases portrayed here, and how certain they present themselves regarding what they believe in. Especially in Berthold's case and, to a lesser degree, also in Heidemarie's, the security in faith comes with a certain defensiveness, perhaps connected to an avoidant or dismissive attachment style rendering them less open to explorations of ideas other than their own (Greenwald, et al., 2018). This can also be seen in atheist Isabella who seems rather set in her stance and, like Berthold and Heidemarie, does not allow much doubt and, going along with that, displays lower openness toward the strange, especially when the strange is a different religion (this is in contrast to her moderate to high scores on *openness to experience* in the survey). The other cases seem to be less defensive when explaining their religiosity or worldview which may lead to the conclusion that they feel more secure, more settled in their respective stance. An interesting difference can be observed when comparing Nadine and Petra: while Nadine seems to be fine with the boundaries of her knowledge-based approach and trusting her experience,

Petra tries to explore these boundaries. The searching movements are quite different, too: While Petra seems to relish this exploration ("There are so many variables!", searching out of curiosity), Nadine acknowledges opportunities for nuance and exploration, but does not seem particularly happy about the overabundance of options, yet accepts them as something challenging that she, however, has learnt to deal with. So, obviously, atheism, or, more general, non-belief, manifests differently in the three women portrayed here: It is interesting to note that although Petra characterizes herself as an atheist in the surveys (at times 1 and 2), this does not seem to play such a big role in how she displays her identity in the interviews; rather, she is engaged in intellectual honesty. For her, the focal point seems to be that she criticizes religion, and she does not focus as much on the affirmative part of an atheist community like we see in Isabella, who we see moving from being a staunch atheist to adopting a more pragmatic approach. Nadine has the most experience-based approach of these three and has come to accept and integrate her dreams and visions.

Moreover, searching movements can also be found in the interviews of Gisela and George. Gisela has, after a short period of doubt, found a new variety of faith and enjoys the community, while also searching for more scientific approaches to religion which she finds in university courses, as well as a more reflected approach to her faith. George's searching movements touch the fields of philosophy and humanism with the effort to integrate these into his own form of spirituality. Gisela is open and tolerant for other religions while Berthold and Heidemarie view every religion that deviates from their Christian belief as false and leading to hell (more in Berthold's case). In terms of the attachment approach Gisela and George might be more open to exploration because they feel secure in their respective faiths, while Berthold and Heidemarie rather seem to hold on what they have accepted as reliable. Gisela's portrait shows her as committed to a deep as well as broad and encompassing faith, while Heidemarie's faith might be characterized as deep as well as focused, which comes across as a rather narrow faith which cannot acknowledge other faiths. On the other hand, Heidemarie and Gisela show similar images of God— "God is love"—and thus god as part of the inner self, which hints to a similarity in depth, possibly in the field of personal experience.

Dealing with Death and Dying
The exploration of human or one's own mortality and dying is addressed in the FDI, so people will talk about their experiences, their fears and their ideas. However, in some cases, this topic takes up more space than in others, or is even discussed in parts of the interview which do not necessarily elicit thoughts about death. Thus, it emerges as an important part of meaning making, be it more or less religious, spiritual, or else.

As became apparent in the case study comparing Nadine and Isabella, for both those non-religious young women the question of what happens to us when we die is of importance. Nadine allegedly has just accepted death as a biological necessity that doesn't bother her too much. On the other hand, most of the spiritual experiences she reports seem to occur when she is faced with the possibility of death; be it her own (in form of suicidal thoughts) or that of others. Isabella is outright scared, as she admits openly, in her first two interviews. In those interviews, the fact that she does not have anything to believe in when it comes to her own mortality is quite upsetting for her. However, in her third interview she seems to convey that death ends everything, even concern with death. Petra, interestingly, shows admiration toward the beauty of the organic process happening after death, an admiration that seems similarly directed toward a horizontal transcendence—which is defined as "the experiential dimension to human life of interconnectedness that is profound, exceptional, and wondrous while requiring no religious, spiritual, or theistic framework [...]" (Coleman et al., 2013, p. 11, see also: Kalton, 2000; Streib & Hood, 2011; Mercadante, 2014; Streib & Hood, 2016b). While being quite aware of the scientific basis of the process, for her, there is still room for curiosity and amazement, as well as some sort of trust in complex processes. Both Isabella and Petra try to find beauty in small things, which might also serve as a means of coping with the question of what happens after death; maybe Isabella will, getting older, realize that in a similar fashion. She does not explicate her fear of death as much in her third interview already.

In the case study presenting Gisela and George, death is not made an explicit topic. Having dealt with depression and severe life crises, Gisela states that she believes in a continuation after death involving light and the love of God which is why she is not afraid of dying. George, having had his fair share of grief in life as well, also holds the belief that he "will be taken care of"; however, his elaborations are less personal and contain a number of references to philosophy and other religions, especially in his third interview. Berthold and Heidemarie display a similar certainty, both being rather calm about the prospect of dying since "they know where they are going," which may support their insistence on their way being the only true way. Berthold's high scores on the *interpretation* subscale of the M-scale may point to a "depth" in faith based on trust in his religious tradition. Here, dialog with research on attachment needs to be continued. This will shed light on defensive vs. open sharing of personal transcendent experiences in the interviews as well as on difference in adherence to one's own tradition and willingness to accept "other" religious options as something that can have value.

Comparing the three non-religious persons with those who follow a religion, a point could be made that the non-religious relate to experiences and notions of horizontal transcendence and try to find happiness in the here and now instead of in the afterworld. In contrast, Heidemarie and Berthold seem to focus more on life after death than their current lives; accordingly, they can serve as an example for a belief in a vertical transcendence, which might also be said for Gisela. For George, the situation is less clear, even though he seems to show signs of favoring a horizontal transcendence over the vertical. Another point could be made that the non-religious presented here are also younger, and we are looking at members of different cohorts as well as persons confronted with different developmental tasks: Focusing on the here and now may be functional for the younger in different ways than for the older interviewees. The younger may feel they have a life to live, including commitments to others, the older may invest themselves in their faith according to their traditions, and find more or less explicit ideas of an afterworld that will be open to them, perhaps offering re-unification with lost loved ones. Moreover, in terms of subjective functionality, development might, for example for Berthold, involve going back to the notions of *the substantially ethnocentric type*, promising reliable rewards—or, in attachment terms, finally a safe haven. Together with his high scores on the *interpretation* subscale of the M-scale, this might be a configuration to be explored further. It remains to be seen if the difference documented here between the atheist younger and the pious older persons also holds for persons in highly religious contexts, or in contexts where death and dying are not as highly correlated to old age as in industrialized Western countries?

The Meaning of Community

Last but not least, the role of community shall serve as another example of how interindividual themes emerge from a coding procedure that is as open and as thorough as the one used here for all interviews. The case who puts the most focus on the importance of groups is Gisela. It becomes clear in her interviews that she values her parish and sees the communal practice as an important element of her faith. Additionally, the young students she met while taking courses at university have offered the opportunity to widen her horizon. In a similar manner, Isabella talks about the atheist/humanist groups that were of importance to her in her 20s, when perhaps her (non-)religious identity was an issue to be explored. Discussing topics related to atheism as well as other shared interests were what constituted the meaning found in these groups. However, at time 3, this community seems to have lost the importance it used to have. Heidemarie reports the value of community as well, however understanding it as referring to those of her tradition, those having the right faith, not a special parish in which she participates. The contrast between Heidemarie (and, to a lesser degree, Berthold) on the one hand and Gisela and Isabella on the other is apparent: while the latter seem to cherish the vivid relationships they experience within their communities, making those encounter a great part of the value those groups constitute for them, Heidemarie's focus is on the one interpretation of God's word which excludes her from communal experiences, but connects her on a higher level to those who believe like her. For George, it seems as if the communal and welfare aspects of his parish are the main reasons why he is still part of it. Nadine and Petra, at the other end of the spectrum, do not seem to need a community; rather, they refer to discussions with single individuals while being skeptical toward groups.

Summed up, we see here that the function of community differs inter-individually. While two of the three non-theists portrayed here do not look to groups for support so much, Isabella makes it clear in her interviews that for her the lack of a community was one of the downsides of being an atheist; therefore, she explicitly looked for groups that would satisfy her need for an exchange with like-minded people. For the other cases, community is important, yet what is defined as community may differ, ranging from a rather abstract community of the faithful to a very concrete parish in which events are organized and faith is lived communally. And perhaps, those who quote from theology and philosophy see themselves as parts of an intellectual community?

Perspectives on Morality

While the investigation of morality as one of the aspects of faith development is included in the structural analysis of the interviews, we can also enrich this evaluation by focusing on thematic and narrative accounts by which the participants ground and justify their morality. When attending to content, we gain insight into different subjective ways of constructing morality. Thereby, our interpretation includes assumptions of moral foundations (Graham et al., 2011).

In all of the case studies we have found, in one way or another, discussions of moral questions. For the atheists Isabella and Petra, we found a hedonist orientation that is focused on their here and now, yet Petra has a clear focus also on society and the welfare of others, while Isabella talks rather vaguely about humanist values. For Petra and George, morality seems to be a dimension of spirituality; while George sees religion as a repository for humanity's collective wisdom, Petra defines her own spirituality as radical honesty and knowledge seeking. George's quote, "come to a position that seems to you to be most reasonable in light of the available evidence" might be something that Petra could have said as well. The term intellectual humility applies to both Petra and George, yet Petra explicitly refers to Metzinger's "intellectual honesty," while George argues in a more elaborated and open way, which may resonate with his higher scores for xenosophia. So, interestingly, Petra and George seem to come to quite similar conclusions when thinking about moral questions, both showing a reflective morality, even though they come from thoroughly different backgrounds, Petra being raised in the religious diaspora of a strictly secular state and later abandoning religious means of explanation, and George being a Protestant in the US with some affiliation to the church, however, with an intellectual and philosophical approach.

When looking at the decidedly faithful and religious part of the case studies, it has been carved out that Gisela displays a harm/care orientation in relation to fellow humans, while toward God she shows more loyalty and an orientation toward an ingroup. Berthold and Heidemarie, in contrast, do not seem to look beyond their sacred texts at all, thus showing a tendency toward sanctity/purity.

Gisela and Petra refer to integrity as a moral obligation, George stresses being faithful and honest. In Chapter 7, based on a network analysis of Petra's interviews, Authenticity/Honesty/Integrity is discussed as additional moral foundation assuming that, as in the words of Graham and colleagues, authenticity certainly looks like "some major island to be named" (Graham, et al., 2011, p. 382).

Emerging Themes and an Emerging Typology

What do we learn for the study of personality development and faith development? We were able to attend to processes of negotiations of personal myths and master narratives, and on subjective evaluations of development. Our data allowed to do that a) in a longitudinal perspective for the individual case, b) in inter-individual comparison of single trajectories, and c) in a research setting that allows for cross-cultural comparison. This gives us the unique opportunity to outline actual development and generalizable trajectories which eventually lead to a detailed and multi-layered map of (religious) development over the lifespan.

Our case studies that were presented in this volume are also an inspiration to advance our work on the typology of religious change and faith development. The synoptic view on the cases in section 1.2 of this chapter allows for reflection on typologies that derived from the studies thus far. Overarching themes—and inter-individual differences between the cases—have emerged when looking at the interviews with an idiothetic perspective, as was laid out in the previous paragraphs. These themes are like axes that help us construct and refine a typology, covering key perspectives for faith development. They included the following typological differences:

- Trust, commitment, and certainty versus search of meaning, exploration, and doubt;
- Vertical versus horizontal transcendence in developing answers for questions of death, dying, and afterlife;
- High versus low desire for, and importance of, community for identity construction;
- Hedonistic versus humanist grounding of morality, but also the polarity of whether morality is embedded in the participant's individual spirituality versus part of collective or tradition-based wisdom.

The inter-individual difference in these themes, which could be carved out in the previous section, but are without any claim to comprehensiveness, have an overlap with the typology developed on the basis of an interpretation of many interviews in the Deconversion Study. This can now be advanced to capture typological structural differences in a wide range of people's understanding their own worldview, more religious, spiritual or non-theist. Here is a proposal:

- *Pursuit of autonomy*: Originally described as the "long-term gradual process of stepping away from the previously taken-for-granted religious environment into which a person was born or brought by the parents as a child" (Streib et al., 2009, p. 221), characterized by the need to question structures and developing further as a person, with the consequence that groups or institutions are abandoned when they do not fit anymore, we have found multiple examples in our case studies that may hint to varieties of this kind of trajectory. The example of Isabella has shown here that this type is also applicable for non-religious trajectories, with the *focus on a scientific worldview*. The *experience-based horizontal transcendence* that we see in Nadine's case can be classified as another form of pursuit of autonomy, and it is characterized not only as not belonging to any organized form of religion or other worldview, but also as embracing experiences of transcendence as they happen. It may be hypothesized that we will find this trajectory in other autobiographies, especially in, but not limited to, those who do not identify as religious. In the religious part of the cases, we found, in George, another variety based on *reflective faith*, which takes scientific discussions and humanitarian interests into consideration. What these people have in common is also that they display the characteristics of at least *the predominantly individuative-reflective type*, which is consistent with the finding from *Deconversion Revisited* that individuals with this kind of trajectory are often found to show a predominantly individuative-reflective style (Keller et al., 2022).
- *Life-long quest for meaning*: The motif of a life-long quest was already found in the original Deconversion Study, the accumulative heretic (Streib, 1998) as one variant of it described as being "on a journey of a life-long quest, [...] a project of intelligent customers on the religious market in search for the product which best serves their needs" (Streib et al., 2009, p. 225). Petra fits this description well (for, as she says herself, "there is always something to add"), albeit outside of the religious context, and therefore rather on an ongoing quest for meaning in a horizontal transcendence,

368 Part D: Conclusion

with a religious type that, in her last two interviews, was categorized as *emerging dialogical-xenosophic*.

- *Overcoming doubt and rediscovering faith:* This is a trajectory that has been introduced as "overcoming doubt" to capture the follow-up of the trajectories of "traditionalists" from the seminal Deconversion Study. It refers to "those who live through a crisis upon which they deepen their faith and their ties to the community" (see Keller et al., 2022, p. 295). However, it may be applicable to other "traditionalists," i.e. religious or non-religious people who experience times of doubt which are overcome, leading, in consequence to a deeper and firmer faith, worldview, or frame of reference.
- *Holding on to faith:* This trajectory resonates with "growing in faith," described for "traditionalists" who report, for example, a deepened attachment to God (see Keller et al., 2022, p. 296). It can be mostly found in the deeply religious and, supposedly, in those with religious types 1 and 2. It is associated with a rather fundamentalist and exclusivist form of faith or worldview, with notions of depth as deepening of commitment to or immersion in one´s tradition, and seems to go along with rather low scores for *openness to experience* and high scores on ttt.

Having now laid out how bottom-up procedures may lead to new insights and offer new possibilities to sort the cases, we will, in the next section, turn to main findings from the quantitative analysis. To emphasize our mixed-methods approach, those findings will be enriched with examples from the case studies as well, showing that there is idiothetic potential also in the more quantitatively oriented analyses presented in section B of this book.

Conclusion for the Quantitative Results with Focus on Faith Development

Our commitment to an idiographic/idiothetic approach is complemented by the statistical analysis of data from our questionnaires. We have used the quantitative data to look for correlates, predictors, and outcomes of changes in faith development (Streib et al., 2021), more spiritual than religious self-identification (Chen et al., 2023), or deconversion (see Chapter 8, this volume). This part of the concluding chapter summarizes and highlights some most recent results based on quantitative data that eventually connect to findings from the case studies. The most general and most central question of our line of research regards the longitudinal observation of the development of faith according to the hierarchy of religious styles and religious types. Therefore, we begin with a discussion of new findings.

The Longitudinal Documentation of Faith Development
—New Findings, New Questions

We have worked with concurrent inter-individual differences in faith development right from the beginning of our series of projects, documenting, for example, higher faith development in deconverts in comparison with stable members (see Streib et al., 2009). After we moved on to include a longitudinal line of research and completed one re-interview with the same person, these two-wave cases already opened new perspectives not only on intra-individual differences (stability, progress, regression), but also on rather complex interactions of inter-individual and intra-individual differences in change and development (see Streib et al., 2022). Consistent with Fowler we argue for genuine faith development that would be empirically problematic if styles or types did not change at all. Further, these changes regard both interindividual and intraindividual individual differences. And it is important to note that change in religious belief or in affiliation is not the same as religious development in the sense of the structural model of religious styles.

Including data from Wave 3 presented in this volume, we can with greater confidence and in much more detail document the directions of change: progression and regression in terms of the hierarchy of styles and types. We have carefully operationalized both these terms so that their identification is purely statistical and the measurement ordinal, but we are cognizant that we propose a model that is normative. Thus, we are able, based on three-wave Faith Development Interviews, to give answers to the questions whether faith includes development, and which directions are prevalent. In the case studies we attend to subjective functionality, thus contending that "regression" in terms of the hierarchy may be an important developmental step in terms of subjective functionality.

In a research report that is published as journal article (Streib, Chen, et al., 2021), we could, for the first time in research with the Faith Development Interview, demonstrate that there *is* faith development as slightly progressive change to higher religious types over the average time distance of ten years. Further, progressive faith development was predicted by higher scores in *openness to experience* (NEO-FFI; Costa & McCrae, 1985) and lower scores on the subscale *truth of texts and teachings* of the Religious Schema Scale (Streib et al., 2010). These preregistered hypotheses were supported.

We have already noted that we have stayers (those who do not change) and movers downward (those that regress) and movers upward (those that progress in religious type) (Streib et al., 2020; Streib, Chen, et al., 2021; see also Chapter 5, this volume). The study by Streib, Chen, and Hood (2021) revealed a variety of trajectories between Wave 1 and Wave 3: 25 (33.3%) are stayers, 34 (45.3%) are movers upward and 16 (21.3%) are movers downward. With such high portion of down-movers, this study contradicts cognitive-structural assumptions of a mono-directional, sequential and irreversible developmental line. Now, the question is on the table: What exactly do progression and regression, upward and downward movements in faith development mean?

The question is in fact even more complicated: With every additional wave of data collection and Faith Development Interviewing, the individual trajectory is becoming more complex. At the idiographic and idiothetic level we may engage in precisely tracking the trajectories of progressions and regressions based upon all unique comparisons. We have presented these more detailed results for the case studies in Table 14.1 in this chapter. A special, and very interesting trajectory is detected when one and the same person's biography includes changes of moving up and down, progress and regress in religious types. This is, of course, a challenge for interpretation. The inspection of biographical events and turning points, and the inspection of the person's questionnaire data at each turning point, as demonstrated in the case studies, may give us a clue to this person's faith development trajectory—even if it may appear incomprehensible at first.

As can be seen in Table 14.1, in most cases portrayed here, there is some movement. Isabella is the only one who does not display major changes in the structure of her answers, accordingly staying within the *predominantly individuative-reflective type*. Gisela, George, and Heidemarie all show a similar direction of development, yet from different starting points and toward different recent styles: Gisela seems to have achieved, entering old age a level of reflection that allows her to also look critically on her own religion, while at the same time being convinced of what she believes in, expressed in her being categorized as *predominantly individuative-reflective*. George's development has been toward a rather solid *emerging dialogical-xenosophic type*, showing genuine interest for and understanding of other religions and worldviews. Heidemarie, having started as a *substantially ethnocentric type* with a literal-mythical understanding of her beliefs, has in old age reached a rather conventional and group-oriented approach. All of these developments seem to be functional for the individual, perhaps accounting for changes in their environment and/or a more thorough engagement with one's own religion. For Berthold, the downward movement indicating that his faith has, with old age, become more literal, more fundamentalist, may be functional in that it gives him something to rely on when he envisions the end of his life. Drawing on the discussions of "breadth" and "depth," on *openness* and *Mysticism* as co-ordinates, and on life-span trajectories as involved in the development of religion and worldview, we may conclude: Movements up or down in the hierarchy of the styles and types may involve personality (*openness to experiences*), or characteristic experiences (mysticism), or current developmental tasks—and all of this is embedded in specific times and places. In longitudinal perspective we may observe regressions in terms of the religious styles or types, which may precede as well as prepare future progress in terms of the hierarchy, and which will be subjectively functional at a given point in one's personal development. Also, we want to explore how "breadth" and "depth" may manifest and follow each other or interact in a given trajectory.

Given that we are engaged in adding a fourth wave of interviewing that will include Faith Development Interviews with individuals at four points in time, there are numerous possibilities for individual change. Closer inspection and interpretation of individual cases and their different faith development trajectories over three and four times of interviewing is a desideratum that needs to be addressed in future research.

Aspect-specific Faith Development

Calculating the religious type as total score (Streib et al., 2020) is one way to come to a conclusion with the 25 assignments of religious styles in one Faith Development Interview. This procedure is especially helpful for an overall indication which religious style may play the predominant or most important role in a person's worldview. And it allows easier statistical modeling. The downside is a loss of variance, or, with respect to the architecture of *aspects of faith* (see also Table 1.1 in Chapter 1 of this volume), the potential risk of concealing a more differentiated insight in faith development.

This was the reason why we started to analyze faith development *aspect-specific* using our three-wave sample. Results (presented in Chapter 5 of this volume) indicate that, unexpectedly, progressive development in religious type appears to take place only in the aspects of *perspective-taking*, followed by the aspect of *social horizon*, while in the aspects of *morality, locus of authority, world coherence*, and *symbolic function* faith development was not clearly indicated. This study also included an analysis of predictors for faith development, when modeled aspect-specific. The most remarkable and thought-provoking result is that scores on the subscale *xenosophia/inter-religious dialog* of the Religious Schema Scale (Streib et al., 2010) and the scores on *pluralism* (from Religion Monitor; Huber, 2007; 2009) have emerged as (strong resp. still significant) predictors for faith development in the aspect of perspective-taking.

One conclusion is this: When the aspects of *perspective-taking* and *social horizon* can be understood as meta-cognitive preconditions for faith development, we may have a clue to answer the question about the motor of development: *Perspective-taking* appears as strongest driving force, followed by *social horizon*. This might point to the importance of this particular aspect, now formulated as drawing on cognitive as well as affective development involved in understanding oneself and others. An alternative explanation may focus on the difference in developmental speed between the domains resp. aspects of faith. Thus, the study presented in Chapter 5 makes a contribution to the identification of driving forces, differences in developmental speed, and aspect-specific predictors for faith development, but certainly suggests replication of these results in future research. There is likely some way to go before we arrive at a more comprehensive conclusion about the meaning of the difference and commonalities between the aspects in faith and their development.

Conclusion for Faith Development Research

The completion of the third wave of interviewing and data collection has opened the door to conclusive longitudinal modeling of faith development. This is new, and our studies are indeed the first in investigating faith development with the Faith Development Interview *longitudinally*. These first longitudinal studies allow to put to the test what previously was strongly or exclusively based on conceptual considerations—which in Fowler's case were considerably influenced by structural-developmental assumptions as developed in Kohlberg's moral development theory, but remained primarily on the conceptual level also in the critical-constructive modification and advancement by the religious styles perspective. Now, previous conclusions about faith development that were based on relatively unpretentious analyses of cross-sectional data can and must be reconsidered and reanalyzed using longitudinal data and sophisticated modeling. This regards the simple question whether there *is* faith development, but immediately, as indicated by our results, rather complex questions arise about the different trajectories of moving up and down in faith development, and the potential differences between the aspects. Our current results need replication, and new questions call for more detailed analyses—and all of this can hopefully be based on a larger sample of Faith Development Interviews when our fourth wave is completed.

Outlook on Future Research and on Interdisciplinary Perspectives

This concluding chapter is also the prolegomenon to a book to come. The new research phase that started in 2022 continues our longitudinal mixed methods approach and will extend our data with another, a fourth, wave. In both Germany and the USA, all available previous interviewees are invited for another interview (FDI) and questionnaire participation. The questionnaire retains quantitative measures from Wave 3 (see Appendix A, this volume) but adds scales for intellectual humility (Krumrei-Mancuso & Rouse, 2016) and for group-focused enmity and prejudice (Zick et al., 2008; Zick et al., 2011) to address the outcomes of faith in development. The new questionnaire will also include two new free text entries, one on the participants' subjective definition of wisdom, and another field with an invitation to note any recent global events which have an impact on the participants' life or worldview. Thus, the data from this fourth wave will increase power and depth in both qualitative and quantitative assessment of religious change in a variety of perspectives, including our key perspective on faith development in terms of religious styles and religious types. We expect, for example, that correlates and predictors for faith development such as *openness to experience* and *Mysticism* (NEO-FFI, Costa & McCrae, 1985, Hood's M-Scale, Streib, et al., 2021) together with *truth of texts and teaching* (RSS, Streib et al., 2010) can be evidenced and expanded further. But beyond replication and extension of current results as reported in this volume and elsewhere, this new data will allow new perspectives that were not possible to analyze because of insufficient sample sizes.

In particular, our expectation is that we will be able to provide answers to the questions: where does faith development lead to, and what are the outcomes of faith development? Thereby, the question about the outcome of faith development has a focus on xenosophia and prejudice reduction, on the development of wisdom, and on respective changes in the image of God or the divine. The aim of faith development is defined as development towards openness for dialog. As specified in Chapter 1 (this volume), faith development aims at the readiness for mutual learning and at responsive receptiveness toward the Unknown/Alien. Thus, we expect that results with the Intellectual Humility Scale will make this case even stronger and profile the outcome of wisdom as xenosophia. But we also expect that the increase in xenosophia and readiness for dialog is reflected by lower inclination for prejudice and xenophobia. This can be tested using the scale for Group-focused Enmity. Finally, these results may be echoed in the representation of God and the divine, for example in a decline of the image of God as authoritarian. Complementarily we will continue dialog with research in attachment, especially for the exploration of experience-based mysticism and attachment-based exploration, but also for the study of God as attachment figure. Also, we may model breadth and depth in faith development in terms of quantitative analyses as well as on the level of single cases using *openness* and *mysticism* for longitudinal predictions.

These expectations for quantitative modeling may be deepened and extended by innovative approaches to analyze content in the interview texts: As demonstrated in Chapter 7 in this volume, Network Analysis with content codings in subsequent interviews with the same person can be used for visualizing hubs of content codings, how they are connected, and how the patterns change from one interview in one wave to the next wave. This can greatly assist the interpretation of which contents may be important for the interviewee and how these are changing over time. Another approach, which is inspired by research on personal wisdom (Mickler & Staudinger, 2005) and research on self-transcendence and life-story (Reischer et al., 2020), is our project for wisdom-related narrative themes; with focus on a concept of wisdom as xenosophia, it combines content ratings of wisdom-related themes in narratives of the interview with subsequent statistical modeling. This may help to more systematically identify wisdom in our data and may result in a contribution to wisdom research.

Of course, reconstructing religious change and faith development in a sample that includes a fourth wave allows, on the individual as well as on the inter-individual level, for drawing new maps and lining out trajectories in higher degrees of resolution. We will be able to capture dynamics across time and across different life phases, in different and changing social and historical contexts, putting a special focus on differences between and commonalities of the German and the US landscape. More longitudinal observations will add additional material for the construction of typologies, of course going along with additional complexity. Thus, the challenge for future research will be to identify typical longitudinal trajectories while finding new means to map and visualize these; and eventually network analysis can be used here, as has been shown in Chapter 7.

But also new avenues open. In particular, we may focus more on exploring the changing configurations of interactions between different aspects of faith development, and interactions between religious styles and other markers of religious experience such as mysticism or personality traits. Also, a thematic focus on humility, honesty, and wisdom might be strengthened, further revising and updating earlier efforts to conceptualize the cognitive and emotional variables involved in faith development and to explore psychological variables which are connected to the development of religious styles and types.

Our future research on change and development should clearly continue to focus on the consideration of *within-person differences* using an *idiographic* approach (Revelle & Wilt, 2021). Thus, our research, which is strongly based on interviews with narrative content, is clearly concerned with the *within-person differences* in narrative identity development in diachronic perspective. Nevertheless, we regard our research a demonstration of the integration of nomothetic and idiographic approaches and of the dynamics and processes in the adult lifespan. For an integration of our research perspectives, qualitative and quantitative, we may, as noted in Chapter 1 in this volume, consider McAdams's (2013; 2015) model of personality development that distinguishes three lines of development: the self as *actor*, as *agent*, and as *author*. The three lines of personality in McAdams's (2013) conceptualization roughly parallel the three sorts of data we have in our data base and the corresponding levels of analysis: (a) data on personality, which in our data include not only the "Big Five" personality traits, but also a variety of other aspects, including mystical experiences; these correspond to the *self as actor*; (b) data about worldview and meaning-making, which result from faith development evaluation (styles, types, and schemata) and are primarily related to agentic commitment to life projects; and (c) data on narrative identity, which result from the analysis of autobiographical narratives in the interviews and correspond to the *self as author*.

Thus, research on narrative identity and personality development in general are important neighboring disciplines. Especially narrative identity was inspiring and a key dimension for our qualitative work with the interviews from the start with the Deconversion Study at the beginning of this century. Now, with more quantitative and qualitative and results, including new coding schemes and specified methods of how to construct case studies, we may be in the position of returning the gift and making a useful contribution to research in narrative identity and personality development.

Necessarily, the further we advance our knowledge about faith development as observed and as reconstructed, the more we encounter complex interactions inspiring new questions that may suggest even more detailed analyses and more specific hypotheses for future research. In particular, we make a strong point for triangulation of different types of data and different types of methods for analyses and argue for the continuation of our mixed-methods approach in longitudinal perspective. In concluding, we hope that this current finale will be used as overture for future research and invite participation.

Finally, we should mention a neighboring discipline that we are beginning to engage in dialog more intensely: wisdom research. Of course, research in faith development is not identical with wisdom research. But faith development may have some overlap with wisdom. And a dialog is mutual: Possibly, our focus on worldview, spirituality, religion and faith in development calls attention to a perspective that is not a primary focus of wisdom research. But there is more: We suppose that *xenosophia* may be an interesting perspective to consider in wisdom research. We have integrated xenosophia conceptually, and xenosophia is included in the names of a subscale (Streib et al., 2010) and a religious type (Streib, et al., 2020). We regard xenosophia an integral aspect and aim of faith development (see more details in Chapter 1, this volume). The proposal is that xenosophia may be an important aspect of wisdom.[4] We expect an interesting, perhaps controversial, but hopefully innovative discussion.

Wisdom research has inspired our conceptualization and analyses of faith development from the start in the Deconversion Study—in a time, when the Berlin model (Baltes et al., 2002) was in the focus of the wisdom discussion. And, as we conclude our third wave of research, we think that wisdom needs to be included more intensely and explicitly in our future research. How can we model correlates and outcomes of faith development as an increase in wisdom? Variables that were already included in our questionnaire such as *openness to experience*, *intolerance of ambiguity*, *truth of texts and teachings*, *xenosophia/inter-religious dialog*, and the newly included measure for *intellectual humility* identify correlates of wisdom. This is a promising beginning. But now we plan to focus on wisdom-related narrative themes—which means that we evaluate narrative parts of the Faith Development Interviews for wisdom-related themes "bottom up" in the extensive subjective reconstructions of experiences and worldview that are elicited in the Faith Development Interviews. We hope to report results in a while.

We may conclude our chapter with a note on the necessity of wisdom—considered as a joint concern of faith development research and wisdom research: In a world severely infected by othering, even toxic othering and xenophobia, the dynamic development that we target in our research on faith in development dovetails with wisdom research. Sternberg (2018) has proposed to consider as opposite to wisdom not foolishness, but toxicity.

---

4   This would imply a balancing of the φρόνησις tradition with the σοφία tradition of wisdom, and a more decisive attention to the way we encounter the other as an unknown (το ξένο = the Unknown, the Alien).

This mirrors our conviction that xenophobia and xenosophia are opposites. Xenophobia and toxicity are lethal threats for interpersonal, societal, and global relations. An escalation of xenophobia generates hate (Sternberg, 2005; 2020), violence, and war, including the potential to terminate the human species as inhabitants of our planet by nuclear annihilation. How high this risk may become, is currently demonstrated in the Russian war against the Ukraine—a war that demonstrates the vicious circle of xenophobia on all levels.

When we suggest a dynamic development from ethnocentric through a conventional embeddedness and an autonomous-individuative reflection to receptive and unprejudiced openness for the other, we outline the dynamics of change and development that suggests common ground on the outlook for a better world. The development of wisdom and faith development describe the progress from the negative to the positive: from toxicity to wisdom, from xenophobia to xenosophia, from prejudice and othering to receptivity and responding, from irresponsive neglect to concern for the common good of all creatures.

References

Ammerman, N. T. (2013). Spiritual but not religious? Beyond binary choices in the study of religion. *Journal for the Scientific Study of Religion*, 52(2), 258–278. http://dx.doi.org/10.1111/jssr.12024

Baltes, P. B., Glück, J., & Kunzmann, U. (2002). Wisdom. Its structure and function in regulating successful life span development. In C. R. Snyder & S. J. Lopez (Eds.), *Handbook of positive psychology* (pp. 327–347). Oxford UP.

Berghuijs, J., Pieper, J., & Bakker, C. (2013). Conceptions of spirituality among the Dutch population. *Archive for the Psychology of Religion*, 35(3), 369–397. https://doi.org/10.1163/15736121-12341272

Chen, Z., Cowden, R. G., & Streib, H. (2023). More spiritual than religious: Concurrent and longitudinal relations with personality traits, mystical experiences, and other individual characteristics. *Frontiers in Psychology*, 13, Article 1025938. https://doi.org/10.3389/fpsyg.2022.1025938

Coleman III, T. J., Silver, C. F., & Holcombe, J. (2013). Focusing on horizontal transcendence: Much more than a "non-belief." *Essays in the Philosophy of Humanism*, 21(2), 1–18. http://dx.doi.org/10.1558/eph.v21i2.1

Costa, P. T., & McCrae, R. R. (1985). *Revised NEO Personality Inventory (NEO PI-R) and NEO Five-Factor-Inventory (NEO-FFI). Professional manual.* Psychological Assessment Resources 1992.

Eisenmann, C., Klein, C., Swhajor-Biesemann, A., Drexelius, U., Streib, H., & Keller, B. (2016). Dimensions of "spirituality:" The semantics of subjective definitions. In H. Streib & R. W. Hood (Eds.), *Semantics and psychology of "Spirituality." A cross-cultural analysis* (pp. 125–151). Springer International Publishing Switzerland. https://doi.org/10.1007/978-3-319-21245-6_9

Farias, M., & Coleman III, T. J. (2021). Non-religion, atheism, and mental health. In A. Moreira-Almeida, B. P. Mosqueiro, & D. Bhugra (Eds.), *Spirituality and mental health across cultures* (pp. 259–276). Oxford University Press.

Gooren, H. (2011). Review essay on: Deconversion: Qualitative and quantitative results from cross-cultural research in Germany and the United States. *Pastoral Psychology*, 60(4), 609–617. https://doi.org/10.1007/s11089-011-0369-0

Graham, J., Nosek, B. A., Haidt, J., Iyer, R., Koleva, S., & Ditto, P. H. (2011). Mapping the moral domain. *Journal of Personality and Social Psychology*, 101(2), 366–385.

Greenwald, Y., Mikulincer, M., Granqvist, P., & Shaver, P. R. (2021). Apostasy and conversion: Attachment orientations and individual differences in the process of religious change. *Psychology of Religion and Spirituality*, 13(4), 425–436. https://doi.org/10.1037/rel0000239

Habermas, T., & Köber, C. (2015). Autobiographical reasoning is constitutive for narrative identity: The role of the life story for personal continuity. In K. C. McLean & M. Syed (Eds.), *Oxford library of psychology. The Oxford handbook of identity development*. Oxford University Press.

Hood, R. W. (1975). The construction and preliminary validation of a measure of reported mystical experience. *Journal for the Scientific Study of Religion*, 14, 29–41. https://doi.org/10.2307/1384454

Huber, S. (2007). *Gutachten zum geplanten Religionsmonitor der Bertelsmann-Stiftung*.

Huber, S. (2009). Religion Monitor 2008: Structuring principles, operational constructs, interpretive strategies. In F. Bertelsmann (Ed.), *What the world believes: Analysis and commentary on the Religion Monitor 2008* (pp. 17–51). Verlag Bertelsmann Stiftung.

Kalton, M. C. (2000). Green spirituality: Horizontal transcendence. In P. Young-Eisendrath & M. E. Miller (Eds.), *The psychology of mature spirituality: Integrity, wisdom, transcendence* (pp. 187–200). Routledge.

Keller, B., Bullik, R., Steppacher, A., Streib, H., & Silver, C. F. (2022). Following deconverts and traditionalists. Longitudinal case study construction. In H. Streib, B. Keller, R. Bullik, A. Steppacher, C. F. Silver, M. Durham, S. B. Barker, & Hood, Jr., Ralph W. (Eds.), *Deconversion revisited. Biographical studies and psychometric analyses ten years later* (pp. 83–108). Vandenhoeck & Ruprecht. https://doi.org/10.13109/9783666568688.83

Keller, B., Bullik, R., Streib, H., Steppacher, A., & Hood, R. W. (2022). Deconversion typologies revisited: Biographical trajectories ten years later. In H. Streib, B. Keller, R. Bullik, A. Steppacher, C. F. Silver, M. Durham, S. B. Barker, & Hood, Jr., Ralph W. (Eds.), *Deconversion revisited. Biographical studies and psychometric analyses ten years later* (pp. 287–300). Vandenhoeck & Ruprecht. https://doi.org/10.13109/9783666568688.287

Keller, B., Hood, R. W., & Streib, H. (2016). Mapping the varieties of "spiritual" biographies. In H. Streib & Hood, Jr., Ralph W. (Eds.), *Semantics and psychology of spirituality: A cross-cultural analysis* (pp. 275–280). Springer. https://doi.org/10.1007/978-3-319-21245-6_17

Keller, B., Streib, H., & Hood, R. W. (2016). Redrawing the map: Varieties of "spiritual," "religious" and "secular" lives. In H. Streib & J. R. W. Hood (Eds.), *Semantics and psychology of spirituality: A cross-cultural analysis* (pp. 373–380). Springer. https://doi.org/10.1007/978-3-319-21245-6_23

Keller, B., Streib, H., Silver, C. F., Klein, C., & Hood, R. W. (2016). Design, methods, and sample characteristics of the Bielefeld-based cross-cultural study of "spirituality." In H. Streib & R. W. Hood (Eds.), *Semantics and psychology of "spirituality." A cross-cultural analysis* (pp. 39–51). Springer International Publishing Switzerland. https://doi.org/10.1007/978-3-319-21245-6_4

Kindt, W. (1992). Argumentation und Konfliktaustragung in Äußerungen über den Golf-krieg. *Zeitschrift Für Sprachwissenschaft*, 11(2), 189–215.

Klein, C., Silver, C. F., Coleman, T. J., Streib, H., & Hood, R. W. (2016). "Spirituality" and mysticism. In H. Streib & R. W. Hood (Eds.), *Semantics and psychology of "Spirituality." A cross-cultural analysis* (pp. 165–187). Springer International Publishing Switzerland. https://doi.org/10.1007/978-3-319-21245-6_11

Köber, C., Kuhn, M. M., Peters, I., & Habermas, T. (2018). Mentalizing oneself: Detecting reflective functioning in life narratives. *Attachment & Human Development*, 1–19. https://doi.org/10.1080/14616734.2018.1473886

Krumrei-Mancuso, E. L., & Rouse, S. V. (2016). The development and validation of the comprehensive Intellectual Humility Scale. *Journal of Personality Assessment*, 98(2), 209–221. https://doi.org/10.1080/00223891.2015.1068174

la Cour, P., Ausker, N. H., & Hvidt, N. C. (2012). Six understandings of the word spirituality in a secular country. *Archive for the Psychology of Religion*, 34(1), 63–81. https://doi.org/doi:10.1163/157361212X649634

Labov, W., & Waletzky, J. (1967). Narrative analysis: Oral versions of personal experience. *Journal of Narrative and Life History*, 7(1–4), 3–38. https://doi.org/10.1075/jnlh.7.02nar

Lamiell, J. T. (1981). Toward an idiothetic psychology of personality. *American Psychologist*, 36(3), 276–289. https://doi.org/10.1037/0003-066X.36.3.276

Lamiell, J. T. (2019). *Psychology's misuse of statistics and persistent dismissal of its critics*. Palgrave Macmillan.

McAdams, D. P. (2013). The psychological self as actor, agent, and author. *Perspectives on Psychological Science*, 8(3), 272–295. https://doi.org/10.1177/1745691612464657

McAdams, D. P. (2015). Tracing three lines of personality sevelopment. *Research in Human Development*, 12(3–4), 224–228. https://doi.org/10.1080/15427609.2015.1068057

McLean, K. C., Lilgendahl, J. P., Fordham, C., Alpert, E., Marsden, E., Szymanowski, K., & McAdams, D. P. (2018). Identity development in cultural context: The role of deviating from master narratives. *Journal of Personality*, 86(4), 631–651. https://doi.org/10.1111/jopy.12341

Mercadante, L. (2014). *Belief without borders: Inside the minds of the spiritual but not religious*. Oxford University Press. https://doi.org/10.1093/acprof:oso/9780199931002.001.0001

Mickler, C., & Staudinger, U. M. (2005). Manual for the assessment of self-related wisdom. Jacobs Center, International University Bremen.

Palitsky, R., Sullivan, D., Young, I. F., & Schmitt, H. J. (2020). Religion and the construction of identity. In K. E. Vail & C. Routledge (Eds.), *The science of religion, spirituality, and existentialism* (pp. 207–222). Academic Press. https://doi.org/10.1016/b978-0-12-817204-9.00016-0

Reischer, H. N., Roth, L. J., Villarreal, J. A., & McAdams, D. P. (2020). Self-transcendence and life stories of humanistic growth among late-midlife adults. *Journal of Personality*. (ARTN e12583). https://doi.org/10.1111/jopy.12583

Revelle, W., & Wilt, J. (2021). The history of dynamic approaches to personality. In J. F. Rauthmann (Ed.), *The handbook of personality dynamics and processes* (pp. 3–31). Academic Press. https://doi.org/10.1016/B978-0-12-813995-0.00001-7

Schlehofer, M. M., Omoto, A. M., & Adelman, J. R. (2008). How do "religion" and "spirituality" differ? Lay definitions among older adults. *Journal for the Scientific Study of Religion*, 47(3), 411–425.

Steensland, B., Wang, X., & Schmidt, L. C. (2018). Spirituality: What does it mean and to whom? *Journal for the Scientific Study of Religion*, 57(3), 450–472. https://doi.org/10.1111/jssr.12534

Sternberg, R. J. (2018). Wisdom, foolishness, and toxicity in human development. *Research in Human Development*, 15(3–4), 200–210. https://doi.org/10.1080/15427609.2018.1491216

Sternberg, R. J. (Ed.). (2005). *The psychology of hate*. American Psychological Association. https://doi.org/10.1037/10930-000.

Sternberg, R. J. (Ed.). (2020). *Perspectives on hate. How it originates, develops, manifests, and spreads*. American Psychological Association. https://doi.org/10.1037/0000180-000.

Streib, H. (1998). Milieus und Organisationen christlich-fundamentalistischer Prägung. In Deutscher Bundestag, Enquete-Kommission „Sogenannte Sekten und Psychogruppen" (Ed.), *Neue religiöse und ideologische Gemeinschaften und Psychogruppen. Forschungsprojekte und Gutachten der Enquete-Kommission ‚Sogenannte Sekten und Psychogruppen'* (pp. 107–157). Hoheneck-Verlag. https://doi.org/10.13140/2.1.4115.2329

Streib, H., & Chen, Z. J. (2021). Evidence for the brief mysticism scale: Psychometric properties, and moderation and mediation effects in predicting spiritual self-identification. *International Journal for the Psychology of Religion*, 31(3), 165–175. https://doi.org/10.1080/10508619.2021.1899641 (post-print at: https://doi.org/10.31234/osf.io/6bx2s)

Streib, H., Chen, Z. J., & Hood, R. W. (2020). Categorizing people by their preference for religious styles: Four types derived from evaluation of faith development interviews. *International Journal for the Psychology of Religion*, 30(2), 112–127. https://doi.org/10.1080/10508619.2019.1664213 (post-print at: https://doi.org/10.31234/osf.io/d3kbr)

Streib, H., Chen, Z. J., & Hood, R. W. (2021). Faith development as change in religious types: Results from three-wave longitudinal data with Faith Development Interviews. *Psychology of Religion and Spirituality*, online-first, 1–10. https://doi.org/10.1037/rel0000440 (post-print at: https://doi.org/10.31234/osf.io/qrcb2)

Streib, H., & Hood, R. W. (2011). "Spirituality" as privatized experience-oriented religion: Empirical and conceptual perspectives. *Implicit Religion*, 14(4), 433–453. https://doi.org/10.1558/imre.v14i4.433

Streib, H., & Hood, R. W. (2013). Modeling the religious field: Religion, spirituality, mysticism and related world views. *Implicit Religion*, 16(3), 137–155. https://doi.org/10.1558/imre.v16i2.133

Streib, H., & Hood, R. W. (Eds.). (2016a). *Semantics and psychology of spirituality. A cross-cultural analysis.* Springer International Publishing Switzerland. https://doi.org/10.1007/978-3-319-21245-6.

Streib, H., & Hood, R. W. (2016b). Understanding "Spirituality" – Conceptual considerations. In H. Streib & R. W. Hood (Eds.), *Semantics and psychology of "Spirituality." A cross-cultural analysis* (pp. 3–17). Springer International Publishing Switzerland. https://doi.org/10.1007/978-3-319-21245-6_1

Streib, H. & Hood, R. W.(2016c) Coordinates for mapping "Spirituality." In H. Streib & R. W. Hood (Eds.), *Semantics and psychology of "Spirituality." A cross-cultural analysis* (pp. 219–235). Springer International Publishing Switzerland. DOI 10.1007/978-3-319-21245-6_14

Streib, H., Hood Jr., R. W., & Klein, C. (2010). The Religious Schema Scale: Construction and initial validation of a quantitative measure for religious styles. *International Journal for the Psychology of Religion*, 20(3), 151–172. https://doi.org/10.1080/10508619.2010.481223

Streib, H., Hood, R. W., Keller, B., Csöff, R.-M., & Silver, C. (2009). *Deconversion. Qualitative and quantitative results from cross-cultural research in Germany and the United States of America.* Vandenhoeck & Ruprecht. https://doi.org/10.13109/9783666604393

Streib, H., & Keller, B. (2022). Quantitative perspectives on deconverts and traditionalists revisited. In H. Streib, B. Keller, R. Bullik, A. Steppacher, C. F. Silver, M. Durham, S. B. Barker, & R. W. Hood Jr (Eds.), *Deconversion revisited. Biographical studies and psychometric analyses ten years later* (pp. 59–82). https://doi.org/10.13109/9783666568688.59

Streib, H., Klein, C., Keller, B., & Hood, R. W. (2021). The Mysticism Scale as measure for subjective spirituality: New results with Hood's M-Scale and the development of a short form. In A. L. Ai, K. A. Harris, R. F. Paloutzian, & P. Wink (Eds.), *Assessing spirituality in a diverse world* (pp. 467–491). Springer Nature Switzerland. https://doi.org/10.1007/978-3-030-52140-0_19 (post-print at: https://doi.org/10.31234/osf.io/gwj2c)

Zick, A., Küpper, B., & Hövermann, A. (2011). *Intolerance, prejudice and discrimination. A European report*. Friedrich-Ebert-Stiftung. http://www.uni-bielefeld.de/ikg/zick/ZicketalGFEengl.pdf

Zick, A., Wolf, C., Küpper, B., Davidov, E., Schmidt, P., & Heitmeyer, W. (2008). The syndrome of Group-Focused Enmity: The interrelation of prejudices tested with multiple cross-sectional and panel data. *Journal of Social Issues*, 64(2), 363–383.

Zinnbauer, B. J., Pargament, K. I., Cole, B., Rye, M. S., Butter, E. M., Belavich, T. G., Hipp, K. M., Scott, A. B., & Kadar, J. L. (1997). Religion and spirituality: Unfuzzying the fuzzy. *Journal for the Scientific Study of Religion*, 36(4), 549–564.

APPENDIX A: Sample and Measures in the Three-Wave Longitudinal Data[1]

Heinz Streib, Ralph Hood, Barbara Keller, Ramona Bullik, Matthew Durham, and Zhuo Job Chen

1. Sample

Almost all studies published in this book are based on the three-wave longitudinal sample of $n = 75$ participants who completed a Faith Development Interview (FDI) in all three waves. In this interviewee sample, $n = 68$ answered our comprehensive questionnaire at each time of interviewing, $n = 74$ participated in two waves, and only one participant did not answer the questionnaire at all. In all research projects we have simultaneously collected data in Germany ($n = 59$ or 78.7%) and the USA ($n = 16$ or 21.3%). Basic demographics further include:

- Gender: 35 (46.7%) identified as female, 40 (53.3 %) as male;
- Age: Mean age at Wave 1 was 45.8 years (range: 18 to 76 years), mean age at Wave 3 was 57.0 years (range: 27 to 85 years);
- Education: From the assessment of school education and vocational training, cultural capital (education) was calculated according to the International Standard Classification of Education 1997 (UNESCO Institute for Statistics, 2006) and the OECD (2009; 2017) Factbooks. This resulted for Wave 1 in 4.2% below secondary education, 29.6% upper secondary, but not tertiary education, and 66.2 % tertiary education participants; at Wave 3, we document 23.9 upper secondary, but not tertiary education and 76.1% tertiary education.
- Per-capita income was reported at Wave 3 with a mean of 38,010 ($SD = 25,243$) USD p.a.

All $n = 75$ participants completed their first interview and survey (Wave 1) in either the Deconversion Study (2002–2005; Streib et al., 2009) or the Spirituality Study (2009–2012; Streib & Hood, 2016) with totals of $n = 272$ and $n = 108$ FDI interviewees, respectively. Both

---

1   This document is also available at https://osf.io/92u8a/.

studies used convenience sampling through media such as paper adds, radio, or websites for reaching out to participants. Problems with locating participants at still valid addresses and getting consent for re-interviewing has limited re-participation in Wave 2 (2014–2017) to 24.5%, but re-participation rate (of re-interviewees in Wave 1 and Wave 2) in Wave 3 (2018–2020) was 80.6%. Time lag between the initial FDI at Wave 1 and the second FDI at Wave 2 is 6.9 years—with a subgroup difference: participants with their first FDI in the Deconversion Study ($n = 34$) have a time lag of 10.1 years (range: 6.1 to 13.4 years), while participants with their first FDI in the Spirituality Study have 4.3 years (range: 3.9 to 5.3 years) between first and second FDI. Mean time lag between the Wave 2 FDI and Wave 3 FDI is 3.6 years (range: 2.08 to 5.05 years). The mean time lag between the first interview at Wave 1 and the last interview at Wave 3 is 10.47 years (range: 6.53 to 16.36 years).

2. Measures

2.1 The Faith Development Interview

The FDI is a semi-structured interview that may last between 30 minutes and 2 hours. The interview format (for wording of interview questions asked in these FDIs and for evaluation prescription, see Fowler et al., 2004; Streib & Keller, 2018) consists of 25 questions (including associated follow-up questions) that address *life review* (Sample question: *"Reflecting on your life, identify its major chapters"*), *relationships* (*"Focusing now on the present, how would you describe your parents and your current relationship to them?"*), *present values and commitments* (*"Are there any beliefs, values, or commitments that seem important to your life right now?"*) and finally *religion and world view* (*"Do you consider yourself a religious, spiritual or faithful person?"*). Evaluation of the FDI is an interpretative process of identifying, in the responses to the respective FDI question, the structural pattern as described in detail in the *Coding Manual* (Streib & Keller, 2018). This evaluation concludes with the assignment of one of the styles to the respective interacts in the FDI transcript that contain the answers of the interviewees to each of the 25 questions. After entering evaluation results into the quantitative data base, this results in 25 variables with integers for the style assignments. FDI rating checks by a second blind rater in random subsamples of ca. 17% of Wave 1 and Wave 2 FDIs resulted in inter-rater agreement of 80% and 69%, respectively. The inter-rater agreement between three independent raters for the entire Wave 3 FDI sample was 79%.

Our method of constructing the final total FDI score is the religious type (Streib, Chen, & Hood, 2020). To construct a summary evaluation of one FDI, the type is constructed according to the following algorithm: Out of the 25 rating variables, if frequency of Style 2 rating is equal to or more than 5 (20%), a person's religious type will be regarded as *substantially ethnocentric* type; if frequency of Style 5 rating is equal to or more than 5 (20%), the type is decided as *emerging dialogical-xenosophic* type; else, the type is *predominantly conventional* if frequency of Style 3 rating is greater than that of Style 4 rating, or the *predominantly individuative-reflective* type if frequency of Style 4 rating is greater than that of Style 3 rating. A specific rule is set in place to break the ties introduced by an identical frequency of Style 3 and Style 4 ratings, and/or both Style 2 and Style 5 ratings exceed 20%. For these situations, the case should be associated with the higher type.

The algorithm used for calculation the religious types as final FDI score for entire interview (Streib et al., 2020) was used also for the calculation of the aspect-specific types in Chapter 5. This made the aspect-specific types more sensitive for ratings of the instrumental-reciprocal style (Style 2) and the dialogical Style (Style 5), since the Style 2 or Style 5 rating of one answer can determine the type assignment of the aspect. We think that this weighting procedure is justified, when the aim is to prevent averaging out the still substantial presence of Style 2 or the emerging development of Style 5 in an interview.

2.2 Scales Included in the Questionnaires

We describe all measure that were included three times of at least twice in our questionnaires (see Table A.1). They constitute the basis for longitudinal modelling. The items in English can be seen from a copy of our Wave 3 questionnaire at https://osf.io/64dcu/. Means, standard deviations, and Cronbach's alphas for all three waves are presented in Table 2.

Personality factors were assessed in all samples with the *NEO Five Factor Inventory* (NEO-FFI, Costa & McCrae, 1985) in the English version of the questionnaires. For the German versions, the translation by Borkenau and Ostendorf (1993) was used. The 60-item measure assesses the Big Five personality traits (12 items each): neuroticism (e.g., "At times I have been so ashamed I just wanted to hide"), extraversion (e.g., "I really enjoy talking to people"), openness to experience (e.g., "I have a lot of intellectual curiosity"), agreeableness (e.g., "I would rather cooperate with others than compete with them"), and conscientiousness (e.g., "I try to perform all the tasks assigned to me conscientiously"). Participants responded to the items using a five-point scale ranging from 1 (Strongly disagree) to 5 (Strongly agree).

Psychological Well-being was measured using the *Psychological Well-Being and Growth Scale* (Ryff, 2010; Ryff & Singer, 1996). The German version has been validated and used in the Berlin Aging Study (Smith et al., 2002). The measure (see also Ryff, 1989; Ryff & Singer, 1998a, 1998b) assesses six dimensions of psychological well-being (7 items each): autonomy (e.g., "My decisions are not usually influenced by what everyone else is doing"), environmental mastery (e.g., "In general, I feel I am in charge of the situation in which I live"), positive relations with others (e.g., "I know that I can trust my friends, and they know they can trust me"), personal growth (e.g., "I have the sense that I have developed a lot as a person over time"), purpose in life (e.g., "Some people wander aimlessly through life, but I am not one of them") and self-acceptance (e.g., "When I look at the story of my life, I am pleased with how things have turned out"). Participants responded to the items using a five-point scale ranging from 1 (Strongly disagree) to 5 (Strongly agree).

For the assessment of *generativity* we included the 20-item Loyola Generativity Scale (LGS; McAdams & de St. Aubin, 1992; McAdams et al., 1993; McAdams et al., 1997; McAdams et al., 1998), which measures the extent to which someone reports to take care of the next generation (e.g., "I have made and created things that have had an impact on other people"). For the German sample we used the translation reported by Hofer et al. (2008). Rating scale was from 1 for "never applies to me" to 4 for "applies to me very often or nearly always." The 4-point scale was transformed in a 5-point-rating scale for calculations.

The *Religious Schema Scale* (RSS, Streib et al., 2010) was included also in all three samples. This scale consists of 15 items and measures three religious schemata in subscales: The schema that features an exclusivist and authoritative understanding of one's own sacred texts is assessed by the subscale *truth of texts and teachings (ttt)* (Sample item: *"What the texts and stories of my religion tell me is absolutely true and must not be changed"*). For the assessment of the opposite notion, the appreciation of difference, of the other, and of dialog, the subscale *xenosophia/inter-religious dialog (xenos)* was constructed (Sample item: *"We need to look beyond the denominational and religious differences to find the ultimate reality"*). A third religious schema is called *fairness, tolerance and rational choice (ftr)* (Sample item: "We should resolve differences in how people appear to each other through fair and just discussion."). Items were rated on five-point scales scale ranging from 1 (Definitely not true) to 5 (Definitely true).

Mysticism was assessed in the questionnaires using Hood's (1975) Mysticism Scale (M-Scale). The German translation was completed in preparing our Spirituality Project and published in Streib and Keller (2015). The three scales of the M-Scale correspond to its three-factor structure (see also Table 1 in Chapter 2 of this volume) (Streib & Chen, 2021; Streib et al., 2021; Chen, Hood, et al., 2011; Chen, Qi, et al., 2011; Chen et al., 2012; Hood et al., 2001) which is based on eight experiential facets: *Introvertive mysticism* is composed of ego loss, timelessness/spacelessness, and ineffability, denoting an inward unitary consciousness beyond time and space (sample item: "I have had an experience that was both timeless and spaceless"). *Extrovertive mysticism* is framed by unity and inner subjectivity, implying an outward merging with the wholeness of all existence (sample item: "I have had an experience in which all things seemed to be aware"). *Interpretation* incorporates positive affect, sacredness, and noetic quality that qualifies both types of mysticism (sample item: "I have had an experience in which a new view of reality was revealed to me"). Items of the M-scale were rated on a 5-point scale from 1 = "very inaccurate" to 5 = "very accurate."

Intolerance of Ambiguity. Intolerance for Ambiguity was assessed using Budner's (1962) scale (Sample item: "What we are used to is always preferable to what is unfamiliar."). This scale was rated on the 7-point scale from "strongly disagree" to "strongly agree." The 7-point scale was transformed in a 5-point-rating scale for calculations.

For the assessment of *Need for Cognition* we used the 18-item scale of Cacioppo et al. (1984). The German translation was completed for the Wave 2 questionnaire by Barbara Keller using J. Keller, Bohner and Erb (2000). A sample item reads: "I really enjoy a task that involves coming up with new solutions to problems."

Religious Fundamenalism and Religious Pluralism was assessed using the items that Huber (2009) has included in the Religion Monitor questionnaire. Sample item for findamentalism: "For my religiousness it is important that I resolutely fight against evil." and for pluralism: "I believe that one should be open to all religions." Ratings were on a 5-point scale from "totally disgree" to "totally agree." After a summary overview of the scales used longitudinal in Table 1, we describe means, standard deviations and Crobach's Alphas in Table 2.

Table A.1: Quantitative Measures in our Longitudinal Faith-in-development Data

Construct	Measure	Wave 1	Wave 2	Wave 3
personality	NEO-FFI (Costa & McCrae, 1985)	X	X	X
well-being	Psychological Well-being and Growth Scale (Ryff, 1989; Ryff & Singer, 1996, 1998a, 1998b)	X	X	X
generativity	Loyola Generativity Scale (LGS, McAdams & de St. Aubin, 1992; McAdams et al., 1993)	X	X	X
religious schemata	Religious Schema Scale (RSS, Streib et al., 2010)	X	X	X
mystical experiences	Mysticism Scale (Hood, 1975; Streib et al., 2021)	X	X	X
intolerance ambiguity	Intolerance for Ambiguity Scale (Budner, 1962)		X	X
need for cognition	Need for Cognition Scale (Cacioppo et al., 1984)		X	X
fundamentalism	items from the Religion Monitor questionnaire (Huber, 2009)		X	X
pluralism	items from the Religion Monitor questionnaire (Huber, 2009)		X	X

Table A.2: Means, Standard Deviations and Cronbach's Alphas for All Scales in the Three-wave Longitudinal Data

	Wave 1			Wave 2			Wave 3		
	M	SD	α	M	SD	α	M	SD	α
NEO-FFI									
neuroticism	2.60	0.82	.91	2.60	0.74	0.89	2.59	0.70	0.89
extraversion	3.29	0.62	.83	3.28	0.66	0.87	3.19	0.65	0.85
openness to experience	3.92	0.49	.72	3.89	0.50	0.72	4.00	0.55	0.79
agreeableness	3.75	0.46	.74	3.75	0.49	0.75	3.85	0.52	0.82
conscientiousness	3.69	0.55	.82	3.73	0.53	0.80	3.79	0.54	0.84
Well-being (Ryff-Scale)									
autonomy	3.69	0.58	.66	3.32	0.49	0.36	3.31	0.53	0.54
environmental mastery	3.65	0.75	.85	3.67	0.63	0.76	3.66	0.67	0.79
personal growth	4.31	0.48	.69	4.14	0.49	0.65	4.28	0.52	0.73
positive relations with others	3.89	0.67	.77	3.91	0.68	0.77	4.00	0.62	0.83
purpose in life	3.80	0.68	.81	3.78	0.63	0.71	3.72	0.62	0.72

	Wave 1			Wave 2			Wave 3		
	M	*SD*	α	*M*	*SD*	α	*M*	*SD*	α
self-acceptance	3.75	0.77	.87	3.82	0.69	0.85	3.87	0.67	0.85
Generativity (range: 1–4)	2.99	0.49	.89	2.88	0.42	0.83	2.93	0.50	0.91
Religious Schema Scale									
truth of texts and teachings	2.53	1.14	0.88	2.35	1.13	0.88	2.55	1.12	0.84
fairness, tolerance & ratl. choice	4.38	0.38	0.35	4.35	0.51	0.65	4.59	0.40	0.52
xenosophia/inter-religious dialog	3.64	0.82	0.72	3.58	0.78	0.61	3.77	0.78	0.69
Mystical experiences									
introvertive	3.52	1.16	0.93	3.60	1.03	0.90	3.40	1.05	0.91
extrovertive	3.45	1.19	0.92	3.46	1.06	0.89	3.29	1.23	0.92
interpretation	3.65	1.11	0.93	3.72	1.02	0.92	3.63	1.01	0.92
Intolerance of ambiguity				2.63	0.43	0.67	2.54	0.43	0.60
Need for cognition				3.55	0.44	0.75	3.53	0.45	0.78
Religious Fundamentalism				2.44	0.85	0.88	2.53	0.85	0.88
Religious Pluralism				3.91	1.09	0.81	3.63	1.01	0.71

References

Borkenau, P., & Ostendorf, F. (1993). *NEO-Fünf-Faktoren-Inventar (NEO-FFI) nach Costa und McCrae: Handanweisung*. Hogrefe, Verlag für Psychologie.

Budner, S. (1962). Intolerance of ambiguity as a personality variable. *Journal of Personality*, 30(1), 29–50. https://doi.org/10.1111/j.1467-6494.1962.tb02303.x

Cacioppo, J. T., Petty, R. E., & Kao, C. F. (1984). The efficient asessment of need for cognition. *Journal of Personality Assessment*, 48(3), 306–307. https://doi.org/10.1207/s15327 752jpa4803_13

Chen, Z., Hood, R. W., Yang, L., & Watson, P. J. (2011). Mystical experience among Tibetan Buddhists: The common core thesis revisited. *Journal for the Scientific Study of Religion*, 50(2), 328–338. https://doi.org/10.1111/j.1468-5906.2011.01570.x

Chen, Z., Qi, W., Hood, R. W., & Watson, P. J. (2011). Common core thesis and qualitative and quantitative analysis of mysticism in Chinese Buddhist monks and nuns. *Journal for the Scientific Study of Religion*, 50(4), 654–670. https://doi.org/10.1111/j.1468-5906.20 11.01606.x

Chen, Z., Zhang, Y., Hood, R. W., & Watson, P. J. (2012). Mysticism in Chinese Christians and Non-Christians: Measurement invariance of the Mysticism Scale and implications for the mean differences. *International Journal for the Psychology of Religion*, 22(2), 155–168. https://doi.org/10.1111/j.1468-5906.2011.01570.x

Costa, P. T., & McCrae, R. R. (1985). *Revised NEO Personality Inventory (NEO PI-R) and NEO Five-Factor-Inventory (NEO-FFI)*. *Professional Manual*. Psychological Assessment Resources 1992.

Fowler, J. W., Streib, H., & Keller, B. (2004). *Manual for faith development research* (3rd ed.). Research Center for Biographical Studies in Contemporary Religion, Bielefeld; Center for Research in Faith and Moral Development, Emory University. https://doi.org/10.13140/2.1.4232.4804

Hofer, J., Busch, H., Chasiotis, A., Kartner, J., & Campos, D. (2008). Concern for generativity and its relation to implicit pro-social power motivation, generative goals, and satisfaction with life: a cross-cultural investigation. *J Pers, 76*(1), 1–30. https://doi.org/10.1111/j.1467-6494.2007.00478.x

Hood, R. W., Ghorbani, N., Watson, P. J., Ghramaleki, A. F., Bing, M. N., Davison, H. K., Morris, R. J., & Williamson, W. P. (2001). Dimensions of the Mysticism Scale: Confirming the three-factor-structure in the United States and Iran. *Journal for the Scientific Study of Religion, 40*(4), 691–705. https://doi.org/10.1111/0021-8294.0008

Huber, S. (2009). Religion Monitor 2008: Structuring principles, operational constructs, interpretive strategies. In F. Bertelsmann (Ed.), *What the world believes: Analysis and commentary on the Religion Monitor 2008* (pp. 17–51). Verlag Bertelsmann Stiftung.

Keller, J., Bohner, G., & Erb, H.-P. (2000). Intuitive und heuristische Urteilsbildung – verschiedene Prozesse? Präsentation einer deutschen Fassung des "Rational-Experiential Inventory" sowie neuer Selbstberichtskalen zur Heuristiknutzung. *Zeitschrift fur Sozialpsychologie, 31*, 87–101.

McAdams, D. P., & de St Aubin, E. D. (1992). A Theory of generativity and its assessment through self-report, behavioral acts, and narrative themes in autobiography. *Journal of Adult Development, 62*, 1003–1015. https://doi.org/10.1037/0022-3514.62.6.1003

McAdams, D. P., de St. Aubin, E., & Logan, R. L. (1993). Generativity among young, midlife, and older adults. *Psychology and Aging, 8*(2), 221–230. https://doi.org/10.1037/0882-7974.8.2.221

McAdams, D. P., Diamond, A., de St Aubin, E. D., & Mansfield, E. (1997). Stories of commitment: The psychosocial construction of generative lives. *Journal of Personality and Social Psychology, 72*(3), 678–694. https://doi.org/10.1037/0022-3514.72.3.678

McAdams, D. P., Hart, H. M., & Maruna, S. (1998). The anatomy of generativity. In D. P. McAdams & E. D. de St Aubin (Eds.), *Generativity and Adult Development. How and Why We Care for the Next Generation* (pp. 7–43). American Psychological Association.

OECD. (2009). *Education at a Glance 2009.* http://www.oecd.org/dataoecd/41/25/43636332.pdf

OECD. (2017). *Education at a Glance 2017. OECD Indicators.* https://doi.org/10.1787/eag-2017-en

Ryff, C. D. (1989). Happiness is everything, or is it? Explorations on the meaning of psychological well-being. *Journal of Personality and Social Psychology, 57*(6), 1069–1081. https://doi.org/10.1037/0022-3514.57.6.1069

Ryff, C. D. (2010). *Documentation of psychosocial constructs and composite variables in MIDUS II Project 1.* University of Wisconsin, Institute of Aging.

Ryff, C. D., & Singer, B. H. (1996). Psychological well-being: Meaning, measurement, and implications for psychotherapy research. *Psychotherapy and Psychosomatics, 65*(1), 14–23. https://doi.org/10.1159/000289026

Ryff, C. D., & Singer, B. H. (1998a). The contours of positive human health. *Psychological Inquiry, 9*(1), 1–28. https://doi.org/10.1207/s15327965pli0901_1

Ryff, C. D., & Singer, B. H. (1998b). The role of purpose in life and growth in positive human health. In P. T. P. Wong & P. S. Fry (Eds.), *The human quest for meaning. Handbook of psychological research and clinical applications* (pp. 213–235). Lawrence Erlbaum Associates.

Smith, J., Maas, I., Mayer, K. U., Helmchen, H., Steinhagen-Thiessen, E., & Baltes, P. B. (2002). Two-wave longitudinal findings from the berlin aging study: Introduction to a collection of articles. *Journal of Gerontology: Psychological Sciences*, 57B(6), P471–P473.

Streib, H., & Chen, Z. J. (2021). Evidence for the brief Mysticism Scale: Psychometric properties, and moderation and mediation effects in predicting spiritual self-identification. *International Journal for the Psychology of Religion*, 31(3), 165–175. https://doi.org/10.1080/10508619.2021.1899641 (post-print at: https://doi.org/10.31234/osf.io/6bx2s)

Streib, H., Chen, Z. J., & Hood, R. W. (2020). Categorizing people by their preference for religious styles: Four types derived from evaluation of faith development interviews. *International Journal for the Psychology of Religion*, 30(2), 112–127. https://doi.org/10.1080/10508619.2019.1664213 (post-print at: https://doi.org/10.31234/osf.io/d3kbr)

Streib, H., Hood Jr., R. W., & Klein, C. (2010). The Religious Schema Scale: Construction and initial validation of a quantitative measure for religious styles. *International Journal for the Psychology of Religion*, 20(3), 151–172. https://doi.org/10.1080/10508619.2010.481223

Streib, H., & Hood, R. W. (Eds.). (2016). *Semantics and psychology of spirituality. A cross-cultural analysis*. Springer International Publishing Switzerland. https://doi.org/10.1007/978-3-319-21245-6

Streib, H., Hood, R. W., Keller, B., Csöff, R.-M., & Silver, C. (2009). *Deconversion. Qualitative and quantitative results from cross-cultural research in Germany and the United States of America*. Vandenhoeck & Ruprecht. https://doi.org/10.13109/9783666604393

Streib, H., & Keller, B. (2015). *Was bedeutet Spiritualität? Befunde, Analysen und Fallstudien aus Deutschland*. Vandenhoeck & Ruprecht.

Streib, H., & Keller, B. (2018). *Manual for the assessment of religious styles in faith development interviews (Fourth, revised edition of the Manual for Faith Development Research)*. Bielefeld University/readbox unipress. https://doi.org/10.4119/unibi/2920987

Streib, H., Klein, C., Keller, B., & Hood, R. W. (2021). The Mysticism Scale as measure for subjective spirituality: New results with Hood's M-Scale and the development of a short form. In A. L. Ai, K. A. Harris, R. F. Paloutzian, & P. Wink (Eds.), *Assessing spirituality in a diverse world* (pp. 467–491). Springer Nature Switzerland. https://doi.org/10.1007/978-3-030-52140-0_19 (post-print at: https://doi.org/10.31234/osf.io/gwj2c)

Unesco Institute for Statistics. (2006). *International standard classification of education (ISCED 1997)*. UNESCO Institute for Statistics.

APPENDIX B: The Bielefeld Narrative and Content Coding Scheme (BiNCCS)

Anika Steppacher, Barbara Keller, & Ramona Bullik

The Bielefeld Narrative and Content Coding Scheme (BiNCCS) has been developed in the past years answering to the demand for an instrument to capture the diverse content of the Faith Development Interviews. While the standard structural evaluation method following the instructions of the Manual for the Assessment of Religious Styles (Streib & Keller, 2018) pays attention to the structure of what is being said, a comprehensive instrument for the evaluation of content and narrative particularities was missing. So, as introduced in Chapter 4, we created a coding guideline both bottom-up and top-down: bottom-up, when we were going through interviews and noting meaningful themes our interviewees talked about; and top-down, when we applied pre-existing categories (such as the exit trajectories, see Streib et al., 2009, or autobiographical arguments, see Köber et al., 2018). By combining these two approaches, we wanted to make sure we rediscovered categories from previous research while not missing out on the unique features the interview material has to offer. The fact that we found interesting codes on the content as well as the narrative level made it necessary to split the guideline into two parts to make it easier to handle. The BiNNCS was used in this volume in its current form, even though it is still under construction by carefully evaluating the codes in a bi-national process with the aim to create a culture-sensitive guideline. The following tables show excerpts (a) from the content coding guideline focusing on some bottom-up codes created in the category "BZ: Relationships" and (b) the narrative coding guideline exemplified by Köber and colleagues' autobiographical arguments sorted into the category "CAMOCO: Causal-motivational coherence."

Sub-Category	Code	Description
Children	Disappointment	Description of children's behavior as disappointing.
	End of relationship	E.g. loss because of contact termination
	Generativity	Raising children, transferring knowledge, and being positively remembered for the impact on younger people (see, for example, Erikson, 1982; Klein, Keller, Silver, Hood, & Streib, 2016)
	Giving meaning	E.g. having children and being a parent structures biography, and the meaning of one's children as part of one's identity is emphasized.
	New definition/development of relationship	The relationship to one's children changes because they grow up, move away, or a crisis forces a new approach to the relationship. Dealing with puberty can be an important topic here.
	Support/friendship	One's children are seen as friends, and offer support and advice.
	Unfulfilled wish to have a child	The person expresses the wish to have children, but is not (yet) a parent.
Parents/Caregivers	Ambivalent relationship	Interviewee describes the relationship to the parent as challenging, difficult or ambivalent.
	Deprivation	Lack or loss of caregivers as felt and reported by the interviewee. Parent is emotionally and/or physically not available to the child. Not the same as critical perspective on parents.
	Improvement of relationship	A formerly difficult relationships becomes better and the interviewee feels closer to the parent. This can for example manifest in seeing parents as people in their own right, accepting differences or forgiving failures of the parent.

Sub-Category	Code	Description
	Parents as authoritarian/ strict	Parent is described as strict and enforcing rules.
	Parents as ideologues	Parents are described as insisting on/promoting a doctrine or ideological framework, e.g. religious fanatics; politically extreme.
	Parents as perpetrators	Parents are made out as the source of suffering
	Parents as pleasant people	Character traits of parents are described as pleasant which allows for a loving and harmonious relationship
	Parents as victims	E.g. due to illness, fragility, biographies, etc.
	Role models/ orientation	Parents behavior or character is presented as recommendable and something the interviewee him or herself aspires to.
	Seeking independence from parents	Discussion of efforts for independence from parents and striving for autonomy.
	Support and good caregivers	Parents fulfilled their role in a sufficient way
	Termination of contact	The interviewee describes that he or she is no longer on speaking terms with his/her parent(s) which is due to a deliberate decision by the interviewee, e.g., because of a so felt toxic relationship that he or she no longer wants to burden her or himself with.

Category	Sub-Category	Code	Description
CAMOCO: Causal-Mo-tivational Coherence	Autobiogra-phical Argu-ments	Biographical Back-ground	A biographical information serves as argument. Example from Köber et al: "I really had problems with my teacher, she was my Physics teacher and today, out of defiance, I'm studying Physics." (Köber et al., 2018, p. 8)
		Developmental Status	Developmental status as argument. Example from Köber et al.: "Because at the time I was still too young, I wasn't aware of any of that." (Köber et al., 2018, p. 8)
		Formative Experience	An experience that is presented as the reason for changing ones way of life. Example from Köber et al.: "My burn-out has led me to no longer attach so much importance to money today." (Köber et al., 2018, p. 8)
		Generalized Insights	Orientation towards normative assumptions. Example from Köber et al.: "I was missing him for many months. Pro-bably it's always like that, when it's the first kiss." (Köber et al., 2018, p. 8)
		Lessons Learned	A lesson learnt. Example from Köber et al.: "After that I told myself, next time when I fall in love, I must take care that school doesn't suffer from that." (Köber et al., 2018, p. 8)
		Turning Points	Talking about profound changes. Example from Köber et al.: "The fact that all of a sudden the child was there turned my life upside down." (Köber et al., 2018, p. 8)
		contamination story	This code is an addition to causal-motivational-coherence according to Köber et al. It refers to McAdams redempti-on/contamination-coding that is defined as follows: "To receive a score of +1 for contamination, the account had to explicitly state that the beginning of the episode in question was affectively positive and that this positive state was followed by a clearly negative outcome." (McAdams et al., 2001 p. 479)
		redemption story	This code is an addition to causal-motivational-coherence according to Köber et al. It refers to McAdams redempti-on/contamination-coding that is defined as follows: "A redemption sequence was defined as an explicit transforma-tion in the story from a decidedly negative affect state to a decidedly positive-affect state. Evidence for the negative state had to be clear and explicit. The participant needed to describe some situation, period, or event in life in which he or she suffered in some way and experienced pain, fear, sadness, anguish, and so on. To score for a redemption sequence, furthermore, the decidedly negative situation needed either (a) to change into a decidedly positive situa-tion or (b) to produce a positive outcome of some kind. […] Note that the positive outcome need not be stronger in magnitude than the negative event." (McAdams et al., 2001, p. 478)

References

Köber, C., Kuhn, M. M., Peters, I., & Habermas, T. (2018). Mentalizing oneself: Detecting reflective functioning in life narratives. *Attachment & Human Development*, 1–19. https://doi.org/10.1080/14616734.2018.1473886

McAdams, D. P., Reynolds, J., Lewis, M., Patten, A. H., Bowman, P. J. (2001). When bad things turn good and good things turn bad: Sequences of redemption and contamination in life narrative and their relation to psychosocial adaptation in midlife adults and in students. *Personality and Social Psychology Bulletin*, 27 (4), 474–485. https://doi.org/10.1177/0146167201274008

Streib, H., Hood, R. W., Keller, B., Csöff, R.-M., & Silver, C. (2009). *Deconversion. Qualitative and quantitative results from cross-cultural esearch in Germany and the United States of America*. Vandenhoeck & Ruprecht. https://doi.org/10.13109/9783666604393

Streib, H., & Keller, B. (2018). *Manual for the assessment of religious styles in Faith Development Interviews (Fourth, revised edition of the Manual for Faith Development Research)*. Bielefeld University/readbox unipress. https://doi.org/10.4119/unibi/2920987

Printed in the USA
CPSIA information can be obtained
at www.ICGtesting.com
JSHW050742170824
68284JS00006B/40